EU ASYLUM PROCEDURES AND THE RIGHT TO AN EFFECTIVE REMEDY

Adequate and fair asylum procedures are a precondition for the effective exercise of rights granted to asylum applicants, in particular the prohibition of *refoulement*. In 1999 the EU Member States decided to work towards a Common European Asylum System. In this context the Procedures Directive was adopted in 2005 and recast in 2013. This directive provides for important procedural guarantees for asylum applicants, but also leaves much discretion to the EU Member States to design their own asylum procedures.

This book examines the meaning of the EU right to an effective remedy in terms of the legality and interpretation of the Procedures Directive in regard to several key aspects of asylum procedure: the right to remain on the territory of the Member State, the right to be heard, the standard and burden of proof and evidentiary assessment, judicial review and the use of secret evidence.

Volume 46 in the series Modern Studies in European Law

Modern Studies in European Law
Recent titles in this series:

Toward a Prosecutor for the European Union Volume 1: A Comparative Analysis
Edited by Katalin Ligeti

Empowerment and Disempowerment of the European Citizen
Edited by Michael Dougan, Niamh Nic Shuibhne and Eleanor Spaventa

Legal Reasoning and the European Court of Justice
Gunnar Beck

Lawyering Europe: European Law as a Transnational Social Field
Edited by Antoine Vauchez and Bruno de Witte

Services and the EU Citizen
Edited by Frank S Benyon

The Accession of the European Union to the European Convention on Human Rights
Paul Gragl

Normative Patterns and Legal Developments in the Social Dimension of the EU
Edited by Ann Numhauser-Henning and Mia Rönnmar

The European Neighbourhood Policy and the Democratic
Values of the EU: A Legal Analysis
Nariné Ghazaryan

EU Security and Justice Law: After Lisbon and Stockholm
Edited by Diego Acosta Arcarazo and Cian C Murphy

EU Environmental Law, Governance and Decision-Making
Maria Lee

Shaping the Single European Market in the Field of Foreign Direct Investment
Philip Strik

Nationalism and Private Law in Europe
Guido Comparato

For the complete list of titles in this series, see 'Modern Studies in European Law' link at www.hartpub.co.uk/books/series.asp

EU Asylum Procedures and the Right to an Effective Remedy

Marcelle Reneman

·HART·
PUBLISHING

OXFORD AND PORTLAND, OREGON
2016

Published in the United Kingdom by Hart Publishing Ltd
16C Worcester Place, Oxford, OX1 2JW
Telephone: +44 (0)1865 517530
Fax: +44 (0)1865 510710
E-mail: mail@hartpub.co.uk
Website: http://www.hartpub.co.uk

Published in North America (US and Canada) by
Hart Publishing
c/o International Specialized Book Services
920 NE 58th Avenue, Suite 300
Portland, OR 97213-3786
USA
Tel: +1 503 287 3093 or toll-free: (1) 800 944 6190
Fax: +1 503 280 8832
E-mail: orders@isbs.com
Website: http://www.isbs.com

First published in hardback 2014
Paperback edition, 2016

Hart Publishing is an imprint of Bloomsbury Publishing plc.

British Library Cataloguing in Publication Data
Data Available

ISBN: HB: 978-1-84946-545-8
PB: 978-1-50990-742-7

Typeset by Compuscript Ltd, Shannon
Printed and bound in Great Britain by
Lightning Source UK Ltd

Acknowledgements

The adventure of writing this book started in 2006, when I was working as a policy officer at the Dutch Council for Refugees. The topic I intended to research, the meaning of the right to an effective remedy for asylum procedures, followed logically from my work at the Dutch Council for Refugees. The previous years I had focused on the Dutch asylum procedure, in particular the problems encountered by asylum applicants and their lawyers in the Netherlands as a result of, amongst others, the 48-hour accelerated procedure, the limited intensity of judicial review and the strict requirements for new evidence imposed by the case law of the Council of State.

There are many things I learned during the process of writing this book. Probably most important to me was my discovery of the potential impact of EU law on national asylum procedures. I never imagined that it would be that relevant and inspiring to read EU Courts' judgments concerning competition law, tax law or agricultural policies. It became clear to me that the same procedural questions arise in all kinds of cases and that EU law provides similar answers to these questions. Hopefully this book will inspire lawyers working in the field of asylum law to use EU law in order to improve procedural guarantees for asylum applicants in Europe.

I am very grateful to my supervisors, Pieter Boeles and Thomas Spijkerboer for their invaluable insights, guidance and support. It was amazing to notice how their comments resulted in great improvements, not only in the content of the research, but also to the readability and accessibility of the book. Their positive criticism and reassurances gave me the energy to review and restructure the chapters of this book time and time again.

I would like to thank my colleagues at the Institute of Immigration Law in Leiden Law School, Peter Rodrigues, Gerrie Lodder, Maarten den Heijer, Mark Klaassen, Kees Wouters, Brigitte Straathof, Ciara Smith, Christian Mommers and Suzanne Guèvremont. In our office under the roof of the Law Faculty, we had many inspired discussions and I have always felt supported in my work. I am very happy that the Institute has continued and is now full of new energy and initiatives. I want to thank the members of the Department of Constitutional and Administrative Law and in particular the Migration Law Section of the VU University in Amsterdam for providing a most inspiring and enjoyable working environment.

As a starting lawyer I was privileged to work with many interesting, inspiring people. Thanks to them I developed a passion for asylum law and got the opportunity to grow as a lawyer and as a person. In particular I am grateful to my colleagues at the aliens chamber of the Council of State, the policy unit of the

Dutch Council for Refugees, the editorial boards of the Nieuwsbrief Asiel- and Vluchtelingenrecht, Asiel & Migrantenrecht and AB Rechtspraak Bestuursrecht, the Advisory Committee of the Dutch Council for Refugees and the Meijers Committee.

I also found an invaluable sparring partner in René Bruin. Thank you for always being prepared to read and discuss the annotations or articles I wrote. Dana Baldinger, Karen Geertsema and Hannah Helmink, I have enjoyed the many interesting meetings we had on procedural topics and your feedback on several chapters of this book was very useful.

I am grateful to the members of the PhD committee, professors Tom Barkhuysen, Hemme Battjes, Peter Rodrigues, Jens Vedsted-Hansen and Rob Widdershoven, for reviewing the manuscript and providing useful feedback. Kees Wouters and Maarten den Heijer, thank you for the support during the PhD defence.

The research for this book was funded by The Netherlands Organisation for Scientific Research (NWO) via a grant under the MaGW Open Competition. The assistance of Hart Publishing throughout the editing and production process of this book was invaluable.

Finally, I want to thank my family and friends for their support, encouragements and confidence. Mum, Dad, Lotte, thanks for being there for me during all the ups and downs. And then of course my dearest three men, Gilles, Yves and Xavier, you are the ones I always long to come home to.

Table of Contents

List of Abbreviations

Adm	admissibility decision
AG	Advocate General
CAT	United Nations Convention against Torture and Other Cruel, Inhuman or Degrading Treatment or Punishment
CEAS	Common European Asylum System
CFI	Court of First Instance
Charter	Charter of Fundamental Rights of the European Union
CRC	United Nations Convention on the Rights of the Child
ComAT	Committee against Torture
ComRC	Committee on the Rights of the Child
Court of Justice	Court of Justice of the European Union
EASO	European Asylum Support Office
EC	European Community
EC Treaty	Treaty Establishing the European Community
ECHR	European Convention on Human Rights
ECtHR	European Court of Human Rights
EComHR	European Commission of Human Rights
EEA	European Economic Area
EU	European Union
EXCOM	Executive Committee of the Programme of the High Commissioner
GC	Grand Chamber (European Court of Human Rights)
HBRB	Housing Benefit and Council Tax Review Board
HRC	Human Rights Committee
ICCPR	International Covenant on Civil and Political Rights
ICJ	International Court of Justice
MoU	Memorandum of Understanding
NGO	non-governmental organisation
Plen	plenary session
RCD	Reception Conditions Directive (2003/9/EC)
Refugee Convention (1951 Geneva Convention)	United Nations Convention relating to the Status of Refugees
SIAC	Special Immigration Appeal Commission
TEU	Treaty on European Union
TFEU	Treaty on the Functioning of the European Union
TPD	Temporary Protection Directive (2001/55/EC)
UN	United Nations
UNHCR	United Nations High Commissioner for Refugees
UNWRA	United Nations Relief and Works Agency for Palestine Refugees

1

Introduction: In Search of EU Standards for Asylum Procedures

THIS INTRODUCTORY CHAPTER starts by sketching the field of investigation and the nature of the issues to be scrutinised. This will lead to the formulation of a research question and an outline of this book.

1.1 ADEQUATE AND FAIR ASYLUM PROCEDURES IN THE EU: STATE OF THE ART

Adequate and fair procedures are a precondition for the effective exercise of rights.[1] In the context of EU law it is generally recognised that the rights granted by EU law to individuals would be worthless if they could not be enforced in national administrative proceedings[2] and in particular before national courts.[3] The importance of procedural rights is acknowledged by the Charter of Fundamental Rights of the European Union (the Charter) as it has accorded fundamental rights status to procedural rights, such as the right to an effective remedy and the right to good administration, on an equal footing with substantive rights.[4]

In asylum cases a lack of procedural guarantees may undermine the EU rights usually claimed by asylum applicants: the right not be expelled or extradited to a country where they face the risk of being subjected to human rights violations (the principle of *non-refoulement*)[5] and the right to asylum. The need for fair

[1] See, eg ECtHR 10 January 2012, *GR v the Netherlands*, no 22251/07, where the ECtHR ruled that the extremely formalistic attitude of the Dutch authorities prevented the applicant from seeking recognition of his arguable claim under Art 8 of the ECHR.

[2] J Ponce, 'Good Administration and Administrative Procedures' (2005) 12 *Indiana Journal of Global Legal Studies* 551, 577; and J Schwartze, 'Judicial Review of European Administrative Procedure' (2004) 68 *Law and Contemporary Problems* 85, 97.

[3] See, eg M Accetto and S Zlepnig, 'The Principle of Effectiveness: Rethinking Its Role in Community Law' (2005) 11 *European Public Law* 375, 380; and K Kańska, 'Towards Administrative Human Rights in the EU. Impact of the Charter of Fundamental Rights' (2004) 10 *European Law Journal* 296, 301.

[4] Kańska, 'Towards Administrative Human Rights in the EU', ibid, 302. Procedural rights can also be seen as an end in themselves. They aim to 'protect an individual and to ensure fairness of proceedings'. Ponce, 'Good Administration' (n 2) 552–53. See also Kańska, ibid, 301.

[5] CW Wouters *International Legal Standards for the Protection from Refoulement* (Antwerp, Intersentia, 2009) 1.

asylum procedures is recognised in the light of both the 'grave consequences of an erroneous determination for the applicant'[6] and the vulnerable situation in which asylum applicants often find themselves.[7]

Making a considered decision on an asylum case is not easy. The task of assessing fear of persecution and future risk of harm poses unique challenges which, as Costello remarks, 'requires both sensitive communicative approaches and objective risk assessment'.[8] This is to a large extent due to the fact that in most asylum cases there is a lack of documentary evidence and, therefore, the asylum applicant's statements may be the only evidence available. Thomas even states that:

> There can be little doubt that asylum decision-making, involving an assessment of future risk for the claimant often on the basis of limited information, is amongst the most problematic, difficult and complex forms of decision-making in the modern state. Decision-makers may feel pulled in different directions in light of both the considerable evidential uncertainty and a complex combination of facts pointing both ways in favour of awarding or refusing international protection.[9]

The examination of the credibility of the applicant's asylum account plays a central role in many asylum decisions.[10] As a result, rules regarding judicial review of the evidentiary assessment of asylum claims are crucial for the outcome of the case. Furthermore, factors such as the quality of the personal interview, the speed of the asylum procedure, and the asylum applicants' access (or lack of access) to legal aid and interpretation services may increase or decrease an applicant's chance of success. This book examines which procedural guarantees are required by EU law in asylum cases.

Rights Claimed by Asylum Applicants: The Prohibition of Refoulement and the Right to Asylum

The prohibition of *refoulement*, explicitly laid down in the United Nations Convention relating to the Status of Refugees (Refugee Convention, also often referred to as the 1951 Geneva Convention) and the United Nations Convention against Torture and Other Cruel, Inhuman or Degrading Treatment or Punishment (CAT), and recognised under the European Convention on Human Rights (ECHR) and the International Covenant on Civil and Political

[6] See EXCOM, *The Problem of Manifestly Unfounded or Abusive Applications for Refugee Status or Asylum*, 20 October 1983, No 30 (XXXIV) 1983, sub (e).

[7] UNHCR, *Handbook on Procedures and Criteria for Determining Refugee Status* (1979, new edition 1992) para 190, available at www.refworld.org/docid/3ae6b3314.html accessed 25 September 2013.

[8] C Costello, 'The European Asylum Procedures Directive in Legal Context, New Issues in Refugee Research, Research Paper No 134' (Geneva, UNHCR, 2006) 2.

[9] R Thomas 'Assessing the Credibility of Asylum Claims, EU and UK Approaches Examined' (2006) 8 *European Journal of Migration and Law* 79, 84.

[10] G Noll, *Proof, Evidentiary Assessment and Credibility in Asylum Procedures* (Leiden/Boston, Martinus Nijhoff, 2005) 1–6; TP Spijkerboer and BP Vermeulen, *Vluchtelingenrecht* (Nijmegen, Ars Aequi Libri, 2005) 261.

Rights (ICCPR), is the cornerstone of international refugee and asylum law.[11] The fundamental nature of the prohibition of *refoulement* is stressed by the European Court of Human Rights (ECtHR) in its case law. In the ECtHR's view, the prohibition of torture and inhuman or degrading treatment or punishment guaranteed by Article 3 ECHR enshrines one of the fundamental values of democratic societies. Protection against the treatment prohibited by Article 3 is absolute. As a result, that provision imposes an obligation not to extradite or expel any person who, in the receiving country, would run a real risk of being subjected to such treatment. According to the ECtHR there can be no derogation from that rule, even if the person concerned acts undesirably or dangerously.[12] The principle of *non-refoulement* requires that a State must assess a person's claim that he is in need of international protection, particularly if this State intends to expel or extradite that person.[13]

The prohibition of *refoulement* is also recognised as an EU fundamental right in Article 19 of the Charter which provides:

> No one may be removed, expelled or extradited to a State where there is a serious risk that he or she would be subjected to the death penalty, torture or other inhuman or degrading treatment or punishment.[14]

According to the Court of Justice, the assessment of the extent of the risk of *refoulement* relates 'to the integrity of the person and to individual liberties, issues which relate to the fundamental values of the Union'.[15] In *Elgafaji* the Court of Justice considered that the fundamental right guaranteed under Article 3 ECHR forms part of the general principles of EU law, observance of which is ensured by the Court.[16] The Court of Justice recognised in *Schmidberger* that the prohibition of torture and inhuman or degrading treatment or punishment laid down in Article 3 ECHR is absolute. It considered:

> [U]nlike other fundamental rights enshrined in that Convention, such as the right to life or the prohibition of torture and inhuman or degrading treatment or punishment, which admit of no restriction, neither the freedom of expression nor the freedom of

[11] Art 33 Refugee Convention, Art 3 CAT, Art 3 ECHR and Art 7 ICCPR.

[12] ECtHR (GC) 28 February 2008, *Saadi v Italy*, no 37201/06, paras 137–38. The prohibitions of *refoulement* guaranteed by the CAT and ICCPR are also absolute, see HRC 15 June 2004, *Ahani v Canada*, no 1051/2002, para 10 and ComAT 20 May 2005, *Agiza v Sweden*, no 233/2003, para 13.8. The Refugee Convention allows for exceptions to the prohibition of *refoulement*, according to Art 33(2).

[13] I Staffans, 'Judicial Protection and the New European Asylum Regime' (2010) 12 *European Journal of Migration and Law* 273, 275; Wouters, *International Legal Standards* (n 5) 164; and E Lauterpacht and D Bethlehem, 'The scope and content of the principle of non-refoulement' in E Feller, V Türk and F Nicholson (eds), *Refugee Protection in International Law, UNHCR's Global Consultations on International Protection* (Cambridge, Cambridge University Press, 2003) 118.

[14] The principle of *non-refoulement* is also recognised in Art 21(1) Dir 2011/95/EU.

[15] Joined Cases C-175/08, C-176/08, C-178/08 and C-179/08 *Salahadin Abdulla* [2010] ECR I-1493, para 90.

[16] Case C-465/07 *Elgafaji* [2009] ECR I-921, para 28.

assembly guaranteed by the ECHR appears to be absolute but must be viewed in relation to its social purpose.[17]

EU law not only provides for a prohibition of *refoulement* but also for a right to asylum in Article 18 of the Charter. This provision states that the right to asylum shall be guaranteed with due respect for the Refugee Convention and in accordance with the Treaty on European Union (TEU) and the Treaty on the Functioning of the European Union (TFEU). The Court of Justice has not yet explained how this right to asylum should be interpreted.[18] It may be argued that it includes the right to asylum status.[19] This right is reflected in Directive 2011/95/EU (the Qualification Directive), which provides that a person who qualifies as a refugee or is eligible for subsidiary protection in accordance with the Directive, should be granted refugee status or subsidiary protection status.[20] In his Opinion in *Puid* AG Jääskinen stated that Article 18 of the Charter does 'not create for asylum seekers a substantive right to be granted asylum'. He does recognise, however, that a subjective right to refugee status is provided for in the Qualification Directive.[21] The EU right to asylum status is not absolute. A refugee may be refused refugee status, for example where there are reasons to believe that he has committed a serious crime outside the country of refuge, if there are reasonable grounds to consider him to be a danger to the security of the Member State, or if he constitutes a danger to the community of that Member State.[22] A person who is in need of subsidiary protection may be refused asylum status on similar grounds.[23] Balancing of interests may thus take place in cases in which only the refusal of an asylum status is under dispute. International treaties such as the ECHR do not provide for a right to asylum status.[24]

Lack of Harmonisation of Standards for Asylum Procedures at the International Level

Although the importance of fair asylum procedures for the effective exercise of the prohibition of *refoulement* is widely recognised, the level of harmonisation of standards for such procedures at the international level is remarkably low.[25]

[17] Case C-112/00 *Schmidberger* [2003] ECR I-5659, para 80.

[18] Questions regarding the interpretation of Art 18 of the Charter have been referred to but were not answered by the Court of Justice in Case C-528/11 *Halaf* [2013].

[19] See also UNHCR, *Statement on the right to asylum, UNHCR's supervisory responsibility and the duty of States to cooperate with UNHCR in the exercise of its supervisory responsibility* (August 2012) 13, available at www.refworld.org/docid/5017fc202.html accessed 29 September 2013.

[20] Dir 2011/95/EU of 13 December 2011 on standards for the qualification of third-country nationals or stateless persons as beneficiaries of international protection, for a uniform status for refugees or for persons eligible for subsidiary protection, and for the content of the protection granted [2011] OJ L337/9. See Arts 13 and 18 of the Directive. See also *Elgafaji* (n16) Opinion of AG Maduro, para 21.

[21] Case C-4/11 [2013] *Puid*, Opinion of AG Jääskinen, paras 49–50.

[22] See Arts 12(2) and 14(4) and (5) Dir 2011/95/EU.

[23] Art 17 Dir 2011/95/EU.

[24] See, eg ECtHR 20 July 2010, *A v the Netherlands*, no 4900/06, paras 152–53.

[25] See Costello, 'The European Asylum Procedures Directive' (n 8) 3.

Most importantly, the Refugee Convention does not contain any standards for refugee status determination proceedings. The UN High Commissioner for Refugees (UNHCR) and the Executive Committee of the Programme of the High Commissioner (EXCOM) have adopted guidelines regarding asylum procedures.[26] However, these guidelines are not binding and provide only limited guidance, as they assume that States are free to choose their own procedural system.[27] The ECtHR has set important requirements for procedures in which claims based on the prohibition of *refoulement* are assessed in its case law under the right to an effective remedy recognised in Article 13 ECHR. However, it is not possible to derive a comprehensive set of standards from this case law, as it only addresses a limited number of procedural issues and leaves many questions unanswered. In addition, the (non-binding) views of other supervising bodies such as the Human Rights Committee (HRC) and the Committee against Torture (ComAT) only provide very limited guidance.

As a result of the lack of international standards, asylum procedures adopted by States vary considerably.[28] Costello notes that governments have taken advantage of the leeway allowed by international law 'and manipulated asylum procedures in order to pursue manifold objectives, from deterring and deflecting asylum seekers, to ensuring that failed asylum seekers will be deportable'.[29] Indeed, many States have decided to take measures in reaction to, for example, large influxes of asylum applicants or the political demand for the prevention of abuse of the asylum procedure. In 2001 the UNHCR noted within the Member States of the EU

> a gradual shift of emphasis away from the identification of persons in need of protection towards the deterrence of real or perceived abuse, if not sheer deterrence of arrivals of asylum applicants. Concern about growing backlogs and the difficulty of agreeing on burden-sharing formulas have resulted in policies of deflection, with less attention paid to key issues of responsibility and international solidarity.[30]

Many of the measures taken by EU Member States lead to diminishing safeguards in the asylum procedure. Arguably, one of the most far-reaching is the introduction of accelerated asylum procedures in many Member States. Procedures in these countries are similar in that applications are dealt with within a very short period of time and are often offered limited procedural safeguards.

[26] See, eg UNHCR, *Handbook* (n 7) and EXCOM Conclusion no 8 (XXVIII) 1977, Determination of Refugee Status.

[27] Noll, *Proof, Evidentiary Assessment and Credibility* (n 10) 5.

[28] See UNHCR, *Handbook* (n 7) paras 191–92, and B Gorlick, 'Common Burdens and Standards: Legal Elements in Assessing Claims to Refugee Status' (2003) 15 *International Journal of Refugee Law* 357, 357–58.

[29] Costello (n 8) 3.

[30] UNHCR, *Observations on the European Commission's proposal for a Council Directive on minimum standards on procedures for granting and withdrawing refugee status, COM(2000) 578 final 20 September 2000* (July 2001) para 5, available at www.refworld.org/docid/3f2fd59b4.html accessed 29 September 2013.

EU Standards for Asylum Procedures

The lack of harmonisation of procedural standards in asylum cases (and migration cases in general) as well as the tendency to curtail procedural guarantees in national legal systems was noted by Pieter Boeles in 1997.[31] At the time Boeles concluded that there was a lacuna in legal protection of immigrants at the Community level. The only measure then available was the Council Resolution on minimum guarantees for asylum procedures of 1995.[32]

Since the conclusion of Boeles' research on procedural standards in immigration proceedings, some major developments have taken place at the European level. In 1999 the European Council recognised that the issues of asylum and migration call for the development of a common EU policy. In that year the European Council decided during the summit in Tampere to work towards a Common European Asylum System (CEAS). This system should, according to the Presidency Conclusions, include 'standards for a fair and efficient asylum procedure'. It was even decided that EU legislation should in the longer term lead to a common asylum procedure.[33]

The First Phase: Directive 2005/85/EC

After lengthy and difficult negotiations, Council Directive 2005/85/EC on minimum standards on procedures in Member States for granting and withdrawing refugee status (Directive 2005/85/EC) was adopted.[34] This directive contains minimum standards for the examination of asylum applications at first instance as well as at appeal. The goal of the approximation of rules on the procedures for granting and withdrawing refugee status was to limit the secondary movements of applicants for asylum between Member States where such movement would be caused by differences in legal frameworks.[35] Nevertheless, the minimum set of standards laid down in Directive 2005/85/EC leaves much discretion to the participating Member States, as it contains a large number of vaguely defined concepts and has failed—due to political differences in opinion—to provide clear-cut answers to a number of core issues in procedural asylum law.[36] It therefore did not succeed in

[31] P Boeles, *Fair Immigration Proceedings in Europe* (The Hague/Boston, Martinus Nijhof Publishers,1997), ch 19.

[32] Council Resolution of 20 June 1995 on minimum guarantees for asylum procedures [2006] OJ C274/13.

[33] Presidency Conclusions of the Tampere European Council 15–16 October 1999 (SN 200/99) paras 14–15.

[34] Council Dir 2005/85/EC on minimum standards on procedures in Member States for granting and withdrawing refugee status [2005] OJ L326/13.

[35] Recital 6 Preamble Dir 2005/85/EC. See also Commission, 'Towards a common asylum procedure and a uniform status, valid throughout the Union, for persons granted asylum' COM (2000) 755 final.

[36] According to Michelogiannaki, the negotiations 'were proved to be the most intense, lengthy and difficult negotiations compared to any other that had taken place in the past, regarding the asylum agenda'. M Michelogiannaki, 'The Negotiations of Directive 2005/85/EC' in K Zwaan (ed), *The Procedures Directive, Central Themes, Problem Issues and Implementation in Selected Member States*

effectively harmonising procedural standards.[37] According to Vedsted-Hansen, the Member States' unwillingness to achieve a higher level of harmonisation on asylum procedures could be explained by the fact that non-compliance with administrative and procedural matters 'will be readily discovered both by the affected individuals and by those bodies controlling the implementation of EU law'.[38]

Arguably, the common standards on asylum procedures were also meant to serve the general objective of CEAS, namely the full and inclusive application of the Refugee Convention and safeguards maintaining the *non-refoulement* principle.[39] However, according to the UNHCR and various NGOs, the minimum standards contained in the Directive violated international human rights standards and reflected a race to the bottom. Just before political agreement on the proposed directive was reached, 10 NGOs even asked EU Commissioner for Justice and Home Affairs Vitorino to withdraw the proposal.[40]

The Second Phase: Directive 2013/32/EU

The European Council in The Hague Programme of 2004[41] and the Stockholm Programme of 2009[42] committed itself to establishing a common area of protection and solidarity based on a common asylum procedure and a uniform status for those granted international protection. The deadline for the completion of the second phase of the CEAS was initially 2010 but was later extended to 2012.[43]

According to the Stockholm Programme, the CEAS should be based on high standards of protection. At the same time it must give due regard to fair and effective procedures capable of preventing abuse. The second phase of the CEAS also seeks to achieve a higher level of harmonisation. The European Council stated that it is crucial that individuals, regardless of the Member State in which their application for asylum is lodged, are offered an equivalent level of treatment as regards, for example, procedural arrangements and status determination. 'The

(Nijmegen, Wolf Legal Publishers, 2008) 21. For further discussion of the Procedures Directive see ch 2, section 2.2 in this volume.

[37] See also J Vedsted-Hansen, 'Common EU Standards on Asylum—Optional Harmonisation and Exclusive Procedures?' (2005) 7 *European Journal of Migration and Law* 369, 371.

[38] Ibid, 374.

[39] Ibid, 370.

[40] European Council for Refugees and Exiles, Amnesty International and Human Rights Watch, *Refugee and Human Rights Organisations across Europe Call on EU to Scrap Key Asylum Proposal* (29 March 2004) available at www.ecre.org/media/news/press-releases.html accessed 29 September 2013. See also UNHCR, *UNHCR regrets missed opportunity to adopt high EU asylum standards* (30 April 2004) available at www.unhcr.org/40921f4e4.html accessed 29 September 2013.

[41] Council of the European Union, The Hague Programme: Strengthening Freedom, Security and Justice in the European Union [2005] OJ C53/1.

[42] Council of the European Union, The Stockholm Programme—An open and secure Europe serving and protecting the citizen [2010] OJ C115/1, para 6.2.1.

[43] See also Council of the European Union, Council Conclusions on Borders, Migration and Asylum, Stocktaking and the way forward, 3096th Justice and Home Affairs Council meeting Luxembourg, 9 and 10 June 2011, 4.

objective should be that similar cases should be treated alike and result in the same outcome.'[44]

In order to realise the second phase of the CEAS the Commission issued proposals for recasts of the asylum directives and regulations. The proposal for the recast of Directive 2005/85/EC was introduced by the Commission in 2009.[45] However, as the negotiations in the Council were difficult and did not result in an agreement, the Commission decided to come up with an amended recast proposal in June 2011.[46] The amended proposal aimed to address the concerns of the Member States by recognising the need for flexibility, cost-effectiveness, simplification of rules and the prevention of abuse. The level of protection offered by the recast proposal was lower than that in the original proposal and during the subsequent negotiations some safeguards, in particular for vulnerable groups of asylum applicants, were further decreased. In June 2013 the recast of Directive 2005/85/EC, Directive 2013/32/EU on common procedures for granting and withdrawing international protection status, was finally adopted. The Directive is due to be transposed in the Member States before 20 July 2015. Directive 2005/85/EC is repealed for the Member States bound by this Directive with effect from 21 July 2015. The United Kingdom and Ireland do not take part in Directive 2013/32/EU and remain bound by Directive 2005/85/EC. Where this study uses the term 'Procedures Directive', it refers to the Procedures Directive in general, which includes the texts of both Directive 2005/85/EC and Directive 2013/32/EU.

Directive 2013/32/EU contains a number of improvements in comparison to Directive 2005/85/EC.[47] However, some critics are also disappointed. Peers states that:

> Member States still retain a good deal of flexibility to set fairly low standards as regards the special procedures and in a couple of respects (as regards new listings of 'super-safe third countries' and a new exception from the right to legal aid) standards have been lowered.[48]

Is the European Harmonisation of Asylum Procedures a Failure?

It is questionable whether the attempt to develop common standards for asylum procedures at EU level should be considered a failure, or even harmful, both

[44] The Stockholm Programme (n 42) para 6.2.

[45] European Commission, 'Proposal for a Directive of the European Parliament and of the Council on minimum standards on procedures in Member States for granting and withdrawing international protection (Recast)' COM (2009) 554.

[46] European Commission, 'Amended proposal for a Directive of the European Parliament and of the Council on minimum standards on procedures in Member States for granting and withdrawing international protection (Recast)' COM (2011) 319.

[47] See, eg UNHCR, *Moving further toward a Common European Asylum System, UNHCR's statement on the EU asylum legislative package* (June 2013) available at www.refworld.org/docid/51de61304.html accessed 26 September 2013.

[48] See, S Peers, 'The second phase of the Common European Asylum System: A brave new world—or lipstick on a pig?' April 2013, www.statewatch.org.

from a human rights perspective and from the perspective of harmonising such procedures. In this book it is argued that it should not. In spite of its shortcomings the Procedures Directive could enhance the position of persons who apply for asylum in one of the Member States and lead to at least some form of harmonisation of standards on asylum procedures within the EU. This is not only because the Procedures Directive provides important safeguards in national asylum procedures. More importantly, the Directive has brought many aspects of national asylum procedures within the scope of EU law. As a result, the Charter of Fundamental Rights of the EU and general principles of EU law, such as the right to an effective remedy and the principle of effectiveness, apply. These rights and principles will be used by the Court of Justice of the European Union (Court of Justice) and national courts to interpret the provisions of the Procedures Directive and to test their legality. On the basis of these rights the courts may limit the discretion of Member States and even require the application of additional procedural safeguards that are not included in the Directive. The Charter and general principles of EU law also come into play because of the clear rights included in the Qualification Directive: the right to refugee status for those who qualify as a refugee; the right to subsidiary protection status for those who are in need of subsidiary protection; and the right to be protected against *refoulement*. The principle of effectiveness abolishes procedural hurdles which render the exercise of these rights practically impossible or excessively difficult.

Through the Charter and principles of EU law, the Procedures Directive may, therefore, provide more procedural safeguards to asylum applicants than many had expected at the time of its adoption. Costello explained in 2006, shortly after the adoption of Directive 2005/85/EC, that this 'new legal context and the general principles it incorporates, as well as the inevitable intervention of another supranational jurisdiction, the European Court of Justice, may well thwart the race to the bottom more than the negotiators anticipated'.[49] Of course, the extent to which the Court will be able to do this largely depends on the national courts' willingness to refer questions regarding the interpretation of the Procedures Directive to the Court for preliminary ruling and to interpret these directives in the light of EU fundamental rights and general principles. It should be noted, however, that EU fundamental rights are not only enforced by the Court of Justice and the national courts but also as a result of their incorporation into EU legislation. Indeed, as will be shown later, some of the safeguards following from the EU right to an effective remedy have already been incorporated in Directive 2013/32/EU. Both the initial and the amended proposal for the recast of Directive 2005/85/EC were 'informed by developing case law of the Court of Justice of the European Union and the European Court of Human Rights, especially concerning the right to an effective remedy'.[50]

[49] Costello (n 8) 6.

[50] Amended proposal (n 46) 4 and Initial proposal (n 45) 6.

1.2 IN SEARCH OF EU STANDARDS FOR ASYLUM PROCEDURES

This study focuses on the potential meaning of EU procedural rights, in particular the right to an effective remedy for the asylum procedures of EU Member States. EU Courts have developed an important body of case law on procedural guarantees. Now that national asylum procedures also fall within the scope of EU law, in principle this case law is also applicable to those procedures. It is expected that, when applying EU procedural rights and principles to asylum cases, the Court of Justice will be inspired by relevant international treaties and the judgments and views of the bodies supervising those treaties. This study aspires to derive from EU legislation and (the case law relating to) EU fundamental rights and general principles a set of EU procedural standards for several important issues in national asylum procedures.

1.2.1 Protection of Fundamental Rights in the EU Legal Order

Until the entry into force of the Treaty of Lisbon on 1 December 2009, fundamental rights, including the right to an effective remedy, were mainly protected in the EU as general principles of EU law by the Court of Justice.[51] In its case law the Court of Justice has developed an 'unwritten charter of rights'.[52] Many of the most far-reaching decisions of the Court of Justice in the field of fundamental rights have been the result of preliminary references by national courts.[53]

Murray states that the Member States have so far actively endorsed the approach of the Court of Justice with regard to human rights protection, by including provisions requiring respect for human rights in successive treaties.[54] Article 6(3) TEU states that fundamental rights, as guaranteed by the ECHR and as they result from the constitutional traditions common to the Member States, shall constitute general principles of EU law.

Many of the fundamental rights recognised by the Court of Justice were incorporated in the Charter of Fundamental Rights of the EU. The Charter's Preamble states:

> This Charter reaffirms, with due regard for the powers and tasks of the Union and for the principle of subsidiarity, the rights as they result, in particular, from the constitutional

[51] For the history and development of EU fundamental rights and general principles of EU law, see, eg B de Witte, 'The Role of the ECJ in Human Rights' in P Alston, MR Bustelo and J Heenan (eds), *The EU and Human Rights* (Oxford, Oxford University Press, 1999) 859–97; P Craig, *EU Administrative Law* (Oxford, Oxford University Press, 2006) 484–86; and JL Murray, 'Fundamental Rights in the European Community Legal Order' (2008) 32 *Fordham International Law Journal* 531–50.

[52] Craig, ibid, 484.

[53] Murray, 'Fundamental Rights in the European Community Legal Order' (n 51) 535 and K Lenaerts and JA Gutiérrez-Fons, 'The Constitutional Allocation of Powers and General Principles of EU Law' (2010) 47 *Common Market Law Review* 1629, 1635.

[54] Murray, 'Fundamental Rights' (n 51) 536; see also Lenaerts and Gutiérrez-Fons, 'The Constitutional Allocation of Powers', ibid, 1633.

> traditions and international obligations common to the Member States, the European Convention for the Protection of Human Rights and Fundamental Freedoms, the Social Charters adopted by the Union and by the Council of Europe and the case-law of the Court of Justice of the European Union and of the European Court of Human Rights.

The Charter thus made EU fundamental rights, including general principles of EU law, more visible.[55] The Procedures Directive states in its preamble that it respects fundamental rights and observes the principles recognised in particular by the Charter.[56]

Although until 1 December 2009 the Charter had no binding force, it did play a role in the EU Courts' case law.[57] The Court referred to the Charter mainly in order to reaffirm the existence of a general principle of EU law.[58] Since the entrance into force of the Treaty of Lisbon, the Charter has become binding.[59] The Court of Justice has in its case law referred to the binding force of the Charter.[60] According to Iglesias Sánchez, this is 'an emphatic sign of acknowledgement, highlighting the relevance of the changes in the legal framework after a long period of uncertainty'.[61] In some cases, however, it still only mentioned the Charter in order to reaffirm an existent general principle of EU law[62] or to support its textual interpretation of a provision of an EU directive.[63] In other cases the Court attached much more weight to the Charter. In *DEB*, for example, the Court of Justice considered that the principle of effective judicial protection is enshrined in Article 47 of the Charter and focused on the interpretation of this provision (instead of that of the principle).[64] In this case even though the referring court asked about the compliance with national rules with the principle of effectiveness, the Court of Justice 'promptly placed the Charter at the core of its reasoning'.[65] Iglesias Sánchez considers the judgment in *DEB* to be 'an example of a discernible trend to resort to the Charter rather than to general principles if possible'.[66] He also notes the value of the Charter in governing and inspiring

[55] According to the preamble to the Charter 'it is necessary to strengthen the protection of fundamental rights in the light of changes in society, social progress and scientific and technological developments by making those rights more visible in a Charter'. See also Lenaerts and Gutiérrez-Fons (n 53) 1656.

[56] Recital 8 Preamble Dir 2005/85/EC.

[57] S Iglesias Sánchez, 'The Court and the Charter: The Impact of the Entry into Force of the Lisbon Treaty on the ECJ's Approach to Fundamental Rights' (2012) 49 *Common Market Law Review* 1565, 1569–73.

[58] See, eg Case C-432/05 *Unibet* [2007] ECR I-2271, para 37, Case C-303/05 *Advocaten voor de Wereld* [2007] ECR I-3633, para 46 and Case C-450/06 *Varec* [2008] ECR I-581, para 48.

[59] Art 6(1) TEU.

[60] See, eg Case C-555/07 *Kücüdeveci* [2010] ECR I-365, para 22 and Case C-578/08 *Chakroun* [2010] ECR I-1839, para 44.

[61] S Iglesias Sánchez, 'The Court and the Charter' (n 57)1565, 1576.

[62] See *Kücüdeveci* (n 60) paras 21–22 and Joined Cases C-317/08, C-318/08, C-319/08 and C-320/08 *Alassini et al* [2010] ECR I-2213, para 61.

[63] Case C-403/09 PPU *Deti ek* [2010] ECR I-12193, paras 53–59.

[64] Case C-279/09 *DEB* [2010] ECR I-13849, para 33 *et seq.*

[65] Iglesias Sánchez, (n 57) 1579.

[66] Ibid, 1580.

the interpretation of EU norms in the field of the Area of Freedom, Security and Justice, including asylum.[67]

General Principles of EU Law Recognised by the Court of Justice
Various lists can be found in legal literature of the general principles recognised by the Court of Justice.[68] These include: the principle of equality; the principle of proportionality; the *non bis in idem* principle; the principle of legal certainty and legitimate expectations; the right to an effective remedy; and the principle of good administration. Many of these general principles of EU law are relevant in the context of asylum procedures.

Rights Included in the Charter
The Charter consists of five chapters: Dignity, Freedoms, Equality, Solidarity and Citizen's Rights. Some of the core rights of the ECHR are included in the Charter, such as the right to life, the prohibition of torture and slavery, the right to respect for private life, and the freedom of religion, expression, assembly and association. The Charter also contains economic and social rights, such as the right to education and the right to social security and social assistance.

The Charter lists many rights which may be of particular relevance for asylum cases, such as the right to asylum (Article 18) and the prohibition of *refoulement* and collective expulsions (Article 19). With respect to asylum procedures, Article 47 of the Charter on the right to an effective remedy, and Article 41 on the right to good administration, are particularly relevant.

1.2.2 Scope of Application of the Charter and General Principles of EU Law

For the purpose of this study it is necessary to know when the Member States should abide by the Charter and general principles of EU law. Are they only bound by EU fundamental rights and principles when implementing the Procedures Directive or do these also apply when taking decisions on individual asylum cases which fall within the scope of this directive or other provisions of EU law?

According to Article 51(1) of the Charter, the provisions of the Charter are first of all addressed to the institutions, bodies, offices and agencies of the EU. Furthermore, the Member States are bound by the Charter 'only when they are implementing Union law'. The EU Institutions and the Member States shall

[67] Ibid, 1577.

[68] For a list of procedural guarantees, see CS Kerse, 'General Principles of Community Law: Procedural Guarantees' in U Bernitz and J Nergelius (eds), *General Principles of European Community Law* (The Hague, Kluwer Law International. 2000) 208. For a comprehensive discussion on the most important principles, see T Tridimas, *The General Principles of Community Law* (Oxford, Oxford University Press, 2006) and X Groussot, *General Principles of Community Law* (Groningen, Europa Law Publishing, 2006).

'respect the rights, observe the principles and promote the application' of the Charter in accordance with their respective powers and respecting the limits of the powers of the Union as conferred on it by the Treaties.

The question arises as to when Member States are 'implementing Union law'. According to the Court of Justice, 'the applicability of European Union law entails applicability of the fundamental rights guaranteed by the Charter'.[69] This means that these rights apply where national legislation falls within the scope of EU law. The scope of application of the Charter is thus the same as that of general principles of EU law.[70] The following categories of national measures fall within the scope of EU law and may therefore fall to be tested against general principles of EU law as well as the Charter:[71]

— measures implementing EU law;[72]
— measures adopted under an EU derogation in order to justify a measure which restricts one of the fundamental freedoms protected by the Treaty;[73] and
— measures which otherwise fall within the scope of EU law.[74]

The Court of Justice generally seems to be willing to accept that a sufficient EU law context exists.[75] Nevertheless, several examples can be found in the Court of Justice's case law of cases where the Court considered that the situation fell out of the field of application of EU law.[76] Matters of pure national law are not governed by the Charter and EU general principles.

For the purpose of this study it is important to note that the fact that procedural issues are not governed by EU legislation does not mean that EU fundamental rights do not apply. EU procedural rights and principles, such as the fundamental right to an effective remedy, require that EU rights are effectively protected in national proceedings. If a person claims a right provided for by EU law in national asylum proceedings, those rights and principles may set

[69] Case C-617/10 *Åkerberg* [2013] para 21. This could have been derived from Case C-256/11 *Dereci et al* [2011] para 72.

[70] Explanations relating to the Charter of Fundamental Rights (2007/C 303/02) OJ 14 December 2007, C 303/32. Some authors believe that the Charter's scope of application is more limited than the scope of application of EU general principles. See Lenaerts and Gutiérrez-Fons (n 53) 1657–59.

[71] HG Schermers and DF Waelbroeck, *Judicial Protection in the European Union* (The Hague, Kluwer, 2001), 36, Tridimas, *The General Principles of Community Law* (n 68) 36–42, S Prechal, 'Competence Creep and General Principles of Law' (2010) 3 *Review of European Administrative Law* 8.

[72] See, eg Case 5/88 *Wachauf* [1989] ECR 2609, para 19. 'Implementation' should be understood in a broad sense. See Prechal, 'Competence Creep', ibid, 8.

[73] See, eg Case C-260/89 *ERT* [1991] ECR I-2925, para 43.

[74] Lenaerts and Gutiérrez-Fons (n 53) 1639, state that general principles are applicable where some specific substantive EU rule is applicable to the situation in question.

[75] See, eg *Åkerberg* (n 69) para 21, Joined Cases C-411/10 and C-493/10 *NS and ME et al* [2011] paras 64–69 and *Kücüdeveci* (n 60) paras 23–26. Tridimas notes that there is 'a clear and, indeed, remarkable tendency towards the broad application of general principles, in particular fundamental rights'. Tridimas (n 68) 39.

[76] Case C-299/95 *Kremzow* [1997] ECR I-2629, paras 16–18 and Case C-144/95 *Maurin* [1996] ECR I-2909. Further examples are mentioned in Prechal (n 72) 11 and Iglesias Sánchez (n 57) 1588–90.

requirements as to these proceedings.[77] With regard to national procedural rules, the scope of EU law is therefore also determined by the substantive right claimed in the national procedure.

Since the inclusion of Title IV in the EC Treaty and the adoption of the various directives on asylum, national measures in the field of asylum often fall within the field of application of EU law. Asylum issues that the Directives did not aim to harmonise will fall outside the scope of EU law and therefore remain out of the reach of EU fundamental rights.[78] Section 2.4.2 discusses the scope of application of EU fundamental rights with respect to national asylum procedures. The Procedures Directive provides the Member States with wide discretion with respect to many issues. Therefore section 2.4.2 addresses the question of whether Member States are bound by EU fundamental rights when making use of their discretionary power.

1.2.3 Function of EU Fundamental Rights and General Principles

EU fundamental rights and general principles have been applied by the national courts and the EU Courts for different purposes. First, these courts use those rights and principles to review the legality of EU legislation. The Court of Justice considered that 'respect for human rights is a condition of the lawfulness of Community acts … and that measures incompatible with respect for human rights are not acceptable in the Community'.[79]

EU fundamental rights and general principles can be invoked under Article 263 or Article 267 TFEU to obtain the annulment of an EU measure. An individual may question the legality of an EU measure before a national court on grounds of infringement of EU fundamental rights and general principles. If the national court considers that an EU measure is invalid on this ground, it should refer to the Court of Justice for a preliminary ruling.[80] The Court of Justice has in several cases declared a provision of secondary EU law to be invalid because it infringed a provision of the Charter[81] or a principle of EU law.[82] Section 2.4.1 examines

[77] See Prechal (n 72) 11–13.

[78] Examples may include national rules concerning special protection policies for unaccompanied minors, humanitarian cases and the prohibition of expulsion for medical reasons based on Art 3 ECHR. See H Battjes, *European Asylum Law and International Law* (Leiden/Boston, Martinus Nijhoff, 2006) 88.

[79] Joined Cases C-402/05 P and C-415/05 P *Kadi and Al Barakaat v Council and Commission* [2008] ECR I-6351, para 284. See also para 285.

[80] Case 314/85 *Foto-Frost* [1987] ECR 4199, paras 17–20. See also Tridimas (n 68) 31 and 35. For more detail see ch 2, section 2.5.1 in this volume.

[81] See, eg Case C-236/09 *Association Belge des Consommateurs Test-Achats et al* [2011] para 32 and Joined Cases C-92/09 and C-93/09 *Volker und Marcus Schecke GbR and Hartmut Eifert* [2010] ECR I-11063.

[82] See, eg Case C-25/02 *Rinke* [2003] ECR I-8349, para 27 and Case C-120/86 *Mulder* [1988] ECR I-2321.

the question of whether the standards included in the Procedures Directive are capable of infringing EU fundamental rights and general principles. This question is relevant because Directive 2005/85/EC and Directive 2013/32/EU both allow Member States to provide a higher level of protection than that offered by the standards of the Directive. Arguably, Member States are never forced by those standards to violate EU fundamental rights, as they are generally allowed to introduce or maintain more favourable provisions.[83]

Secondly, the national courts of the Member States and the Court of Justice use the Charter and general principles of EU law to interpret EU legislation.[84] The Court has held that EU legislation cannot be interpreted in such a way that it disregards a fundamental right included in the Charter.[85] Furthermore, it has considered that where an EU measure must be interpreted, preference must be given as far as possible to the interpretation that renders it compatible with general principles of EU law.[86] National rules and practice will be tested against this interpretation of EU law.[87] Finally, the EU Courts have used general principles of EU law to fill in gaps in EU legislation and to supplement the provisions of written EU law.[88]

In summary, EU fundamental rights and general principles may require that relevant EU legislation is set aside and may set additional standards to those explicitly included in EU legislation. In order to discover which requirements are set by EU law for national asylum procedures, therefore, it is necessary to have regard not only to the Procedures Directive, but also to relevant EU fundamental rights and general principles. This book attempts to define the meaning and content of the EU fundamental right to an effective remedy and related rights and general principles for the legality and interpretation of EU legislation on asylum procedures.

1.2.4 Sources of Inspiration of EU Fundamental Rights and General Principles

Both the EU Charter and general principles of EU law have several sources of inspiration, in particular the constitutional traditions and international

[83] See, eg Art 5 Dir 2005/85/EC and Art 5 Dir 2013/32/EU.

[84] The Court has interpreted provisions of secondary EU legislation in the light of the Charter. See *Chakroun* (n 60) para 44 and *Salahadin Abdulla* (n 15) para 54.

[85] *Detiček* (n 63) para 55. This case concerned the compatibility of a regulation with the rights of the child set out in Art 24 of the Charter.

[86] Tridimas (n 68) 29. He refers to several cases including Case C-314/89 *Rauh* [1991] ECR I-1647.

[87] Lenaerts and Gutiérrez-Fons (n 53) 1650.

[88] As to the triple function of general principles of EU law, see Lenaerts and Gutiérrez-Fons ibid, 1629–31.

obligations common to the Member States.[89] Secondary EU legislation[90] and EU soft law[91] may also serve as a source of inspiration for EU fundamental rights and general principles. However, as secondary legislation and EU soft law play only a minor role in this study they will not be addressed in this section.[92] For the purpose of this study by far the most weight is attached to international law as a source of inspiration.

International Law as a Source of Inspiration

Article 6(2) TEU states that the EU shall accede to the ECHR.[93] The EU could also become a party to other human rights treaties.[94] At the time of writing, however, the EU, unlike its Member States, is not a party to human rights treaties such as the ECHR or the ICCPR.[95] The EU is therefore not directly bound by human rights treaties. Although the wording of the case law sometimes suggests differently, the EU Courts therefore have generally not directly applied these treaties.[96] Instead they use human rights treaties as a source of inspiration for EU fundamental rights and general principles of EU law. The following standard consideration has been used by the Court of Justice:

> Fundamental rights form an integral part of the general principles of law the observance of which the Court ensures. For that purpose, the Court draws inspiration from the constitutional traditions common to the Member States and from the guidelines supplied

[89] See the Preamble to the Charter and Art 6(3) TEU.

[90] See Case T-228/02 *Organization des Modhahedines du peuple d'Iran v Council* [2006] ECR II-4665, para 149 and Case T-47/03 *Sison v Council* [2007] ECR II-73, para 204. See also B Kunoy and B Mortansson, 'Case C-578/08, *Chakroun* [2010]' (2010) 47 *Common Market Law Review* 1815, 1825.

[91] See Case C-322/88 *Grimaldi* [1989] ECR 4407, paras 18–19, Case C-188/91 *Deutsche Shell* [1993] ECR I-363 and *Alassini et al* (n 62) para 40. Several Advocates General are of the opinion that the *Grimaldi* obligation should also apply to the EU Courts. See Case C-450/93 *Kalanke* [1995] ECR I-3051, Opinion of AG Tesauro, para 20 and Case C-76/97 *Tögel* [1998] ECR I-5357, Opinion of AG Fennelly, para 34. See also L Senden, *Soft Law in Community Law* (Oxford and Portland OR, Hart Publishing, 2004) 399.

[92] The following Resolutions are relevant: Council Resolution of 20 June 1995 on minimum guarantees for asylum procedures [2006] OJ C274/13; Council Resolution of 26 June 1997 on unaccompanied minors who are nationals of third countries [1997] OJ C221/23; and Council Resolution of 30 November 1992 on manifestly unfounded applications for asylum (not published in the Official Journal).

[93] In April 2013 the draft accession agreement of the EU to the ECHR was finalised. See www.coe.int/t/dghl/standardsetting/hrpolicy/Accession/Meeting_reports_en.asp accessed 29 September 2013.

[94] The Stockholm Programme (n 42) para 6.2.1 mentions a possible accession to the Geneva Convention and its 1967 Protocol.

[95] In Opinion 2/94 the Court of Justice held that the European Community had no competence to accede to the ECHR. According to Groussot, Opinion 2/94 marked the start of an extensive use of the ECtHR's jurisprudence and acceleration in the shaping of fundamental rights. Groussot, *General Principles of Community Law* (n 68) 61.

[96] See, eg Case C-199/11 *Europese Gemeenschap v Otis* [2012] para 47 and Case T-112/98 *Mannesmannröhren-Werke v Commission* [2001] ECR II-729, para 59. *Cf* Case C-60/00 *Carpenter* [2002] ECR I-6279 and Case C-413/99 *Baumbast* [2002] ECR I-7091 where the Court of Justice directly applied Art 8 ECHR. See Groussot, 'UK Immigration Law under Attack and the Direct Application of Article 8 ECHR by the Court of Justice' (2003) 3 *Non state actors and International Law* 199.

> by international instruments for the protection of human rights on which the Member States have collaborated or to which they are signatories.[97]

International law also inspired the drafters of the Charter. The Preamble of the Charter states that the Charter reaffirms rights including those which result from the international obligations common to the Member States and the ECHR as well as from the ECtHR's case law. Many of the rights included in the Charter are clearly based (partly or wholly) on the ECHR. When interpreting the fundamental rights included in the Charter the Court of Justice has relied on the ECtHR's case law.[98]

The Court of Justice has recognised several international treaties as sources of inspiration for EU fundamental rights and general principles of EU law.[99] Among those treaties are the ECtHR, the Refugee Convention,[100] the ICCPR[101] and the UN Convention on the Rights of the Child (CRC)[102] which play a significant role in the context of this study. According to Article 6(3) TEU, the Charter[103] and the Court of Justice's case law, the ECHR has special significance for the development of EU fundamental rights and general principles.[104] Therefore, in many cases in which the Court of Justice applies EU fundamental rights or general principles, it refers to the ECHR and/or the ECtHR's case law. The CAT, which will also be included in this study as a source of inspiration, has so far not been recognised as such by the EU Courts. However, it may be expected that the Court of Justice will recognise it in the future as all Member States are parties to this convention.[105]

Chapter three will further address the Court of Justice's use of international treaties as sources of inspiration for EU fundamental rights and principles. It will in particular explain the (relative) weight which should be given to these sources of inspiration *for the purpose of this study.*

The Constitutional Traditions of the Member States

Although the constitutional traditions of the Member State may be relevant in defining the meaning of the EU right to an effective remedy, they are not included in this study (see section 1.4). The reason for this is that it is very difficult to identify principles which are common to the constitutional traditions of the

[97] Case C-540/03 *Parliament v Council* [2006] ECR I-5769, para 35.

[98] See, eg *DEB* (n 64) where the Court of Justice interpreted Art 47 of the Charter in the light of the ECtHR's case law concerning Art 6 ECHR.

[99] The European Social Charter in Case C-438/05 *Viking Line* [2007] ECR I-10779, para 44 and Case 149/77 *Defrenne* [1978] ECR 1365, para 28 and the ILO Conventions in *Defrenne*, para 28.

[100] *Salahadin Abdulla* (n 15) paras 51–53 and Joined Cases C-57/09 and C-101/09 *B and D* [2010] ECR I-10979, paras 76–78.

[101] Case C-347/87 *Orkem* [1989] ECR I-1083 and *Parliament v Council* (n 97).

[102] *Parliament v Council* (n 97), see also Case C-244/06 *Dynamic Medien* [2008] ECR I-505.

[103] See the Preamble and Art 52(3) of the Charter. Other human rights conventions such as the ICCPR or the CAT are not explicitly mentioned by the Charter.

[104] Case C-222/84 *Johnston* [1986] ECR 1651, see also *Parliament v Council* (n 97) para 35.

[105] See Battjes, *European Asylum Law* (n 76) 85.

Member States. First, in order to discover such principles we would need to assess the legislation of the 27 Member States, which would be complicated and time-consuming. This may also be the reason why, in practice, the Court of Justice does not often enter into a comparative analysis of the constitutions of the Member States.[106] Secondly, the EU Courts have not set out any criteria on the basis of which it should be decided whether a constitutional tradition is common to the EU Member States.[107]

Arguably, an EU general principle is common to the constitutional traditions of the Member States if it is laid down in a treaty of which the Member States are signatories. Groussot states that the most common approach is to let the use of the constitutional traditions come after international law. The reason is that international law is appraised as having a unifying potential. International obligations are also easier to identify than the common constitutional traditions of the Member States. Thus only if the international treaties do not provide any guidance, may the absence of an assessment of the constitutional traditions of the Member States be problematic.[108] In such a situation the Court of Justice could accept a certain interpretation of an EU fundamental right or general principle on the basis of the common constitutional traditions of the Member States alone.[109]

1.3 AIM OF THE STUDY

The purpose of this study is generally to examine the potential meaning of EU fundamental rights and general principles for national asylum procedures. In particular, it aims to derive a set of EU procedural standards for several key issues of asylum procedures from EU legislation and/or the EU right to an effective remedy. This study addresses the meaning of the EU right to an effective remedy in its broadest sense and also takes into account requirements following from EU procedural rights and principles which are included in or strongly connected to

[106] See, eg S Douglas-Scott, 'A Tale of Two Courts: Luxembourg, Strasbourg and the Growing European Rights *Aquis*' (2006) 43 *Common Market Law Review* 629, 658; de Witte, 'The Role of the ECJ in Human Rights' (n 51) 878; and Murray (n 51) 537. The Advocates General usually analyse the constitutional traditions of the Member States rather than the Court of Justice.

[107] See AL Young, 'The Charter, Constitution and Human Rights: Is this the Beginning of the End for Human Rights Protections by Community Law' (2005) 11 *European Public Law* 219, 223–24; Groussot (n 68) 50. The Court of Justice's considerations in Joined Cases C-46/87 and C-227/88 Hoechst [1989] ECR I-2859, para 17 seem to point in the direction of an evaluative approach and to exclude the possibility of the minimalist approach. In Case C-144/04 *Mangold* [2005] ECR I-9981, however, the Court of Justice accepted a general principle, which was not obviously (or even obviously not) common to the constitutional traditions of the Member States. D Schiek, 'The ECJ Decision in *Mangold*: A Further Twist on Effects of Directives and Constitutional Relevance of Community Equality Legislation' 35 *Industrial Law Journal* 329, 329–41. For an overview of other critics, see Lenaerts and Gutiérrez-Fons (n 53) 1654.

[108] See also section 1.4.

[109] The *Mangold* case (n 107) concerning the prohibition of age discrimination, may be an example. See Schiek 'The ECJ Decision in *Mangold*' (n 107) 329–41.

the right to an effective remedy. Examples of such rights and principles include: the right to a fair trial; the principle of effectiveness; and the right to good administration.[110] The study aims to define the meaning of the EU right to an effective remedy for the following procedural topics:

1. the right to remain on the territory during asylum proceedings in first instance and appeal;
2. the asylum applicant's right to be heard in first instance and appeal; and
3. questions relating to evidence in asylum procedures:
   - the standard and burden of proof and evidentiary assessment;
   - judicial review of the establishment and qualification of the facts; and
   - the use of secret evidence.

The book is divided in three parts. Part one addresses several preliminary issues which are necessary to define the meaning of EU right to an effective remedy for national asylum proceedings. Part two then examines the requirements following from the EU right to an effective remedy for the three specific procedural topics mentioned above. In part three conclusions are drawn.

Preliminary Issues (Part I)

Chapter two introduces the CEAS and, in particular, the Procedures Directive. It also examines the potential impact and the scope of application of EU fundamental rights in asylum cases taking into account the particular characteristics of the Procedures Directive. Chapter three discusses the Court of Justice's use of international treaties as sources of inspiration for EU fundamental rights. In particular, it examines the (relative) weight which should be accorded to the ECHR, the Refugee Convention, the CAT, the ICCPR and the CRC as a source of inspiration for the EU right to an effective remedy when applied in the context of asylum procedures. Chapter four introduces the EU procedural rights, which will be used in this study in order to build a set of EU standards for the themes discussed in later chapters. It shows how EU fundamental rights have limited the procedural autonomy of the Member States. In addition, this chapter explains how EU procedural rights and principles are interlinked and it discusses their general content. It also gives an overview of the specific provisions of international treaties, which may inspire the Court of Justice when defining the meaning and content of the EU right to an effective remedy in the context of asylum. Finally, three basic concepts are introduced which may help to explain the case law of the Court of Justice as well as the case law of the ECtHR and predict how they will rule on procedural issues in the future. Chapter five draws conclusions as to the preliminary issues discussed and explains the methodology applied in the following chapters.

[110] See further ch 4.

Key Issues of Asylum Procedures (Part II)

Chapter six addresses the question whether, according to EU law, Member States are required to allow asylum applicants to remain on their territory during first instance proceedings and the appeal procedure. In addition, it examines whether the Member States must grant applicants the opportunity to lodge an appeal against this expulsion before being expelled. Chapter seven addresses the EU standards with regard to the asylum applicant's right to be personally heard on his asylum motives in first instance and appeal proceedings. The statements of the claimant play an essential role in the assessment of whether this person runs a risk of *refoulement* upon return to his country of origin. Chapter eight examines the EU requirements with regard to the standard and burden of proof and the evidentiary assessment in asylum cases. Chapter nine concerns the standard of judicial review in asylum cases. It examines in particular whether the (first instance) courts of some Member States can defer (more or less) to the authorities' decision on the establishment of the facts, or whether they are required to apply a full judicial review to the asylum decision. Chapter ten considers the use of secret information in asylum proceedings. This chapter specifically addresses procedural safeguards applying to asylum cases in which (part of) the establishment of the facts is based on evidence gathered by the authorities, which is not made available to the asylum applicant himself or his legal representative.

Conclusions (Part III)

Chapter eleven recapitulates the methodology used in this study. It draws some conclusions as to the achievements of the Procedures Directive up to the time of writing and its potential impact for the future. It also contains a list of procedural standards which were derived from the Procedures Directive and the EU right to an effective remedy described in chapters six to ten.

1.4 SCOPE AND LIMITATIONS OF THE STUDY

The section will set out the scope and limitations of the study and explain some of the choices which have been made in order to clearly define the research topic.

Focus on EU Law

As is apparent from the central research question described in section 1.3, this study focuses primarily on EU law. Its purpose is to develop a set of EU procedural standards for several important issues in national asylum procedures. International law (the ECtHR, the Refugee Convention, the ICCPR, the CAT and the CRC) is only included in this study as a source of inspiration for EU fundamental rights. It is, therefore, only in this context that the study assesses the requirements for asylum procedures which follow from those treaties.

No Assessment of National Law

This study does not include an assessment of the national law and practices of Member States. It only briefly refers to European Commission evaluations and UNHCR research, which examined the implementation of the Procedures Directive in the Member States, in order to show how certain procedural aspects addressed in this study cause problems or are discussed in practical and not just in theoretical terms. However, a set of EU standards for national asylum procedures has been developed in the abstract on the basis of EU legislation, the EU Courts' case law and relevant sources of inspiration.

Asylum Procedures Governed by the Procedures Directive

This study only assesses which EU standards should apply to asylum procedures which fall within the scope of the Procedures Directive. Asylum applications governed by the Procedures Directive (procedural standards) are also governed by the Qualification Directive (substantive standards).[111] The standards laid down by the Qualification Directive are relevant for the purpose of this study for two reasons. First, it defines the content of the substantive EU rights claimed by asylum applicants: the right to asylum and the prohibition of *refoulement*. National procedural rules which render the effective exercise of these rights impossible or excessively difficult are contrary to EU law. Furthermore, it will be argued in section 4.5.3.1 that the nature of the substantive EU rights claimed by a person defines to a certain extent the level of procedural protection which must be offered to that person. Secondly, the Qualification Directive contains standards regarding several evidentiary issues which are addressed in chapter seven. The standard of proof which must be met in asylum cases should be derived from the criteria for qualifying as a refugee or a person eligible for subsidiary protection included in the Directive. Moreover, Article 4 of the Qualification Directive provides for standards concerning the burden of proof and evidentiary assessment. For these reasons the Qualification Directive is included in this study where it is relevant.

This study does not address the procedural guarantees applicable when a person claims that his expulsion, extradition or transfer to another country will violate the prohibition of *refoulement* in a procedure governed by an EU measure other than the Procedures Directive. A claim of a risk of *refoulement* may be made in the context of a refusal of entry to the EU at the border under the Schengen Borders Code,[112] a transfer to another Member State on the basis of the Dublin Regulation or a return procedure governed by the Return Directive.[113] In such procedures,

[111] See Arts 2(b) and 3(1) Dirs 2005/85/EC and 2013/32/EU and Art 1 and 2(g) Dir 2011/95/EU.

[112] Reg (EC) No 562/2006 of the European Parliament and of the Council of 15 March 2006 establishing a Community Code on the rules governing the movement of persons across borders [2006] OJ L105/1.

[113] Dir 2008/115/EC of the European Parliament and of the Council of 16 December 2008 on common standards and procedures in Member States for returning illegally staying third-country nationals [2008] OJ L348/98.

the risk of a violation of the prohibition of *refoulement* should also be assessed. Arguably, many of the standards which apply to asylum procedures governed by the Procedures Directive should also apply to those procedures. However, border, Dublin or return proceedings have different characteristics to asylum procedures, which may influence the level of procedural protection which should be offered to the individual. In Dublin cases the asylum applicant will be transferred to another EU Member State, which may impact on, for example, the burden of proof. A return procedure may follow an asylum procedure, which could have implications for the procedural safeguards which need to be offered. If a person first claims a violation of the prohibition of *refoulement* when a decision to refuse entry at the border or to return him to his country of origin is taken, the most logical step would be to lodge an asylum claim. From the moment the asylum claim is lodged the Procedures Directive applies.

Directive 2005/85/EC and Directive 2013/32/EU

The study will define the meaning of the EU right to an effective remedy for the interpretation and validity of Directive 2005/85/EC and its recast Directive 2013/32/EU. Member States remain bound by Directive 2005/85/EC until they have transposed Directive 2013/32/EU or the time limit for transposing Directive 2013/32/EU has passed on 20 July 2015. After this date the UK and Ireland will remain bound by Directive 2005/85/EC as they are not taking part in the adoption of Directive 2013/32/EU. The conclusions with regard to the interpretation and validity of Directive 2005/85/EC will thus remain relevant after 20 July 2015.

No Questions Concerning the Exclusion from an Asylum Status and Detention

This study only concerns the assessment of the question whether a person falls within the scope of the EU prohibition of *refoulement*, according to the criteria laid down in the Qualification Directive. Most persons who have a well-founded fear of persecution or run a real risk of serious harm are not only protected by the prohibition of *refoulement* but will also be granted asylum status on the basis of Article 13 or 18 of the Qualification Directive. However, some persons in need of protection will be excluded from such a status, for example, because they have committed serious crimes in their country of origin or because they constitute a danger to the national security or community of the Member State to which they have moved.[114] EU procedural standards which apply to the decision to refuse a person asylum status or to withdraw asylum status for reasons other than that protection against expulsion is no longer necessary, will not be examined in this study. The reason for this is that the nature of the EU right involved in such a decision (the right to asylum) is different from the EU right to protection against

[114] Arts 12(2) and 14(4) and (5) and 18 Dir 2011/95/EU.

refoulement. While the EU right to asylum may be subject to limitations, the EU prohibition of *refoulement* is absolute. Before refusing or withdrawing asylum status for national security reasons, the interests of the person concerned should be balanced against the interests of the State. This has implications for the level of procedural protection which should be offered and specific procedural questions may arise.[115] For example, the burden of proof and the required intensity of judicial review is different in the case of a balancing test in the context of a decision as to whether asylum status may be refused for reasons of national security, to that in the case of a decision regarding the existence of a real risk of *refoulement* upon return to the country of origin. In addition, procedural guarantees applicable to detention cases falling within the scope of Article 18 of Directive 2005/85/EC and Article 26 of Directive 2013/32/EU will not be assessed.

Limited Number of Procedural Topics

The procedural topics which will be examined in the second part of this book were chosen because the way they are regulated in a Member State arguably determines to a significant extent the fairness of the asylum procedure. Another reason to choose these particular topics was the assumption that they cause problems in practice in at least some Member States. Several important procedural topics, such as the right of access to the asylum procedure, the right to (free) legal assistance and interpretation services, the application of safe country of origin, first country of asylum and safe third-country concepts, and the use of very speedy (accelerated) procedures, will not be discussed in this book. It should be noted that these procedural topics are also governed by the Procedures Directive and, as a result, by the EU right to an effective remedy and related procedural rights. The methodology used in this study to discover the meaning of the EU procedural right to an effective remedy can, therefore, also be applied to these procedural topics.[116]

[115] See also ch 4, section 4.5.3.1 in this volume.

[116] For the right of access to (free) legal assistance in relation to the right of access to court, see AM Reneman, 'Access to an Effective Remedy before a Court or Tribunal in Asylum Cases' in E Guild and P Minderhoud (eds), *The First Decade of EU Migration and Asylum Law* (Leiden/Boston, Martinus Nijhoff, 2011) 401.

Part I

Preliminary Issues

2

The Common European Asylum System and the Applicability of EU Procedural Standards

IN ORDER TO be able to interpret the Procedures Directive and to test the legality of its provisions, it is necessary to know more about the context in which it was adopted, its purposes, its system and the character of its norms. This chapter will therefore consider the Common European Asylum System (CEAS) of which the Procedures Directive is part (section 2.1) as well as Directives 2005/85/EC and 2013/32/EU (section 2.2).

Relevance of the Qualification Directive

When assessing the procedural guarantees which apply to asylum procedures one cannot ignore the importance of the Qualification Directive. This directive defines the content of the right to asylum and the prohibition of *refoulement*, the substantive EU rights usually claimed by asylum applicants during the asylum procedure. National procedural rules should not undermine the effective exercise of these rights. These substantive rights also determine, to some extent, the level of procedural protection which should be offered.[1] Furthermore, the Qualification Directive contains minimum standards for the evidentiary issues which will be discussed in chapter eight.[2] This directive will be introduced in Section 2.3.

Potential Impact and Scope of Application of EU Fundamental Rights

The Procedures Directive allows that Member States can offer a higher level of protection than that required by its standards, and leaves discretion to the Member States in designing their asylum procedure. This raises two important questions relating to the potential impact and scope of application of EU fundamental rights. These questions must be addressed in order to define the meaning and content of EU procedural rights for the themes which will be addressed in chapters six to ten.

[1] See further ch 4, section 4.5.3 in this volume.

[2] See also ch 1, section 1.5 in this volume.

Testing the Legality of the Procedures Directive's Provisions
First, we need to consider whether the standards included in the Procedures Directive are capable of infringing EU fundamental rights. Both Directive 2005/85/EC (which contains minimum standards) and Directive 2013/32/EU allow Member States to introduce or maintain more favourable provisions than the standards included in the Directive, provided that those provisions are compatible with the Directive. Arguably, Member States are, therefore, never forced by those standards to violate EU fundamental rights. Section 2.4.1 explains that the Court of Justice is competent to test the legality of the standards included in the Procedures Directive against EU fundamental rights, and sets out circumstances in which these standards should be considered invalid.

Applying EU Fundamental Rights to National Asylum Procedures
Secondly, questions arise with regard to the *scope of application* of EU fundamental rights in the context of the Procedures Directive. Directives 2005/85/EC and 2013/32/EU allow exceptions to the procedural safeguards which should be offered to asylum applicants and many vague terms are used.[3] Member States may argue that they are not bound by EU fundamental rights when making use of their discretionary power, because the national measures implementing this discretionary power fall outside the scope of EU law. It is contended in section 2.4.2 that this line of reasoning is not compatible with the case law of the Court of Justice. According to the Court of Justice, Member States are bound by EU fundamental rights when making use of the discretion allowed by EU legislation.

The Role of the National Courts and the Court of Justice
Finally, it is relevant to examine how questions regarding the interpretation and legality of the provisions of the Procedures Directive may be may be brought before the national courts and the Court of Justice. This issue is addressed in section 2.5.

2.1 THE COMMON EUROPEAN ASYLUM SYSTEM AND ITS LEGAL BASIS

2.1.1 Legal Basis of EU Asylum Legislation

With the Treaty of Amsterdam, which was concluded in 1997, asylum and immigration was moved from the third pillar to the first pillar of the European Union. The relevant provisions with regard to this area were laid down in Title IV of Part Three of the former EC Treaty (Articles 61 to 69). Article 63 of the former EC

[3] See further section 2.2.3.

Treaty required the Council to adopt the following measures within a period of five years after the entry into force of the Treaty of Amsterdam:[4]

- measures on asylum;
- measures on refugees and displaced persons;
- measures on immigration policy; and
- measures defining the rights and conditions under which nationals of third countries who are legally resident in a Member State may reside in other Member States.

The Procedures Directive, together with the Qualification Directive, is based on Article 63(1) of the former EC Treaty.

Since the entry into force of the Treaty of Lisbon, the legal basis for EU policies on border checks, asylum and immigration can be found in chapter two of Title V of the Treaty on the Functioning of the European Union (TFEU) (Articles 77 to 80). Article 78 TFEU states that the EU shall develop a common policy on asylum, subsidiary protection and temporary protection with a view to offering appropriate status to any third-country national requiring international protection and ensuring compliance with the principle of *non-refoulement*. Like Article 63 of the former EC Treaty, this provision states that EU asylum policy must be in accordance with the Refugee Convention and other relevant treaties.

2.1.2 Policy Framework: The Common European Asylum System

The Procedures Directive, together with the Qualification Directive, the Dublin Regulation, the Reception Conditions Directive (RCD)[5] and arguably the Temporary Protection Directive (TPD)[6] are part of the CEAS. It was decided to work towards establishing a CEAS during a special meeting held on 15 and 16 October 1999 in Tampere. The CEAS was to be established as part of the European Council's objective to develop the EU as an area of freedom, security and justice. It was agreed that this system should include a clear and workable determination of the State responsible for the examination of an asylum application, common standards for a fair and efficient asylum procedure, common minimum conditions of reception of asylum applicants, and the approximation of rules on the recognition

[4] Measures to be adopted pursuant to points 2(b), 3(a) and 4 of Art 63 were not subject to this five-year period. According to Art 67 of the former EC Treaty, during the initial period of five years after the entry into force of the Treaty of Amsterdam, these measures had to be adopted according to the consultation procedure. After this period, measures based on Art 63 EC Treaty had to be adopted according to the co-decision procedure.

[5] Council Dir 2003/9/EC of 27 January 2003 laying down minimum standards for the reception of asylum seekers [2003] OJ L31/18, based on Art 63(1)(b) EC Treaty.

[6] Council Dir 2001/55/EC of 20 July 2001 on minimum standards for giving temporary protection in the event of a mass influx of displaced persons and on measures promoting a balance of efforts between Member States in receiving such persons and bearing the consequences thereof [2001] OJ L212/12, based on Art 63(2)(a) EC Treaty.

and content of the refugee status. These measures had to be completed with measures on subsidiary forms of protection offering an appropriate status to any person in need of such protection. It was agreed that in the longer term, EU rules should lead to a common asylum procedure and a uniform status for those who are granted asylum valid throughout the Union.[7] This aim was reaffirmed in The Hague Programme of 2004[8] and The Stockholm Programme of 2009.[9] For this purpose a recast of the Qualification Directive was adopted in 2011.[10] The recasts of the Procedures Directive,[11] the RCD[12] and the Dublin Regulation[13] followed in June 2013.

Objectives

The main objective of the first phase measures constituting the CEAS was simply to lay down minimum standards.[14] The second phase of the CEAS aimed to achieve a higher level of harmonisation. The preambles of all the first phase and second measures of CEAS state that they aim to preclude secondary movements of third-country nationals.[15] Differences in protection or reception standards between Member States may encourage persons to move from one Member State to another. Therefore, harmonisation of those standards is deemed necessary. The European Council stated with respect to the second phase of CEAS that it is crucial that individuals, regardless of the Member State in which their application for asylum is lodged, are offered an equivalent level of treatment including in procedural arrangements and status determination. 'The objective should be that similar cases should be treated alike and result in the same outcome.'[16]

Another main objective of CEAS is to ensure respect for the fundamental rights of third-country nationals.[17] In the Presidency Conclusions of the Tampere summit, the European Council reaffirmed the importance the EU and Member

[7] See also recital 3 Preamble Dir 2005/85/EC.

[8] Council of the European Union, The Hague Programme: Strengthening Freedom, Security and Justice in the European Union [2005] OJ C53/1.

[9] Council of the European Union, The Stockholm Programme—An open and secure Europe serving and protecting the citizen [2010] OJ C115/1, para 6.2.1.

[10] Dir 2011/95/EU of the European Parliament and of the Council of 13 December 2011 on standards for the qualification of third-country nationals or stateless persons as beneficiaries of international protection, for a uniform status for refugees or for persons eligible for subsidiary protection, and for the content of the protection granted [2011] OJ L337/9.

[11] Dir 2013/32/EU of 26 June 2013 on common procedures for granting and withdrawing international protection (recast) [2013] OJ L180/60.

[12] Dir 2013/33/EU of 26 June 2013 laying down standards for the reception of applicants for international protection (recast) [2013] OJ L180/96.

[13] Reg (EU) No 604/2013 of 26 June 2013 establishing the criteria and mechanisms for determining the Member State responsible for examining an application for international protection lodged in one of the Member States by a third-country national or a stateless person (recast) [2013] OJ L180/31.

[14] See, eg recital 5 Preamble and Art 1 Dir 2005/85/EC.

[15] See, eg recital 6 Preamble Dir 2005/85/EC and recital 13 Preamble Dir 2013/32/EU.

[16] The Stockholm Programme (n 9) para 6.2.

[17] See H Battjes, *European Asylum Law and International Law* (Leiden/Boston, Martinus Nijhoff, 2006) 201.

States attach to absolute respect for the right to seek asylum.[18] The conclusions, moreover, state that the CEAS should be based on the full and inclusive application of the Refugee Convention, thus ensuring that nobody is sent back to a country where they would suffer persecution, that is, it maintains the principle of *non-refoulement*.[19] This was confirmed in the Stockholm Programme. According to this programme, the CEAS should be based on high protection standards. At the same time it must give due regard to fair and effective procedures capable of preventing abuse.[20]

The aim of ensuring respect for human rights is reflected in Article 63(1) of the former EC Treaty, Article 78 TFEU and the preambles of the measures adopted under CEAS, which refer to the fact that CEAS is based on respect for the Refugee Convention.[21] In addition, the preambles of all first phase and second phase measures except the TPD state that they respect fundamental rights and observe the principles specifically recognised by the Charter.[22]

Applicability to Third-Country Nationals Only

All first phase and second phase measures adopted under the CEAS are only applicable to asylum applications lodged by third-country nationals.[23] Asylum applications submitted by EU nationals thus fall outside the scope of the CEAS.

Character of the Norms

The level of harmonisation achieved by directives adopted under the first phase of CEAS is rather limited, because the standards laid down in those directives are minimum standards.[24] This means that Member States may introduce or maintain more favourable standards, in so far as these standards are compatible with the Directive.[25] The aim of the second phase measures was to raise the level of harmonisation and strictly speaking they no longer contain minimum standards.[26] However, the Directives still include a provision which allows Member States to introduce or maintain more favourable standards, insofar as those standards are compatible with the Directives.[27] Section 2.4.1 examines whether, and if so in which circumstances, these (minimum) standards are capable of infringing EU fundamental rights.

[18] See also recital 10 Preamble Dir 2004/83/EC and recital 5 Preamble Dir 2003/9/EC.

[19] Presidency Conclusions of the Tampere European Council 15–16 October 1999 (SN 200/99) para 13.

[20] The Stockholm Programme (n 9) para 6.2.1.

[21] See, eg recital 2 Preamble Dir 2005/85/EC and recital 3 Preamble Dir 2013/32/EU.

[22] See, eg recital 8 Preamble Dir 2005/85/EC and recital 60 Preamble Dir 2013/32/EU.

[23] Arts 1 and 2(c) Dir 2001/55/EC, Art 3(1) Dir 2003/9/EC and Art 3(1) Dir 2013/33/EU, Art 1 Reg 343/2003 and Art 1 Reg 604/2013, Art 1 Dir 2004/83/EC and Art 1 Dir 2011/95/EU, Art 2(b) and (c) Dir 2005/85/EC and Art 2(b) and (c) Dir 2013/32/EU.

[24] See Art 63(1) and (2)(a) of the former EC Treaty.

[25] Art 5 Dir 2005/85/EC; Art 3 2004/83/EC; Art 4 Dir 2003/9/EC; and Art 5 Dir 2001/55/EC.

[26] Art 78 TFEU.

[27] See, eg Art 5 Dir 2013/32/EU and Art 3 Dir 2011/95/EU.

Relation between the Measures Adopted under the CEAS

The fact that the measures adopted under the CEAS are constituents of a system implies that all their provisions must be read conjointly.[28] In these measures common definitions are used. An important example is the term 'application for asylum', which can be found in the Procedures Directive, the Dublin Regulation and the RCD.[29] Furthermore, several cross-references can be found in the measures of the CEAS. The Procedures Directive refers several times to provisions of the Qualification Directive. For example, Article 10(1)(a) of Directive 2005/85/EC, which includes the duty to inform the asylum applicant of his obligations, refers to Article 4 of the Qualification Directive. Article 4 imposes a duty upon the asylum applicant to submit all elements needed to substantiate the application for international protection.

Relation with Other Measures Adopted on the Basis of Article 63 of the Former EC Treaty

The measures adopted under the Common Asylum System are not only linked to each other, but also to other measures adopted on the basis of Article 63 EC Treaty. These include EU measures constituting the EU removal and repatriation policy[30] such as the Return Directive adopted in 2008.[31] Other measures which have been adopted on the basis of Article 63 EC Treaty, which are also relevant for asylum applicants, include the Directives regarding family reunification[32] and human trafficking.[33]

2.2 THE PROCEDURES DIRECTIVE

Directive 2005/85/EC

Directive 2005/85/EC introduces a minimum framework in the EU for procedures for granting and withdrawing refugee status. According to the Tampere conclusions, these procedures need to be fair and efficient.[34] The legal basis for the

[28] Battjes, *European Asylum Law* (n 17) 211. This is what the Court of Justice did in Case C-179/11 *Cimade and GISTI* [2012].

[29] Battjes, ibid, 206–207.

[30] Para 1.6.4 of The Hague Programme (n 8) called for the establishment of an effective removal and repatriation policy based on common standards for persons to be returned in a humane manner and with full respect for their human rights and dignity.

[31] Dir 2008/115/EC of the European Parliament and of the Council of 16 December 2008 on common standards and procedures in Member States for returning illegally-staying third-country nationals [2008] OJ L348/98. For example, Art 13(4) Dir 2008/115/EC refers to Art 15 Dir 2005/85/EC.

[32] Council Dir 2003/86/EC of 22 September 2003 on the right to family reunification [2003] OJ L251/12, based on Art 63(3)(a) of the former EC Treaty.

[33] Dir 2004/81/EC on the residence permit issued to third-country nationals who are victims of trafficking in human beings or who have been the subject of an action to facilitate illegal immigration, who cooperate with the competent authorities [2004] OJ L261/19, based on Art 63(3) EC Treaty.

[34] Presidency Conclusions of the Tampere European Council 15–16 October 1999 (SN 200/99) para 14.

Directive is Article 63 (1)(d) of the former EC Treaty. The Directive was adopted by the Council on 13 December 2005 as the final asylum measure of the legislative programme.

The directive was the result of lengthy and difficult negotiations.[35] Negotiations with regard to the first proposal for the Directive came to a standstill and the proposal was withdrawn. The Commission issued a new proposal in June 2002. The process progressed slowly, as Member States wanted to adhere to the special characteristics of their asylum procedures. Article 39 on appeal procedures and suspensive effect, for example, was discussed extensively, because national procedures differed widely on this point. Furthermore, in several countries the national asylum policy was revised and the relation of these changes to the proposal of the Directive had to be analysed.

On 29 April 2004 a political agreement on the Directive was reached.[36] After the political agreement the negotiations on the minimum common list of safe countries of origin were continued. The Directive was published on 15 December 2005 and had to be transposed in the Member States before 1 December 2007.[37] Article 15 on the right to legal aid and representation had to be implemented by 1 December 2008.

The proposal for the Directive was subjected to heavy criticism. The European Parliament had proposed a list of 102 amendments to the Directive.[38] None of these amendments was taken into account by the Council.[39] The amendments related to the right to remain in the Member State during the appeals procedure, the right to free legal aid, detention of an asylum applicant and a duty for the Member States to give notice of the decision on the asylum application within a time limit of six months.

The United Nations High Commissioner for Refugees (UNHCR) and several NGOs expressed fundamental criticism of the proposal. Just before political agreement on the proposed directive was reached, 10 NGOs asked EU Commissioner for Justice and Home Affairs Vitorino to withdraw the proposal. The organisations were concerned that proposals to designate certain countries as 'safe countries of origin' or 'safe third countries', and the absence of a guaranteed right for all

[35] M Michelogiannaki, 'The Negotiations of Directive 2005/85/EC' in K Zwaan (ed), *The Procedures Directive, Central Themes, Problem Issues and Implementation in Selected Member States* (Nijmegen, Wolf Legal Publishers, 2008) 21.

[36] See for the negotiation process, D Ackers, 'The Negotiations on the Asylum Procedures Directive' (2005) 7 *European Journal of Migration and Law* 1 and Michelogiannaki, 'The Negotiations of Directive 2005/85/EC' (n 35).

[37] Art 43 Dir 2005/85/EC.

[38] European Parliament, 'Legislative resolution on the amended proposal for a Council directive on minimum standards on procedures in Member States for granting and withdrawing refugee status' (14203/2004 – C6-0200/2004 – 2000/0238(CNS)).

[39] Michelogiannaki (n 35) 21.

asylum applicants to remain in a country of asylum pending an appeal, violated EU Member States' international obligations.[40]

The European Parliament challenged the legality of several provisions of Directive 2005/85/EC before the Court of Justice. It asked for the annulment of Articles 29(1) and (2) and 36(3) of the Directive, which lay down the procedures for adopting and amending common minimum lists of safe countries of origin (Article 29) and European safe countries (Article 36). The European Parliament argued that, according to Article 67(5) of the EC Treaty, those lists should be adopted and amended according to the co-decision procedure of Article 251 of the former EC Treaty. The challenged provisions only envisaged a consultative role for the European Parliament in adopting the lists. The Court of Justice deemed Parliament's appeal to be well founded and annulled the challenged provisions in a judgment of 6 May 2008.[41]

Directive 2013/32/EU

The recast proposal of Directive 2005/85/EC was introduced by the Commission in 2009.[42] The main objective of this proposal was to 'ensure higher and more coherent standards on procedures for granting and withdrawing international protection that would guarantee an adequate examination of the protection needs of third country nationals or stateless persons in line with international and Community obligations of Member States'.[43] The proposal also aimed to simplify and consolidate procedural notions and devices and improve coherence between asylum instruments.[44] The proposal introduced a single asylum procedure with the same minimum guarantees for refugee and subsidiary protection claims. It contained detailed standards with respect to, for instance, the training of personnel examining applications and taking decisions on international protection, the use of medico-legal reports, and the examination of applications of persons with special needs. It also removed many of the opportunities to derogate from procedural guarantees which had been included in the Directive, such as the right to a personal interview and the right to free legal aid. In addition, the proposal limited the number of situations in which asylum proceedings could be accelerated. Finally, it provided for the right to an effective remedy with automatic suspensive effect, which provides for a full and *ex nunc* examination of both facts and points of law.

[40] European Council for Refugees and Exiles, Amnesty International and Human Rights Watch, *Refugee and Human Rights Organisation across Europe Call on EU to Scrap Key Asylum Proposal* (29 March 2004) available at www.ecre.org/media/news/press-releases.html accessed 29 September 2013.

[41] Case C-133/06 *Parliament v Council* [2008] ECR I-3189.

[42] Commission, 'Proposal for a Directive of the European Parliament and of the Council on minimum standards on procedures in Member States for granting and withdrawing international protection (recast)' COM (2009) 554.

[43] Ibid, 4.

[44] Ibid, 5.

The proposal was welcomed by the UNHCR[45] and was generally supported by the European Parliament.[46] However, the discussions in the Council were difficult and the Council was unable to reach a position. In order to boost the work to achieve a CEAS, the Commission issued an amended recast proposal in June 2011.[47] The amended proposal aims to address the concerns of the Member States by recognising the need for flexibility, cost-effectiveness, the simplification of rules, and the prevention of abuse. The Commission made changes in the amended proposal to ensure that the proposal was 'more compatible with the variety of legal systems and other arrangements in different Member States'.[48] This necessarily resulted in a lower level of harmonisation than that envisaged by the initial proposal. Provisions were inserted in the amended proposal in order to enable Member States to deal with a large number of simultaneous asylum claims.[49] In order to prevent abuse of the asylum system, the amended proposal reintroduced two grounds for applying an accelerated procedure.[50] In addition, some of the procedural guarantees introduced in the initial proposal were weakened.[51] The recast was finally adopted in June 2013. Its legal basis can be found in Article 78(2)(a) TFEU. Directive 2013/32/EU needs to be transposed in the Member States before 20 July 2015. Only Article 31(3), (4) and (5) of the Directive containing maximum time limits for the administrative phase in asylum proceedings should be transposed before 20 July 2018.

2.2.1 Scope of Application

Both Directive 2005/85/EC and Directive 2013/32/EU apply to applications for asylum made on the territory of the Member States and to the withdrawal

[45] UNHCR, 'Comments on the European Commission's proposal for a Directive of the European Parliament and of the Council on minimum standards on procedures in Member States for granting and withdrawing international protection' (COM (2009) 554, 21 October 2009) (August 2010) available at www.refworld.org/docid/4c63ebd32.html accessed 29 September 2013.

[46] European Parliament, 'Legislative resolution of 6 April 2011 on the proposal for a directive of the European Parliament and of the Council on minimum standards on procedures in Member States for granting and withdrawing international protection (recast)' COM (2009)0554 – C7-0248/2009 – 2009/0165(COD).

[47] Commission, 'Amended proposal for a Directive of the European Parliament and of the Council on minimum standards on procedures in Member States for granting and withdrawing international protection (recast)' COM (2011) 319.

[48] Ibid, 5. For an overview of the changes see the annex to the amended proposal.

[49] See, eg Art 6(4) allowing an extension of the time limit within which an asylum application must be registered and Art 14 allowing the temporary involvement of personnel of an authority other than the determining authority in conducting interviews in the situation of a large influx of applicants.

[50] Art 31(6)(e) and (g) of the 'Amended proposal' (n 47). 'Amended proposal' (n 47) 5.

[51] For example, the proposal no longer included a right to free legal assistance in first instance proceedings, but only the right to free legal and procedural information (Art 20). It also stated that Member States should make 'a thorough report containing all substantial elements' instead of a 'transcript' of the personal interview (Art 17).

of refugee status.[52] This includes asylum applications made at the border or in transit zones. Directive 2013/32/EU also applies to asylum applications made in the territorial waters of the Member States. Persons who are present in the territorial waters of a Member State and who wish to apply for international protection should be disembarked on land and have their applications examined in accordance with this Directive. The Directives do not apply in cases of requests for diplomatic or territorial asylum submitted to representations of Member States.[53] They also do not apply to procedures which are governed by the Dublin Regulation.[54]

The United Kingdom and Ireland take part in the application of Directive 2005/85/EC, but not Directive 2013/32/EU. These Member States will continue to be bound by Directive 2005/85/EC until they notify their wish to accept the new measure. Neither Directive applies to Denmark.[55]

In principle, Directive 2005/85/EC is only applicable to procedures in which a person's right to a refugee status is assessed.[56] In practice, almost all requests for international protection need to be assessed according to the minimum standards of Directive 2005/85/EC. The most important reason for this is that where Member States have one procedure, in which a person's right to both refugee status and to subsidiary protection status is assessed, the Member State shall apply Directive 2005/85/EC throughout the procedure.[57] In 2010 all Member States except Ireland employed this single asylum procedure. Thus Directive 2005/85/EC applies to the assessment of the right to subsidiary protection status in 26 Member States.[58] Directive 2013/32/EU introduces a single asylum procedure as it applies to both the assessment of refugee status and subsidiary protection.[59]

2.2.2 Overview of the Provisions of the Procedures Directive

The Procedures Directive consists of six chapters. Chapter I contains some general provisions on the purpose and scope of the Directive and definitions. Chapter II consists of a list of basic principles and guarantees. First, the right of access to the asylum procedure is guaranteed.[60] This chapter also grants some important rights to asylum applicants, including: the right to remain on the territory of the

52 Art 3(1) Dir 2005/85/EC and Art 3(1) Dir 2013/32/EU.
53 Art 3(2) Dir 2005/85/EC and Art 3(2) Dir 2013/32/EU.
54 Recital 29 Preamble Dir 2005/85/EC and recital 53 Preamble Dir 2013/32/EU.
55 Recitals 32–34 Preamble Dir 2005/85/EC, recitals 58 and 59 Preamble Dir 2013/32/EU.
56 This follows from Art 2(b) Dir 2005/85/EC.
57 Art 3(3) Dir 2005/85/EC.
58 Commission, 'Report from the Commission to the European Parliament and the Council on the application of Directive 2005/85/EC' COM (2010) 465 final, 3. Art 3(4) Dir 2005/85/EC states that Member States may decide to apply this Directive in procedures for deciding on applications for any kind of international protection.
59 Recital 11 Preamble Dir 2013/32/EU.
60 Art 6 Dir 2005/85/EC and Art 6 Dir 2013/32/EU.

Member State pending the examination of the asylum application;[61] the right to be informed of the procedure to be followed, of rights and obligations and of the result of the decision on the application;[62] the right to interpretation services[63] and legal aid and assistance;[64] the right to a personal interview;[65] and the right to contact the UNHCR.[66] Special guarantees are provided for unaccompanied minors.[67] Directive 2013/32/EU also contains provisions regarding medical examinations[68] and applicants in need of special protection.[69] Chapter II also sets out requirements for the examination of and decisions on asylum applications.[70] It also states which obligations may be imposed on asylum applicants, such as the obligation to hand over documents in their possession relevant to the examination of the asylum application.[71] Finally, Chapter II contains provisions regarding detention,[72] (implicit) withdrawal of the asylum application,[73] the role of UNHCR,[74] and a provision which seeks to prevent actors of persecution from being informed of the asylum application of an asylum applicant.[75]

Chapter III sets out standards for procedures at first instance. Member States are obliged to process asylum applications in a procedure which is in accordance with the principles and guarantees laid down in Chapter II.[76] Both Directive 2005/85/EC and Directive 2013/32/EU outline situations in which Member States may derogate from those principles and guarantees. Such derogations are allowed in subsequent asylum applications,[77] applications submitted at the border (only Directive 2005/85/EC)[78] and cases in which the asylum applicant seeks to enter or has entered the territory illegally from a European safe third country.[79] Chapter III furthermore covers the prioritisation and acceleration of the examination procedure.[80] It also sets out the conditions on which applications may be declared inadmissible[81] or unfounded.[82] Chapter III finally contains minimum standards

[61] Art 7 Dir 2005/85/EC and Art 9 Dir 2013/32/EU.
[62] Art 10(1)(a), (d) and (e) Dir 2005/85/EC and Arts 8(1) and 12(1)(a) and (f) Dir 2013/32/EU.
[63] Art 10(1)(b) Dir 2005/85/EC and Art 12(1)(b) Dir 2013/32/EU.
[64] Arts 15 and 16 Dir 2005/85/EC and Arts 19–23 Dir 2013/32/EU.
[65] Art 12 Dir 2005/85/EC and Art 14 Dir 2013/32/EU.
[66] Art 10(1)(c) Dir 2005/85/EC and Art 12(1)(c) Dir 2013/32/EU.
[67] Art 17 Dir 2005/85/EC and Art 25 Dir 2013/32/EU.
[68] Art 18 Dir 2013/32/EU.
[69] Art 24 Dir 2013/32/EU.
[70] Arts 8 and 9 Dir 2005/85/EC and Arts 10 and 11 Dir 2013/32/EU.
[71] Art 11 Dir 2005/85/EC and Art 13 Dir 2013/32/EU.
[72] Art 18 Dir 2005/85/EC and Art 26 Dir 2013/32/EU.
[73] Arts 19 and 20 Dir 2005/85/EC and Arts 27 and 28 Dir 2013/32/EU.
[74] Art 21 Dir 2005/85/EC and Art 29 Dir 2013/32/EU.
[75] Art 22 Dir 2005/85/EC and Art 30 Dir 2013/32/EU.
[76] Art 23 Dir 2005/85/EC and Art 31(1) Dir 2013/32/EU.
[77] Arts 24(1)(a) and 32–34 Dir 2005/85/EC and Arts 40–42 Dir 2013/32/EU.
[78] Arts 24(1)(b) and 35 Dir 2005/85/EC.
[79] Arts 24(1)(c) and 36 Dir 2005/85/EC and Art 39 Dir 2013/32/EU.
[80] Art 23(3) and (4) Dir 2005/85/EC and Art 31(7) and (8) Dir 2013/32/EU.
[81] Art 25 Dir 2005/85/EC and Art 33 Dir 2013/32/EU.
[82] Art 28 Dir 2005/85/EC and Art 32 Dir 2013/32/EU.

as regards four concepts of safe countries: first country of asylum, safe third country, safe country of origin and European safe third country.[83]

Chapter IV contains rules regarding the withdrawal of refugee status. Chapter V consists of one provision, which grants asylum applicants the right to an effective remedy before a court or tribunal against a negative decision on his asylum application.[84] Finally Chapter VI contains some general and final provisions.

2.2.3 Level of Harmonisation and Discretion of Member States

The minimum standards included in Directive 2005/85/EC allow Member States wide discretion. First, as mentioned in the previous section, the Directive provides for the opportunity to employ specific procedures which may derogate from the basic principles and guarantees of Chapter II of the Directive. Secondly, the basic principles and guarantees themselves contain many options for derogation. Examples include Article 12, which allows for exceptions to the right to a personal interview, and Article 15, which provides for several opportunities to limit the right to free legal aid in the event of a negative decision on the asylum application. Finally, the derogation provisions included in the Directive contain many vague terms, which need to be interpreted by the Member States. Article 12(3) of Directive 2005/85/EC states, for example, that a personal interview may be omitted, amongst other situations, where it is 'not reasonably practicable', in particular where the competent authority is of the opinion that the applicant is 'unfit or unable to be interviewed owing to enduring circumstances beyond his/her control'.

Directive 2013/32/EU aims to further develop the standards for procedures in Member States for granting and withdrawing international protection with a view to establishing a common asylum procedure in the EU. Nevertheless, the Directive still allows Member States to derogate from many of the basic principles and guarantees included in Chapter II and provides for flexibility in designing the asylum procedure.

The fact that the Procedures Directive leaves wide discretion for Member States may have consequences for the application of EU fundamental rights. As was shown in section 1.2.1, these EU fundamental rights and general principles of EU law only apply to issues which fall within the scope of EU law. The question whether Member States are acting within the scope of EU law when they make use of the opportunities for derogation offered by the Directive, will be addressed in section 2.4.2.

[83] Arts 26, 27, 29–31 and 36 Dir 2005/85/EC and Arts 35–39 Dir 2013/32/EU.

[84] Art 39 Dir 2005/85/EC and Art 46 Dir 2013/32/EU.

2.3 THE QUALIFICATION DIRECTIVE

Directive 2004/83/EC

Directive 2004/83/EC was based on Article 63(1)(c) of the former EC Treaty. The Directive has been described as the heart of the CEAS, because of its subject matter.[85] It lays down the criteria for the qualification for two statuses: refugee status and subsidiary protection status. Furthermore, the Directive sets out which rights should be granted to persons eligible for these statuses. The Directive seeks to ensure full respect for human dignity and the right to asylum of applicants for asylum and their accompanying family members.[86]

Directive 2004/83/EC was adopted by the Council on 27 April 2004 and published on 30 September 2004. It was the result of 'intense and protracted negotiations'.[87] The level of protection offered by the Directive has been criticised[88] and it has been argued that some of the provisions of the Directive infringe the international obligations of the Member States.[89] The provisions of the Directive had to be implemented in the Member States by 10 October 2006.

Directive 2011/95/EU

In December 2011 Directive 2011/95/EU, a recast of Directive 2004/83/EC, was adopted.[90] The Directive had to be implemented in the Member States by 21 December 2013.[91] On this date Directive 2004/83/EC was repealed.[92] Many of the provisions of Directive 2004/83/EC, such as Article 4 regarding evidentiary issues, have remained unchanged in Directive 2011/95/EU. However, the new directive contains a number of changes to Directive 2004/83/EC. It pays more attention to gender issues and children's rights.[93] Moreover, it contains more safeguards with regard to the application of the internal flight alternative;[94] requires effective and

[85] Battjes (n 17) 197.

[86] See recital 10 Preamble Dir 2004/83/EC.

[87] The inclusion of non-state agents of persecution, the definition of subsidiary protection, and the exclusion clauses were all controversial issues. S Peers and N Rogers (eds), *EU Immigration and Asylum Law: Text and Commentary* (Leiden/Boston, Martinus Nijhoff, 2006) 323. For more information on the background and legislative history of the Directive, see ibid 326–33.

[88] J McAdam, 'The Qualification Directive, An Overview' in K Zwaan (ed), *The Qualification Directive: Central Themes, Problem Issues and Implementation in Selected Member States* (Nijmegen, Wolf Legal Publishers, 2007) 9.

[89] See Peers and Rogers (n 88) 334–40, and Battjes (n 17) 275.

[90] Dir 2011/95/EU of the European Parliament and of the Council of 13 December 2011 on standards for the qualification of third-country nationals or stateless persons as beneficiaries of international protection, for a uniform status for refugees or for persons eligible for subsidiary protection, and for the content of the protection granted [2011] OJ L337/9.

[91] Art 39 Dir 2011/95/EU.

[92] Art 40 Dir 2011/95/EU.

[93] See Arts 9(2)(f) and 10(1)(d) for gender issues and recitals 18, 19, 28, 38 Preamble and Art 2(j), 9(2)(f) for children's rights, 31 Dir 2011/95/EU.

[94] Art 8 Dir 2011/95/EU.

durable protection against persecution or serious harm in the country of origin;[95] and it has brought several provisions of the Directive more closely into line with the Refugee Convention.[96] Furthermore, persons eligible for subsidiary protection are now granted the same secondary rights as persons who are recognised as refugees according to the Qualification Directive.[97]

2.3.1 Scope of Application

The Qualification Directive is silent on its territorial scope of application. Battjes argues that it is hardly likely that the Community legislator intended to harmonise the criteria for dealing with asylum applications lodged outside the territory of the Member States of the EU.[98]

The Qualification Directive does not apply to Denmark. Ireland and the UK do not follow Directive 2011/95/EU but remain bound by Directive 2004/83/EC.[99]

2.3.2 Overview of the Qualification Directive's Provisions

There are nine chapters in the Directive. The first chapter contains provisions regarding the subject and scope of the Directive, definitions, and more favourable standards. The second chapter covers the assessment of applications for international protection. This chapter applies to the examination of the right to both refugee status and subsidiary protection. Article 4 on the assessment of facts and circumstances in applications for international protection is particularly relevant for this study. It contains important rules of evidence, including rules concerning the burden of proof, evidentiary assessment and the granting of the benefit of the doubt.[100]

Chapter III lays down the criteria for qualification as a refugee, while Chapter V sets out the criteria for subsidiary protection. It is of crucial importance that Articles 13 and 18 of the Qualification Directive provide that a person who qualifies as a refugee, or is eligible for subsidiary protection in accordance with the Directive, should be granted refugee status or subsidiary protection status. Arguably, these provisions reflect the EU fundamental right to asylum laid down in Article 18 of the Charter. Usually persons applying for asylum in EU Member States will claim the EU right to asylum status. According to the EU principle of effectiveness, hurdles in national asylum procedures which render the exercise of these rights practically impossible or excessively difficult are not allowed.

[95] Art 7(2) Dir 2011/95/EU.

[96] Arts 9(3) and 11(3) Dir 2011/95/EU.

[97] Art 20(2) Dir 2011/95/EU.

[98] Battjes (n 17) 209–10 and 474. See also M den Heijer, *Europe and Extraterritorial Asylum* (Oxford and Portland, OR, Hart Publishing, 2012) 203–204.

[99] Recitals 38–40 Preamble Dir 2011/95/EU.

[100] See ch 8 of this volume.

The right to asylum status is neither absolute nor permanent. Chapters III and V contain provisions regarding the cessation of and exclusion from, international protection. Chapters IV and VI provide rules for granting and withdrawing refugee and subsidiary protection status. Chapter VII lists the rights which should be granted to persons eligible for international protection.[101] The obligation for Member States to respect the principle of *non-refoulement*, laid down in Article 21 of the Qualification Directive, which arguably reflects Article 19 of the Charter, is of particular importance for this study. Finally, Chapters VIII and IX contain rules regarding administrative cooperation and final provisions.

2.4 APPLICABILITY OF EU FUNDAMENTAL RIGHTS

This section answers the following questions:

1. Is the Court of Justice competent to test the legality of the provisions of the Procedures Directive against EU fundamental rights, and if so, what could be the result of this legality test? (section 2.4.1)
2. Are Member States bound by EU fundamental rights when making use of the discretionary powers offered by the Procedures Directive to make exceptions to rights included in that Directive? (section 2.4.2)

2.4.1 Testing the Legality of (Minimum) Standards

According to Article 263 TFEU, the Court of Justice is competent to review the legality of acts of EU institutions, including EU legislation such as directives and regulations. This provision also states the grounds on which such an act may be deemed illegal: lack of competence; infringement of an essential procedural requirement; infringement of the Treaties or of any rule of law relating to their application; and misuse of powers. The Court of Justice also has the power to test the legality of provisions of EU legislation against EU fundamental rights and general principles of EU law.[102] If the Court of Justice concludes that an action on grounds of illegality is well founded, Article 264 TFEU requires it to declare that act to be void.

The question arises whether the Court of Justice is also competent to review the legality of (minimum) standards or provisions which afford Member States wide discretion to derogate from the rights included in the Procedures Directive in light of the EU right to an effective remedy. It could be argued that Directive 2005/85/EC and Directive 2013/32/EU both enable Member States to retain or adopt national

[101] It includes the right to a residence permit and to travel documents and contains rules concerning access to employment, education, social welfare, health care, accommodation and integration facilities.

[102] Arts 51(1) and 52(5) of the Charter. See also Battjes (n 17) 85.

provisions compatible with respect for fundamental rights and thus Member States cannot infringe EU fundamental rights. At the same time, provisions adopted and applied by Member States which might be contrary to EU fundamental rights do not constitute acts of EU Institutions the legality of which, according to Articles 263 and 267 TFEU, can be reviewed by the Court of Justice.[103]

The judgment in *Parliament v Council*,[104] which concerned the Family Reunification Directive,[105] shows that the Court of Justice is indeed competent to test the legality of the minimum standards or provisions allowing for derogation. In this procedure, which was brought by the European Parliament, annulment was sought of provisions which derogated from the obligations imposed on Member States by the Family Reunification Directive. The Court of Justice decided that it was competent to review the legality of provisions in the Family Reunification Directive which allow Member States to derogate from basic rules laid down in that Directive:

> [T]he fact that the contested provisions of the Directive afford the Member States a certain margin of appreciation and allow them in certain circumstances to apply national legislation derogating from the basic rules imposed by the Directive cannot have the effect of excluding those provisions from review by the Court of their legality as envisaged by Article 230 EC.[106]

It should be observed that in *Parliament v Council* the Court of Justice took into account that the provisions concerned derogated from a 'basic rule'.[107] The Court of Justice did not give a definition of the term 'basic rule'. Arguably, the provisions in the Procedures Directive which reflect the right to access to asylum procedures and the right to an effective remedy, such as the procedural standards laid down in Chapter II of the Directive, should be basic rules.[108] The right to effective access to asylum procedures[109] and the right to an effective remedy[110] lie at the basis of the Procedures Directive. The observance of these rights is necessary in the interest of a correct recognition of those persons in need of protection as refugees within the meaning of the Refugee Convention and the Qualification Directive.[111] It is thus conceivable that the Court of Justice is, according to Article 263 TFEU, competent to review the legality of the provisions in the Procedures Directive that derogate from the standards reflecting the right to access to asylum procedures and the right to an effective remedy.

[103] This was argued by the Council with regard to the competence of the Court of Justice to review the legality of the provisions of the Family Reunification Directive in Case C-540/03 *Parliament v Council* [2006] ECR I-5769, para 16.

[104] *Parliament v Council*, ibid.

[105] Dir 2003/86/EC (n 32).

[106] *Parliament v Council* (n 104) para 22. Art 230 of the former EC Treaty has been replaced by Art 263 TFEU.

[107] In this case the provisions concerned derogated from the right of family reunification, which is the basis of the Family Reunification Directive.

[108] See recital 13 Preamble Dir 2005/85/EC and recital 25 Preamble Dir 2013/32/EU.

[109] See recital 13 Preamble Dir 2005/85/EC and recital 25 Preamble Dir 2013/32/EU.

[110] Recital 27 Preamble Dir 2005/85/EC and recital 50 Preamble Dir 2013/32/EU.

[111] Recital 13 Preamble Dir 2005/85/EC.

Like the Procedures Directive, the Family Reunification Directive allows Member States to adopt or maintain more favourable provisions than those laid down in the Directive.[112] In *Parliament v Council* the Court of Justice tested some of these provisions against EU fundamental rights. It should, therefore, be derived from this judgment that the Court of Justice is also competent to test the legality of the (minimum) standards included in the Procedures Directive.

Potential Results of the Legality Test

The next question is whether (minimum) standards or provisions allowing for derogation can be at odds with EU fundamental rights. It may be argued that such standards or provisions are not capable of infringing fundamental rights. The Procedures Directive allows Member States to maintain or introduce more favourable standards, insofar as those standards are compatible with the Directive.[113] Member States may make use of this possibility where the (minimum) standard offers a level of protection which is lower than the level required by EU fundamental rights, in order to avoid acting in violation of EU fundamental rights. In the same vein, Member States are free not to make use of provisions allowing for derogation in order to prevent a violation of EU fundamental rights.

In *Parliament v Council* the Court of Justice indicated that minimum standards or provisions allowing for derogation could infringe fundamental rights and should thus be considered invalid. It considered that a provision of an EU Act could in itself fall short of respecting fundamental rights 'if it required, or expressly or impliedly authorised' Member States to adopt or retain national legislation not respecting those rights.[114]

The (minimum) standards of the Procedures Directive do not require Member States to violate fundamental rights.[115] However, it could be argued that minimum standards which offer less protection than the standards required by EU fundamental rights 'expressly or impliedly authorise' Member States to act in violation of those fundamental rights. The same applies to provisions that allow for derogation by the Member States of basic rights of a directive.

A reading of the minimum standards and provisions allowing for derogation which authorises Member States to disrespect fundamental rights would, however, oppose one of the main objectives of a CEAS: ensuring the fundamental rights of third-country nationals.[116] This objective is also reflected in the TFEU and the preamble and provisions of the Procedures Directive.[117] The references to international human rights treaties and the fundamental rights laid down in

[112] Art 3(5) Dir 2003/86/EC.

[113] See Art 5 Dir 2005/85/EC and Art 5 Dir 2013/32/EU.

[114] *Parliament v Council* (n 104) para 23.

[115] See Battjes (n 17) 556. He concludes that for that reason minimum standards cannot be at variance with international law.

[116] See also Battjes (n 17) 201.

[117] See recital 2 Preamble Dir 2005/85/EC.

the Charter show that the EU legislator did not envisage authorising the Member States to disrespect fundamental rights.[118]

It is, therefore, submitted here that it is likely that the Court of Justice will interpret minimum standards and provisions allowing for derogation in the light of fundamental rights, thus avoiding violations of those rights. This is what the Court of Justice did in *Parliament v Council*. The laws and decisions of Member States may subsequently be tested against this interpretation of EU legislation. However, if no interpretation in conformity with EU fundamental rights is possible the Court of Justice should declare a provision void.[119]

2.4.2 Interpreting and Filling in Gaps in EU Asylum Legislation

In this section it is argued that Member States are bound by EU fundamental rights when making use of the discretionary power, offered in particular, by the Procedures Directive, to make exceptions to rights included in that Directive.[120] National legislation which is based on this discretionary power falls within the scope of EU law and can, therefore, be tested against EU law by national courts and the Court of Justice. This follows from the *Parliament v Council* judgment mentioned above.[121] In this judgment the Court of Justice made clear that Member States are not allowed to infringe general principles of EU law by making use of the possibility to derogate from the right to family reunification. This also applies if the derogation provision contains terms which are not defined. The Court's considerations concerning Article 4 of the Family Reunification Directive are most important in this regard. This provision allows Member States to derogate under certain conditions from the parents' right to family reunification with their child, if that child does not meet a condition for integration provided for by national legislation.[122] The Court of Justice held:

> The fact that the concept of integration is not defined cannot be interpreted as authorising the Member States to employ that concept in a manner contrary to general principles

[118] The Court of Justice in *Parliament v Council* also took into account the objectives of Dir 2003/86/EC in its ruling that its provisions did not infringe EU fundamental rights. These objectives are to promote family life and to ensure that the best interests of the child are taken into account. *Parliament v Council* (n 104) paras 73 and 87.

[119] See also I de Jesús Butler and O de Schutter, 'Binding the EU to International Human Rights Law' (2007) 26 *Yearbook of European Law* 277, 295, where they state that 'Community legislation will be valid as long as it can be interpreted in conformity with the general principles'.

[120] See section 2.2.3.

[121] See also Joined Cases C-411/10 and C-493/10, *NS and ME et al* [2011] para 69, where the Court of Justice held that a Member State is implementing EU law and is therefore bound by the Charter when it makes use of the discretionary power granted by Art 3(2) of the Dublin Regulation to examine an asylum application, which is not its responsibility according to the criteria laid down in the regulation.

[122] Derogation is possible if the child is aged over 12 years and arrives independently from the rest of his family.

> of Community law, in particular to fundamental rights. The Member States which wish to make use of the derogation cannot employ an unspecified concept of integration, but must apply the condition for integration provided for by their legislation … in order to examine the specific situation of a child over 12 years of age arriving independently from the rest of his or her family. Consequently, the final subparagraph of Article 4(1) of the Directive cannot be interpreted as authorising the Member States, expressly or impliedly, to adopt implementing provisions that would be contrary to the right to respect for family life.[123]

Member States are thus bound by general principles of EU law, and in particular by EU fundamental rights, when making use of a derogation provision and when interpreting an undefined term included in the derogation provision.[124] This implies that the Member States' discretion when making use of the possibilities for derogation offered by the Procedures Directive is limited by EU fundamental rights, such as the right to an effective remedy.[125] Therefore, it is very likely that national measures that fall within the scope of a derogation provision provided by the Procedures Directive can be tested against this right.

2.5 THE ROLE OF NATIONAL COURTS AND THE COURT OF JUSTICE

This section examines how questions regarding the legality and interpretation of the provisions of the Procedures Directive may be brought before, and assessed by national courts and the Court of Justice.

2.5.1 Legality Review of EU Legislation

Actions on grounds of the illegality of EU legislation may be brought before the Court of Justice by a Member State, the European Parliament, the Council or the Commission. Such action must be instituted within two months of the publication of the measure.[126] As noted in section 2.2, the European Parliament successfully challenged the legality of several provisions of the Procedures Directive.[127]

Natural or legal persons cannot directly challenge the legality of the Procedures Directive before the Court of Justice. According to Article 263 TFEU, any natural or legal person may only institute proceedings against an act addressed to that person or which is of direct and individual concern to them, and against a regulatory

[123] *Parliament v Council* (n 104) para 70.

[124] See also S Iglesias Sánchez, 'The Court and the Charter: The Impact of the Entry into Force of the Lisbon Treaty on the ECJ's Approach to Fundamental Rights' (2012) 49 *Common Market Law Review* 1565, 1585–86.

[125] Case 222/86 *UNECTEF v Heylens et al* [1987] ECR 4097; see also Case C-340/89 *Vlassopoulou* [1991] ECR I-2357.

[126] Art 263 TFEU.

[127] *Parliament v Council* (n 41).

act which is of direct concern to them and does not entail implementing measures. The Court of Justice ruled in *UPA* that the principle of effective judicial protection cannot have the effect of setting aside the condition of 'direct and individual concern' expressly laid down in the Treaty, without going beyond the jurisdiction conferred by the Treaty on the EU Courts.[128]

An individual should plead the illegality of the Procedures Directive before the national courts, for example, in the appeal against a negative asylum decision.[129] He may contest the legality of the provisions of EU legislation on which the decision is based, for example, on the ground that an EU fundamental right has been violated. The following example illustrates how such a situation may occur. The asylum applicant's asylum request is rejected on the basis of information which is not disclosed to him or the court assessing the appeal against this rejection for national security reasons. Such practice is allowed by Article 16(1) of Directive 2005/85/EC. The applicant argues before the national court that Article 16(1) of Directive 2005/85/EC should be considered invalid, at least as far as it permits the determining authorities[130] to withhold information underlying the asylum decision to the national court, because it infringes the EU right to an effective remedy.[131]

National courts may consider the legality of a provision of EU legislation and reject the grounds put forward by the parties in support of illegality, concluding that the measure is completely valid, if they consider those grounds to be unfounded. However, national courts do not have jurisdiction to declare a provision of EU law invalid. The reasons for this are set out by the Court of Justice in *Foto Frost*.[132] First, this rule seeks to ensure the unity of EU law and the principle of legal certainty. If national courts were competent to declare an EU act invalid, this could lead to divergences between those courts as to the legality of such acts. Such divergences would be liable to place in jeopardy the very unity of the EU legal order and detract from the fundamental requirement of legal certainty. Moreover Article 264 TFEU gives the Court of Justice exclusive competence to declare an act of an EU Institution void. The coherence of the system, therefore, requires that the power to declare such an act invalid must also be reserved to the Court of Justice. Furthermore, the Court of Justice is in the best position to decide on the legality of EU legislation, because EU Institutions are entitled to participate in proceedings before the Court in order to defend the legality of the acts in

[128] Case C-50/00P *Union de Pequeños* [2002] ECR I-6677, para 44.

[129] Art 277 TFEU states that notwithstanding the expiry of the period laid down in Art 263 TFEU, any party may, in proceedings in which an act of general application adopted by an EU Institution, body, office or agency is at issue, plead the grounds specified in Art 263 TFEU, in order to invoke before the Court of Justice the inapplicability of that act.

[130] In this study 'determining authority' means: the quasi-judicial or administrative body in a Member State responsible for examining applications for asylum and competent to take decisions at first instance in such cases. See Art 2(e) Dir 2005/85/EC and Art 2(f) Dir 2013/32/EU.

[131] See on this issue ch 10 in this volume on the use of secret information in asylum cases.

[132] Case 314/85 *Foto-Frost* [1987] ECR 4199, paras 17–20.

question.[133] This implies that the individual concerned needs to ask the national court to make a reference for a preliminary ruling on the legality to the Court of Justice.[134] According to Article 267 TFEU, the Court of Justice has jurisdiction to give preliminary rulings regarding the legality of acts of EU Institutions, bodies, offices or agencies.

2.5.2 Interpretation of EU Law

Lower national courts as well as the highest national court may interpret the provisions of the Procedures Directive when deciding on higher appeals against asylum decisions. They may use EU fundamental rights to find such an interpretation. The national courts decide whether national (implementing) legislation breaches an EU fundamental right. The courts will, if they deem it necessary, be guided by the Court of Justice under the preliminary ruling proceedings.[135] In *Samba Diouf* the Court of Justice interpreted Directive 2005/85/EC in the light of the EU right to an effective remedy for the first time.[136]

The competence of the Court of Justice to give preliminary rulings on questions regarding the interpretation of the Treaty or EU legislation is laid down in Article 267 TFEU. This competence includes answering questions regarding the conformity with EU law of Member States' acts which fall within the scope of EU law. Such questions may arise, for example, if an individual argues that EU fundamental rights require a certain interpretation of a provision of EU legislation and that a national act violates this (interpretation of that) legislation. He could state, for example, that Article 39 of Directive 2005/85/EC read in the light of the EU right to an effective remedy is a remedy with automatic suspensive effect. A national remedy without such suspensive effect would then violate EU law.[137]

2.5.3 The Important Role of the National Courts as EU Courts

Until the entry into force of the Treaty of Lisbon, Article 68 of the former EC Treaty denied lower courts the opportunity to make references for preliminary rulings with regard to the measures adopted under Title IV of the former EC

[133] However, Ward writes: 'While the Court of Justice has developed an impressive range of substantive rules against which the legality of EC measures can be tested, they rarely result in a declaration of invalidity in cases arising from Article 234 reference from national courts.' A Ward, *Judicial Review and the Rights of Private Parties in EU Law* (Oxford, Oxford University Press, 2007) 12.

[134] T Tridimas, *The General Principles of Community Law* (Oxford, Oxford University Press, 2006) 31 and 35.

[135] Ibid, 38.

[136] Case C-69/10 *Samba Diouf* [2011]. See further ch 9 of this volume.

[137] See further ch 6, section 6.3 in this volume.

Treaty such as the Procedures Directive and Qualification Directive.[138] Potentially as a result of this limited role no questions regarding the legality and few regarding the interpretation of EU measures adopted under Title IV had been referred to the Court of Justice until 1 December 2010. The Court of Justice's role in assessing the legality of and interpreting measures adopted under Title IV of the former EC Treaty was therefore limited.

The Treaty of Lisbon repealed Article 68.[139] As a result, the rules laid down in Article 267 TFEU on preliminary rulings also apply to asylum measures. However, following the Treaty of Lisbon, it is still the national courts which in practice play the most important role in interpreting the Procedures Directive and testing its legality. Only in very few of the asylum cases pending before the national courts of Member States will a reference for preliminary ruling be made to the Court of Justice.[140]

The general rule is that any national court or tribunal of a Member State *may* request the Court of Justice to give a preliminary ruling regarding questions on the legality of an act of an EU Institution, if it considers that a decision on the question is necessary to enable it to give a judgment. Where any such question is raised in a case pending before a court or tribunal of a Member State against whose decisions there is no judicial remedy under national law, that court or tribunal is *required* to bring the matter before the Court of Justice.[141] However, it is up to the national court to decide whether it is necessary to refer a question to the Court of Justice for preliminary ruling. National courts may be hesitant to refer questions, for example because it involves a lot of work or because it takes the Court of Justice a long time to answer the questions, which may lead to considerable delay of many asylum cases in which the same question is at issue. Thus Individuals always depend on the willingness of national courts to refer a question to the Court of Justice. If the national court refuses to refer a question, the individual does not have a remedy against that decision.[142]

It should be concluded that it depends to a large extent on the national courts whether the procedural issues addressed in this study will ever be put before the Court of Justice. The national courts have an important responsibility in guaranteeing the EU right to an effective remedy and related procedural rights in asylum cases.[143]

[138] This provision presumably was aimed at preventing the overburdening of the Court of Justice. See Battjes (n 17) 572.

[139] Treaty of Lisbon amending the Treaty on European Union and the Treaty establishing the European Community, 2007/C 306/01, 17 December 2007, Art 2 sub 67.

[140] The Court of Justice has recognised the importance of the role of the national courts as 'guardians' of the EU legal order and 'ordinary' courts in the EU legal order in its Opinion 1/09 of 8 March 2011. See R Baratta, 'National Courts as "Guardians" and "Ordinary" Courts of EU Law: Opinion 1/09 of the ECJ' (2011) 38 *Legal Issues of Economic Integration* 297.

[141] Art 267 TFEU.

[142] See also B de Witte 'The Role of the ECJ in Human Rights' in P Alston, MR Bustelo and J Heenan (eds), *The EU and Human Rights* (Oxford, Oxford University Press, 1999), 877.

[143] See also ch 11, section 11.4 in this volume.

3

The Subsidiary Role of International Treaties as Sources of Inspiration for EU Fundamental Rights

INTERNATIONAL TREATIES CONTAINING human rights and fundamental freedoms, in particular the European Convention on Human Rights (ECHR), are an important source of inspiration for EU fundamental rights.[1] Therefore, these treaties and the views of their supervising bodies will play a crucial role in this study's attempt to define the meaning of the EU right to an effective remedy. In this chapter a few important questions will be addressed regarding the potential use of these treaties by the Court of Justice in the context of the Common European Asylum System (CEAS). The consequences of this for the way in which this study is conducted will also be discussed.

The Level of Protection Offered by EU Fundamental Rights

The first question to be answered is whether the fact that international treaties are only used as sources of inspiration and not directly applied by the EU Courts, may result in EU fundamental rights offering a lower level of protection than international treaties. It is concluded in section 3.1 that this is generally not the case. It is possible, however, that EU fundamental rights require broader protection than that offered by international treaties. The standards following from international treaties thus indicate the minimum level of protection which should be guaranteed by EU fundamental rights.

The Role and Significance of International Treaties in the Context of the CEAS

This study takes into account the ECHR, the Refugee Convention, the International Covenant on Civil and Political Rights (ICCPR), the UN Convention against Torture and Other Cruel, Inhuman or Degrading Treatment or Punishment (CAT) and the UN Convention on the Rights of the Child (CRC) and the views of their supervising bodies. Section 3.2 will show that these international treaties have been, or should be, recognised as a source of inspiration in general, and in

[1] Art 6(3) TEU, Arts 52 and 53 of the Charter.

particular in the context of the CEAS. It follows from Article 63(1) of the former EC Treaty and Article 78(1) TFEU that EU asylum legislation must be 'in accordance' with these treaties. Section 3.2.6 addresses the question whether this requirement means that international treaties should be directly applied by the Court of Justice and not only used as sources of inspiration.

The Relative Weight of International Treaties

Finally, section 3.3 examines the relative weight which should be attached to the treaties taken into account in this study. It is argued that in practice the importance of a treaty for the development of EU fundamental rights seems to relate primarily to the authority of the judgments or views of its sources of interpretation. It will be shown that the Court of Justice attaches great weight to the (binding) judgments issued by the European Court of Human Rights (ECtHR). The Court of Justice is much more reluctant to base its interpretation of EU fundamental rights on the non-binding views of other monitoring bodies. For this reason, in this study most weight will be accorded to the case law of the ECtHR, while the non-binding views of other monitoring bodies will only play a complementary role.

3.1 INTERNATIONAL TREATIES VERSUS EU FUNDAMENTAL RIGHTS

An important question which will be addressed in this section, is whether EU fundamental rights could offer a different level of protection than human rights recognised in international treaties.

3.1.1 Might EU Fundamental Rights provide a Lower Level of Protection?

Both the Charter and the case law of the EU Courts (which will be discussed in more detail in section 3.3) show that, in principle, EU fundamental rights do not provide less protection than international treaties. Article 52(3) of the Charter provides that, in so far as the Charter contains rights which correspond to rights guaranteed by the ECHR, 'the meaning and scope of those rights shall be the same as those laid down by the said Convention'.[2] According to the Explanations, Article 52(3) of the Charter is intended to ensure the necessary consistency between the Charter and the ECHR and its Protocols.[3] The meaning and scope of the

[2] The explanations contain a list of rights which may, without precluding developments in the law, legislation and the Treaties, be regarded as corresponding to rights in the ECHR. Explanations relating to the Charter of Fundamental Rights (2007/C 303/02), OJ 14 December 2007, 33–34.

[3] See also the Joint communication from the Presidents of the ECtHR and the Court of Justice, Costa and Skouris, of January 2011 in which they state with regard to the relationship between the ECHR and the Charter that 'it is important to ensure that there is the greatest coherence between

guaranteed rights are determined not only by the text of the ECHR, but also by the case law of the ECtHR. The explanations state that 'in any event, the level of protection afforded by the Charter may never be lower than that guaranteed by the ECHR'.[4]

Article 53 of the Charter provides more generally that nothing in the Charter shall be interpreted as restricting or adversely affecting human rights and fundamental freedoms as recognised by international law, including the ECHR. According to the Explanations relating to the Charter, this provision is intended to maintain the level of protection currently afforded within their respective scope by international law.[5]

Level of Protection Offered According to the Case Law of the Court of Justice
Some authors argue that general principles of EU law as applied by the EU Courts allow, by their very nature, the balancing of human rights with competing principles in cases where the underlying provisions of international law do not.[6] However, most scholars seem to be of the opinion that the indirect application of international treaties does not result in less protection than their direct application. Groussot states that 'once the ECHR has been "filtered" by the ECJ through the general principles, the end result is much the same as if the Community was formally bound by the ECHR'.[7] Battjes notes that it is questionable whether one can conclude on the basis of the mere phrasing of the Court that the application of human rights law via general principles offers less protection. He refers to the judgments in *Steffensen* and *Akrich* where the Court seems to consider that human rights treaties must be complied with within the EU legal order.[8] In *Steffensen* the Court states:

> According to the Court's case-law, where national legislation falls within the field of application of Community law, the Court, in a reference for a preliminary ruling, must give the national court all the guidance as to interpretation necessary to enable it to assess the compatibility of that legislation with the fundamental rights—as laid down, in particular, in the European Convention for the Protection of Human Rights and Fundamental Freedoms—whose observance the Court ensures.[9]

In *Akrich* the Court observed that the right to respect for family life as enshrined in Article 8 ECHR 'is among the fundamental rights which, according to the

the Convention and the Charter insofar as the Charter contains rights which correspond to those guaranteed by the Convention'. In their view a 'parallel interpretation' of the two instruments could prove useful.

[4] Explanations relating to the Charter (n 2).
[5] Ibid.
[6] H Battjes, *European Asylum Law and International Law* (Leiden/Boston, Martinus Nijhoff, 2006) 92.
[7] X Groussot, *General Principles of Community Law* (Groningen, Europa Law Publishing, 2006) 71.
[8] Battjes, *European Asylum Law* (n 6) 92.
[9] Case C-276/01 *Steffensen* [2003] ECR I-3735, para 70. See also Case C-260/89 *ERT* [1991] ECR I-2925, para 42.

Court's settled case-law, restated by the preamble to the Single European Act and by Article 6(2) EU, are protected in the Community legal order'.[10] Section 3.3.1 will show that, when actually interpreting EU fundamental rights and principles, the Court of Justice also complies with the standards following from the case law of the ECHR and the ECtHR.

3.1.2 Might EU Fundamental Rights provide Broader Protection?

EU fundamental rights cannot offer less protection than international law, but they may offer broader protection.[11] This may be derived from Article 52(3) of the Charter which states that this provision shall not prevent EU law providing more extensive protection than the ECHR.[12] Iglesias Sánchez states that this provision 'constitutes a manifestation of the autonomy of the EU system'.[13] Advocate General Cruz Villalón considered in his Opinion in *Samba Diouf* that

> the right to effective judicial protection, as expressed in Article 47 of the [Charter of the Fundamental Rights of the European Union] CFREU, has, through being recognised as part of European Union law by virtue of Article 47, acquired a separate identity and substance under that article which are not the mere sum of the provisions of Articles 6 and 13 of the ECHR.[14]

It will be shown in this book that on several points Article 47 does indeed provide broader protection than Article 6 and 13 ECHR. Several other examples of a broader interpretation of a fundament right can be found in the case law of the Court of Justice.[15] In its judgment in *McB*, however, the Court of Justice considered that Article 7 of the Charter corresponds with Article 8 ECHR and must therefore be given the same meaning and the same scope as Article 8(1) ECHR.[16]

[10] Case C-109/01 *Akrich* [2003] ECR I-9607. See also Case C-60/00 *Carpenter* [2002] ECR I-6279, para 41 and Case C-482/01 *Orfanopoulos* [2004] ECR I-5257, para 98.

[11] The Court of Justice has held that the nature and scope of EU fundamental rights must be determined autonomously and may thus differ from fundamental rights recognised in the ECHR. See JL Murray, 'Fundamental Rights in the European Community Legal Order' (2008) 32 *Fordham International Law Journal* 531, 538.

[12] See also Case C-465/07 *Elgafaji* [2009] ECR I-921, Opinion of AG Maduro, para 23.

[13] S Iglesias Sánchez, 'The Court and the Charter: The Impact of the Entry into Force of the Lisbon Treaty on the ECJ's Approach to Fundamental Rights' (2012) 49 *Common Market Law Review* 1565, 1600.

[14] See Case C-69/10 *Samba Diouf* [2011] Opinion of AG Cruz Villalón, para 39. Kunoy and Mortansson state that in Case C-578/08 *Chakroun* [2010] ECR I-1839 the Court of Justice declined the invitation to emancipate the Charter from the ECHR. B Kunoy and B Mortansson, 'Case C-578/08, *Chakroun* [2010]' (2010) 47 *Common Market Law Review* 1815, 1826 and 1829–30.

[15] Bronckers writes that the Court of Justice reserves for itself the opportunity to give its own, diverging interpretation of the Convention's fundamental rights as incorporated in general principles of EC law. MCEJ Bronckers, 'The Relationship of the EC Courts with other International Tribunals: Non-committal, Respectful or Submissive?' (2007) 44 *Common Market Law Review* 601. See also P van Cleynenbreugel, 'Case C-69/10, *Samba Diouf* [2011]' 49 *Common Market Law Review* 327, 344. See further section 3.3.1.

[16] Case C-400/10 PPU *McB* [2010] ECR I-8965, para 53.

Here, the Court thus seems to exclude the possibility of Article 7 of the Charter offering broader protection than Article 8 ECHR.[17]

3.2 INTERNATIONAL TREATIES AND THE COMMON EUROPEAN ASYLUM SYSTEM

Article 63(1) of the former EC Treaty requires the asylum measures based on that provision, such as Directive 2005/85/EC, are 'in accordance with the Geneva Convention of 28 July 1951 and the Protocol of 31 January 1967 relating to the status of refugees and other relevant treaties'. Article 78 TFEU also states that the common policy on asylum, subsidiary protection and temporary protection must be in accordance with those treaties. This section will explain that besides the Refugee Convention, to which the mentioned provisions explicitly refer, the ECHR, the ICCPR, the CAT and the CRC should also be considered 'relevant treaties' in the context of the CEAS. Furthermore, it shows that all these treaties have been, or should be, recognised as sources of inspiration for the interpretation of EU fundamental rights.

The requirement of being in 'accordance with' international law mentioned in Article 63(1) of the former EC Treaty and Article 78 TFEU is almost unique in EU law.[18] It raises the question whether, on the basis of these provisions, the Court of Justice should apply the Refugee Convention and other relevant international treaties directly, instead of using them as sources of inspiration. Section 3.2.6 briefly addresses this question and explains why this study uses international treaties only as sources of inspiration for the EU right to an effective remedy and not as a separate category of norms.

3.2.1 The European Convention on Human Rights

The ECHR contains a set of civil and political rights which apply to every person within the jurisdiction of the High Contracting Parties irrespective of that person's nationality or legal status.[19] According to Article 6(3) TEU, the Charter[20] and the case law of the Court of Justice, the ECHR has special significance for the

[17] See also M den Heijer, 'Joined Cases C-411 & 493/10, *NS and ME and Others v Refugee Applications Commissioner, Minister for Justice, Equality and Law Reform* [2011]' (2012) 49 *Common Market Law Review* 1735, 1749.

[18] Battjes (n 6) 97.

[19] CW Wouters, *International Legal Standards for the Protection from Refoulement* (Antwerpen, Intersentia, 2009) 202.

[20] The Charter specifically states that it reaffirms the rights included in the ECHR and following from the case law of the ECtHR. See Art 52(3) of the Charter.

development of EU fundamental rights.[21] In the context of the CEAS, the ECHR should also be considered a 'relevant treaty' within the meaning of Article 63(1) of the former EC Treaty and Article 78 TFEU. This is due to the fact that Article 3 ECHR contains by far the most developed prohibition on *refoulement*.[22] Article 2 and Article 1 of Protocols 6 and 13 and, in exceptional cases, Article 6 ECHR, also contain prohibitions of *refoulement*.[23] The grounds for qualification as a person in need of subsidiary protection laid down in Article 2(e) in conjunction with Article 15 of the Qualification Directive are partly based on the case law of the ECtHR under Article 2 and 3 ECHR.[24] It will be argued in section 4.3.1 that the procedural guarantees following from Articles 3, 6, 13 and 35 ECHR inspire the EU right to an effective remedy in the context of the CEAS.

3.2.2 The Refugee Convention

The Refugee Convention 'provides the most comprehensive codification of the rights of refugees at the international level'.[25] The most important right granted to a refugee is the right to be protected from *refoulement*, as laid down in Article 33 of the Convention.

The relevance of the Refugee Convention for the CEAS has been explicitly recognised in Article 63(1) of the former EC Treaty and Article 78 TFEU. The preamble and the text of the Procedures Directive also refer to the Refugee Convention.[26] The Refugee Convention itself does not contain any provisions relating to refugee determination procedures.[27]

The Refugee Convention is most relevant for the interpretation of the criteria for qualification as a refugee laid down in the Qualification Directive which

[21] Case C-222/84 *Johnston* [1986] ECR 1651; see also Case C-540/03 *Parliament v Council* [2006] ECR I-5769, para 35.

[22] Wouters, *International Legal Standards* (n 19) 187.

[23] Ibid, 187. See also M den Heijer, 'Whose Rights and Which Rights? The Continuing Story of *Non-Refoulement* under the European Convention on Human Rights' (2008) 10 *European Journal of Migration and Law* 277.

[24] There are several other ECHR provisions which are relevant in the asylum context. See, eg Art 5 ECHR, which provides for rules for the detention of asylum applicants, and Art 4 of Protocol No 4, which prohibits collective expulsion of aliens.

[25] See UNHCR, *Introductory note to the Refugee Convention by the Office of the United Nations High Commissioner for Refugees* (August 2007) www.unhcr.org/3b66c2aa10.pdf accessed 29 September 2013, and the Preamble to the Refugee Convention.

[26] Recitals 2, 7, 13 Preamble and Art 2(a)(b) and (f), Art 3(3), Art 21(1)(c), Art 27(1)(b) and (d) and Art 36(2)(a) and (4) Dir 2005/85/EC and recitals 3, 25, 2(a), 29(1)(c), 38(1)(c) and (e) and 39(2)(a) Dir 2013/32/EU.

[27] UNHCR, *Handbook on Procedures and Criteria for Determining Refugee Status* (1979, new edition 1992) available at www.refworld.org/docid/3ae6b3314.html accessed 25 September 2013, para 191, refers to the fact that asylum procedures are not specifically regulated by the Refugee Convention and that, as a result, asylum procedures in State parties vary considerably. See also I Staffans, 'Judicial Protection and the New European Asylum Regime' (2010)12 *European Journal of Migration and Law* 273, 275.

are directly based on, and are often exactly the same as, those laid down in the Refugee Convention.[28] In particular, where the criteria is exactly the same the Qualification Directive should be considered to have the same meaning as the Refugee Convention.[29] According to recital 4 of the preamble of the Qualification Directive, 'the Geneva Convention and Protocol provide the cornerstone of the international legal regime for the protection of refugees'. The Court of Justice has referred to this recital in several cases in which it was asked to interpret provisions of the Qualification Directive, which are directly based on the Refugee Convention. It considered that the provisions of the Qualification Directive must be interpreted while respecting the Geneva Convention.[30]

3.2.3 The International Covenant on Civil and Political Rights

The ICCPR contains a list of civil and political rights, which apply to all persons irrespective of their nationality or legal status, including asylum applicants and refugees.[31] The Court of Justice has recognised the ICCPR as a source of inspiration for EU fundamental rights.[32] Furthermore, the ICCPR should be considered a relevant treaty in the sense of Article 63(1) of the former EC Treaty and Article 78 TFEU, as it contains prohibitions of *refoulement* in Article 6 (the right to life)[33] and Article 7 (prohibition of torture and cruel, inhuman or degrading treatment or punishment).[34] With respect to asylum procedures, Article 2(3) ICCPR, which obliges State parties to ensure that any person whose rights or freedoms as herein recognised are violated shall have an effective remedy, is most relevant.[35]

3.2.4 The UN Convention against Torture

The UN Convention against Torture and Other Cruel, Inhuman or Degrading Treatment or Punishment (CAT) seeks to 'make more effective the struggle against torture and other cruel, inhuman or degrading treatment or punishment throughout the world'.[36] In order to achieve this objective the Convention contains a set of obligations for the State parties, including the obligation to take

[28] See in particular, Arts 2(c), 11, 12 and 14 Dir 2011/95/EU.

[29] See Case C-31/09 *Bolbol* [2010] ECR I-5539, Opinion of AG Sharpston, para 92.

[30] See, eg Joined Cases C-175/08, C-176/08, C-178/08 and C-179/08 *Salahadin Abdulla* [2010] ECR I-1493, paras 52–53 and *Bolbol* (n 29) paras 37–38.

[31] See Art 2(1) ICCPR, HRC General Comment No 31 (2004, CCPR/C/21/Rev1/Add.13) para 10. See also Wouters (n 19) 362.

[32] *Parliament v Council* (n 21) para 37.

[33] See, eg HRC 20 October 2003, *Judge v Canada*, no 829/1998.

[34] See, eg HRC 10 November 2006, *Alzery v Sweden*, no 1416/2005.

[35] See further ch 4, section 4.3.1 in this volume.

[36] For the aims of the CAT, see M Nowak and E McArthur, *The United Nations Convention against Torture: A Commentary* (Oxford, Oxford University Press, 2008) 595.

effective legislative, administrative, judicial or other measures to prevent acts of torture in any territory under its jurisdiction.[37]

The CAT has not yet been recognised as a source of inspiration for EU fundamental rights by the Court of Justice. However, the CAT is expected to be so recognised in the future because all EU Member States are a party to this Convention. Article 3 CAT contains an explicit prohibition of *refoulement*,[38] which is guaranteed to all individuals, including stateless persons and illegal aliens.[39] Therefore, the CAT should be considered to be a relevant treaty in the meaning of Article 63(1) of the former EC Treaty and Article 78 TFEU. The CAT does not have an 'effective remedy provision' which is comparable to Article 13 ECHR or Article 2(3)(a) ICCPR. However, the Committee against Torture (ComAT) has derived a right to an effective remedy from the absolute prohibition of *refoulement* laid down in Article 3.[40]

3.2.5 The UN Convention on the Rights of the Child

The UN Convention on the Rights of the Child (CRC) contains a set of civil, social, cultural and economic rights, which shall be ensured to each child[41] within the State parties' jurisdiction without discrimination of any kind.[42] The Committee on the Rights of the Child (ComRC) has identified four general principles of the CRC: the right to non-discrimination; the primary consideration of the child's best interests; the right to life and development; and the right to be heard.[43]

The CRC has been recognised as a source of inspiration for EU fundamental rights by the Court of Justice.[44] Furthermore, it should be considered a relevant treaty for the purposes of Article 78 TFEU and Article 63 of the former EC Treaty for several reasons. First, the preambles of the measures adopted in the context of the second phase of CEAS explicitly refer to the CRC.[45] Secondly, the preambles of the first phase and second phase measures state that the fundamental rights and principles recognised by the Charter should be respected. Article 24 of the Charter includes the requirement that the child's best interests be a primary consideration in all actions relating to children. The Procedures Directive reflects

[37] See Wouters (n 19) 427.

[38] Art 3 CAT states that 'no State Party shall expel, return ("refouler") or extradite a person to another State where there are substantial grounds for believing that he would be in danger of being subjected to torture'.

[39] Wouters (n 19) 435.

[40] ComAT 20 May 2005, *Agiza v Sweden*, no 233/2003, para 13.6. See further ch 4, section 4.3.1 in this volume.

[41] According to Art 1 CRC a child means every human being below the age of 18 years unless under the law applicable to that child, majority is attained earlier.

[42] Art 2 CRC.

[43] ComRC General Comment No 5 (2003, CRC/GC/2003/5) para 12.

[44] *Parliament v Council* (n 21) para 37.

[45] See, eg recital 26 Preamble Dir 2013/32/EU and recital 18 Preamble Dir 2011/95/EU.

this fundamental right while stating that the best interests of the child 'shall be a primary consideration' for Member States when implementing the provisions of the Directive.[46] The 'best interests' principle included in Article 24 of the Charter and the Procedures Directive is based on Article 3 CRC. Other provisions of the Procedures Directive clearly affect children's rights although they are not directly based on one of the rights laid down in the CRC. Article 17 of Directive 2005/85/EC states, for example, that Member States must ensure that a representative acts for and/or assists the unaccompanied minor with respect to the examination of the asylum application. This representative must be able to inform the minor about and prepare him for the personal interview. Arguably these provisions should be interpreted in the light of the relevant provisions of the CRC. Article 22 CRC specifically addresses the rights of refugee and asylum-seeking children. Moreover, the CRC contains certain provisions which should be considered relevant for asylum procedures in particular, such as the State parties' duty to give due weight to the views of the child in accordance with the age and maturity of the child (Article 12 CRC).[47]

3.2.6 Direct Application of International Treaties?

The Court of Justice normally uses international treaties as sources of inspiration for the interpretation of EU fundamental rights. Arguably, this should be different when ruling in asylum cases. The text of Article 63(1) of the former EC Treaty and Article 78 TFEU suggests that the Court of Justice must apply relevant international treaties directly, instead of using them as sources of inspiration.[48] This means that the Court of Justice should test the legality of the Procedures Directive against human rights treaties and interpret its provisions in the light of these treaties. Arguably, the Court of Justice may also test national measures implementing the measures adopted under Article 63(1) directly against the relevant treaties mentioned in Article 63(1).[49] Direct application of international treaties by the Court of Justice could also be based on references to these treaties in secondary EU legislation, such as the text and preamble of the Procedures Directive, which refer to the Refugee Convention. The Court of Justice considered in several cases that the Qualification Directive, which also refers to the Refugee Convention, must 'be interpreted in the light of its general scheme and purpose, and in a manner consistent with the 1951 Geneva Convention and the other relevant treaties referred to in point (1) of the first paragraph of Article 63 EC, now Article 78(1)

[46] Recital 18 Preamble Dir 2011/95/EU, Art 17(6) Dir 2005/85/EC and recital 26 Preamble and Art 25 Dir 2013/32/EU.

[47] See further ch 7 of this volume on the asylum applicant's right to be heard on his asylum motives.

[48] See Battjes (n 6) 100–101.

[49] Ibid, 98–99.

TFEU'.[50] Furthermore, the Court of Justice in *Salahadin Abdulla* and *B and D* seems to consider the Refugee Convention and the Charter separate instruments for the interpretation of the Qualification Directive.[51]

However, it was concluded in section 3.1.1 that EU fundamental rights guarantee that the treaties mentioned in Article 63(1) of the former EC Treaty and 78 TFEU are fully respected. For this reason, it is not likely that the direct application of those treaties would result in a higher level of protection than the indirect application of international treaties as sources of inspiration of EU fundamental rights.[52] In this study international treaties will, therefore, not be treated as a separate category of norms, but only as sources of inspiration.

3.3 THE WEIGHT OF INTERNATIONAL TREATIES IN THE CASE LAW OF THE COURT OF JUSTICE

It is relevant to know whether the international treaties taken into account for the purpose of this study all have equal weight as sources of inspiration. What should be done if several relevant sources of inspiration or the views of their supervising bodies contradict each other? Could the interpretation of the EU fundamental rights and general principles be based on the non-binding view of supervising bodies alone?

Arguably, it follows from the specific references to the ECHR and the Refugee Convention in the Treaties, the Charter, and EU legislation that these treaties have special significance. Nothing can be found in those instruments as to the relative weight which should be attached to the ICCPR, the CRC or the CAT. It will be shown in this section that, in practice, the ECHR is by far the most important source of inspiration for EU fundamental rights. Much less weight is attributed to other international treaties. Murray states that the ECHR

> has played, and was bound to play, an increasingly central role in the Court's case law as a source from which inspiration may be drawn in fundamental rights cases, in comparison to which other international sources of inspiration referred to, such as various Council of Europe instruments and those emanating from the United Nations and the International Labour Organisation ('ILO') have played bit parts.[53]

The Authority of a Treaty's Sources of Interpretation

The importance of a treaty for the development of EU fundamental rights seems to relate primarily to the authority of the judgments or views of its sources

[50] *Salahadin Abdulla* (n 30) para 53 and Joined Cases C-57/09 and C-101/09 *B and D* [2010] ECR I-10979, para 78. The Court based this consideration on Art 63(1) of the EC Treaty and recitals 13, 16 and 17 Preamble Dir 2004/83/EC. See also *Bolbol* (n 29) Opinion of AG Sharpston, para 36.

[51] *B and D* (n 50) para 78 and *Salahadin Abdulla* (n 30) paras 53–54.

[52] See Battjes (n 6) 104.

[53] Murray 'Fundamental Rights' (n 11) 538.

of interpretation. The judgments of the ECtHR are binding and provide clear guidance as to the interpretation of the rights included in the Convention.[54] This makes it a suitable source of inspiration for EU fundamental rights. Section 3.3.1 will give an overview of the use of ECtHR case law by the Court of Justice.

It will be demonstrated in sections 3.3.2 to 3.3.4 that the EU Courts attach much less weight to non-binding views of other bodies, such as the institutions of the Council of Europe and the bodies supervising the Refugee Convention, the ICCPR, the CAT and the CRC. The Refugee Convention does not have a supervising court or any other legally binding sources for interpretation.[55] Guidance for the interpretation of the Refugee Convention is provided by the UN High Commissioner for Refugees (UNHCR)[56] and the Executive Committee of the Programme of the High Commissioner (EXCOM). The UNHCR has given its view on the application and interpretation of the Refugee Convention, including procedural issues, in the *Handbook on Procedures and Criteria for Determining Refugee Status* (UNHCR *Handbook*)[57] and its guidelines on international protection. EXCOM has issued several EXCOM Conclusions regarding requirements for national asylum procedures. The UNHCR's view[58] and EXCOM Conclusions[59] are not formally binding, but they do have authority.

The implementation of the ICCPR, the CAT and the CRC is supervised by the Human Rights Committee (HRC), the ComAT, and the ComRC respectively

[54] According to Art 46 ECHR, the judgments of the ECHR are legally binding on the State party to the case. However, the Court's judgments are also important for other State parties to the Convention. ECtHR (Plen) 18 January 1978, *Ireland v the United Kingdom*, no 5310/71, para 154 and ECtHR 24 July 2003, *Karner v Austria*, no 40016/98, para 26. See also JH Gerards, 'Judicial Deliberations in the European Court of Human Rights' in N Huls, M Adams and J Bomhof (eds), *The Legitimacy of Highest Court's Rulings* (The Hague, TMC Asser Press) 408–409.

[55] According to Art 38 of the Refugee Convention, the ICJ may be asked to interpret the Convention. However, at the time of writing, no referral to the ICJ has yet been made. There is no other body which is competent to provide legally binding decisions on the interpretation of the Refugee Convention. Wouters (n 19) 37.

[56] For the supervising role of UNHCR see the preamble and Art 35 of the Refugee Convention and Art 8(a) of the Statute of the office of the United Nations High Commissioner for Refugees. See also V Türk, *UNHCR's Role in Supervising International Protection Standards in the Context of its Mandate* (Geneva, UNHCR, 2010).

[57] UNHCR *Handbook* (n 27).

[58] W Kälin, 'Supervising the 1951 Convention Relating to the Status of Refugees: Article 35 and Beyond' in E Feller, V Türk and F Nicholson (eds), *Refugee Protection in International Law: UNHCR's Global Consultations on International Protection* (Cambridge, Cambridge University Press, 2003) 619 and 625–27; Battjes (n 6) 20. According to Hathaway, there is 'a traditional practice of giving particular weight to UNHCR's Handbook'. JC Hathaway, *The Rights of Refugees under International Law* (Cambridge, Cambridge University Press, 2005) 114–16. Several authors have contended that the authority of UNHCR guidelines is undermined because of their number, level of detail and varying objectives, formats and discourse. Ibid, 118, Wouters (n 19) 42.

[59] Hathaway, *The Rights of Refugees* (n 58) 113; Wouters (n 19) 45–46. Courts and tribunals in a range of jurisdictions use EXCOM Conclusions as soft law instruments for persuasive and even authoritative sources on matters of policy, legal practice or interpretation. B Deschamp and R Dowd, 'Review of the use of UNHCR Executive Committee Conclusions on International Protection' (Geneva, UNHCR, 2008) 22–27.

(in this study these Committees are also referred to as the UN Committees).[60] The views of the UN Committees, included in General Comments, Concluding Observations regarding State parties[61] and rulings in individual cases[62] do not bind the State parties.[63] However, the Committees' views on interpreting an application of the Convention should be considered as an authoritative interpretation.[64]

The following sections of this chapter will examine the Court of Justice's use of documents issued by the institutions of the Council of Europe (section 3.3.2), the UNHCR (section 3.3.3) and the views of the UN Committees (section 3.3.4). In section 3.3.5 it will be argued that the Court of Justice should, like the ECtHR, take account of non-binding but authoritative views of supervising bodies in its case law.

3.3.1 The Judgments of the ECtHR

The expansion of the European Union's areas of competence has resulted in the spheres of activity of the Luxembourg and Strasbourg courts progressively converging on each other. Asylum law is a very clear example of an area in which the competences of the Court of Justice and the ECtHR overlap.[65] It would be problematic if the two courts developed diverging case law on similar human rights issues. For this reason, the courts need to cooperate and take each other's judgments into account.[66]

The EU Courts have regularly referred to the case law of the ECtHR when applying general principles of EU law as well as the fundamental rights included in the Charter.[67] Douglas-Scott notes, however, that the citation of ECtHR case law

[60] Art 28 ICCPR, Art 17 CAT and Art 43 CRC.

[61] For the procedure followed by the Committees, see S Joseph, J Schultz and M Castan, *The International Covenant on Civil and Political Rights: Cases, Material and Commentary* (Oxford, Oxford University Press, 2004) 19 (HRC) and Nowak and McArthur, *The UN Convention against Torture* (n 36) 648 (ComAT). For the procedure followed by ComRC, see Rule 75 of its Rules of Procedure.

[62] See the Optional Protocol with the ICCPR and Art 22 CAT.

[63] For the HRC see Battjes (n 6) 21; Wouters (n 19) 365; and A Conte and R Burchill, *Defining Civil and Political Rights: The Jurisprudence of the United Nations Human Rights Committee* (Aldershot, Ashgate, 2009) For ComAT Nowak and McArthur (n 36) 777 and Battjes (n 6) 22.

[64] For the HRC see, eg I Boerefijn, *The Reporting Procedure under the Covenant on Civil and Political Rights, Practice and Procedures of the Human Rights Committee* (Antwerp/Groningen/Oxford, Intersentia/Hart Publishing, 1999) 300. With regard to ComAT, see Nowak and McArthur (n 36) 12; and Wouters (n 19) 431.

[65] See G Harpaz, 'The European Court of Justice and its Relations with the European Court of Human Rights: The Quest for Enhanced Reliance, Coherence and Legitimacy' (2009) 46 *Common Market Law Review* 105, 119.

[66] See JP Costa, 'The Relationship between the European Convention on Human Rights and European Union Law—A Jurisprudential Dialogue between the European Court of Human Rights and the European Court of Justice' (Lecture at the King's College London, 7 October 2008).

[67] See, eg the extensive references to the ECtHR's case law in Case C-279/09 *DEB* [2010] ECR I-3849, para 46 *et seq* and Joined Cases C-402/05 P and C-415/05 P *Kadi and Al Barakaat* [2008] ECR I-6351,

is a relatively new phenomenon, which started in the late 1980s with the Opinions of Advocates General and only occurred in a judgment by the Court of Justice in 1996.[68] He recognises two trends: the Court of Justice has in recent years referred to the case law of the ECtHR more frequently than before. Secondly, while earlier references to Strasbourg case law tended to be brief, more recent references are usually more reliant on this case law as a ground of justification, especially if they are made in Opinions of Advocates General.[69] Douglas-Scott states that references to Strasbourg case law continue to be relatively brief, but increasingly cite Strasbourg case law as an unqualified authority. Scott-Douglas points to a lack of coherence and method when the Court of Justice refers to Strasbourg case law.[70]

The Case Law of the ECtHR as Minimum Standard

The Court of Justice has not explicitly pronounced on the weight which should be attached ECtHR case law.[71] It has never explicitly accepted that it is bound by this case law.[72] However, the Court of Justice usually ensures that the level of protection offered by EU fundamental rights is not lower than that offered by the case law of the ECtHR.[73] In some cases the Court stressed that its interpretation is fully compatible with the ECHR, including the case law of the ECtHR.[74] The Court of Justice strongly reacts to the Strasbourg Court's findings on interpretation and level of protection.[75] In some cases, however, it is not clear whether the Court of Justice complies with ECtHR case law. The *NS* judgment on the Dublin Regulation, for example, extensively referred to the ECtHR's judgment in *MSS*.[76]

paras 310–14, 344, 360–63 and 368. An example of an asylum case is *Elgafaji* (n 12) para 27. See also Joined Cases C-411/10 and C-493/10 *NS and ME et al* [2011] Opinion of AG Trstenjak, para 147.

[68] S Douglas-Scott, 'A Tale of Two Courts: Luxembourg, Strasbourg and the Growing European Rights *Aquis*' (2006) 43 *Common Market Law Review* 629, 644. See also B de Witte, 'The Role of the ECJ in Human Rights' in P Alston, MR Bustelo and J Heenan (eds), *The EU and Human Rights* (Oxford, Oxford University Press, 1999) 878.

[69] Douglas-Scott, ibid, 645. See also Murray (n 11) 538.

[70] Douglas-Scott, ibid, 656.

[71] Ibid, 649 and 651; Harpaz, 'The ECJ and its Relations with the ECtHR' (n 65) 109–110.

[72] However, the CFI stated in Case T-69/04 *Schunk and Schunk Kohlenstoff-Technik v Commission* [2008] ECR II-2567, para 32: '[T]here is nothing which would justify the Court of First Instance giving a different interpretation of the principle of legality, which is a general principle of Community law, from that resulting from the Strasbourg Court's case-law.' Bronckers states that the EU Courts use the ECtHR's case law to 'bolster the persuasive force of their own rulings'. Bronckers, 'The Relationship of the EC Courts' (n 15) 601.

[73] Battjes (n 6) 94; Douglas-Scott (n 68) 650; and D Spielmann, 'Human Rights Case Law in the Strasbourg and Luxembourg Courts: Conflicts, Inconsistencies, and Complementarities' in P Alston, MR Bustelo and J Heenan (eds), *The EU and Human Rights* (Oxford, Oxford University Press, 1999) 770. See also section 3.1.

[74] See *Elgafaji* (n 12) para 44.

[75] Gerards states that she expects an extension of the scope of the rights laid down in the ECHR in the Strasbourg context, to be reflected in the Luxembourg case law. JH Gerards, 'Fundamental Rights and other Interests: Should it really make a Difference?' in E Brems (ed), *Conflicts between Fundamental Rights* (Antwerp, Intersentia, 2008) 655, 667 and 672.

[76] ECtHR (GC) 21 January 2011, *MSS v Belgium and Greece*, no 30696/09.

Commentators doubt, however, whether the criteria set out by the Court of Justice are in full conformity with the judgment of the ECtHR in *MSS*. The Court of Justice's definition of circumstances that give rise to a prohibition of transfer (systemic deficiencies in the asylum procedure and in the reception conditions of asylum seekers in the receiving Member State) seems to be more restrictive than that applied by the ECtHR.[77]

Although the Court of Justice has (generally) shown that it does not offer less protection than the ECtHR under the ECHR, the Court finds that it is free to offer its own divergent jurisprudence of EU law.[78] Advocate General Maduro stated in his Opinion in the *Elgafaji* case that: 'Community provisions, irrespective of which provisions are concerned, are given an independent interpretation which cannot therefore vary according to and/or be dependent on developments in the case-law of the European Court of Human Rights'.[79] He added that the interpretation of the Convention by the ECtHR is dynamic and always changing. He argued that it is not for the EU Courts to determine the interpretation of Article 3 ECHR which should prevail. However, he did recognise in this same Opinion that

> although the case-law of the Strasbourg court is not a binding source of interpretation of Community fundamental rights, it constitutes none the less a starting point for determining the content and scope of those rights within the European Union. Taking that case-law into account is, moreover, essential to ensure that the Union, founded on the principle of respect for human rights and fundamental freedoms, will contribute to extending the protection of those rights in the European area.[80]

The independent interpretation of EU provisions thus only seems to result in broader, and not more limited, protection than under the ECHR.[81]

Several examples can be found in the case law of the Court of Justice in which the Court adopted a more generous interpretation of a fundamental right than the ECtHR. Douglas Scott refers to the judgments in *Carpenter*[82] and *Akrich*,[83] in which the Court gave a very generous interpretation of the ECtHR's judgment in *Boultif*.[84] Some commentators refer to the judgment in *Parliament v Council*, in which the Court of Justice recognised a 'right to live with one's close family',[85] and

[77] den Heijer, 'Joined Cases C-411 & 493/10' (n 17) 1747; C Costello, 'Dublin-case NS/ME: Finally, an end to blind trust across the EU?' (2012) 3 *Asiel & Migrantenrecht* 83, 89.

[78] Harpaz (n 65) 112.

[79] *Elgafaji* (n 12) Opinion of AG Maduro, para 19. See also *NS and ME* (n 67) Opinion of AG Trstenjak, para 146 and *Samba Diouf* (n 14) Opinion of AG Cruz Villalón, para 39.

[80] The Court of Justice itself seems to suggest in *Elgafaji* (n 12) para 28 that the interpretation of the scope of EU provisions which correspond to rights laid down in the ECHR (in this case Article 15(b) Dir 2004/83/EC) must be carried out on the basis of the ECtHR's case law.

[81] This also follows from *Elgafaji* (n 12) para 28.

[82] *Carpenter* (n 10).

[83] *Akrich* (n 10).

[84] ECtHR 2 August 2001, *Boultif v Switzerland*, no 54273/00.

[85] *Parliament v Council* (n 21) para 52.

stated that it follows from the Family Reunification Directive[86] that applications for family reunification should be examined with a view to promoting family life.[87] Both formulations seem to offer more protection than the standing case law by the ECtHR under Article 8 ECHR.[88] In the cases mentioned the Court has not given any reasons for a broader interpretation.[89]

Possible Situations of the Court of Justice Providing a Lower Level of Protection than the ECtHR

Three situations may be distinguished in which the Court of Justice has adopted, or may adopt, a different view on a human rights issue to the ECtHR, which results in a lower standard of protection. First, the Court of Justice may have to apply existing Strasbourg case law to a new situation on which the Strasbourg court has not yet ruled. Then, the Court of Justice has to give its own interpretation of an EU fundamental right which corresponds to a right laid down in the ECHR. In these types of situations the Court of Justice has adopted a different, more restrictive view on the content of such a right, than the view of the ECtHR in later case law.[90] The Court of Justice was prepared to reconsider its own case law in view of subsequent developments in Strasbourg.[91]

Secondly, the ECtHR may change its standing case law concerning an issue after a judgment of the Court of Justice on the same issue. As Maduro noted in his Opinion in *Elgafaji*, the interpretation of the Convention by the Strasbourg Court is dynamic and changes over time.[92] This because the ECtHR considers the Convention to be 'a living instrument', which must be interpreted in the light of current conditions.[93] Therefore, the ECtHR may adopt a broader view on a particular issue than that of the Court of Justice, which was based on the 'old' case law of the ECtHR. On the basis of Article 52(3) of the Charter and the standing case law of the Court of Justice, it is likely that in this situation too the Court

[86] Council Dir 2003/86/EC of 22 September 2003 on the right to family reunification [2003] OJ L251/12.

[87] *Parliament v Council* (n 21) para 88.

[88] P Boeles, 'Case C-540/03, *Parliament v Council* [2006]' (2006) *Jurisprudentie Vreemdelingenrecht*, no 2006/313; Kunoy and Mortansson, 'Case C-578/08, *Chakroun*' (n 14) 1825. See also Case C-404/92P *X v Commission* [1994] para 17, where the Court of Justice held that the right to respect for private life, embodied in Art 8 of the ECHR and deriving from the common constitutional traditions of Member States includes in particular a person's right to keep his state of health secret. See Spielmann 'Human Rights Case Law' (n 73)1999 775–76.

[89] Bulterman argues that the Court of Justice has to reason why a specific human right which can be found in the ECHR should be given a more favourable interpretation when it is applied as a fundamental principle of EU law. M Bulterman, 'Case C-540/03, *Parliament v Council* [2006]' (2008) 45 *Common Market Law Review* 245, under 5.3.

[90] Douglas-Scott refers to Case C-347/87 *Orkem* [1989] ECR I-1083 and Case 227/88 *Hoechst* [1989]. Douglas-Scott (n 68) 645.

[91] Costa, 'The Relationship between the ECHR and EU Law' (n 66). See also Murray (n 11) 543.

[92] *Elgafaji* (n 12) Opinion of AG Maduro, para 20.

[93] See, eg ECtHR (GC) 4 February 2005, *Mamatkulov and Askarov v Turkey*, no 46827/99, para 121.

of Justice will reconsider its case law in the light of subsequent developments in Strasbourg.

Thirdly, it is possible that the Court of Justice could misunderstand the ECtHR's case law and, as a result, adopt a different view than the ECtHR. Arguably, the Court of Justice misunderstood the ECtHR's judgment in *NA* in its ruling in the *Elgafaji* case.[94] In this case the Court of Justice considered that the serious harm defined in paragraphs (a) and (b) of Article 15 of the Qualification Directive, which are based on Articles 2 and 3 ECHR and the case law of the ECtHR, required a clear degree of individualisation of the risk of serious harm. However, the ECtHR had ruled less than a year before the judgment in *Elgafaji*, in its judgment in *NA*, that Article 3 ECHR may also apply in extreme cases of general violence, where there is a real risk of ill-treatment simply by virtue of an individual being exposed to such violence on return.[95] Therefore, under Article 3 ECHR in a situation of extreme general violence no 'individualisation' is required. Although the Court of Justice referred to *NA* in its judgment it did not seem to recognise this. Errors, such as the one in *Elgafaji*, should be considered as incidents which do not detract from the fact that in principle the Court of Justice abides by the ECtHR's case law. The error in *Elgafaji* did not result in a lower level of protection than that guaranteed by the ECtHR.[96]

3.3.2 Council of Europe Documents

Texts adopted by the Institutions of the Council of Europe have played a marginal role in the EU Courts' case law. The Court of First Instance referred to guidelines by the Committee of Ministers in *Sison* in order to support its position that a right to an effective remedy should be provided particularly in the context of measures to freeze the funds of persons or organisations suspected of terrorist activities.[97] In *Parliament v Council*, the European Parliament invoked two Committee of Minister Recommendations in support of its appeal.[98] However, the Court did

[94] *Elgafaji* (n 12). See, eg TP Spijkerboer, 'Case C-465/07, *Elgafaji* [2009]' (2009) *Jurisprudentie Vreemdelingenrecht*, no 2009/111.

[95] ECtHR 17 July 2008, *NA v the United Kingdom*, no 25904/07, para 115.

[96] According to the Court of Justice, Art 15(c) Dir 2004/83/EC/Dir 2011/95/EU covers risks of serious harm which result from the general human rights situation in the country of origin.

[97] Case T-47/03 *Sison v Council* [2007] ECR II-73, paras 157–58; see also Case T-228/02 *Organisation des Modjahedines du peuple d'Iran v Council* [2006] ECR II-4665, paras 111 and 135. In Case C-421/09 *Humanplasma GmbH* [2010] ECR I-12869 the reference in the applicable EU legislation to a specific Council of Europe document was the reason to take it into account.

[98] Committee of Ministers of the Council of Europe, Recommendation No R (94) 14 on coherent and integrated family policies (22 November 1994) available at wcd.coe.int/com.instranet.InstraServlet?command=com.instranet.CmdBlobGet&InstranetImage=534811&SecMode=1&DocId=515750&Usage=2 accessed 29 September 2013; and Recommendation No R (99) 23 on family reunion for refugees and other persons in need of international protection (15 December 1999) available at wcd.coe.int/com.instranet.InstraServlet?command=com.instranet.CmdBlobGet&InstranetImage=540364&SecMode=1&DocId=428672&Usage=2 accessed 29 September 2013.

not include these recommendations in its judgment.[99] The Advocates General have referred to recommendations of the Committee of Ministers and the Parliamentary Assembly in some of their Opinions.[100]

3.3.3 UNHCR Documents and EXCOM Conclusions

In its case law the Court of Justice has taken account of, or made reference to, the UNHCR's view in its recent judgment in *HID*.[101] It considered that the UNHCR endorsed the interpretation by the Irish Government of Article 23(3) of Directive 2005/85/EC on accelerated procedures. In *NS* the Court of Justice considered the observations submitted on behalf of the UNHCR as well as Amnesty International and the AIRE Centre.[102] In several other cases the Court of Justice refrained from explicitly taking into account the UNHCR's view although it had the opportunity to do so.[103] Several cases concerned the interpretation of provisions of EU law which were directly based on the Refugee Convention. Furthermore, in some of these cases the applicant relied on the UNHCR's view.[104] Finally, the UNHCR issued statements in the context of these cases in which it set out its views on the questions referred to the Court of Justice.[105] In *Salahadin Abdullah* the Court of Justice adopted a different interpretation of the cessation clauses provided by the Qualification Directive to that proposed by the UNHCR. The Court ruled that refugee status ceases to exist when, having regard to a change of circumstances of a significant and non-temporary nature in the third country concerned, the circumstances which justified the person's fear of persecution on the basis of which refugee status was granted no longer exist and that person has no other reason to fear 'persecution'. According to the UNHCR, the cessation clauses should only apply when the applicant is effectively protected in his country of origin, which entails more than the absence of a fear of persecution, namely a respect for human rights, including the right to a basic livelihood.[106]

[99] *Parliament v Council* (n 21) para 33.

[100] See, eg Case C-353/99 P *Hautala* [2001] ECR I-9565, Opinion of AG Léger para 62; Case C-105/03 *Pupino* [2005] ECR I-5285, Opinion of AG Kokott, para 55; and Case C-270/99 P *Z v Parliament* [2001] ECR I-9197, Opinion of AG Jacobs, para 40.

[101] Case C-175/11 *HID and BA* [2013] para 55.

[102] *NS and ME* (n 67). The AIRE Centre is a specialist charity whose mission is to promote awareness of European law rights and assist marginalised individuals and those in vulnerable circumstances to assert those rights.

[103] The UK Government has argued before the Court of Justice that the UNHCR Guidelines are not binding on Member States as a matter of international law and have not been incorporated into Community law. See *Salahadin Abdulla* (n 30) Opinion of AG Mázak, para 36.

[104] See, eg ibid, para 32.

[105] In reference to Dir 2005/85/EC, see UNHCR, 'Statement on the right to an effective remedy in relation to accelerated asylum procedures' (21 May 2010) available at www.refworld.org/docid/4bf67fa12.html accessed 29 September 2013.

[106] See UNHCR, 'Statement on the "Ceased Circumstancese Clause of the EC Qualification Directive' (August 2008) available at www.refworld.org/docid/48a2f0782.html accessed 29 September 2013, para 4.1.2.

The Advocates General have paid more attention to UNHCR documents in their Opinions.[107] In the *Bolbol* case concerning the criteria for excluding Palestinians from refugee status, AG Sharpston considered that 'the UNHCR occasionally makes statements which have persuasive, but not binding, force'.[108] In her Opinion she disagreed with the interpretation put forward by the Office of the UNHCR because she was guided primarily by the clear text of the provision of the Refugee Convention, which has not been amended in over 50 years. She stated: 'In contrast, it seems to me that the UNHCR's reading has varied over time, reflecting the intractable nature of the Palestine problem.'[109] Advocate General Mengozzi wrote in his Opinion in *B and D* which concerned the interpretation of the EU criteria for excluding a person from refugee status that guidance for interpreting provisions of the Qualification Directive which have their origin in the text of the Refugee Convention is provided by the EXCOM Conclusions, the UNHCR *Handbook* and UNHCR's Guidelines on International Protection. He also referred to the fact that UNHCR's view is not always clear, as UNHCR documents sometimes contradict each other.[110] AG Mengozzi in his Opinion made extensive references to UNHCR documents, such as the UNHCR *Handbook* and Guidelines as well as the document specifically drawn up by UNHCR for the purposes of the case before the Court of Justice.[111]

3.3.4 The Views of the UN Committees

The views of UN Committees have played a minor role in the case law of the Court of Justice.[112] The Court only ruled on the relevance of the HRC's view in its judgment in *Grant*.[113] So far, the Court of Justice has not addressed the relevance of General Comments or Concluding Observations of the Human Rights Committee, or of the views of the ComAT or ComRC in its case law. The considerations in *Grant* may, however, also apply to those sources of interpretation.

In *Grant* the applicant argued before the Court of Justice that Article 119 of the former EC Treaty, which prohibited discrimination on the basis of sex, should

[107] In Joined Cases C-356/11 and C-357/11 *O, S and L* [2012] AG Bot referred in his Opinion to UNHCR Guidelines on Determining the Best Interests of the Child, and in his Opinion in Case C-277/11 *MM v Minister for Justice, Equality and Law Reform Ireland* [2012] he referred to the UNHCR *Handbook* (n 27) and UNHCR's annotated comments on Dir 2004/83/EC.

[108] *Bolbol* (n 29) Opinion of AG Sharpston, para 16.

[109] Ibid, para 76.

[110] *B and D* (n 50) Opinion of AG Mengozzi, para 43.

[111] In the Opinions in *Salahadin Abdulla* (n 30) para 32; and *Elgafaji* (n 12) the AG did not take UNHCR's view into account.

[112] I de Jesús Butler and O de Schutter, 'Binding the EU to International Human Rights Law' (2007) 26 *Yearbook of European Law* 277, 282–83.

[113] Case C-249/96 *Grant* [1998] ECR I-621, paras 44–47.

include discrimination on the basis of sexual orientation.[114] She referred to a view of the HRC in an individual complaint, according to which the term 'sex' mentioned in the prohibitions of discrimination laid down in Articles 2(1) and 26 ICCPR includes the meaning 'sexual orientation'.[115]

The Court of Justice reiterated that the Covenant is one of the international instruments relating to the protection of human rights of which the Court takes account in applying the fundamental principles of EU law. However, it considered that the HRC is not a judicial institution and that its findings have no binding force in law. It furthermore noted that the HRC's view did not in any event appear to reflect the interpretation so far generally accepted of the concept of discrimination based on sex which appeared in various international instruments concerning the protection of fundamental rights. In this regard, it referred to ECtHR case law, which stated that homosexual relationships did not fall within the scope of Articles 8 and 12 ECHR.[116] Furthermore, the Court took into account that the laws of the Member States did not generally treat same-sex relationships in the same way as marriages between persons of the opposite sex. The Court concluded that the HRC's view could not constitute a basis for the Court to extend the scope of Article 119 of the former EC Treaty to include sexual orientation. Butler and de Schutter state that the *Grant* case underlines the lack of faith that the Court of Justice places in the interpretations of international human rights law issued by the monitoring bodies responsible for supervising the correct implementation of these treaties. In their view, the Court of Justice ignores the generally accepted view that the UN monitoring bodies' interpretation of the treaties should be treated as authoritative.[117]

One may conclude from this judgment that the view of the HRC (or the ComAT or the ComRC) alone cannot provide sufficient basis for extensive interpretation of a Treaty provision. However, the Court did not exclude the possibility that those views may inspire the Court in future cases.[118] This could be the case especially where they corroborate the case law of the ECtHR and/or other treaty

[114] Ms Grant was refused travel benefits for her female partner by her employer, while those benefits were granted to persons of opposite sex, who were married or involved in a meaningful relationship.

[115] HRC 31 March 1994, *Toonen v Australia*, no 488/1992. The Court of Justice remarks that the HRC, as it stated itself without giving specific reasons, confined itself to 'noting … that in its view the reference to "sex" in Articles 2, paragraph 1, and 26 is to be taken as including sexual orientation'. *Grant* (n 113) para 46.

[116] Spielmann notes, however, that the Court of Justice omitted to have a close look at the ECtHR's case law on Art 8 ECHR, in particular the so-called 'positive obligations' theory imposing concrete action on public authorities. Spielmann (n 73) 774.

[117] Butler and de Schutter, 'Binding the EU' (n 112) 284–85.

[118] The fact that Advocates General have referred to the views of the HRC in several Opinions may indicate that the UN supervising bodies' views may be taken into account by the Court in future cases. See Case C-436/04 *van Esbroeck* [2006] Opinion of AG Ruiz-Jarabo Colomer (interpretation of the *ne bis in idem* principle), *Parliament v Council* (n 21) Opinion of AG Kokott (the right to family life); and Case C-357/09 PPU *Kadzoev* [2006] Opinion of AG Mazák (possibilities of detention of asylum applicants).

bodies and/or the interpretation stemming from the laws of the Member States.[119] The Court of Justice may be more willing to follow the UN Committees' views when interpreting secondary EU legislation than when determining the meaning of a Treaty provision. Some Advocates General have referred to the view of the HRC in their Opinions.[120]

3.3.5 Should Non-binding Documents be taken into Account?

There are strong arguments that the non-binding views of the Institutions of the Council of Europe, the UNHCR and the UN Committees should be taken into account by the Court of Justice. The weight which should be attached to those views depends on their quality of reasoning.[121] Most importantly, it would be inconsistent for the Court of Justice to recognise a treaty as a source of inspiration, while ignoring the views of the body supervising this treaty which are generally considered to be an important subsidiary means of interpretation of those treaties. Furthermore, systematic interpretation of a fundamental right may be facilitated by a comparative analysis of international or regional human rights treaties which include a similar right.[122] An interesting development in this regard is the current trend in the case law of the ECtHR case law to use soft law standards as a source of interpretation.[123] This could prompt the Court of Justice to do the same, particularly when interpreting EU fundamental rights corresponding to rights recognised in the ECHR.

The ECtHR, when interpreting the rights laid down in the Convention, takes into account 'any relevant rules and principles of international law applicable in relations between the Contracting Parties'.[124] In *Demir and Baykara* the ECtHR considered that in interpreting the Convention it

> can and must take into account elements of international law other than the Convention, the interpretation of such elements by competent organs, and the practice of European States reflecting their common values. The consensus emerging from specialised international instruments and from the practice of Contracting States may constitute a relevant consideration for the Court when it interprets the provisions of the Convention in specific cases.[125]

[119] See also Butler and de Schutter (n 112) 283. They state that the cases of the Court of Justice imply that the Court will rely primarily on the ECHR, and while it may draw on other treaties to complement its analysis, it may not draw on them where they appear to go beyond the ECHR, except when there appears to be some support for this in the EC or EU Treaty.

[120] See Joined Cases C-71/11 and C-99/11 *Y and Z* [2012], Opinion of AG Bot (reference to General Comment No 22) and *O, S and L* (n 107) Opinion of AG Bot (reference to General Comment No 17).

[121] See Battjes (n 6) 22.

[122] Wouters (n 19) 12; and Nowak and McArthur (n 36) 12.

[123] See T Barkhuysen and ML van Emmerik, 'Ongebonden binding, Verwijzing naar soft law-standaarden in uitspraken van het EHRM' (2010) 35 *NTM/NJCM-Bulletin* 827.

[124] ECtHR (GC) 29 January 2008, *Saadi v the United Kingdom*, no 13229/03, para 62. See also ECtHR 12 March 2003, *Öcalan v Turkey*, no 46221/99, para 190.

[125] ECtHR (GC) 12 November 2008, *Demir and Baykara v Turkey*, no 34503/97, para 85.

The ECtHR has mentioned many different sources which may be relevant, including the ICCPR, CAT, CRC and the Refugee Convention.[126] In its case law the Court regularly refers to non-binding documents such as views in individual cases[127] or General Comments and Concluding Observations of UN supervising bodies.[128] The ECtHR also takes into account UNHCR documents, such as the UNHCR *Handbook*,[129] EXCOM Conclusions and Guidelines.[130] Council of Europe documents, such as the recommendations, resolutions or guidelines of the Committee of Ministers and the Parliamentary Assembly were taken into account in several cases, including some asylum cases.[131] The ECtHR does not seem to have developed clear guidelines for using non-binding documents for its interpretation of the Convention. Its case law does not show when such documents should be taken into account and the weight which should be granted to them.[132] The ECtHR seems to regard the views adopted by supervisory bodies to international treaties as a relevant consideration for the ECtHR. However, it does not always follow such views.[133]

3.4 THE RELATIVE WEIGHT OF INTERNATIONAL TREATIES AS SOURCES OF INSPIRATION

It should be expected on the basis of the existing case law of the Court of Justice that, in the context of asylum procedures too, the Court of Justice will attach by far the most weight to the ECHR and the case law of the ECtHR when looking for inspiration for the interpretation of EU fundamental rights. This is not only the result of the 'special significance' granted to the ECHR by Article 6(3) TEU and the Charter. It is also due to the fact that the most important source of interpretation of the ECHR, the judgments of the ECtHR, are all binding upon the

[126] Ibid, paras 69–86 and ECtHR 28 October 2010, *Fawsie v Greece*, no 40080/07, para 38 (Refugee Convention).

[127] See *Saadi* (n 124) paras 31–32. In *Öcalan* (n 124) paras 60–62 and 203, the ECtHR used the view of the HRC to support its ruling that the implementation of the death penalty in respect of a person who has not had a fair trial would not be permissible under Art 2 ECHR.

[128] ECtHR (GC) 19 February 2009, *A et al v the United Kingdom*, no 3455/05, paras 110 and 178, ECtHR (GC) 23 June 2008, *Maslov v Austria*, no 1638/03, para 83 read in conjunction with 37–38, ECtHR 12 October 2006, *Mubilanzila Mayeka and Kaniki Mitunga v Belgium*, no 13178/03, para 40 and ECtHR 10 February 2011, *Soltysyak v Russia*, no 4663/05, para 51.

[129] ECtHR 2 September 2010, *YP and LP v France*, no 32476/06, para 73.

[130] *Saadi* (n 124) paras 34–35. The Court rejected a narrow interpretation of Art 5(1)(f) ECHR amongst other reasons because such an interpretation would be inconsistent with EXCOM Conclusion no 44 (XXXVII) 1986, the UNHCR's Guidelines and a Recommendation of the Committee of Ministers of the Council of Europe.

[131] ECtHR 26 April 2007, *Gebremedhin v France*, no 25389/05, para 58, ECtHR (Adm) 2 December 2008, *KRS v the United Kingdom*, no 32733/08; ECtHR 23 October 2008, *Soldatenko v Ukraine*, no 2440/07, para 30.

[132] See Barkhuysen and van Emmerik, 'Ongebonden binding' (n 123) 834–35.

[133] See, eg *A et al* (n 128) paras 110 and 178. In *Saadi* (n 124) the ECtHR does not seem to follow the HRC's views regarding detention of aliens under Art 9 ICCPR.

State parties to the ECHR and constitute an extensive body of case law. The non-binding recommendations and resolutions issued by Council of Europe institutions have played a marginal role in the case law of the EU Courts.

In asylum cases, the Refugee Convention also seems to have a special status as a source of inspiration, because of its explicit recognition as a 'relevant treaty' in the asylum context by Article 63 of the former EC Treaty and Article 78 TFEU as well as the preambles and texts of the EU measures adopted under this provision. The Court of Justice interprets EU asylum legislation, as well as probably EU fundamental rights, in the light of the Refugee Convention. However, this is difficult if the relevant provisions of the Refugee Convention need interpretation, because the Convention lacks a supervising body, which is competent to provide legally binding decisions on the interpretation of its provisions. With regard to procedural issues, the Refugee Convention does not provide much guidance, as it does not contain any provisions which cover refugee determination procedures. The Court of Justice can only rely on (non-binding) UNHCR documents and EXCOM Conclusions when examining the procedural requirements following from the Refugee Convention. However, those documents have so far not played a very visible role in the case law of the Court of Justice. In fact, the Court of Justice itself has arguably become the most important source of interpretation of the Refugee Convention.

The potential impact of the UN treaties on the development of EU fundamental rights, including the right to an effective remedy, seems to be limited. This is due to the fact that the Court is clearly hesitant to take into account the non-binding views of the UN supervising bodies, which may provide guidance as to the interpretation of those treaties. The UN Conventions have played a minor role in the case law of the Court of Justice. It should be concluded from *Grant* and the lack of references to the non-binding views of UN supervising bodies that the Court of Justice is not easily persuaded to follow those views. This seems to be specifically the case when this view is not sustained by ECtHR case law, the constitutional traditions of the Member States, or potentially non-binding views of other supervising bodies.

However, the non-binding views of institutions of the Council of Europe, UNHCR and the UN Committees could serve as sources of inspiration in future asylum cases. It was even argued in section 3.3.5 that the Court of Justice should take into account these authoritative views and attach weight to them according to their quality of reasoning. Such practice would correspond with the current trend in the case law of the ECtHR to use 'soft law standards' as a source of interpretation.

Consequences for the Way this Study is Conducted

In this study international treaties are not treated as a separate category of norms, which should be directly applied by the Court of Justice in the asylum context. They are only used as sources of inspiration for the EU right to an effective remedy. As was explained in section 3.1.1, it is expected that this will have no consequences for the way the EU right to an effective remedy will be interpreted.

For the purpose of finding the content and meaning of the EU right to an effective remedy in the context of asylum, the following assumptions will be used as to the relative weight which should be granted to the different sources of inspiration included in this study.

— The ECHR and the ECtHR's case law have most significance as a source of inspiration for EU fundamental rights.
— Where the ECtHR's view is corroborated by the non-binding views of other supervising bodies, an even more solid basis for the interpretation of EU fundamental rights is provided.
— Where the ECtHR's case law and the non-binding view of another supervising body conflict, the Court of Justice generally follows the ECtHR.
— The Court of Justice does not seem to be prepared to adopt a far-reaching interpretation of an EU fundamental right on the basis of the non-binding view of one supervising body alone.
— If the views of more supervising bodies (for example, the HRC, the ComAT and the UNHCR) agree, the Court of Justice may be more inclined to follow these views.

In this study the ECHR and the case law of the ECtHR will thus play a central role as a source of inspiration for the interpretation of the EU right to an effective remedy. Where the ECtHR's case law is clear on a certain issue, the non-binding views of other supervising bodies will only be briefly addressed. Where the ECtHR's case law does not set clear requirements, more attention will be paid to such non-binding views. The weight which is attached to these non-binding views depends on their quality of reasoning. This study will be reluctant to base the interpretation of the EU right to an effective remedy on non-binding views alone.

4

The EU Right to an Effective Remedy and Related Procedural Rights and Principles

THIS CHAPTER WILL address the scope of application and the general content and meaning of the EU right to an effective remedy. It will also introduce the procedural rights included in or linked to this right, such as the right to a fair trial, the principle of effectiveness, and the right to good administration, as well as the specific rights they encompass (sections 4.3 to 4.4). These EU rights and principles will be used in this study to build a set of EU standards for the themes discussed in chapters six to ten. This chapter also establishes the specific sources of international law inspiring these EU procedural rights.

At the time of writing, the Court of Justice has only recognised Articles 6 and 13 European Convention on Human Rights (ECHR) as sources of inspiration for the EU right to an effective remedy. However, it is argued in this chapter that in the asylum context the case law of the European Court of Human Rights (ECtHR) regarding substantive provisions such as the prohibition of *refoulement* and provisions regarding the exhaustion of domestic remedies, should also be considered relevant for the development of EU procedural rights. Furthermore, it is expected that other provisions of international law, which also include a right to an effective remedy or a right to a fair hearing, such as Articles 2(3) and 14 International Covenant on Civil and Political Rights (ICCPR) and Article 3 UN Convention against Torture and Other Cruel, Inhuman or Degrading Treatment or Punishment (CAT), will serve as sources of inspiration for EU fundamental rights.[1]

Before introducing the EU rights to effective judicial protection and the right to good administration, two important issues will be addressed. Section 4.1 concerns the potential impact of EU procedural rights on national procedural systems. It shows that Court of Justice case law on EU procedural rights, in particular the right to an effective remedy, has considerably limited what is often called the principle of procedural autonomy of the Member States. It may, therefore, be expected

[1] It was argued in ch 3, sections 3.2.3 and 3.2.4 in this volume that the ICCPR and the CAT should be considered as sources of inspiration for EU fundamental rights in the asylum context.

that the EU right to an effective remedy will limit the Member States' discretion to design their asylum procedures.

Section 4.2 addresses the interrelationship between the different EU procedural rights. It contends that all EU procedural rights discussed in this study are interlinked. Therefore, it is sometimes difficult to establish which procedural right should be applied to a particular procedural issue. The EU Courts do not give clear guidance in this respect. It is argued, however, that it is not necessary for the purpose of this study to define the exact relationship between the EU procedural rights discussed in this chapter. With regard to each of the themes addressed in chapters six to ten, the relevant case law of the EU Courts will be examined, irrespective of the procedural right applied by these courts. EU procedural rights are thus treated as a category of rights, which overlap and complement each other.

Finally, it will be explained in section 4.5 that three 'basic concepts' emerge from the case law of the Court of Justice as well as the ECtHR regarding procedural rights. These concepts will be used to analyse the case law examined in the thematic chapters six to ten and to develop a set of EU procedural standards for the procedural topics discussed in some of these chapters.

1. When assessing whether EU procedural rights have been infringed, interests must often be balanced against each other.
2. When determining whether a procedure should be considered fair, regard should be had to all aspects and instances of this procedure: the overall fairness of a procedure must be examined.
3. The subject matter of the procedure influences the level of procedural protection which must be offered to the applicant.

4.1 LIMITATIONS TO THE PROCEDURAL AUTONOMY OF MEMBER STATES

The Court of Justice, when assessing national procedural rules which are not governed by EU law, takes national procedural autonomy as a starting point.[2] It considers:

> In the absence of EU rules governing the matter, it is for the legal system of each Member State to designate the courts and tribunals having jurisdiction and to lay down the detailed procedural rules governing actions for safeguarding rights which individuals derive from EU law.[3]

[2] M Accetto and S Zlepnig, 'The Principle of Effectiveness: Rethinking Its Role in Community Law' (2005) 11 *European Public Law* 375, 396. The Court of Justice has explicitly referred to the principle of procedural autonomy in Case C-201/02 *Wells* [2004] ECR I-723, para 67; Case C-212/04 *Adeneler* [2006] ECR I-6057, para 95; and Case C-314/09 *Strabag et al* [2010] ECR I-8769, para 34.

[3] See, eg Case C-115/09 *Trianel Kohlekraftwerk Lünen* [2011] ECR I-3673, para 43. Schwartze notes that the principle of the administrative autonomy is explicitly stipulated in Art 291(1) TFEU. See J Schwartze, 'European Administrative Law in the Light of the Treaty of Lisbon' (2012) 18 *European Public Law* 285, 292.

The idea which is underlying the principle of national procedural autonomy is consistent with the principle of subsidiarity and recognises that 'national procedural rules may reflect deep-seated cultural and ethical values and should not be lightly set aside'.[4] Indeed, sometimes the EU Courts seem reluctant to impose obligations on Member States with regard to procedural guarantees or remedies. The Court of Justice, for example, refrained from imposing the conditions for granting interim protection at the national level where compatibility of national law with EU law is concerned. It did so only for cases before the national courts in which the legality of EU law was contested.[5]

Much has been written on the principle of national procedural autonomy and it is not feasible to give an extensive overview of relevant literature in this section.[6] However, it should be noted here that there seems to be a broad consensus among scholars that, as a result of the case law of the Court of Justice, the national procedural autonomy of Member States is, in practice, very limited. This limitation is the result of the important role of national legal systems to implement and enforce EU law.[7] According to Trstenjak and Beysen,

> the concept of procedural autonomy of the Member States does not imply the existence of a general principle of EU law, according to which each Member State has the right to preserve a nucleus of national procedural rules with regard to the enforcement of rights derived from EU law.[8]

Schwartze states that 'notwithstanding national autonomy, the need for equity and effectiveness has led to considerable Community influence on national administrative law and procedure'.[9] The national procedural framework for the enforcement of EU law must comply with several EU rights and principles such as the EU right to an effective remedy, the right to a fair trial, the principle of effectiveness, and the right to good administration. Schwartze notes that the general principles of administrative law as elaborated by the Court of Justice have thus become an instrument and promoter of an evolution of a common European administrative law.[10] These rights and principles will be discussed in the following sections of this chapter.

[4] A Arnull, 'The Principle of Effective Judicial Protection in EU Law: An Unruly Horse?' (2011) 36 *European Law Review* 51, 52. See also Accetto and Zlepnig, 'The Principle of Effectiveness' (n 2) 395; and JS Delicostopoulos, 'Towards European Procedural Primacy in National Legal Systems' (2003) 9 *European Law Journal* 599, 603.

[5] G Anagnostaras, 'The Incomplete State of Community Harmonization in the Provision of Interim Protection by the National Courts' (2008) 33 *European Law Review* 586, 597. See further ch 6 in this volume on the right to remain.

[6] For an overview, see Accetto and Zlepnig (n 2) 395–97.

[7] Accetto and Zlepnig (n 2) 394.

[8] V Trstenjak and E Beysen, 'European Consumer Protection Law: Curia Semper Dabit Remedium?' (2011) 48 *Common Market Law Review* 95, 98–99.

[9] J Schwartze, 'Judicial Review of European Administrative Procedure' (2004) 68 *Law and Contemporary Problems* 85, 87.

[10] Schwartze, 'European Administrative Law' (n 3) 289.

Traditionally, it is thought that the principle of effectiveness must be balanced against the national procedural autonomy of the State.[11] Some authors, however, suggest that EU procedural rights have become hierarchically superior to the principle of national procedural autonomy.[12] Haapaniemi suggests that 'to speak about national procedural autonomy is, … at least today, much more about lip service than reality'.[13] Kakouris even argues that procedural autonomy does not exist and that national procedural rules have become ancillary EU law. He states that national procedural law is there to serve EU law. 'Its provisions only apply insofar as they contribute to the effective application of Community law. Where they do not they must be set aside.' According to Kakouris, therefore, there is no question of balancing the principle of effectiveness against the procedural autonomy of the Member States.[14] In his view, Member States only have institutional autonomy, freedom in organising their legal system, the jurisdictional hierarchy of the courts and the division of competence between and amongst the courts.[15]

This study contains numerous examples of cases in which the Court of Justice has limited Member States' discretion to design their national procedures. In its judgment in *Factortame*, for example, discussed in chapter six, the Court of Justice held that the national court should be able to grant interim relief if this is necessary to ensure the effectiveness of a judgment on the existence of the rights claimed under EU law. This applies even if the court does not have the power to grant interim relief under national law.[16] In chapter eight it is explained that any requirement of proof, which has the effect of making it virtually impossible or excessively difficult to exercise a right granted by EU law, would be incompatible with EU law. In *Danfoss* and other cases the Court of Justice made clear that the principle of effectiveness requires a shift of the burden of proof from one party to the other if this is necessary to ensure the effectiveness of EU law.[17]

In the field of asylum procedures, Directives 2005/85/EC and 2013/13/EU limit the procedural autonomy of Member States. It was even decided that EU legislation should in the longer term lead to a common asylum procedure.[18] However, as the Directives do not address every aspect of asylum procedures and include many exceptions to the main rules and many vague norms, it leaves Member States scope to design their own asylum procedure. Directive 2005/85/EC explicitly states in its

[11] Accetto and Zlepnig (n 2) 397 and 401.

[12] Arnull, 'The Principle of Effective Judicial Protection in EU Law' (n 4) 68. See also Accetto and Zlepnig (n 2) 397.

[13] P Haapaniemi, 'Procedural Autonomy: A Misnomer' in L Ervo, M Gräns and A Jokela (eds), *Europeanization of Procedural Law and the New Challenges to Fair Trial* (Groningen, Europa Law Publishing, 2009) 119.

[14] CN Kakouris, 'Do the Member States Posses Judicial Procedural Autonomy?' (1997) 34 *Common Market Law Review* 1389, 1390 and 1408.

[15] Ibid, 1394 and 1411.

[16] Case C-213/89 *Factortame* [1990] ECR I-2433. See ch 6, section 6.3.1.1 in this volume.

[17] See ch 8, section 8.3.1 in this volume.

[18] Presidency Conclusions of the Tampere European Council 15–16 October 1999 (SN 200/99) paras 14–15.

Preamble that Member States have discretion in organising their asylum system and legal remedies.[19] This study shows that EU procedural rights and principles will potentially set considerable additional requirements for national asylum procedures and will thus further limit the Member States' discretion in laying down national procedural rules. The principle approach taken in this study is that national procedural rules should ensure the effectiveness of the right to asylum and the prohibition of *refoulement*. In the absence of requirements set by the Procedures Directive, Member States are free to decide how they comply with that duty so long as they do so. This approach thus resembles the approach taken by Kakouris.

A first sign that in asylum cases the Court of Justice is willing to limit national procedural autonomy in favour of the EU right to an effective remedy is the judgment in *Samba Diouf*.[20] In this judgment the Court of Justice held that the intensity of judicial review in asylum cases falls within the scope of the EU right to an effective remedy.[21] Furthermore, it held that the time limit for lodging an appeal in an accelerated procedure should be set aside if that time limit proves, in a given situation, to be insufficient in view of the circumstances.[22] Van Cleynenbreugel writes that the Court of Justice

> thus directly interferes with Member States' discretion to adapt their national systems in conformity with newly identified EU adequate judicial protection requirements. In so doing, *Samba Diouf* challenges the classic division of procedural competences between the EU and its Member States.[23]

4.2 THE LINK BETWEEN EU PROCEDURAL RIGHTS AND PRINCIPLES

The right to an effective remedy encompasses several rights and principles such as the right to a fair trial, the right to access to court, and the principles of equality of arms and adversarial proceedings.[24] Furthermore, procedural guarantees are offered by the right to good administration which in its turn comprises several rights and obligations such as the right to be heard and the obligation to state reasons. All these rights and principles will be separately addressed in the following sections. Finally, the Court of Justice has also derived procedural guarantees directly from the principle of full effectiveness of EU law, such as with regard to the burden of proof in equal pay cases.[25]

[19] See recital 11 Preamble Dir 2005/85/EC. See also Case C-69/10 *Samba Diouf* [2011] paras 29–30.

[20] See P van Cleynenbreugel, 'Case C-69/10, *Samba Diouf* [2011]' (2012) 49 *Common Market Law Review* 327, 344–45.

[21] See also RJGM Widdershoven, 'Case C-69/10, *Samba Diouf* [2011]' (2011) *AB Rechtspraak Bestuursrecht* no 2011/304, para 3.

[22] *Samba Diouf* (n 19) para 68.

[23] van Cleynenbreugel, 'Case C-69/10' (n 20) 337.

[24] Case C-199/11 *Europese Gemeenschap v Otis NV* [2012] para 48.

[25] Case C-109/88 *Danfoss* [1998] ECR 3199. See further ch 8, section 8.2.1 in this volume.

In their case law the EU Courts have addressed the same procedural issues under different EU procedural rights.[26] An example is the case law of the Court of Justice with regard to the right to interim relief. In *Factortame* the Court held that the national court should be able to grant interim relief in order to ensure *full effectiveness of Community law*[27] while in *Unibet* it based the requirement to grant interim relief on the *principle of effective judicial protection*.[28] The Court of Justice does not usually explain its choice to apply a particular EU procedural right or principle. Therefore, the exact relationship between certain EU principles, in particular between the right to an effective remedy and the principle of effectiveness, has remained unclear.[29]

The Right to an Effective Remedy and the Principle of Effectiveness

In literature, different views can be found on the relationship between the right to an effective remedy and the principle of effectiveness. Some consider the right to an effective remedy to be only one feature of the overarching obligation on the Member States stemming from the principle of effectiveness.[30] Others see the principle of effective judicial protection as the overarching principle of which effectiveness is one aspect.[31]

In the judgment in *Impact* the Court of Justice explains the relationship between (1) the principle that rules of EU law must be fully effective; (2) the right to an effective remedy; and (3) the principles of equivalence and effectiveness:

> It is the responsibility of the national courts in particular to provide the legal protection which individuals derive from the rules of Community law and to ensure that those rules are fully effective …
>
> In that regard, it is important to note that the principle of effective judicial protection is a general principle of Community law …

[26] In some cases it is not entirely clear which principle is used by the Court of Justice, mainly because it uses different terminology for the same principle. The Court uses the words 'effective protection of fundamental rights' (Case C-340/89 *Vlassopoulou* [1991] ECR I-2357), 'the legal protection which persons derive from the direct effect of provisions of Community law' (*Factortame* (n 16)), or 'requirements of sufficiently effective protection' (Case C-136/03 *Dörr and Ünal* [2005] ECR I-4659).

[27] *Factortame* (n 16) para 21.

[28] Case C-432/05 *Unibet* [2007] ECR I-2271, para 83. See also S Prechal and RJGM Widdershoven, 'Redefining the Relationship between "Rewe-effectiveness" and Effective Judicial Protection' (2011) 4 *Review of European Administrative Law* 31, 33.

[29] See also P Oliver, 'Case C-279/09, DEB [2010]' (2011) 48 *Common Market Law Review* 2023, 2038; and Prechal and Widdershoven (n 28) 39.

[30] Accetto and Zlepnig, (n 2) 388. According to Prechal and Shelkoplyas it can usually be said that the principle of effective judicial protection expands the 'old' principle of effectiveness. S Prechal and N Shelkoplyas, 'National Procedures, Public Policy and EC Law. From Van Schijndel to Eco Swiss and Beyond' (2004) 5 *European Review of Private Law* 589, 591.

[31] Accetto and Zlepnig (n 2) 385. P Haapaniemi, 'Procedural Autonomy: A Misnomer' in L Ervo, M Gräns and A Jokela (eds), *Europeanization of Procedural Law and the New Challenges to Fair Trial* (Groningen, Europa Law Publishing, 2009) 108–109. He states that 'the principle of effective judicial protection is a cardinal principle, whereas the principles of effectiveness and equivalence, under the *Rewe* jurisprudence, can be seen as sub principles of it.' See also Joined Cases C-411/10 and C-493/10 *NS and ME et al* [2011], Opinion of AG Trstenjak, para 161.

> The Court has consistently held that, in the absence of Community rules governing the matter, it is for the domestic legal system of each Member State to designate the courts and tribunals having jurisdiction and to lay down the detailed procedural rules governing actions for safeguarding rights which individuals derive from Community law …
>
> The Member States, however, are responsible for ensuring that those rights are effectively protected in each case …
>
> On that basis, as is apparent from well-established case-law, the detailed procedural rules governing actions for safeguarding an individual's rights under Community law must be no less favourable than those governing similar domestic actions (principle of equivalence) and must not render practically impossible or excessively difficult the exercise of rights conferred by Community law (principle of effectiveness) …
>
> Those requirements of equivalence and effectiveness, which embody the general obligation on the Member States to ensure judicial protection of an individual's rights under Community law, apply equally to the designation of the courts and tribunals having jurisdiction to hear and determine actions based on Community law.
>
> A failure to comply with those requirements at Community level is—just like a failure to comply with them as regards the definition of detailed procedural rules—liable to undermine the principle of effective judicial protection.[32]

From these considerations it may be derived that the overarching principle is the principle that EU rules should be fully effective in the national legal order. This principle seeks to protect the interests of the EU. It is based on the direct effect of EU law and promotes the effective enforcement of EU law in national courts.[33] Under this principle Member States may not apply rules which are liable to jeopardise the achievement of the objectives pursued by a directive and, therefore, deprive it of its effectiveness.[34] This follows from Article 4(3) TEU (the principle of sincere cooperation) which requires the Member States to

> take any appropriate measure, general or particular, to ensure fulfilment of the obligations arising out of the Treaties or resulting from the acts of the institutions of the Union. The Member States shall facilitate the achievement of the Union's tasks and refrain from any measure which could jeopardise the attainment of the Union's objectives.

The right to an effective remedy follows from the principle of full effectiveness of EU law. Article 4(3) TEU requires national courts and tribunals to apply EU law in full and to protect the rights it confers on individuals.[35] The national procedural rules governing actions for safeguarding an individual's rights under EU law before the national courts must comply with the principles of effectiveness and equivalence. Other case law, however, implies another relationship between the

[32] Case C-268/06 *Impact* [2008] ECR I-2483, paras 42–48.

[33] Case C-6/90 *Francovich* [1991] ECR I-5357, paras 33–34.

[34] See, eg Case C-104/10 *Kelly* [2001] ECR I-6813, para 33. According to the Court this follows from Art 4(3) TEU.

[35] Case C-312/93 *Peterbroeck* [1995] ECR I-4599, para 12. See also Trstenjak and Beysen (n 8) 97.

right to an effective remedy and the principles of effectiveness and equivalence. In *Mono Car Styling*, for example, the Court of Justice seems to suggest that national rules on an individual's standing and legal interest in bringing proceedings must be tested against both the principle of effectiveness and effective judicial protection.[36] Prechal and Widdershoven argue that this is the right approach. They point to the different purposes of the principle of effectiveness and the right to an effective remedy. The principle of effectiveness aims to guarantee the effective application of substantive EU law, while the right to an effective remedy 'is intimately linked to the right of access to court and, ultimately, to the idea of the "Rechtstaat"'.[37] While those two interests may overlap, this is not necessarily the case.[38] Prechal and Widdershoven contend that the test applied under the principle of effectiveness is less demanding than that applied under the right to an effective remedy.[39]

The EU Right to an Effective Remedy and the Right to Good Administration

It follows from the case law of the EU Courts that the specific rights following from the right to an effective remedy, the right to a fair trial and the right to good administration interrelate, overlap and complement each other. According to the EU Courts, for example, the rights of the defence and the right to good administration are intertwined or complementary. The Charter has codified the right to be heard and the right of access to the file, often regarded to be rights of the defence under the right to good administration.[40] In the *Modjahedines* case the Court of First Instance (CFI) addressed the close relation between the right to a fair hearing and the obligation to state reasons and the right to an effective remedy:

> It is appropriate to begin by examining, together, the pleas alleging infringement of the right to a fair hearing, infringement of the obligation to state reasons and infringement of the right to effective judicial protection, which are closely linked. First, the safeguarding of the right to a fair hearing helps to ensure that the right to effective judicial protection is exercised properly. Second, there is a close link between the right to an effective judicial remedy and the obligation to state reasons. As held in settled case-law, the Community institutions' obligation under Article 253 EC to state the reasons on which

[36] Case C-12/08 *Mono Car Styling* [2009] ECR I-6653, paras 47–49.

[37] Prechal and Widdershoven (n 28) 50. See also 45.

[38] Ibid, 42. The principle of effectiveness may, for example, require the imposition of sanctions on individuals or the recovery of illegal State aid. In the field of asylum procedures it is hard to imagine a situation in which the effective enforcement of EU law is not in the interest of the individual asylum applicant.

[39] Ibid, 39–40. See also S Iglesias Sánchez, 'The Court and the Charter: The Impact of the Entry into Force of the Lisbon Treaty on the ECJ's Approach to Fundamental Rights' (2012) 49 *Common Market Law Review* 1565, 1579–80.

[40] E Barbier de La Serre, 'Procedural Justice in the European Community Case-law concerning the Rights of the Defence: Essentialist and Instrumentalist Trends' (2006) 12 *European Public Law* 225, 234–36.

> a decision is based is intended to enable the Community judicature to exercise its power to review the lawfulness of the decision and the persons concerned to know the reasons for the measure adopted so that they can defend their rights and ascertain whether or not the decision is well founded … Thus, the parties concerned can make genuine use of their right to a judicial remedy only if they have precise knowledge of the content of and the reasons for the act in question …[41]

For the purpose of this study it is not necessary to define the exact relationship between all relevant EU procedural rights and principles. It is sufficient to note that all these principles set requirements for national proceedings. In the following thematic chapters all relevant case law with regard to certain procedural topics will be assessed, regardless of which right or principle was used by the EU Court. The right to an effective remedy, the principle of effectiveness and related procedural rights are taken as a category of procedural norms.[42]

Provisions of International Law inspiring EU Procedural Rights

Like the EU procedural rights, the procedural rights guaranteed by international law which inspire the interpretation of those EU rights also overlap and complement each other. Provisions of international law which may inspire the interpretation of EU procedural rights in the context of the Common European Asylum System (CEAS) could be divided into four categories: (1) provisions guaranteeing the right to an effective remedy; (2) provisions regarding the right to a fair trial; (3) substantive provisions, in particular those containing a prohibition of *refoulement*, of which the effective protection requires certain procedural guarantees; and finally (4) provisions aimed at ensuring the subsidiary role of human rights mechanisms. The ECtHR, like the Court of Justice, addresses the same procedural issues under different provisions. The obligation of a rigorous scrutiny of a risk of *refoulement*, for example, has been derived from both Article 3 ECHR and Article 13 ECHR. The use of secret information has been addressed under the right to family life guaranteed by Article 8 ECHR as well as several procedural rights (Articles 5(4), 6 and 13 ECHR).[43] The ECtHR usually does not explain in its judgments why it addresses a procedural issue under a certain provision. For these reasons the procedural rights recognised by the ECHR as well as other treaties are for the purpose of this study (like procedural rights recognised by EU law) considered to be one category of procedural rights which are all interlinked. In the thematic chapters six to ten the relevant case law and views of the supervising bodies with regard to each theme is taken into account, irrespective which provision was applied.

[41] Case T-228/02 *Organisation des Modhahedines du peuple d'Iran v Council* [2006] ECR II-4665, para 89.

[42] See also Accetto and Zlepnig (n 2) 385.

[43] See ch 10, section 10.5.1 in this volume.

4.3 THE EU RIGHT TO AN EFFECTIVE REMEDY

Article 47 of the Charter states: 'Everyone whose rights and freedoms guaranteed by the law of the Union are violated has the right to an effective remedy before a tribunal in compliance with the conditions laid down in this Article.' Furthermore according to Article 19(1) TEU: 'Member States shall provide remedies sufficient to ensure effective legal protection in the fields covered by Union law.'[44] These articles codify the general principle of effective judicial protection which has been considered a principle of EU law and a fundamental right by the Court of Justice.[45] According to the Court of Justice, the right to an effective remedy[46] reflects a general principle of EU law stemming from the constitutional traditions common to the Member States and enshrined in Articles 6 and 13 ECHR.[47]

It follows from the text of Article 47 of the Charter and the case law of the Court of Justice that the EU right to an effective remedy comprises the right to a fair trial.[48] Article 47 states:

> Everyone is entitled to a fair and public hearing within a reasonable time by an independent and impartial tribunal previously established by law. Everyone shall have the possibility of being advised, defended and represented. Legal aid shall be made available to those who lack sufficient resources in so far as such aid is necessary to ensure effective access to justice.

The objective of the right to an effective remedy is to secure for the individual effective protection of the (fundamental) rights granted by EU law.[49] The Court of Justice has held that it is particularly important for judicial protection to be effective, when the measures challenged by the individual have serious consequences.[50]

The Court of Justice has stressed the significance of the requirements following from Article 47 of the Charter. Furthermore, it has pointed at the fact that limitations to the right to an effective remedy should respect the essence of this right and, subject to the principle of proportionality, must necessary and genuinely

[44] Haapaniemi states that this provision gives a solid legal basis to interfere, under EU law, with the national law of remedies and therefore, it cures the problem that such a firm basis for intervention was missing before. Haapaniemi, 'Procedural Autonomy' (n 31) 120.

[45] See Case T-111/96 *ITT Promedia v Commission* [1998] ECR II-2937, para 60 (the right of access to the Court), Case C-105/03 *Pupino* [2005] ECR I-5285, para 58; Case C-305/05 *Ordre des barreaux francophones et germanophones* [2007] ECR I-5305, para 29 (the right to a fair trial); and Case C-28/05 *Dokter* [2006] para 75 (rights of the defence).

[46] The Court uses different terminology for the same principle such as 'the right to an effective judicial remedy' (Case 222/84 *Johnston* [1986] ECR 1651), 'the principle of effective judicial control' (Case C-185/97 *Coote* [1998] ECR I-5199), 'the requirement for judicial review' (Case C-459/99 *MRAX* [2002]), or the requirement of judicial control (Case C-269/99 *Kühne et al* [2001] ECR I-9517).

[47] Case 222/86 *UNECTEF v Heylens et al* [1987] ECR 4097, para 14.

[48] The Court of Justice often refers to the right to a fair trial guaranteed by Art 6 ECHR when applying the principle of effective judicial protection.

[49] *UNECTEF* (n 47) and *Vlassopoulou* (n 26).

[50] Case C-229/05 P *PKK/KNK v Council* [2006] ECR I-439, para 110.

meet objectives of general interest recognised by the EU in accordance with Article 52(1) of the Charter.[51]

4.3.1 Provisions of International Law inspiring the EU Right to an Effective Remedy

The (case law concerning) various provisions of international law may inspire the EU right to an effective remedy and fair trial in the context of the CEAS. Obviously these provisions contain a right to an effective remedy or a right to a fair trial. Furthermore, the procedural guarantees are derived from the principle that the prohibition of *refoulement* and other substantive rights should be effectively protected, and rights derived from the subsidiary role of human rights mechanisms should be considered sources of inspiration. In the following sections the procedural requirements following from these sources of inspiration will be further elaborated on.

The Right to an Effective Remedy

Article 13 ECHR and Article 2(3) ICCPR require State parties to provide an effective remedy to any person whose rights included in the Convention and the Covenant respectively are violated.[52] The Committee against Torture (ComAT) has derived a right to an effective remedy from Article 3 CAT.[53] According to the ECtHR the right to an effective remedy serves two purposes. The first is comparable to the objective of the EU principle of effective judicial protection: to secure for the individual effective protection of the rights granted by the treaties concerned.[54] Secondly, the right to an effective remedy aims to preserve the subsidiary nature of the treaty system.[55] It gives direct expression to the States' obligation to protect human rights first and foremost within their own legal system.[56]

The Right to a Fair Trial

Article 6(1) ECHR and Article 14(1) ICCPR guarantee the right to a fair and public hearing by a competent, independent and impartial tribunal established by law. The right to a fair trial is intended to secure the interests of the parties and those

[51] Case C-300/11 *ZZ* [2013] para 51.

[52] Art 5(4) ECHR and Art 9(4) ICCPR require judicial review of detention measures. Art 5(4) ECHR and Art 9(4) ICCPR play only a minor role in this study. Therefore, the specific requirements set by these provisions will not be further addressed.

[53] See ComAT 20 May 2005, *Agiza v Sweden*, no 233/2003.

[54] See ECtHR (GC) 26 October 2000, *Kudla v Poland*, no 30210/96, para 152.

[55] See, eg ECtHR 5 February 2002, *Conka v Belgium*, no 51564/99, para 33.

[56] *Kudla* (n 54) para 152 and ECtHR (GC) 10 May 2001, *Z et al v UK*, no 29392/95, para 103, where the ECtHR emphasised that Art 13 takes on a crucial function in ensuring the supervisory role of the ECtHR.

of the proper administration of justice.[57] According to the ECtHR, the right to a fair trial holds a prominent place in a democratic society.[58]

Effectiveness of the Prohibition of Refoulement and Other Substantive Rights

Not only under EU law, but also under international law, procedural safeguards have been derived from the principle that substantive rights must be effectively protected. Procedural safeguards may be derived from the principle that the prohibition of *refoulement* laid down in Article 33 Refugee Convention must be effectively protected.[59] Hathaway, for example, states that 'a fair assessment of refugee status is the indispensable means by which to vindicate Convention rights'.[60] The EXCOM and the UNHCR have developed procedural guidelines which seek to promote the fair determination of refugee status. These may inspire the EU procedural rights and principles in the asylum context.

The ComAT has applied the principle of effectiveness to the principle of *non-refoulement* by recognising that Article 3 CAT entails a right to an effective remedy. In *Agiza* the ComAT observed

> that the right to an effective remedy for a breach of the Convention underpins the entire Convention, for otherwise the protections afforded by the Convention would be rendered largely illusory … In the Committee's view, in order to reinforce the protection of the norm in question and understanding the Convention consistently, the prohibition on refoulement contained in article 3 should be interpreted the same way to encompass a remedy for its breach, even though it may not contain on its face such a right to remedy for a breach thereof … The nature of refoulement is such, however, that an allegation of breach of that article relates to a future expulsion or removal; accordingly, the right to an effective remedy contained in article 3 requires, in this context, an opportunity for effective, independent and impartial review of the decision to expel or remove, once that decision is made, when there is a plausible allegation that article 3 issues arise.[61]

The ECtHR has derived procedural guarantees directly from Article 3 ECHR. The clearest example of the application of the principle of effectiveness can be found in *Jabari*. In this case the complainant was denied any scrutiny of the factual basis of her fears about being removed to Iran because she failed to comply with the requirement to submit her asylum application within five days of her arrival in Turkey. The Court considered that the automatic and mechanical application of

[57] ECtHR 27 January 1997, *Nideröst-Huber v Switzerland*, no 18990/91, para 30. According to HRC General Comment No 32 (2007, CCPR/C/GC/32) para I sub 2, Art 14 ICCPR 'aims at ensuring the proper administration of justice, and to this end guarantees a series of specific rights'.

[58] ECtHR 9 October 1979, *Airey v Ireland*, no 6289/73, para 24.

[59] See, eg EXCOM Conclusion no 71 ((XLIV) 1993, para (i).

[60] J Hathaway, *The Rights of Refugees under International Law* (Cambridge, Cambridge University Press, 2005) 630. See also Wouters, *International Legal Standards for the Protection from Refoulement* (Antwerpen, Intersentia, 2009) 164–65; GS Goodwin-Gill and J McAdam, *The Refugee in International Law* (Oxford, Oxford University Press, 2007) 530–31; and P Boeles, *Fair Immigration Proceedings in Europe* (The Hague/Boston, Martinus Nijhoff, 1997) 66–69.

[61] *Agiza* (n 53).

this time limit for submitting an asylum application was 'at variance with the protection of the fundamental value embodied in Article 3 of the Convention'.[62]

The ECtHR has also derived procedural rules from other substantial provisions of the Convention, notably Article 8 ECHR on the right to private and family life. An important procedural issue addressed under Article 8 ECHR is the use of secret evidence in the context of measures affecting national security.[63] In asylum cases similar procedural issues as those addressed under Article 8 ECHR may arise.[64] The case law concerning the procedural safeguards which follow from Article 8 ECHR should therefore also be considered relevant in asylum cases.[65]

The Subsidiary Role of Human Rights Mechanisms

It is first and foremost up to the State Parties, including their national courts, to guarantee the rights included in international human rights treaties.[66] The ECtHR, Human Rights Committee (HRC) and the ComAT cannot be regarded as courts of fourth instance; they play only a subsidiary role. As President Costa stated in 2011 in his statement concerning requests for interim measures:

> [T]he Court is not an appeal tribunal from the asylum and immigration tribunals of Europe, any more than it is a court of criminal appeal in respect of criminal convictions. Where national immigration and asylum procedures carry out their own proper assessment of risk and are seen to operate fairly and with respect for human rights, the Court should only be required to intervene in truly exceptional cases.[67]

It follows from this subsidiary role that national authorities must provide for effective remedies against expulsion measures.[68] These remedies must be exhausted by applicants before they turn to the ECtHR or the UN Committees.[69] This means in general that the complainant must have appealed to the highest national authority and that the complaint must have been made before the national authority at least

[62] ECtHR 11 July 2000, *Jabari v Turkey*, no 40035/98, para 40. See also ECtHR 22 September 2009, *Abdolkhani and Karimnia v Turkey*, no 30471/08, para 115.

[63] See, eg ECtHR 8 June 2006, *Lupsa v Romania*, no 10337/04 and ECtHR 6 December 2007, *Liu and Liu v Russia*, no 42086/05.

[64] Ch 10 will discuss the use of secret information. In this context references will be made to the case law of the ECtHR regarding the right to adversarial proceeding under Art 8 ECHR.

[65] The procedural requirements for Art 3 ECHR cases are normally more strict than those for Art 8 ECHR cases. See ECtHR (GC) 25 October 1996, *Chahal v the United Kingdom*, no 22414/93, para 150.

[66] The ECtHR states that the machinery of protection established by the Convention is subsidiary to the national systems safeguarding human rights. ECtHR (GC) 28 July 1999, *Selmouni v France*, no 25803/94, para 74.

[67] Statement Issued by the President of the ECtHR concerning Requests for Interim Measures (Rule 39 of the Rules of Court) (11 February 2011) available at www.coe.int/t/dghl/standardsetting/cddh/gt-gdr-c/GT-GDR-C(2012)005_Statement%20of%20the%20ECtHR%20President%20on%20Interim%20Measures.pdf accessed 30 September 2013.

[68] See, eg ECtHR (GC) 21 January 2011, *MSS v Belgium and Greece*, no 30696/09, paras 286–87.

[69] Art 35(1) ECHR, Arts 2 and 5(2)(b) of the Optional Protocol to the ICCPR and Art 22(5)(b) CAT.

in substance.[70] Only the ineffectiveness of the domestic remedy, the fact that this remedy was bound to fail, or the particular circumstances of the case may absolve a person from the obligation to exhaust domestic remedies.[71] In assessing whether domestic remedies have been exhausted, the ECtHR and UN Committees thus regularly examine the effectiveness of those remedies. Their case law with regard to the requirement to exhaust domestic remedies in asylum cases is therefore relevant in order to discover what procedural guarantees are necessary in such cases.

Secondly it may be argued that it follows from the subsidiary role of supervising bodies that the way in which those bodies assess claims under the substantive provisions of the treaties is indicative of the way in which the national courts should assess such claims. In particular, it is contended that the scope and intensity of judicial review performed by national courts should not be more limited than the review performed by the supervising bodies. Spijkerboer argues with regard to the ECtHR that in asylum cases national authorities 'should operate in such a way as to ensure that the national remedy provides scrutiny of at least as good a quality as that provided by the Court'.[72] The same may be true for the scrutiny applied by the HRC or the ComAT. For this reason, in chapter nine the case law under Article 3 ECHR, Article 7 ICCPR and Article 3 CAT will be used as a source of inspiration for the EU right to an effective remedy, in particular when assessing its meaning and content for the scope and intensity of judicial review by national courts in asylum cases.

4.3.2 Application to Asylum Cases

The scope of application of the EU right to an effective remedy and the right to a fair trial is broader than the same rights guaranteed by international treaties. The right to an effective remedy and the right to a fair trial recognised by the ECHR and other treaties do inspire the Court of Justice when applying the EU right to an effective remedy and fair trial in all cases falling within the scope of EU law.[73] This means that, indirectly, the scope of application of the right to a fair trial recognised under international law is extended through EU law. More important for the purpose of this study is that, even in asylum cases, the EU right to an effective

[70] ECtHR (GC) 16 September 1996, *Akdivar v Turkey*, no 21893/93, para 66. HRC 28 April 2009, *Moses Solo Tarlue v Canada*, no 1551/2007, para 7.5. For application of this rule in an asylum case, see ECtHR 19 February 1998, *Bahaddar v the Netherlands*, no 25894/94.

[71] *Selmouni* (n 66) para 77, ECtHR 11 January 2007, *Salah Sheekh v the Netherlands*, no 1948/04, para 50. See also HRC 5 April 1995, *Griffin v Spain*, no 493/1992, para 6.1, HRC 28 April 2008, *Lnenicka v Czech Republic*, no 1484/2006, para 6.3, ComAT 9 June 1995, *Parot v Spain*, no 6/1990, para 6 and ComAT 22 February 1996, *RK v Canada*, no 42/1996, para 7.2.

[72] TP Spijkerboer, 'Subsidiarity and "Arguability": the European Court of Human Rights' Case Law on Judicial Review in Asylum Cases' (2009) 21 *International Journal of Refugee Law* 48, 52.

[73] Case C-327/02 *Panayotova* [2004] ECR I-11055, para 27 (a migration case). See S Peers and N Rogers (eds), *EU Immigration and Asylum Law: Text and Commentary* (Leiden/Boston, Martinus Nijhoff, 2006) 120–21.

remedy and a fair trial may be inspired by the case law of the ECtHR concerning Article 6 ECHR. It would not make sense if in migration cases the EU right to a fair trial is inspired by Article 6 ECHR, but not by ECtHR case law in which this provision is interpreted. Widdershoven argues that the Court of Justice in the asylum case of *Samba Diouf* indeed (implicitly) interpreted the EU right to an effective remedy in the light of the case law of the ECtHR under Article 6 which requires a court or tribunal to have full jurisdiction.[74]

Asylum Procedures must Comply with the EU Right to a Fair Trial

The EU right to a fair trial applies to all claims under EU law, including asylum cases. The explanations of the Charter state:

> In Union law, the right to a fair hearing is not confined to disputes relating to civil law rights and obligations. That is one of the consequences of the fact that the Union is a community based on the rule of law. Nevertheless, in all respects other than their scope, the guarantees afforded by the ECHR apply in a similar way to the Union.[75]

Article 6 ECHR and Article 14 ICCPR are limited to cases which concern the determination of a person's civil rights and obligations or any criminal charge.[76] Both the ECtHR and the HRC ruled that the right to a fair trial does not apply to proceedings concerning the entry, stay and deportation of aliens.[77]

No Need for an Arguable Claim

The EU right to an effective remedy has a broader scope of application than the right to an effective remedy guaranteed by Article 13 ECHR, Article 2(3) ICCPR and Article 3 CAT because it does not require an 'arguable claim' of a violation of an EU fundamental right. The EU right to an effective remedy implies the right to effective judicial scrutiny of the decisions of the EU Institutions[78] or national authorities[79] taken pursuant to the applicable provisions of EU law. Article 39 of Directive 2005/85/EC and Article 46 of Directive 2013/32/EU show that the EU right to an effective remedy also applies to asylum claims which had been rejected as inadmissible or manifestly unfounded.

[74] Widdershoven, 'Case C-69/10' (n 21) para 4. It should also be noted that some important rights following from Art 6, such as the right of access to a remedy and the right to legal assistance, have also been brought within the scope of Art 13 ECHR by the ECtHR. See ECtHR 10 January 2012, *GR v the Netherlands*, no 22251/07, paras 49–50 and ECtHR 2 February 2012, *IM v France*, no 9152/09, para 151.

[75] See the Explanations relating to the Charter of Fundamental Rights (2007/C 303/02) OJ 14 December 2007, C303/17. See also A Ward, *Judicial Review and the Rights of Private Parties in EU Law* (Oxford, Oxford University Press, 2007) 174.

[76] The applicability of the right to a fair trial guaranteed in Art 14 ICCPR is limited to 'rights and obligations in a suit at law'.

[77] ECtHR (GC) 5 October 2000, *Maaouia v France*, no 39652/98, para 40; HRC 4 April 2007, *Ernst Zundel v Canada*, no 1341/2005, para 6.8; and *Moses Solo Tarlue* (n 70) para 7.8.

[78] *Organization des Modhahedines du peuple d'Iran v Council* (n 41) para 110.

[79] Case C-226/99 *Siples* [2001] ECR I-277, para 17 and *Panayotova* (n 73) para 27.

The right to an effective remedy guaranteed by Article 13 ECHR and Article 2(3) ICCPR can only be invoked in conjunction with one of the substantive rights included in those treaties.[80] There must be an *arguable claim* of a treaty violation.[81] Both the ECtHR and the HRC recognised that a State party cannot reasonably be required to make an effective remedy available no matter how unmeritorious a claim of such violation may be.[82] Also the scope of application of the right to an effective remedy under Article 3 CAT is limited to a 'plausible allegation' of a violation of Article 3 CAT.[83]

Only Applicable to Decisions with Legal Effect

The EU right to an effective remedy does not apply where the contested decision is without legal effect and therefore not capable of infringing any rights guaranteed by EU law.[84] Furthermore, the Court of Justice held in *Samba Diouf* specifically with regard to asylum procedures, that decisions that are preparatory to the decision on the substance or decisions pertaining to the organisation of the procedure are not covered by the right to an effective remedy laid down in Article 39 of Directive 2005/85/EC.[85] In that case it concerned the decision to process an asylum claim in an accelerated procedure. The Court considered that it follows from the EU right to an effective remedy that asylum applicants should be able to effectively challenge the reasons for the decision to accelerate the procedure in the context of the appeal against the decision to reject the asylum application.[86]

4.3.3 Effectiveness

According to the case law of the Court of Justice EU law requires 'that national legislation does not undermine the right to an effective judicial protection'.[87] In its case law the Court of Justice has tested national procedural rules, including

80 P van Dijk et al (eds), *Theory and Practice of the European Convention on Human Rights* (Antwerp/Oxford, Intersentia, 2006) 998. According to the ECtHR, Art 13 guarantees the availability at national level of a remedy 'to enforce the substance of the Convention rights and freedoms in whatever form they might happen to be secured in the domestic legal order'. *Jabari* (n 62) para 48.

81 Concerning the ECHR, see Spijkerboer, 'Subsidiarity and "Arguability"' (n 72) 50. The HRC has considered that the right to an effective remedy would be void, if it were not available where a violation of the Covenant had not yet been established. See HRC 19 September 2003, *George Kazantzis v Cyprus*, no 972/2001, para 6.6.

82 ECtHR (Plen) 27 April 1988, *Boyle and Rice v the United Kingdom*, no 9659/82, para 52 and *George Kazantzis* (n 81) para 6.6.

83 *Agiza* (n 53) para 13.7. ComAT has not explained when an allegation or claim is plausible. CW Wouters, *International Legal Standards for the Protection from Refoulement* (Antwerpen, Intersentia) 517.

84 Case T-276/02 *Forum 187 v Commission* [2003] ECR II-2075, para 50.

85 *Samba Diouf* (n 19) para 43.

86 Ibid, para 58.

87 See, eg Case C-87/90 *Verholen* [1991] ECR I-3757, para 24; Case C-13/01 *Safalero* [2003] ECR I-8679, para 50; and *Mono Car Styling* (n 36) para 49.

technical rules which affect the accessibility of a remedy, against the principle of effectiveness. This principle prohibits national procedural rules which render virtually impossible or excessively difficult the exercise of rights conferred by EU law.[88] The principle of effectiveness seeks to ensure the effective enforcement of EU law in national courts. As Accetto and Zlepnig state:

> Effectiveness may … be eroded by specific substantive and procedural hurdles at the national level that are not immediately apparent: subtle procedural rules, administrative practices adopted by national authorities, or systemic failures in the institutional set-up of authorities in charge of ensuring the proper application of Community law.[89]

When assessing whether a national procedural rule renders the exercise of an EU right excessively difficult 'a comprehensive review in which all particularities of national legal systems must be taken into account' is required.[90] The Court of Justice considered:

> Each case which raises the question whether a national procedural provision renders application of Community law impossible or excessively difficult must be analysed by reference to the role of that provision in the procedure, its progress and its special features, viewed as a whole, before the various national instances. In the light of that analysis the basic principles of the domestic judicial system, such as protection of the rights of the defence, the principle of legal certainty and the proper conduct of procedure, must, where appropriate, be taken into consideration.[91]

The Court of Justice has assessed many types of national procedural rules in the light of the principle of effectiveness. In chapters six to ten the content and meaning of the principle with regard to certain procedural issues in the context of the CEAS will be examined.

Effectiveness of Remedies under International Law

The effectiveness of a remedy within the meaning of Article 13 ECHR does not depend on the certainty of a favourable outcome for the applicant.[92] The remedy concerned must be able to prevent the alleged violation or its continuation, or provide adequate redress for any violation that has already occurred.[93] Article 13 ECHR does not go so far as to require any particular form of remedy.[94] The Contracting States are afforded some discretion as to the manner in which they conform to their Convention obligations under Article 13 ECHR.[95] In cases

[88] Case 33/76 *Rewe* [1976] ECR 1989, para 5 and *Safalero* (n 87) para 49.
[89] Accetto and Zlepnig (n 2) 376.
[90] Trstenjak and Beysen (n 8) 102.
[91] See, eg *Peterbroeck* (n 35) para 14 and Case C-276/01 *Steffensen* [2003] ECR I-3735, para 66.
[92] See, eg ECtHR (Plen) 7 July 1989, *Soering v the United Kingdom*, no 14038/88, para 122.
[93] *Kudla* (n 54) para 158, *Jabari* (n 62) para 48. van Dijk et al, *Theory and Practice of the ECHR* (n 80) 1006.
[94] ECtHR 30 October 1991, *Vilvarajah et al v the United Kingdom*, nos 13163/87, 13164/87, 13165/87, 13447/87, 13448/87, para 122.
[95] See, eg *Z et al* (n 56) para 163.

concerning the expulsion of asylum applicants, the main concern of the ECtHR is whether there are effective guarantees to protect the applicant against arbitrary *refoulement*, be it direct or indirect, to the country from which he or she has fled.[96]

The obligation to exhaust domestic remedies is limited to making use of those remedies which can be considered effective and available.[97] The requirement of effectiveness for domestic remedies under the requirement to exhaust domestic remedies and the right to an effective remedy are very similar. This follows most clearly from the case law of the ECtHR which states that Article 35 has 'a close affinity' with Article 13 ECHR.[98] The case law on Articles 35(1) and 13 ECHR to a certain extent run parallel.[99] In order to be considered effective, domestic remedies must offer sufficient safeguards.[100] The ECtHR has, for example, held under Article 35(1) ECHR that the domestic remedy must be accessible for the person concerned[101] and that the remedy must have automatic suspensive effect in case of a claim of a risk of *refoulement*.[102]

4.3.4 Institutions Responsible for Providing Effective Remedies

It is the national courts which need to provide natural or legal persons with an effective remedy against a decision by the EU Institutions or national authorities taken pursuant to the applicable provisions of EU law.[103] Therefore, 'it is for the Member States to establish a system of legal remedies and procedures which ensure respect for the right to effective judicial protection'.[104] The Court of Justice held that the right to an effective remedy 'affords an individual a right of access to a court or tribunal but not to a number of levels of jurisdiction'.[105]

The EU right to an effective remedy provides broader protection than Article 13 ECHR, Article 2(3) ICCPR and Article 3 CAT. These provisions require an effective

[96] *MSS* (n 68) para 286.

[97] *Selmouni* (n 66) para 75. For the ICCPR see, eg HRC 26 August 2004, *Madafferi v Australia*, no 1011/2001, para 8.4. See also Art 22(5)(b) CAT and M Nowak and E McArthur, *The United Nations Convention against Torture: A Commentary* (Oxford, Oxford University Press, 2008) 796.

[98] *Selmouni* (n 66) para 74.

[99] TP Spijkerboer, 'Case C-465/07, *Elgafaji* [2009]' (2009) 111 *Jurisprudentie Vreemdelingenrecht* no 2009/111 51; DJ Harris, M O'Boyle, C Warbrick and E Bates (eds), *Law of the European Convention on Human Rights* (Oxford, Oxford University Press, 2009) 562. In some cases the preliminary objection regarding the alleged non-exhaustion of domestic remedies and the complaint of a violation of Art 13 ECHR are assessed together by the ECtHR. See, eg *MSS* (n 68) paras 336–37. Arguably, a clear parallel also exists between the right to an effective remedy and the obligation to exhaust domestic remedies included in the ICCPR and CAT.

[100] ECtHR 23 October 2008, *Soldatenko v Ukraine*, no 2440/07, para 49.

[101] ECtHR 8 January 2004, *Sardinas Albo v Italy*, no 56271/00.

[102] ECtHR (Adm) 20 September 2007, *Sultani v France*, no 45223/05, para 51. See also HRC 1 November 1985, *Arzuaga Gilboa v Uruguay*, no 147/1983.

[103] See ch 2, section 2.5 in this volume.

[104] C-50/00P *Union de Pequeños* [2002] ECR I-6677, para 41.

[105] *Samba Diouf* (n 19) para 69.

remedy before an independent and impartial authority, which does not need to be a judicial authority.[106] Both Article 6(1) ECHR and Article 14(1) ICCPR require a fair trial before an independent and impartial court or tribunal.

Criteria Court or Tribunal

When examining whether a national body can be regarded as a court or tribunal, the Court of Justice takes several factors into account, such as whether the body concerned is established by law, whether it is permanent, whether its jurisdiction is compulsory, whether its procedure is *inter partes*, and whether it applies rules of law. Furthermore, a court or tribunal must be independent and impartial.[107]

The factors used by the ECtHR and the HRC in order to establish whether a national body should be considered as a court or tribunal are similar to those used by the Court of Justice.[108] Article 6(1) ECHR also demands that the court or tribunal have 'full jurisdiction'. This means that it must be able to quash the challenged decision in all respects, on questions of fact and law.[109]

4.3.5 Effect in the National Legal Order

What needs to be done if a national procedural rule does not comply with the EU right to an effective remedy? First, the national court should try to interpret national procedural rules in conformity with EU rules.[110] This may avoid a breach of the right to an effective remedy. In *Unibet* the Court considered:

> [I]t is for the national courts to interpret the procedural rules governing actions brought before them … in such a way as to enable those rules, wherever possible, to be implemented in such a manner as to contribute to the attainment of the objective … of ensuring effective judicial protection of an individual's rights under Community law.[111]

[106] See, eg ECtHR 11 January 2007, *Musa et al v Bulgaria*, no 61259/00, HRC 10 November 2006, *Alzery v Sweden*, no 1416/2005, para 11.8. Art 13 ECHR speaks of a 'national authority', Art 2(3) ICCPR requires a competent judicial, administrative or legislative authority, or any other competent authority provided for by the legal system of the State. ComAT decided in *Agiza* (n 53) para 13.7 that the review required under Art 3 CAT can be provided by a judicial or independent administrative authority.

[107] Case C-175/11 *HID and BA* [2013] para 83; and Case C-506/04 *Wilson* [2006] ECR I-8613, paras 47–53.

[108] ECtHR (GC) 6 May 2003, *Kleyn et al v the Netherlands*, nos 39343/98, 39651/98, 43147/98 and 46664/99, paras 190–91. With regard to Art 14 ICCPR see, eg HRC 10 November 1993, *Oló Bahamonde v Equatorial Guinea*, no 468/1991, para 9.4 and HRC 3 November 2008, *Castedo v Spain*, no 1122/2002, paras 9.5–9.8 and General Comment No 32 (n 57) para III, sub 19–21.

[109] See, eg ECtHR 28 September 1995, *Schmautzer v Austria*, no 15523/89, para 36. See further ch 9 on judicial review of the establishment and qualification of the facts.

[110] Haapaniemi (n 31) 96–97 and Arnull (n 4) 55.

[111] *Unibet* (n 28) para 44. See also *Union de Pequeños* (n 104) para 42 and *Samba Diouf* (n 19), para 60.

If consistent interpretation is not possible, a national procedural rule which breaches the EU right to an effective remedy should be set aside.[112]

No New Remedies?

An important question is whether EU law requires a Member State to introduce new remedies, if no effective remedy is available. The judgment of the Court of Justice in *Rewe-Handelsgesellschaft Nord v Hauptzollamt Kiel* suggested that the Court accepts that no such requirement exists. The Court considered that the EC-Treaty 'was not intended to create new remedies in the national courts to ensure the observance of Community law other than those already laid down by national law'.[113]

For a long time it remained uncertain whether Member States could be obliged to introduce new remedies under EU law. Several judgments seemed to undermine the no new remedies statement in *Rewe*.[114] In *Unibet* the Court finally made clear that Member States may be exceptionally required to create new national remedies if this is necessary to ensure the EU fundamental right to an effective remedy.[115] This right thus entails negative as well as positive obligations.[116] In *Unibet* the Court considered:

> Although the EC Treaty has made it possible in a number of instances for private persons to bring a direct action, where appropriate, before the Community Court, it was not intended to create new remedies in the national courts to ensure the observance of Community law other than those already laid down by national law … It would be otherwise only if it were apparent from the overall scheme of the national legal system in question that no legal remedy existed which made it possible to ensure, even indirectly, respect for an individual's rights under Community law …[117]

Applicants cannot insist on a particular remedy where alternative remedies exist in the national legal system, which comply with the principles of effectiveness and equivalence.[118]

[112] Haapaniemi (n 31) 96–97.

[113] Case 158/80 *Rewe-Handelsgesellschaft Nord v Hauptzollamt Kiel* [1981] ECR 1805, para 6.

[114] P Craig and G de Búrca, *EU Law* (Oxford, Oxford University Press, 2003) 237–38. They refer amongst others to *Factortame* (n 16). See also ch 6, section 6.3.1.1 in this volume. Groussot refers to Case C-424/99 *Commission v Austria* [2001] ECR I-9285, paras 39–47 and Case C-97/91 *Borelli* [1991] ECR I-6313, para 13. X Groussot, *General Principles of Community Law* (Groningen, Europa Law Publishing, 2006) 338.

[115] Arnull (n 4) 56; Haapaniemi (n 31) 107–108; and Trstenjak and Beysen (n 8) 105–106.

[116] Prechal and Widdershoven (n 28) 41–42.

[117] *Unibet* (n 28) paras 40–41.

[118] *Samba Diouf* (n 19) para 54; *Unibet* (n 28) para 65; and Case C-326/96 *Levez* [1998] para 53. See also on this issue, Arnull (n 4) 58–62.

4.3.6 The Right of Access to a Court or Tribunal

Article 19(1) EU Treaty and Article 39 of Directive 2005/85/EC require the *existence* of an effective remedy before national courts, but do not explicitly require that such remedy is accessible to the individual. It should, however, be derived from Article 47 of the Charter that the EU right to an effective remedy includes a right of *access* to such a remedy.[119] Article 47 requires that free legal aid be provided when necessary to ensure effective access to justice.[120] This implies that the remedy required by Article 47 should be accessible. Furthermore, the Court of Justice has considered that Article 47 comprises the right of access to a court or tribunal.[121] It has ruled in several cases that national procedural rules limiting access to a remedy were contrary to the principle of effectiveness as they rendered the right to an effective remedy virtually impossible or excessively difficult.[122]

Access to Court under International Law

It also follows from the sources of inspiration for the interpretation of the EU right to an effective remedy that access to court should be guaranteed. The ECtHR and the HRC have ruled that the remedy required by Article 13 ECHR[123] and Article 2(3) ICCPR must be accessible for the individual.[124] According to the ECtHR this means in particular that the exercise of the remedy must not be unjustifiably hindered by the acts or omissions of the authorities of the respondent State.[125] This follows from the fact that the remedy required by Article 13 must be effective in practice as well as in law. Furthermore, both Article 6(1) ECHR and Article 14 ICCPR include a right of access to court.[126] According to the ECtHR this implies, for example, that free legal assistance should be granted to a person if, without the assistance of a lawyer, this person would not be able to present her case properly and satisfactorily before the court.[127] It also prohibits blocking of

[119] See M Dougan, *National Remedies Before the Court of Justice, Issues of Harmonisation and Differentiation* (Oxford and Portland, OR, Hart Publishing, 2004) 4–5.

[120] See also Case C-279/09 *DEB* [2010] ECR I-13849, para 29.

[121] *Europese Gemeenschap v Otis NV* (n 24) para 49 and *DEB* (n 120) para 60.

[122] See, eg Case C-459/99 *MRAX* [2002] ECR I-6591, paras 102–103; Case C-78/98 *Preston and Fletcher* [2000] ECR I-3201; and Case C-255/00 *Grundig Italiana* [2002] ECR I-8003.

[123] *MSS* (n 68) para 318.

[124] The HRC ruled that Art 2(3) ICCPR requires State parties to ensure that individuals have accessible, effective and enforceable remedies to uphold the rights protected by the Covenant. HRC 16 August 2007, *Kimouche v Algeria*, no 1328/2004, para 7.10; and *George Kazantzis* (n 81) para 6.6.

[125] van Dijk et al (n 80) 1006. See, eg ECtHR 12 April 2005, *Shamayev et al v Georgia and Russia*, no 36378/02, para 447.

[126] ECtHR (Plen) 21 February 1975, *Golder v the United Kingdom*, no 4451/70, and HRC 10 November 1993, *Oló Bahamonde* (n 108) para 9.4. See also HRC General Comment No 32 (n 57) para II sub 9.

[127] ECtHR 9 October 1979, *Airey* (n 58) para 24.

access to a court due to narrow time limits for lodging the appeal[128] or procedural rules which amount to excessive formalism.[129]

4.3.7 The Right to Equality of Arms and Adversarial Proceedings

The principle of equality of arms and the right to adversarial proceedings are often linked to each other and to other elements of the right to a fair trial or the right to an effective remedy, such as the right of the defence, the right to be heard, or the duty to give reasons for a decision.[130] The principle of equality of arms and the right to adversarial proceedings are also guaranteed by the right to a fair hearing or fair trial included in Article 6 ECHR and Article 14 ICCPR. Chapter ten discusses the meaning of the principle of equality of arms and the right to adversarial proceedings in cases where the (asylum) decision is based on secret evidence. In this section some general remarks will be made concerning these rights.

The Right to Equality of Arms

The Court of Justice has recognised that the principle of effective judicial protection laid down in Article 47 of the Charter comprises the principle of equality of arms.[131] Although this EU principle is based on Article 6 ECHR which only applies to procedures before courts, it seems to also apply to administrative proceedings.[132] According to the Court of Justice, the principle of equality of arms implies 'that each party must be afforded a reasonable opportunity to present his case, including his evidence, under conditions that do not place him or her at a substantial disadvantage vis-à-vis his opponent'.[133] This interpretation is in conformity with Article 6 ECHR and Article 14 ICCPR.[134] According to the Court of Justice 'the aim of equality of arms is to ensure a balance between the parties to proceedings, guaranteeing that any document submitted to the court may be examined and challenged by any party to the proceedings'.[135] The Court of Justice has derived procedural guarantees from this principle, in particular in competition cases. These rights often relate to the right of access to the file. The Court held, for example, that the principle of equality of arms presupposes that in a

[128] ECtHR 28 October 1998, *Pérez de Rada Cavanilles v Spain*, no 28090/95.

[129] See, eg ECtHR 28 June 2005, *Zednik v Chech Republic*, no 74328/01, para 29.

[130] See, eg Case T-36/91 *Imperial Chemical Industries v Commission* [1995] ECR II-1847.

[131] *Europese Gemeenschap v Otis NV* (n 24) para 48.

[132] See, eg Case C-63/01 *Evans* [2003] ECR I-14447, paras 74–78; Case T-9/99 *HFB et al v Commission* [2002] ECR I-1487, para 330; and Case T-232/00 *Chef Revival USA v OHIM* [2002] ECR II-2749, para 42, where it concerned translation of documents in the administrative phase before an EU Institution.

[133] *Europese Gemeenschap v Otis NV* (n 24) para 71.

[134] ECtHR 27 October 1993, *Dombo beheer v the Netherlands*, no 14448/88, para 33. See with regard to the ICCPR, HRC 28 July 1989, *Morael v France*, no 207/86, para 9.3 and General Comment No 32 (n 57) para II, sub 8 and 13.

[135] *Europese Gemeenschap* (n 24) para 72.

competition case the knowledge which the undertaking concerned has of the file used in the proceeding is the same as that of the Commission.[136]

The Right to Adversarial Proceedings

Closely linked to the principle of equality of arms is the right to adversarial or *inter partes* proceedings. The Court of Justice has also referred to this right particularly in competition cases. The adversarial principle means, as a rule, that the parties have a right to a process of inspecting and commenting on the evidence and observations submitted to the court.[137] It also requires that in proceedings before EU courts, the parties must be appraised of and be able to debate and be heard on, the matters of fact and of law which will determine the outcome of the proceedings.[138] This also implies a right for the parties to be apprised of pleas in law raised by the court of its own motion, on which it intends to base its decision, and to discuss them.[139]

These requirements are very similar to those following from the right to adversarial proceedings guaranteed by Article 6 ECHR and Article 14 ICCPR.[140] In addition, the right to an effective remedy guaranteed by Article 13 ECHR includes the right to adversarial proceedings.[141]

4.4 THE EU RIGHT TO GOOD ADMINISTRATION

Article 41 of the Charter includes the right of every person to have his or her affairs handled impartially, fairly and within a reasonable time (the right to good administration). This right includes the right to be heard, the right of access to the file, and the duty to state reasons for a decision. Kańska mentions that this provision is the first official attempt at a positive definition of the meaning of 'good administration'.[142] Part of the rights of Article 41 of the Charter are based on rights which were already included in the former EC Treaty (the duty to state reasons, the right to reparation of damages, and the right to write to the institutions).

[136] *Imperial Chemical Industries* (n 130) para 93.

[137] Case C-450/06 *Varec* [2008] ECR I-581, para 47.

[138] Case C-89/08 P *Commission v Ireland et al* [2009] ECR I-11245, para 56.

[139] Case C-472/11 *Banif Plus Bank Zrt* [2013] para 30.

[140] According to the ECtHR, this right requires in principle, the opportunity for the parties to a trial to have knowledge of and comment on all evidence adduced or observations filed, with a view to influencing the court's decision. ECtHR (GC) 22 January 1996, *Lobo Machado v Portugal*, no 15764/89, para 31. See also HRC *Morael* (n 134) para 9.3 and General Comment No 32 (n 57) para II.

[141] See ECtHR 20 June 2002, *Al-Nashif v Bulgaria*, no 50963/99, para 137.

[142] K Kańska, 'Towards Administrative Human Rights in the EU. Impact of the Charter of Fundamental Rights' (2004) 10 *European Law Journal* 296, 303. See also J Dutheil de la Rochère, 'The EU Charter of Fundamental Rights, Not Binding but Influential: The Example of Good Administration' in A Arnull, P Eeckhout and T Tridimas (eds), *Continuity and Change in EU Law* (Oxford, Oxford University Press, 2008) 168.

However, Article 41 is mainly inspired by the case law of the EU Courts.[143] The EU principle of good administration is an umbrella principle which comprises more rights and obligations than those included in Article 41 of the Charter, such as the duty of care[144] and the right to transparency other than the right of access to the file.[145]

Applicability to National Administrative Proceedings

It follows from the text of Article 41 that it does not apply to pure national administrative proceedings. However, recital 39 of the Preamble to Directive 2013/32/EU states that Member States should comply with Article 41 of the Charter when postponing the conclusion of the asylum procedure. Furthermore, the Court of Justice has considered in its judgment in *MM* that Article 41 of the Charter is 'of general application'.[146] It stated that the right of the applicant for asylum to be heard following from this provision 'must apply fully to the procedure in which the competent national authority examines an application for international protection pursuant to rules adopted in the framework of the Common European Asylum System'.[147] The Court of Justice had already ruled prior to *MM* that national authorities are required under EU law to state the reasons for their decisions and to hear persons adversely affected by a decision during the administrative phase.[148] Some aspects of the principle of good administration are codified in the Procedures Directive. Articles 8(2) of Directive 2005/85/EC and 10(3) of Directive 2013/32/EU, for example, contain a duty for the decision-making authorities to conduct an appropriate examination of the asylum claim. This could be regarded as a codification of the duty of care. Articles 16(1) of Directive 2005/85/EC and 23(1) of Directive 2013/32/EU guarantee access to the applicant's file for the applicant's lawyer. Several rights included in Article 41 of the Charter play a role in this study. In the following sections the right to be heard and the duty to state reasons will be introduced more in detail.

[143] Kańska, ibid, 303–304. See also Schwartze (n 3) 298–99.

[144] See, eg Joined Cases T-3/00 and T-337/04 *Pitsiorias v Council and ECB* [2007] ECR II-4779, para 163.

[145] Kańska (n 142) 305 and 322–23; Dutheil de la Rochère, 'The EU Charter of Fundamental Rights' (n 142) 169.

[146] Case C-277/11 *MM v Minister for Justice, Equality and Law Reform Ireland* [2012] para 84. See also Case C-75/08 *Mellor* [2009], Opinion of AG Kokott, para 33. The Court of Justice seemed to be of a different opinion in Case C-482/10 *Cicale* [2011] para 28.

[147] *MM*, ibid, para 89.

[148] Kańska (n 142) 309 and Dutheil de la Rochère 'The EU Charter of Fundamental Rights' (n 145) 170.

4.4.1 Provisions of International Law inspiring the EU Right to Good Administration

Although according to its text Article 13 ECHR only applies to proceedings before an independent and impartial authority, the ECtHR has also derived guarantees for administrative proceedings from this provision. In *MSS* the ECtHR concluded that Article 13 ECHR had been violated as a result of the deficiencies in the Greek authorities' examination of the applicant's asylum request (insufficient information about the asylum procedure, difficult access to the asylum procedure, shortage of interpreters and lack of training of the staff responsible for conducting the individual interviews, lack of legal aid, and excessively lengthy delays in receiving a decision). Furthermore, it took into account the risk the applicant faced of being returned to his country of origin without any serious examination of the merits of his asylum application and without having access to an effective remedy.[149]

Arguably, the case law regarding Article 6 ECHR and Article 14 ICCPR may also inspire the EU right to good administration laid down in Article 41 of the Charter.[150] The ECtHR has, for example, recognised in the context of Article 6 ECHR that the fact that a decision is not reasoned may render it impossible to bring a meaningful action before a court.[151] Moreover, as mentioned in section 4.3.7, the Court of Justice seems to apply the principle of equality of arms to the administrative phase.

4.4.2 The Right to be Heard

According to Article 41 of the Charter the right to good administration includes the right of every person to be heard, before any individual measure which would affect him or her adversely is taken.[152] The right to be heard (also seen as part of the rights of the defence) applies to decisions taken by national authorities, including asylum decisions.[153] It may be assumed that the EU Courts' case law regarding the right to be heard on decisions by EU Institutions is also relevant for the interpretation of the right to be heard in the national context. This also follows from the fact that the Court of Justice in its judgment in *MM*, which concerned

[149] *MSS* (n 68) paras 301–20. See also *Abdolkhani* (n 62) paras 111–17.

[150] Kańska states that 'the right to good administration, as expressed by the Charter, mirrors the principles of fair trial (or due process) guaranteed by the Convention' Kańska (n 142) 306.

[151] ECtHR 10 July 2012, *KMC v Hungary*, no 19554/11, para 34.

[152] Schwartze mentions that the right to be heard is probably the most important principle of administrative procedure. Schwartze 'Judicial Review' (n 9) 91.

[153] *MM* (n 146) para 89 and *Dokter* (n 45) para 74. See also J Reichel, 'Between Supremacy and Autonomy' in U Bernitz, J Nergelius and C Cardner (eds), *General Principles of EC Law in a Process of Development* (Alphen aan den Rijn, Kluwer Law International, 2008) 243, 266.

asylum proceedings, referred to this case law.[154] This case law will, therefore, be briefly discussed in this section.

According to the standing case law of the EU Courts, the right to be heard is a fundamental principle of EU law in all proceedings initiated against a person which might culminate in a measure adversely affecting that person.[155] The right to be heard must be guaranteed even in absence of any rules governing the procedure in question or where legislation existed but did not take sufficient account of that right.[156] A violation of the right to be heard will only lead to the annulment of the contested decision if, in the absence of this irregularity, the procedure could have lead to a different decision.[157]

The right to be heard requires that the addressees of decisions which significantly affect their interests be placed in a position in which they may effectively make known their views on the evidence on which the decision is based[158] and the relevant facts and circumstances.[159] This implies that the parties concerned must be informed of the evidence adduced against them[160] or that a draft decision is submitted to this party.[161] According to the EU Courts' settled case law the right of access to the file is one of the procedural safeguards which ensure that the right to be heard can be exercised effectively.[162] The right of every person to have access to his or her file is laid down in Article 41(2) of the Charter. The right to be heard also 'requires the authorities to pay due attention to the observations thus submitted by the person concerned, examining carefully and impartially all the relevant aspects of the individual case and giving a detailed statement of reasons for their decision'.[163]

The safeguarding of the right to be heard in the context of the administrative procedure itself is to be distinguished from that resulting from the right

[154] *MM* (n 146) paras 85–88.

[155] See, eg *Dokter* (n 45) para 74.

[156] *MM* (n 146) para 86 and, eg *Organisation des Modjahedines du peuple d'Iran* (n 41) para 91 and P Craig, *EU Administrative Law* (Oxford, Oxford University Press, 2006) 519.

[157] Joined Cases C-191/09 P and C-200/09 P, *Council and Commission v Interpipe Niko Tube and Interpipe NTRP* [2012] para 79.

[158] See, eg *Dokter* (n 45) para 74 and Case C-32/95P *Commission v Lisrestal et al* [1996] ECR I-5373, para 21. On the scope of application of the right to be heard included in Art 41 of the Charter, see I Rabinovici, 'The Right to Be Heard in the Charter of Fundamental Rights of the European Union' (2012) 18 *European Public Law* 149.

[159] *MM* (n 146) para 87 and Case C-269/90 *Technische Universität München* [1991] ECR I-5469, para 25.

[160] *Organisation des Modjahedines du peuple d'Iran* (n 41) para 93. Case C-32/95P *Commission v Lisrestal et al* [1996] ECR I-5373, para 41. See also T-49/88, *Al-Jubail Fertilizer* v *Council* [1991] para 17.

[161] Case C-462/98 P *Mediocurso v Commission* [2000] ECR I-7183, para 42. The right to be heard does not extend to the final decision which an administrative authority intends to adopt. See, eg Case T-262/09 *Safariland v OHIM* [2011] para 80.

[162] See, eg Case T-170/06 *Alrosa v Commission* [2007] ECR II-2601, para 197. It also follows from this judgment that the relevant documents should be made accessible to the party concerned at a moment where the right to be heard can still be exercised. See para 201. See also Kańska (n 142) 318.

[163] *MM* (n 146) para 88.

to an effective judicial remedy against the act having adverse effects which may be adopted at the end of that procedure.[164] The party must generally be able to exercise the right to be heard before the administrative decision is adopted[165] and a reasonable period should be afforded to effectively put forward his views.[166] In *Hercules Chemicals NV* the Court of Justice considered that an infringement of the right to be heard had not been remedied by the mere fact that access to the relevant files was made possible after the decision, in particular during the judicial proceedings relating to an action in which annulment of the contested decision was sought.[167]

The right to be heard may be restricted, provided that the restrictions correspond to objectives of general interest pursued by the measure in question and that they do not constitute, with regard to the objectives pursued, a disproportionate and intolerable interference which infringes upon the very substance of the rights guaranteed.[168] The EU Courts have, for example, accepted that the right to be heard may be restricted in the context of measures against foot and mouth disease[169] and decisions to freeze funds of persons, groups or entities identified as being involved in terrorist acts.[170] In such cases, the authorities who took the decision may be obliged to hear this party as soon as possible after the adoption of the decision[171] or in subsequent proceedings.[172]

The right to be heard will play a significant role in chapter seven on the asylum applicant's right to be heard on his asylum motives, and in chapter ten on the use of secret information.

4.4.3 The Duty to State Reasons

According to Article 296 TFEU[173] and Article 41(2) of the Charter, the bodies of the EU are obliged to state reasons for their legal acts or decisions. The Court of Justice regards this obligation as an essential procedural requirement[174] which

[164] Ibid, para 87, *Organisation des Modjahedines du peuple d'Iran* (n 41) para 94; and Case T-372/00 *Campolargo v Commission* [2002] ECR II-223, para 36.

[165] *MM*, ibid, para 87, Case C-269/90 *Technische Universität München* [1991] ECR I-5469, para 25; Joined Cases C-379/08 and C-380/08 *ERG et al* [2010] ECR I-2007, paras 54–56 and *Dokter* (n 45) para 74.

[166] Case C-462/98 P *Mediocurso v Commission* [2000] ECR I-7183, para 38.

[167] Case C-51/92 P *Hercules Chemicals v Commission* [1999] ECR I-4235, paras 78–79. See also section 4.5.2.

[168] *Dokter* (n 45) para 75.

[169] Ibid, para 76.

[170] The Court stated that an initial measure to freeze funds must be able to benefit from a surprise effect and to be applied with immediate effect. *Organisation des Modjahedines du peuple d'Iran* (n 41) para 127. See also Case C-111/02 P *Parliament v Reynolds* [2004] ECR I-5475, paras 57–60.

[171] See, eg Case T-211/98 *F v Commission* [2000] ECR II-471, para 34.

[172] *Dokter* (n 45) para 76, *Organisation des Modjahedines du peuple d'Iran* (n 41) para 130.

[173] Art 253 of the former EC Treaty.

[174] Case C-17/99 *France v Commission* [2001] ECR I-2481, para 35.

may only be derogated from for compelling reasons.[175] The plea of absence of, or inadequate statement of, reasons is a plea involving a matter of public policy which may, and even must, be raised by the EU judicature of its own motion.[176]

Article 296 TFEU and Article 41(2) of the Charter are directed towards the Institutions of the EU. However, it follows from the case law of the Court of Justice that the duty to state reasons also applies to national authorities taking a decision on the basis of EU legislation.[177] The duty of national authorities to state reasons is also laid down in Article 9 of Directive 2005/85/EC and Article 11 of Directive 2013/32/EU.

The Court of Justice has not ruled whether the requirements under the duty to state reasons are the same for national authorities and EU Institutions.[178] However, it may be assumed that the Courts' case law regarding the obligation to state reasons for the EU Institutions is relevant for the interpretation of the duty to state reasons in the national context. This is supported by the fact that several EU measures seem to have codified the case law of the EU Courts regarding the EU Institutions' duty to state reasons in EU legislation containing requirements for national authorities.[179]

The duty to state reasons is closely connected to the right to an effective remedy.[180] This right can only be effectively exercised if the person concerned knows the reasons underlying the negative decision.[181] Compliance with the obligation to state reasons is all the more important if the party concerned is not afforded the opportunity to be heard before the adoption of the initial decision. In that situation the obligation to state reasons constitutes the sole safeguard enabling the party concerned, especially after the adoption of that decision, to make effective use of the legal remedies available to it to challenge the lawfulness of that decision.[182] Furthermore, the statement of reasons must enable the court to review the decision.[183] Finally, the statement of reasons serves transparency and may raise the quality of decision-making.[184]

[175] See, eg T-390/08 *Bank Melli Iran v Council* [2009] ECR II-3967, para 80.

[176] C-89/08 P *Commission v Ireland et al* [2009] ECR I-11245, para 34.

[177] *UNECTEF* (n 47), para 15 and Case C-239/05 *BVBA Management, Training en Consultancy* [2007] ECR I-1455, para 36. See also Reichel, 'Between Supremacy and Autonomy' (n 153) 265.

[178] See Reichel, ibid, 265–67.

[179] See, eg Art 30 of Dir 2004/38/EC of the European Parliament and of the Council of 29 April 2004 on the right of citizens of the EU and their family members to move and reside freely within the territory of the Member States amending Reg (EEC) No 1612/68 and repealing Dirs 64/221/EEC, 68/360/EEC, 72/194/EEC, 73/148/EEC, 75/34/EEC, 75/35/EEC, 90/364/EEC, 90/365/EEC and 93/96/EEC [2004] OJ L158/77.

[180] See also section 4.2.

[181] J Ponce, 'Good Administration and Administrative Procedures' (2005) 12 *Indiana Journal of Global Legal Studies* 551, 574.

[182] Case C-417/11 P *Council v Bamba* [2012] para 51.

[183] The statement of reasons must enable the EU judicature to exercise its power of review. See Case T-111/96 *ITT Promedia v Commission* [1998] ECR II-2937; Joined Cases T-110/03, T-150/03 and T-405/03 *Sison v Council* [2005] ECR II-1429, para 59; and *Organisation des Modjahedines du peuple d'Iran* (n 41) para 89. See Kańska (n 142) 320.

[184] See also Reichel (n 153) 252 and *Mellor* (n 146) Opinion of AG Kokott.

The duty to state reasons must ensure that the party concerned can defend an EU right under the best possible conditions and that this person is able to decide, with a full knowledge of the relevant facts, whether there is any point in his applying to the court.[185] In its judgment in *MM*, the Court of Justice considered that 'the obligation to state reasons for a decision which are sufficiently specific and concrete to allow the person to understand why his application is being rejected is thus a corollary of the principle of respect for the rights of the defence'.[186] The statement of reasons for a decision required by Article 296 TFEU must be appropriate to the act at issue and must disclose in a clear and unequivocal fashion the reasoning followed by the EU Institution which adopted the measure in question.[187] General reasons, which do not contain any specific information relating to the case at issue are not sufficient.[188] The EU Institutions are not obliged to adopt a position on all the arguments relied on by the parties concerned in support of their case nor on all the relevant facts and points of law.[189] They need only to set out the facts and legal considerations of decisive importance to their decision.[190] This includes the factual and legal elements which provide the legal basis leading to the adoption of the decision[191] and the assessment of the essential complaints made by the parties.[192]

The requirements under the duty to state reasons vary according to the circumstances of the case. In *France v Commission* the Court of Justice stated that the duty to state reasons

> must be appraised by reference to the circumstances of each case, in particular the content of the measure in question, the nature of the reasons given and the interest which the addressees of the measure, or other parties to whom it is of direct and individual concern, may have in obtaining explanations.[193]

Moreover, the degree of precision of the statement of the reasons for a decision must be weighed against practical realities and the time and technical facilities available for making the decision.[194]

The statement of reasons must be notified to the person concerned, as far as possible, at the same time as the act adversely affecting him, or as soon as possible

[185] *UNECTEF* (n 47) para 15 and Case C-70/95 *Sodemare* [1997] para 19.

[186] *MM* (n 146) para 88.

[187] Case C-41/00P *Interporc v Commission* [2003] ECR I-2125, para 55.

[188] Case T-132/03 *Casini v Commission* [2005] ECR II-1169, para 35.

[189] *ITT Promedia* (n 183) para 79 and Case T-387/94 *Asia Motor France v Commission* [1996] ECR II-961, para 104; and *Sison v Council* (n 183) para 59.

[190] *ITT Promedia*, ibid, para 79 and *Asia Motor France v Commission*, ibid, para 104.

[191] Joined Cases T-346/02 and T-347/02 *Cableuropa et al v Commission* [2003] ECR II-4251, para 232.

[192] Joined Cases T-371/94 and T-394/94 *British Airways and British Midland Airways v Commission* [1998] ECR II-2405, para 64.

[193] *France v Commission* (n 174) para 36 and Case T-70/05 *Evropaïki Dynamiki v EMSA* [2010] ECR II-313, para 171. See also Reichel (n 153) 253.

[194] *Organisation des Modjahedines du peuple d'Iran* (n 41) para 141 and Case T-237/00 *Reynolds v Parliament* [2004] para 102.

after the decision has been taken.[195] According to the CFI, the failure to state the reasons for a decision cannot be remedied by the fact that the person concerned learns the reasons for the act during the proceedings before the judicature.[196] '[T]he possibility of remedying the total absence of a statement of reasons after an action has been brought would prejudice the rights of the defence because the applicant would only have the reply in which to set out his pleas contesting the reasons which he would not know until after he had lodged his application. The principle of equality of the parties before the EU judicature would accordingly be adversely affected.'[197]

The EU duty to state reasons plays an important role in chapter ten of this study on the use of secret information.

4.5 THREE BASIC CONCEPTS

For the purpose of this study a large number of judgments of the Court of Justice and the ECtHR have been assessed. It is contended here that from this case law three 'basic concepts' emerge:

1. When assessing whether EU procedural rights have been infringed interests must often be balanced against each other.
2. When determining whether a procedure should be considered fair, regard should be had to all aspects and instances of this procedure: the overall fairness of a procedure must be examined.
3. The subject matter of the procedure influences the level of procedural protection which must be offered to the applicant.

These ideas seem to play a role in many of the cases in which procedural rules are tested against procedural rights and principles. Therefore, they may be helpful on the one hand to explain some of the choices made by the Court of Justice and the ECtHR, and on the other hand to predict the approach of these courts in new situations. These concepts will therefore be used as a tool to analyse the case law examined in the thematic chapters six to ten and to develop a set of EU procedural standards for the procedural topics discussed. The three basic principles will be further explained in this section.

[195] Joined Cases C-402/05 P and C-415/05 P *Kadi and Al Barakaat v Council and Commission* [2008] ECR I-6351, para 336.

[196] See, eg *Bank Melli Iran* (n 175) para 80 and *Organisation des Modjahedines du peuple d'Iran* (n 41) para 139.

[197] Case T-253/04 *KONGRA-GEL et al v Council* [2008] ECR II-46, para 101 and *Organisation des Modjahedines du peuple d'Iran* (n 41) para 139, 165. In *Casini* (n 188) para 33 the Court stated that insufficiency of the statement of reasons can be compensated during the appeal stage. In *Reynolds v Parliament* (n194) paras 97 and 101, however, the Court stated that this applies only in exceptional cases.

4.5.1 Balancing of Interests

The EU Courts have recognised that Member States are allowed to limit EU procedural rights, such as the right to an effective remedy, the right to be heard, or the duty to state reasons. In that situation the interest of the party concerned must often be balanced against the interests of the State or other parties in such limitations. The right of access to court, for example, may be limited by the imposition of time limits for bringing proceedings in the interest of legal certainty.[198] The right of one company to be heard may be limited in order to ensure the right of protection of business secrets of another company.[199] The State's interest assessing an asylum claim as quickly as possible in order to remove persons who have no right to stay could result in lesser procedural guarantees for the applicant.[200]

The Court of Justice has held that in the assessment of the effectiveness of national procedural rules 'the basic principles of the domestic judicial system, such as protection of the rights of the defence, the principle of legal certainty and the proper conduct of procedure, must, where appropriate, be taken into consideration'.[201] The Court examines which aim underlies the national procedural rule which limits a party's procedural right. Often these underlying aims, such as legal certainty, are also recognised as EU general principles. The Court then strikes a balance between this underlying aim of the national procedural rule and the need for effectiveness.[202] Some authors call this the 'procedural rule of reason' test.[203]

The procedural rule of reason test has been criticised because it leads to a lack of predictability and legal certainty, as it is applied on a case-by-case basis. Using case law as a guideline is therefore complicated.[204] Haapaniemi remarks that in its case law the Court of Justice has not repeated the procedural rule of reason test in every case where it applied the principle of effectiveness and equivalence, but has referred to it from time to time. He states, however, that 'reconciliation of the interests the national provision represents and the exigencies of EU law are at any rate intrinsic in the *Rewe/Comet* jurisprudence' without any explicit reference to the balancing test.[205] Prechal and Widdershoven argue that the balancing test performed by the Court of Justice under the principle of effectiveness is less intense than that applied when the EU right to an effective remedy is at stake.[206]

198 See, eg Case C-63/08 *Pontin* [2008] ECR I-10467, para 48.

199 See, eg *Varec* (n 137) para 51 and Case C-438/04 *Mobistar* [2006] ECR I-6675, para 40. See also Schwartze (n 9) 96.

200 *Samba Diouf* (n 19) para 65.

201 *Peterbroeck* (n 35) para 14.

202 J Engström, 'National Courts' Obligation to Apply Community Law Ex Officio—The Court Showing New Respect for Party Autonomy and National Procedural Autonomy?' (2008) 1 *Review of European Administrative Law* 67, 68. See also Trstenjak and Beysen (n 8) 103.

203 Engström, ibid, 68. Prechal and Shelkoplyas, 'National Procedures' (n 30) 593.

204 Engström, ibid, 71. See also Prechal and Shelkoplyas, ibid, 593.

205 Haapaniemi (n 31) 98.

206 Prechal and Widdershoven (n 28) 43–44.

Balancing of Interests in the Case Law of the ECtHR

The ECtHR has held with regard to Article 13 ECHR that the context in which an alleged violation occurs may entail inherent limitations on the conceivable remedy.[207] The ECtHR has, for example, accepted limitations to the right to an effective remedy in circumstances where national security considerations did not permit the divulging of certain sensitive information.[208] Furthermore, the right to a court guaranteed by Article 6 ECHR, of which the right of access is one aspect, is not absolute. It is subject to limitations permitted by implication, in particular where the conditions of admissibility of an appeal are concerned, since by its very nature it calls for regulation by the State. However, these limitations must not restrict or reduce a person's access in such a way, or to such an extent, that the very essence of the right is impaired. Such limitations will not be compatible with Article 6(1) if they do not pursue a legitimate aim or if there is not a reasonable relationship of proportionality between the means employed and the aim pursued.[209] Furthermore, the right to a public hearing may in exceptional circumstances be dispensed with.[210] Finally, the ECtHR has recognised that the right to adversarial proceedings may be limited, for example, in order to preserve the fundamental rights of another individual or to safeguard an important public interest, which justifies a limitation of this right.[211]

4.5.2 Assessing the Overall Fairness of a Procedure

Asylum procedures and other procedures usually consist of several phases, such as an administrative phase, an appeal phase and a higher appeal phase. Within those phases several procedural steps may be taken. The administrative phase of an asylum procedure, for example, may consist of several interviews with the asylum applicant, gathering of additional evidence or information, contacts between the applicant and his lawyer, and taking the decision. Generally, shortcomings in one phase or step of the procedure may be compensated for or repaired in another step or phase of the same procedure or even in a subsequent procedure. Shortcomings in the assessment of evidence during the administrative phase may, for example, be repaired by a full judicial review of the facts. In such a situation

[207] *Kudla* (n 54) para 151.

[208] *Al-Nashif v Bulgaria* (n 141). See also HRC 15 June 2004, *Ahani v Canada*, no 1051/2002, where the HRC considered that in the circumstances of national security involved, it was not persuaded that the process was unfair to the applicant. See further ch 10, section 10.5 in this volume.

[209] See, eg ECtHR 15 February 2000, *Garcia Manibardo v Spain*, no 38695/97, para 36 and ECtHR 10 July 1998, *Tinnelly & Sons v the United Kingdom*, no 20390/92 and 21322/92, para 72. See also HRC General Comment No 32 (n 57) para II, sub 9.

[210] ECtHR (GC) 23 November 2006, *Jussila v Finland*, no 73053/01, para 41 and ECtHR (GC) 11 July 2002, *Göç v Turkey*, no 36590/97, para 47.

[211] See, eg ECtHR (GC) 16 February 2000, *Fitt v the United Kingdom*, no 29777/96, para 45.

the violation of a procedural right or principle may be prevented. It is, therefore, the fairness of a procedure as a whole which should be assessed.

In cases where it assesses national procedural rules in the light of the principle of effectiveness, the Court of Justice has considered that:

> each case which raises the question whether a national procedural provision renders application of Community law impossible or excessively difficult must be analysed by reference to the role of that provision in the procedure, its progress and its special features, viewed as a whole, before the various national instances.[212]

This implies that the fairness of a national procedural rule should not be assessed in a vacuum but in the context of the national procedure as a whole.[213] Recital 27 of the Preamble of the Procedures Directive reflects this case law, while stating that the effectiveness of a national remedy, also with regard to the examination of the relevant facts, depends on the administrative and judicial system of each Member State seen as a whole.[214] The Court of Justice referred to this recital in its judgment in *HID and BA* In this case it was argued before the Court of Justice that the Irish Refugee Appeal Tribunal, which reviews first instance asylum decisions, could not be considered independent. The Court considered that the Irish judicial system fulfilled the requirements of an effective remedy within the meaning of Article 39 PD. The Court found that the opportunity to appeal decisions of the Refugee Appeals Tribunal before the High Court and the Supreme Court was 'capable of protecting the Refugee Appeal Tribunal against potential temptations to give in to external intervention or pressure liable to jeopardise the independence of its members'.[215]

Overall Fairness in the Case Law of the ECtHR

According to the ECtHR 'even if a single remedy does not by itself entirely satisfy the requirements under Article 13, the aggregate of remedies provided for under domestic law may do so'.[216] Furthermore, the ECtHR has explicitly considered under Article 6 that it 'always tries to take into account the "proceedings as a whole" before deciding whether or not there has been a violation of the Convention in respect of a specific episode'.[217] Guarantees offered in one instance of the procedure may justify lesser safeguards in further instances.

[212] See, *Evans* (n 132) para 46. See also, *Peterbroeck* (n 35) para 14.

[213] Accetto and Zlepnig (n 2) state that the Court of Justice confirmed in *Evans* (n 132) that the negative impact of a national procedural provision on the application of EU law must be analysed in the light of the domestic judicial system as a whole. Accetto and Zlepnig (n 2) 391.

[214] Recital 27 Preamble Directive 2005/85/EC.

[215] *HID and BA* (n 107) paras 102–103.

[216] *MSS* (n 68) para 289. See also ECtHR 26 March 1987, *Leander v Sweden*, no 9248/81, para 84. See also *HID and BA* (n 107) Opinion of AG Bot, para 93.

[217] ECtHR 11 December 2008, *Mirilashvili v Russia*, no 6293/04, para 164. See also ECtHR 13 October 2009, *Salontaji-Drobnjak v Serbia*, no 36500/05, para 128 and ECtHR 22 November 1995, *Bryan v the United Kingdom*, no 19178/91, paras 45–46 and Harris, O'Boyle and Warbrick, *Law on the EC Convention on Human Rights* (n 99) 246.

Article 6 ECHR applies to appeal and cassation procedures. In its assessment of the fairness of such proceedings, the ECtHR takes into account the guarantees offered in first instance proceedings.[218] Furthermore, the possibility exists that a higher tribunal may, in certain circumstances, make reparation for an initial violation of Article 6 ECHR. Such a violation cannot be remedied at a later stage of the procedure if any prejudice suffered in the meantime has become irreversible.[219] Alternatively, the ECtHR may rule that domestic proceedings had been unfair 'because of the cumulative effect of various procedural defects'. In such a situation each defect, taken alone, would not have convinced the ECtHR that the proceedings were unfair, but their coexistence is the factor that leads to a finding of a violation of Article 6.[220]

No Possible Reparation for Procedural Flaws

It is, however, also possible that a procedural rule or practice on its own amounts to a violation of a procedural right or principle. The CFI has, for example, held that a violation of the right to be heard during the administrative procedure cannot be repaired during the appeal phase.[221] In *Hercules Chemicals* the Court of Justice considered that the disclosure during the appeal phase of relevant documents underlying a Commission decision to impose a fine or penalty, cannot remedy a breach of the rights of the defence caused by the non-disclosure of those documents during the administrative phase.[222] The Court stated:

> Although belated disclosure of documents in the file allows the undertaking that has support of the forms of order it is seeking, it does not put the undertaking back into the situation it would have been in if it had been able to rely on those documents in presenting its written and oral observations to the Commission.[223]

Furthermore, procedural rules which effectively block access to a court or tribunal in themselves often violate the right to an effective remedy or fair trial.[224]

4.5.3 The Subject Matter of the Procedure

When assessing procedural matters the Court of Justice and the ECtHR often take the individual circumstances of the case into account.[225] Factors which may

[218] According to the ECtHR 'the manner in which Article 6 applies to courts of appeal or of cassation must depend on the special features of the proceedings concerned and account must be taken of the entirety of the proceedings conducted in the domestic legal order and the court of cassation's role in them'. See, eg ECtHR 22 March 2007, *Sialkowska v Poland*, no 8932/05, para 104.

[219] ECtHR 14 June 2011, *Mercieca et al v Malta*, no 21974/07, para 49.

[220] *Mirilashvili v Russia* (n 217) para 165.

[221] *KONGRA-GEL et al v Council* (n 197) para 101 and *Organisation des Modjahedines du peuple d'Iran* (n 41) para 139.

[222] *Hercules Chemicals v Commission* (n 167) paras 77–79.

[223] Ibid, para 79.

[224] *Johnston* (n 46) and ECtHR 28 October 1998, *Pérez de Rada Cavanilles v Spain* (n 128).

[225] See, eg Barbier de la Serre, 'Procedural Justice' (n 40) 248–49.

influence the level of procedural protection which should be granted include the nature of the rights claimed by the applicant and the personal circumstances of the applicant. Arguably, the required level of procedural protection depends on the interests at stake for the party concerned. Furthermore, the characteristics of the person concerned may require more or fewer procedural guarantees. As a result, one must be careful not to apply judgments of the EU Courts and the ECtHR mechanically to other fields of EU law.[226]

Asylum cases have a few characteristics which distinguish them from most other cases falling within the scope of EU law. These relate first to the fundamental and even absolute nature of the rights claimed, and secondly to the special and often vulnerable situation in which asylum applicants find themselves. The Court should take these characteristics into account when interpreting the Procedures Directive and assessing national procedural rules in the light of EU procedural rights and principles. Other factors may also influence the level of procedural guarantees offered. Both the Court of Justice and the ECtHR have, for example, accepted that the level of discretion left to the decision-making authorities determines the standard of judicial review which is required.[227]

4.5.3.1 The Nature of the Rights Claimed

Unlike issues of State aid, mergers or agriculture, asylum is not an economic but a human rights issue, in which the absolute EU prohibition of *refoulement* and the right to asylum play a crucial role. The fact that the principle of *non-refoulement* is absolute will potentially play an important role in cases regarding procedural guarantees for asylum applicants. A lack of procedural guarantees or the balancing of interests may never lead to a violation of this principle. Therefore, it is not unlikely that in asylum cases the Court of Justice will require more procedural guarantees than in cases involving fundamental rights, which allow for derogations and demand a balance of interests.[228] The Court of Justice has held that the assessment of the extent of the risk of *refoulement* 'must, in all cases, be carried out with vigilance and care, since what are at issue are issues relating to the integrity of the person and to individual liberties, issues which relate to the fundamental

[226] See Case C-473/00 *Cofidis* [2002] ECR I-10875, para 37.

[227] See further ch 9 in this volume on judicial review of the establishment and qualification of the facts.

[228] Staffans states that the vast interests embedded in asylum procedures on the side of the State as well as the applicant require real, objective and effective possibilities for review and remedy. I Staffans, 'Judicial Protection and the New European Asylum Regime' (2010) 12 *European Journal of Migration and Law* 273–97.

values of the Union'.[229] The fundamental nature of the right to asylum, although not absolute, will potentially also require high procedural standards.[230]

The Court of Justice has also shown in its case law on other fields of EU law that it takes into account what is at stake for an individual when deciding on the effectiveness of national procedural rules. In *Visciano*, for example, the Court of Justice took into account, when assessing a time limit set by national law in the light of the principle of effectiveness, that the case concerned a claim for payment of salary. According to the Court, such claims are by their very nature, of great importance to the individual concerned.[231] The Court of Justice also held that the duty to state reasons must be appraised by reference to the circumstances of each case, in particular the content of the measure in question, the nature of the reasons given, and the interest which the addressees of the measure, or other parties to whom it is of direct and individual concern, may have in obtaining explanations.[232]

The same approach can be found in the case law of the ECtHR. This court has considered that the scope of the obligation to provide an effective remedy under Article 13 ECHR varies according to the nature of the applicant's complaint under the Convention.[233] The absolute nature of the right safeguarded under Article 3 has implications for Article 13 ECtHR.[234] It held that 'in view of the importance which the Court attaches to Article 3 of the Convention and the irreversible nature of the damage which may result if the risk of torture or ill-treatment materialises', the effectiveness of a remedy within the meaning of Article 13 requires close scrutiny by a national authority, independent and rigorous scrutiny of any claim that there are substantial grounds for fearing a real risk of treatment contrary to Article 3, and access to a remedy with automatic suspensive effect.[235] The HRC considered in *Ahani* that 'where one of the highest values protected by the Covenant, namely the right to be free from torture, is at stake, the closest scrutiny should be applied to the fairness of the procedure applied to determine whether an individual is at a substantial risk of torture.[236] When assessing the fairness of the proceedings under Article 6 ECHR, the ECtHR also takes into account what is at stake for the person concerned. The Court allows greater latitude when dealing

[229] Joined Cases C-175/08, C-176/08, C-178/08 and C-179/08, *Salahadin Abdulla* [2010] ECR I-1493, para 90.

[230] *MM* (n 146) Opinion of AG Bot, para 43.

[231] Case C-69/08 *Visciano* [2009] ECR I-6741, para 44. See also *Dokter* (n 45) para 74.

[232] *France v Commission* (n 174) para 36 and *Evropaïki Dynamiki v EMSA* (n 193) para 171.

[233] According to the EctHR, the scope of the obligation under Art 13 varies according to the nature of the applicant's complaint under the Convention. See ECtHR 20 June 2002, *Al-Nashif* (n 141) para 136.

[234] See, eg *MSS* (n 68) para 288.

[235] Ibid, para 293.

[236] HRC *Ahani* (n 208) para 10.5. See also HRC 19 August 1997, *Vincente et al v Colombia*, no 612/1995.

with civil cases than when dealing with criminal cases.[237] In several cases in which the right to adversarial proceedings was limited as a result of the use of secret evidence, the Court stressed the need for procedural safeguards while referring to the serious consequences of the contested decision for the applicant.[238]

4.5.3.2 General Circumstances of the Party Concerned

The Court of Justice takes into account the general characteristics of the (legal or natural) persons involved in the procedure when assessing procedural rules. Short time limits may, for example, be justified in cases in which the parties concerned are (legal) professionals, who are familiar with the procedure.[239]

On the other hand, the Court of Justice seems to be inclined to protect parties which find themselves in a weak legal position. In several decisions concerning procedural guarantees in consumer cases the Court of Justice had regard to the fact that the consumer may be unaware of his rights or may encounter difficulties in enforcing them.[240] The Court concluded in those cases that national courts must assess the fairness of a contract term of their own motion in order to ensure consumer protection envisaged by the relevant directive. Trstenjak and Beysen state that the Court of Justice resorted to 'a consumer-oriented interpretation' of the concepts of procedural and remedial autonomy of the Member States. 'By emphasizing the weak position of the consumer the ECJ implicitly raised the effectiveness threshold which national procedural rules for the enforcement of rights under the consumer protection directives must meet.'[241] In *Pontin* the Court considered that a 15-day period for bringing an action for nullity of a dismissal and reinstatement of a pregnant woman must be regarded as being particularly short and appeared to infringe the principles of effectiveness 'in view inter alia of the situation in which a woman finds herself at the start of her pregnancy'. It also took into account that it would be 'very difficult for a female worker dismissed during her pregnancy to obtain proper advice and, if appropriate, prepare and bring an action within the 15-day period'.[242]

When assessing asylum procedures in the light of the EU right to an effective remedy the difficult position in which asylum applicants often find themselves should be taken into account. AG Bot in his Opinion in *MM v the Minister for Justice, Quality and Law Reform* concerning asylum applicant's right to be

[237] See, eg *Dombo* (n 134) para 32.

[238] ECtHR 24 April 2007, *Matyjek v Poland*, no 38184/03, para 59; ECtHR 31 October 2006, *Aksoy v Turkey*, no 59741/00, para 27; and ECtHR 19 October 2010, *Özpinar v Turkey*, no 20999/04, para 78.

[239] ECJ Case C-349/07 *Sopropé* [2008] ECR I-10369, para 41. The case concerned an application for post-clearance recovery of a customs debt established following an investigation into the origin of goods imported into Portugal by Sopropé.

[240] See, eg Joined Cases C-240/98 to C-244/98 *Océano Grupo Editorial and Salvat Editores* [2000] ECR I-4941, para 26.

[241] Trstenjak and Beysen (n 8) 121.

[242] *Pontin* (n 198) paras 62 and 65.

heard took into account 'the state of not only material, but also psychological deprivation in which an applicant for asylum is likely to find himself'.[243] The ECtHR has considered that asylum seekers are a particularly underprivileged and vulnerable population group in need of special protection.[244] Asylum applicants generally do not speak the language of the Member State, are not familiar with the legal system in the Member State and do not have any resources to pay for legal aid. Furthermore, as mentioned above, asylum applicants often arrive without documentation to support their asylum account. Therefore, interpreters, information on the asylum procedure or free legal aid may be essential in order to guarantee a fair asylum procedure.[245] The ECtHR has underlined the importance of information on the asylum procedure and accessibility of linguistic and legal aid in several judgments in asylum cases.[246]

4.5.3.3 Personal Circumstances of the Party Concerned

The Court of Justice requires national courts to take into account the personal circumstances of the party concerned when assessing national procedural rules in the light of the EU right to an effective remedy. The Court of Justice itself generally assesses in the abstract whether a procedural rule, taking into account the rights claimed by the party concerned and the specific features of the procedure, is reasonable and proportionate. The Court has made clear, however, that the application in a particular case of a procedural rule, which was generally considered reasonable and proportionate, may violate the EU right to an effective remedy. In *Samba Diouf*, for example, the Court of Justice considered a time limit of 15 days for bringing an appeal against the rejection of the asylum application in the accelerated procedure sufficient in the light of the EU right to an effective remedy. The Court did not exclude, however, that, while a time limit may be considered generally reasonable, it may be insufficient in the individual circumstances of the case. Whether this is the case, is up to the national court to decide.[247]

Certain groups of specifically vulnerable asylum applicants are in need of extra procedural safeguards.[248] This applies, for example, to unaccompanied minor asylum applicants.[249] Victims of torture may be afraid to speak freely to the

[243] *MM* (n 146) Opinion of AG Bot, para 66.

[244] *MSS* (n 68) para 251.

[245] Ibid, paras 304–11, 319.

[246] ECtHR (GC) 23 February 2012, *Hirsi Jamaa et al v Italy*, no 27765/09, para 204; *MSS* (n 68) paras 301 and 304 and *IM* (n 74) paras 145, 151 and 155.

[247] *Samba Diouf* (n 19) paras 66–68. See also *Sopropé* (n 239) para 44.

[248] Art 21 Dir 2013/33/EU and Art 20(3) Dir 2011/95/EU mention categories of persons which should be considered vulnerable. Some of these categories may be in need of extra procedural guarantees.

[249] According to recital 14 Preamble Directive 2005/85/EC 'specific procedural guarantees for unaccompanied minors should be laid down on account of their vulnerability'.

authorities of the State of refuge.[250] Victims of human trafficking may need time to deprogramme and escape the influence of the trafficker.[251] Special provisions may be necessary to enable such applicants to tell their asylum story in the best possible way.[252] Asylum applicants may have psychological or physical problems, which impede a normal examination of their case.[253] These circumstances may require, for example, that the burden of proof normally incumbent upon the applicant be lightened, or 'different techniques of examination' be used by the authorities.[254]

[250] UNHCR, *Handbook on Procedures and Criteria for Determining Refugee Status* (1979, new edition 1992) available at www.refworld.org/docid/3ae6b3314.html accessed 25 September 2013, para 198.

[251] In the Netherlands unaccompanied minors who are potentially the victims of human trafficking must follow a deprogramming course prior to the start of the asylum procedure. See Parliamentary Papers II 2007–2008, 19 637, no 1174.

[252] See, eg J Herlihy, 'Evidentiary Assessment and Psychological Difficulties' in G Noll (ed), *Proof, Evidentiary Assessment and Credibility in Asylum Procedures* (Leiden/Boston, Martinus Nijhoff, 2005) 123–37.

[253] UNHCR *Handbook* (n 250) para 207.

[254] Ibid, paras 207 and 210.

5

Preliminary Conclusions and Methodology used for the Following Chapters

IN ORDER TO be able to understand the potential significance of the right to an effective remedy and related procedural rights in the context of asylum, several preliminary issues have been addressed in chapters one to four. The following conclusions are the most important for the purpose of this study:

- Asylum procedures are now governed by the Procedures Directive and thus fall within the scope of EU law.
- The Court of Justice and national courts may test the validity of the minimum standards of the Procedures Directive against the EU right to an effective remedy. Those standards should be considered invalid if they require or expressly or impliedly authorise Member States to adopt or retain legislation which does not respect the EU right to an effective remedy.
- The Court of Justice and national courts may also use the EU right to an effective remedy to interpret the provisions of the Procedures Directive.
- Member States are bound by the EU right to an effective remedy when acting within the scope of EU law. They should observe this right even when making use of the discretionary powers afforded to them by the Procedures Directive. As a result, the discretion retained by Member States to design their asylum system may be significantly limited. The Court of Justice has shown in its case law in other fields of EU law that the EU right to an effective remedy greatly limits the procedural autonomy of Member States.
- Asylum legislation is a relatively new phenomenon within the EU and there is little case law concerning the meaning of the EU right to an effective remedy for asylum procedures. However, the Court of Justice has developed an important body of case law concerning the EU right to an effective remedy in its judgments on other fields of EU law. The principles emerging from this case law are applicable in all fields of EU law, including asylum law.
- The EU right to an effective remedy includes rights such as the right to a fair trial, the right of access to court, the right to equality of arms and the right to adversarial proceedings. Furthermore, it is closely linked to the right to good administration, which embodies the right to be heard and the duty to state

the reasons for a decision. The exact relationship between the EU right to an effective remedy and the principle of effectiveness, which also sets standards for national procedures, remains unclear. For the purpose of this study, the case law of the EU Courts regarding all these rights and principles will be taken into account.

— The interpretation of EU fundamental rights is inspired by international treaties. In the context of asylum the European Convention on Human Rights (ECHR), the Refugee Convention, the UN Convention against Torture (CAT), the International Covenant on Civil and Political Rights (ICCPR) and the UN Convention on the Rights of the Child (CRC) are particularly relevant. The EU right to an effective remedy is inspired by Articles 6 and 13 ECHR, Article 3 CAT, and Articles 2(3) and 14 ICCPR. The Court of Justice attaches by far most weight to the ECHR and the judgments of the European Court of Human Rights (ECtHR) as a source of inspiration. However, the authoritative but non-binding views of other supervising bodies such as the UNHCR, the CAT, the Human Rights Committee (HRC) and the Committee on the Rights of the Child (ComRC) should be also taken into account. For the purpose of this study the case law of the ECtHR plays a prominent role, while the non-binding views of other monitoring bodies are used as complementary sources of inspiration.

— EU fundamental rights, such as the right to an effective remedy, may not offer a lower level of protection than international treaties. The Court of Justice has shown in its case law that it scrupulously interprets EU fundamental rights to conform with the case law of the ECtHR. It follows from the text of the Charter as well as from the case law of the Court of Justice that EU fundamental rights may offer broader protection than international treaties.

— The EU right to a fair trial applies to all cases falling within the scope of EU law including asylum cases. Even though the ECtHR has ruled that Article 6 ECHR does not apply to asylum cases falling within the scope of application of the ECHR, its case law concerning Article 6 ECHR may very well inspire the EU right to a fair trial, including when it is applied in the context of asylum.

— From the case law of the EU Courts and the ECtHR concerning the right to an effective remedy and fair trial three basic concepts emerge, which may be helpful to explain the choices made by these courts when deciding on procedural issues and predicting these courts' approach in new situations:

  1. Procedural rights may be limited. It is often necessary to balance conflicting interests of the parties involved in the procedure.
  2. The overall fairness of a procedure should be assessed.
  3. The courts should have regard to the subject matter of the procedure, in particular the nature of the rights claimed and particular vulnerability of the person concerned.

5.1 METHOD FOR DEFINING THE MEANING OF THE EU RIGHT TO AN EFFECTIVE REMEDY

The following chapters will examine the potential meaning of EU fundamental rights and general principles for a number of key issues of asylum procedures: the right to remain on the territory of Member States during first instance and appeal asylum proceedings (chapter six); the asylum applicant's right to be heard on his asylum motives in first instance and appeal proceedings (chapter seven); and questions relating to evidence in asylum procedures (chapters eight to ten).

For many of these topics Directive 2005/85/EC and/or Directive 2013/32/EU do not provide for minimum standards. The applicable standards leave the Member States a wide discretion or are in need of interpretation. The chapters examine whether the EU right to an effective remedy sets additional standards, limits Member States' discretion or prescribes a certain interpretation of the Directives. With regard to some minimum standards the question is raised (and answered) whether they violate the EU right to an effective remedy and should be considered invalid.

The following method is used in order to define the meaning of the EU right to an effective remedy:

— Most of the topics which will be discussed are not specifically addressed by Articles 41 and 47 of the Charter. The meaning of the EU right to an effective remedy is therefore derived from the case law of the EU Courts and from relevant sources of inspiration, in particular the case law of the ECtHR.
— The case law of the Court of Justice with regard to the specific meaning of the EU right to an effective remedy for asylum procedures is still very limited. However, the EU Courts have addressed many of these topics in the context of other fields of EU law, such as competition law, equal treatment law or EU sanctions. As was concluded above the procedural principles emerging from this case law are applicable to asylum procedures.
— The ECtHR's case law regarding Articles 6 and 13 ECHR with regard to non-asylum cases is taken into account when examining which procedural principles follow from the EU right to an effective remedy. With regard to some topics, such as the use of secret information, the standards set out in the ECtHR's case law complement the principles emerging from the EU Courts' case law.
— When applying these procedural principles to the asylum context the special features of asylum procedures should be taken into account (see the three basic concepts mentioned above). The ECtHR in its case law under Articles 3 and 13 ECHR concerning asylum cases and the UNHCR and the UN Committees in their views concerning asylum procedures provide important guidance for the way in which the EU right to an effective remedy should be interpreted in the asylum context.

— With regard to some issues discussed in the chapters six to ten, such as the assessment of the credibility of the asylum applicant's asylum account or the right to an oral hearing before a court or tribunal, no relevant case law of the EU Courts is available. In this situation the meaning of the EU right to an effective remedy is largely defined on the basis of the case law of the ECtHR and the (complementary) views of UNHCR and the UN-Committees concerning this issue.

For the purpose of this method the following steps will be taken in each of the following chapters:[1]

1. identification of the provisions of Directive 2005/85/EC and Directive 2013/32/EU applicable to the specific procedural issue discussed;
2. assessment of the existing case law of the EU Courts concerning the specific topic;
3. examination of the case law of the ECtHR and the non-binding views of the UNHCR, the ComAT, the HRC and the ComRC which inspire the EU right to an effective remedy;
4. conclusion as to the meaning of the EU right to an effective remedy for the specific aspect of the asylum procedure; and
5. application of the provisions of Directive 2005/85/EC and Directive 2013/32/EU.

The result of this exercise is a set of EU procedural standards with regard to the key issues discussed in the following chapters.

[1] See also ch 1, section 1.4 in this volume.

Part II

Key Issues of Asylum Procedures

6

*The Right to Remain on the Territory of the Member State**

THIS CHAPTER ADDRESSES three questions which relate to the asylum applicant's right to remain on the territory of the Member State from where he is applying for asylum:

1. Should an asylum seeker be allowed to stay in the State where he applied for asylum during first instance proceedings?
2. Are Member States required to grant applicants the time and opportunity to lodge an appeal against their expulsion before being expelled?
3. Must Member States refrain from expelling the applicant until the decision on the appeal against the asylum decision has been taken?

Several international monitoring bodies have addressed these questions over the past years. Most importantly, the European Court of Human Rights (ECtHR) ruled that Article 13 European Convention on Human Rights (ECHR) requires State Parties to provide for a remedy with automatic suspensive effect in the case of an arguable claim that the person concerned will be subjected to torture or ill-treatment upon return to his country of origin.

It is argued in this chapter that the effective protection of the prohibition of *refoulement* and the right of (access to) an effective remedy require Member States to refrain from expulsion while asylum proceedings (first instance and appeal) are still pending. Expulsion of an asylum applicant before the determining authorities, and/or the court or tribunal within the meaning of Article 39 of Directive 2005/85/EC or Article 46 of Directive 2013/32/EU, have assessed the risk of *refoulement* entails a risk of irreparable harm: the asylum applicant may be subjected to persecution or serious harm upon expulsion. Furthermore, the European Union right of access to a court or tribunal requires that the asylum applicant be offered sufficient time and opportunity to lodge an appeal against a negative asylum decision.

* Part of this chapter has been published as AM Reneman, 'An EU Right to Interim Protection during Appeal Proceedings in Asylum Cases?' (2010) 12 *European Journal of Migration and Law* 407–34.

6.1 THE RIGHT TO REMAIN DURING THE EXAMINATION OF THE ASYLUM CLAIM

Directive 2005/85/EC

According to Article 7(1) of Directive 2005/85/EC Member States must allow asylum applicants to remain on their territory, for the sole purpose of the procedure, until the determining authority has made a decision in accordance with the procedures at first instance set out in Chapter III of the Directive.[1] However, the second limb of Article 7 permits Member States to make an exception to this rule in two situations. First, the right to remain does not apply where, in accordance with Articles 32 and 34, a subsequent application will not be further examined. According to these provisions such further examination does not need to take place if no new elements or findings relating to the examination of whether he/she qualifies for asylum status have arisen or have been presented by the asylum applicant.[2]

Secondly, the applicant may be expelled during the first instance asylum procedure where the Member State will surrender or extradite a person either to another Member State pursuant to obligations in accordance with a European arrest warrant or otherwise, to a third country, or to international criminal courts or tribunals. The Commission reported in 2010 that Member States adopt divergent approaches with respect to these surrender or extradition-related exceptions. In some Member States such exceptions are allowed.[3]

Directive 2013/32/EU

Article 9 of Directive 2013/32/EU also states as a general rule that States must allow asylum applicants to remain on their territory for the sole purpose of the asylum procedure, until the determining authority has made a decision on the asylum application. An exception can be made in three situations. The first concerns persons who make a first subsequent application, merely in order to delay or frustrate the enforcement of a decision which would result in his imminent removal from that Member State and this application is not further examined pursuant to Article 40(5) and is considered inadmissible in accordance with Article 33(2)(d) of the Directive.[4] The second concerns persons who make a second or

[1] See also Council resolution regarding minimum guarantees for asylum procedures of 20 June 1995 [1996] OJ C274, para 12 and Commission, 'Report from the Commission to the European Parliament and the Council on the application of Directive 2005/85/EC' COM (2010) 465 final, 4.

[2] According to the UNHCR, many Member States provide for a right to remain during subsequent asylum procedures. In Germany and the Netherlands the right to remain is not guaranteed by law or the status of persons awaiting the decision on a subsequent application is unclear. UNHCR, *Improving Asylum Procedures: Comparative Analysis and Recommendations for Law and Practice* (Geneva, March 2010) available at www.refworld.org/docid/4c63e52d2.html accessed 25 September 2013, s 14, 42–43.

[3] The Commission mentioned Austria, Cyprus, the Czech Republic, France, Germany, Ireland, Italy, Luxemburg, Malta, Poland, Romania and Sweden (only in cases of terrorism). Commission Report on the application of Directive 2005/85/EC (n 1) 4–5.

[4] Arts 9(2)(a) and 41(5)(a) Dir 2013/32/EU.

further subsequent asylum application in the same Member State, following a final decision to consider a first subsequent application inadmissible pursuant to Article 40(5) or after a final decision to reject that application as unfounded.[5] Finally, the right to remain may not apply if the Member State surrenders or extradite a person to another Member State, a third country or international criminal courts or tribunals.[6]

Article 9(3) of Directive 2013/32/EU includes a new provision that a Member State may extradite an applicant to a third country only 'where the competent authorities are satisfied that an extradition decision will not result in direct or indirect *refoulement* in violation of international obligations of the Member State'. Furthermore, Article 41(1)(b) of the Directive states that Member States may make an exception to the right to remain in case of subsequent applications 'only where the determining authority considers that a return decision will not lead to direct or indirect *refoulement* in violation of international and Union obligations of that Member State'.

The Case Law of the Court of Justice

Although the Court of Justice has not yet addressed the matter, it is clear that expulsion or extradition before an assessment of the merits of the asylum claim has taken place would seriously undermine the effectiveness of the (absolute) EU principle of *non-refoulement*.[7]

Obligations Stemming from the Refugee Convention, ECHR, CAT and ICCPR

It follows from the case law under Articles 3 and 13 ECHR that an asylum applicant may not be expelled or extradited to his country of origin or a third country before his claim that he will be subjected to a treatment contrary to Article 3 ECHR in that country has been scrutinised closely and rigorously by the national authorities.[8] According to the ECtHR there must be effective guarantees to protect the applicant against arbitrary *refoulement*, be it direct or indirect, to the country from which he or she has fled.[9] This means that the applicant must also be granted the opportunity to have the 'arguability' of his claim of a risk of *refoulement*

[5] Arts 9(2)(a) and 41(5)(b) Dir 2013/32/EU.

[6] Art 9(2)(b) Dir 2013/32/EU.

[7] The Court of Justice did rule that Art 7(1) Dir 2005/85/EC provides asylum applicants with the right to remain in the territory of the Member State where they are subject to a Dublin procedure. Case C-179/11 *Cimade and Gisti* [2012] paras 46–48.

[8] See, eg ECtHR (GC) 23 February 2012, *Hirsi Jamaa et al v Italy*, no 27765/09, para 205; ECtHR (GC) 21 January 2011, *MSS v Belgium and Greece*, no 30696/09, para 293; ECtHR 22 September 2009, *Abdolkhani and Karimnia v Turkey*, no 30471/08, para 113; ECtHR 13 April 2010, *Charahili v Turkey*, no 46605/07, paras 57–58; and ECtHR 21 October 2010, *Gaforov v Russia*, no 25404/09, paras 122–27.

[9] *MSS* (n 8) para 286.

assessed by an independent and impartial authority within the meaning of Article 13 ECHR before being expelled or extradited.[10]

The ECtHR explicitly ruled on the right to remain during first instance asylum procedures in the case of *Mohammed*. In this case the applicant's first asylum claim lodged in Austria was rejected because Hungary was responsible for examining the asylum application according to the Dublin Regulation. Almost a year later, the applicant lodged a second asylum claim and stated that his transfer to Hungary would lead to a violation of Article 3 ECHR. He based his claim on a number of reports on reception conditions and access to asylum proceedings in Hungary as well as the Austrian Asylum Court's own case law. According to Austrian law a person whose asylum claim has been rejected pursuant to lack of jurisdiction under the Dublin Regulation is not entitled to protection against deportation in the event that he lodges a second asylum application. The ECtHR found in this case that, at the time of the second asylum application, there was an arguable claim of a violation of the prohibition of *refoulement* upon transfer to Hungary. It considered that Austrian law did not afford the applicant protection from forced transfer 'and thus deprived him of a meaningful substantive examination of both the changed situation and his arguable claim under Article 3 concerning the situation of asylum-seekers in Hungary'.[11] Therefore, the law denied the applicant access to an effective remedy against the enforcement of the order for his forced transfer. It concluded that Article 13 ECHR had been violated. The ECtHR in this case remarked that Mohammed's second application 'cannot *prima facie* be considered abusively repetitive or entirely manifestly ill-founded'.[12] Furthermore, it pointed at the specific circumstances of the case, namely the fact that almost a year elapsed had between the transfer order and its enforcement and the change of circumstances manifesting itself during that time. This may imply that the ECtHR leaves open the possibility of refusing the right to remain in subsequent asylum applications which can prima facie be considered abusively repetitive or entirely manifestly ill-founded. It should be noted, however, that this is a very high standard which will not be easily met.

In 2010 the Committee against Torture (ComAT) also expressed concern in respect of the Austrian asylum law, in particular the provision which stated that persons basing their repeat applications for international protection on new grounds cannot be granted a stay of their expulsion if they lodge their application within two days prior to the date set for deportation. According to the Committee, those asylum applicants may, consequently, be at risk of *refoulement*.[13]

[10] See, eg ECtHR 19 November 2009, no 41015/04, *Kaboulov v Ukraine*, para 119. See further section 6.3.

[11] ECtHR 6 June 2013, no 2283/12, *Mohammed v Austria*, para 81

[12] ECtHR 6 June 2013, *Mohammed v Austria*, no 2283/12, para 81. See also *MSS* (n 8) para 315 where the ECtHR was concerned because of the risks of *refoulement* the applicant faced in practice before any decision was taken on the merits of his case.

[13] ComAT, 'Concluding Observations on Austria', 20 May 2010, CAT/C/AUT/CO/4–5, para 13.

It also follows from the effective protection of the principle of *non-refoulement* under the Refugee Convention that States should determine whether a person qualifies as a refugee before expelling that person.[14] The principle of effectiveness requires that during the determination process this person should be allowed to remain on the territory.[15] According to the UNHCR *Handbook* and Executive Committee of the Programme of the High Commissioner (EXCOM) Conclusion No 8 the asylum applicant's right to remain in the country pending a decision on his initial request for a refugee status is a 'basic requirement' of an asylum procedure. Only if it is established that this request is clearly abusive, may the applicant be expelled before a decision on the request has been taken.[16]

Conclusion

It should be concluded that the effective protection of the EU prohibition of *refoulement* requires that all asylum applicants be allowed to stay on the territory of the Member States until their claim of a risk of *refoulement* has been closely and rigorously assessed by the determining authority. It follows from the ECtHR's judgment in *Mohammed* that subsequent asylum applications should first be assessed in the light of all facts or evidence supporting the existence of a risk of *refoulement*, which have not been taken into account in the previous asylum procedure(s). Only if the subsequent application can prima facie be considered abusively repetitive or entirely manifestly ill-founded may the State make an exception to the right to remain.[17] Moreover, if an asylum applicant claims to risk *refoulement* or onward removal to a country where he risks *refoulement* as a result of his surrender or extradition to another Member State, a third country, or to an international criminal court or tribunal, Member States should always rigorously assess this claim.

This does not mean, however, that the applicant may be expelled or extradited immediately after a rigorous assessment of the risk of *refoulement* has been made by the determining authority, before a decision has been taken. The EU right to an effective remedy requires that an applicant should be able to appeal the outcome of this assessment and the decision to expel or extradite him before a court or tribunal. This implies that the Member State must offer the applicant sufficient time and opportunity to lodge an appeal in accordance with Article 39 of Directive 2005/85/EC and Article 46 of Directive 2013/32/EU (see section 6.2).

[14] See, eg GS Goodwin-Gill and J McAdam, *The Refugee in International Law* (Oxford, Oxford University Press) 528; JC Hathaway, *The Rights of Refugees under International Law* (Cambridge, Cambridge University Press, 2005) 158–60; and CW Wouters, *International Legal Standards for the Protection from Refoulement* (Antwerpen, Intersentia, 2009) 164.

[15] Hathaway, ibid, 303–304.

[16] EXCOM Conclusion no 8 (XXVIII) 1977, para (e) and UNHCR, *Handbook on Procedures and Criteria for Determining Refugee Status* (1979, new edition 1992) available at www.refworld.org/docid/3ae6b3314.html accessed 25 September 2013, para 192.

[17] See also ch 9, section 9.3 in this volume.

Furthermore, as will be argued in section 6.3, this appeal should have automatic suspensive effect.

Articles 9(3) and Article 41(1)(b) of Directive 2013/32/EU explicitly state that no exceptions to the right to remain may be made if this would lead to a violation of the prohibition of *refoulement*. Reading these provisions in the light of ECtHR case law, this implies that the determining authority should always rigorously assess the risk of *refoulement* before making use of these exceptions.

The question remains, however, whether Article 7(2) of Directive 2005/85/EC should be declared invalid. This is hard to determine. Potentially, there are situations in which the EU principle of *refoulement* and the EU right to an effective remedy do not prohibit expulsion or extradition of an applicant during first instance asylum proceedings, even though such situations will be rare. It is not excluded for example, that an asylum applicant claims to fear persecution or to risk serious harm upon return to his country of origin, but does not oppose expulsion or extradition to a third country or an international court or tribunal.

6.2 THE RIGHT TO REMAIN DURING THE TIME NECESSARY TO LODGE THE APPEAL

Swift expulsion after the asylum decision may render the right of access to court illusory or excessively difficult. First, the applicant may have no opportunity to file the appeal, for example, because he has not been informed that he is going to be deported and is not able to reach his lawyer in time to appeal. Secondly, when expulsion is imminent the applicant may be forced to immediately lodge an appeal and, if necessary, a request for interim protection. This may not allow him time to take all the required procedural steps in order to submit the appeal, such as consulting a lawyer. The United Nations High Commissioner for Refugees (UNHCR) mentioned in 2010 that in Finland the expulsion order may be executed immediately upon the decision being taken. According to the UNHCR this means that the appellant would not have an effective opportunity to apply to the Helsinki District Court to suspend enforcement.[18]

Directive 2005/85/EC and Directive 2013/32/EU

Directive 2005/85/EC does not regulate the right to remain in the Member State in order to exercise the right of appeal. Article 46(5) of Directive 2013/32/EU provides that Member States shall allow applicants to remain on the territory until the time limit within which the applicant must exercise his right to an effective remedy has expired.

[18] UNHCR, *Improving Asylum Procedures* (n 2) s 16, 42.

The Case Law of the Court of Justice

The Court of Justice has not yet addressed the question whether an asylum applicant should be allowed to stay on the territory of the Member State for the time necessary to lodge an appeal against a negative asylum decision. However, the Court of Justice seemed to recognise in *Pecastaing* that such right to remain should be accorded to nationals of the Member States who made use of their right to free movement and who are going to be expelled. The Court of Justice considered that expulsion of such nationals may take place immediately after the expulsion order has been taken 'subject always to the right of this person to stay on the territory for the time necessary to avail himself of the remedies accorded to him'.[19] The accessibility of the remedy should thus be guaranteed. It follows from the case law of the ECtHR and the views of the UN Committees that this should also apply to asylum cases.

Obligations Stemming from the ECHR, CAT and ICCPR

The ECtHR ruled in several cases that Article 13 ECHR was violated when the person claiming that his expulsion or extradition would violate Article 3 ECHR, did not have the time and opportunity to appeal against the expulsion or extradition decision before this decision was enforced. In *Shamayev and others* the ECtHR stated:

> [W]here the authorities of a State hasten to hand over an individual to another State two days after the date on which the order was issued, they have a duty to act with all the more promptness and expedition to enable the person concerned to have his or her complaint under Articles 2 and 3 submitted to independent and rigorous scrutiny and to have enforcement of the impugned measure suspended. The Court finds it unacceptable for a person to learn that he is to be extradited only moments before being taken to the airport, when his reason for fleeing the receiving country has been his fear of treatment contrary to Article 2 or Article 3 of the Convention.[20]

The Court concluded that Article 13 ECHR had been violated because neither the applicants nor their lawyers had been informed of the extradition orders issued in respect of the applicants and the competent authorities unjustifiably hindered the exercise of the right of appeal that might have been available to them, at least theoretically.[21]

The UN Committees also ruled in a few cases that expulsion before a person could avail himself of an effective remedy violated the right to an effective

[19] Case 98/79 *Pecastaing* [1980] ECR 691, para 18. A right to a remedy was provided in this case in Art 8 of Council Dir 64/221/EEC of 25 February 1964 on the coordination of special measures concerning the movement and residence of foreign nationals which are justified on grounds of public policy, public security or public health [1964] OJ 056/850.

[20] ECtHR 12 April 2005, *Shamayev et al v Georgia and Russia*, no 36378/02, para 460.

[21] Ibid, para 461. See also ECtHR 7 June 2007, *Garabayev v Russia*, no 38411/02; and ECtHR 10 August 2006, *Olaechea Chuas v Spain*, no 24668/03.

remedy.[22] The Human Rights Committee (HRC) considered in *Alzery* that by the nature of *refoulement*, effective review of a decision to expel must take place prior to expulsion, in order to avoid irreparable harm to the individual and rendering the review otiose and devoid of meaning.[23] In *Judge* the HRC was even of the opinion that the State must give the applicant the opportunity to lodge a further appeal before being expelled.[24] Finally UNHCR stated that access to an effective remedy is best guaranteed by ensuring by law that deportation orders are not issued or cannot be executed within the time-limit to lodge an appeal.[25]

The right of access to an effective remedy following from Article 39 of Directive 2005/85/EC and Article 46 of Directive 2013/32/EU, read in the light of the *Pecastaing* judgment, the ECtHR's judgment in *Shamayev* and the UN Committees' views, requires that an asylum applicant be allowed to stay on the territory for the time necessary to avail himself of this remedy. This means that the applicant must be informed of the imminent expulsion in time to consult his lawyer. The time limit for lodging the appeal indicates the time necessary for lodging the appeal. Article 46(5) of Directive 2013/32/EU, therefore, does not allow the applicant to be expelled before the time limit for filing the appeal has expired. Arguably, such a prohibition also follows from Article 39 of Directive 2005/85/EC read in the light of the EU right to an effective remedy.

6.3 THE RIGHT TO REMAIN DURING APPEAL PROCEEDINGS

Once the appeal against the negative asylum decision has been lodged, the question arises whether the asylum applicant is allowed to await the decision of the court or tribunal on the territory of the Member State. This question will be addressed in this section.

Directive 2005/85/EC

The issue of suspensive effect of the asylum appeal was heavily discussed by the Member States during the drafting of Directive 2005/85/EC.[26] The result of these

[22] ComAT 5 June 2000, *Josu Arkauz Arana v France*, no 63/1997, para 11.5. See also ComAT 3 May 2005, *Iratxe Sorzábal Díaz v France*, no 194/2001, para 6.1. ComAT also stated in its Annual Report 2006 that 'the requirement of exhaustion of domestic remedies can be dispensed with, if … there is a risk of immediate deportation of the complainant after the final rejection of his or her asylum application'. ComAT, 'Annual Report 2006', A/61/44, para 61.

[23] HRC 10 November 2006, *Alzery v Sweden*, no 1416/2005, para 11.8.

[24] HRC 20 October 2003, *Judge v Canada*, no 829/1998, para 10.8–10.9. The Committee held that the decision to deport the author to the United States, where he was under sentence of death, without affording him the opportunity to avail himself of an available appeal, was taken arbitrarily and in violation of Art 6, and Art 2(3) ICCPR.

[25] UNHCR *Improving Asylum Procedures* (n 2) s 16, 38.

[26] M Michelogiannaki, 'The Negotiations of Directive 2005/85/EC' in K Zwaan (ed), *The Procedures Directive, Central Themes, Problem Issues and Implementation in Selected Member States* (Nijmegen, Wolf Legal Publishers, 2008) 25.

discussions was a clear compromise: the Directive does not oblige the Member States to attach suspensive effect to the asylum appeal required by Article 39 of Directive 2005/85/EC. Article 39(3) of the Directive leaves this issue to the discretion of the Member States.[27] This provision states that the Member States shall, where appropriate, provide for rules *in accordance with their international obligations* dealing with the question of whether the remedy shall have the effect of allowing applicants to remain in the Member State concerned pending its outcome. If the remedy does not have suspensive effect, the Member States shall provide for rules to deal with the possibility of legal remedy or protective measures.

According to the Commission report concerning the implementation of Directive 2005/85/EC of 2010, automatic suspensive effect is attached to all first instance appeals against asylum decisions in Bulgaria, Hungary, Ireland, Lithuania, Luxembourg and Portugal. In Greece and Spain, automatic suspensive effect was not afforded to any appeals.[28] In other Member States, applicable exceptions vary widely and concern decisions not to further examine a subsequent application, a refusal to reopen the examination, decisions taken in border procedures, inadmissibility decisions, decisions taken in an accelerated procedure, applications deemed manifestly unfounded, and decisions concerning applicants in detention. Where an appeal does not have suspensive effect, interim measures are generally available. However, the right to remain pending the outcome of the procedure for interim measures is not guaranteed by law in the Czech Republic, Greece or Sweden. In other Member States the request for an interim measure does not have suspensive effect in certain categories of cases.[29]

The UNHCR mentioned in its report of 2010 that many refugees are only recognised following an appeal process. UNHCR estimated that in 2007 around 14 per cent of persons, who were recognised as refugees or received a complementary form of protection, initially received a negative decision which was subsequently overturned during the appeal stage. In some States, such as the United Kingdom, around 20 per cent of asylum decisions are overturned in appeal.[30] These figures indicate the need to allow asylum applicants to remain on the territory of the Member State during appeal proceedings, in order to prevent irreparable harm.

Directive 2013/32/EU

Article 46 of Directive 2013/32/EU provides much more clarity and higher standards with regard to the right to an appeal with suspensive effect than Article 39 of Directive 2005/85/EC. Article 46(5) of Directive 2013/32/EU provides as a general

[27] In this chapter the term 'interim protection' is used as a general term covering both the question whether an appeal should have suspensive effect and the question whether an applicant should be able to request interim relief (in asylum cases usually the suspension of the expulsion measure).

[28] Commission Report (n 1) 14. See also UNHCR *Improving Asylum Procedures* (n 2) s 16, 38.

[29] Commission Report (n 1) 14–15. See also UNHCR *Improving Asylum Procedures* (n 2) s 16, 44.

[30] UNHCR *Improving Asylum Procedures* (n 2) s 16, 36–37.

rule that Member States shall allow applicants to remain on the territory pending the outcome of the remedy, when the right to an effective remedy has been exercised within the time limit. It follows from Article 46(6) and (7) of the Directive that an exception to this rule may be made in situations including cases considered manifestly unfounded or inadmissible and decisions taken in accelerated proceedings. In such a situation a court or tribunal shall have the power to rule whether or not the applicant may remain on the territory of the Member State, either upon the request of the concerned applicant or acting on its own motion. According to Article 46(8), the Member States must allow the applicant to remain on the territory pending the outcome of the procedure to rule whether or not the applicant may remain. Article 46(7) of Directive 2013/32/EU states that where in border procedures an exception is made to the right to a remedy with automatic suspensive effect, two further conditions apply:

(a) the applicant has the necessary interpretation, legal assistance and at least one week to prepare the request and submit to the court or tribunal the arguments in favour of granting him/her the right to remain on the territory pending the outcome of the remedy
(b) in the framework of the examination of the request for interim relief the court or tribunal examines the negative decision of the determining authority in terms of fact and law.

6.3.1 The Right to Interim Protection

This section will argue that EU law requires that the appeal within the meaning of Article 39 2005/85/EC has automatic suspensive effect. Article 46 of Directive 2013/32/EU requires that the appeal itself or the request for interim relief have automatic suspensive effect. Section 6.3.2 will examine the required form of the interim protection which should be offered. Should the lodging of the appeal automatically entail that the asylum applicant is allowed to stay on the territory of the Member State? Or is a system allowed in which the asylum applicant needs to apply to the national court for interim relief? This question is relevant for the interpretation of both Article 39 of Directive 2005/85/EC and Article 46 of Directive 2013/32/EU.

6.3.1.1 The Case Law of the Court of Justice

The Court of Justice ruled on the right to interim protection in a number of cases. In some of them, such as the *Siples* case, which will be discussed later in this section, the Court was asked to interpret EU legislation which specifically addressed the right to interim protection. In the most important cases, however, no relevant EU legislation existed with regard to this issue. In those cases the Court judged that the principle of effectiveness[31] or the right to an effective remedy[32] may nevertheless oblige national courts to provide interim protection. Important examples of the latter category are the judgments in *Factortame* and *Zuckerfabrik*, which will be discussed at greater length in this section. In all cases the Court of Justice has recognised the significance of the right to interim protection. It held that interim protection should be provided by the national court if necessary to ensure the full effectiveness of its judgment on the existence of a right guaranteed by EU law.

The Court of Justice has not yet ruled on interim protection in issues of asylum. However, taking into account the fundamental nature of the rights claimed during asylum proceedings, there is no reason to believe that the *Factortame* standards will not apply in asylum cases. Thus, it may be assumed that Article 39 of Directive 2005/85/EC, read in the light of the EU right to an effective remedy, demands that interim protection be granted in asylum cases if it is necessary to ensure the full effectiveness of the judgment by the national court regarding the question whether the applicant's expulsion would violate the prohibition of *refoulement*. It is, therefore, important to examine whether, and if so under which circumstances, interim protection is necessary in asylum cases to ensure the effectiveness of the remedy available and to avoid irreparable harm to the applicant. For this purpose the case law of the Court of Justice in cases concerning expulsion of EU citizens and the requirements following from the ECHR, the International Covenant on Civil and Political Rights (ICCPR) and the UN Convention against Torture (CAT) should be considered relevant. The case law of the Court of Justice with regard to the necessity of interim protection against expulsions of EU citizens during the proceedings against the expulsion measure will be discussed in this section, while the case law of the ECtHR and the views of the UN Committees and the UNHCR will be examined in section 6.3.1.2 below.

Factortame, Zuckerfabrik *and* Siples

According to the Court of Justice, interim protection must be provided if it is necessary to ensure the effectiveness of EU law. The most fundamental case in this respect is *Factortame*.[33] In *Factortame*, fishing companies questioned the compatibility with Community law of a British act which prohibited them from fishing. They asked for interim relief until such time as final judgment was given on their application for judicial review. The question put before the Court of Justice by the

[31] Case C-213/89 *Factortame* [1990] ECR I-2433, paras 20–21. See D Sinaniotis, *The Interim Protection of Individuals before the European and National Courts* (Alphen aan de Rijn, Kluwer, 2006) 65, where he states: 'It should be emphasized that the essential legal basis for which interim relief was acknowledged in the instant case is the principle of effectiveness of Community law.'

[32] Joined Cases C-143/88 and C-92/89 *Zuckerfabrik Süderdithmarschen and Zuckerfabrik Soest* [1991] ECR I-415, paras 16–17 and Case C-432/05 *Unibet* [2007] ECR I-2271, para 72.

[33] *Factortame* (n 31). See also *Unibet* (n 32).

House of Lords was whether Community law obliges the national court to grant interim protection of the rights claimed. Under national law the English courts had no power to grant interim relief in a case such as the one before it. The Court of Justice referred to its judgment in *Simmental* where it held that

> any provision of a national legal system and any legislative, administrative or judicial practice which might impair the effectiveness of Community law by withholding from the national court having jurisdiction to apply such law the power to do everything necessary at the moment of its application to set aside national legislative provisions which might prevent, even temporarily, Community rules from having full force and effect are incompatible with those requirements, which are the very essence of Community law … .[34]

Then the Court of Justice went on to consider that

> the full effectiveness of Community law would be just as much impaired if a rule of national law could prevent a court seised of a dispute governed by Community law from granting interim relief in order to ensure the full effectiveness of the judgment to be given on the existence of the rights claimed under Community law. It follows that a court which in those circumstances would grant interim relief, if it were not for a rule of national law, is obliged to set aside that rule.[35]

The Court left the conditions for granting interim relief up to the national courts. It considered, however, in line with the *Rewe* judgment,[36] that these national procedural rules should not be less favourable than those for the enforcement of national law rights, nor should they render the exercise of the right to interim protection practically impossible or excessively difficult.[37]

According to Sinaniotis the judgment in *Factortame* is revolutionary because it established interim protection as part of the principle of effectiveness of Community rights, by imposing on the national judge dealing with interim relief the task of acting as a Community judge.[38] Toth wrote that as a result the national courts are able to 'provide immediate protection to individuals by '"freezing" … national laws, whose compatibility with Community law is challenged, thereby saving them from irreparable loss, and possibly from economic ruin, which might otherwise occur while their Community rights are being determined'.[39] According to Toth the obligation to grant interim relief had been implicitly present in some fundamental principles of Community law, namely the principle of supremacy of

[34] *Factortame* (n 31) para 20. The Court of Justice referred to Case 106/77 *Amministrazione delle finanze dello Stato v Simmenthal* [1978] ECR 629, paras 22–23.

[35] Ibid, para 21.

[36] Case 33/76 *Rewe* [1976] ECR 1989.

[37] Sinaniotis, *The Interim Protection of Individuals* (n 30) 95. In *Unibet* (n 32) the Court also refrained from providing the national courts with conditions for granting interim relief. The Court followed the Opinion of AG Sharpston that in cases which concern the validity of a national measure, there is no reason to depart from the general rule of procedural autonomy. See A Arnull, 'Case C-432/05 *Unibet* [2007]' (2007) 44 *Common Market Law Review* 1763 1777–78.

[38] Sinaniotis (n 30) 61.

[39] AG Toth, 'Case C-213/89 *Factortame I* [1990]' (1990) 27 *Common Market Law Review* 573, 583.

Community law, the principle of complete and effective judicial protection, and the principles of effectiveness and equivalence.[40]

Factortame did not explicitly answer the question whether the Court requires a national court to create a new remedy in order to be able to grant interim relief.[41] The Court only obliged the national court to set aside a national procedural rule which precludes the national court from granting interim relief. However, the problem in *Factortame* was that in the UK no legal basis for granting interim relief was available under national law. Therefore, the national court could comply with the Court's judgment only by creating a new remedy. According to Craig and de Búrca, *Factortame* weakened the force of the Court's previous statement that, in the absence of harmonisation, EC law does not oblige national courts to create new remedies which would not be available under national law.[42] In its later judgment in *Unibet* the Court of Justice made clear that Member States are exceptionally required to create new national remedies if this is necessary to ensure the EU fundamental right to an effective remedy.[43]

In *Zuckerfabrik*[44] it was the deficiency not of national law but of Community law which was at issue. In this case the Court accepted that, under certain conditions, interim relief can be granted by a national court in a case in which the applicant's claim is based on the alleged invalidity of Community legislation. The applicants contested a decision before the national court, which required them to pay an amount of money in respect of a special elimination levy for the 1986/87 sugar-marketing year. The applicants argued that this levy was based on a Community regulation, which was in their opinion contrary to Community law. They asked the national court to suspend the contested decision.

The national court asked the Court of Justice whether national courts may suspend an administrative measure by way of an interim measure, based on a regulation, and if so, under what conditions. The possible barrier against the interim measure was not national law, as in *Factortame*, but Community law itself. By temporarily not applying a rule of Community law by way of interim measure, the national court could violate the principle of priority of Community law and the monopoly of the Court to decide upon its legality.

The Court considered that interim legal protection which Community law ensures for individuals before national courts, must remain the same, irrespective of whether courts contest the compatibility of national legal provisions with Community law or the validity of secondary Community law, because the dispute

[40] Ibid, 583–84.

[41] See *Factortame* (n 31) Opinion of AG Bot; Sinaniotis (n 30) 61; and V Trstenjak and E Beysen, 'European Consumer Protection Law: Curia Semper Dabit Remedium?' (2011) 48 *Common Market Law Review* 95, fn 38.

[42] P Craig and G de Búrca, *EU* Law (Oxford, Oxford University Press, 2003) 237–38. However, in his comment on *Factortame* that the Court does not require the courts to devise an interim relief where none exists. Toth) 'Case C-213/89' (n 38) 586.

[43] *Unibet* (n 32) paras 40–41. See further ch 4, section 4.3.5 in this volume.

[44] *Zuckerfabrik Süderdithmarschen and Zuckerfabrik Soest* (n 32) paras 16–33.

in both cases is based on Community law itself. By granting interim relief in a case where the validity of a Community measure is contested, the national court temporarily disapplies a Community measure, and so the Court in *Zuckerfabrik* set conditions to the national courts for granting interim relief in such cases.[45] The national courts may grant interim relief only if the conditions applied by the Court of Justice when deciding on applications to it for interim measures pursuant to Articles 278 and 279 TFEU, are satisfied.[46] First, the national court should entertain serious doubts as to the validity of the Community measure. Secondly, it must refer the question on the validity of the Community measure to the Court of Justice for preliminary ruling. Finally, the situation must be urgent and a threat of serious and irreparable damage to the applicant and the national court should take due account of the Community's interests.[47]

In *Zuckerfabrik* the Court expressly accepted the national judiciary's role in Community legal protection. Schermers considers *Zuckerfabrik* to be a landmark case because it so clearly placed the protection of the individual in the foreground, even before the question of priority of Community law.[48]

Provisions of secondary EU law may not prevent national courts from providing interim protection, in order to ensure the full effectiveness of the judgment to be given on the existence of the rights claimed under EU law. This was decided in the *Siples* judgment.[49] In this case the Court was asked to interpret Article 244 of the Customs Code which confers power to suspend implementation of the contested decision exclusively on the customs authorities.[50] The Court ruled, while referring to *Factortame*, that this provision meant that both the customs authorities and the courts have the power to suspend a customs decision.

The Right to Interim Protection in Cases Concerning EU Citizens

The Court of Justice seems to be of the opinion that the fact that a person is expelled before a decision on the appeal against the expulsion measure has been given, does not automatically render his right to an appeal ineffective. This may be derived from a few expulsion cases concerning EU citizens and their family

45 According to AG Sharpston, there is a clear Community interest in having uniform strict criteria for granting interim relief in this situation. See also Arnull, 'Case C-432/05' (n 36) 1777–78.

46 JH Jans, R de, Lange, S Prechal and RJGM Widdershoven, *Europeanisation of Public Law* (Groningen, Europe Law Publishing, 2007) 248 and 278.

47 Whether there is a threat of serious and irreparable damage should be decided on the basis of the circumstances of the case. According to the court, purely financial damage cannot be regarded in principle as irreparable. *Zuckerfabrik Süderdithmarschen and Zuckerfabrik Soest* (n 32) para 29.

48 HG Schermers, 'Joined Cases C-143/88 and C-92/89, *Zuckerfabrik Süderdithmarschen* and *Zuckerfabrik Soest* [1991]' (2006) 29 *Common Market Law Review* 133, 136–37. See also Sinaniotis (n 30) 68.

49 Case C-226/99 *Siples* [2001] ECR I-277, paras 16–19. See also Case C-1/99 *Kofisa Italia* [2001] ECR I-207, paras 48–49.

50 Council Reg (EEC) No 2913/92 of 12 October 1992 establishing the Community Customs Code [1992] OJ L302/1.

members, falling within the scope of former Directive 64/221/EEC.[51] According to this Directive the general rule was that the court deciding on the appeal against the expulsion measure had suspensive effect. However, Article 9 of this Directive provided for the possibility of omitting the suspensive effect of this appeal on the condition that the expulsion decision would not be taken by the administrative authority until an opinion had been obtained from a competent authority of the host country.[52] In cases of urgency this opinion could be omitted. In *Dörr and Ünal* the Court seemed to accept that these provisions provided sufficient legal protection. Expulsion of the person concerned before the decision on the appeal against the expulsion measure had been taken was thus allowed, if the opinion of the competent authority had been obtained or in cases of urgency.[53]

Article 31 of Directive 2004/38/EC, which replaced Directive 64/221/EEC gives as the general rule:

> Where the application for appeal against or judicial review of the expulsion decision is accompanied by an application for an interim order to suspend enforcement of that decision, actual removal from the territory may not take place until such time as the decision on the interim order has been taken.[54]

The request for interim relief should thus have suspensive effect. There are a few possibilities of deviating from this general rule, namely: where the expulsion decision is based on a previous judicial decision; where the person concerned has had previous access to judicial review; or where the expulsion decision is based on imperative grounds of public security.

It should be concluded that the general rule which follows from Directive 64/221/EEC and Directive 2004/38/EC is that EU citizens should be allowed to await the decision on their appeal against the expulsion decision or their request to suspend the expulsion measure for the duration of the appeal proceedings. These Directives, as well as the judgment of the Court of Justice in *Dörr and Ünal*, allow expulsion before the decision on the appeal regarding the expulsion measure under certain conditions. However, it is not excluded that, even if these

[51] Council Dir 64/221/EEC on the coordination of special measures concerning the movement and residence of foreign nationals which are justified on grounds of public policy, public security or public health [1964] OJ 056/850.

[52] The Directive did not set any requirements for the competent authority, except that it shall not be the same as the authority empowered to take the decision refusing renewal of the residence permit or ordering expulsion. According to the Court of Justice, the independent authority, mentioned in Art 9 of Dir 64/221/EEC, needed to examine all the facts and circumstances and the expediency of the expulsion measure before the final decision was adopted. See Case C-136/03 *Dörr and Ünal* [2005] ECR I-4759, paras 48–51 and 55.

[53] *Dörr and Ünal*, ibid and *Pecastaing*, ibid, para 19, which referred to *Dörr and Ünal*, para 55. Whether there was a case of urgency was for the administrative authority to decide.

[54] Dir 2004/38/EC of the European Parliament and of the Council of 29 April 2004 on the right of citizens of the Union and their family members to move and reside freely within the territory of the Member States amending Reg (EEC) No 1612/68 and repealing Dirs 64/221/EEC, 68/360/EEC, 72/194/EEC, 73/148/EEC, 75/34/EEC, 75/35/EEC, 90/364/EEC, 90/365/EEC and 93/96/EEC [2004] OJ L158/77.

conditions were fulfilled, the Court would have required suspensive effect of the appeal, if an applicant could show that his expulsion would render his right to an appeal ineffective.

Neither does *Dörr and Ünal* exclude that the Court may require that a national court be able to grant interim relief or that a remedy have (automatic) suspensive effect in asylum cases.[55] The fact that expulsion of an asylum seeker to his country of origin may lead to irreparable harm (such as torture or ill-treatment), should urge the Court of Justice to require more safeguards regarding interim protection in asylum cases than in cases of EU citizens. Furthermore, it is conceivable that while EU citizens may be able to exercise their right to an effective remedy from abroad, this is often more problematic in asylum cases.

6.3.1.2 Obligations Stemming from the ECHR, the ICCPR, CAT and the Refugee Convention

This section will assess the national courts' obligations regarding interim protection by examining ECtHR case law as well as the UN Committees' views regarding the right to an effective remedy and the obligation to exhaust national remedies. Furthermore, the interim measures granted by the ECtHR, the ComAT and the HRC will be briefly examined, as these give an indication of the situations in which these bodies consider interim protection against expulsion to be essential. It will be argued on the basis of this case law and these views that in an asylum case a judicial remedy without automatic suspensive effect cannot be considered effective.

The Right to Remain under the Right to an Effective Remedy and the Obligation to Exhaust Domestic Remedies

The ECtHR has laid down clear standards with regard to the suspensive effect of asylum appeals in asylum cases under Articles 13 and 35 ECHR. In *Gebremedhin* the ECtHR ruled for the first time that Article 13 ECHR requires that an asylum seeker have access to a remedy with automatic suspensive effect if a State decides to expel him to a country where he runs a real risk of becoming a victim of treatment contrary to Article 3 ECHR.[56] The ECtHR incorporated the principle of automatic suspensive effect as an absolute safeguard based upon the possible irreversible consequences of a deportation in violation of Article 3 ECHR.[57] Even

[55] See also Council resolution regarding minimum guarantees for asylum procedures (n 1) para 17.

[56] ECtHR 26 April 2007, *Gebremedhin v France*, no 25389/05. See also ECtHR 11 December 2008, *Muminov v Russia*, no 42502/06, para 100 and *Abdolkhani and Karimnia* (n 8) para 108. Automatic suspensive effect only needs to be guaranteed in one instance. See ECtHR 22 September 2011, *HR v France*, no 64780/09, paras 78–80.

[57] R Byrne, 'Remedies of Limited Effect: Appeals under the Forthcoming Directive on EU Minimum Standards on Procedures' (2005) 7 *European Journal of Migration and Law* 71, 80. See *Abdolkhani and Karimnia* (n 8) para 108.

if, after expulsion, a violation of Article 3 ECHR is found, according to the ECtHR it is hard to see how this court can still offer the asylum applicant suitable redress as required by Article 13 ECHR.[58]

The applicant in *Gebremedhin* had been refused access to France at Paris Charles de Gaulle Airport upon arrival in June 2005. The French authorities deemed his application for permission to enter France for asylum reasons manifestly unfounded because of inconsistencies in his asylum account. He appealed to the urgent applications judge of the Administrative Court. During the appeal procedure, France tried but failed to expel him. The Administrative Court dismissed his appeal. Less than a week later the ECtHR accepted the applicant's request for an interim measure and indicated to the French Government that it was not desirable to remove the applicant to Eritrea prior to the forthcoming meeting of the appropriate Chamber. Following this interim measure, the French authorities granted the applicant leave to enter France and granted the applicant refugee status in November 2005.[59]

The two judicial remedies at the applicant's disposal (an appeal against the refusal of entry and a request for interim relief) which provided, according to the ECtHR, 'solid guarantees', both lacked automatic suspensive effect.[60] The applicant could be legally expelled before the judgment by the court. The ECtHR concluded that Gebremedhin did not have access to a remedy with automatic suspensive effect in the transit zone and therefore Article 13 ECHR had been violated.

The judgment by the ECtHR in *Gebremedhin* was affirmed by many later cases, including *Sultani* in which the effectiveness of the remedy was assessed in the light of Article 35(1) ECHR.[61] The Court stated, even more explicitly than in *Gebremedhin*, that a remedy without suspensive effect cannot be considered effective where an individual complains that his expulsion would expose him to treatment which is contrary to Article 3 ECHR.[62] It should be noted that the Court does not seem to consider the existence of an arguable claim of a violation of Article 3 ECHR a prerequisite for the applicability of this rule.[63] The ECtHR may, therefore, be of the opinion that in all cases in which an applicant complains of a violation of Article 3 ECHR, a national remedy without automatic suspensive

[58] *MSS* (n 8) para 393.

[59] The fact that the Court decided on the complaint regarding Art 13 ECHR, while the complaint regarding Art 3 ECHR had been declared inadmissible because of the granting of a residence permit, shows that the Court apparently deemed the complaint regarding the lack of interim protection to be very serious. For a different view, see ECtHR 31 January 2008, *Mir Isfahani v the Netherlands*, no 31252/03, which was declared inadmissible because the applicant received a permit. The applicant complained under Art 13 ECHR about the limited scope of judicial review by the national court.

[60] *Gebremedhin* (n 55) para 65.

[61] ECtHR (Adm) 20 September 2007, *Sultani v France*, no 45223/05, paras 50–52. See also ECtHR 4 December 2008, *Y v Russia*, no 20113/07, para 70; and ECtHR 18 November 2010, *Boutagni v France*, no 42360/08, paras 35–37.

[62] *Sultani* ibid, para 50.

[63] See TP Spijkerboer, 'ECtHR 20 September 2007, *Sultani v France*, no 45223/05' *Jurisprudentie Vreemdelingenrecht* 462.

effect cannot be regarded as effective. Important reasons for the ineffectiveness of remedies without suspensive effect, other than the risk of irreparable harm, are that after being expelled (ex-)asylum applicants may not be able to keep in touch with their lawyer or the authorities in the Member State.[64] This makes it complex, if not impossible, to substantiate their case.[65] Furthermore, it might be impossible to trace asylum applicants in their country of origin, which prevents their return to the Member State should the remedy be successful.[66]

The Court established in *Sultani* that the remedies pending did not have suspensive effect and concluded that they did not need to be exhausted in order for the complaint to be admissible.[67] Asylum applicants who do not have a remedy with automatic suspensive effect at their disposal thus can complain directly at the ECtHR and request an interim measure in order to prevent expulsion during the proceedings before the Court. In 2011 the President of the ECtHR requested the State Parties to the ECHR to provide national remedies with suspensive effect in the context of the high numbers of requests for interim measures which had been submitted to the ECtHR in the previous years.[68]

The requirement of a remedy with automatic suspensive effect not only applies in cases in which Article 3 ECHR is invoked but also where it concerns complaints under Article 2 ECHR and Article 4 of Protocol No 4 ECHR. The ECtHR held in the case of *De Souza Ribeiro* that a remedy with automatic suspensive effect is not obligatory where expulsions are challenged on the basis of alleged interference with private and family life.[69] However, in this case a violation of Article 13 ECHR was found because the applicant was expelled shortly after he lodged the appeal against his expulsion, which rendered the possibility of a serious examination of the circumstances and legal arguments either in favour or against a violation of Article 8 ECHR impossible.

[64] See by analogy, ECtHR 17 January 2006, *Aoulmi v France*, no 50278/99, where the ECtHR considered with regard to the effectiveness of its interim measure: 'In the present case, as the applicant was expelled by France to Algeria, the level of protection that the Court was able to afford the rights which he was asserting under Article 3 of the Convention was irreversibly reduced. In addition, as the applicant's lawyer has lost all contact with him since his expulsion, the gathering of evidence in support of the applicant's allegations has proved more complex.' See also *Hirsi Jamaa* (n 8) para 206 and ECtHR 5 April 2011, *Toumi v Italy*, no 25716/09, paras 72–76.

[65] See also the decision of the German *Bundesverfassungsgericht* to grant interim protection to an asylum seeker who would be transferred to Greece under the Dublin Regulation. The court took into account that the asylum seeker substantiated that it would be impossible for him to register in Greece and that he would become homeless. In this situation it would be very difficult to contact him during the proceedings before the court. BVerfG, 2 BvQ 56/09, 8 September 2009, Absatz-Nr (1–6).

[66] See, eg ECtHR 23 June 2011, *Diallo v Czech Republic*, no 20493/07, para 44.

[67] See also *Olaechea Chuas* (n 21) para 35; and ECtHR 23 October 2008, *Soldatenko v Ukraine*, no 2440/07, para 49.

[68] Statement issued by the President of the ECtHR concerning Requests for Interim Measures (Rule 39 of the Rules of Court) (11 February 2011) www.coe.int/t/dghl/standardsetting/cddh/gt-gdr-c/GT-GDR-C(2012)005_Statement%20of%20the%20ECtHR%20President%20on%20Interim%20Measures.pdf accessed 30 September 2013.

[69] ECtHR 13 December 2012, *De Souza Ribeiro v France*, no 22689/09, para 83.

In their views in individual cases, the ComAT and the HRC have not explicitly addressed the question whether the right to an effective remedy guaranteed by Article 3 CAT and Article 2(3) ICCPR requires that an asylum applicant be allowed to remain on the territory of the State during appeal proceedings. However, both Committees in their Concluding Observations with regard to several State Parties did stress that remedies against expulsion orders should have suspensive effect[70] or even automatic suspensive effect.[71]

In *Alzery* the HRC considered that there must be an opportunity for effective review of a decision to expel to an arguable risk of torture prior to expulsion, in order to avoid irreparable harm to the individual and render the review otiose and devoid of meaning. The absence of any opportunity for effective, independent review of the decision to expel in *Alzery* accordingly amounted to a breach of Article 7, read in conjunction with Article 2 ICCPR.[72] One may conclude from this consideration that there must be a possibility for interim protection during the proceedings before a national court reviewing the decision regarding the risk of *refoulement*.

Both the ComAT and the HRC have considered, in the light of the requirement to exhaust domestic remedies, that a remedy which does not suspend the asylum seeker's expulsion cannot be deemed effective.[73] In some of these cases, national proceedings were still pending;[74] in others the complainant had been deported before the decision on the remedy had been concluded.[75] The reason for the ineffectiveness is that irreparable harm cannot be averted if the domestic remedy subsequently yields a decision favourable to the complainant.[76]

The Refugee Convention does not provide for a right to a remedy with suspensive effect. However, such a right may be derived from the principle that the rights granted by the Convention should be effectively protected. UNHCR is of the opinion that an applicant for refugee status should in principle be permitted to

[70] ComAT, 'Concluding Observations on Austria' (15 December 2005, CAT/C/AUT/CO/3) Belgium (27 May 2003, CAT/C/CR/30/6), Finland (29 June 2011, CAT/C/FIN/CO/5-6), France (3 April 2006, CAT/C/FRA/CO/3 and 20 May 2010, CAT/C/FRA/CO/4-6), Ireland (17 June 2011, CAT/C/IRL/CO/1), Slovenia (20 June 2011, CAT/C/SVN/CO/3) and Switzerland (25 May 2010, CAT/C/CHE/CO/6). HRC, 'Concluding Observations' on Belgium (12 August 2004, CCPR/CO/81/BEL), Finland (2 December 2004, CCPR/CO/82/FIN), Germany (12 November 2012, CCPR/C/DEU/CO/6) and Lithuania (31 August 2012, CCPR/C/LTU/CO/3).

[71] ComAT, 'Concluding Observations' on Austria (20 May 2010, CAT/C/AUT/CO/4–5) and Monaco (28 May 2004, CAT/C/CR/32/1).

[72] *Alzery* (n 23) para 11.8.

[73] ComAT stated in its Annual Report 2006: 'The requirement of exhaustion of domestic remedies can be dispensed with, if the only remedies available to the complainant are without suspensive effect, i.e. remedies that do not automatically stay the execution of an expulsion order'. ComAT, 'Annual Report 2006' A/61/44, para 61.

[74] See ComAT 16 May 2007, *Nadeem Ahmad Dar v Norway*, no 249/2004, paras 6.2–6.5 and ComAT 17 December 2004, *Falcon Rios v Canada*, no 133/1999, para 7.3.

[75] See also ComAT 11 May 2007, *Adel Tebourski v France*, no 300/2006, para 7.3 and ComAT 15 May 2001, *ZZ v Canada*, no 123/1998, para 8.2.

[76] ComAT 24 May 2005, *Mafhoud Brada v France*, no 195/2002, para 7.7 and HRC 15 May 2003, *Weiss v Austria*, no 1086/2002, para 8.2.

remain in the country while an appeal to a higher administrative authority or to the court is pending.[77] If an applicant is not permitted to await the outcome of an appeal against a negative decision at first instance on the territory of the Member State, the remedy against a decision is ineffective according to the UNHCR.[78]

Interim Protection by the ECtHR, the ComAT and the HRC

The ECtHR has not only stressed the importance of interim protection to prevent irreparable harm in asylum cases in its case law, but also by calling for (binding) interim measures in a large number of expulsion and extradition cases pending before it.[79] In cases 'where there is plausibly asserted to be a risk of irreparable damage to the enjoyment by the applicant of one of the core rights under the Convention, the object of an interim measure is to maintain the status quo pending the Court's determination of the justification for the measure'.[80] Indications of interim measures given by the Court permit it to carry out an effective examination of the application and to ensure that effective protection is afforded to the applicant by the Convention.[81] The ECtHR has considered that although the assessment of a real risk of ill-treatment is to some degree speculative, the Court has always been very cautious, carefully examining the material placed before it in the light of the requisite standard of proof before indicating an interim measure under Rule 39.[82]

In practice, the Court has granted requests for interim measures in many asylum cases to prevent expulsion to the asylum seeker's country of origin. The Court has even called for interim measures for certain groups of asylum applicants, such as Somali asylum applicants in 2004,[83] Tamils from Sri Lanka in 2007[84] and

[77] UNHCR EXCOM Conclusion no 8 (n 16) para (e) and UNHCR, *Handbook* (n 16) para 192.

[78] UNHCR, *Observations on the European Commission's Proposal for a Directive on common standards and procedures in Member States for returning illegally staying third-country nationals* (16 December 2005) www.refworld.org/docid/43a2a58f4.html accessed 25 September 2013.

[79] In 2008–2012 the ECtHR granted a total of 3290 interim measures. See ECtHR, 'Rule 39 requests granted and refused in 2008, 2009 and 2010, 2011 and 2012 by responding state' www.echr.coe.int/Documents/Stats_art_39_2008_2012_ENG.pdf accessed 25 September 2013. Interim measures are usually granted in expulsion or extradition cases. For an overview, see also C Burbano Herrera and Y Haeck, 'Staying the Return of Aliens from Europe through Interim Measures: The Case-law of the European Commission and the European Court of Human Rights' (2011) 13 *European Journal of Migration and Law* 31.

[80] ECtHR (GC) 4 February 2005, *Mamatkulov and Askarov v Turkey*, nos 46827/99 and 46951/99, para 108.

[81] ECtHR (GC) 4 February 2005, *Mamatkulov and Askarov v Turkey*, nos 46827/99 and 46951/99, para 108, ECtHR (Adm) 20 February 2007, *Al-Moayad v Germany*, no 35865/03, paras 119–20 and 125 and *Toumi* (n 64) paras 69–71.

[82] ECtHR (GC) 28 February 2008, *Saadi v Italy*, no 37201/06, para 142.

[83] The Court granted interim measures in at least 11 complaints against the Netherlands in Somalian cases.

[84] By October 2007 the Court had applied Rule 39 in 22 cases where Tamils sought to prevent their removal to Sri Lanka from the UK. ECtHR 17 July 2008, *NA v the United Kingdom*, no 25904/07, para 21.

Afghan asylum applicants[85] and applicants who were to be transferred to Greece in 2008.[86]

Like the ECtHR, the ComAT[87] and the HRC[88] regularly request the State Party concerned not to deport or extradite the complainant while his complaint is being considered. They call for an interim measure, when they consider that there is a risk of irreparable harm if the complainant were to be expelled.

The ECtHR,[89] the ComAT[90] and the HRC[91] have ruled that interim measures are binding for the State Party concerned. It is their view that, by ignoring a request for an interim measure, the State Party undermines the protection offered by the ECHR, the CAT or the ICCPR and therefore commits a breach of its obligations under those treaties.

6.3.1.3 Subconclusion: The Right to Interim Protection

The Court of Justice attaches great importance to the effectiveness of a judgment on the existence of the rights claimed under EU law. The national court should be able to grant interim relief if this is necessary to ensure effectiveness, even if the court does not have the power to grant interim relief under national law. Whether interim relief should be considered necessary depends on the nature of the case lying before the court. Furthermore, the Court accepted that under strict conditions the national court may grant an interim measure which involves the (temporary) disapplication of EU legislation. EU legislation may further not prevent a national court from granting interim relief, if this is necessary to ensure the effectiveness of its judgment.

In cases concerning the expulsion of EU citizens, the general rule is that the EU citizens should be allowed to await the decision on the appeal against the expulsion measure or his request for interim relief on the territory of the Member State. Article 31 of Directive 2004/38/EC, as well as the case law of the Court of Justice allow, under certain conditions, that EU citizens are expelled before the decision on the appeal regarding the expulsion measure has been taken. It is apparently accepted that the expulsion of an EU citizen while the remedy against the expulsion measure is still pending, does not automatically render this remedy

[85] In a press release of 18 November 2008 the ECtHR announced that it indicated interim measures in 11 cases to the French Government in order to prevent removal to Afghanistan.

[86] ECtHR (Adm) 2 December 2008, *KRS v the United Kingdom*, no 32733/08 mentions that between 14 May 2008 and 16 September 2008 Rule 39 was applied in a total of 80 cases.

[87] ComAT 24 May 2005, *Mafhoud Brada v France*, no 195/2002, para 7.7. See ComAT, 'Annual Report 2006' (n 73) para 61, which states that 'a complaint must have a substantial likelihood of success on the merits for it to be concluded that the alleged victim would suffer irreparable harm in the event of his or her deportation'.

[88] See, eg *Weiss* (n 76); HRC 15 June 2004, *Ahani v Canada*, no 1051/2002.

[89] ECtHR (GC) 4 February 2005, *Mamatkulov and Askarov v Turkey*, nos 46827/99 and 46951/99.

[90] *Mafhoud Brada* (n 76) and ComAT 29 May 2007, *Elif Pelit v Azerbaijan*, no 281/2005.

[91] *Weiss* (n 76); *Ahani* (n 88) paras 8.1–8.2.

ineffective. The Court seems to be of the opinion that the person concerned can pursue the proceedings from abroad.

It follows from the case law of the ECtHR and the views of the HRC, the ComAT and the UNHCR that the approach of the Court of Justice should be different in asylum cases from cases concerning the expulsion of EU citizens. It follows from the ECtHR's case law, as well as the views of the HRC, the ComAT and the UNHCR that a remedy before a national authority cannot be considered effective if the expulsion of an asylum seeker takes place before the final decision of this authority, mainly because this expulsion may lead to irreparable harm.[92] The need for interim protection in cases in which a risk of *refoulement* is claimed is also underlined by the fact that the ECtHR, the HRC and the ComAT deemed it necessary to grant requests for interim measures in many expulsion and extradition cases in order to protect the applicant against irreparable harm and to ensure the effectiveness of their judgment or view.

The case law of the ECtHR and the views of the UN Committees also indicate that the effectiveness of the judgment on the expulsion measure against an asylum seeker can never be ensured if expulsion takes place prior to this judgment, even if no arguable claim is present. In *Sultani* the ECtHR stated in general terms that a remedy without suspensive effect cannot be regarded as effective. Moreover, the ComAT and the HRC did not limit their recommendation to attach (automatic) suspensive effect to remedies against expulsion orders to 'arguable claims'. The reason for this may be that the applicant is not able to effectively continue the appeal procedure from the country to which he has been expelled.

It should be reiterated that the EU right to an effective remedy guaranteed by Article 39 of Directive 2005/85/EC and 46 of Directive 2013/32/EU applies to all asylum cases, including asylum applications deemed inadmissible or manifestly unfounded.[93] It is, therefore, conceivable that the obligation to provide for a remedy with automatic suspensive effect also applies in all asylum cases.

Article 46(5) of Directive 2013/32/EU provides as a general rule an appeal with automatic suspensive effect for asylum cases and therefore seems to be in line with the EU right to an effective remedy and international law. However, with respect to certain categories of cases Article 46(6) to (8) allows a system in which interim relief should be requested before a court, while this request automatically suspends the expulsion. The question is whether such a system is in line with the requirement to offer a remedy with *automatic suspensive effect* and if so, under which conditions. The next section will address this question and assess how interim protection should be guaranteed. Does it need to be provided by law or do practical arrangements suffice? All these questions are also relevant for the interpretation of Article 39 of Directive 2005/85/EC.

[92] It is much less likely that the expulsion of an EU citizen during appeal proceedings will lead to irreparable harm.

[93] See also ch 4, section 4.3.2 in this volume.

6.3.2 The Meaning of Automatic Suspensive Effect

Interim protection can be provided in a national legal order in several ways. Two important characteristics of the national system determine the level of protection offered to an asylum seeker. The first is whether the lodging of the appeal in itself has suspensive effect or whether the asylum seeker has to apply to the national court for interim relief. A system in which national law provides for an appeal against an asylum decision which automatically suspends the expulsion decision, offers most guarantees. Potentially, less protection is offered by a system in which interim relief may be granted on request by the national court, while the mere fact that such a request has been lodged suspends the expulsion decision. Often the judge deciding on the request for interim relief does not perform a test of the risk of *refoulement* which is as rigorous as the test performed in the appeal; time limits are shorter and the applicant has fewer procedural rights. As mentioned above, Article 39(3) of Directive 2005/85/EC refers to both systems and Article 46 of Directive 2013/32/EU allows for both systems.

Even fewer guarantees are offered by a system in which the asylum seeker is not protected against expulsion while the request for interim relief is pending. It follows from the ECtHR's judgment in *Gebremedhin* that such a system violates the EU right to an effective remedy.

The second characteristic of the national system which determines the level of protection offered to an asylum seeker relates to the way in which interim protection is provided. If national authorities have only agreed in practice to await the decision on the request for interim relief, this offers fewer guarantees than where the suspensive effect of such request is provided for by law.

The question is what level of protection is required in asylum cases by EU law. In order to answer this question this section will examine the case law of the Court of Justice and the ECtHR. The HRC and the ComAT have not addressed this question.

6.3.2.1 The Case Law of the Court of Justice

It is not clear from the case law of the Court of Justice whether in asylum cases Member States are required to attach suspensive effect to the appeal itself or whether they may demand that the applicant lodge a request for interim relief. The judgment of the Court of Justice in *Dörr and Ünal* seems to imply that, according to the Court, an appeal with automatic suspensive effect provides for more protection than a system in which interim relief should be requested. It held that the safeguard of the right of appeal with suspensive effect guaranteed by Article 9 of Directive 64/221/EEC in cases of expulsion of EU citizens, required—in principle—automatic suspensive effect:

> In order to be regarded as having a suspensory effect in terms of that article, the appeal available to persons covered by Directive 64/221 must have an automatic suspensory

> effect. It is not sufficient for the court having jurisdiction to have the authority, upon application by the person concerned and under certain conditions, to stay implementation of the decision ending that person's residence. The assertion by the Austrian Government that suspension of such a decision may in fact be obtained as a matter of course from the Austrian courts is not such as to vitiate that conclusion.[94]

As was pointed out in section 6.3.1.1, the Court of Justice did allow that no automatic suspensive effect was attached to the appeal if an opinion had been obtained from a competent authority within the meaning of Article 9 of Directive 64/221/EEC or in cases of urgency.[95]

Article 31 of Directive 2004/38/EC, which replaced Directive 64/221/EEC, does not guarantee a remedy with suspensive effect in cases of expulsion of EU citizens. It does provide that, if the appeal against an expulsion decision is accompanied by a request for application for an interim order to suspend enforcement of this decision, no removal from the territory may take place until the decision on this application has been taken. The request for application of interim relief thus needs to have automatic suspensive effect.

6.3.2.2 Obligations Stemming from the ECHR

The term 'automatic suspensive effect' suggests that suspensive effect should be attached to the appeal against the asylum or expulsion decision. However, the case law of the ECtHR seems to indicate that the Court is of the opinion that a system in which automatic suspensive effect is attached to the applicant's request for interim relief (suspension of the expulsion decision) is also allowed under Article 13 ECHR.[96] In *Grebremedhin*, the Court examined whether the appeal, as well as the possibility of requesting the administrative court for interim relief could be regarded as an effective remedy. This would have been unnecessary if Article 13 could only be complied with if the appeal itself had automatic suspensive effect. Similarly, in *MSS* the ECtHR examined the effectiveness of the Belgian extremely urgent procedure in which the applicant could have applied for a stay of execution of the order to leave the country.[97]

[94] *Dörr and Ünal* (n 52) para 51.

[95] Ibid, paras 48–51 and 55.

[96] *Abdolkhani and Karimnia* (n 8) seems to indicate that the ECtHR requires that the appeal itself has automatic suspensive effect. The ECtHR concluded in para 108 that Art 13 was violated 'since an application for annulment of a deportation order does not have suspensive effect, unless the administrative court specifically orders a stay of execution of that order'. See also S Peers and N Rogers (eds), 'EU Immigration and Asylum Law: Text and Commentary' (Leiden/Boston, Martinus Nijhoff, 2006) 408.

[97] *MSS* (n 8) paras 386–96. For the procedure, see paras 138–40 of the judgment. In ECtHR 11 January 2007, *Salah Sheekh v the Netherlands*, no 1948/04, para 154 the ECtHR ruled that a procedure in which the applicant could ask the provisional-measures judge to stay the expulsion pending a decision on his objection against the manner in which his expulsion was to be carried out, complied with Art 13 ECHR.

Close and Rigorous Scrutiny

In *MSS* the ECtHR made clear that the judge who is examining the request for interim relief should apply close and rigorous scrutiny to the claim of a risk of *refoulement*. Furthermore, it showed that important procedural rights such as the rights of the defence should be respected in such a procedure and that the burden to prove the need to suspend the expulsion decision may not be set too high. The ECtHR considered that

> the requirement flowing from Article 13 that execution of the impugned measure be stayed cannot be considered as a subsidiary measure, that is, without regard being had to the requirements concerning the scope of the scrutiny. The contrary would amount to allowing the States to expel the individual concerned without having examined the complaints under Article 3 as rigorously as possible.[98]

The extremely urgent procedure in Belgium did not comply with the requirements of Article 13 ECHR because it reduced the rights of the defence and the examination of the case to a minimum. According to the ECtHR, the examination of the complaints under Article 3 carried out by the Aliens Appeals Board in the extremely urgent procedure was not thorough. The Alien Appeals Board limited its examination to verifying whether the persons concerned had produced concrete proof of the irreparable nature of the damage that might result from the alleged potential violation of Article 3. According to the ECtHR it thereby increased the burden of proof to such an extent as to hinder the examination on the merits of the alleged risk of a violation.[99] It follows from this judgment that Member States cannot circumvent the requirement of a rigorous scrutiny and other important procedural safeguards, by choosing a system in which interim relief should be requested, instead of an appeal with automatic suspensive effect. Furthermore, the ECtHR's judgment in *IM* makes clear that short time limits for preparing a remedy and receiving legal and linguistic assistance may seriously affect the accessibility of this remedy.[100] If the applicant is expected to lodge a fully substantiated request for interim relief within a very short period of time this would be problematic under Article 13 ECHR. However, the fact that the decision on the request for interim protection is taken after a very long period of time may also contribute to a violation of Article 13 ECHR.[101]

Guarantees Instead of Practical Arrangements

It follows from the fact that the requirements of Article 13 take the form of a guarantee that suspensive effect of a remedy must be provided for by law or other

[98] *MSS* (n 8) paras 387–88. For the standard of judicial review, see ch 9 in this volume.

[99] Ibid, paras 389–90.

[100] ECtHR 2 February 2012, *IM v France*, no 9152/09, para 150.

[101] ECtHR 25 September 2012, *Ahmade v Greece*, no 50520/09, para 115. In this case the procedure took almost two years.

clear rules. Practical arrangements with regard to interim protection in asylum cases are thus not sufficient.[102] In *Čonka* the ECtHR held that the extremely urgent procedure before the *Conseil d'Etat* which existed in Belgium before 2006, did not comply with Article 13 ECHR, because it was not guaranteed in fact and in law that an application for interim relief would suspend the enforcement of the expulsion measure. A few factors lead to this conclusion. First, the authorities were not required to stay the deportation while an application under the extremely urgent procedure was pending, even for a minimum reasonable period to enable the Council of State to decide on the application. Moreover, in practice it was up to the Council of State to ascertain the authorities' intentions regarding the proposed expulsions and to act accordingly. However, the Council of State did not appear to be obliged to do so. Finally, it was merely on the basis of internal directions that the registrar of the Council of State, acting on the instructions of a judge, contacted the authorities for that purpose, and there was no indication of what the consequences might be should he omit to do so. Ultimately, the alien had no guarantee that the Council of State and the authorities would comply in every case with that practice, that the Council of State would deliver its decision, or even hear the case, before his expulsion, or that the authorities would allow a minimum reasonable period of grace.[103]

6.3.2.3 Subconclusion: The Meaning of Automatic Suspensive Effect

On the basis of the case law of the Court of Justice and the ECtHR it is conceivable that Article 39(3) of Directive 2005/85/EC read in the light of the EU right to an effective remedy allows for two systems. The first is a system in which the remedy mentioned in Article 39(1) itself has suspensive effect. This option generally offers most protection and would be in line with the Court of Justice's interpretation of the term remedy with 'suspensory effect' in *Dörr and Ünal.* The second system is a national system in which provisional measures may be taken by national courts on request. Article 46(6) to (8) allows for exceptions to the right to an appeal with automatic suspensive effect, but requires that if such exceptions are applied automatic suspensive effect is attached to the request for interim protection. It should be concluded that this conforms with the EU right to an effective remedy.

A system in which the suspension of the expulsion should be requested is, however, only compatible with the EU right to an effective remedy if certain conditions are fulfilled. The fact that the asylum applicant must apply separately for interim protection may not put up barriers which render the exercise of the EU right to an effective remedy virtually impossible or excessively difficult. It can be

[102] ECtHR 5 February 2002, *Čonka v Belgium*, no 51564/99, para 83, ECtHR 23 July 2013, *MA v Cyprus*, no 41872/10, paras 136–38.

[103] *Čonka* (n 102) para 83. See also ECtHR 7 June 2011, *RU v Greece*, no 2237/08, para 77.

derived from the case law of the ECtHR that the following important procedural guarantees must be put in place:

— the request for interim protection has automatic suspensive effect;
— sufficient time is offered to the applicant to prepare the request for interim relief, if necessary with the help of a lawyer and/or interpreter;
— the standard of proof with respect to the need to suspend the expulsion decision is not set too high; and
— the judge deciding on the request performs close and rigorous scrutiny of the claim of a risk of *refoulement*.

Article 46(7) of Directive 2013/32/EU provides that some of these conditions must be met if Member States wish to make an exception to the right to an appeal with suspensive effect with respect to cases rejected in a border procedure. According to this provision:

— the applicant must have the necessary interpretation and legal assistance;
— the applicant should be granted at least one week to prepare the request and submit to the court or tribunal the arguments in favour of granting him or her the right to remain on the territory pending the outcome of the remedy; and
— the court or tribunal should examine the negative decision of the determining authority in terms of fact and law.

Arguably these conditions should not only apply to cases rejected in a border procedure, but also to the other cases mentioned in Article 46(6) of Directive 2013/32/EU in which an exception to the right to an appeal with automatic suspensive effect may be made.

Giving the Member States the opportunity to choose between the two systems would respect the procedural autonomy of the Member States. However, given the fact that both systems should offer similar procedural guarantees, a system in which interim relief is granted on request does not seem to enable Member States to process asylum cases much more expeditiously than a system in which the appeal has automatic suspensive effect.

On the basis of the ECtHR's judgment in *Čonka* it is contended that Article 39(3) of Directive 2005/85/EC and Article 46(5) to (8) of Directive 2013/32/EU require that Member States provide for clear entitlements regarding interim protection. Practical arrangements which allow asylum applicants to await the appeal on the territory of the receiving Member State do not provide sufficient guarantees.

6.4 SYNTHESIS OF FINDINGS

The effectiveness of the EU prohibition of *refoulement* would be seriously undermined if an asylum applicant was expelled or extradited before he has had the opportunity to have his asylum claim closely and rigorously assessed by the determining authority as well as the national court or tribunal. Early expulsion could result in the asylum applicant being subjected to irreparable harm (that is, persecution or serious harm). Furthermore, expulsion during the appeal proceedings will render ineffective the judgment of the national court concerning the existence of an EU right to be protected against *refoulement* or the right to asylum. Therefore, the asylum applicant should be allowed to remain on the territory of the Member State

— until the determining authority in first instance has carried out a close and rigorous assessment of the asylum claim.[104] This means that in practice the derogation from the right to remain during first instance asylum proceedings provided for in Article 7(2) of Directive 2005/85/EC and Articles 9(3) and 41(1)(b) of Directive 2013/32/EU can only be applied in exceptional circumstances. An example of such exceptional circumstance may be a subsequent asylum claim which can prima facie be considered abusively repetitive or entirely manifestly ill-founded. This is a very high standard which will not be easily met;
— for the time necessary to avail himself of the effective remedy before a court or tribunal in the meaning of Article 39(1) of Directive 2005/85/EC and Article 46(1) of Directive 2013/32/EU. Access to this remedy may not be blocked as a result of the swift expulsion of the asylum applicant after the negative asylum decision. The applicant should be informed of the imminent expulsion in time, leaving him sufficient time and opportunity to consult his lawyer.[105] Article 46(5) of Directive 2013/32/EU in line with the case law of the ECtHR grants the right to remain until the time limit for lodging the appeal has expired; and
— during the course of the appeal proceedings, until rigorous scrutiny of the claim of a risk of *refoulement* has been performed by the court or tribunal.

The following conclusions should be drawn with specific reference to the right to interim protection during appeal proceedings:

— Article 39(3) of Directive 2005/85/EC is very unlikely to be declared invalid by the Court of Justice because of violation of the EU right to an effective remedy, as this provision expressly requires national legislation concerning interim protection to be in accordance with international law.[106]
— It follows from the case law of the Court of Justice and the ECtHR as well as the views of the UN Committees that a remedy cannot be considered effective when irreparable harm may be done before the final judgment has been reached. In asylum cases expulsion of the asylum seeker before the court has reached a final judgment against the expulsion order or negative asylum

[104] See *Hirsi Jamaa* (n 8) para 205; and *MSS* (n 8) paras 286 and 293.
[105] *Pecastaing* (n 53) and *Shamayev* (n 2) paras 460–61.
[106] See also ch 2, section 2.4.1 in this volume.

decision may lead to such irreparable harm.[107] The remedy is also rendered ineffective by the real chance that asylum applicants who are expelled to their country of origin lose contact with their lawyers and disappear or face difficulties substantiating their case. Granting interim protection against expulsion during the proceedings before the court is therefore essential.

— Article 39(3) of Directive 2005/85/EC, read in the light of the EU right to an effective remedy, thus requires that interim protection against expulsion be granted *in all asylum cases*, including, for example, manifestly unfounded cases. Article 46(5) to (8) of Directive 2013/32/EU explicitly provides for such a requirement.

As to the required form of interim protection it was concluded that:

— Article 39 of Directive 2005/85/EC, read in the light of the EU right to an effective remedy, requires that automatic suspensive effect be attached either tp the appeal itself or to a request for interim relief.[108] Article 46(5) to (8) of Directive 2013/32/EU provides for such requirement.
— It follows from the ECtHR's judgment in *MSS* that the procedure in which interim relief may be granted by the national court or tribunal on request (as mentioned in Article 46(6) to (8) of Directive 2013/32/EU) can only be considered an effective remedy if it complies with important procedural guarantees. These include the rights of the defence, a reasonable burden of proof and a rigorous scrutiny of a claim of a risk of refoulement.[109] Arguably, therefore, the procedural guarantees mentioned in Article 46(7) of Directive 2013/32/EU, which only apply to a request for interim protection in cases rejected in border procedures, should apply to all cases in which an exception to the right to an appeal with automatic suspensive effect is made.
— Article 39(3) of Directive 2005/85/EC and Article 46(5) to (8) of Directive 2013/32/EU, read in the light of the EU right to an effective remedy, requires that Member States provide for clear entitlements regarding interim protection. Practical arrangements which allow asylum applicants to await the appeal on the territory of the receiving Member State are not sufficient.[110]

[107] See notably *Factortame* (n 31) paras 20–21; *Gebremedhin* (n 56); *Mafhoud Brada* (n 76) para 7.7; and *Weiss* (n 76) para 8.2.
[108] This may be derived from the fact that the ECtHR assessed in *Gebremedhin* (n 56) and *MSS* (n 8) whether the request for interim relief had automatic suspensive effect.
[109] *MSS* (n 8) paras 387–88.
[110] *Čonka* (n 102) para 83.

7

The Asylum Applicant's Right to be Heard on his Asylum Motives

THE ASYLUM APPLICANT should be allowed to remain on the territory of the Member State until his asylum claim has been closely and rigorously assessed, in order to effectively guarantee the prohibition of *refoulement*. Moreover, a rigorous assessment of the asylum claim is not possible without the presence of the asylum applicant in the Member State. The statements of the asylum applicant play an essential role in assessing whether he runs a risk of *refoulement* upon return to his country of origin. This is due to the fact that in many asylum cases there is a lack of documentary evidence to support the asylum claim. The assessment of the credibility of the applicant's asylum account is often decisive for the outcome of the case.[1] It is, therefore, crucial that claimants are given sufficient opportunity to present their case to the determining authorities and a personal interview is often necessary to achieve this. Furthermore, it may be considered necessary for the applicant to be able to respond to allegations made against him and to the evidence underlying the asylum decision.

In chapter nine it will be argued that the judicial review required by Article 39 of Directive 2005/85/EC and Article 46 of Directive 2013/32/EU must cover the establishment and qualification of the facts. In this light it is relevant to examine whether European Union law also demands that the national courts hear the applicant and/or his legal representative at a public hearing.

This chapter addresses the EU standards with regard to the asylum applicant's right to be personally heard on his asylum motives in first instance and appeal proceedings.

The Right to a Personal Interview

It is generally recognised that asylum applicants should have the right to a personal interview. Directive 2005/85/EC allows for a number of exceptions to this right and does not describe the necessary conditions for a personal interview. Directive 2013/32/EU has reduced the number of exceptions to the right to a personal

[1] See also ch 8 in this volume.

interview and this Directive contains more detailed provisions concerning the way the personal interview should be conducted.

The Court of Justice in the case of *MM* made clear that the EU right to be heard applies to asylum procedures.[2] This chapter contends, mainly on the basis of the case law of the European Court of Human Rights (ECtHR) and non-binding sources of inspiration, that the EU right to be heard and the full effectiveness of the principle of *non-refoulement* set additional standards to those laid down in Directive 2005/85/EC. In section 7.1 it is argued on the basis of these principles that a personal interview may only be omitted in exceptional circumstances. Section 7.2 discusses the requirements for the way the interview is conducted.

The Right to be Heard Following the Personal Interview

Directive 2005/85/EC does not require Member States to offer the asylum applicant the opportunity to comment on the contents of the report of the interview or to respond to the determining authority's conclusions as to the fact-finding and the assessment of the risk of *refoulement.* Directive 2013/32/EU provides for a right to comment on the report of the interview, but does not contain a right to be heard on a concept asylum decision.

Section 7.3 addresses the applicant's right to be heard following the personal interview. It examines in particular whether the applicant has the right to comment on the report of the interview and on the conclusions of the determining authority concerning the merits of the asylum claim.

The Right to be Heard by the National Court

Does EU law require that the asylum applicant and/or his legal representative be heard by the court during a public hearing? Or may the appeal against the asylum decision within the meaning of Article 39 of Directive 2005/85/EC and Article 46 of Directive 2013/32/EU also be decided on the basis of only written documents? As there is no case law from the EU Courts on this issue, this question will be addressed in this chapter mainly on the basis of the ECtHR's case law regarding Article 6 European Convention on Human Rights (ECHR), which incorporates the right to an oral hearing before a court. It is contended that an oral hearing of the asylum applicant before the court can only be omitted in exceptional circumstances, given the fact that the credibility of the asylum applicant's account and the applicant's personal fear of persecution or serious harm are generally crucial for the asylum decision and the fundamental rights at stake for the applicant.

[2] Case C-277/11 *MM v Minister for Justice, Equality and Law Reform Ireland* [2012] para 89.

7.1 THE RIGHT TO A PERSONAL INTERVIEW IN FIRST INSTANCE PROCEEDINGS

Directive 2005/85/EC

Directive 2005/85/EC as a general rule provides for a right to a personal interview in all asylum cases including those assessed in border procedures.[3] However, the Directive allows Member States to omit an interview on several grounds. The absence of a personal interview in asylum cases may limit the applicant's ability to substantiate his asylum claim.[4] Article 12(4) of Directive 2005/85/EC states that the absence of a personal interview in accordance with Article 12 of the Directive shall not prevent the determining authority from taking a decision on an application for asylum. Some applicants may thus only get the opportunity to submit written information to substantiate their asylum claim.

The first ground for making an exception to the right to a personal interview is that the determining authority is able to take a positive decision on the basis of the evidence available.[5] The absence of an interview in such cases may prove problematic if the asylum status is withdrawn in a later stage. In cases of withdrawal of asylum status a personal interview is not obligatory. The person concerned may only be given the opportunity to submit the reasons as to why his or her refugee status should not be withdrawn in a written statement.[6] It is thus possible for an asylum status to be granted and withdrawn, without the asylum applicant being given the opportunity to explain his reasons for requesting asylum in an interview.

Secondly, Member States may refrain from conducting a personal interview if the competent authority has already had a meeting with the applicant for the purpose of assisting him with completing his application and submitting the essential information regarding the application.[7] Thirdly, an interview may be omitted if the determining authority, on the basis of a complete examination of information provided by the applicant, considers the application to be unfounded under certain circumstances which may also be a reason to accelerate the procedure. These circumstances apply where the applicant:

- only raised issues that are not relevant or are of minimal relevance to the examination of whether he or she qualifies as a refugee;
- is considered to be from a safe country of origin;

[3] See Art 12 Dir 2005/85/EC in normal asylum cases and Art 35(3)(d) Dir 2005/85/EC in border procedures.

[4] The fact that Art 12(5) Dir 2005/85/EC provides that the absence of a personal interview pursuant to Art 12(2)(b) and (c) and Art 12(3) shall not adversely affect the decision of the determining authority, does not prevent that Costello states that if the apparent discretion afforded by Art 12 of the Directive were exploited by decision-makers, it would lead to *refoulement*. C Costello, 'The European Asylum Procedures Directive in Legal Context, New Issues in Refugee Research, Research Paper No 134' (Geneva, UNHCR, 2006) 24.

[5] Art 12(2)(a) Dir 2005/85/EC.

[6] Art 38(1)(b) Dir 2005/85/EC.

[7] Art 12(2)(b) Dir 2005/85/EC.

— can be returned to a safe third country;
— has made inconsistent, contradictory, improbable or insufficient representations;
— has submitted a subsequent application which does not raise any relevant new elements; or
— is making an application merely in order to delay or frustrate his removal.[8]

According to Article 34(2)(c) of Directive 2005/85/EC the preliminary examination in subsequent asylum applications may be conducted solely on the basis of written submissions without a personal interview.

The fourth ground to omit a personal interview is that the interview is not reasonably practicable, in particular where the competent authority is of the opinion that the applicant is unfit or unable to be interviewed owing to enduring circumstances beyond his or her control. When in doubt, Member States may require a medical or psychological certificate.[9] If the interview is omitted on this ground, reasonable efforts shall be made to allow the applicant or the dependant to submit further information. Finally, the Member States have the discretion to omit an interview in the case of dependent adults and minors. The right of these two groups to an interview will be addressed separately in sections 7.1.1 and 7.1.2.

According to information from the European Commission in 2009, 10 Member States have provided for a possibility to derogate from the right to a personal interview in asylum cases in their national legislation.[10] In addition, the United Nations High Commissioner for Refugees (UNHCR) mentions in its report of 2010 concerning the implementation of Directive 2005/85/EC that several of the Member States surveyed allow that a personal interview be omitted in specific cases.[11] Slovenia, for example, usually omits a personal interview when an asylum application is assessed in the accelerated procedure.[12] In France, a personal interview may be omitted, for example, in cases in which the asylum applicant is a national of a country to which Article 1C of the Refugee Convention applies, where the elements underlying the asylum claim are manifestly unfounded or where medical reasons prevent the interview.[13]

[8] Art 12(2)(c) and Art 23(4)(a), (c), (g), (h) and (j) Dir 2005/85/EC.

[9] Art 12(3) Dir 2005/85/EC.

[10] Commission, 'Staff Working Document accompanying the Proposal for a Directive of the European Parliament and of the Council on minimum standards on procedures in Member States for granting and withdrawing international protection' COM (2009) 554, SEC (2009) 1377, 13. According to the Commission up to 111,650 applicants (40% of the total number of asylum applicants) might potentially be targeted by this derogation. See also Commission, 'Report from the Commission to the European Parliament and the Council on the application of Directive 2005/85/EC' COM (2010) 465 final, 6.

[11] UNHCR mentions Finland, France, Greece, Slovenia and the United Kingdom. UNHCR, *Improving Asylum Procedures: Comparative Analysis and Recommendations for Law and Practice* (March 2010) www.refworld.org/docid/4c63e52d2.html accessed 25 September 2013 s 4, 33–39.

[12] Ibid, s 4, 6 and s 9, 27.

[13] Ibid, s 4, 37, s 9, 25.

Directive 2013/32/EU

Under Directive 2013/32/EU too, the general rule is that applicants are granted the opportunity to present their asylum claim during a personal interview. In addition, before deciding that an asylum application is inadmissible in accordance with Article 33 of the Directive, Member States should hear an applicant at a personal interview.[14]

Exceptions to the right to a personal interview are limited to two situations described in Article 14(2) of the Directive. The first is the situation in which the determining authority is able to take a positive decision with regard to refugee status on the basis of evidence available. It is thus not allowed to forgo a personal interview where the authorities intend to grant a subsidiary protection status. Secondly, the authority may refrain from interviewing the applicant where it believes that the applicant is unfit or unable to be interviewed owing to enduring circumstances beyond his or her control. If there is any doubt, the determining authority shall consult a medical professional to establish whether the condition that makes the applicant unfit or unable to be interviewed is temporary or of an enduring nature. Article 14(3) provides that the absence of a personal interview in accordance with Article 14 of the Directive shall not prevent the determining authority from taking a decision on an asylum application.

The Directive allows two further exceptions to the right to a personal interview in specific categories of asylum cases. First, Article 42(2)(b) of the Directive states that an interview may be omitted in a subsequent asylum application, which is subject to a preliminary examination. This exception does not apply to first asylum applications of dependent adults or minors lodged after an asylum application had been made on their behalf.[15] Secondly, it follows from Article 45(1)(b) that Member States are not required to offer a personal interview in cases in which asylum status has been withdrawn.

The Importance of a Personal Interview under EU Law

The question should be raised whether the absence of a personal interview undermines the effectiveness of the right to asylum or the principle of *non-refoulement*. The Court of Justice has not yet addressed this issue. As the right to a personal interview is the general rule, it may be expected that the Court will interpret any exceptions to this rule restrictively and in the light of the principle of effectiveness.[16]

The right to an interview should be considered as essential to ensure an appropriate examination of a claim of *refoulement* within the meaning of Article 8(2) of Directive 2005/85/EC and Article 10(3) of Directive 2013/32/EU and therefore for the effective exercise of the right to asylum or the prohibition of *refoulement*

[14] Art 34(1) Dir 2013/32/EU.

[15] See Arts 42(2)(b) and 40(6) Dir 2013/32/EU.

[16] See, eg Case C-578/08 *Chakroun* [2010] ECR I-1839, para 43.

for the following reasons. It will be shown in chapter eight that EU law requires that the claim of *refoulement* be assessed on an individual basis and be subjected to rigorous scrutiny. This means that claimants must be able to submit relevant information and to substantiate their claim of *refoulement*. In exceptional cases it may be possible to do this by submitting only written statements and evidence. This may, for example, be the case where the asylum applicant has submitted only that he fears serious harm as a result of the general human rights situation in his country of origin. Such a case may be decided on the basis of country of origin information provided by governments, UN bodies or NGOs. However, the asylum applicant himself will generally be the most important source of information, at least with regard to the personal risk of persecution or serious harm. This is especially the case when the applicant does not have sufficient evidence to support his claim. Furthermore, as is recognised in Article 4(3) of Directive 2011/95/EU, the individual position and personal circumstances of the applicant, including factors such as background and gender, should be taken into account in the assessment whether, on the basis of the applicant's personal circumstances, the acts to which the applicant has been or could be exposed would amount to persecution or serious harm. This information is best obtained by a personal interview of the individual concerned. Moreover, an interview is necessary to test the credibility of the applicant's account. As was stated in the explanations with the amended proposal for Directive 2005/85/EC:

> Since in most if not all asylum cases the determining authorities must assess the credibility of statements and/or of the applicant on the basis of all available facts, it is imperative for a proper assessment that applicants have, as much as possible, the opportunity to bring these forward in a personal manner, ie in an interview.[17]

Finally, a personal interview may be necessary to allow the applicant to exercise his EU right to be heard. The applicant may, for example, clarify any alleged discrepancies, inconsistencies or omissions in an initial written or oral account, give his view on evidence relied on by the determining authorities, or rebut the presumption of safety of his country of origin or a third country.[18]

A meeting, as mentioned in Article 12(2)(b) of Directive 2005/85/EC, should not be considered an appropriate alternative to a personal interview. This meeting serves to assist the applicant with completing his application and to submit the essential information regarding the application mentioned in Article 4(2) of the Qualification Directive. Battjes notes that this meeting does not address the assessment of the applicant's credibility. The interview allows the applicant to

[17] Commission, 'Amended proposal for a Council Directive on minimum standards on procedures in Member States for granting and withdrawing refugee status' COM (2002) 326 final, 7–8.

[18] Costello, 'The European Asylum Procedures Directive' (n 4) 24 and H Battjes, *European Asylum Law and International Law* (Leiden/Boston, Martinus Nijhoff, 2006) 313. See also UNHCR, *Handbook on Procedures and Criteria for Determining Refugee Status* (1979, new edition 1992) www.refworld.org/docid/3ae6b3314.html accessed 25 September 2013, para 109.

present the grounds for their application in a comprehensive manner and the determining authority to assess the credibility of the asylum account.[19]

Obligations Stemming from the European Convention on Human Rights, the Convention Against Torture and the Refugee Convention

The ECtHR has stressed the importance of the personal interview in several asylum cases and attaches much weight to the assessment of the credibility of the applicant's asylum account by an authority who has heard the applicant in person. In *RC* the ECtHR held that, as a general principle, the national authorities are best placed to assess not just the facts, but, more particularly, the credibility of witnesses 'since it is they who have had an opportunity to see, hear and assess the demeanour of the person concerned'.[20] In *EG* the Secretary of State had in a subsequent asylum procedure disregarded the fact that the Adjudicator had accepted in the first asylum procedure that the applicant had been detained and ill-treated in the past. The ECtHR considered: 'It is unfortunate, in the Court's view, that the Secretary of State did not consider the findings of the Adjudicator who had had the opportunity to see the applicant give evidence in person.' As a result, the Secretary of State did not take into account an important risk factor in this case.[21] In cases in which the national authorities failed to assess the asylum claim of the applicant and thus to conduct a personal interview, the ECtHR relied heavily on the opinion of the UNHCR. It stressed that the UNHCR interviewed the person concerned and thus had the opportunity to test the credibility of his fears and the veracity of his account of the circumstances in his home country.[22]

When assessing the quality of the national decision-making process the Court takes into account that the applicant was interviewed by the national authorities or was granted 'ample opportunity to state his case and to submit whatever he found relevant for the outcome'.[23] On the other hand, in *Charahili* the Court referred to the fact that the Turkish Government failed to submit any document to the Court demonstrating that the applicant had been interviewed in relation to his asylum request.[24] In *IM* when assessing the quality of the French accelerated procedure the ECtHR took into account that the personal interview with the applicant only lasted half an hour. The ECtHR noted in this context that it concerned a first asylum application.[25]

[19] See Art 13(3) Dir 2005/85/EC. See also Battjes, *European Asylum Law* (n 18) 313.

[20] ECtHR 9 March 2010, *RC v Sweden*, no 41827/07, para 52.

[21] ECtHR 31 May 2011, *EG v the United Kingdom*, no 41178/08, para 72.

[22] See, eg ECtHR 15 June 2010, *MB et al v Turkey*, no 36009/08, para 33; ECtHR 15 June 2010, *Ahmadpour v Turkey*, no 12717/08, para 39; ECtHR 13 April 2010, *Charahili v Turkey*, no 46605/07, para 59; ECtHR 19 January 2010, *ZNS v Turkey*, no 21896/08, para 48; and ECtHR 22 September 2009, *Abbdolkhani and Karimnia v Turkey*, no 30471/08, para 82.

[23] See, eg ECHR (Adm) 16 March 2004, *Nasimi v Sweden*, no 38865/02; ECtHR (Adm) 24 June 2004, *Kandomabadi v the Netherlands*, no 6276/03; ECtHR (Adm) 1 October 2002, *Tekdemir v the Netherlands*, nos 46860/99 and 49823/99.

[24] *Charahili* (n 22) para 57. See also *Ahmadpour* (n 22) para 38.

[25] ECtHR 2 February 2012, *IM v France*, no 9152/09, para 155.

The significance of the personal interview is also recognised in several non-binding views of human rights bodies. For example, in its Concluding Observations on France of 2006, the Committee against Torture (ComAT) recommended

> that the situations covered by article 3 of the Convention should be the subject of a more thorough risk assessment in accordance with the provisions of article 3, including by systematically holding individual interviews to better assess the personal risk to the applicant, and by providing free interpretation services.[26]

In the case of *Ke Chun Rong* ComAT found a violation of Article 3 of the Convention Against Torture (CAT) because the Australian authorities failed to verify the complainant's allegations and evidence. The Committee considered that the authorities based their decision predominantly on the content of the applicant's initial application for a Protection Visa, which he filed shortly after arriving in the country, without knowledge or understanding of the system. It further observed that the complainant was not interviewed in person either by the immigration department, which rejected his initial application, or by the Refugee Review Tribunal, 'and therefore he did not have the opportunity to clarify any inconsistencies in his initial statement'.[27]

Both the Committee of Ministers and the Parliamentary Assembly of the Council of Europe have recommended the governments of the Member States of the Council of Europe to ensure the right of all asylum applicants to a personal interview when accelerated procedures are applied.[28] Finally, the UNHCR Executive Committee of the Programme of the High Commissioner (EXCOM) Conclusion no 30 requires a complete personal interview by a fully qualified official in cases deemed manifestly unfounded or abusive.[29] UNHCR states in its *Handbook* that basic information, frequently given, in the first instance, by completing a standard questionnaire, will not normally be sufficient to enable the examiner to reach a decision, and that one or more personal interviews will be required.[30]

Subconclusion: The Right to a Personal Interview

Article 12 of Directive 2005/85/EC and Article 14 of Directive 2013/32/EU read in the light of the principle of effectiveness as well as the right to be heard, require in principle that a personal interview is held in each first asylum procedure. They

[26] ComAT, Concluding Observations on France (3 April 2006, CAT/C/FRA/CO/3) para 6.

[27] ComAT 7 February 2013, *Ke Chun Rong v Australia*, no 416/2010, para 7.5.

[28] Committee of Ministers of the Council of Europe, *Guidelines on human rights protection in the context of accelerated asylum procedures* (1 July 2009) www.refworld.org/docid/4a857e692.html accessed 25 September 2013, para IV 1.d and Parliamentary Assembly of the Council of Europe, *Resolution 1471 (2005) on accelerated asylum procedures in Council of Europe member states* (7 October 2005) www.refworld.org/docid/43f349e04.html accessed 25 September 2013, para 8.10.2.

[29] EXCOM Conclusion no 30 (XXXIV) 1983, on the problem of manifestly unfounded or abusive applications for refugee status or asylum.

[30] UNHCR, *Handbook* (n 18) para 199.

preclude whole categories of cases from being excluded from a right to a personal interview on the basis of the possibilities for derogation mentioned notably in Article 12 of Directive 2005/85/EC. The absence of a personal interview is only justified in exceptional cases, where it is established that this absence does not make it impossible for the claimant to substantiate his case or for the examining authorities to take a considered decision. Where the interview is omitted, the examining authorities should ensure that sufficient information is gathered to accurately assess the risk of *refoulement*, in particular when the person concerned is not able to be interviewed because of their mental condition.

7.1.1 Dependent Adults

Persons (mostly women), on whose behalf an asylum application is made by another person, may have independent asylum motives.[31] If an interview of these persons is omitted, there is a risk that these motives will not come to the fore. The woman may be afraid to talk about her experiences, such as sexual abuse, to her husband or he may not want to mention those experiences to the determining authorities.[32] She may be willing to express her personal fear of persecution or serious harm in a confidential interview with the authorities. Article 12(1) of Directive 2005/85/EC leaves it to the Member States to decide whether dependent adults are offered a personal interview.[33] Article 14(1) of Directive 2013/32/EU on the other hand, states that dependent adults shall be given the opportunity to receive a personal interview.

The ECtHR and the UN Committees have not specifically addressed the right to an interview of dependent adults. The UNHCR is of the opinion that the determining authority should meet with each dependant adult individually to ensure that they understand the grounds for protection and their procedural rights.[34] In order to ensure that gender-related claims, particularly of women, are properly considered in the refugee status determination process, female asylum-seekers should be interviewed separately, without the presence of male family members, in order to ensure that they have an opportunity to present their case. It should be explained to them that they may have a valid claim to asylum in their own right.[35]

[31] Dependent adults must consent to the lodging of the application on their behalf, failing which they shall have an opportunity to make an application on their own behalf. See Arts 6(3) Dir 2005/85/EC and 7(2) Dir 2013/32/EU.

[32] For an example, see ComAT 22 January 2007, *VL v Switzerland*, no 262/2005.

[33] According to the UNHCR report of 2010 there was an opportunity for adult dependents to have a personal interview in 10 of the 12 Member States of focus. UNHCR, *Improving Asylum Procedures* (n 11) s 4, 16.

[34] UNHCR, *Improving Asylum Procedures* (n 11) s 4, 15.

[35] UNHCR, *Guidelines of International Protection: Gender-Related Persecution within the context of Article 1A(2) of the 1951 Convention and/or its 1967 Protocol relating to the Status of Refugees* (7 May 2002, HCR/GIP/02/01) www.refworld.org/docid/3d36f1c64.html accessed 25 September 2013, para 36.

It may thus be argued that, in the context of Article 12 of Directive 2005/85/EC, the determining authorities should investigate whether the dependent adult has an independent claim of *refoulement*. This is best done during a personal meeting with the dependent adult without the presence of family members. Where there is an independent claim, the omission of a personal interview may undermine the effectiveness of the right to asylum or the prohibition of *refoulement*.

7.1.2 Accompanied and Unaccompanied Minor Asylum Applicants

The asylum claim of an accompanied child will often be directly related to the claims of their parents or other accompanying family members. In such a case the parents may well be able to represent the child in the asylum procedure and to present their and their child's asylum motives in their personal interview. This may be different, however, if the accompanied child has independent asylum motives. The child may, for example, fear persecution due to his sexual orientation or religious beliefs. Furthermore, he may fear child-specific forms of persecution such as under-age recruitment, child trafficking, female genital mutilation, family and domestic violence, forced or underage marriage, bonded or hazardous child labour, forced labour, forced prostitution or child pornography.[36] The child's parents may not be aware of these independent asylum motives or may be unwilling to mention them to the determining authorities. The child may, for example, conceal homosexual feelings, because he fears being disowned or the parents may be involved in practices such as forced marriage, female genital mutilation or forced labour. In such cases a personal interview with the child would be the only way for the determining authorities to be informed about the child's asylum motives.[37] Furthermore, even if the asylum claim of the child is directly related to the claim of his parents, it is possible that the child may have important additional information which supports these asylum claims. The child may, for example, have personally experienced persecution or serious harm in his country of origin as a result of the political activities of his parent(s).

Directive 2005/85/EC and Directive 2013/32/EU

Article 12(1) of Directive 2005/85/EC and Article 14(1) of Directive 2013/32/EU leave it to the discretion of Member States to determine in which cases a

[36] See UNHCR EXCOM Conclusion no 107 (LVIII) 2007, para (g) (viii) and UNHCR, *Guidelines on international protection: Child Asylum Claims under Articles 1(A)2 and 1(F) of the 1951 Convention and/or 1967 Protocol relating to the Status of Refugees* (22 December 2009, HCR/GIP/09/08) www.refworld.org/docid/4b2f4f6d2.html acessed 25 September 2013, para 18. See also Art 9(2)(f) Dir 2011/95/EU.

[37] UNHCR, *Guidelines on Child Asylum Claims* (n 36) para 70, 'A child's own account of his/her experience is often essential for the identification of his/her individual protection requirements and, in many cases, the child will be the only source of this information.'

minor shall offered a personal interview. This applies to both accompanied and unaccompanied minors.[38] Thus, even though in an asylum procedure an unaccompanied minor is often the most important source of information, the Procedures Directive does not provide him with a right to a personal interview.[39]

The Commission reported in 2010 that applications made by parents generally cover dependent minors. It mentions that in three Member States (Germany, Greece and the Netherlands) the right to lodge an application is recognised for minors of a certain age. Furthermore, in a number of Member States a guardian or other representative is considered competent to lodge an application for an unaccompanied minor.[40]

It is argued in this section that Article 12 of Directive 2005/85/EC and Article 14 of Directive 2013/32/EU, read in the light of Article 24 of the Charter, require that every child who is sufficiently mature must be informed about the asylum process and in particular on options to present his own asylum claim. This would also be in line with the asylum seeker's right to information guaranteed by Article 10(1) of Directive 2005/85/EC and Article 12(1) of Directive 2013/32/EU. If the child wants to be interviewed personally on his asylum motives he must be given this opportunity.

Interviewing Children and Article 24 of the Charter

Articles 12(1) of Directive 2005/85/EC and 14(1) of Directive 2013/32/EU should be read in the light of Article 24(1) and (2) of the Charter and Article 12 of the UN Convention on the Rights of the Child (CRC).[41] According to Article 24(1) of the Charter, children may express their views freely. Such views shall be taken into consideration on matters which concern them in accordance with their age and maturity. Furthermore, Article 24(2) provides that in all actions relating to children, whether taken by public authorities or private institutions, the child's best interests must be of primary consideration. The best interests principle is also mentioned in Article 17(6) of Directive 2005/85/EC and 25(6) of Directive 2013/32/EU concerning the rights of unaccompanied minors.

The Child's Right to be Heard According to the Court of Justice

The Court of Justice has made clear in *Aguirre Zarraga* that Article 24 of the Charter requires that a child be able to express his views in legal proceedings. However, each case must be assessed individually as to how the right to be heard should be exercised, taking account of the age and maturity of the child as well as

[38] Art 17 Dir 2005/85/EC and Art 25 Dir 2013/32/EU on unaccompanied minors do not state whether such a minor should be given a personal interview, but they do set out minimum standards where an interview is conducted.

[39] UNHCR, *Guidelines on Child Asylum Claims* (n 36) para 70.

[40] Commission Report (n 10) 4.

[41] See also UNHCR, *Improving Asylum Procedures* (n 11) s 4, 19–20.

their best interests. This case concerned a child who illegally remained with her mother in Germany instead of staying with her father in Spain. According to EU law, the German court was bound by the Spanish court's judgment which awarded sole custody of the child to the Spanish father and ordered the return of the child to Spain.[42] One of the preliminary questions put before the Court of Justice was whether the German court should enforce the Spanish judgment even though the Spanish court had not heard the child's view on the case before rendering its judgment. In this context the Court of Justice considered that it is for the court which has to rule on the return of a child to assess whether an oral hearing of the child is appropriate. The Court noted that conflicts which lead to child custody cases and the associated tensions

> create situations in which the hearing of the child, particularly when, as may be the case, the physical presence of the child before the court is required, may prove to be inappropriate, and even harmful to the psychological health of the child, who is often exposed to such tensions and adversely affected by them. Accordingly, while remaining a right of the child, hearing the child cannot constitute an absolute obligation, but must be assessed having regard to what is required in the best interests of the child in each individual case, in accordance with Article 24(2) of the Charter of Fundamental Rights.[43]

According to the Court of Justice it is not a necessary consequence of the right of the child to be heard that a hearing before the court of the Member State of origin take place. However, that right does require that legal procedures and conditions are made available to that child to enable the child to express his or her views freely and that those views are obtained by the court.[44]

Obligations Stemming from the Convention on the Rights of the Child

Article 24 of the Charter is based on several provisions of the CRC, including Article 12 CRC which provides that the child 'shall be provided the opportunity to be heard in any judicial and administrative proceedings affecting the child, either directly, or through a representative or an appropriate body, in a manner consistent with the procedural rules of national law'.[45] Article 12 CRC applies, according to its text, to all judicial and administrative proceedings affecting the child, and thus also to asylum procedures.[46]

The Committee on the Rights of the Child (ComRC) is of the opinion that Article 12 CRC requires that in the case of an asylum claim, 'the child must ...

[42] Art 42 of Council Reg (EC) No 2201/2003 of 27 November 2003 concerning jurisdiction and the recognition and enforcement of judgments in matrimonial matters and the matters of parental responsibility [2003] OJ L338/1. This provision also states that the court deciding on the custody of the child should give the child an opportunity to be heard, unless a hearing was considered inappropriate having regard to his or her age or degree of maturity.

[43] Case C-491/10 PPU, *Aguirre Zaraga* [2010] ECR I-14247, para 64.

[44] Ibid, para 65.

[45] Explanations relating to the Charter of Fundamental Rights (2007/C 303/02), OJ 14 December 2007, C 303/25.

[46] ComRC, General Comment No 12 (2009, CRC/C/GC/12) para 32.

have the opportunity to present her or his reasons leading to the asylum claim'.[47] It also stated with regard to unaccompanied and separated children that 'where the age and maturity of the child permits, the opportunity for a personal interview with a qualified official should be granted before any final decision is made'.[48] In order to be able to exercise its right to be heard the child must be informed about the asylum process.[49] According to the ComRC there can be no correct application of the best interests of the child principle laid down in Article 3 CRC if the components of Article 12 are not respected.[50]

Article 12 CRC applies to all minors capable of forming their own views, irrespective of their age.[51] The ComRC stated that States parties are obliged

> to assess the capacity of the child to form an autonomous opinion to the greatest extent possible. This means that States parties cannot begin with the assumption that a child is incapable of expressing her or his own views. On the contrary, States parties should presume that a child has the capacity to form her or his own views and recognise that she or he has the right to express them; it is not up to the child to first prove her or his capacity.[52]

The Committee points to the fact that children are able to form views from a very young age, even if they are unable to express them verbally. It states that, consequently, full implementation of Article 12 CRC 'requires recognition of, and respect for, non-verbal forms of communication including play, body language, facial expressions, and drawing and painting, through which very young children demonstrate understanding, choices and preferences'.[53] Furthermore, State parties are under an obligation to ensure the implementation of the right to be heard for children experiencing difficulties in making their views heard. For instance, efforts must be made 'to recognise the right to expression of views for minority, indigenous and migrant children and other children who do not speak the majority language'.

According to the ComRC children should never be coerced into expressing views against their wishes.[54] If the child wishes to be heard, he or she will have to decide how to be heard: directly or through a representative or appropriate body. The representative can be the parent(s), a lawyer or another person (such as a social worker). The Committee recommends that, wherever possible, the child must be given the opportunity to be directly heard in any proceedings.[55]

[47] Ibid, para 123. See also paras 32 and 67.

[48] ComRC, General Comment No 6 (2005, CRC/GC/2005/6) para 71. See also UNHCR, *Improving Asylum Procedures* (n 11) s 4, 18.

[49] ComRC, General Comment No 12 (n 46) and General Comment No 6 (n 48) para 25.

[50] ComRC, General Comment No 12 (n 46) para 74 and General Comment No 14 (2013, CRC/C/GC/14) paras 43–45. See also UNHCR EXCOM Conclusion no 107 (n 36) on Children at Risk.

[51] See Art 12(1) CRC and ComRC, General Comment No 12 (n 46) para 21.

[52] ComRC, General Comment No 12, ibid, para 20.

[53] Ibid, para 21.

[54] Ibid, para 134(b).

[55] Ibid, paras 35–36.

The Committee emphasises that a child should not be interviewed more often than necessary, in particular when harmful events are explored. According to the Committee the hearing of a child is a difficult process that can have a traumatic impact on the child.[56]

Subconclusion: Minor's Right to a Personal Interview

It should be concluded that Member States do not have full discretion when setting out rules regarding interviewing minors. It follows from Article 12 of Directive 2005/85/EC and Article 14(1) of Directive 2013/32/EU, read in the light of Article 24 of the Charter which should in turn be interpreted in conformity with Article 12 CRC, that each child must in some way be put in a position to be able to present their asylum claim. For that purpose children should be informed about the asylum process in conformity with Article 10(1)(a) of Directive 2005/85/EC and Article 12(1)(a) of Directive 2013/32/EU.

If the child is unaccompanied or if it has individual asylum motives or important information in support of his and his parents' asylum claim, it should be decided whether the age and maturity of the child allows the child to be interviewed about their asylum motives. If this is the case, the child should, in principle, be personally interviewed if he so wishes. However, it should always be noted that an interview in an asylum procedure can be stressful for a child, as she may be asked to talk about traumatic events she experienced in her country of origin. As in child abduction cases such as *Aguirre Zarraga*, it should therefore be assessed whether an asylum interview is inappropriate, or even harmful to the psychological health of the child. If interviewing the child would indeed be inappropriate or harmful, the interview should be omitted. In analogy with Article 12(3) of Directive 2005/5/EC and Article 14(2) of Directive 2013/32/EU reasonable efforts shall be made to allow the child to submit further information, for example through his guardian or legal representative.

7.2 REQUIREMENTS AS TO THE CONDUCT OF THE INTERVIEW

According to the Procedures Directive, personal interviews should take place under conditions which ensure appropriate confidentiality.[57] Furthermore, Member States should take appropriate steps to ensure that personal interviews are conducted under conditions which allow applicants to present the grounds for their applications in a comprehensive manner.[58] According to Article 16 of Directive 2013/32/EU the applicant should be given an adequate opportunity to present

[56] Ibid, para 24.

[57] Arts 13(2) Dir 2005/85/EC and 15(2) Dir 2013/32/EU.

[58] Arts 13(3) Dir 2005/85/EC and 15(3) Dir 2013/32/EU. This provision also applies to interviews in border procedures (Art 35(3)(d) Dir 2005/85/EC) and where refugee status is withdrawn (Arts 38 (1)(b) Dir 2005/85/EC and 45(1)(b) Dir 2013/32/EU).

elements needed to substantiate the application in accordance with Article 4 of the Qualification Directive as completely as possible. 'This shall include the opportunity to give an explanation regarding elements which may be missing and/or any inconsistencies or contradictions in his/her statements.'

Important guarantees in this regard include that the interview is conducted in a language which the person concerned understands or that he or she is assisted by an interpreter. Furthermore, it is essential that the interviewer is competent and able to gain the trust of the applicant. In particular, Directive 2005/85/EC does not guarantee these safeguards in all asylum cases. Therefore, these issues will be addressed in this section. Other circumstances which also determine the quality of the interview, which will not be discussed in this section, are the confidentiality of the interview, the time and assistance available for the asylum applicant to prepare for the interview, the environment in which the interview takes place, and the time allocated for and duration of the personal interview.[59]

In 2010 the UNHCR pointed out that in several Member States the quality of personal interviews was not guaranteed. It observed, for example, that in some Member States the confidentiality of the interview was not ensured[60] and that interviews were conducted by officers who were not properly trained. Furthermore, the UNHCR research revealed widespread misconduct involving interpreters in personal interviews, such as a lack of competence and impartiality. Finally, the UNHCR noted that in some Member States as a result of a shortage of interpreters in a certain language interviews may not take place in a language the applicant actually understands.[61] Conditions such as those described by the UNHCR may impede the applicant from fully presenting his asylum claim and thus undermine the effectiveness of the right to a personal interview.

7.2.1 Language of the Interview

Article 13(3)(b) of Directive 2005/85/EC states that communication during the personal interview 'need not necessarily take place in the language preferred by the applicant for asylum if there is another language which he/she may reasonably be supposed to understand and in which he/she is able to communicate'. With regard to language, Directive 2013/32/EU provides for more guarantees. According to Article 15(3)(c) the communication shall take place 'in the language preferred by the applicant unless there is another language which he or she understands and in which he or she is able to communicate clearly'.

[59] UNHCR, *Improving Asylum Procedures* (n 11) s 5.

[60] UNHCR states in its report *Improving Asylum Procedures* (n 11) s 5, 10, that it observed interviews in Greece, Spain and Italy which took place in conditions which breached Art 13(2) Dir 2005/85/EC. See also Commission Report (n 10) 6.

[61] UNHCR, *Improving Asylum Procedures* (n 11) s 5.

According to the UNHCR's research of 2010 most interviews were conducted in the mother tongue of the applicant or in another language chosen by the applicant. However, in some cases the applicant was interviewed in a language he was supposed to, but did not actually understand, most often as a result of a shortage of interpreters in particular languages.[62]

It may be argued that the effectiveness of the right to a personal interview, and consequently the right to asylum or the prohibition of *refoulement*, are undermined when there is no certainty that the person concerned is actually able to explain his asylum motives or objections against transfer or expulsion in an interview.[63] It should be remembered that the credibility of the account of the person concerned is assessed on the basis of often very detailed information, gathered during the interview. If a person does not understand exactly what the interviewer is asking him, or is not able to respond to questions in detail, this may work to his detriment and lead to the conclusion that the account should be deemed not credible.

The Court of Justice, the ECtHR and the UN Committees have not addressed this issue. Both the Parliamentary Assembly of the Council of Europe and the UNHCR stress that Member States must ensure the right of all asylum applicants to a personal interview in a language they understand.[64] The UNHCR is of the opinion that an interview in the language the applicant understands is a pre-requisite for a fair procedure. When it is not fulfilled any evidence gathered in the course of the personal interview may be unreliable.[65] Furthermore, the UNHCR stresses that there is a difference between the basic ability to make oneself understood in a language and the ability to present a complex account which may include difficult or painful events in that language.[66] The UNHCR notes that assumptions that an asylum seeker speaks or understands the official language of his or her country of origin may be incorrect. As a matter of principle, bearing in mind the need to prevent deliberate obstruction, every effort should be undertaken in this regard by the countries of asylum.[67]

Arguably, the principle of effectiveness thus requires Member States to ascertain that the person concerned is actually able to understand the language chosen for the interview and that he can express himself effectively in that language. If the claimant does not understand the interviewer, an interpreter should be used to facilitate communication. If such an interpreter is not available (for example,

[62] Ibid, 45. See also Commission Report (n 10) 7.

[63] Doornbos notes in her research that asylum applicants often hesitate to let the interviewer know that they do not understand the interviewer or the interpreter. N Doornbos, *Op verhaal komen, Institutionele communicatie in de asielprocedure* (Nijmegen, Wolf Legal Publishers, 2006) 274.

[64] Parliamentary Assembly of the Council of Europe, *Resolution 1471* (n 28) para 8.10.2.

[65] UNHCR, *Improving Asylum Procedures* (n 11) s 5, 29.

[66] Ibid, s 5, 44.

[67] UNHCR, *Provisional Comments on the Proposal for a Council Directive on Minimum Standards on Procedures in Member States for Granting and Withdrawing Refugee Status* (Council Document 14203/04, Asile 64, of 9 November 2004) (10 February 2005) www.refworld.org/docid/42492b302.html accessed 25 September 2013, 13.

because the language spoken by the claimant is very uncommon) the authorities should take this into account when examining the case and taking a decision on the credibility of the claimant's account.

7.2.2 The Right to a Free and Competent Interpreter

If the language chosen for the interview is not understood by the asylum applicant, free interpretation services should be provided in a language this person understands. This follows from Article 10(1)(b) of Directive 2005/85/EC and Article 12(1)(b) of Directive 2013/32/EU, which grant asylum applicants the right to an interpreter for submitting their case to the competent authorities whenever this is necessary.[68] According to these provisions Member States shall consider it necessary to provide the services of an interpreter at least when the determining authority calls upon the applicant to be interviewed, and appropriate communication cannot be ensured without such services. Interpreters used at the interview and in other cases where the competent authorities call upon the applicant shall be paid for out of public funds.[69] Article 13(3)(b) of Directive 2005/85/EC and Article 15(3)(c) of Directive 2013/32/EU require Member States to select an interpreter who is able to ensure appropriate communication between the applicant and the person who conducts the interview. It may be derived from these provisions that Member States need to ensure that interpreters are competent[70] and qualified and that the languages spoken by the interpreter are understood by both the person who is interviewed and the interviewer.[71]

The UNHCR mentions in its report of 2010 that a number of Member States face shortages of interpreters in particular languages or in particular regional locations. This problem is sometimes solved by using interpreters in other Member States via a video-conference call.[72] The UNHCR also states that in some Member States no specific professional qualifications are required for interpreters and that in the 12 Member States of focus the provision of training for interpreters is at best limited and in many cases non-existent.[73] Finally, the UNHCR's research revealed widespread misconduct involving interpreters in personal interviews, and serious shortcomings in the ability of interviewers to work effectively with or manage the conduct of interpreters.[74]

[68] This right also applies in border procedures. See Arts 35(3)(c) Dir 2005/85/EC and 43(1) Dir 2013/32/EU.

[69] See also Council resolution of 20 June 1995 on minimum guarantees for asylum procedures, OJ 19 September 1996, C 274 , 13–17, para 13.

[70] See also UNHCR, *Improving Asylum Procedures* (n 11) s 5, 42.

[71] Ibid, s 5, 28–29.

[72] Ibid, s 5, 32–33.

[73] Ibid, s 5, 35–36.

[74] Ibid, s 5, 38. UNHCR mentions examples at 38–40.

The right to an interpreter is considered an important procedural safeguard in asylum proceedings by several sources of inspiration.[75] In *MSS* the ECtHR took into account a number of deficiencies in the Greek asylum procedure which together lead to a violation of Article 13 ECHR. One of those deficiencies was the shortage of interpreters.[76] In *IM* the ECtHR recognised that a lack of linguistic aid may affect the asylum applicant's ability to present his asylum claim.[77] In its Concluding Observations of 2006 regarding France, the ComAT recommended

> that the situations covered by article 3 of the Convention should be the subject of a more thorough risk assessment in accordance with the provisions of article 3, including by systematically holding individual interviews to better assess the personal risk to the applicant, *and by providing free interpretation services* (emphasis added).[78]

With regard to the competence of the interpreter it is interesting to note that the ECtHR has recognised that in order for the right of every defendant to the free assistance of an interpreter of Article 6(3)(e) ECHR 'to be practical and effective, the obligation of the competent authorities is not limited to the appointment of an interpreter but, if they are put on notice in the particular circumstances, may also extend to a degree of subsequent control over the adequacy of the interpretation provided'.[79] On the basis of this judgment it may be argued that in order to comply with their obligation under Article 13(3)(b) of Directive 2005/85/EC and Article 15(3)(c) of Directive 2013/32/EU, the Member State authorities should control the quality of the interpretation offered by the State.

7.2.3 The Competence of the Interviewer

Under Directive 2005/85/EC a personal interview should be conducted by a person competent under national law and not necessarily by the determining authority. Article 13(3)(a) of Directive 2005/85/EC states that Member States must ensure that the person who conducts the interview is 'sufficiently competent' to take account of the personal *or* general circumstances surrounding the application, including the applicant's cultural origin or vulnerability, insofar as it is possible to do so. These are not particularly high standards. The UNHCR observed

[75] See, eg Parliamentary Assembly of the Council of Europe, *Resolution 1471* (n 28) para 7 and Parliamentary Assembly of the Council of Europe, *Recommendation 1236 (1994) on the right of asylum* (12 April 1994) assembly.coe.int/Main.asp?link=/Documents/AdoptedText/ta94/EREC1236.htm accessed 25 September 2013.

[76] ECtHR (GC) 21 January 2011, *MSS v Belgium and Greece*, no 30696/09, para 301.

[77] *IM* (n 25) para 145.

[78] ComAt, Concluding Observations on France (n 26).

[79] ECtHR (GC) 18 October 2006, *Hermi v Italy*, no 18114/02, para 70.

in its report of 2010 that Greece, Italy and Spain did not provide for formal and compulsory specialist training for all interviewers upon recruitment.[80]

Standards with regard to the competence of the interviewer have been raised in Directive 2013/32/EU. According to Article 14(1) of this directive, interviews on the substance of the asylum application shall be conducted by the personnel of the determining authority. It follows from Article 4(3) of the Directive that this personnel must receive relevant training, which includes training on international and EU asylum law, the examination of applicants of vulnerable asylum applicants with specific needs, interviewing techniques, expert medical and legal reports and country of origin information.[81] Furthermore, personnel who are interviewing applicants need to have acquired a general knowledge of problems which could adversely affect the applicant's ability to be interviewed, such as indications of past torture. Personnel of another authority may only conduct personal interviews when a large number of asylum applicants simultaneously request international protection. These personnel should receive, in advance, training similar to the interviewers of the determining authority.[82] Article 15(3)(a) of Directive 2013/32/EU provides that the person who conducts the interview must be 'competent to take account of the personal and general circumstances surrounding the application'.

The ECtHR recognised the importance of training for interviewers in asylum cases in *MSS*. In this case it considered the 'lack of training of the staff responsible for conducting the individual interview' to be one of the deficiencies in the Greek asylum procedure which lead to a violation of Article 13 ECHR.[83] The UNHCR stresses that the task of the interviewer is 'hugely challenging and complicated'.[84] According to the UNHCR *Handbook* it will be necessary for the examiner to gain the confidence of the applicant in order to assist the latter in putting forward his case and in fully explaining his opinions and feelings.[85]

Arguably, in order to ensure the effectiveness of the right to a personal interview and as a result of the EU prohibition of *refoulement*, Article 13 of Directive 2005/85/EC should be considered to include a requirement to give proper training to interviewers. Article 4(3) of Directive 2013/32/EU specifies what kind of training is necessary for interviewers.[86]

[80] UNHCR, *Improving Asylum Procedures* (n 11) s 5, 12–25.

[81] See Art 6(4) of Reg (EU) No 439/2010 of 19 May 2010 establishing a European Asylum Support Office [2010] OJ L132/11.

[82] See Art 14(2) Dir 2013/32/EU, this provision also refers to Art 6(4) of Reg 439/2010.

[83] *MSS* (n 76) para 301.

[84] UNHCR, *Improving Asylum Procedures* (n 11) s 5, 12.

[85] UNHCR, *Handbook* (n 18) para 200.

[86] See also UNHCR, *Improving Asylum Procedures* (n 11) s 5, 12–13.

7.2.4 Gender Sensitive Interviews

Some persons claiming a risk of *refoulement*, in particular victims of sexual violence, may feel apprehensive of talking about their experiences. According to the ComAT:

> It is well-known that the loss of privacy and prospect of humiliation based on revelation alone of the acts concerned may cause both women and men to withhold the fact that they have been subject to rape and/or other forms of sexual abuse until it appears absolutely necessary.[87]

It may be argued that Article 13(3) of Directive 2005/85/EC requires the use of an interviewer and interpreter of the same sex as the claimant if helps the applicant to present the grounds for his application in a comprehensive manner. When interpreters of the same sex are not available, it may be argued that the examining authorities should take this into account when taking the decision and/or when assessing the value of late statements in first or subsequent asylum procedures.[88]

Article 15(3)(b) and (c) of Directive 2013/32/EU provides that Member States should, where possible, provide for an interviewer and an interpreter of the same sex if the applicant so requests, unless the determining authority has reason to believe that this request is based on grounds which are not related to the difficulties of the applicant to present the grounds of his application in a comprehensive manner. Furthermore, Article 15(3)(a) states that the interviewer should be competent to take account of the applicant's gender.

Several non-binding sources of inspiration have stressed the importance of the involvement of female interviewers and interpreters in interviews with women. The Council resolution on minimum guarantees for asylum procedures provides that Member States must endeavour to involve skilled female employees and female interpreters in the asylum procedure where necessary, particularly where female asylum seekers find it difficult to present the grounds for their application in a comprehensive manner owing to the experiences they have undergone or to their cultural origin.[89] The Human Rights Committee (HRC) in its Concluding Observations regarding Austria noted with concern that women seeking asylum were not automatically interviewed by female asylum officers and assisted by female interpreters. The Committee recommended that the State party should adopt a gender-sensitive approach to refugee status determination by automatically assigning female interviewers and interpreters to women seeking asylum.[90]

[87] *VL* (n 32) para 8.8.

[88] For late statements see also ch 8, section 8.4 in this volume.

[89] Council resolution on minimum guarantees for asylum procedures (n 69) 13–17, para 28.

[90] HRC Concluding Observations on Austria (30 October 2007, CCPR/C/AUT/CO/4) para 18. See also ComAT, Concluding Observations on Austria (15 December 2005, CAT/C/AUT/CO/3) and Parliamentary Assembly of the Council of Europe, *Recommendation 1374 (1998) on the situation of refugee women in Europe* (26 May 1998) www.refworld.org/docid/47fdfb36f.html accessed 25 September 2013.

Furthermore, the UNHCR stressed the importance of the use of female interpreters in interviews with female asylum applicants in EXCOM Conclusion no 64.[91]

7.2.5 Child-friendly Interviews

Article 17 of Directive 2005/85/EC and Article 25 of Directive 2013/32/EU provide for special provisions concerning the interview of unaccompanied minors. They state that the Member State should ensure that the minor's representative is given the opportunity to inform the unaccompanied minor about the meaning and possible consequences of the personal interview and, where appropriate, how to prepare himself or herself for the personal interview.[92] Furthermore, Article 17(1)(b) of Directive 2005/85/EC requires Member States to allow the representative to be present at that interview, while Article 25(1)(b) of Directive 2013/32/EU states that Member States should ensure the presence of a representative and/or legal adviser or other counsellor. The Directives both state that such representatives (or counsellors) should be able to ask questions or make comments, within the framework set by the person who conducts the interview. Moreover, interviews with unaccompanied minors should be conducted by a person who has the necessary knowledge of the special needs of minors.[93]

These special guarantees do not apply to the interviews with accompanied minors. Article 15(3)(e) of Directive 2013/32/EU provides that interviews with minors should be conducted in a child-appropriate manner. It may be argued, on the basis of the Court of Justice's judgment in *Aguirre Zarraga*, as well as from the views of the ComRC and the UNHCR, that Article 17(4) of Directive 2005/85/EC and Article 25 of Directive 2013/32/EU should be applied by analogy to such interviews. Such application would ensure the child-appropriate nature of the interview. Furthermore, it would be in line with the requirement that personal interviews must be conducted under conditions which allow applicants to present the grounds for their applications in a comprehensive manner and that the person who conducts the interview be sufficiently competent to take account of the personal circumstances of the applicant including his vulnerability.[94]

The UNHCR reported in 2010 that several Member States did not provide special training for interviewing children.[95] Only four of the 12 Member States of focus in the UNHCR's research of 2010 had specific guidelines on interviewing children.[96]

[91] EXCOM Conclusion no 64 (XLI) 1990, on Refugee Women and International Protection (1990) and UNHCR, *Guidelines on Gender-Related Persecution* (n 35) para 36.

[92] Arts 17(1)(b) Dir 2005/85/EC and 25(1)(b) Dir 2013/32/EU.

[93] Arts 17(4)(a) Dir 2005/85/EC and 25(3)(a) Dir 2013/32/EU.

[94] Arts 13(3) Dir 2005/85/EC and 15(3) Dir 2013/32/EU.

[95] UNHCR, *Improving Asylum Procedures* (n 11) s 5, 22–23.

[96] Ibid, s 5, 61.

Interviewing in a Child-friendly Manner

The Court of Justice has recognised that Article 24 of the Charter requires that the State authorities should ensure that a hearing of the child should be conducted in a child-friendly manner. In *Aguirre Zarraga* it considered that where a court decides to hear the child, Article 24 of the Charter requires the court 'to take all measures which are appropriate to the arrangement of such a hearing, having regard to the child's best interests and the circumstances of each individual case, in order to ensure the effectiveness of those provisions, and to offer to the child a genuine and effective opportunity to express his or her views'.[97]

According to the ComRC interviews with children should take place in a friendly and safe atmosphere.[98] 'A child cannot be heard effectively where the environment is intimidating, hostile, insensitive or inappropriate for her or his age.'[99] Furthermore, it stated that 'the context in which a child exercises her or his right to be heard has to be enabling and encouraging, so that the child can be sure that the adult who is responsible for the hearing is willing to listen and seriously consider what the child has decided to communicate'.[100] In order to be able to express its views effectively the child should, according to the Committee, be well prepared for the interview. The decision-maker 'should provide explanations as to how, when and where the hearing will take place and who the participants will be, and has to take account of the views of the child in this regard'.[101]

Training of Interviewers

The ComRC believes that officials working with separated and unaccompanied children and dealing with their cases should be trained in appropriate interview techniques.[102] According to the Committee, interviews of unaccompanied minors in the context of the asylum procedure should be conducted by representatives of the refugee determination authority who will take into account the special situation of unaccompanied children in order to carry out the refugee status assessment and apply an understanding of the history, culture and background of the child.[103]

It is the UNHCR's position that 'personal interviews of children—whether they are accompanied, unaccompanied or separated—should be carried out by an interviewer who has special training and knowledge regarding the psychological and emotional development and behaviour of children'.[104] The UNHCR mentions that the training of the personnel of the determining authority charged with

[97] *Aguirre Zaraga* (n 43) para 66.

[98] ComRC, General Comment No 6 (n 48) para 20. See also UNHCR, *Guidelines on Child Asylum Claims* (n 36) para 72.

[99] ComRC, General Comment No 6 (n 48) para 34.

[100] ComRC, General Comment No 12 (n 46) paras 23 and 42.

[101] Ibid, para 41.

[102] ComRC, General Comment No 6 (n 48) para 96.

[103] Ibid, para 72.

[104] UNHCR, *Improving Asylum Procedures* (n 11) s 5, 21.

conducting the personal interview of children should include relevant human rights norms, standards and principles, including: the rights of the child; the impact and consequences of persecution, serious harm and trauma on children; and understanding of the effect of the child's age and stage of development on the child's recall of events and knowledge of conditions in the country of origin. Interviewers should furthermore have appropriate adult–child communication skills and must be able to use interview techniques that minimise trauma to the child while maximising the quality of information received from the child. Interviewers must finally have the skills to deal with children in a sensitive, understanding, constructive and reassuring manner.[105]

7.3 THE ASYLUM APPLICANT'S RIGHT TO BE HEARD FOLLOWING THE PERSONAL INTERVIEW

The question which will be addressed in this section is whether the asylum applicant's right to be heard under EU law is completely fulfilled by the personal interview. Should he also be offered the opportunity to add information to the report of the interview or to correct mistakes? Must he be able to comment on conclusions of the determining authority with regard to the credibility of his account, the value of other evidence underlying the assessment of the asylum claim and the risk of *refoulement* before the decision on the asylum application will be taken?

It is argued in this section that, although the Procedures Directive does not require the determining authorities to give the asylum applicant this opportunity, the EU right to be heard does. It follows from the EU right to be heard that the addressees of decisions which significantly affect their interests, such as asylum decisions, should be placed in a position in which they may effectively make known their views on the evidence on which the decision is based and the relevant facts and circumstances.[106] This implies that the asylum applicant should not only be able to present his asylum motives during the personal interview, but also to express his views regarding the fact-finding and assessment of the risk of *refoulement* by the determining authorities.

7.3.1 The Right to Comment on the Report of the Interview

Directive 2005/85/EC

Article 14(1) of Directive 2005/85/EC requires Member States to ensure that a written report of the personal interview be made 'containing at least the essential

[105] UNHCR, Improving Asylum *Procedures* (n 11) s 5, 21–22.

[106] See, eg Case C-28/05 *Dokter* [2006] ECR I-5431, para 74 and Case C-269/90 *Technische Universität München* [1991] ECR I-5469, para 25. See further ch 4, section 4.4.2 in this volume.

information regarding the application, as presented by the applicant'.[107] In this context, the provision refers to Article 4(2) of the Qualification Directive, which mentions the elements needed to substantiate the asylum claim: statements concerning the applicant's age, background (including that of relevant relatives), identity, nationality, country(ies) and place(s) of previous residence, previous asylum applications, travel routes, identity and travel documents and the reasons for applying for international protection. In many cases this report forms, together with the evidence submitted by the asylum applicant and the determining authorities as well as country of origin information, the basis of the decision on the asylum claim.[108] Directive 2005/85/EC does not give the applicant the right to comment on the contents of the report of the interview.[109] Article 14(3) of the Directive only states that Member States may request the applicant's approval of the contents of the report of the personal interview. Where an applicant refuses to approve the contents of the report, the reasons for this refusal shall be entered into the applicant's file.

The UNHCR stated in 2010 that practice with regard to checking the accuracy and changing the content of the report of the personal interview varies between Member States.[110] In some Member States the report is printed out immediately after the interview and read back to the applicant before he or she is asked to sign the document to confirm approval. In other Member States applicants are asked to sign the report, without being given the opportunity to read it or to have it read back to them.[111] In several Member States the written report of the interview is provided after the asylum decision has been taken.[112] The Commission noted in 2010 that the accuracy of records therefore varies.[113]

Directive 2013/32/EU

Article 17(1) of Directive 2013/32/EU obliges Member States to make a thorough and factual report containing all substantial elements or a transcript of every personal interview. Member States may choose to make an audio or audio-visual recording of the interview. The applicant shall be granted the opportunity to make comments and/or to provide clarification with regard to any mistranslations or misconceptions appearing in the report or the transcript. Such opportunity

[107] This provision also applies to interviews held in the context of border procedures (Art 35(3)(d) Dir 2005/85/EC) or procedures in which a refugee status is withdrawn (Art 38(1)(b)) as well as in cases in which a meeting was held with the applicant for the purpose of assisting him/her with completing his/her application and submitting the essential information regarding the application referred to in Art 12(2)(b) Dir 2005/85/EC (see Art 14(4) Dir 2005/85/EC).

[108] See further on evidentiary assessment ch 8, sections 8.4–8.5 in this volume.

[109] Commission Staff Working Document (n 10) 13.

[110] UNHCR, *Improving Asylum Procedures* (n 11) s 6, 11.

[111] Ibid, s 6, 12–17.

[112] The Commission mentions Belgium, Cyprus, France, Greece and Romania. Commission Report COM (2010) 465 final, 7. See also UNHCR, *Improving Asylum Procedures* (n 11) s 6, 19–20.

[113] Commission Report COM (2010) 465 final, 7. See also UNHCR, *Improving Asylum Procedures*, ibid, s 6.

should be given at the end of the personal interview or within a specified time limit before the asylum decision is made. To that end the applicant must be 'fully informed of the content of the report or the substantial elements of the transcript with the assistance of an interpreter if necessary'. No opportunity to provide comments or clarifications needs to be offered if the Member State provides for a transcript and a recording of the interview. Member States shall request the applicant to confirm that the content of the report or the transcript correctly reflects the interview.[114] Where the applicant refuses to do so, the reasons for this should be entered on the applicant's file.[115] Member States do not need to request such confirmation if the audio(-visual) recording is admissible as evidence.[116]

The EU Right to be Heard

In the light of the crucial role of the statements of the asylum applicant as evidence in the asylum procedure, it is of utmost importance for the quality of the decision that the written report of the personal interview is complete and that the information contained in it is accurate.[117] Gaps or mistakes in the report may occur as a result of disturbed communication, faults or omissions by interpreters or the person drawing the report.[118] In order to ensure the accuracy and completeness of the report and thus an adequate examination of the case within the meaning of Article 8 of Directive 2005/85/EC and Article 10(3) of Directive 2013/32/EU, it may be considered necessary for the person concerned or his representative to be able to examine this report and correct mistakes or fill in gaps.

Arguably, Article 14(3) of Directive 2005/85/EC read in the light of the EU right to be heard requires that the applicant be granted the opportunity to comment on the report of the interview, in particular when the determining authority intends to reject the asylum application on the basis of the information included in the report. If, for example, the determining authority finds the statements of the applicant as written down in the report inconsistent, contradictory, vague or incomplete and thus not credible, the applicant should be able to respond to those allegations.

Access to the Report or Transcript

The EU right to be heard requires that the parties concerned must be informed of the evidence adduced against them.[119] Article 14(2) of Directive 2005/85/

[114] Art 17(3) Dir 2013/32/EU.

[115] Art 17(4) Dir 2013/32/EU.

[116] Art 17(3) Dir 2013/32/EU.

[117] See also UNHCR, *Improving Asylum Procedures* (n 11) s 6, 2.

[118] Doornbos, *Op verhaal komen* (n 63) 45. She states that research from States other than the Netherlands are critical of the quality of reports of the interview. The UNHCR in 2010 expressed grave concerns about the quality of the reports of interviews in Greece. It found during its observations of interviews in Athens that the written summary reports made of personal interviews did not reflect the oral evidence given by the applicant at all. UNHCR, *Improving Asylum Procedures* (n 11) s 6, 7–9.

[119] Case T-228/02 *Organisation des Modjahedines du peuple d'Iran v Council* [2006] ECR II-4665, para 93. Case C-32/95P *Commission v Lisrestal et al* [1996] ECR I-5373, para 41. See also Case T-49/88 *Al-Jubail Fertilizer v Council* [1991] para 17.

EC requires that Member States ensure that applicants have timely access to the report of the personal interview. However, this provision allows that access to the report is only granted after the decision on the application. If the Member State chooses to make use of this option, access must be made possible as early as necessary for allowing an appeal to be prepared and lodged in due time.[120] Such late provision of the report of the interview may infringe the EU right to be heard, as the person concerned must, in principle, according to the standing case law of the Court of Justice, be able to exercise this right before the administrative decision is adopted.[121] Furthermore, it should be derived from this case law that the person concerned must be afforded a reasonable period to put forward his views effectively.[122] The content of the report of the interview should thus be made known to the applicant while he is still able to effectively exercise his right to be heard.

Article 17(5) of Directive 2013/32/EU better ensures the effective exercise of the EU right to be heard as it requires in principle that the applicant and his legal adviser or other counseller have access to the report, the transcript and/or the recording of the interview before the asylum decision is taken. However, in accelerated proceedings, the determining authority may only provide access to the report, transcript or recording at the same time as the decision is made. Furthermore, recordings may be made available only during the appeal proceedings if the applicant has been provided with a transcript of the interview. In particular, the first exception to the rule of access to the report or transcript in accelerated proceedings may infringe the EU right to be heard.

7.3.2 The Right to Comment on the Fact-finding and Risk Assessment

After the personal interview(s) the determining authority will establish the facts and assess the credibility of the asylum account. Following the establishment of the facts, it is decided whether there is a real risk of *refoulement* upon return to the country of origin or transfer to a third country. The determining authority may include evidence in these assessments on which the applicant has not had the opportunity to comment. The question arises whether the claimant should be heard on the conclusions of the decision-making authority concerning fact-finding and risk assessment. This could be done, for example, by offering the claimant the opportunity to comment on these conclusions (and the evidence on which they are based) in an oral hearing or by submitting written observations.

[120] According to the explanations of the Commission with the amended proposal for the Procedures Directive this provision reflects the principle of a fair and effective procedure. It is meant to enable the applicant to exercise his appeal rights properly and to enable appellate bodies, where appropriate, to verify whether the decision is based on relevant information. Amended proposal (n 17) 8–9.

[121] *Technische Universität München* (n 106) para 25, Joined Cases C-379/08 and C-380/08 *ERG et al* [2010] paras 54–56 and *Dokter* (n 106) para 74.

[122] Case C-462/98 P *Mediocurso v Commission* [2000] ECR I-7183, para 38.

The Procedures Directive does not provide for a right to be heard on the conclusions reached by the determining authority. Article 16 of Directive 2013/32/EU provides that during the personal interview the applicant must be offered the opportunity to give an explanation regarding elements which may be missing and/or any inconsistencies or contradictions in his or her statements.

A right to be informed of and comment on the fact-finding and risk assessment by the determining authority may be derived from Article 4(1) of the Qualification Directive, which states that the Member State has a duty to assess the relevant elements of the application in cooperation with the applicant.[123] According to Noll, this provision entails far-reaching obligations to communicate, for both the Member State and the applicant. The Member State should allow the applicant to participate in the assessment of the evidence.[124]

The Case Law of the Court of Justice

In the case of *MM* the Court of Justice was asked whether the duty of cooperation laid down in Article 4(1) of the Qualification Directive entails an obligation for the Member States to supply the applicant, before the adoption of the negative decision on that application with the elements on which it intends to base its decision and to seek the applicant's observations in that regard. The Court answered the question in the negative. It considered that the assessment of the asylum claim takes place in two stages.

> The first stage concerns the establishment of the factual circumstances which may constitute evidence that supports the application, while the second stage relates to the legal appraisal of that evidence, which entails deciding whether, in the specific circumstances of the case the substantive conditions … for the grant of international protection are met.[125]

The Court finds that the duty of cooperation only relates to the first stage of the procedure, while the question put before the Court in *MM* related to the second stage. In this second stage a duty to cooperate is, according to the Court of Justice, of no relevance. The Court adds that the Qualification Directive does not seek to determine the procedural guarantees which must be provided to asylum applicants. At the same time, however, the Court stressed that observance of the EU right to be heard must be ensured. In Ireland where the case of *MM* was processed, separate procedures exist for the examination of eligibility for refugee status and subsidiary protection. The applicant had been heard in the context of the refugee status determination procedure, but not in the second procedure regarding his application for subsidiary protection. For the purpose of the second procedure the applicant only filled out a questionnaire. The Court of Justice did

[123] Battjes (n 18) 226.

[124] G Noll, *Evidentiary Assessment and the EU Qualification Directive, New Issues in Refugee Research, Working Paper No 117* (Geneva, UNHCR, 2005) 4.

[125] *MM* (n 2) para 64.

not agree with the view of the Irish authorities and the referring court that where an applicant is heard in the first procedure, it is not necessary to hear him again in the second procedure. The Court of Justice stated that the applicant's right to be heard, given its fundamental nature, should be fully respected in both procedures. The Court pointed at the fact that the conditions which must be fulfilled for the grant of refugee status and for the awarding of subsidiary protection status as well as the nature of the rights attaching to them are different. It leaves it to the national court to decide whether the EU right to be heard is respected in the procedure in which the application for subsidiary protection was assessed.[126] The Court of Justice thus did not exclude the possibility that the fact that the applicant did not have the opportunity to respond to the elements on which the determining authority intends to base its decision, may violate the EU right to be heard.

In this regard it should be noted that it may be derived from the EU Courts' case law concerning the EU right to be heard discussed in section 4.4.2 that the addressee of an asylum decision has a right to effectively make known his views on the evidence on which this decision is based and the relevant facts and circumstances taken into account, before the decision is taken. The EU right to be heard may require that a draft decision is submitted to the party concerned.[127] Therefore, arguably the EU right to be heard requires that the applicant be heard on important evidence relied on and the main conclusions reached by the determining authority. If the applicant did not have the opportunity to comment on such evidence and conclusions during the personal interview, in response to the written report of the personal interview or otherwise, he should be granted this opportunity before the negative decision is taken. This is especially the case if the applicant's comments concerning the fact-finding or credibility assessment cannot be fully taken into account in the appeal phase as a result of a limited judicial review of the fact-finding by the national court.[128]

Obligations Stemming from the ECHR

This view is supported by the ECtHR's judgment in *IM* In this case the applicant's asylum application was rejected in essence because his statements during the interview were very imprecise and inaccurate with regard to his ethnic origin and his family's origin from the Darfur region. According to the French determining authority the applicant's origin could, therefore, not be established. Furthermore, it was stated in the decision that the applicant's statements regarding the applicant's involvement in a student movement, the circumstances of his arrest, the conditions of his detention, and the reasons for his release were not sufficiently precise and credible. The fact that the applicant was not granted the opportunity

[126] *MM* (n 2) paras 81–94.

[127] *Mediocurso* (n 122) para 42.

[128] See ch 9, section 9.2 in this volume. It is argued in this section that Arts 39 Dir 2005/85/EC and 46 Dir 2013/32/EU require a thorough judicial review of the asylum decision.

to dispute these allegations orally or in writing, even though he could have explained alleged inconsistencies and submitted missing documents, was one of the factors leading to a violation of Article 13 ECHR in this case.[129]

Furthermore, the ECtHR has held that asylum applicants must be in a position to effectively comment on the decision-making authority's conclusions as to the credibility of the asylum account or the authenticity of the documents submitted by the applicant. According to the ECtHR the individual must provide a satisfactory explanation for the alleged discrepancies, when the examining authorities present information which gives strong reason to question the veracity of an asylum applicant's submissions.[130] Furthermore, it ruled that when the authorities examined documents adduced by the applicant and give detailed reasons why they consider these documents to be forgeries, the applicant has to contest these allegations.[131] This implies that the applicant must be in a position to present its views on the authority's conclusions during the asylum proceedings.

Conclusion

On the basis of the ECtHR's case law the EU right to be heard should potentially be considered to include a right to contest the decision-making authorities' main conclusions as to the credibility of the asylum account, the assessment of the evidence and the existence of a risk of *refoulement* upon return. The EU right to be heard also requires that the determining authority's conclusions be made available to the applicant and that the applicant have access to the evidence underlying the (concept) asylum decision.

7.4 THE RIGHT TO AN ORAL HEARING BEFORE A COURT OR TRIBUNAL

In chapter nine it will be concluded that the right to an effective remedy guaranteed by Article 39 of Directive 2005/85/EC and Article 46 of Directive 2013/32/EU requires a thorough judicial review of the asylum decision. This entails the national courts reviewing asylum decisions on points of fact as well as points of law. Furthermore, it implies as a minimum that the national court or tribunal assesses the claim of a risk of *refoulement* on its merits. It should carefully examine the facts and evidence underlying the asylum claim.

The question which will be addressed in this section is whether the national court is obliged to hear the asylum applicant in the context of his appeal against the refusal of his asylum claim. It will be argued that Article 39 of Directive 2005/85/EC and Article 46 of Directive 2013/32/EU read in the light of Article 47 of the Charter requires that the asylum applicant is heard in an oral hearing by the

[129] *IM* (n 25) para 147.

[130] See *RC* (n 20) para 50, ECtHR (Adm) 8 March 2007, *Collin and Akaziebie v Sweden*, no 23944/05.

[131] ECtHR (Adm) 21 June 2005, *Matsiukhina and Matsiukhin v Sweden*, no 31260/04.

court or tribunal assessing the appeal against the negative asylum decision if this court decides on factual issues, including the credibility of the applicant's asylum account. According to the UNHCR report of 2010 in several Member States the national court may decide on the appeal against the negative asylum decision without holding an oral hearing.[132]

Article 39 of Directive 2005/85/EC and Article 46 of Directive 2013/32/EU do not contain standards with regard to the right to a public and oral hearing. Article 47 of the Charter provides that everyone is entitled to a fair and public hearing by an independent and impartial tribunal. The Court of Justice has not yet interpreted the EU right to a public hearing. No judgments were found in the context of this study which addressed the right to an oral hearing in the light of the right to an effective remedy. However, the ECtHR has developed an extensive body of case law regarding the right to an oral hearing under Article 6 ECHR. It is argued here that Article 47 of the Charter should be interpreted in conformity with this case law.

Obligations Stemming from the ECtHR

The ECtHR has not ruled on the question whether Article 13 ECHR requires that asylum applicants be heard by an independent authority. However, it should be reiterated that the ECtHR has recognised the importance of an oral hearing particularly for the assessment of the credibility of the asylum applicant's statements.[133]

Like Article 47 of the Charter, Article 6 ECHR provides for a right to a 'fair and public hearing'. According to the standing case law of the ECtHR the right to a public hearing includes the right to an oral hearing before a court or tribunal.[134] The ECtHR is of the opinion that the right to a public hearing, which applies in both criminal and civil cases, is a right of a fundamental nature.[135]

The obligation to hold a hearing is not absolute. A hearing may be dispensed with if a party unequivocally waives his or her right thereto and there are no questions of public interest to make a hearing necessary.[136] Furthermore, the ECtHR assesses the overall fairness of the procedure. An oral hearing does not have to take place in every instance before a court or tribunal. The absence of a hearing before a second or third instance may be justified by the special features of the proceedings at issue,[137] in particular the fact that the appellate or cassation court

[132] UNHCR, *Improving Asylum Procedures* (n 11) s 16, 58–60.

[133] See further section 7.1.

[134] ECtHR (GC) 23 November 2006, *Jussila v Finland*, no 73053/01, para 40.

[135] ECtHR (GC) 11 July 2002, *Göç v Turkey*, no 36590/97, para 46; *Jussila* (n 134) para 40.

[136] A waiver can be made explicitly or tacitly, in the latter case, for example, by refraining from submitting or maintaining a request for a hearing. See, eg ECtHR 12 November 2002, *Döry v Sweden*, no 28394/95, para 37.

[137] See, eg *Döry* ibid, para 39.

is only competent to review questions of law.[138] The absence of an oral hearing may, however, not undermine the right to adversarial proceedings and the principle of equality of arms.[139]

The complete absence of an oral hearing before a court or tribunal in a procedure can only be justified in exceptional circumstances.[140] The circumstances that may justify dispensing with an oral hearing depend on the type of the issues to be decided by the competent national court. The frequency of these situations is not relevant: Article 6(1) ECHR does not mean that the absence of an oral hearing may only be justified in rare cases.[141] The Court has accepted exceptional circumstances in cases where proceedings concerned exclusively legal or highly technical questions. The ECtHR held, for example, 'that disputes concerning benefits under social-security schemes are generally rather technical and their outcome usually depends on the written opinions given by medical doctors. Many such disputes may accordingly be better dealt with in writing than in oral argument'.[142]

Furthermore, an oral hearing may be dispensed with when a case 'raises no questions of fact or law which cannot be adequately resolved on the basis of the case-file and the parties' written observations'.[143] As an example of such cases the ECtHR mentions cases 'where there are no issues of credibility or contested facts'.[144] In *Jussilla* the ECtHR considered that 'checking and ensuring that the taxpayer has given an accurate account of his or her affairs and that supporting documents have been properly produced may often be more efficiently dealt with in writing than in oral argument'. It was not persuaded by the applicant that in this particular case any issues of credibility arose in the proceedings which required oral presentation of evidence or cross-examination of witnesses.[145]

If questions concerning facts or credibility are at issue in the first instance or second instance appeal procedure, the ECtHR is generally of the opinion that an oral hearing should be held.[146] The ECtHR ruled on the necessity of an oral hearing in several cases in which the applicant had claimed compensation before the national court for damage suffered as a result of alleged unlawful detention. In these cases, when deciding on the level of compensation, the national court had regard to a series of personal factors, namely the financial and social status

[138] According to the ECtHR 'proceedings for leave to appeal or proceedings involving only questions of law, as opposed to questions of fact, may comply with the requirements of Article 6 even where the appellant was not given an opportunity of being heard in person by the appeal or cassation court'. ECtHR (GC) 26 July 2002, *Meftah et al v France*, nos 32911/96, 35237/97 and 34595/97, para 41. See also ECtHR (Plen) 26 May 1988, *Ekbatani v Sweden*, no 10563/83, para 32.

[139] ECtHR 25 March 1998, *Belziuk v Poland*, no 23103/93, para 39.

[140] See, eg *Döry* (n 136) para 39.

[141] *Jussila* (n 134) para 42.

[142] *Döry* (n 136) para 41.

[143] Ibid, para 37.

[144] *Jussila* (n 134) para 41.

[145] Ibid, para 47.

[146] ECtHR (GC) 12 July 2001, *Malhous v the Czech Republic*, no 33071/96, para 60, ECtHR 25 April 1995, *Fischer v Austria*, no 16922/90, para 44 and ECtHR 12 February 2013, *Krastev v Bulgaria*, no 26524/04, para 63.

of the applicant and, in particular, the extent of the emotional suffering which he endured during the period of his detention. According to the ECtHR, an oral hearing could not be dispensed with in these cases because of 'the essentially personal nature of the applicant's experience, and the determination of the appropriate level of compensation'. It considered:

> While it is true that the fact of the applicant's detention and the length of that detention as well as his financial and social status could be established on the basis of the report drawn up by the judge rapporteur and without the need to hear the applicant ... different considerations must apply to assessment of the emotional suffering which the applicant alleged he endured. In the Court's opinion, the applicant should have been afforded an opportunity to explain orally to the Karşıyaka Assize Court the moral damage which his detention entailed for him in terms of distress and anxiety.[147]

In the ECtHR's view the administration of justice and the accountability of the State would have been better served in the applicant's case by affording him the right to explain his personal situation in a hearing before the domestic court subject to public scrutiny.[148]

When deciding whether the omission of an oral hearing is justified, the ECtHR takes into account the interests at stake for the applicant. In *Fischer*, for example, it had due regard 'to the importance of the proceedings in question for the very existence of Mr Fischer's tipping business'.[149] However, the ECtHR also held that 'the fact that proceedings are of considerable personal significance to the applicant, as in certain social insurance or benefit cases, is not decisive for the necessity of a hearing'.[150]

Furthermore, the ECtHR has acknowledged that the national authorities may have regard to the demands of efficiency and economy.[151] Systematically holding hearings could, for instance, be an obstacle to the particular diligence required in social security cases.[152] In determining the necessity of a public hearing at stages in the proceedings subsequent to the trial at first instance considerations such as the right to trial within a reasonable time and the related need for expeditious handling of the courts' case load must be taken into account.[153] In the cases mentioned above in which compensation was claimed for damage suffered as a result of unlawful detention, the ECtHR held that the interests served by an oral hearing outweighed the considerations of speed and efficiency on which the absence of an oral hearing was based.[154] Furthermore, where the party concerned is detained,

[147] *Göç* (n 135) para 51.
[148] Ibid, para 51; ECtHR 20 October 2005, *Ozata v Turkey*, no 19578/02, para 36.
[149] *Fischer* (n 146) para 44. See also ECtHR (Plen) 29 October 1991, *Helmers v Sweden*, no 11826/85, para 38, where the ECtHR referred to the seriousness of what was at stake for the applicant, namely his professional reputation and career.
[150] *Jussila* (n 134) para 44.
[151] Ibid, para 42.
[152] *Döry* (n 136) para 41.
[153] *Helmers* (n 149) para 36.
[154] *Göç* (n 135) para 51.

the applicant's participation in the proceedings may also be ensured by holding a session by way of a video link or in the detention facility, in so far as it is possible under the rules on court jurisdiction.[155]

Finally, it is relevant to note that the ECtHR has ruled in criminal cases that Article 6 ECHR also includes the right of the person concerned to hear and follow the proceedings before the court or tribunal and generally to participate effectively in them.

> Such rights are implicit in the very notion of an adversarial procedure and can also be derived from the guarantees contained in sub-paragraphs (c), (d) and (e) of paragraph 3 of Article 6 … 'to defend himself in person', 'to examine or have examined witnesses', and 'to have the free assistance of an interpreter if he cannot understand or speak the language used in court'.[156]

The ECtHR considered that in the case of a child, it is essential that he be dealt with in a manner which takes full account of his age, level of maturity and intellectual and emotional capacities, and that steps are taken to promote his ability to understand and participate in the proceedings.[157] The right to adversarial proceedings also applies in civil law cases as well as cases falling within the scope of Articles 5 and 13 ECHR.[158] It is, therefore, conceivable that the right to participate effectively in a hearing before a court or tribunal also applies in such cases.

Application to Asylum Cases

On the basis of the case law of the ECtHR it may be argued that the right to a public hearing within the meaning of Article 47 of the Charter should include the right to an oral hearing. The absence of an oral hearing, particularly in first instance appeal proceedings, is only allowed in exceptional cases. The ECtHR's case law indicates that an oral hearing is necessary in cases in which a court or tribunal needs to decide on factual issues, in which the credibility of the person concerned is disputed or in which the personal experiences of the person concerned play an important role.

As mentioned earlier, asylum cases often hinge on the credibility of the applicant's asylum account. Furthermore, the personal experiences of the asylum applicant in the country of origin are important for the assessment of his individual risk of *refoulement* upon return.[159] It should be derived from the ECtHR's case law that a court which reviews the asylum decision on such factual grounds should in principle hold an oral hearing. The fact that in asylum cases the fundamental nature of the EU right to asylum and the prohibition of *refoulement* are at stake

[155] ECtHR 10 January 2012, *Valsilyev v Russia*, no 28370/05, para 84.

[156] ECtHR 23 February 1994, *Stanford v the United Kingdom*, no 16757/90, para 26.

[157] ECtHR 16 December 1999, *V v the United Kingdom*, no 24888/94, para 86 and ECtHR 15 June 2004, *SC v the United Kingdom*, no 60958/00, para 28.

[158] See further ch 10, section 10.5 in this volume.

[159] See further ch 8, sections 8.1 and 8.2.1 in this volume.

adds to the need for an oral hearing. For example, an oral hearing is less crucial if the disputed facts do not concern the individual asylum seeker, but only the seriousness of the general human rights situation in his country of origin. The court may include in its decision whether to hold an oral hearing, the interest of both Member States and applicants for asylum in deciding on applications for asylum as promptly as possible.[160] It should thus be concluded that there are strong arguments that Article 39 of Directive 2005/85/EC and Article 46 of Directive 2013/32/EU, read in the light of Article 47 of the Charter, generally require an oral hearing before the (first instance) court or tribunal hearing the appeal against the rejection of the asylum claim.

Furthermore, it should be derived from the ECtHR's case law under Article 6 ECHR that the right to an oral hearing can only be effectively exercised if the person concerned is able to hear and follow the proceedings before the court or tribunal and generally to participate effectively in them. Therefore, arguably the EU right to a fair trial requires, for example, that in asylum cases free interpretation services are available for asylum applicants who do not understand the language spoken in the court.[161]

7.5 SYNTHESIS OF FINDINGS

Asylum applicants must be granted sufficient opportunity to substantiate their claim that their return will violate the prohibition of *refoulement*. Often these applicants are themselves the most important source of information as to the risk of *refoulement*, for example because there is no evidence supporting the claim and/or because their personal experiences play an important role in the assessment of this risk. The following conclusions have been drawn in this chapter with regard to the asylum applicant's right to be heard.

The Right to a Personal Interview

— A personal interview is indispensable in order to fulfil the requirement to carry out an appropriate examination of the asylum claim within the meaning of Article 8(2) of Directive 2005/85/EC and Article 10(3) of Directive 2013/32/EU. The ECtHR's case law indicates that a personal interview with the applicant is crucial for the assessment of the credibility of the applicant's asylum account. According to the ECtHR, the absence of such an interview is a factor which may contribute to a violation of Articles 3 and 13 ECHR.[162] Other sources of inspiration have also pointed to the importance of a

[160] Recital 11 Preamble Dir 2005/85/EC and recital 18 Preamble Dir 2013/32/EU.

[161] See also ComAT, Concluding Observations on France (20 May 2010, CAT/C/FRA/CO/4–6) para 15.

[162] *Charahili* (n 22) para 57 and *IM* (n 25) para 155.

personal interview in all asylum cases, including cases considered manifestly unfounded and/or examined in an accelerated procedure.[163]

- Therefore, exceptions to the right to a personal interview, in particular those allowed for by Article 12(2) of Directive 2005/85/EC, may only be applied in exceptional cases.
- The determining authority of the Member State should ensure that the EU right to *refoulement* will not be undermined as a result of the absence of an interview. The asylum applicant should be given sufficient opportunity to substantiate his asylum claim, for example, by submitting written information.
- Article 12 of Directive 2005/85/EC leaves it to the Member States to decide when dependent adults are offered a personal interview. Nevertheless, it may be argued that the determining authorities should investigate whether dependent adults have independent asylum motives which could best be explained in a personal interview.[164] Under Directive 2013/32/EU dependent adults have a right to a personal interview.
- Article 24 of the Charter limits the Member State's discretion to interview minor asylum applicants. A minor asylum applicant should in principle be interviewed if he so wishes and if the age and maturity of the child permits. Only if an interview is not considered to be in the best interests of the child, for example, because it would cause harm to the child, should an interview be omitted.[165]

Requirements as to the Conduct of the Interview

- It follows from Article 13(3) of Directive 2005/85/EC and Article 15(3) of Directive 2013/32/EU, as well as several (non-binding) sources of inspiration, that the right to a personal interview can only be exercised effectively if the conditions under which interviews are conducted allow applicants to present the grounds for their applications in a comprehensive manner.
- This means that the interviewer should be able to communicate effectively with the applicant. The principle of effectiveness requires the determining authority to ascertain that the applicant is actually able to understand the language chosen for the interview and that he can express himself effectively in that language.[166]

[163] See notably Committee of Ministers of the Council of Europe, Guidelines on human rights protection in the context of accelerated asylum procedures (n 28) para IV 1.d and Parliamentary Assembly of the Council of Europe, *Resolution 1471* (n 28) para 8.10.2 and EXCOM Conclusion no 30 (n 29).

[164] UNHCR, *Improving Asylum Procedures* (n 11) s 4, 15; UNHCR, *Guidelines on Gender-Related Persecution* (n 35) para 36.

[165] *Aguirre Zaraga* (n 43) paras 64–65; ComRC, General Comment No 12 (n 46) para 123; and General Comment No 6 (n 48) para 71.

[166] Parliamentary Assembly of the Council of Europe, *Resolution 1471* (n 28) para 8.10.2; UNHCR, *Improving Asylum Procedures* (n 11) s 5, 29 and 44; and UNHCR *Provisional Comments* (n 67) 13.

- If the applicant does not understand the language of the interview the Member State should provide a competent and qualified interpreter free of charge to facilitate communication. If no such interpreter is available, the determining authority should take this into account when examining the case.[167]
- The interviewer must be competent and properly trained to interview asylum applicants.
- On the basis of several non-binding sources of inspiration it may be argued that Article 13 of Directive 2005/85/EC means that interviews be conducted in a gender-sensitive manner.[168] Article 15(3) of Directive 2013/32/EU contains several important guarantees with regard to the gender-sensitivity of the interview, such as an interviewer of the same sex.
- It follows from the Court of Justice's judgment in *Aguirra Zarraga*, as well as the views of the Committee on the Rights of the Child and the UNHCR, that Article 24 of the Charter requires that minors be heard in a child-friendly manner.[169] This obligation also follows from Article 15(3)(e) of Directive 2013/32/EU.

The Asylum Applicant's Right to be Heard Following the Personal Interview

- The fact that the applicant was interviewed about his reasons for seeking asylum is not necessarily enough for the Member State to comply with the EU right to be heard.
- It is conceivable that the EU right to be heard requires that the applicant be granted the opportunity to comment on the report of the personal interview. This is so particularly if the determining authority intends to reject the asylum application on the basis of the information contained in the report and the applicant was not able to comment on this information during the interview. Such a right has been included in Article 17 of Directive 2013/32/EU for the first time. The applicant should have timely access to the report of the interview in order to be able to exercise his right to be heard.[170]
- The EU right to be heard obliges the Member States at one stage of the administrative procedure to hear the asylum applicant on its main conclusions regarding the fact-finding (including the assessment of the credibility of the asylum account) and the assessment of the risk of *refoulement* as well

[167] Arts 10(1)(b) and 13(3)(b) Dir 2005/85/EC and Arts 12(1)(b) and 15(3)(c). See also *MSS* (n 76) para 301 and *IM* (n 25) para 145.

[168] Council resolution on minimum guarantees for asylum procedures (n 69) para 28, EXCOM Conclusion no 64 (n 91), HRC Concluding Observations on Austria 2007 (n 90) para 18 and ComAT, Concluding Observations on Austria 2005 (n 90).

[169] *Aguirre Zaraga* (n 43) para 66, ComRC, General Comment No 6 (n 48) paras 20 and 34, UNHCR, *Guidelines on Child Asylum Claims* (n 36) para 72.

[170] The EU right to be heard requires that the parties concerned be informed of the evidence adduced against them. See, eg *Organisation des Modjahedines du peuple d'Iran* (n 119) para 93.

as important pieces of evidence on which these conclusions are based. This is particularly relevant if the applicant's comments concerning the fact-finding or credibility assessment cannot be fully taken into taken into account in the appeal phase as a result of a limited judicial review of the fact-finding by the national court.[171]

The Right to a Hearing before a Court or Tribunal

— It follows from the ECtHR's case law under Article 6 ECHR that the right to a public hearing guaranteed by Article 47 includes the right to an oral hearing before a court or tribunal.[172]
— Article 39 of Directive 2005/85/EC and Article 46 of Directive 2013/32/EU read in the light of Article 47 of the Charter arguably requires that in principle an oral hearing be held before the first instance court or tribunal reviewing the negative decision on the asylum claim.
— The ECtHR's case law indicates that an oral hearing is especially indispensable when the court decides on important questions of fact or the credibility of the applicant and where the applicant's personal experiences play an important role.[173]
— It should be derived from the ECtHR's case law under Article 6 ECHR that Article 47 of the Charter requires the Member States to ensure that the applicant is able to hear and follow the proceedings before the court or tribunal and generally to participate effectively in them.[174]

[171] *MM* (n 2); *IM* (n 25) para 147.
[172] *Jussila* (n 134) para 40.
[173] Ibid, paras 41 and 47 and *Göç* (n 135) para 51.
[174] *Stanford* (n 156) para 26.

8

The Burden and Standard of Proof and Evidentiary Assessment

ON THE BASIS of the applicant's statements made during the personal interview and the other evidence available, the determining authority shall assess whether the applicant is in need of international protection and whether he qualifies as a refugee or as a person eligible for subsidiary protection. Establishing the facts in asylum cases is not easy. In most asylum cases there is a lack of documentary evidence with regard to the asylum applicant's personal situation. Often the applicant's statements are the only evidence available. The assessment of the credibility of the applicant's asylum account is therefore usually an important part of the decision-making process. Cultural and linguistic differences between the applicant and the examining authorities may complicate the establishment of the facts. Furthermore, the determining authorities need to assess whether there is a future risk of *refoulement*. This means that there are no certainties which can be established.[1]

Evidentiary rules for asylum cases vary considerably among Member States of the EU, in particular between common law and civil law systems.[2] Rules concerning the standard and burden of proof and evidentiary assessment are decisive for the outcome of asylum proceedings. It is argued in this chapter that evidentiary rules or practices which make unreasonable demands on the asylum applicant undermine the effective exercise of the EU right to asylum and the prohibition of *refoulement*. Examples of such rules and practices include: a standard of proof which is set too high; the authorities' refusal to apply the benefit of the doubt; their unwillingness to share the burden of proof; the use of presumptions which are (practically) impossible for the applicant to rebut; a credibility assessment on the basis of details which are not part of the core of the asylum account; and a failure to take into account or to recognise the value of certain types of evidence.

[1] See I Staffans, *Evidence in European Asylum Procedures* (Leiden/Boston, Martinus Nijhoff, 2012) 42–50 and R Thomas, 'Assessing the Credibility of Asylum Claims, EU and UK Approaches Examined' (2006) 8 *European Journal of Migration and Law* 79, 84.

[2] See, eg UNHCR, *Note on Burden and Standard of Proof in Refugee Claims* (16 December 1998) www.refworld.org/docid/3ae6b3338.html accessed 25 September 2013, para 3; B Gorlick, 'Common Burdens and Standards: Legal Elements in Assessing Claims to Refugee Status' (2003) 15 *International Journal of Refugee Law* 357, 361.

This chapter examines which standards relating to the standard and burden of proof and evidentiary assessment follow from EU law. In particular, in Article 4 of the Qualification Directive (concerning the assessment of facts and circumstances) and Article 8(2) of Directive 2005/85/EC and Article 10(3) of Directive 2013/32/EU (requirement of an appropriate and careful examination of the asylum claim), aim to harmonise the Member State's legislation as regards evidence. However, they leave many important evidentiary issues untouched. It may be assumed in the light of the importance of evidentiary rules for the effective exercise of the prohibition of *refoulement* that evidentiary issues which are not explicitly governed by the Qualification Directive or Procedures Directive also fall within the scope of EU law. They may therefore be addressed by the Court of Justice in the light of the principle of effectiveness. It follows from the case law of the Court of Justice that any requirement of proof which has the effect of making it virtually impossible or excessively difficult to exercise a right granted by EU law would be incompatible with EU law.[3] The Court of Justice has assessed national evidentiary rules in the light of this principle in several fields of EU law such as equal treatment, State aid and the Member State's duty to repay charges levied contrary to EU law. The underlying principles emerging from this case law should be considered relevant in asylum cases.

It is conceivable, however, that the specific nature of asylum cases requires special evidentiary rules. Therefore, in this chapter the case law of the European Court of Human Rights (ECtHR) and other supervising bodies, which specifically addresses evidentiary issues in asylum cases is considered significant. The ECtHR has held that Article 6(1) European Convention on Human Rights (ECHR) does not lay down any rules on the admissibility of evidence as such, which is therefore primarily a matter for regulation under national law.[4] For this reason no attention is paid to the ECtHR's case law under that provision.

The issues addressed in this chapter are all interlinked and sometimes overlap. It is useful, therefore, to make some preliminary remarks as to their mutual relationship. Section 8.1 on the standard of proof addresses the question what needs to be proved. In asylum cases the most important question is how likely the risk of future harm should be in order for the applicant to qualify as a refugee or a person in need of subsidiary protection.[5] Section 8.2 regarding the burden of proof examines who bears the risk (the applicant or the State) if the standard of proof is not met and who bears the burden of producing evidence in support of the asylum claim. A particularly heavy burden of proof is placed on the applicant when the Member State makes use of certain presumptions. In section 8.3 the use of such presumptions is examined in the light of the duty to conduct an individual examination of the asylum claim. Finally, sections 8.4 and 8.5 address the assessment of the evidence produced by the applicant and the State in the

[3] Case C-199/82 *SpA San Giorgio* [1983] ECR I-3595, para 14.
[4] ECtHR 18 March 1997, *Mantovanelli v France*, no 21497/93, para 34.
[5] See also Staffans, *Evidence* (n 1) 97.

context of the asylum application. They examine which types of evidence should be taken into account and what value should be attributed to them. Section 8.4 specifically concerns the statements of the applicant. It addresses, amongst other issues, the question when the determining authority should grant the applicant the benefit of the doubt in the assessment of the credibility of the asylum account. Section 8.5 covers other types of evidence such as documentary evidence and expert reports. Some aspects of the asylum claim may have consequences for several of the issues mentioned. For example, if the applicant was persecuted or had been subjected to serious harm in his country of origin the standard of proof is (nearly) met and at the same time the burden of proof shifts from the applicant to the State. Furthermore, the importance which should be attributed to this fact arguably requires that evidence, such as medical reports supporting past torture or ill-treatment, may not be ignored by the determining authority.

8.1 THE STANDARD OF PROOF

This section examines the standard of proof which should be met in order to qualify for asylum status or to be protected from *refoulement*. The central questions with regard to the standard of proof in asylum cases are first how likely the risk of persecution or serious harm must be,[6] and secondly which indicators should be taken into account in order to assess this risk.

The Qualification Directive does not provide standards with regard to the likelihood of the risk.[7] Therefore, Member States are in principle allowed to maintain or introduce their own national requirements regarding the standard of proof. However, it is submitted in this section that EU law prohibits Member States from setting the standard of proof too high, because this will undermine the full effectiveness of the EU prohibition of *refoulement* and the right to asylum.[8] It follows from the principle of effectiveness that Member States cannot require asylum applicants to prove something which is impossible or excessively difficult to prove.[9] In particular, it is argued that Member States may not require that a future risk of persecution or serious harm be *proved*. Moreover, the standard of

[6] G Noll (ed), *Evidentiary Assessment and the EU Qualification Directive, New Issues in Refugee Research, Working Paper No 117* (Geneva, UNHCR, 2005) 3; and Gorlick, 'Common Burdens' (n 2) 367.

[7] Noll, *Evidentiary Assessment* ibid, 3. The proposal for Dire 2004/83/EC provided that there had to be a 'reasonable possibility' of persecution or serious harm. This was, however, deleted during the negotiations because the Member States could not agree on a risk criteria. K Hailbronner, *EU Immigration and Asylum Law, Commentary on EU Regulations and Directives* (Munich, CH Beck/Hart Publishing/Nomos, 2010) 1026–27.

[8] See also V Trstenjak and E Beysen, 'European Consumer Protection Law: *Curia Semper Dabit Remedium*?' (2011) 48 *Common Market Law Review* 95, 101.

[9] See Case C-435/03 *British American Tobacco and Newman Shipping* [2005] ECR I-7077, para 28; and Case C-31/09 *Bolbol* [2010] ECR I-5539, Opinion of AG Sharpston, para 95, where she stated that 'the State may not lay down unrealistic standards for the evidence required'.

proof cannot be raised in cases where the applicant is considered a danger to national security.

It is also submitted in this section that the principle of effectiveness requires that all relevant risk factors be taken into account individually as well as cumulatively. Furthermore, Member States may not always expect an asylum applicant to substantiate that he runs an *individual* risk of serious harm as such risk can (in exceptional circumstances) also emanate from the *general situation* in the country of origin alone. The individual risk should always be assessed in the light of the general situation in the country of origin.

Relevant Provisions of the Qualification Directive

According to the Qualification Directive, a person must have a 'well-founded fear of being persecuted for reasons of race, religion, nationality, political opinion or membership of a particular social group' in order to be considered a refugee.[10] This definition refers directly to the refugee definition in the Refugee Convention.[11] For this reason the interpretation of the standard of proof under the Refugee Convention may be considered a source of inspiration to the Court of Justice when addressing the standard of proof for qualification as a refugee under the Qualification Directive.[12] For this purpose, the view of the United Nations High Commissioner for Refugees (UNHCR) as well as legal doctrine will be examined in this section.

According to Article 2(e) of the Qualification Directive, a person is eligible for subsidiary protection when 'substantial grounds have been shown' for believing that, if returned to his country of origin he 'would face a real risk of suffering serious harm'. Article 15 of the Qualification Directive defines the term 'serious harm; as: (a) death penalty or execution; or (b) torture or inhuman or degrading treatment or punishment of an applicant in the country of origin; or (c) serious and individual threat to a civilian's life or person by reason of indiscriminate violence in situations of international or internal armed conflict. These provisions refer to the standard of proof following from the ECtHR's case law[13] and the views of the Committee against Torture (ComAT) and the Human Rights Committee (HRC). It may, therefore, be assumed that the standard of proof required under EU law may not be set higher than the standard of proof applied by these bodies.[14] This also follows from the judgment of the Court of Justice in *Elgafaji*, where it considered that the fundamental right guaranteed under Article 3 ECHR forms part

[10] Art 2(d) Dir 2011/95/EU.

[11] See also Hailbronner, *EU Immigration and Asylum Law* (n 7) 1026.

[12] See also I Staffans, 'Evidentiary Standards of Inquisitorial versus Adversarial Asylum Procedures in the Light of Harmonization' (2008) 14 *European Public Law* 615, 638.

[13] See also Hailbronner (n 7) 1026.

[14] It should, however, be noted that the case law of the ECtHR, ComAT and HRC only considers the principle of *non-refoulement*, while the fact that a person is eligible for subsidiary protection (also) gives him a right to asylum status.

of the general principles of EU law, observance of which is ensured by the Court, and that the case law of the ECtHR is taken into consideration in interpreting the scope of that right in the EU legal order.[15]

Applicants who risk persecution or serious harm upon return may be excluded from the right to an asylum status, for example, because they constitute a danger to the community of the Member State.[16] Such applicants will, however, be protected against expulsion by the EU prohibition of *refoulement*, laid down in Article 21(1) of the Qualification Directive. This provision does not mention the requirements which should be met in order to be protected by this prohibition. It only states that States should respect the principle of *non-refoulement* in accordance with their international obligations. This provision should be interpreted in the light of Article 19 of the Charter, which provides that no-one may be removed, expelled or extradited to a State where there is a 'serious risk' that he or she would be subjected to the death penalty, torture or other inhuman or degrading treatment or punishment. On first sight this provision seems to require a higher degree of forseeability of the risk of *refoulement* (serious risk) than the ECtHR (real risk) does.[17] However, it follows from Article 52(3) of the Charter, as well as the explanations with Article 19 of the Charter that the EU prohibition of *refoulement* incorporates the ECtHR's case law regarding Article 3 ECHR.[18] Furthermore, as mentioned above, the Court of Justice has recognised the principle of *non-refoulement* guaranteed by Article 3 ECHR as a principle of EU law. This implies that the standard of proof under Article 21(1) of the Qualification Directive is the same, or at least not more restrictive, than the standard of proof required under Articles 2(c) and 15 of the Qualification Directive.[19]

Likeliness of the Risk of Persecution or Serious Harm

It is argued by the UNHCR as well as legal scholars that an applicant should not be required to *prove* a well-founded fear of persecution in order to qualify as a refugee. According to the UNHCR *Handbook* an applicant's fear of persecution 'should be considered well-founded if he can establish, *to a reasonable degree*, that his continued stay in his country of origin has become intolerable to him for the reasons stated in the [refugee] definition, or would for the same reasons be intolerable if he returned there' (emphasis added).[20] In its 'Note on Burden and

[15] Case C-465/07 *Elgafaji* [2009] ECR I-921, para 28.

[16] Arts 12, 14, 17 and 19 Dir 2011/95/EU.

[17] H Battjes, *European Asylum Law and International Law* (Leiden/Boston, Martinus Nijhoff, 2006) 115.

[18] Explanations relating to the Charter of Fundamental Rights (2007/C 303/02) OJ 14 December 2007, C 303/24.

[19] See also Staffans, *Evidence* (n 1) 99.

[20] UNHCR, *Handbook on Procedures and Criteria for Determining Refugee Status* (1979, new edition 1992) www.refworld.org/docid/3ae6b3314.html accessed 25 September 2013, para 42. See also UNHCR, *Note on Burden and Standard of Proof in Refugee Claims* (n 2) para 17; and Gorlick (n 2) 369–70.

Standard of Proof in Refugee Claims' the UNHCR states that a substantial body of jurisprudence 'largely supports the view that there is no requirement to prove well-foundedness conclusively beyond doubt, or even that persecution is more probable than not'.[21] Furthermore, several scholars contend that the 'reasonable possibility test' is the appropriate test for assessing the risk of persecution.[22] In their view, the more restrictive 'balance of probabilities standard', which requires the applicant to establish that persecution will probably take place or is reasonably likely or more likely than not to occur, should be rejected.[23]

On the basis of the foregoing it may be argued that the full effectiveness of the EU right to a refugee status would be undermined if Member States required applicants to prove a well-founded fear of persecution instead of granting refugee status when such a fear is established to a reasonable degree. As will be shown below, the binding judgments of the ECtHR confirm the non-binding view of the UNHCR that an asylum applicant should not be required to prove a future risk of a certain treatment.

Article 3 ECHR,[24] Articles 6 and 7 ICCPR[25] and Article 3 CAT[26] prohibit expulsion by a Contracting State where *substantial grounds* have been shown for believing that the person in question, if deported, would face a treatment contrary to these provisions in the receiving country. The applicant is not expected to *prove* that he will be treated in violation of the prohibition of *refoulement*.[27] The ECtHR is of the opinion that 'requesting an applicant to produce "indisputable" evidence of a risk of ill-treatment ... would be tantamount to asking him to prove a future event, which is impossible, and would place a clearly disproportionate burden on him'.[28] It considers that a claim of a risk of *refoulement*

> always concerns an eventuality, something which may or may not occur in the future. Consequently, such allegations cannot be proven in the same way as past events. The

[21] On the standard of proof in several countries, see S Norman, 'Assessing the Credibility of Refugee Applicants: A Judicial Perspective' (2007) 19 *International Journal of Refugee Law* 279–80; and Staffans (n 1).

[22] JC Hathaway, *The Law of Refugee Status* (Toronto/Vancouver, Butterworths, 1991) 79–80. See also CW Wouters, *International Legal Standards for the Protection from Refoulement* (Antwerp, Intersentia, 2009) 84–85.

[23] Wouters, *International Legal Standards* (ibid) 85; Hathaway, *The Law of Refugee Status*, ibid, 79; GS Goodwin Gill and J McAdam, *The Refugee in International Law* (Oxford, Oxford University Press, 2007) 234.

[24] See, eg ECtHR (GC) 28 February 2008, *Saadi v Italy*, no 37201/06, para 125. In several cases the ECtHR applied a higher standard of proof, namely 'beyond reasonable doubt'. See Wouters (n 22) 269–70. He refers to ECtHR 12 April 2005, *Shamayev et al v Russia*, no 36378/02, para 338 and ECtHR 7 June 2007, *Garabayev v Russia*, no 38411/02, para 76. More recent examples are ECtHR (Adm) 10 July 2007, *Achmadov and Bagurova v Sweden*, no 34081/05 and ECtHR 23 September 2010, *Iskandarov v Russia*, no 17185/05. The 'beyond reasonable doubt' standard is used by the Court in cases under Art 3 ECHR, which do not involve *refoulement*.

[25] HRC, General Comment No 31 (2004, CCPR/C/21/Rev1/Add.13) para 12.

[26] See Art 3 CAT.

[27] See ECtHR (Plen) 7 July 1989, *Soering v the United Kingdom*, no 14038/88, where the ECtHR found a violation of Art 3 because the likelihood of the feared exposure of the applicant to the 'death row phenomenon' had been shown to be such as to bring Art 3 ECHR into play.

[28] ECtHR 3 July 2012, *Rustamov v Russia*, no 11209/10, para 117.

> applicant must only be required to show, with reference to specific facts relevant to him and to the class of people he belonged to, that there was a high likelihood that he would be ill-treated.[29]

In *MSS* the ECtHR held that persons engaged in an extremely urgent procedure before the Belgian Aliens Appeals Board were prevented from establishing the arguable nature of their complaints under Article 3 of the Convention because they were required to produce 'concrete proof of the irreparable nature of the damage that might result from the alleged potential violation of Article 3'. According to the ECtHR the Aliens Appeal Board thereby increased the burden of proof to such an extent as to hinder the examination on the merits of the alleged risk of a violation.[30]

Article 3 ECHR requires the decision-maker to focus on the 'foreseeable consequences of removal' for each individual applicant.[31] The mere possibility of ill-treatment on account of an unsettled situation in the receiving country does not in itself give rise to a breach of Article 3.[32] The ComAT is of the opinion that the risk of torture must be assessed on grounds that go beyond mere theory or suspicion. The risk of torture must be foreseeable, real and personal. However, the risk does not have be highly probable.[33]

It is not always easy to predict on the basis of the facts whether the ECtHR will consider the standard of proof to be met. In some cases the ECtHR seems to apply a higher standard of proof than in others. In *SH* the Court accepted that there were substantial grounds for believing that there was a real risk that the applicant would be subjected to ill-treatment if returned to Bhutan, although there was little evidence to support this risk. The Court considered that none of the experts who had written reports on the applicant's request were able to predict precisely what would happen to the applicant on his return. It took into account that there was no evidence that the situation of the ethnic Nepalese in Bhutan had improved following the adoption of the Constitution.[34] In *BA* on the other hand, the Court seems to apply a fairly high standard of proof. The Court held that there was no real risk of *refoulement* although it accepted that the applicant was a deserter and that deserters were severely repressed in Chad, the applicant's country of origin. The Court reproached the applicant for not having submitted any documents which concerned him personally and which could prove that the authorities in Chad were still looking for him six years after he left the country.[35]

[29] ECtHR 18 April 2013, *Azimov v Russia*, no 67474/11, para 128.

[30] ECtHR (GC) 21 January 2011, *MSS v Belgium and Greece*, no 30696/09, para 389.

[31] ECtHR 28 June 2011, *Sufi and Elmi v the United Kingdom*, nos 8319/07 and 11449/07, para 249. The ECtHR often assesses itself whether the 'foreseeable consequences' of extradition or expulsion are such as to bring Art 3 ECHR into play. ECtHR 12 May 2010, *Khodzayev v Russia*, no 52466/08, para 91, ECtHR 20 July 2010, *N v Sweden*, no 23505/09, para 54.

[32] See, eg ECtHR 10 February 2011, *Dzhaksybergenov v Ukraine*, no 12343/10, para 35.

[33] ComAT, General Comment No 1 (1997, A/53/44) paras 6–7 and ComAT 16 May 2008, *ZK v Sweden*, no 301/2006, para 8.3.

[34] ECtHR 15 June 2010, *SH v the United Kingdom*, no 19956/06, para 71.

[35] ECtHR 2 December 2010, *BA v France*, no 14951/09, para 44. The arrest warrant submitted by the applicant only stated that he had committed a grave fault and not that he was a deserter.

Likeliness of a Risk of Refoulement *in Cases of Danger of National Security*

The UK has argued that in cases in which an asylum status was refused on national security grounds a higher standard of proof should apply in order for the person concerned to be protected under the prohibition of *refoulement.* This means that, if the State adduces evidence that there is a threat to national security, the individual concerned must prove that it is 'more likely than not' that he would be subjected to treatment prohibited by Article 3.[36] The ECtHR has ruled that such an approach is contrary to Article 3 ECHR. As a result it should also be considered as undermining the full effectiveness of the EU prohibition of *refoulement.*

The ECtHR observed that requiring a higher standard of proof in cases in which national security concerns are involved is not compatible with the absolute nature of the protection afforded by Article 3 ECHR. It amounts to asserting that, in the absence of evidence meeting a higher standard, protection of national security justifies accepting more readily a risk of ill-treatment to the individual. The ECtHR therefore sees 'no reason to modify the relevant standard of proof … by requiring in cases like the present that it be proved that subjection to ill-treatment is "more likely than not"'. The Court

> reaffirms that for a planned forcible expulsion to be in breach of the Convention it is necessary and sufficient for substantial grounds to have been shown for believing that there is a real risk that the person concerned will be subjected in the receiving country to treatment prohibited by Article 3.[37]

Indicators of a Future Risk of Persecution or Serious Harm

There are various factors which may indicate that a future risk of persecution or serious harm exists. It is argued here that the duty to perform an appropriate and careful examination of the asylum claim laid down in Article 8(2) of Directive 2005/85/EC and Article 10(3) of Directive 2013/32/EU requires that all relevant factors be taken into account.[38] These factors must examined together and not simply in isolation.

A very important indicator of a future risk of persecution or serious harm is the fact that an applicant was persecuted or suffered serious harm in the past on the condition that such past persecution or serious harm is connected to the grounds on which the applicant claims to fear persecution or risk serious harm in the future.[39] This follows from Article 4(4) of the Qualification Directive which applies to the assessment of both refugee and subsidiary protection status. This provision

[36] *Saadi* (n 24) para 122.

[37] Ibid, para 140.

[38] The ECtHR has emphasised that the assessment of whether there is a real risk must be made on the basis of all relevant factors which could increase the risk of ill-treatment. ECtHR 17 July 2008, *NA v the United Kingdom*, no 25904/07, para 130; and ECtHR 31 May 2011, *EG v the United Kingdom*, no 41178/08, para 72.

[39] See Joined Cases C-175/08, C-176/08, C-178/08 and C-179/08 *Salahadin Abdulla* [2010] ECR I-1493, para 94 and ECtHR 6 December 2012, *DNW v Sweden*, no 29946/10, para 41.

states that the fact that an applicant has already been subject to persecution or to direct threats of persecution is a serious indication of the applicant's well-founded fear of persecution, unless there are good reasons to consider that such persecution will not be repeated. Several authors mention that this provision implies that previous (threats of) persecution or serious harm give rise to a refutable presumption that the applicant qualifies for refugee or subsidiary protection.[40]

The importance of the fact that a person was persecuted, tortured or ill-treated in the past when assessing a future risk of such treatment is confirmed in the case law of the ECtHR and the ComAT.[41] In *Salah Sheekh*, for example, the ECtHR established that the applicant suffered inhuman treatment in the past. It considered:

> Having regard to the information available … the Court is far from persuaded that the situation has undergone such a substantial change for the better that it could be said that the risk of the applicant being subjected to this kind of treatment anew has been removed or that he would be able to obtain protection from the (local) authorities. There is no indication, therefore, that the applicant would find himself in a significantly different situation from the one he fled.[42]

The fact that past persecution is an important indicator for a well-founded fear of persecution in the future is recognised by the UNHCR *Handbook*[43] as well as legal scholars.[44]

In the case law of the ECtHR and the ComAT past torture or ill-treatment does not automatically make the existence of a future risk of such treatment plausible. The following circumstances may warrant the conclusion that no such future risk exists:

— the conditions in the country of origin have changed significantly;[45]
— the abuses were applied by individuals and not condoned by the authorities;[46]

[40] See Battjes, *European Asylum Law* (n 17) 227, Hailbronner (n 7) 1037; Staffans, 'Evidentiary Standards' (n 12) 638.

[41] See, eg ComAT 30 November 2010, *Said Amini v Denmark*, no 339/2008, para 9.8. See also ComAT, General Comment No 1 (n 33) para 8(b). In ComAT 14 December 2005, *MSH v Sweden*, no 235/2003, para 6.5, however, the Committee considered that according to General Comment No 1, 'previous experience of torture is but one consideration in determining whether a person faces a personal risk of torture upon return to his country of origin'.

[42] ECtHR 11 January 2007, *Salah Sheekh v the Netherlands*, no 1948/04, paras 146–47. See also ECtHR 9 March 2010, *RC v Sweden*, no 41827/07, para 55.

[43] UNHCR, *Handbook* (n 20) para 45. See also UNHCR, *Note on Burden and Standard of Proof in Refugee Claims* (n 2) para 19.

[44] A Grahl-Madsen, *The Status of Refugees in International Law* (Leiden, Sijthoff, 1966) 176. See also Hathaway (n 22) 88.

[45] *Salah Sheekh* (n 42) para 147 and ECtHR 2 September 2010; *YP and LP v France*, no 32476/06, para 71. See also ComAT 27 March 2002, *YHA v Australia*, no 162/2000, para 7.4; UNHCR, *Note on Burden and Standard of Proof in Refugee Claims* (n 2) para 19; and Hailbronner (n 7) 1037–38.

[46] ECtHR (Adm) 27 March 2008, *Hakizimana v Sweden*, no 37913/05.

— the applicant has stayed in the country of origin without problems after the torture or ill-treatment;[47] and
— the persecution or torture occurred a long time ago,[48]

Arguably these factors may be considered 'good reasons' that no risk of future persecution or serious harm exists within the meaning of Article 4(4) of the Qualification Directive.

Other factors, such as the applicant's high profile,[49] the fate of his family members, friends or members of the same racial or social group,[50] or the existence of systematic human rights violations in the country of origin[51] are indicators of a future risk of persecution or serious harm. On the basis of the ECtHR's case law, the UNHCR *Handbook*, and the view of the ComAT it should be concluded that the duty to perform an appropriate examination of the asylum claim laid down in Article 8(2) of Directive 2005/85/EC and 10(3) of Directive 2013/32/EU, requires that risk factors should be taken together and not (only) be assessed in isolation.[52] According to the ECtHR:

> [D]ue regard should also be given to the possibility that a number of individual factors may not, when considered separately, constitute a real risk; but when taken cumulatively and when considered in a situation of general violence and heightened security, the same factors may give rise to a real risk.[53]

In the ECtHR's view both the need to consider all relevant factors and the need to give appropriate weight to the general situation in the country of destination derive from the obligation to consider all the relevant circumstances of the case.[54]

Individual Risk or General Risk

The determining authorities in Member States may expect an asylum applicant to substantiate that he has a well-founded fear of persecution or faces a real risk of suffering serious harm on individual grounds. Furthermore, they may assess the risk emanating from the individual situation of the applicant and that emanating

[47] *DNW* (n 39) para 42.

[48] See, eg *ZK* (n 33) para 8.4 and ComAT 19 May 2008, *RK v Sweden*, no 309/2006, para 8.5. In *YP and LP* (n 45) para 71, the ECtHR considered that the passage of time did not diminish the risk of *refoulement*.

[49] See, eg ECtHR (GC) 25 October 1996, *Chahal v the United Kingdom*, no 22414/93, para 106 and ComAT 7 July 2011, *Harminder Singh Khalsa et al v Switzerland*, no 336/2008, para 11.5.

[50] See, eg *YP and LP* (n 45) para 73.

[51] See, eg ECtHR 21 October 2010, *Gaforov v Russia*, no 25404/09, para 130.

[52] UNHCR, *Handbook* (n 20) paras 53 and 201.

[53] *NA* (n 38) para 130. For an example where the ComAT considered that cumulative factors established a real and foreseeable risk of torture, see ComAT 7 July 2011, *Mondal v Sweden*, no 338/2008, para 7.7.

[54] *NA* (n 38) para 130. See also *N v Sweden* (n 31) para 62 and UNHCR, *Handbook* (n 20) para 201.

from the general situation in the country of origin separately, instead of taking them together.[55]

It is true that applicants who fear becoming a victim of the general situation of indiscriminate violence in their country of origin will not qualify as a refugee under the Qualification Directive without a persecution ground.[56] However, members of a particular group which is systematically persecuted because of its race, religion, ethnicity or other persecution ground, should be considered refugees, without being further singled out.[57]

It follows from the case law of the Court of Justice and the ECtHR that requiring individual grounds for a risk of serious harm in each case undermines the full effectiveness of the EU right to subsidiary protection and the prohibition of *refoulement*. This case law shows that a real risk of suffering serious harm may also emanate from the fact that a person belongs to a special vulnerable group or, in exceptional situations, even from the general situation in the applicant's country or region of origin. In the assessment of the risk of serious harm individual factors, as well as the general situation in the country of origin, should be taken into account. This case law will now be further examined.

The Court of Justice held in *Elgafaji* that the terms 'death penalty', 'execution' and 'torture or inhuman or degrading treatment or punishment of an applicant in the country of origin', used in Article 15(a) and (b) of the Qualification Directive cover situations in which the applicant for subsidiary protection is specifically exposed to the risk of a particular type of harm. Article 15(c) of the Qualification Directive on the other hand, covers a more general risk of harm.[58] This provision covers

> harm to civilians irrespective of their identity, where the degree of indiscriminate violence characterising the armed conflict taking place reaches such a high level that substantial grounds are shown for believing that a civilian, returned to the relevant country or, as the case may be, to the relevant region, would, solely on account of his presence on the territory of that country or region, face a real risk of being subject to the serious threat referred in Article 15(c) of the Directive.[59]

According to the Court of Justice, collective factors play a significant role in the application of Article 15(c) of the Directive, 'in that the person concerned belongs, like other people, to a circle of potential victims of indiscriminate violence in situations of international or internal armed conflict'.[60] In order to meet the standard of proof required under Articles 2(e) and 15 of the Qualification Directive, the

[55] TP Spijkerboer and BP Vermeulen, *Vluchtelingenrecht* (Amsterdam/Leersum, Nederlands Centrum Buitenlanders, 1995) 91–93.

[56] Wouters (n 22) 71.

[57] Hathaway (n 22) 90–94; Wouters (n 22) 88; and Goodwin Gill and McAdam, *The Refugee in International Law* (n 23) 128–29.

[58] *Elgafaji* (n 15) paras 32–33.

[59] Ibid, para 35.

[60] Ibid, para 38.

grounds substantiating the risk of suffering the serious harm within the meaning of Article 15(c) may thus focus (at least to a large extent) on the general situation in the country of origin. According to the Court, the rule described in Article 15 of the Qualification Directive entails a sliding scale where 'the more the applicant is able to show that he is specifically affected by reason of factors particular to his personal circumstances, the lower the level of indiscriminate violence required for him to be eligible for subsidiary protection'.[61] It may be assumed that the opposite is also true: the higher the level of indiscriminate violence in the country of origin, the less important it is for the applicant to show that he is specifically affected by reason of his individual circumstances.

The approach taken by the Court of Justice is similar to that of the ECtHR.[62] The ECtHR accepted that, if the existence of a real risk of treatment contrary to Article 3 ECHR is established, 'the applicant's removal would necessarily breach Article 3, regardless of whether the risk emanates from a general situation of violence, a personal characteristic of the applicant, or a combination of the two'.[63] In *Sufi and Elmi* the ECtHR held that the level of violence in Mogadishu was of sufficient intensity to pose a real risk of treatment reaching the Article 3 threshold to anyone in that city. In its assessment of the situation in Mogadishu, the ECtHR took into account the indiscriminate bombardments and military offensives carried out by all parties to the conflict, the unacceptable number of civilian casualties, the substantial number of persons displaced within and from the city, and the unpredictable and widespread nature of the conflict.[64] The ECtHR also recognised that persons belonging to a group systematically exposed to a practice of ill-treatment face a real risk of *refoulement*. The protection of Article 3 ECHR comes into play when an applicant establishes that there are serious reasons to believe in the existence of such practice of ill-treatment and proves that he is a member of the group concerned.[65] To insist in such cases that the applicant show the existence of special distinguishing features would render the protection offered by Article 3 illusory. Moreover, such a finding would call into question the absolute nature of Article 3.[66] The applicant need show the existence of 'further special distinguishing features' only if the level of violence in the country is not sufficiently intense and an individual is not a member of a vulnerable group. The

[61] Ibid, para 39. See also the Opinion of AG Maduro in this case, paras 36 and 41.

[62] In *Sufi and Elmi* (n 31) para 225, the ECtHR considered that it was not persuaded that Art 3 ECHR does not offer comparable protection to that afforded under Dir 2004/83/EC. Art 3 CAT does not cover cases of risk of harm due to indiscriminate violence. See, eg *RK* (n 48) para 8.2.

[63] *Sufi and Elmi* (n 31) para 218.

[64] Ibid, para 248.

[65] Zahle calls these two evidentiary aspects of a refugee case 'risk-group existence' and 'risk-group affiliation'. H Zahle, 'Competing Patterns for Evidentiary Assessments' in G Noll (ed), *Proof, Evidentiary Assessment and Credibility in Asylum Procedures* (Leiden/Boston, Martinus Nijhoff, 2005) 18.

[66] *Sufi and Elmi* (n 31) para 217.

focus then lies on the individual asylum account of the applicant, which should be assessed in the light of the general situation in the country of origin.[67]

8.2 THE BURDEN OF PROOF

This section considers which party in asylum proceedings (the asylum applicant or the determining authority) bears the burden of proof. The concept 'burden of proof' has different meanings. First, it may refer to the *objective burden* of proof which determines which party bears the negative consequences if the required standard of proof in the individual case is not met.[68] It may also refer to a *subjective burden* of proof which determines the responsibility to produce evidence.[69] In this section both issues will be addressed. It is assumed for the purpose of this section that in assessing whether a person qualifies as a refugee or as a person eligible for subsidiary protection, the same EU standards regarding the burden of proof apply. This also follows from the fact that Article 4 of the Qualification Directive, which concerns the assessment of facts and circumstances, applies to both issues. Therefore, the standards which may be derived from the Refugee Convention and those which follow from the ECHR, ICCPR and CAT are discussed together.

8.2.1 Adducing Evidence and Dispelling Doubts

The Qualification Directive does not explicitly mention that the asylum applicant bears the risk if the standard of proof for qualification as a refugee or person eligible for subsidiary protection is not met.[70] However, it may be assumed, in particular on the basis of the case law of the Court of Justice,[71] State practice and principles of international law[72] that the objective burden of proof is on the applicant.[73] This section only addresses the general burden of proof with regard to the risk of *refoulement* upon return. The burden of proof with regard to more specific aspects of the assessment of the asylum claim, such as the reliance on a

[67] ECtHR (GC) 4 February 2005, *Mamatkulov and Askarov v Turkey*, no 46827/99, para 67.

[68] See Staffans (n 12) 629. See also A Popovic, 'Evidentiary Assessment and Non-Refoulement' in G Noll (ed), *Proof, Evidentiary Assessment and Credibility in Asylum Procedures* (Leiden/Boston, Martinus Nijhoff, 2005) 36.

[69] See Staffans (n 12) 630. See also UNHCR, *Note on Burden and Standard of Proof in Refugee Claims* (n 2) para 5.

[70] See Staffans, *Evidence* (n 1) 72 and Noll (n 6) 5.

[71] See, eg Case C-381/99 *Brunhofer* [2001] ECR I-4961, para 52; Case C-127/92 *Enderby* [1993] ECR I-5535, para 13.

[72] See, eg *Saadi* (n 24) para 129, ComAT, General Comment No 1 (n 33), para 5; and UNHCR, *Handbook* (n 20) para 196.

[73] See Staffans (n 12) 629.

safe country of origin, a safe third country, an internal flight alternative or the effectiveness of diplomatic assurances will not be examined.[74]

The case law of the Court of Justice, which will be addressed below, shows that the principle of full effectiveness of EU law may require a shift of the burden of proof from the applicant to another party, even if no EU legislation with regard to the burden of proof exists. Furthermore, the ECtHR's recent case law has made clear that in *refoulement* cases the burden of proof needs to shift to the determining authority if the applicant has adduced evidence capable of proving that there are substantial grounds for believing that there is a real risk of treatment in violation with Article 3 ECHR upon return. The ComAT and the HRC also apply such a shift of the burden of proof where the applicant has substantiated (an important part) of the asylum claim. On the basis of this case law it is argued in this section that the full effectiveness of the EU right to asylum and the prohibition of *refoulement* require a shift of the burden of proof to the determining authority in a number of specific situations.

Shifting the Burden of Proof in EU Equal Treatment Cases

The Court of Justice has recognised in several cases that national rules concerning the burden of proof are capable of undermining the full effectiveness of EU law. According to the Court, Member States may be obliged to apply and interpret their national rules on the burden of proof in the light of the purpose of the applicable EU legislation.[75] In equal treatment cases (usually concerning equal pay between men and women) the Court requires a shift of the burden of proof from the applicant (the worker) to the defending party (the employer) in order to guarantee the full effectiveness of the right to equal treatment, where there is a prima facie case of discrimination.[76] The employer then has to show that there are objective reasons for the difference in pay. There is a prima facie case of discrimination, for example, when significant statistics disclose an appreciable difference in pay between two jobs of equal value, one of which is carried out almost exclusively by women and the other predominantly by men.[77] Statements from the employer may also amount to facts from which it may be presumed that there has been discrimination.[78]

[74] For safe countries of origin, see Art 31(1) Dir 2005/85/EC and Art 36(1) Dir 2013/32/EU; for safe third countries and first countries of asylum, see Arts 27(1) and 26 Dir 2005/85/EC and Arts 38 and 35 Dir 2013/32/EU, and for internal flight alternatives, see Art 8 Dir 2011/95/EU.

[75] Joined Cases C-253/96 to C-258/96 *Kampelmann et al* [1997] ECR I-6907, paras 32–34 and Case C-350/99 *Lange* [2001] ECR I-1061, paras 31–32. Note that in these cases Council Dir 91/533/EEC of 14 October 1991 on an employer's obligation to inform employees of the conditions applicable to the contract or employment relationship [1991] OJ 288/32 provided that the Directive shall be without any prejudice to national law and practice concerning proof as regards the existence and content of a contract or employment relationship.

[76] *Enderby* (n 71) para 18, *Brunnhofer* (n 71) para 58. In Case C-54/07 *Feryn* [2008] ECR I-5187, para 31, which concerned discrimination on the grounds of racial or ethnic origin a 'presumption of a discriminatory recruitment policy' caused the shift of the burden of proof.

[77] *Enderby* (n 71) para 19.

[78] Case C-81/12, *Asociaţia ACCEPT* [2013] paras 46–53.

When establishing whether a there is prima facie case of discrimination, the Court of Justice takes into account difficulties encountered by the applicant in adducing evidence of discrimination. In *Danfoss*, for example, the employer applied a system of pay which was wholly lacking in transparency, which made it very difficult for female employees to prove that they were paid less than their male colleagues, who were doing the same work and that this was at variance with the Equal Pay Directive.[79] Female employees could establish differences only so far as average pay was concerned. The Court therefore required a shift of the burden of proof to the employer if a female worker established, in relation to a relatively large number of employees, that the average pay for women was less than that for men. The employer had to prove that the differentiation in pay between men and women was not the result of discrimination.[80] The Court considered that the concern for effectiveness which underlies the Equal Pay Directive 'means that it must be interpreted as implying adjustments to national rules on the burden of proof in special cases where such adjustments are necessary for the effective implementation of the principle of equality'.[81]

A prima facie case of discrimination may be refuted by the employer with 'a body of consistent evidence'. This was considered by the Court of Justice in a case concerning alleged discrimination on the basis of sexual orientation by a football club in recruiting new players. The claim of discrimination was based on statements made by a shareholder and patron of the football club. In this case the Court of Justice stated that a body of consistent evidence could have included a 'reaction by the employer concerned clearly distancing itself from public statements on which the appearance of discrimination is based, and the existence of express provisions concerning its recruitment policy aimed at ensuring compliance with the principle of equal treatment'.[82]

The case law of the Court of Justice in equal treatment cases has been codified in EU legislation, in particular in a special directive on the burden of proof in cases of discrimination based on sex.[83]

[79] Council Dir 75/117/EEC of 10 February 1975 on the approximation of the laws of the Member States relating to the application of the principle of equal pay for men and women [1975] OJ L045/19.

[80] See also Case C-196/02 *Nikoloudi v Organismos Tilepikonion Ellados AE* [2005] ECR I-1789, para 74 and Case C-400/93 *Specialarbejderforbundet i Danmark* [1995] ECR I-1275, paras 24–27. In *Brunnhofer* (n 71) para 58 the normal burden of proof applied because there were no special circumstances such as those established in C-109/88, *Danfoss* [1989] ECR I-3199. The worker had to prove that the pay she received was less than that of her chosen comparator and that she did the same work or work of equal value comparable to that performed by him.

[81] *Danfoss* (n 80) para 14. Art 6 of the Equal Pay Directive provides that Member States must, in accordance with their national circumstances and legal systems, take the measures necessary to ensure that the principle of equal pay is applied and that effective means are available to ensure that it is observed.

[82] *Asociaţia ACCEPT* (n 78) paras 56–57.

[83] Council Dir 97/80/EC of 15 December 1997 on the burden of proof in cases of discrimination based on sex [1997] OJ L14/6. See also Art 8 of Council Dir 2000/43/EC of 29 June 2000 implementing the principle of equal treatment between persons irrespective of racial or ethnic origin [2000] OJ

Cases before the ECtHR, ComAT and HRC

In the case law of the ECtHR, ComAT and HRC it is accepted that the burden of proof should shift from the asylum applicant to the determining authority when the applicant has made out a prima facie case of a risk of *refoulement*.[84] The burden of proof returns to the applicant if these authorities have sufficiently disputed the evidence or arguments submitted by the applicant. The ECtHR uses the following standard as regards the burden of proof:

> It is in principle for the applicant to adduce evidence capable of proving that there are substantial grounds for believing that, if the measure complained of were to be implemented, he would be exposed to a real risk of being subjected to treatment contrary to Article 3. ... Where such evidence is adduced, it is for the Government to dispel any doubts about it.[85]

It is impossible to state exactly when the burden of proof shifts to the determining authority. In most *refoulement* cases the ECtHR, ComAT or HRC did not indicate that the burden of proof had shifted or any reasons for the shift.[86] However, on the basis of their judgments several circumstances can be identified which may trigger a shift of the burden of proof.

Past Persecution or Serious Harm

One example is where the applicant had been subjected to ill-treatment in the past. In the previous section it was noted that past ill-treatment or torture is an important factor which indicates that a future risk of persecution or serious harm exists. It follows from Article 4(4) of the Qualification Directive as well as the case law of the ECtHR and ComAT that this factor generally also requires a shift of the burden of proof to the decision-making authorities.[87] In *RC* the ECtHR considered:

> Having regard to its finding that the applicant has discharged the burden of proving that he has already been tortured, the Court considers that the onus rests with the State to dispel any doubts about the risk of his being subjected again to treatment contrary to Article 3 in the event that his expulsion proceeds.[88]

L180/22 and Art 10 of Council Dir 2000/78/EC of 27 November 2000 establishing a general framework for equal treatment in employment and occupation [2000] OJ L303/16.

[84] See also Spijkerboer, 'Subsidiarity and "Arguability": the European Court of Human Rights' Case Law on Judicial Review in Asylum Cases' (2009) 21 *International Journal of Refugee Law* 48, 61–62.

[85] See, eg *Saadi* (n 24) para 129.

[86] In non-asylum cases under Arts 2 and 3 ECHR the ECtHR did set out more precisely which circumstances lead to a shift of the burden of proof to the State authorities. See, eg ECtHR (GC) 6 July 2005, *Nachova et al v Bulgaria*, nos 43577/98 and 43579/98, para 157. See also HRC 16 August 2007, *Kimouche v Algeria*, no 1328/2004.

[87] See also Noll (n 6) 8 and Staffans, *Evidence* (n 1) 72.

[88] *RC* (n 42) para 55. See also ECtHR 10 December 2009, *Koktysh v Ukraine*, no 43707/07, para 64.

The Court then assessed the future risk of a treatment in violation of Article 3 ECHR in the light of the very tense situation in Iran at the time. Furthermore, the Court considered that the applicant would face a specific risk upon his return as he could not produce evidence of his having left that country legally. The Court observed that the government had not rebutted the applicant's claim that he left Iran illegally. Therefore, the Court found it probable that the applicant, being without valid exit documentation, would come to the attention of the Iranian authorities and that his past was likely to be revealed. The Court concluded that the expulsion of the applicant to Iran would violate Article 3.

In the ECtHR's judgment in *DNW* the burden of proof did not shift to the State even though it accepted that the applicant had been detained and subjected to ill-treatment in the past. The ECtHR in this judgment did not give reasons for this and did not refer to its considerations in *RC*. It simply considered that it had not been substantiated that the applicant would be at risk of being subjected to ill-treatment in the future. The ECtHR pointed to the fact that the applicant had been travelling around and preaching in public in Ethiopia, his country of origin, after he had escaped from prison and before leaving the country, without the Ethiopian authorities showing any adverse interest in him. Furthermore, it referred to some credibility issues. Two judges dissented in this case and argued that the burden of proof should have shifted to the State.[89]

Plausible Statements and Reliable Proof

The burden of proof may also shift to the determining authority if the applicant was able to substantiate a future risk of *refoulement* by submitting credible statements and/or documents in support of his asylum account. In *SH*, for example, the applicant had adduced several expert reports (from Amnesty International, the Human Rights Council of Bhutan, Human Rights Watch and two individual experts) which supported his claim that he would be at risk of imprisonment and ill-treatment upon return to Bhutan. Furthermore, human rights reports indicated that the ethnic Nepalese in Bhutan suffered discriminatory treatment on account of their ethnicity. The Court was satisfied that there were substantial grounds for believing that there was a real risk that the applicant would be subjected to ill-treatment contrary to Article 3 if returned to Bhutan. It noted that the government had not adduced any evidence capable of dispelling the Court's concerns. In particular, the government had accepted that there was no evidence that the situation of the ethnic Nepalese had improved following the adoption of the Constitution in Bhutan.[90]

[89] *DNW* (n 39).
[90] *SH* (n 34) paras 69–71.

In *Chedli Ben Ahmed Karoui* the ComAT found it impossible to verify the authenticity of some of the documents provided by the complainant.

> However, in view of the substantive reliable documentation he has provided, including medical records, a support letter from Amnesty International, Sweden, and an attestation from the Al-Nahdha chairman, the complainant ... has provided sufficient reliable information for the burden of proof to shift.[91]

Serious Human Rights Violations in the Country of Origin

When reports of human rights organisations, submitted by the applicant or taken into account by the ECtHR on its own initiative, show the existence of serious human rights violations in the country of origin or another country to which the applicant will be expelled, it is up to the determining authority to dispute that information. The burden of proof with regard to the risks emanating from the general situation in the country of origin thus shifts to the State. In *Garayev*, for example, the applicant claimed that he would be tortured in prison upon extradition to Uzbekistan. The ECtHR considered that the government had not adduced any evidence or reports capable of rebutting the credible reports by human rights organisations of torture, routine beatings and use of force against criminal suspects or prisoners by the Uzbek law-enforcement authorities. No evidence had been produced of any fundamental improvement in the protection against torture in Uzbekistan in recent years.[92]

The Applicant belongs to a Group at Risk

It follows from *Sufi and Elmi* that the determining authority should prove that an individual is not at risk when it is established on the basis of human rights reports that the violence in a country or region of origin is of such intensity that in principle anyone in that region or country would be at real risk of treatment prohibited by Article 3 of the Convention. In this case the Court concluded that this situation occurred in Mogadishu. It accepted that some persons who were exceptionally well connected to 'powerful actors' could find protection in Mogadishu. However, it was for the government to show that a person could be afforded protection for this reason.[93] On the basis of this judgment it is conceivable that, if it is established that a person belongs to a group systematically exposed to ill-treatment (such as the Ashraf minority in the case of *Salah Sheekh*[94]), it is for the determining authorities to prove that this person could obtain protection against persecution or serious harm.

[91] ComAT 25 May 2002, *Chedli Ben Ahmed Karoui v Sweden*, no 185/2001, para 10. See also ComAT 15 February 2001, *AS v Sweden*, no 149/1999, para 8.6; and HRC 9 December 2004, *Jonny Rubin Byahuranga v Denmark*, no 1222/2003, paras 11.2–11.4.

[92] ECtHR 10 June 2010, *Garayev v Azerbaijan*, no 53688/08, para 73. See also ECtHR 19 November 2009, *Kaboulov v Ukraine*, no 41015/04, para 111. *Khodzayev* (n 31) para 98.

[93] *Sufi and Elmi* (n 31) paras 249–50. See similarly *MSS* (n 30) para 359 where the Court held that the State authorities should have concluded on the basis of the available human rights reports that the applicant faced a real and individual risk of *refoulement*.

[94] *Salah Sheekh* (n 42).

No Burden of Proving Negative Facts

It could be assumed from *M and others* that the asylum applicant should not be expected to prove negative facts. In this case, the Bulgarian Supreme Court acknowledged the existence of a risk of death and ill-treatment of the applicant, who had converted to Christianity, upon return to Afghanistan. However, it refused the applicant's claim because the applicant had not proved that those risks stemmed from the Afghan authorities and that those authorities would not guarantee his safety. The ECtHR considered under Article 13 ECHR:

> [B]y dealing with such a serious issue summarily and by placing on the first applicant, without any explanation, the burden of proving negative facts, such as the lack of State guarantees in Afghanistan, the court practically deprived Mr M. of a meaningful examination of his claim under Article 3.[95]

This case is quite specific because of the number of deficiencies in the Supreme Court's review of the asylum claim.[96] However, it does show that, particularly when a risk of treatment contrary to Article 3 is found, no burden to prove negative facts can be placed on the applicant.

Shifting the Burden of Proof Back to the Applicant

If the examining authorities provide well-founded reasons to contest the statements or the evidence submitted by the applicant, the burden of proof shifts back to the applicant.[97] The determining authority may, for example, have submitted good reasons to consider that past ill-treatment will not be repeated, by showing that the situation in the country of origin has improved to an important extent.[98] Furthermore, the burden of proof may shift back to the applicant if the determining authority gave strong reasons to question the information submitted by the applicant[99] or the authenticity of documents provided by him.[100]

Subconclusion: The Objective Burden of Proof

It should be derived from the Court of Justice's case law in equal treatment cases that the principle of effectiveness requires a shift of the burden of proof from the applicant to the State if this is necessary to ensure the purpose of the Procedures

[95] ECtHR 26 July 2011, *M et al v Bulgaria*, no 41416/08, para 127. See also ECtHR 24 May 2011, *Abou Amer v Romania*, no 14521/03, para 58.

[96] The Supreme Administrative Court failed to carry out a proper examination of the executive's assertion that the applicant presented a national security risk and it placed excessive reliance on the question whether the ill-treatment risked in the receiving State would emanate from State or non-State sources. Finally, the remedy before the Supreme Court did not have suspensive effect.

[97] See Zahle, 'Competing Patterns for Evidentiary Assessments' (n 65) 19–20.

[98] See Art 4(4) Dir 2011/95/EU, ECtHR (Adm) 4 July 2006, *Karim v Sweden*, no 24171/05 and *YHA* (n 45) para 7.4.

[99] See, eg ECtHR (Adm) 8 July 2008, *AJ v Sweden*, no 13508/07, para 56; ECtHR (Adm) 2 September 2008, *AA v Sweden*, no 8594/04, para 66; *Hakizimana* (n 46).

[100] ECtHR (Adm) 21 June 2005, *Matsiukhina and Matsiukhin v Sweden*, no 31260/04, ComAT 26 November 2008, *MF v Sweden*, no 326/2007, para 7.7.

and Qualification Directive, namely respect for the right to asylum and the prohibition of *refoulement* and the full and inclusive application of the Refugee Convention.[101] It is contended on the basis of the ECtHR's case law that such a shift of the burden of proof is necessary if the applicant adduced evidence capable of proving that he has a well-founded fear of persecution or that there are substantial grounds for believing that he faces a real risk of suffering serious harm. It may be derived from the case law of the ECtHR that this condition is met in the following situations:

— it is established that the applicant has been subjected to torture or ill-treatment in the past;
— the applicant has substantiated to a certain extent that there is a future risk of *refoulement* by submitting credible statements and or documents in support of the asylum account;
— human rights organisations report the existence of serious human rights violations in the applicant's country of origin. In this situation the burden of proof shifts to the State authorities with regard to the risk emanating from the general situation in the country of origin; or
— it is established that in the applicant's country or region of origin the violence is of such intensity that anyone is at risk of torture or ill-treatment or that the applicant belongs to a particularly vulnerable group.

Finally, the ECtHR's judgment in *M and others* may indicate that the applicant may not be required to prove negative facts.

8.2.2 Producing Evidence: A Shared Duty

Most Member States impose upon the applicant the duty to produce evidence in support of his asylum claim.[102] This is allowed by Article 4(1) of the Qualification Directive, which provides that Member States may consider it the duty of the applicant 'to submit as soon as possible all elements needed to substantiate the application for international protection'.[103] According to the case law of the ECtHR[104]

[101] According to recital 8 Preamble Dir 2005/85/EC, recital 60 Preamble Dir 2013/32/EU and recital 16 Preamble Dir 2011/95/EC, these directives aim to ensure the right to asylum and the prohibition of *refoulement* laid down in the Charter. See also ch 2, section 2.1.2 in this volume.

[102] According to the Commission in 2010 Art 4(1) first sentence was transposed by all Member States except for Belgium, Cyprus, the Czech Republic, Finland, Hungary, Lithuania and Romania. Commission, 'Report from the Commission to the European Parliament and the Council on the application of Directive 2005/85/EC' COM (2010) 465 final, 4.

[103] Note that Member States are not *required* to place the burden of proof on the applicant. This also follows from Art 4(5) Dir 2011/95/EU, where rules are provided for the situation where Member States apply Art 4(1) first sentence. See also Hailbronner (n 7) 1027–28.

[104] ECtHR 5 July 2005, *Said v the Netherlands*, no 2345/02, para 49.

and the views of the ComAT,[105] the HRC[106] and the UNHCR[107] the applicant also bears the burden of providing evidence in support of his asylum claim.

This section agues, however, that the Member States' duty to assess the relevant elements of the application in cooperation with the applicant laid down in Article 4(1) of the Qualification Directive[108] as well as the duty to conduct an appropriate examination of the asylum claim[109] entail a positive obligation on Member States to investigate certain aspects of the asylum claim. The Court of Justice considered in its judgment in *MM* that the duty to cooperate

> means, in practical terms, that if, for any reason whatsoever, the elements provided by an applicant for international protection are not complete, up to date or relevant, it is necessary for the Member State concerned to cooperate actively with the applicant, at that stage of the procedure, so that all the elements needed to substantiate the application may be assembled.[110]

Furthermore, the principle of effectiveness and the right to good administration arguably prevent an unreasonable burden of proof being imposed on the applicant.[111]

This interpretation of the duty to cooperate and the duty to conduct an appropriate examination would be in line with the ECtHR's case law concerning Article 3 ECHR. According to the ECtHR, Article 3 ECHR entails an obligation for the State to carry out a meaningful or adequate assessment of the applicant's claim of a risk of *refoulement*.[112] It follows from this obligation that the State authorities must address the applicant's allegations of past torture and the future risk of *refoulement*.[113] In a number of complaints against Turkey, the ECtHR concluded that the State authorities failed to carry out a meaningful assessment of the risk of *refoulement*. Amongst other factors, the ECtHR took into account that the State authorities did not interview the applicants. In these cases the ECtHR concluded, on the basis of the evidence submitted by the applicants and the fact that the UNHCR recognised the applicants as refugees, that expulsion would violate Article 3 ECHR.[114] Furthermore, the State authorities may not disregard important evidence without verifying its authenticity, if such verification is easily done.

[105] See, eg ComAT 2 May 2007, *ERK and YK v Sweden*, no 270 and 271/2005, para 7.4 and ComAT 5 May 2009, *X v Australia*, no 324/2007, para 7.4.

[106] See, eg HRC 28 April 2009, *Moses Solo Tarlue v Canada*, no 1551/2007, para 7.4.

[107] UNHCR, *Handbook* (n 20) para 195.

[108] See also P Boeles, M den Heijer, G Lodder, and K Wouters (2009) *European Migration Law* (Antwerp/Oxford/Portland, Intersentia, 2009) 338.

[109] See Art 8(2) Dir 2005/85/EC and Art 10(3) Dir 2013/32/EU.

[110] Case C-277/11 *MM* [2012] para 66.

[111] See, eg Case T-170/09 *Shanghai Biaowu High-Tensile Fasteners* [2012] paras 105–106.

[112] See, eg *Gaforov* (n 51) para 122; ECtHR 15 June 2010, *Ahmadpour v Turkey*, no 12717/08, para 38; ECtHR 19 January 2010, *ZNS v Turkey*, no 21896/08, para 48; and ECtHR, 11 July 2000, *Jabari v Turkey*, no 40035/98, para 40.

[113] *Gaforov* (n 51) para 123.

[114] See, eg ECtHR 22 September 2009, *Abdolkhani and Karimnia v Turkey*, no 30471/08 and ECtHR 13 April 2010, *Tehrani et al v Turkey*, nos 32940/08, 41626/08 and 43616/08.

In the case of *Singh* the ECtHR found a violation of Article 13 ECHR because the Belgian authorities failed to contact the UNHCR in order to determine whether a UNHCR document submitted by the applicants which stated that the applicants were recognised as refugees in India, was authentic.[115]

This section contends that Member States are obliged under EU law to gather reliable country of origin information from different sources. Furthermore, the State is required to request a medical report by an expert, if the applicant makes a prima facie case that the scars on his body or other medical problems suffered by him are caused by ill-treatment in his country of origin. Finally, it is argued that the determining authority should gather evidence which is only obtainable by this authority and not by the asylum applicant. The authority examining the asylum claim is thus not allowed to limit itself to the assessment of the statements and evidence adduced by the applicant.[116]

The Duty to Gather Reliable Country of Origin/Transit Country Information of Different Sources

Article 8(2)(b) of Directive 2005/85/EC and Article 10(3)(b) of Directive 2013/32/EU state that in the context of their duty to conduct an appropriate examination of the asylum claim Member States must ensure that 'precise and up-to-date information is obtained from various sources', such as the UNHCR and (in the case of Directive 2013/32/EU) the European Asylum Support Office (EASO), 'as to the general situation prevailing in the countries of origin of applicants for asylum and, where necessary, in countries through which they have transited'. Such information should be made available to the personnel responsible for examining applications and taking decisions'.[117] The duty to gather relevant country of origin information is important in all asylum cases and in particular in the context of the assessment of the right to subsidiary protection on the basis of Article 15(c) of the Qualification Directive. In this assessment collective factors play a significant role. The determining authority should examine whether the person concerned 'belongs, like other people, to a circle of potential victims of indiscriminate violence in situations of international or internal armed conflict'.[118]

It also follows from the case law of the ECtHR that the determining authority should carry out an adequate assessment of the situation in the country of origin which is sufficiently supported by domestic evidence as well as by evidence from other reliable and objective sources.[119] The ECtHR has criticised governments

[115] ECtHR 2 October 2012, *Singh v Belgium*, no 33210/11, para 104.

[116] See also Council resolution regarding minimum guarantees for asylum procedures of 20 June 1995 [1996] OJ C274, para 5, which states that 'when examining an application for asylum the competent authority must, of its own initiative take into consideration and seek to establish all the relevant facts'.

[117] See also Art 4(3) Dir 2011/95/EU.

[118] *Elgafaji* (n 15) para 38.

[119] See *Salah Sheekh* (n 42) para 136; and ECtHR 18 September 2012, *Umirov v Russia*, no 17455/11, para 120.

for failing to include any country of origin information in the assessment of the asylum claim or to refer to such information in their asylum decision.[120] In *MSS* the ECtHR considered that the Belgian Government should have been aware of the general situation in Greece and therefore of the applicant's fears of being returned to this country, although the applicant failed to voice those fears at his interview. In this context, the Court referred to the numerous reports concerning the situation in Greece. According to the Court, in this situation the applicant should not be expected 'to bear the entire burden of proof'. The ECtHR did not explain which part of the burden of proof still rested on the applicant.[121] It did address, however, what was expected of the Belgian authorities: the reports concerning the general situation in Greece should have urged them to verify how the Greek authorities applied their legislation on asylum in practice. They could not assume that the applicant would be treated in conformity with the standards of the ECHR.[122] The Court concluded that the Belgian authorities knew or ought to have known that the applicant had no guarantee that his asylum application would be seriously examined by the Greek authorities.[123]

It should be concluded that it follows from Article 8(2)(b) of Directive 2005/85/EC and Article 10(3)(b) of Directive 2013/32/EU read in the light of the ECtHR's case law, that the determining authority should gather and assess on its own initiative reports concerning the general situation in the country of origin (or transit). The value which should be attached to country of origin or transit country information, in particular reports issued by human rights organisations, will be examined in section 8.6.

The Duty to Request Medical Expert Reports

Directive 2005/85/EC does not explicitly require the determining authority of the Member States to request an expert to write a medical report if the applicant claims to have scars or medical problems as a result of past torture or ill-treatment. Article 18(1) of Directive 2013/32/EU provides that Member States shall arrange for a medical examination of the applicant for signs that might indicate past persecution or serious harm, where the determining authority deems it relevant for the assessment of an application for international protection. Member States may also provide that the applicant arranges for such a medical examination. In both situations the medical examination shall be paid for out of public funds. The examination shall only take place with the consent of the applicant.

[120] See, eg ECtHR 16 October 2012, *Makhmudzhan Ergashev v Russia*, no 49747/11, para 70 and *YP and LP* (n 45) para 70. See also ComAT, Concluding Observations on Hungary (6 February 2007, CAT/C/HUN/CO/4) para 10.

[121] See also H Battjes, 'ECtHR 21 January 2011, *MSS v Belgium and Greece*, no 30696/09' (2011) *Jurisprudentie Vreemdelingenrecht* no 2011/68, sub 6.2.1.

[122] *MSS* (n 30) para 359.

[123] Ibid, para 358. See also ECtHR 23 February 2012, *Hirsi Jamaa et al v Italy*, no 27765/09, paras 131–33 and 156–57 and ECtHR 13 December 2012, *El-Masri v the Former Yugoslav Republic of Macedonia*, no 39630/09, para 218.

If the applicant refuses to undergo the examination, this does not prevent the determining authority from taking a decision on the asylum claim.

Even though Directive 2005/85/EC does not provide for a duty to arrange a medical report, it is contended here that such a duty follows from the duty to conduct an adequate examination of the asylum claim laid down in Article 8(2) of Directive 2005/85/EC. This should be derived from the ECtHR's judgment in *RC*. The ECtHR held in this case that the State authorities have a duty to direct that an expert opinion be obtained as to the probable cause of the applicant's scars, if the applicant submitted a medical certificate, which makes out a prima facie case as to the origin of scars on the body of the applicant (namely torture or ill-treatment).[124] Furthermore, the ECtHR made clear in its judgment in *Yoh-Ekale Mwanje* that the State should also arrange for a thorough medical examination if the applicant claims that his expulsion will violate the prohibition of *refoulement* because of his state of health and the lack of appropriate treatment in his country of origin.[125] In section 8.5.3 it will be contended that medical reports should be considered very important evidence for the assessment of the asylum claim.

The Duty to Gather Evidence Obtainable by the State Authorities, but Unavailable to the Applicant

It may be contended on the basis of the case law of the Court of Justice and the ECtHR that the duty to conduct an appropriate examination of the asylum claim, as well as the principle of full effectiveness of EU law, entails a positive obligation for the determining authority to investigate aspects of the asylum claim, where it has access to the relevant information and the asylum seeker does not. For example, arguably, State authorities are better placed than the applicant to produce decisions on the asylum claims of relatives of the applicant in other Member States, information of judicial proceedings against the applicant pending in the country of origin, or information on the fate of returnees to the applicant's country of origin who have been monitored by the State authorities.[126]

The Court of Justice suggested in *MM* that Member States should cooperate actively with the applicant in order to assemble all the elements needed to substantiate the application particularly where the Member State is 'better placed than an applicant to gain access to certain types of documents'.[127] Furthermore, it accepted in its case law that requiring a party to produce evidence which it

[124] *RC* (n 42) para 53. See also ComAT 23 October 1997, *A v the Netherlands*, no 91/1997, para 6.6 where the Committee considered that the State party had failed to explain why the applicant's claims were considered insufficiently substantial as to warrant a medical examination.

[125] ECtHR 20 December 2011, *Yoh-Ekale Mwanje v Belgium*, no 10486/10, para 106.

[126] For example, in the context of Art 8(6) of Dir 2008/115/EC of the European Parliament and of the Council of 16 December 2008 on common standards and procedures in Member States for returning illegally staying third-country nationals [2008] OJ L348/98.

[127] *MM* (n 110) para 66.

cannot obtain is contrary to the principle of effectiveness.[128] The national court should instead use all the procedures available to it, including ordering measures of inquiry, in order to obtain the evidence, for example from third parties. This was decided in the judgment in *Laboratoires Boiron*. In this case Laboratoires Boiron, a pharmaceutical laboratory, claimed the reimbursement of taxes, arguing that wholesale distributors, which were the laboratory's direct competitors, were not liable to pay those taxes. Laboratoires Boiron claimed that this constituted State aid. According to national law it was Laboratoires Boiron's duty to prove this claim. At the same time, the national courts had wide (discretionary) powers to order all measures of inquiry permissible in law on their own initiative. The question before the Court was whether these rules of evidence were in compliance with the principle of effectiveness. The Court considered:

> [I]f the national court finds that the fact of requiring a pharmaceutical laboratory such as Boiron to prove that wholesale distributors are overcompensated, and thus that the tax on direct sales amounts to State aid, is likely to make it impossible or excessively difficult for such evidence to be produced, since inter alia that evidence relates to data which such a laboratory will not have, the national court is required to use all procedures available to it under national law, including that of ordering the necessary measures of inquiry, in particular the production by one of the parties or a third party of a particular document.[129]

The ECtHR has not explicitly considered that the burden of producing evidence should rest with the authorities of the State when they are better placed to obtain certain relevant information in an asylum case. However, the Court in *Singh* did note that it would have been easy for the State authorities to verify with the UNHCR office in New Delhi whether the UNHCR documents submitted by the applicants were authentic. In doing so the State authorities could have removed any doubts as to the existence of a risk of *refoulement*.[130] Furthermore, in *Bader* the ECtHR found it surprising that the first applicant's defence lawyer in Syria was not contacted by the Swedish embassy during their investigation into the case, even though the applicants had furnished the Swedish authorities with his name and address and he could, in all probability, have provided useful information about the case. In this case the applicant had submitted an original judgment of a Syrian Court in which he was sentenced to death *in absentia* for murder.[131]

The UNHCR *Handbook* states that, in some cases, it may be for the examiner to use all the means at his disposal to produce the necessary evidence in support

[128] Case C-310/09 *Accor* [2011] ECR I-8114, para 100.

[129] Case C-526/04 *Laboratoires Boiron SA* [2006] ECR I-7529, para 55. See also para 57 of this judgment. See also Case C-264/08 *Direct Parcel Distribution Belgium* [2010] ECR I-731, paras 31–37.

[130] *Singh* (n 115) para 104.

[131] ECtHR 8 November 2005, *Bader v Sweden*, no 13284/04, para 45. See also Wouters (n 22) 274.

of the application.[132] The UNHCR here seems to refer to cases of minors[133] and mentally disturbed or traumatised persons.[134]

8.3 INDIVIDUAL ASSESSMENT AND THE USE OF PRESUMPTIONS

According to Article 4(3) of the Qualification Directive, Article 8(2)(a) of Directive 2005/85/EC and Article 10(3)(a) of Directive 2013/32/EU, the assessment of an application for international protection is to be carried out on an individual basis.[135] When assessing asylum claims the determining authority of the Member States sometimes applies certain presumptions to groups of asylum applicants. An important example is that of persons originating from a certain country (a safe country of origin) not needing protection.[136]

Directives 2005/85/EC and 2013/32/EU allow for the use of a presumption of safety of countries of origin or third countries under certain conditions.[137] According to Directive 2005/85/EC, for example, Member States are allowed to designate a country as a safe country of origin where it can be shown that there is generally and consistently no persecution as defined in Article 9 of the Qualification Directive, no torture or inhuman or degrading treatment or punishment and no threat by reason of indiscriminate violence in situations of international or internal armed conflict.[138] If a country is designated as a safe country of origin it is presumed that asylum applicants originating from that country do not have a well-founded fear of persecution or face a real risk of serious harm. According to the Directive the presumption of safety of the country of origin may be rebutted by the applicant. The third country designated as a safe country of origin may only be considered as a safe country of origin for a particular applicant if he has not submitted any serious grounds for considering the country not to be

[132] UNHCR, *Handbook* (n 20) para 196. See also Zahle (n 65) 26.

[133] The UNHCR states in its annotated comments on Dir 2004/83/EC that in the case of asylum-seeking children the burden of proof should be applied flexibly and liberally, by fact-finding and gathering supporting evidence in any manner possible. UNHCR, *Annotated Comments on the EC Council Directive 2004/83/EC of 29 April 2004 on Minimum Standards for the Qualification and Status of Third Country Nationals or Stateless Persons as Refugees or as Persons Who Otherwise Need International Protection and the Content of the Protection Granted (OJ L304/12 of 30.9.2004)* (28 January 2005) www.refworld.org/docid/4200d8354.html accessed 25 September 2013, 16.

[134] See UNHCR, *Handbook* (n 20) para 210.

[135] See also Art 19(4) Dir 2011/95/EU, which requires that the State authorities demonstrate on an individual basis that the person concerned has ceased to be or is not eligible for subsidiary protection.

[136] Other presumptions applied in asylum cases which do not fall within the scope of this study are: all Member States operate equivalent protection systems which comply with human rights standards (the presumption underpinning the Dublin Regulation); all members of a certain organisation are individually responsible for actions giving rise to exclusion from an asylum status according to Arts 12 and 17 Dir 2011/95/EU; and all persons convicted to a certain sentence for a particular offence are a danger to the security or community of the Member State. See also Noll (n 6) 8.

[137] Arts 27, 30–31 and 36 Dir 2005/85/EC and Arts 36–39 Dir 2013/32/EU.

[138] See Art 30(1) and Annex II Dir 2005/85/EC.

a safe country of origin in his particular circumstances and in terms of his qualification as a refugee. If the country of origin is considered safe for the individual applicant, this has some serious consequences. The application may be dealt with in an accelerated procedure and/or may be considered manifestly unfounded.[139] This will generally reduce the asylum applicant's chances of rebutting the presumption of safety.

Asylum applicants may in practice find it (almost) impossible to prove that a presumption, such as the one mentioned above, does not apply in his particular case. In several cases the Court of Justice has held that the use of a presumption which is impossible or excessively difficult to rebut, is contrary to the principle of effectiveness. It is argued in this section on the basis of this case law as well as the case law of the ECtHR and the views of the ComAT and the UNHCR that in asylum cases the use of presumptions is permissible, but only if it is possible to rebut them and if the asylum applicant is granted sufficient opportunity to do so.[140] Whether such presumption must be considered rebutted should be examined on a case-by-case basis. The use of conclusive (irrebuttable) presumptions should be considered contrary to the duty of an individual assessment of the asylum claim. Furthermore, such practice should be considered to undermine the effectiveness of the EU right to asylum and the prohibition of *refoulement*.

Case Law by the Court of Justice

The case law of the Court of Justice shows that the principle that asylum claims should be assessed on an individual basis does not preclude the use of presumptions. However, the use of irrebuttable presumptions violates this requirement as well as the principle of effective judicial protection. This should be derived from the case law of the Court of Justice in asylum cases as well as in other fields of EU law. With regard to asylum cases, the Court of Justice held in *Samba Diouf* that in order for the right to an effective remedy to be exercised effectively

> the national court must be able to review the merits of the reasons which led the competent administrative authority to hold the application for international protection to be unfounded or made in bad faith, there being no irrebuttable presumption as to the legality of those reasons.[141]

In this case the Luxembourg authorities and the Luxembourg court disagreed on the extent to which the reasons for rejecting an asylum claim in an accelerated procedure could be reviewed by the national court in the context of the appeal against the final rejection of the claim.

In *NS and ME and others* the Court of Justice recognised the importance of the presumption of compliance by other Member States, with EU law and, in particular, fundamental rights in the context of the EU as well as the Common European

139 Arts 23(4)(c)(i) and 28(2) Dir 2005/85/EC and Arts 31(8)(b) and 32(2) Dir 2013/32/EU.

140 See also Noll (n 6) 8 and Hailbronner (n 7) 1031.

141 Case C-69/10 *Samba Diouf* [2011] ECR I-7151, para 61.

Asylum System (CEAS). However, it considered that an application of the Dublin Regulation on the basis of the conclusive presumption that the asylum seeker's fundamental rights will be observed in the Member State primarily responsible for his application, is incompatible with the duty of the Member State to interpret and apply the Dublin Regulation in a manner consistent with fundamental rights. The asylum applicant must, according to the Court of Justice, be able to submit evidence in order to rebut this presumption.[142]

The Court of Justice addressed the use of a presumption of responsibility for certain crimes which give rise to the exclusion from an EU asylum status on the basis of Article 12 of the Qualification Directive in its judgment in *B and D*. The Court established that the exclusion from refugee status of a person who has been a member of a terrorist organisation is conditional on an individual assessment of the specific facts. The Court accepted that any authority which finds in the course of this assessment that the person concerned has occupied a prominent position within an organisation which uses terrorist methods is entitled to presume that this person has individual responsibility for acts committed by that organisation during the relevant period. Nevertheless, the Court deems it necessary that all the relevant circumstances be examined before a decision excluding that person from refugee status can be adopted.[143] It should thus be derived from this judgment that the requirement of an individual assessment laid down in Article 4(3) of the Qualification Directive, Article 8(2)(a) of Directive 2005/85/EC and Article 10(3)(a) of Directive 2013/32/EU does not preclude the use of presumptions. However, such presumption may not prevent the determining authority from assessing the specific circumstances of the case. This implies that the individual must be able to rebut the presumption while referring to his individual circumstances.

Cases Concerning the Repayment of Charges Levied by a Member State Contrary to EU Law

In several cases concerning the repayment of charges levied by a Member State contrary to EU law the Court of Justice reached the conclusion that a presumption used by State authorities violated the principle of effectiveness, because this presumption could in practice not be rebutted by an individual party.[144] In *SpA San Giorgio* a company brought an action before the Italian court, reclaiming amounts unduly paid. In these proceedings the State invoked Italian law, which stated that import duties or taxes would not be repaid, when the charge in question had been passed on to other persons in any way whatsoever. This charge was

[142] Joined Cases C-411/10 and C-493/10 *NS and ME et al* [2011] paras 99–105 and the Opinion of AG Trstenjak with this case.

[143] Joined Cases C-57/09 and C-101/09 *B and D* [2010] ECR I-10979, paras 94 and 98. See also the Opinion of AG Mengozzi with this case, para 77.

[144] For judgments with regard to other fields of EU law in which the Court of Justice considered that presumptions must be rebuttable, see eg Case C-508/11 P *Eni SpA* [2013] and Case C-137/11 *Partena ASBL* [2012].

presumed to have been passed on, whenever the goods, in respect of which the payment was effected, had been transferred, in the absence of documentary proof to the contrary. SpA San Giorgio questioned whether these provisions were compatible with principles of EU law. The question put before the Court of Justice was whether the requirement of negative documentary proof rendered the exercise of rights, which national courts are under a duty to protect, virtually impossible. The Court of Justice considered that the conditions for repayment of charges levied by a Member State contrary to EU law may not be contrary to the principles of equivalence and effectiveness. The Court recognised that Member States may take certain measures to prevent unjust enrichment of the recipients. The Court considered, however, that

> any requirement of proof which has the effect of making it virtually impossible or excessively difficult to secure the repayment of charges levied contrary to Community law would be incompatible with Community law. That is so particularly in the case of presumptions or rules of evidence intended to place upon the taxpayer the burden of establishing that the charges unduly paid have not been passed on to other persons[145]

The Court thus held that a presumption that the duties and charges unlawfully levied or collected have been passed on to third parties, and the requirement for the plaintiff to rebut that presumption, are contrary to EU law.[146]

Presumptions in the ECtHR's Case Law and the Views of the ComAT and UNHCR

The ECtHR and the ComAT have accepted in its case law that certain rebuttable presumptions may be used in asylum cases. Like the Court of Justice, the ECtHR held that it needs to be presumed that States comply with their obligations under international treaties.[147] In the context of the Dublin Regulation it must be presumed in the absence of any proof to the contrary, that the Member States of the EU will comply with their obligations under the ECHR and under EU law.[148] However, according to the ECtHR, State parties are required to assess on a case-by-case basis whether there is any evidence which rebuts the presumption that the State party will comply with its obligations stemming from international or EU law.[149] The ECtHR held in several cases that the presumption that a State

[145] *SpA San Giorgio* (n 3) para 14. See also Case C-147/01 *Weber's Wine World* [2003] ECR I-11365, paras 109–17.

[146] For comparable judgments, see Case C-343/96 *Dilexport* [1999] ECR I-579, para 48; Joined Cases C-441/98 and C-442/98 *Kapniki Michaïlidis* [2000] ECR I-7145, paras 36–37; and Case C-129/00, *Commission v Italy* [2003] ECR I-14637 paras 36–40.

[147] ECtHR (Adm) 1 September 2009, *Harutioenyan et al v the Netherlands*, no 43700/07 and ComAT 3 September 2000, *SC v Denmark*, no 143/199 and ComAT 28 November 2003, *EJVM v Sweden*, no 213/2002.

[148] *MSS* (n 30) para 345.

[149] Ibid, paras 341–43. The judgment in *RU v Greece* made clear that the ECtHR itself assesses on a case-by-case basis whether such a presumption is rebutted. ECtHR 7 June 2011, *RU v Greece*, no 2237/08, para 79.

Party of the ECHR complies with its obligations under this Convention should be considered rebutted. The most important example of this type of case is the judgment in *MSS*. In this case the Court based its judgment on numerous reports issued by human rights organisations which pointed at human rights violations by Greece (see section 8.3.1).[150] Furthermore, the ECtHR has held in the context of the assessment of the reliability of diplomatic assurances that

> the existence of domestic laws and accession to international treaties guaranteeing respect for fundamental rights in principle are not in themselves sufficient to ensure adequate protection against the risk of ill-treatment where ... reliable sources have reported practices resorted to or tolerated by the authorities which are manifestly contrary to the principles of the Convention.[151]

It may thus not be presumed that a country complies with national law and human rights treaties where reliable sources show the contrary.

Both the ComAT and the UNHCR have criticised the use of presumptions of safety of countries in asylum procedures. They stress the need for an effective opportunity to rebut this presumption and for an individual assessment of the case.[152] The UNCHR states that

> given the need for an individual assessment of the specific circumstances of the case and the complexities of such a decision, best State practice does not apply any designation of safety in a rigid manner or use it to deny access to procedures. Rather, it bases any presumption of safety on precise, impartial and up-to-date information and admits the applicant to the regular asylum procedure, so that s/he has an effective opportunity to rebut any general presumption of safety based on his/her particular circumstances.[153]

8.4 ASSESSING THE CREDIBILITY OF THE APPLICANT'S STATEMENTS

Many asylum applicants arrive in EU Member States without documents or evidence supporting their asylum account.[154] In most cases, therefore, the asylum application should be examined largely on the basis of the statements of the

[150] *MSS* (n 30). See also *Shamayev* (n 24) and *RU* (n 149) para 82.

[151] *Saadi* (n 24) para 147. See also ECtHR 24 March 2009, *O v Italy*, no 37257/06, para 40 and *Khodzayev* (n 31) para 98.

[152] See ComAT, Concluding Observations on Estonia (19 February 2008, CAT/C/EST/CO/4, 3) and France (3 April 2006, CAT/C/FRA/CO/3, p 4); and UNHCR, *Provisional Comments on the Proposal for a Council Directive on Minimum Standards on Procedures in Member States for Granting and Withdrawing Refugee Status (Council Document 14203/04, Asile 64, of 9 November 2004)* (10 February 2005) www.refworld.org/docid/42492b302.html accessed 25 September 2013, 40.

[153] UNHCR, *Global Consultations on International Protection Asylum Processes (Fair and efficient asylum procedures)* (31 May 2001, EC/GC/01/12) www.refworld.org/docid/3b36f2fca.html accessed 25 September 2013, paras 39–40.

[154] See European Migration Network, *Establishing Identity for International Protection: Challenges and Practices* (February 2013) ec.europa.eu/dgs/home-affairs/what-we-do/networks/european_migration_network/reports/docs/emn-studies/establishing-identity/0_emn_id_study_synthesis_migr280_finalversion_2002013_en.pdf accessed 25 September 2013.

asylum applicant and his family members made during interviews or in writing, in the light of the available country of origin information.[155] In these cases the assessment of the credibility of the asylum account is often decisive.[156] Once the credibility of the individual asylum account is (seriously) called in question, it is usually concluded that there is no well-founded fear of persecution or that no substantial grounds have been shown for believing that there is a real risk of serious harm.[157] It is argued below that if the *general credibility* of the applicant is established, the Member States should, according to Article 4(5) of the Qualification Directive, be required to consider the facts stated by the applicant established, even if no evidence is submitted in support of these facts (that is, they should apply the benefit of the doubt).

Assessing the credibility of asylum applicant's account is a very complex and difficult task.[158] EU legislation does not contain any specific standards with regard to the credibility assessment. However, some guidance as to the factors which should be taken into account when performing such an assessment may be derived from Article 23(4) of Directive 2005/85/EC and Article 31(8) of Directive 2013/32/EU. This provision mentions the circumstances in which an asylum application may be processed in an accelerated procedure and may be deemed manifestly unfounded. Member States and human rights bodies such as the ECtHR, HRC and ComAT often take the following circumstances into account when examining the credibility of an asylum account:

— the applicant has misled the authorities by presenting false information or documents or by withholding relevant information or documents with respect to his identity and/or nationality that could have had a negative impact on the decision;
— the applicant has filed another application for asylum stating other personal data;
— the applicant has not produced information establishing with a reasonable degree of certainty his identity or nationality;
— it is likely that, in bad faith, he has destroyed or disposed of an identity or travel document that would have helped establish his identity or nationality; or
— the applicant has made inconsistent, contradictory, improbable or insufficient representations which make his or her claim clearly unconvincing in relation to his having been the object of persecution.[159]

[155] This follows from Art 4(2) and (3) Dir 2011/95/EU. See also J Herlihy, K Gleeson and S Turner, 'What Assumptions about Human Behaviour Underlie Asylum Judgments?' (2010) 22 *International Journal of Refugee Law* 351, 351–52.

[156] See, eg Popovic, 'Evidentiary Assessment and Non-Refoulement' (n 68) 18 and Thomas, 'Assessing the Credibility of Asylum Claims' (n 1) 79.

[157] See UNHCR, *Beyond Proof, Credibility Assessment in EU Asylum Systems* (May 2013) www.refworld.org/docid/519b1fb54.html accessed 25 September 2013, 28–29. This report contains a lot of information on credibility assessment and practice in several EU Member States.

[158] See, eg Thomas (n 1) 96.

[159] Most of these grounds are also mentioned (in similar wording) as grounds for accelerating the procedure in Art 31(8) Dir 2013/32/EU.

It is argued in this section that national procedural rules or practices which have as a consequence that it is concluded too easily that an asylum account is not credible, undermine the full effectiveness of the EU right to asylum and the principle of *non-refoulement*. From the case law of the ECtHR as well as the views of the HRC and the ComAT several standards emerge which should be complied with in order to ensure the effectiveness of the prohibition of *refoulement*. It follows from this case law, which will be examined more extensively later in this section, that the determining authority should focus on the credibility of the essence of the asylum account and that asylum applicants should be granted the opportunity to provide a reasonable explanation for the alleged shortcomings in their account.

Credibility Assessment by the ECtHR, HRC and ComAT

An asylum account is usually deemed credible when the applicant's statements are coherent, detailed and plausible and consistent with information concerning his country of origin.[160] Human rights bodies often consider an asylum account credible when the State authorities have not presented any information which rebuts the applications allegations.[161]

There are many factors which affect the credibility of the asylum account.[162] It is often a combination of these factors which leads to the conclusion that the asylum account is insufficiently substantiated. First, contradictions or inconsistencies in the asylum seeker's statements, which are not satisfactory explained by the applicant,[163] or a lack of detail in the asylum applicant's account are generally considered to undermine the credibility of the applicant's statements.[164] In *SM* the applicant claimed to have been a courier for the Congolese ambassador in Sweden and a friend, transferring money between them. The Court observed in this case that she had only given very general information about this activity and had failed to specify, for example, how she came to be entrusted with such a secret and dangerous task and the circumstances surrounding her arrest, as well as exactly how she had been able to escape from a hospital where she had been guarded by a soldier. This was one of the reasons why the ECtHR concluded in this case that the asylum account was not sufficiently substantiated.[165]

Furthermore, it is accepted that a person's failure to seek asylum immediately after arrival,[166] the use of a false name or false identity documents without

[160] See, eg *RC* (n 42) paras 52 and 54; *Gaforov* (n 51) para 135; and *Garayev* (n 92) para 72. See also UNHCR, *Handbook* (n 20) para 204.

[161] See, eg *YP and LP* (n 45) para 68; and *Jonny Rubin Byahuranga v Denmark* (n 91) para 11.3.

[162] See Thomas (n 1) 81.

[163] See, eg *AJ* (n 99) paras 59–60 and ECtHR 5 March 2002, *Hemat Kar v Sweden*, no 62045/00. See also ComAT, General Comment No 1 (n 33) para 8(g) and ComAT 21 June 1999, *MBB v Sweden*, no 104/1998, para 6.6.

[164] See *Achmadov and Bagurova* (n 24) and ECtHR 20 January 2011, *NS v Denmark*, no 58359/08, para 94.

[165] ECtHR (Adm) 10 February 2009, *SM v Sweden*, no 47683/08, para 33.

[166] *Rustamov* (n 28) para 116.

explanation,[167] or the applicant's failure to submit identity documents or information on the travel route, may undermine the credibility of the asylum account.[168] When documents submitted by the applicant, such as arrest warrants, court summons or judgments, are discovered to be forgeries, this is also generally held against the applicant.[169] In *EN* the ECtHR considered that the applicant gave a false name and date of birth and submitted a forged identity card to the Swedish authorities. Moreover, he alleged that he had used a fake passport and did not know his travel route while, in reality, he had travelled legally to France on his own passport and with a valid entry visa to study in France. 'These untruths clearly affect the applicant's general credibility negatively in the eyes of the Court.'[170]

The applicant is often reproached for a total absence of evidence supporting the asylum claim or of crucial parts of it, in particular when there are already doubts as to the credibility of the asylum account.[171] For example, in *Achmadov and Bagurova* the ECtHR took into account that the applicants were not in possession of any receipts of police reports or any copies of letters to or from public authorities, lawyers or human rights organisations relating to harassment allegedly suffered by them. Nor did they present any medical statements, despite the fact that one of the applicants had visited a doctor after an assault, just weeks before the applicants entered Sweden. The ECtHR found this remarkable. It particularly referred to the fact that one of the applicants and her adult son had had experience with the German and Italian immigration authorities as a result of an earlier asylum application. Therefore, the ECtHR found that they must have been aware that any kind of evidence would have been of significant value to the asylum proceedings.[172] The ComAT has reproached applicants for a lack of medical evidence supporting an account of past torture or ill-treatment.[173] This is, however, problematic as acts of torture or ill-treatment will not always leave traces on a person's body.[174]

Finally, an important factor which is generally considered to undermine the credibility of the asylum account, would be the fact that the asylum applicant submitted new statements or evidence at a late stage of the asylum proceedings.

[167] *AJ* (n 99) para 59 and ECtHR (Adm) 8 December 2009; *EN v Sweden*, no 15009/09, para 30. See, however, ECtHR 18 April 2013, *MOM v France*, no 18372/10, para 41.

[168] *SM* (n 165) para 33.

[169] See, eg *Matsiukhina and Matsiukhin* (n 100) and *MBB* (n 163) para 6.6.

[170] *EN* (n 167) para 30.

[171] *Achmadov and Bagurova* (n 24); ComAT 21 November 2007, *KA et al v Sweden*, no 308/2006, para 7.3; and ComAT 26 November 2008, *LJR v Australia*, no 316/2007, para 7.5. For the ECtHR see also HJM Baldinger, *Rigorous Scrutiny versus Marginal Review* (Nijmegen, Wolf Legal Publishers, 2013) 254.

[172] *Achmadov and Bagurova* (n 24).

[173] ComAT 15 May 2008, *MX v Sweden*, 311/2007, paras 9.4–9.6; ComAT 2 May 2007, *EVI v Sweden*, no 296/2006, para 8.6, *ERK and YK* (n 105) para 7.4; and ComAT 19 May 1998, *ALN v Switzerland*, no 90/1997, para 8.4.

[174] See the Manual on Effective Investigation and Documentation of Torture and Other Cruel, Inhuman or Degrading Treatment or Punishment (Istanbul Protocol) www.ohchr.org/Documents/Publications/training8Rev1en.pdf accessed 25 September 2013, paras 161 and 172; and ECtHR 25 September 2012, *El Haski v Belgium*, no 649/08, para 86.

For example, the ECtHR noted in *AA* that the applicant did not mention being threatened by the LLTE (Liberation Tigers of Tamil Eelam) in his first two interviews with the migration authorities although one of the interviews lasted approximately six hours. It was not until after the Migration Board had refused to grant him asylum that the applicant claimed to be in danger of revenge from the LTTE. More than two years after the refusal of the Swedish authorities to reassess the asylum claim, the applicant submitted some documents which allegedly concerned the threats that he had received from the LTTE. The Court stated that, taking these circumstances into account, it could not but endorse the national authorities' observations as to the applicant's credibility. In the same judgment, the Court also took into account that the applicant had further extended his reasons for seeking asylum, adding that he would be punished as a deserter upon return to Sri Lanka after his asylum application had been rejected twice.[175]

The ECtHR's judgment in *Hilal* shows that the ECtHR does not base its conclusion that the applicant's asylum account is not credible only on the fact that statements or evidence were submitted at a late stage of the procedure. In this case the applicant mentioned that he was tortured in his second interview which took place more than a month after the initial interview. Furthermore, he waited almost two years to submit significant evidence, such as the death certificate of his brother, medical reports and a police summons. The ECtHR found no reason to reject these documents as forged or fabricated, referring to an expert opinion submitted by the applicant which concluded that the documents were genuine. On the basis of these documents and the applicant's statements the ECtHR concluded that there was a real risk of *refoulement*.[176]

Focus on the Core of the Asylum Account

Inconsistencies, vaguenesses or lack of documents and evidence supporting the asylum account cannot always lead to the conclusion that the asylum account should not be believed. The determining authority sometimes puts too much emphasis on minor defects and refuses to recognise that the asylum applicant's basic story is credible and provides substantial grounds for believing that there is a real risk of *refoulement*.[177] The ECtHR considers that the task of the domestic courts

> is not to search for flaws in the alien's account … or to trip him up, but to assess, on the basis of all the elements in their possession, whether the alien's fears as to the possible ill-treatment in the country of destination are objectively justified.[178]

[175] *AA* (n 99) paras 66–68. See also ECtHR 4 December 2008, *Y v Russia*, no 20113/07; *Hakizimana* (n 46) and ECtHR 20 January 2011, *TN v Denmark*, no 20594/08, para 101.

[176] ECtHR 6 March 2001, *Hilal v the United Kingdom*, no 45276/99.

[177] See, eg Wouters (n 22) 268–69; and Gorlick (n 2) 371–72.

[178] *Azimov* (n 29) para 121.

The case law of the ECtHR, the ComAT and the HRC show that the *general credibility* of the asylum account should be assessed, while less weight is attached to inconsistencies, ambiguities or uncertainties in less relevant parts of the account.[179]

In particular, in the ECtHR's case law some important examples can be found in which the Court found a violation of Article 3 ECHR although there were (serious) doubts about certain parts of the applicant's asylum account.[180] In *Said*, for example, the Dutch authorities found the applicant's account of his arrest, the reasons for it and his escape, so implausible as to invalidate his claim of having deserted from the army. However, the ECtHR proceeded to an assessment of the general credibility of the statements made by the applicant before the Dutch authorities and during the proceedings before the ECtHR itself. The Dutch authorities had not disputed that the applicant had served in the Eritrean army following a general mobilisation. The ECtHR considered that a strong indication that the applicant was indeed a deserter lay in the fact that he applied for asylum in the Netherlands at a time when demobilisation had not yet begun and would not begin for another year. It considered that it was difficult to imagine by what means other than desertion the applicant might have left the army. 'Even if the account of his escape may appear somewhat remarkable … it does not detract from the overall credibility of the applicant's claim that he is a deserter.' The ECtHR concluded that being a deserter, Said faced a real risk of *refoulement* upon return to Eritrea.[181]

In *RC* the ECtHR also ignored inconsistencies in the applicant's escape story, although in this case this part of the asylum account could easily be considered essential for the asylum claim. The applicant claimed that friends had helped him to escape from the revolutionary court, where he would be tried for his participation in demonstrations against the Iranian regime. The government questioned this story while referring to international sources which stated that there was very little public control of these courts, that the proceedings were only open to the parties and, exceptionally, to some family members, and that people who entered and exited the court building were carefully checked. The ECtHR found, however, that 'the applicant's basic story was consistent throughout the proceedings and that notwithstanding some uncertain aspects, such as his account as to how he escaped from prison, such uncertainties did not undermine the overall credibility of his story'.[182] In *FN* the ECtHR was of the opinion that the applicants 'maintained the essentials of their story', even though it acknowledged that the applicants had 'given certain contradictory and inconsistent information about

[179] See, eg ComAT 3 June 2010, *Njamba and Balikosa v Sweden*, no 322/2007, para 9.5; ComAT 22 January 2007, *CT and KM v Sweden*, no 279/2005; and HRC 17 January 2012, *X v Sweden*, no 1833/2008. See also ComAT, General Comment No 1 (n 33) para 8(g) and UNHCR, *Handbook* (n 20) para 204.

[180] See also Spijkerboer, 'Subsidiarity and Arguability' (n 84) 59.

[181] *Said* (n 104) paras 50–53. See also *YP and LP* (n 45) para 69.

[182] *RC* (n 42) paras 44 and 52.

what happened to them in Uzbekistan and that they seem to have added to their accounts'. The ECtHR noted that applicants had presented written evidence, of which at least some had to be taken to support their story. The ECtHR concluded that, 'while the applicants cannot be said to have comprehensively substantiated their story, there are elements which call for caution when evaluating whether they can safely return to Uzbekistan'. The ECtHR found that there was a real risk that the applicants would be subjected to ill-treatment upon return.[183]

Finally, in *N* the ECtHR held that the applicant's basic story was credible although it had 'certain reservations' about the applicant's own testimony before the delegates of the ECtHR which it considered to have been evasive on many points. The ECtHR was not prepared to accept every statement of his as fact. In particular, it found the applicant's account of his journey to Finland not credible. One of the reasons that the Finnish authorities had rejected the asylum claim was due to inconsistencies in the applicant's asylum account, which was not supported by documents.[184] Furthermore, the applicant's identity could not be ascertained as the applicant had used several names and had not presented any identity documents.[185]

It should also be noted that when the risk of *refoulement* follows from the general situation in the country of origin, the credibility of the individual asylum account (except for the person's nationality or State of habitual residence) is of no importance.[186] If a person claims to face a real risk of *refoulement* because he belongs to a vulnerable group, it is sufficient to substantiate that there are serious reasons to believe in the existence of a systematic practice of ill-treatment of that group and that he is a member of the vulnerable group concerned to fall within the scope of Article 3 ECHR.[187] In those situations inconsistencies regarding other elements of the asylum account (such as past experiences, age and travel route) cannot lead to refusal of protection.

Explanations for Alleged Inconsistencies or Late Statements

If the examining authorities present information which gives strong reason to question the veracity of an applicant's submissions, the individual must provide a satisfactory explanation for the alleged discrepancies.[188] This implies that the

[183] ECtHR 18 December 2012, *FN v Sweden*, no 28774/09, para 73.

[184] The applicant's statements made during the Finnish asylum procedure differed from his statements made in the context of an earlier asylum procedure in the Netherlands. According to the Finnish authorities, the applicant's statements concerning his role in the overthrowing of President Mobutu and his escape to Finland had been inconsistent and imprecise.

[185] ECtHR 26 July 2005, *N v Finland*, no 38885/02, paras 152–57. Wouters states that in *N v Finland* elements could have seriously undermined the claim. Wouters (n 22) 268.

[186] See *Sufi and Elmi* (n 31) paras 301–304. In this case the ECtHR did not consider relevant whether the applicant made plausible that he belonged to a minority clan.

[187] *Saadi* (n 24) para 132.

[188] See ECtHR (Adm) 8 March 2007, *Collin and Akaziebie v Sweden*, no 23944/05, *RC* (n 42) para 50. See also Gorlick (n 2) 371.

applicant must be offered the opportunity to rebut the determining authority's findings and that his explanations must be seriously assessed. In *Hilal*, for example, the applicant failed to mention the fact that he was tortured in his first interview. The ECtHR accepted the applicant's explanation for his failure, namely that he did not think he had to give all the details until the full interview a month later. The ECtHR considered that this explanation had become more credible in the light of the medical report submitted by the applicant which confirmed that the applicant was tortured.[189] The HRC found a violation of Articles 6 and 7 ICCPR in the case of an Afghan man who claimed, six years after his first asylum claim, that he was bisexual and would for that reason fear ill-treatment in his country of origin. The Swedish authorities did not accept the applicant's reasons for his late statements, namely 'stigma associated with bisexuality and homosexuality, feelings of shame, fear of reprisal, as well as lack of knowledge that sexual orientation would be a valid claim for refugee status and asylum' as a valid excuse for the delay and deemed these statements not credible. The Committee noted that the Swedish authorities focused mainly on inconsistencies in the author's account of specific supporting facts and the low credibility derived from the late submission of the sexual orientation claim. It found that insufficient weight had been given to the author's allegations on the real risk he might face in Afghanistan in view of his sexual orientation.[190]

Psychological Trauma

Notably, it is accepted by the ComAT that inconsistencies or ambiguities in the asylum account may be the result of psychological problems caused by past torture. In that case these inconsistencies may not be held against the asylum applicant. The ComAT has held in many cases that 'complete accuracy is seldom to be expected by victims of torture'.[191] This applies particularly where the asylum seeker is suffering from post-traumatic stress disorder.[192] The fact that it has been claimed or established that a person has been tortured or detained, is also taken into account by the Committee.[193] In this regard the ComAT attaches importance to medical evidence provided by the author.[194] For example, in *Falcon Ríos* the national authorities concluded that the complainant's testimony contained significant gaps.

[189] *Hilal* (n 176) para 64.

[190] *X v Sweden* (n 179). For a different view, see ECtHR 27 June 2013, *MKN v Sweden*, no 72413/10, para 43.

[191] See, eg *CT and KM* (n 179) para 7.6; *Chedli Ben Ahmed Karoui* (n 91) para 10; ComAT 16 December 1998, *Halil Haydin v Sweden*, no 101/97, para 6.6; ComAT 8 May 1996, *Kisoki v Sweden*, no 41/1996, para 9.3; and ComAT 8 May 1995, *Alan v Switzerland*, no 21/1995, para 11.3.

[192] *Halil Haydin* (n 191) para 6.6 and ComAT 15 November 1996, *Kaveh Yaragh Tala v Sweden*, no 43/1996, para 10.3.

[193] *CT and KM* (n 179) paras 7.5–7.6.

[194] *Halil Haydin* (n 191) para 6.6 and ComAT 8 May 1998, *AF v Sweden*, no 89/1997, para 6.5. In ComAT 3 June 1999, *NP v Australia*, no 106/1998, para 6.6 the ComAT held against the applicant that he failed to submit medical evidence, which could have explained the important inconsistencies in the author's statements before the Australian authorities.

The Committee noted that, according to the psychologist's report, the complainant displayed 'great psychological vulnerability' as a result of the torture to which he had allegedly been subjected. The same report stated that Mr Falcon Ríos was 'very destabilized by the current situation, which presents concurrent difficulties', and that he was 'bruised, weakened by the torture he had undergone and events associated with trauma'. In the Committee's view, the vagueness referred to by the State party could be seen as a result of the psychological vulnerability of the complainant mentioned in the report; moreover, the vagueness was not so significant as to lead to the conclusion that the complainant lacked credibility.[195] The ECtHR also acknowledged that complete accuracy as to dates and events cannot be expected in all circumstances from a person seeking asylum.[196] However, the ComAT and ECtHR do not accept that major inconsistencies can be explained by the fact that the person concerned is a victim of torture or ill-treatment.[197]

In addition, the late submission of statements or evidence may be the result of psychological trauma. In that case the tardiness of the submissions does not affect the credibility of the asylum account.[198] The ECtHR has considered that 'it may be an ordeal to talk about experiences of torture'[199] and that it 'would not deny that symptoms of post-traumatic stress disorder may indeed materialise years after events'.[200] However, the ECtHR has decided in several cases that late statements could not be explained by the applicant's psychological problems. In *Cruz Varas* the Court stated that:

> [E]ven if allowances are made for the apprehension that asylum-seekers may have towards the authorities and the difficulties of substantiating their claims with documentary evidence, the first applicant's complete silence as to his alleged clandestine activities and torture by the Chilean police until more than eighteen months after his first interrogation by the Växjö Police Authority casts considerable doubt on his credibility in this respect.[201]

[195] ComAT 17 December 2004, *Enrique Falcon Ríos v Canada*, no 133/99, para 8.5.

[196] ECtHR (Adm) 17 January 2006, *Bello v Sweden*, no 32213/04.

[197] Ibid. See also ComAT 22 November 2004, *SUA v Sweden*, no 223/2002, para 6.5. See also Wouters (n 22) 267.

[198] On this issue, see Bruin and Reneman, 'Supervising bodies and medical reports', in R Bruin, AM Reneman and E Bloemen (eds), *Care Full, Medico-legal reports and the Istanbul Protocol in asylum procedures* (Utrecht/Amsterdam, Pharos/Amnesty International/Dutch Council for Refugees, 2006), 87–109. For the potential influence of psychological factors on a person's ability to recount past events, see E Bloemen, E Vloeberghs and C Smits, 'Psychological and Psychiatric Aspects of Recounting Traumatic Events by Asylum Seekers' in E Bloemen, R Bruin and M Reneman (eds), *Care Full, Medico-legal reports and the Istanbul Protocol* (Pharos/Amnesty International/Dutch Council for Refugees, 2006) 43–85; J Herlihy, 'Evidentiary Assessment and Psychological Difficulties' in G Noll (ed), *Proof, Evidentiary Assessment and Credibility in Asylum Procedures* (Leiden/Boston, Martinus Nijhoff, 2005) 123–37 and D Rhys Jones, 'Medical Evidence in Asylum and Human Rights Appeals' (2004) 16 *International Journal of Refugee Law* 381, 383. See also UNHCR, *Improving Asylum Procedures: Comparative Analysis and Recommendations for Law and Practice* (Geneva, March 2010) www.refworld.org/docid/4c63e52d2.html accessed 25 September 2013, s 5, 23–24.

[199] ECtHR (Adm) 16 March 2004, *Nasimi v Sweden*, no 38865/02.

[200] ECtHR (Adm) 10 November 2005, *Paramsothy v the Netherlands*, no 14492/03.

[201] ECtHR (Plen) 20 March 1991, *Cruz Varas v Sweden*, no 15576/89, para 78.

The applicant in this case stated two years after his asylum application that he had been subjected to sexual abuse. He said that he had tried to suppress this event and that he found it very painful to talk about. Furthermore, he submitted a medical report which concluded that nothing had been established which contradicted the assumption that he had been subjected to such torture and sexual abuse as he alleged and that there were strong indications that he suffered from post-traumatic stress disorder. In more recent cases the ECtHR also refused to recognise that psychological trauma provided an acceptable explanation for new statements which were made considerable time (a year or more) after the first asylum application. In those cases the Court considered that the applicant had not substantiated that his mental problems were caused by experiences in the country of origin.[202]

The ComAT seems to be more sensitive to the circumstances which may prevent victims of sexual violence to talk about their experiences to the authorities examining the asylum claim.[203] In *VL* the ComAT stated in a case of a woman who had submitted almost two years after her arrival in Switzerland that she had been raped in her country of origin:

> The complainant's explanation of the delay in mentioning the rapes to the national authorities is totally reasonable. It is well-known that the loss of privacy and prospect of humiliation based on revelation alone of the acts concerned may cause both women and men to withhold the fact that they have been subject to rape and/or other forms of sexual abuse until it appears absolutely necessary. Particularly for women, there is the additional fear of shaming and rejection by their partner or family members.[204]

The Committee considered in this case that the complainant's allegation that her husband reacted to the complainant's admission of rape by humiliating her and forbidding her to mention it in their asylum proceedings added credibility to her claim. It noted that as soon as her husband left her, the complainant who was then freed from his influence immediately mentioned the rapes to the national authorities. The ComAT considered further evidence of her psychological state or psychological obstacles, as called for by the State party, to be unnecessary. The Committee concluded:

> The State party's assertion that the complainant should have raised and substantiated the issue of sexual abuse earlier in the revision proceedings is insufficient basis upon which to find that her allegations of sexual abuse lack credibility, particularly in view of the fact that she was not represented in the proceedings.[205]

[202] *Paramsothy* (n 200); ECtHR (Adm) 31 May 2005, *Ovdienko v Finland,* no 1383/04; *Nasimi* (n 199).

[203] See also UNHCR, *Handbook* (n 20) para 198.

[204] ComAT 22 January 2007, *VL v Switzerland*, no 262/2005, para 8.8.

[205] Ibid, para 8.8.

The Minor Age of the Applicant

It was argued in sections 7.1.2 and 7.2.5 that Articles 12 of Directive 2005/85/EC and 14 of Directive 2013/32/EU read in the light of Article 24 of the Charter require that unaccompanied as well as accompanied minors have the right to a personal interview in order to present their asylum claim. It also follows from Article 24(1) of the Charter that the statements made by a minor in such an interview should be taken into consideration in accordance with the age and maturity of the child. On the basis of the views of the Committee on the Rights of the Child (ComRC) and the UNHCR it is argued here that account should be taken of the age and maturity of the child when assessing the credibility of the minor's statements. Inconsistencies or vaguenesses in the child's asylum account may well be explained by the child's young age or immaturity.

According to the ComRC the requirement that due weight must be given to the child's views in accordance with his age and maturity means that 'the views of the child have to be seriously considered when the child is capable of forming her or his own views'.[206] This capacity should be assessed on a case-by-case basis. In the context of Article 12 CRC concerning the right to be heard, 'maturity' means 'the capacity of a child to express her or his views on issues in a reasonable and independent manner'.[207] The Committee states: 'The greater the impact of the outcome on the life of the child, the more relevant the appropriate assessment of the maturity of that child.'[208]

In its Guidelines on Child Asylum Claims the UNHCR points to the fact that children recount their experiences differently than adults and that this has implications for the assessment of the credibility of their statements:

> Children cannot be expected to provide adult-like accounts of their experiences. They may have difficulty articulating their fear for a range of reasons, including trauma, parental instructions, lack of education, fear of State authorities or persons in positions of power, use of ready-made testimony by smugglers, or fear of reprisals. They may be too young or immature to be able to evaluate what information is important or to interpret what they have witnessed or experienced in a manner that is easily understandable to an adult. Some children may omit or distort vital information or be unable to differentiate the imagined from reality. They also may experience difficulty relating to abstract notions, such as time or distance. Thus, what might constitute a lie in the case of an adult might not necessarily be a lie in the case of a child. It is, therefore, essential that examiners have the necessary training and skills to be able to evaluate accurately the reliability and significance of the child's account.[209]

[206] ComRC, General Comment No 12 (2009, CRC/C/GC/12) para 28.

[207] Ibid, para 30.

[208] Ibid, para 30.

[209] UNHCR, *Guidelines on International Protection: Child Asylum Claims under Articles 1(A)2 and 1(F) of the 1951 Convention and/or 1967 Protocol relating to the Status of Refugees* (22 December 2009, HCR/GIP/09/08) www.refworld.org/docid/4b2f4f6d2.html accessed 25 September 2013, para 72.

Applying the Benefit of the Doubt

As was stated above a (total) lack of evidence can undermine the credibility of the applicant's asylum account, particularly if no reasonable explanation is offered for such a lack of evidence. However, Member States should not require proof of each and every statement submitted by the applicant.[210] This follows from Article 4(5) of the Qualification Directive, which only applies if the Member State has made use of the option provided for by Article 4(1) of the Qualification Directive to place the burden of producing evidence in support of the asylum claim on the asylum applicant.[211] Under certain conditions the applicant should be granted 'the benefit of the doubt' and his statements should be accepted as fact even if no or insufficient proof is available.[212] Article 4(5) of the Qualification Directive states that where Member States place the burden of proof on the applicant and where aspects of the applicant's statements are not supported by documentary or other evidence, those aspects shall not need confirmation, if the following conditions are met:

(a) the applicant has made a genuine effort to substantiate his application;
(b) all relevant elements, at the applicant's disposal, have been submitted, and a satisfactory explanation regarding any lack of other relevant elements has been given;
(c) the applicant's statements are found to be coherent and plausible and do not run counter to available specific and general information relevant to the applicant's case;
(d) the applicant has applied for international protection at the earliest possible time, unless the applicant can demonstrate good reason for not having done so; and
(e) the general credibility of the applicant has been established.

It is submitted here that a strict application of the conditions mentioned in Article 4(5) of the Qualification Directive is capable of undermining the effectiveness of the EU right to asylum and the prohibition of *refoulement*. It was argued above that the principle of effectiveness requires Member States to focus on the credibility of the core of the asylum account (general credibility of the asylum applicant). The conditions mentioned in Article 4(5)(a) to (d) of the Qualification Directive may affect the general credibility of the asylum applicant, but this is not necessarily the case. The clearest example of a condition which on its own cannot undermine the credibility of the core of the asylum account is the condition mentioned under (d). The fact that the asylum application was not lodged at the earliest possible time does not in itself exclude the possibility that a person has a well-founded fear of persecution or runs a real risk of serious harm.[213]

[210] See also Boeles, *European Migration Law* (n 108) 338.

[211] According to Battjes, this provision means that if the credibility of the applicant's statements has been established, these statements should be accepted as facts for the purpose of the assessment of the asylum claim. If the conditions listed in Art 4(5) Dir 2011/95/EU are not met 'the relevant aspect of the claim may be regarded as not "substantiated"'. Battjes 2006, 228.

[212] According to Gorlick the application of the benefit of the doubt has been widely adopted in national determination procedures and as part of UNHCR's practices in the field. Gorlick (n 2) 366.

[213] See *Khodzayev* (n 31) para 101; and *Rustamov* (n 28) para 116.

It would be contradictory if the Member States are allowed to refuse the benefit of the doubt on (one of) the conditions mentioned under (a) to (d), while they did not consider them to undermine the general credibility of the asylum applicant. Therefore, the only condition which should be considered independent grounds to refuse the benefit of the doubt is the fact that the general credibility of the applicant could not be established.

This explanation would be in line with the views of the ECtHR, the ComAT and the UNHCR.[214] They seem to be of the opinion that the benefit of the doubt should be applied if the asylum account is generally credible or 'sufficiently substantiated and reliable'.[215] The ECtHR acknowledged that 'owing to the special situation in which asylum seekers often find themselves, it is frequently necessary to give them the benefit of the doubt when it comes to assessing the credibility of their statements and the documents submitted in support thereof'.[216] The UNHCR pointed to the fact that, even if the applicant had made genuine efforts to substantiate his story, there may still be a lack of evidence of some of his statements. According to the UNHCR

> it is hardly possible for a refugee to 'prove' every part of his case and, indeed, if this were a requirement the majority of refugees would not be recognized. It is therefore frequently necessary to give the applicant the benefit of the doubt.[217]

The UNHCR states that the benefit of the doubt should only be given if all available evidence has been obtained and checked. This seems to be a procedural requirement, which ensures that a careful examination has been carried out before the benefit of the doubt is applied. The only material condition which must be fulfilled is that the examiner is satisfied as to the applicant's general credibility. 'The applicant's statements must be coherent and plausible, and must not run counter to generally known facts.'[218] The UNHCR mentions that there may be 'good reasons' to refuse the benefit of the doubt even though the applicant's account appears to be credible. It does not explain, however, what these good reasons could be. The UNHCR is of the opinion that a liberal application of the benefit of the doubt may be called for in cases of unaccompanied minors.[219]

NA is an example of a judgment in which the ECtHR seems to have given the benefit of the doubt. In this case the Court accepted that the detention of the applicant was recorded by the authorities in Sri Lanka (one of the risk factors identified by the Court) although there were many uncertainties about this

[214] See, eg *Collin and Akaziebie* (n 188) and *AJ* (n 99) para 56.

[215] ComAT 29 May 1997, *Aemei v Switzerland*, no 34/1995, para 9.6. See also ComAT 3 June 1999, *HD v Switzerland*, no 112/1998, para 6.4.

[216] ECtHR 9 March 2010, *RC v Sweden*, no 41827/07, para 50.

[217] UNHCR, *Handbook* (n 20) para 203.

[218] Ibid, para 204. See also para 196 and UNHCR, *Note on Burden and Standard of Proof in Refugee Claims* (n 2) para 12. See also Gorlick (n 2) 364 and 366.

[219] UNHCR, *Handbook* (n 20) para 218 and UNHCR, *Guidelines on Child Asylum Claims* (n 209) para 73.

record. The document signed by the applicant's father in order to secure his son's release was not available to the parties and therefore its precise nature was not known. The Court held that, whatever the nature of that document, at the very least it amounted to a record of the applicant's detention. The Court took into account in its assessment that the credibility of the applicant's account was not disputed by the government of the State Party.[220] In *Gaforov* the Court accepted as a fact the applicant's submission that he had already experienced ill-treatment at the hands of the Tajikistani law enforcement officials. The Court observed that the applicant did not adduce certain evidence to support his submission, but it considered nonetheless that the applicant's account of events was consistent and detailed.[221] Finally, in *N v Sweden* the government contended that the applicant's claim that her family had rejected her and that she had no social network or male protection in her home country was unsubstantiated. The Court noted, however, that although there were divergences as to whether the applicant's last contact with her family had been in the summer of 2005 or in October 2005, no information had been presented which gave strong reasons to question the veracity of her submissions that she had had no contact with her family for almost five years, which supported her claim that she no longer had a social network or adequate protection in Afghanistan.[222]

Subconclusion: Assessing Credibility

It should be concluded on the basis of the case law examined above that Member States may refuse an asylum claim in case of a lack of evidence and major deficiencies in an applicant's asylum story. However, the full effectiveness of the EU right to asylum and the prohibition of *refoulement* is seriously undermined if Member States focus on marginal issues such as non-compliance with procedural rules or inconsistencies in parts of the applicant's account which do not relate to the essence of the asylum claim.

Asylum applicants should be granted the opportunity to explain the alleged deficiencies in their asylum account. It follows from the case law of the ECtHR and the views of the ComAT that inconsistencies in an asylum account or late statements by the applicant which are caused by psychological trauma, should not be held against the applicant. However, the ECtHR is reluctant to accept that inconsistencies—and in particular late statements—are the result of psychological problems, while the ComAT is more ready to accept such problems as an explanation. It was explained in chapter four that more weight should be given to the ECtHR's case law as a source of inspiration of EU fundamental rights than the views of the ComAT. However, arguably this should be different if it concerns the weight which should be attached to the late statements of persons suffering

[220] *NA* (n 38) para 143.
[221] *Gaforov* (n 51) para 135.
[222] *N v Sweden* (n 31) para 61.

from psychological problems. The ComAT is specialised in the examination of cases of victims of torture, and is therefore potentially more sensitive to the potential difficulties encountered by such persons when talking about their experiences. Furthermore, it should be noted that the ECtHR does not deem an asylum account not credible only because the applicant made new statements concerning his asylum motives or provided evidence at a late stage in the procedure. In the case of *Hilal* the ECtHR was convinced that there was a risk of *refoulement*, even though the applicant had not mentioned that he was tortured in his first interview and had provided crucial evidence on his asylum claim at a considerable time after the asylum application had been lodged. It follows from the views of the ComRC and the UNHCR that account should be taken of the age and maturity of the child when assessing the credibility of the minor's statements.

As soon as the general credibility of the asylum applicant is established according to Article 4(5) of the Qualification Directive, his statements should be accepted as facts, without requiring further evidence. Refusing the benefit of the doubt in such a situation, for example, because the applicant did not comply with certain procedural requirements, should be considered as undermining the effectiveness of the EU right to asylum and the prohibition of *refoulement*.

8.5 EVIDENTIARY ASSESSMENT

Asylum applicants may submit all kinds of documents or evidence in order to support their asylum claim. This section examines the question of which types of evidence should be taken into account in the assessment of the asylum claim and how this evidence must be valued. The determining authority of the Member States may regard certain types of evidence as irrelevant or may attach very limited significance to them. According to Dutch case law, for example, statements of the applicant's family members or friends who are still residing in his country of origin are considered to be of no value because they do not originate from an 'objective source'.[223] Documents the authenticity of which cannot be established by the Dutch authorities, because of a lack of reference documents, are not taken into consideration in subsequent asylum applications as they are not considered to be new facts or circumstances.[224]

In this section it is argued that the automatic exclusion of specific types or forms of evidence or the fact that very little weight is attributed to them, may violate the duty to conduct an appropriate examination of the asylum claim, which

[223] These statements may regard their own observations or experiences or concern the risk the applicant faces upon return. See, eg Administrative Jurisdiction Division of the Council of State 18 November 2008, no 200805862/1, where the court considered that the statements made by the applicant's father could not be regarded as new facts as they did not originate from an objective source and were not supported by any other concrete evidence.

[224] See, eg Administrative Jurisdiction Division of the Council of State 26 May 2009, no 200902200/1/V2.

follows from Article 8(2) of Directive 2005/85/EC and Article 10(3) of Directive 2013/32/EU read in the light of the principle of full effectiveness of EU law.

Section 8.5.1 addresses the weight which must be given to expert reports. In this section two types of expert reports are specifically addressed: country of origin information and medical reports.

EU Standards Regarding Evidentiary Assessment

Article 4 of the Qualification Directive mentions the elements which should be taken into account in the assessment of the asylum claim and therefore also gives some general indications as to which types of documents or other evidence should be considered relevant. It may be derived from Article 4(2), (3) and (4) of the Qualification Directive that evidence concerning the following elements should be considered: the position and personal circumstances of the applicant,[225] in particular the reasons for applying for asylum including previous persecution to which he was exposed,[226] the situation in the country of origin,[227] the applicant's activities in the country of refuge, which may lead to a risk of *refoulement* upon his return to the country of origin[228] and the availability of safe third countries.[229] As the Qualification Directive does not address which specific types of evidence should be included or excluded from the assessment of the asylum claim, the determining authority has wide discretion in the evaluation of all materials adduced by the applicant. However, it is conceivable that the exclusion of relevant evidence from the assessment of the asylum claims, or the fact that little value is attributed to this evidence, is capable of undermining the effectiveness of the EU right to asylum and the principle of *non-refoulement*. Such exclusion should, therefore, be considered contrary to the duty to conduct an appropriate examination of the asylum claim following from Article 8(2) of Directive 2005/85/EC and Article 10(3) of Directive 2013/32/EU and the effectiveness of the EU prohibition of *refoulement* and the right to asylum.

The Court of Justice has ruled in several cases that the requirement of a particular type of evidence in support of a claim may undermine the effectiveness of EU law. In *Bolbol* the Court held that registration with the United Nations Relief and Works Agency for Palestine Refugees (UNWRA) is sufficient proof that a person had availed himself of the assistance of UNWRA. However, as such assistance can be provided even in the absence of such registration, the beneficiary must be permitted to adduce evidence of that assistance by other means.[230] AG Sharpston,

[225] Art 4(3) and (4) Dir 2011/95/EU refers to background, gender and age, identity, nationality, country(ies) and place(s) of previous residence and previous asylum applications.

[226] See Art 4(4) Dir 2011/95/EU.

[227] See Art 4(2) and (3) Dir 2011/95/EU.

[228] Art 4(3) Dir 2011/95/EU mentions 'the applicant's activities since leaving the country of origin' as a relevant element.

[229] Art 4(3) Dir 2011/95/EU mentions 'whether the applicant could reasonably be expected to avail himself of the protection of another country where he could assert citizenship' as a relevant element.

[230] *Bolbol* (n 9) para 52. See also the Opinion of AG Sharpston, para 98.

in her Opinion in this case, stated that 'the State is entitled to insist on some evidence, but not on the best evidence that might be produced in an ideal world'.[231]

The principle that national authorities are not allowed to accept only the best possible evidence in support of a claim under EU law can also be found in the case law concerning other fields of EU law, in particular tax law. In *SpA San Giorgio*, the Court of Justice considered that requirements of proof having the effect of making it virtually impossible or excessively difficult to exercise a Community right may include 'special limitations concerning the form of the evidence to be adduced, such as the exclusion of any kind of evidence other than documentary evidence'.[232] In *Meilicke* the Court of Justice held under the principle of sound administration and the principle of proportionality that the tax authorities of a Member State are entitled to require the taxpayer to provide such proof as they may consider necessary in order to determine whether the conditions for a tax advantage provided for in the legislation applicable to the case at issue have been met and, consequently, whether or not to grant that advantage.[233] However, according to the Court such an assessment must not be conducted too formalistically. The tax authorities of the Member State of taxation should accept documentary evidence which enables them to ascertain, clearly and precisely, whether the conditions for obtaining a tax advantage have been met. Evidence should be taken into account even if it lacks the degree of detail and is not presented in the form of a corporation tax certificate which is usually required. Only if no such evidence is produced may the relevant tax authorities refuse the tax advantage sought.[234] It follows from these judgments that the (automatic) exclusion of particular forms of evidence may be contrary to the principle of effectiveness.[235]

Evidentiary Assessment in Asylum Cases before the ECtHR, ComAT and HRC

More specific guidance as to the relevance and value of certain types of evidence is offered by the case law of the ECtHR, ComAT and HRC. These bodies have not excluded specific types of evidence when ruling in *refoulement* cases.[236] Documents which they considered particularly relevant include: court summons,[237] police

[231] *Bolbol* (n 9) Opinion of AG Sharpston, para 102.

[232] *SpA San Giorgio* (n 3) para 14. See section 8.4 for a description of the case. See also Case C-228/98 *Dounias* [2000] ECR I-577, paras 71–72.

[233] The case concerned a measure ensuring the effectiveness of fiscal supervision which restricted free movement of capital. Such measure is only justified if the principle of proportionality is observed. See paras 40–42 of the judgment.

[234] Case C-262/09 *Meilicke et al* [2011] ECR I-5669, paras 43–47. See also *Accor* (n 128) paras 99–101.

[235] See also Council Resolution on Minimum Guarantees for Asylum Procedures (n 116) para 4, which states that 'recognition of refugee status is not dependent on the production of any particular formal evidence'.

[236] ComAT, General Comment No 1 (n 33) para 7 states that all pertinent information may be introduced by either party in order to establish whether the applicant would be in danger of being tortured.

[237] ComAT 11 May 2007, *AA v Switzerland*, no 268/2005, para 8.5.

summons,[238] judgments entailing a criminal conviction of the applicant,[239] death certificates of family members[240] and UNHCR documents which state that the applicant has been recognised as a refugee by the UNHCR.[241] Letters written by representatives of political parties or other organisations of which the applicant claims to have been a member or for which he claims to have been active have also been taken into account.[242] The same applies to statements by human rights organisations,[243] (expert) witnesses[244] or relatives[245] regarding the position of the applicant. In *Klein* significant weight was attached to a statement of the Vice President of Colombia printed in a Russian newspaper, even though the source of the information was unknown.[246] In *Hilal* and *N* the ECtHR took into account the statements of the applicant's wife.[247]

Like the Court of Justice, the ECtHR seems to be of the opinion that Member States may not expect ideal evidence in asylum cases. In *FN* the Swedish authorities found that the applicants had not established their identities even though they had submitted original employment books and a birth certificate, the authenticity of which was not questioned by the Swedish authorities. The ECtHR considered:

> Although the Court agrees that the best way for asylum seekers to prove their identity is by submitting a passport in original, this is not always possible due to the circumstances in which they may find themselves and for which reason other documents might be used to make their identity probable.[248]

The ECtHR considered that the employment books and the birth certificate as well as copies of a drivers licence could not be ignored as evidence because some of them contained photographs of the applicants and the information included in the documents was consistent.

Documents are only considered relevant if they contain information relating to the applicant personally and support the risk of *refoulement*.[249] In *Mawajedi Shikpohkt and A Makkamat Shole*, the ECtHR noted that the documents which had been submitted in support of the applicant's allegations contained little of

[238] *Hilal* (n 176) para 65.

[239] *Bader* (n 131) para 44; ECtHR 22 June 2006, *D et al v Turkey*, no 24245/03, para 48.

[240] *Hilal* (n 176) para 64.

[241] *Singh* (n 115), para 101.

[242] ComAT 22 January 2007, *El Rgeig v Switzerland*, no 280/2005, para 7.4; ComAT 5 December 2005, *Dadar v Canada*, no 258/2004, para 8.6; and *Chedli Ben Ahmed Karoui* (n 91) para 10.

[243] *YP and LP* (n 45) para 68; *Saadi* (n 24) para 71 and 144, *CT and KM* (n 179) paras 4.7, 5.8 and 7.6; *Chedli Ben Ahmed Karoui* (n 91) para 10.

[244] ECtHR 2 October 2012, *Abdulkhakov v Russia*, no 14743/11, para 148.

[245] *Gaforov* (n 51) para 135.

[246] ECtHR 1 April 2010, *Klein v Russia*, no 24268/08, para 54.

[247] *Hilal* (n 176) para 66. In this case the applicant's wife applied for asylum in the UK several years after the applicant had applied for asylum there. In *N v Finland* (n 185) the ECtHR took statements from the applicant's wife several years after the applicant had applied for asylum in Finland. See also ECtHR 28 March 2013, *IK v Austria*, no 2964/12.

[248] *FN* (n 183) para 72.

[249] ECtHR (Adm) 6 September 2007, *M v Sweden*, no 22556/05, paras 59 and 92; ECtHR (Adm) 16 June 2009; *AM et al v Sweden*, no 38813/08.

any direct relevance to the applicant herself. In so far as they expressed any fears on her behalf, they were, in the ECtHR's view, vague and speculative.[250] In *Minani* the ComAT took into consideration that the letter of the President of a Burundian human rights organisation only mentioned the risk of being detained and not the real and personal risk of the applicant being tortured upon return to Burundi. It concluded that the applicant did not submit objective elements of such real and personal risk.[251]

The ECtHR seems to consider copies of documents less valuable than original documents.[252] However, copies have been taken into account by the supervising bodies.[253] The fact that there is no official translation of a document may also work to the applicant's disadvantage.[254] As was explained in section 8.4, if a document submitted by the applicant turns out to be a forgery, this is taken into account in the assessment of the credibility of the asylum account. The authorities may not disregard documents which lie at the heart of the application without assessing their authenticity.[255] The ECtHR and ComAT attach significant weight to the findings of the examining authorities, often the embassy in the country of origin, as to the veracity of documents.

The timing of submission of documents in the procedure and the way they were obtained by the applicant may raise questions as to the authenticity of those documents. If documents are submitted at a late stage of the asylum proceedings without valid explanation, this generally reduces their value as evidence.[256] In *Nasimi*, for example, the ECtHR took into account that a copy of a purported revolutionary court summons was submitted to the Swedish Aliens Appeals Board one year and eight months after its date of issue. The ECtHR stated that 'notwithstanding the difficulties of obtaining a copy of such a document in Iran, the applicant has acknowledged, in his submissions to the ECtHR, that he was aware of the existence of the summons long before he received a copy of it'. In these circumstances, the ECtHR found it remarkable that the applicant had apparently failed to even mention the document to the immigration authorities earlier. It also noted that the applicant submitted the summons at a time when he had already had two asylum applications rejected.[257] In *AA and others* on the other hand, the ECtHR considered that there were reasons to question the authenticity of a court record submitted by the applicants since the applicants had not presented any information about how they obtained the document within a few weeks of its

[250] ECtHR (Adm) 27 January 2005, *Mawajedi Shikpohkt and Makkamat Shole v the Netherlands*, no 39349/03. See also ComAT 19 May 1998, *KN v Switzerland*, no 94/1997, para 10.3.

[251] ComAT 10 December 2009, *Minani v Canada*, no 331/2007, para 7.7. See also ECtHR (Adm) 20 October 2008, *MH v Sweden*, no 10641/08, para 39.

[252] *SM* (n 165) para 34.

[253] *FN* (n 183) para 72; ComAT 18 November 1994, *Khan v Canada*, no 15/1994, para 12.4.

[254] ECtHR (Adm) 12 October 2010, *AM v France*, no 20341/08.

[255] *Singh* (n 115) para 104.

[256] See, eg *M v Sweden* (n 248) para 92 and ECtHR 26 October 2004, *B v Sweden*, no 16578/03. See also ComAT 16 May 2003, *HBH et al v Switzerland*, no 192/2001, para 6.8.

[257] *Nasimi* (n 199).

issuance.[258] In *DNW* the ECtHR found it improbable that the Ethiopian authorities would hand over an arrest warrant to members of the applicant's church in Sweden who were visiting Ethiopia. It noted that the applicant did not submit any documents or particulars in support of that claim.[259]

When the authorities question the authenticity or evidentiary value of documents or other evidence submitted by the applicant, the applicant must be given the opportunity to contest the authorities' findings. Where these findings are not addressed by the asylum applicants this will usually be considered as undermining the reliability of the evidence concerned.[260] In *Mehdi Zare*, for example, the ComAT noted that the complainant had adduced what he alleged were two summonses to attend a court. According to the Committee, the State party had provided extensive reasons, based on expert evidence obtained by its consular services in Tehran, why it questioned the authenticity of each of the documents. In reply, the complainant argued that, apparently, the criminal procedure was not applied in this case. The Committee considered that the complainant had failed to disprove the State party's findings in this regard, and to validate the authenticity of any of the documents in question.[261]

In some cases the ECtHR and the ComAT, unlike the national authorities, found that the applicant's explanations were plausible. In *FN* the ECtHR considered that 'the applicants' responses to some of the Swedish authorities' grounds for questioning the documents appear credible and are, moreover, supported by information from international sources'. It stated, for example, that the explanation that the medical certificate from a Tashkent hospital did not state that the applicant had been tortured by the Uzbek authorities because the doctor would then be at risk of repercussions from the authorities, 'seems reasonable'. The ECtHR concluded that 'although the certificate cannot be considered as proof of ill-treatment by the authorities, it is an indication that the first applicant was hospitalised at that time'.[262] In *Chahin* the ComAT considered that the complainant had provided satisfactory explanations for the delay in submitting a translation of a court judgment and medical reports. The Committee took into account that the complainant's asylum application had been prepared by a non-lawyer and that it was only after receiving funds that he was able to obtain the translation and the medical reports.[263]

[258] ECtHR 28 June 2012, *AA et al v Sweden*, no 1499/09, para 81.

[259] *DNW* (n 39) para 43.

[260] See, eg *Matsiukhina and Matsiukhin* (n 100). See also Baldinger, *Rigorous Scrutiny versus Marginal Review* (n 171) 258.

[261] ComAT 17 May 2006, *Mehdi Zare v Sweden*, no 256/2004, para 9.5. See also ComAT 8 July 2011, *MSG et al v Switzerland*, no 352/2008, para 11.4; and *EVI* (n 173) para 8.6, *ERK and YK* (n 105) para 7.5; and ComAT 16 December 1998, *JUA v Switzerland*, no 100/1997. For a different view, see ComAT 25 November 2011, *Eftekhary v Norway*, no 312/2007, para 7.8.

[262] *FN* (n 183) para 71.

[263] ComAT 8 July 2011, *Chahin v Sweden*, no 310/2007, para 9.5.

Subconclusion: Evidentiary Assessment
It should be concluded that Article 8(2) of Directive 2005/85/EC, Article 10(3) of Directive 2013/32/EU and Article 4 of the Qualification Directive, read in the light of the principle of effectiveness, require that the determining authority of the Member State take into account all documents or other evidence which concern:

— the position and personal circumstances of the applicant;
— the reasons for applying for asylum, including previous persecution;
— the situation in the country of origin;
— the applicant's activities in the country of refuge, which may lead to a risk of *refoulement*; and
— the availability of safe third countries.

It follows from the case law of the Court of Justice that the principle of effectiveness prevents the assessment of the evidence submitted in an asylum case from being conducted formalistically. The (automatic) exclusion of certain types of relevant and reliable evidence or the fact that they are only given very limited weight should be considered as undermining the effectiveness of the EU right to asylum and the prohibition of *refoulement*. National authorities are not allowed to accept only the best possible evidence in support of an asylum claim, such as a passport to prove the applicant's identity. They must take into account other evidence substantiating the claim. This should be derived from the judgment of the Court of Justice in *Bolbol* and several tax law cases as well as the ECtHR's judgment in *FN*. The case law of the ECtHR and the views of the ComAT and the HRC show that a wide variety of documents and witness statements should be considered capable of substantiating an applicant's claim of a risk of *refoulement*. The only documents which can be excluded from the assessment of the asylum claim are those which are considered forgeries according to an expert report submitted by the State authorities, and this finding is not sufficiently contested by the applicant. The late submission of documents may undermine their credibility but can never lead to their automatic exclusion.

8.5.1 Expert Reports

In asylum proceedings the determining authority as well as the asylum applicant may submit expert reports in order to support or refute the applicants' claims. Examples of such expert reports are language analysis reports, reports in which the authenticity of documents, such as passports or arrest warrants, is assessed, country of origin information reports and medical reports. Some Member States refuse to take certain expert reports adduced by the asylum applicant into account, or attach very little value to them. It is contended in this section that the exclusion from the assessment of the asylum claim of an expert report containing relevant and reliable information in support of the applicant's asylum claim, may render the applicant's EU right to asylum and the prohibition of *refoulement* ineffective.

It is generally recognised that only expert reports which are of sufficient quality should be taken into consideration. EU asylum legislation does not provide any standards for the quality of expert reports.[264] However, the judgment of the Court of First Instance (CFI) in *Pfizer* provides some useful standards which can be applied in asylum cases. These standards will be assessed in this section.

In sections 8.5.2 and 8.5.3 two specific types of expert reports will be addressed: country of origin information reports and medical reports. The status and value of these reports cause discussion in several Member States. It is argued on the basis of the ECtHR's case law and the views of the ComAT that country of origin information reports and medical reports which are reliable and of sufficient quality should be taken into account in the assessment of the asylum claim. Standards for the quality of these reports can be derived from the *Pfizer* judgment. As will be shown below, the ECtHR and the ComAT use similar standards as those laid down by the CFI in *Pfizer* when examining the quality and/or value of country of origin information and medical reports in asylum cases.

The Case Law of the Court of First Instance Regarding Expert Evidence

In *Pfizer* a regulation was contested, by which the authorisation of an additive in feeding stuffs was withdrawn because of the (potential) risk of this additive for human health. In this context a risk assessment had to be carried out in order to assess the degree of probability of the additive having adverse effects on human health and the seriousness of any such adverse effects. For this purpose the Community Institution had to entrust a scientific risk assessment to experts who would give scientific advice. In *Pfizer* the Commission asked the advice of a committee of experts. However, in its decision it disregarded this committee's opinion, while it did use part of this opinion in support of its decision.

In *Pfizer* the CFI gave standards for reviewing the quality of scientific advice. It held that on matters relating to consumer health, expert advice must be based on the principles of excellence, independence and transparency.[265] Where experts carry out a scientific risk assessment, the competent public authority must be given sufficiently reliable and cogent information to allow it to understand the ramifications of the scientific questions raised and decide upon a policy in full knowledge of the facts. The scientific assessment must enable the competent public authority to take its decision on the basis of the best available scientific data and the most recent results of international research.[266]

The CFI stated in *Pfizer* that the competent public authority in its turn is required to ensure that any measures that it takes be based on as thorough a scientific risk assessment as possible, account being taken of the particular

[264] See also G Noll, 'Evidentiary Assessment in Refugee Status Determination and the EU Qualification Directive' (2006) 12 *European Public Law* 295, 298.

[265] Case T-13/99 *Pfizer* [2002] ECR II-1961, paras 158–59.

[266] Ibid, para 162.

circumstances of the case at issue. The competent Community institution first has to prepare for the committee of experts the factual questions which need to be answered before it can adopt a decision and, secondly, assess the probative value of the opinion delivered by the committee. The CFI considered that the Community institution must also ensure that the reasoning in the opinion is full, consistent and relevant.

The CFI considered that the Community Institutions are allowed to disregard the expert opinion requested by them. However, in such a case the institution must provide specific reasons for its findings by comparison with those made in the opinion, and its statement of reasons must explain why it is disregarding the latter. The statement of reasons must be of a scientific level at least commensurate with that of the opinion in question. In such a case, the institution may take as its basis either a supplementary opinion from the same committee of experts, or other evidence the probative value of which is at least commensurate with that of the opinion concerned. In the event that the Community institution disregards only part of the opinion, it may also avail itself of those parts of the scientific reasoning which it does not dispute. In *Pfizer* the CFI concluded that the Community institutions did not make an error when they decided not to accept the conclusions of the committee of expert's opinion.[267]

Arguably, the requirements of excellence, independence and transparency mentioned in *Pfizer* apply to all expert reports, including those used in asylum procedures. Expert reports should be of sufficient quality to ensure that the decision is taken on the basis of reliable information and to prevent arbitrariness.[268] In this context it does not matter whether these reports have been requested by the examining authority or submitted by the asylum applicant. If the examining authorities request the expert opinion it must pose the right questions to the expert and it has the duty to ascertain that the expert report is of sufficient quality. If the determining authority decides to disregard information in the expert report they must justify this decision.

8.5.2 Country of Origin Information Reports

It was concluded in section 8.2.2 that Article 8(2)(b) of Directive 2005/85/EC and Article 10(3)(b) of Directive 2013/32/EU require the determining authority of the Member States to gather and assess country of origin information reports themselves. Determining authorities often use country of origin information reports produced by their own Ministries. The quality and status of those reports

[267] Ibid, paras 193–210.

[268] The CFI stated in para 172 of *Pfizer* (n 265) that in the relevant case a scientific risk assessment, carried out as thoroughly as possible on the basis of scientific advice founded on the principles of excellence, transparency and independence is an important procedural guarantee whose purpose is to ensure the scientific objectivity of the measures adopted and preclude any arbitrary measures.

has been under discussion in several Member States.[269] Asylum applicants often submit reports of (inter)national human rights organisations and UN bodies concerning the general situation in their country of origin in support of their asylum claim. They sometimes use these reports to dispute the conclusions made in the report produced by the State. Member States may, however, disregard country of origin information submitted by the asylum applicant or attach limited weight to it. In the Netherlands, for example, the country of origin reports issued by the Ministry of Foreign Affairs are considered to be expert reports. According to the standing case law, the determining authority may rely on information laid down in such a report, if this report provides information in an impartial, objective and transparent manner. This applies unless the applicant has submitted specific reasons which cast doubt on the reliability or the completeness of the information contained in the report. According to the Dutch courts, country of origin information reports issued by human rights organisation do not generally provide such specific reasons.[270]

It is argued in this section that EU law requires that the determining authority take into account and attach weight to country of origin information provided by different sources, including reputable human rights organisations. The exclusion of relevant and reliable country of origin information from the assessment of the asylum claim is contrary to EU law. Furthermore, the asylum decision should be based on country of origin information which is of sufficient quality. Quality standards are derived from the *Pfizer* judgment as well as the case law of the ECtHR.

Taking into Account Country of Origin Information from Different Sources

Article 8(2)(b) of Directive 2005/85/EC and Article 10(3)(b) of Directive 2013/32/EU explicitly require the determining authority to take into account country of origin information provided by different sources, including the UNHCR and (in the case of Directive 2013/32/EU) EASO. The significance of UNHCR information regarding the situation in countries of origin or transit may also be derived from the judgment of the Court of Justice in *Halaf*. In this case the Court considered that UNHCR documents were among the instruments likely to enable the Member States to assess the functioning of the asylum system in the Member State indicated as responsible by the Dublin Regulation, and therefore to evaluate the risks to which the asylum seeker would actually be exposed were he to be transferred to that Member State. 'Those documents are particularly relevant in that assessment in the light of the role conferred on the UNHCR by the Geneva Convention,

[269] For the UK, see Thomas (n 1) 85–86; and A Good, 'Expert Evidence in Asylum and Human Rights Appeals: An Expert's View' (2004) 16 *International Journal of Refugee Law* 358, 360–61. For the Netherlands, see *Salah Sheekh* (n 42) paras 80–84.

[270] See, eg Administrative Jurisdiction Division of the Council of State 12 October 2001, no 200103977/1. See also Spijkerboer and Vermeulen, *Vluchtelingenrecht* (n 55) 275–76.

in consistency with which the rules of European Union law dealing with asylum must be interpreted …'.[271]

Furthermore, it follows from Article 4(3) of the Qualification Directive that *all relevant facts* as they relate to the country of origin at the time of taking a decision on the application should be taken into account in the assessment of the asylum claim. Asylum decisions should thus not only be based on information gathered by the State itself, but also on information or reports issued by other organisations. Furthermore, these provisions imply that country of origin information reports submitted by the asylum applicant, which contain relevant and reliable information, should not be excluded from the assessment of the asylum claim.

The recent case law of the ECtHR confirms that in asylum cases the determining authority should base its decision on reliable and objective country of origin information and cannot rely only on reports issued by their own Ministry of Foreign Affairs.[272] It needs to include other country of origin information such as reports by human rights organisations in its assessments. The ECtHR considered in *Salah Sheekh* that

> given the absolute nature of the protection afforded by Article 3, it must be satisfied that the assessment made by the authorities of the Contracting State is adequate and sufficiently supported by domestic materials as well as by materials originating from other, reliable and objective sources.[273]

The Court itself does not hesitate to compare information included in country of origin reports used by the determining authority of the State with other information provided by the complainant or gathered by the Court itself. In *Salah Sheekh* the Court considered that it will gather material on its own initiative, in particular where the applicant—or an intervening party—provides reasoned grounds which cast doubt on the accuracy of the information relied on by the respondent government.[274]

The Quality of Country of Origin Information Reports

Asylum decisions should be based on country of origin information which is of sufficient quality. This follows from Article 8(2)(b) of Directive 2005/85/EC and Article 10(3)(b) of Directive 2013/32/EU according to which the country of origin information taken into account by the determining authority should be 'precise and up-to-date'. Furthermore, it may be derived from the CFI's judgment in *Pfizer* that country of origin information reports should also meet the requirements of excellence, independency and transparency. The reports must contain sufficiently reliable and cogent information. Determining authorities requesting a country of

[271] Case C-528/11 *Halaf* [2013] para 44.

[272] See, eg *Rustamov* (n 28) para 119.

[273] *Salah Sheekh* (n 42) para 136. See also Wouters (n 22) 275.

[274] Ibid, para 136, see also ECtHR 24 April 2008, *Ismoilov v Russia*, no 2947/06, para 120, *Khodzayev* (n 31) para 96 and *Gaforov* (n 51) para 129.

origin information report must pose the right questions to the expert and they have a duty to ascertain that the expert report is of sufficient quality. Furthermore, it may be concluded from *Pfizer*, as well as the more general EU duty to state reasons that if the determining authority decides to disregard country of origin information contained in an expert report it must fully explain this decision.

The ECtHR has shown in its case law that it only takes into account country of origin information which meets certain quality criteria. These criteria resemble to some extent the *Pfizer* criteria of excellence, independence and transparency. In *NA* the Court stated:

> [C]onsideration must be given to its source, in particular its independence, reliability and objectivity. In respect of reports, the authority and reputation of the author, the seriousness of the investigations by means of which they were compiled, the consistency of their conclusions and their corroboration by other sources are all relevant considerations.[275]

When assessing the reliability country of origin information reports the ECtHR takes into account whether their conclusions are consistent with each other, whether those conclusions are corroborated in substance by other sources[276] and whether the information has been refuted by the government of the State party.[277] The consistency of a report with information supplied by other sources is particularly important where this report is based on anonymous sources.[278]

Furthermore, consideration must be given to the presence and reporting capacities of the author of the material in the country in question. The Court observed in this respect that States 'through their diplomatic missions and their ability to gather information, will often be able to provide material which may be highly relevant to the Court's assessment of the case before it'. It finds that the same consideration must apply, a fortiori, in respect of UN agencies, particularly given their direct access to the authorities of the country of destination as well as their ability to carry out on-site inspections and assessments in a manner which States and non-governmental organisations may not be able to do. The Court held in *Sufi and Elmi* that it

> appreciates the many difficulties faced by governments and NGOs gathering information in dangerous and volatile situations. It accepts that it will not always be possible for investigations to be carried out in the immediate vicinity of a conflict and, in such cases, information provided by sources with first-hand knowledge of the situation may have to be relied on. The Court will not, therefore, disregard a report simply on account of the

[275] *NA* (n 38) para 120.

[276] See, eg ECtHR 23 October 2008, *Soldatenko v Ukraine*, no 2440/07, para 71 and *Saadi* (n 24), para 143. In *EG* (n 39) para 70, the ECtHR attached limited weight to an expert report because it differed greatly from the rest of the background evidence.

[277] See, eg *SH* (n 34) para 71.

[278] *Sufi and Elmi* (n 31) paras 233–34.

fact that its author did not visit the area in question and instead relied on information provided by sources.[279]

The ECtHR, moreover, attaches greater importance to reports which consider the human rights situation in the country of destination and directly address the grounds for the alleged real risk of ill-treatment in the case before the Court. The weight to be attached to independent assessments must inevitably depend on the extent to which those assessments are couched in terms similar to Article 3. The ECtHR states that it has, therefore, given due weight to the UNHCR's own assessment of an applicant's claims when it determined the merits of a complaint under Article 3.[280] Conversely, where the UNHCR's concerns are focused on general socio-economic and humanitarian considerations, the Court has been inclined to accord less weight to them, since such considerations do not necessarily have a bearing on the question of a real risk to an individual applicant of ill-treatment within the meaning of Article 3.[281]

The ECtHR has in its case law considered several human rights organisations, most importantly Amnesty International[282] and Human Rights Watch,[283] sufficiently independent, reliable and objective.[284] Furthermore, it has taken into account information provided by UNHCR[285] and other UN agencies, such as the United Nations Secretary General,[286] the United Nations High Commissioner for Human Rights,[287] the United Nations Special Rapporteur on Torture[288] and the United Nations Independent Expert on Minority Issues.[289] Finally, it has referred to governmental sources[290] including the US State Department,[291] the Immigration and Refugee Board of Canada[292] and the UK Border Agency.[293] Sometimes the ECtHR also attaches important weight to individual experts.[294]

[279] Ibid, para 232.

[280] *NA* (n 38) para 122. The Court referred to *Jabari* (n 112) para 41. See also *Abdolkhani and Karimnia* (n 114) para 82.

[281] *NA* (n 38) para 122. The Court referred to *Salah Sheekh* (n 42) para 141. See also ECtHR 20 January 2009, *FH v Sweden*, no 32621/06, para 92.

[282] *Saadi* (n 24) para 143 and *Said* (n 104) paras 51 and 54.

[283] *Saadi* (n 24) para 143 and *NA* (n 38) para 127.

[284] The Court has also referred to reports issued by other human rights organisations, such as the Norwegian Organisation for Asylum Seekers, the Norwegian Helsinki Committee, Greek Helsinki Monitor (ECtHR (Adm) 2 December 2008, *KRS v the United Kingdom*, no 32733/08) and the Helsinki Federation for Human Rights (*Kaboulov* (n 92) para 111).

[285] *KRS* (n 284) and *Abdolkhani and Karimnia* (n 114) paras 80–81 and 85–86.

[286] *Ismoilov* (n 274) para 121.

[287] *NA* (n 38) para 132 and *Ismoilov* (n 274) para 122.

[288] See *NA* (n 38) paras 124 and 132; and *Ismoilov* (n 274) paras 121–22. See also *Harminder Singh Khalsa* (n 49) para 11.3.

[289] ECtHR (Adm) 13 October 2009, *Haililova et al v Sweden*, no 20283/09.

[290] These are sources other than the State party in the case lying before the ECtHR and may be Contracting or non-Contracting States. *Ismoilov* (n 274) para 120.

[291] ECtHR 19 June 2008, *Ryabikin v Russia*, no 8320/04, para 113; and *Khodzayev* (n 31) para 93.

[292] *NA* (n 38) para 135, ECtHR 8 April 2008, *Nnyanzi v the United Kingdom*, no 21878/06, para 64.

[293] *Abdolkhani and Karimnia* (n 114) para 79.

[294] See, eg *SH* (n 34) paras 69–71.

The ECtHR has reproached responding governments for not including relevant human rights reports in the assessment of the claim of a risk of *refoulement*.[295]

Subconclusion: Country of Origin Information Reports
Articles 8(2)(b) of Directive 2005/85/EC and 10(3)(b) of Directive 2013/32/EU and Article 4(3) of the Qualification Directive read in the light of the ECtHR's case law require that Member States do not only rely on the information provided by their own ministries but also take into account reports issued by reputable human rights organisations, UN agencies and authorities of other States. It follows from Article 8(2)(b) of Directive 2005/85/EC and Article 10(3)(b) of Directive 2013/32/EU that country of origin information reports taken into account by the determining authority should meet certain quality standards. This provision explicitly mentions that such reports should be precise and up-to-date. Further useful standards for the examination of the quality and relevance of country of origin information reports may be derived from the Court of Justice's judgment in *Pfizer* as well as the case law of the ECtHR. Such reports should be independent, reliable and objective. The weight which should be attached to a country of origin information report depends on the authority and reputation of the author, the seriousness of the investigations by means of which they were compiled, the consistency of their conclusions, and their corroboration by other sources. Reports which specifically address potential violations of Article 3 ECHR should be considered most relevant. On the basis of the ECtHR's case law Member States may accord less weight to reports which focus on the general socio-economic and humanitarian situation in the country of origin.

8.5.3 Medical Evidence

It was explained in section 8.2 that the fact that an applicant who has already been subject to persecution or serious harm or to direct threats of such persecution or such harm should, according to Article 4(4) of the Qualification Directive, be considered a serious indication of the applicant's future risk of persecution or serious harm. Asylum applicants often submit medical reports to support their allegations of past torture. However, some Member States refuse to admit such reports as evidence in asylum procedures or attach limited weight to them. They argue, for example, that no causal link can be established between scars or medical problems and past torture.[296]

[295] *Gaforov* (n 51) para 125, *Klein* (n 246) para 56.

[296] See, eg ComAT, Concluding Observations on the Netherlands (3 August 2007, CAT/C/NET/CO/4), para 8. Some State parties argued before the ECtHR or the ComAT that the applicant's scars could have been caused by other events than torture. See, eg *RC* (n 42); *Khan* (n 252); and ComAT 22 November 2006, *MN v Switzerland*, no 259/2004.

Directive 2013/32/EU

Article 18 of Directive 2013/32/EU explicitly addresses medical examinations (see also section 8.2.2). It provides that Member States shall arrange for a medical examination of the applicant concerning signs that might indicate past persecution or serious harm, where the determining authority deems it relevant for the assessment of the asylum claim in accordance with Article 4 of the Qualification Directive. When no medical examination is carried out by the Member State applicants should be offered the opportunity to arrange for a medical examination concerning signs that might indicate past persecution or serious harm, on their own initiative and at their own cost. Article 18(3) of the Directive requires the determining authority to take into account the results of both kinds of medical examinations.

Directive 2005/85/EC

Directive 2005/85/EC does not include any provisions on medical examinations and the evidentiary value of medical evidence. However, it is submitted in this section that Article 8(2) of Directive 2005/85/EC and Article 4(4) of the Qualification Directive read in the light of the requirement to ensure the full effectiveness of the EU right to asylum and the prohibition of *refoulement* require that medical reports be taken into account in this assessment. Such interpretation is based on the case law of the ECtHR and the views of the ComAT, which indicate that medical evidence should be considered relevant or even very important in the assessment of the asylum claim.[297]

The Importance of Medical Reports According to the ECtHR and the ComAT

The ECtHR's recent case law shows that States should attach significant weight to medical reports submitted by the applicant which support the applicant's account of past torture or ill-treatment. In *RC* the Court even held that the State is obliged to direct that an expert opinion be obtained as to the probable cause of the applicant's scars in circumstances where the applicant has made out a prima facie case as to their origin. In this case the applicant submitted a medical certificate, which according to the Court 'gave a rather strong indication to the authorities that the applicant's scars and injuries may have been caused by ill-treatment or torture'.[298] It is important to note that this certificate was not written by an expert specialising in the assessment of torture injuries. In the State authorities' view this medical certificate provided insufficient proof of torture injuries, as it could not be ruled out that (some of) the injuries found could be caused by other events than torture or ill-treatment of the applicant. The Swedish Government in this context

[297] On this issue, see also Bruin and Reneman (n 198).

[298] *RC* (n 42) para 53.

pointed to the fact that the medical examination had been performed more than seven years after the alleged torture took place and that the applicant had failed to inform the doctor of other possible causes for some of the injures. The ECtHR in this case requested the applicant to submit a forensic medical report. This report documented numerous scars on the applicant's body. The ECtHR recognised that some injuries may have been caused by means other than torture. However, it accepted the report's general conclusion that the injuries, to a large extent, were consistent with having been inflicted on the applicant by other persons and in the manner in which he described, thereby strongly indicating that he had been a victim of torture. The medical evidence thus corroborated the applicant's story. According to the ECtHR, the applicant's account was also consistent with the information available from independent sources concerning Iran. The Court considered, therefore, that the applicant had substantiated his claim that he was detained and tortured by the Iranian authorities.[299] In several other cases the ECtHR has attributed important or even decisive weight to medical reports submitted by the applicant.[300]

The ComAT has recognised the importance of medical evidence for the assessment of claims of *refoulement* in its General Comment No 1[301] and its Concluding Observations[302] as well as in its views in individual cases.[303] It is of the opinion that State parties should take into account medical reports in their assessment of a claim under Article 3 CAT.[304] Both the ECtHR and the ComAT are inclined to follow the conclusions of a medical report if the State party has failed to contest them.[305]

Quality of Medical Reports

Article 18(1) of Directive 2013/32/EU states that medical examinations arranged by the Member State 'shall be carried out by qualified medical professionals'. The ECtHR and the ComAT have not set any standards as to the quality of medical reports. The ECtHR's judgment in *RC* shows that medical reports issued by persons who cannot be considered experts can also establish a prima facie case as to the origin of scars on the body of the applicant. In such a situation the State party should request an expert to write a medical report. In several cases the ECtHR did

299 *RC* (n 42) paras 53–54; *MOM* (n 167) para 40. See also Baldinger (n 171) 264–69.

300 ECtHR 7 June 2011, *RU v Greece*, no 2237/08, paras 81–82; *YP and LP* (n 45) para 68, *Hilal* (n 176) para 64; and ECtHR (Adm) 7 March 2000, *TI v the United Kingdom*, no 43844/98.

301 ComAT, General Comment No 1 (n 33) para 8(c).

302 ComAT, Concluding Observations on the Netherlands 2007 (n 295) para 8.

303 *Enrique Falcon Ríos* (n 195) para 8.4; ComAT 21 March 1997, *IAO v Sweden*, no 65/1997, para 14.3; *Halil Haydin* (n 191) *Chedli Ben Ahmed Karoui* (n 91); ComAT 12 November 1998, *Ayas v Sweden*, no 97/1997. See also Baldinger (n 171) 164–70. She remarks that since 2000 the Committee has given less weight to medical reports than previously.

304 In its views in individual cases the ComAT sometimes remarks that the authorities failed to take into account medical reports. See, eg *CT and KM* (n 179) para 7.5. See also ComAT, Concluding Observations on the Netherlands 2007 (n 296) para 8.

305 *CT and KM* (n 179) para 7.5; *Enrique Falcon Ríos* (n 195) ECtHR 14 October 2008, *Mehmet Eren v Turkey*, no 32347/02.

refer to the expertise and experience of the physician who drafted the report or the way in which the medical examinations were conducted when assessing the significance to be attached to the report.[306]

Recital 31 of Directive 2013/32/EU provides that national measures dealing with identification and documentation of symptoms and signs of torture or other serious acts of physical or psychological violence, including acts of sexual violence in asylum procedures may, inter alia, be based on the Manual on Effective Investigation and Documentation of Torture and Other Cruel, Inhuman or Degrading Treatment or Punishment (Istanbul Protocol). This protocol provides clear guidelines for the impartial and objective documentation of torture and is applicable to asylum procedures.[307] Several bodies which issue medical certificates that are used in asylum procedures to support allegations of past torture work according to the guidelines of this protocol.[308] Both the ECtHR (in non-asylum cases under Article 3 ECHR)[309] and the ComAT[310] have indicated that the Istanbul Protocol could be used as a tool to examine the quality of a medical report.[311] The Istanbul Protocol provides useful standards in assessing the quality of a medical report, which may be used to fill in the *Pfizer* criteria of excellence, independence and transparency. The Istanbul Protocol states that medical evaluation for legal purposes should be conducted with objectivity and impartiality and that the evaluation should be based on the physician's clinical expertise and professional experience. The clinicians who conduct an evaluation must be properly trained. The medical report needs to be factual and carefully worded. Jargon should be avoided and all medical terminology defined so that it is understandable to lay persons. Furthermore, it is the physician's responsibility to discover and report upon any material findings that he or she considers relevant, even if they may be considered irrelevant or adverse to the case of the party requesting the medical examination.[312]

[306] *MOM* (n 167) para 40; *Cruz Varas* (n 201) paras 39 and 77; and *Mehmet Eren* (n 305) para 43.

[307] The introduction to the Protocol states that documentation methods contained in the manual are applicable to 'political asylum evaluations'.

[308] Examples include the Medical Foundation for the Care of Victims of Torture in the United Kingdom and the Institute for Human Rights and Medical Assessment (iMMO) in the Netherlands.

[309] See, eg ECtHR 1 February 2011, *Desde v Turkey*, no 23909/03, para 98; *Mehmet Eren* (n 305) para 41 and ECtHR 3 June 2004; *Bati v Turkey*, no 33097/96 and 57834/00, para 133.

[310] ComAT, Concluding Observations on the Netherlands 2007 (n 296) para 8; and ComAT, Concluding Observations on the Netherlands (20 June 2013, CAT/C/NLD/5–6) para 12.

[311] The Protocol is not binding on States, but it may serve as a means of interpretation of State's obligations under the ECHR, CAT or ICCPR. See H Battjes 'Legal effects of the Istanbul Protocol' in R Bruin, AM Reneman and E Bloemen (eds), *Care Full, Medico-legal reports and the Istanbul Protocol in asylum procedures* (Utrecht/Amsterdam, Pharos/Amnesty International/Dutch Council for Refugees 2006) 20–21 and 27. It was adopted by the UN General Assembly (UNGA Resolution 55/89 of 4 December 2004) and the UN High Commissioner for Human Rights (Resolution 200/43 of 25 January 2001, E/CN.4/2001/66).

[312] Istanbul Protocol (n 174) para 162. See also Rhys Jones, 'Medical Evidence' (n 198) 385.

Conclusiveness of Medical Reports

It follows from Article 18 of Directive 2013/32/EU that a medical examination should 'concern signs that might indicate past persecution or serious harm'. It does not set any standards as to the content of the medical report. It should be derived from the case law of the ECtHR and the views of the ComAT that the medical report should be sufficiently detailed and conclusive as to the origin of the injuries found on the applicant's body.[313] Usually medical reports contain conclusions as to the degree of consistency between a physical or psychological after-effect and the attribution given to it by the patient.[314] In *RC* the ECtHR attached much significance to the forensic medical report submitted on its request, which concluded that causes for the origins of the scars other than torture could not be completely excluded but that experience showed that self-inflicted injuries and injuries resulting from accidents normally had a different distribution to those showed by the applicant. The findings in that case favoured the conclusion that the injuries had been inflicted on the applicant completely or to a large extent by other persons and in the manner claimed by him. According to the report, the findings strongly indicated that the applicant had been tortured.[315] In *Elmuratov* the ECtHR considered that the medical expert examination report submitted by the applicant was not conclusive as to the date the injuries were inflicted and could not in itself serve as evidence of ill-treatment. The medical report concluded that the applicant had numerous scars which were the result of injuries sustained at least 18 months before the examination and that it was impossible to establish more precisely the date the injuries had been incurred.[316] The ComAT has held that past torture cannot be made plausible only on the basis of a medical report which lacks detail or conclusiveness. However, in several cases the Committee did not exclude such reports as evidence of past torture.[317]

Subconclusion: Medical Evidence

Past experiences of torture or ill-treatment are a serious indication of the applicant's well-founded fear of persecution or real risk of suffering serious harm. It follows from Article 18 of Directive 2013/32/EU as well as the case law of the ECtHR and the views of the ComAT that medical reports which assess the degree of consistency between a physical or psychological after-effect and the applicant's asylum account should be regarded as important evidence in support of such past torture or ill-treatment. It should, therefore, be concluded that the requirement of an appropriate assessment of the asylum application of Article 8(2) of

[313] ECtHR 3 March 2011, *Elmuratov v Russia*, no 66317/09, paras 71 and 86, *MN* (n 295); ComAT 3 June 2010, *AM v France*, no 302/2006, para 13.5 and ComAT 4 July 2011, *RT-N v Switzerland*, no 350/2008, para 8.7.

[314] For the terms generally used in medical reports, see Istanbul Protocol (n 174) para 187.

[315] *RC* (n 42) paras 25 and 53. See also *MOM* (n 167) para 40 and *Kaveh Yaragh Tala* (n 192).

[316] *Elmuratov* (n 312) paras 71 and 86. For a different view, see *Chahin* (n 262) para 9.5.

[317] *ZK* (n 33); *RK* (n 48).

Directive 2005/85/EC and Article 4(4) of the Qualification Directive also require that Member States take such medical reports into account. The refusal to take medical reports supporting an account of past torture into consideration or to attach significant weight to them undermines the effectiveness of the EU right to asylum and the principle of *non-refoulement*. The consideration which should be accorded to a medical report depends on its quality and conclusiveness. However, it may be derived from *RC* that even medical reports issued by a physician who is not an expert specialising in the assessment of torture injuries can make out such a prima facie case as to the origin of scars. In such a prima facie case EU law requires State authorities to request an expert report.[318]

8.6 SYNTHESIS OF FINDINGS

Any requirement of proof which has the effect of making it virtually impossible or excessively difficult to exercise the EU right to asylum or the prohibition of *refoulement* would be incompatible with EU law.[319] In the absence of EU asylum legislation specifically governing a certain evidentiary issue, national evidentiary rules should be tested against this general rule. In this chapter several evidentiary issues were discussed in the light of this principle of effectiveness as well as Article 4 of the Qualification Directive concerning the assessment of facts and circumstances and Article 8(2) of Directive 2005/85/EC and Article 10(3) of Directive 2013/32/EU which contain a duty to conduct an appropriate examination of the asylum claim.

In asylum cases, in principle, the normal evidentiary rules which govern (administrative) procedures, may be applied. Article 4 of the Qualification Directive allows Member States to require the asylum applicant to convince the court that he is in need of international protection and to produce evidence substantiating his asylum claim. However, the special nature of the EU fundamental rights at issue, which require a careful and vigilant assessment as well as the special characteristics of asylum cases (the lack of documentary evidence and the emphasis on the credibility assessment) require the determining authority to adopt an active, flexible and open-minded approach and focuses on the core of the asylum account.[320] Sometimes this authority may be expected to assist the applicant in gathering relevant evidence or to ignore his shortcomings or mistakes. No unrealistic evidentiary requirements should be imposed on the asylum applicant. Otherwise, the applicant's effective exercise of the EU right to asylum or the prohibition of *refoulement* may be undermined.

[318] See also section 8.3.2.
[319] *SpA San Giorgio* (n 3) para 14.
[320] *Salahadin Abdulla* (n 39) para 90.

In particular the following conclusions have been drawn in this chapter:

The Standard of Proof

— It follows from the principle of effectiveness that the standard of proof should not be set too high. It may be expected of the applicant to show that there is a 'reasonable possibility' of future persecution or that there are substantial grounds for believing that he faces a real risk of serious harm.[321] Member States may not require the applicant to *prove* that he will be subjected to persecution or serious harm in the future or that such treatment is more probable than not.[322] This also applies when examining whether an applicant, who poses a risk to the national security of the Member State, is in need of subsidiary protection.[323]

— In the examination of the asylum claim all relevant indicators, with regard to the individual applicant as well as the general situation in the country of origin, should be taken into account.[324] The fact that a person has been persecuted or subjected to serious harm in the past is an important indicator of a future risk of such treatment.[325]

The Burden of Proof

— Member States are allowed to place the burden of proof on the asylum applicant.[326]

— It should be derived from the case law of the Court of Justice in equal treatment cases as well as the case law of the ECtHR that certain circumstances should make the burden of proof shift from the applicant to the determining authority.[327] This is particularly so if:
   1. the applicant has shown that he was persecuted or subjected to serious harm in the past;[328]
   2. the applicant substantiated a risk of *refoulement* by submitting credible statements and/or documents;[329]

[321] For refugee status, see UNHCR, *Handbook* (n 20) para 42 and Gorlick (n 2) 369–70. For subsidiary protection, see *Saadi* (n 24) para 125.

[322] *Mawajedi Shikpohkt and Makkamat Shole* (n 249).

[323] *Saadi* (n 24) para 140.

[324] *Elgafaji* (n 15) paras 38–40; *Sufi and Elmi* (n 31) para 218; and *NA* (n 38) para 130.

[325] Art 4(4) Dir 2011/95/EU, *Salah Sheekh* (n 42) paras 146–47; *RC* (n 42) para 55; UNHCR, *Handbook* (n 20) para 45.

[326] Under EU law the claimant normally bears the burden of proof. See, eg *Brunnhofer* (n 71) para 52. See with regard to asylum cases *Saadi* (n 24) para 129; ComAT, General Comment No 1 (n 33) para 5 and UNHCR, *Handbook* (n 20) para 196.

[327] *Danfoss* (n 80) para 14; *Enderby* (n 71) para 18; and *Brunnhofer* (n 71) para 58.

[328] *RC* (n 42) para 55.

[329] *SH* (n 34) paras 69–71 and *Chedli Ben Ahmed Karoui* (n 91) para 10.

3. country of origin information reports show that serious human rights violations occur in the applicant's country of origin;[330] or
4. the applicant has shown that he belongs to a group which is at risk.[331]

— The duty to produce evidence is shared between the applicant and the determining authority. Article 4(1) of the Qualification Directive requires Member States to cooperate actively with the applicant so that all the elements needed to substantiate the application may be assembled, if the elements provided by an applicant for international protection are not complete, up-to-date or relevant.[332]

— The determining authority has a positive obligation to gather precise and up-to-date country of origin information.[333]

— The determining authority must direct that a medical expert report be written if the applicant makes out a prima facie case as to the origin of the scars on his body.[334]

— The determining authority is required to gather evidence which is accessible to it, but not to the applicant.[335]

Individual Assessment and the Use of Presumptions

— The use of presumptions is permissible even though an individual assessment of the case is required according to Articles 4(3) of the Qualification Directive and 8(2)(a) of Directive 2005/85/EC and 10(3)(a) of Directive 2013/32/EU.

— However, it follows, in particular from the Court of Justice's judgment in *NS and ME and others*, *B and D* and *San Giorgio* that presumptions, which are excessively difficult to rebut are capable of undermining the effectiveness the EU right to asylum and the prohibition of *refoulement*.[336]

Assessing the Credibility of the Applicant's Statements

— When assessing the credibility of the applicant's asylum account, the determining authority should focus on the core of the asylum account and should not put decisive weight on marginal issues such as non-compliance with

330 *Garayev* (n 92) para 73.
331 *Sufi and Elmi* (n 31) paras 249–50.
332 *MM* (n 110) para 66.
333 Art 8(2)(b) Dir 2005/85/EC and *MSS* (n 30) para 358–59.
334 *RC* (n 42) para 53.
335 *Singh* (n 115), para 104. See also *Accor* (n 128) para 100 and *Laboratoires Boiron SA* (n 129) paras 55–57.
336 *NS and ME* (n 142) paras 99–105; *B and D* (n 143) paras 94 and 98; and *SpA San Giorgio* (n 3) para 14.

procedural rules or inconsistencies in parts of the applicant's account which do not relate to the essence of the asylum claim.[337]

- Asylum applicants should be granted the opportunity to explain the alleged deficiencies in the asylum account.[338]
- Inconsistencies in an asylum account or late statements by the applicant, which are caused by psychological trauma or by the minor age of the applicant, should not be held against the applicant.[339]
- As soon as the general credibility of the asylum applicant is established, his statements should according to Article 4(5) of the Qualification Directive be accepted as facts, without requiring further evidence. Refusing the benefit of the doubt in such a situation should be considered to undermine the effectiveness of the EU right to asylum and the prohibition of *refoulement*.

Evidentiary Assessment

- When examining the (documentary) evidence submitted by the asylum applicant, the determining authority should not take a formalistic approach, requiring or excluding specific forms of evidence.[340] All relevant and reliable evidence should be taken into account in the assessment of the asylum claim. This may be derived from the Court of Justice's case law in tax law cases as well as the ECtHR's case law and the views of the ComAT and the HRC, which show that a wide variety of evidence is capable of substantiating an applicant's claim of a risk of *refoulement*.[341]
- It should be derived from the CFI's judgment in *Pfizer* that expert reports must fulfil the requirements of excellence, independence and transparency.[342] Country of origin information reports and medical reports are expert reports which should, according to Article 4 of the Qualification Directive and Articles 8(2) of Directive 2005/85/EC and 10(3) of Directive 2013/32/EU as well as the ECtHR's case law, be accorded important weight in asylum cases.
- Member States may not only rely on country of origin information provided by their own Ministries but should also take into account reports issued by reputable human rights organisations, UN agencies and authorities of other States. It follows from the case law of the ECtHR that the weight which should be attached to a country of origin information report depends on the authority and reputation of the author, the seriousness of the investigations

[337] See, eg *RC* (n 42) paras 44 and 52; *N v Finland* (n 185) paras 152–57; and *Said* (n 104) paras 50–53.

[338] *RC* (n 42) para 50.

[339] With regard to trauma, see particularly the views of ComAt eg in *CT and KM* (n 179) para 7.6 and *VL* (n 204) para 8.8. With regard to children, see ComRC, General Comment No 12 (n 206) paras 28 and 30 and UNHCR, *Guidelines on Child Asylum Claims* (n 209) para 72.

[340] See, eg *FN* (n 183).

[341] *SpA San Giorgio* (n 3) para 14, *Meilicke* (n 233) paras 43–47.

[342] *Pfizer* (n 265) paras 158–59.

by means of which they were compiled, the consistency of their conclusions, and their corroboration by other sources.[343]

— It follows from Article 18 of Directive 2013/32/EU and the case law of the ECtHR and the ComAT that medical reports establishing a link between medical sequelae and the applicant's asylum story should be taken into account when examining the asylum claim in conformity with Article 4 of the Qualification Directive. The weight which should be accorded to a medical report depends on its quality and conclusiveness.[344] However, it may be derived from the judgment of the ECtHR in *RC* that medical reports issued by a physician who is not an expert specialising in the assessment of torture injuries can make out a prima facie case as to the origin of scars.[345]

343 *Salah Sheekh* (n 42), para 136, *NA* (n 38), para 120–122.

344 This follows from the *Pfizer* criteria. See for quality criteria the Istanbul Protocol (n 174) s 8.5.3. See with regard to conclusiveness *Elmuratov* (n 313) paras 71 and 86 and *AM* (n 313) para 13.5.

345 *RC* (n 42) para 53.

9

Judicial Review of the Establishment and Qualification of the Facts

THE ESTABLISHMENT AND qualification (assessment) of the facts is generally considered to be the task of the determining (administrative) authorities. National rules concerning the standard of the judicial review of the facts, including the credibility assessment, depend on the Member State's vision on the division of tasks between the legislator, administration and judiciary. Spijkerboer notes that the national courts 'will generally avoid taking substantive decisions, and merely supervise (a) correct interpretation of the law; (b) the reasonableness of decisions; and (c) conformity with procedural requirements'.[1] However, there are significant differences in the standard (scope and intensity)[2] of judicial review applied by the national courts in the Member States.[3] The (first instance) courts of some Member States consider the determining authorities best placed to establish the facts and therefore pay (more or less) deference to these authorities' decision. The courts of other Member States apply a full judicial review to the asylum decision and replace the findings of the determining authorities with their own findings of fact.[4]

Directive 2005/85/EC does not provide for minimum standards concerning the standard of judicial review. However, in *Samba Diouf* the Court of Justice considered that in order for the European Union right to an effective remedy to be exercised effectively, 'the national court must be able to review the merits of the

[1] TP Spijkerboer, 'Subsidiarity and "Arguability": the European Court of Human Rights' Case Law on Judicial Review in Asylum Cases' (2009) 21 *International Journal of Refugee Law* 48, 52.

[2] The *scope* of judicial review determines which issues are included by the court in its assessment of the case. The review may for instance be limited to questions of law and leave out questions of fact. The *intensity* of judicial review relates to how rigorous the court scrutinises a certain issue. Does the court eg pay deference to the part of the decision in which the credibility of the asylum account is assessed or does it carry out its own credibility assessment?

[3] See also Costello, who states that the deferent standard of judicial review in the Netherlands is incompatible with Art 13 ECHR and EC law while the 'most anxious scrutiny test', which is the standard for the UK judiciary, appears to meet those standards. C Costello, 'The European Asylum Procedures Directive in Legal Context, New Issues in Refugee Research, Research Paper No 134' (Geneva, UNHCR, 2006) 30.

[4] UNHCR, *Improving Asylum Procedures, Comparatative Analyses and Recommendations for Law and Practice*, (Geneva, March 2010) www.refworld.org/docid/4c63e52d2.html accessed 25 September 2013, 461–63.

reasons which led the competent administrative authority to hold the application for international protection to be unfounded or made in bad faith.'[5] The legality of the final decision adopted in an accelerated asylum procedure, and, in particular, the reasons which led the competent authority to reject the application for asylum as unfounded should be the subject of a 'thorough review' by the national court.[6] The Court of Justice has not explained exactly what is meant by a 'thorough review'. Article 46(3) of Directive 2013/32/EU in line with the judgment in *Samba Diouf* provides that Member States should ensure that an effective remedy before a court or tribunal of first instance 'provides for a full and *ex nunc* examination of both facts and points of law'. This should include, where applicable, an examination of the international protection needs pursuant to the Qualification Directive.

In this chapter it is argued that the EU right to an effective remedy sets limits to the Member States' discretion with respect to the standard of judicial review of the fact-finding in asylum cases. The right to an effective remedy precludes that the appeal against the first instance asylum decision is limited to points of law. Furthermore, this chapter contends that EU law requires *rigorous* and *ex nunc* judicial scrutiny of the facts by the national courts in asylum cases. This is based on an examination of the case law of the EU Courts and the European Court of Human Rights (ECtHR) and the views of the UN Committees. It also explores what a 'full' or 'thorough' and *ex nunc* judicial review actually means.

This chapter limits itself to the standard of judicial review of the assessment of the facts in asylum cases. Other issues with regard to the standard of judicial review, such as the possible obligation of national courts to apply EU law *ex officio* or the judicial review of points of law, will not be addressed in this chapter. The question whether EU law requires that the asylum applicant be heard by the national court was examined in chapter seven on the asylum applicant's right to be heard on his asylum motives in first instance and appeal proceedings.

The structure of this chapter is as follows. Section 9.1 argues that the EU right to an effective remedy requires the national court or tribunal to address both of points of law and points of fact. Section 9.2 addresses the required intensity of judicial review of the fact-finding, including the assessment of the credibility of the asylum claim, by the court or tribunal within the meaning of Article 39 of Directive 2005/85/EC and Article 46(3) of Directive 2013/32/EU. Finally, section 9.3 argues that the national court or tribunal should at one stage of the asylum procedure, before the expulsion of the applicant, review the asylum decision on the basis of all relevant available facts and evidence. Conclusions will be drawn in section 9.4.

[5] Case C-69/10 *Samba Diouf* [2011] ECR I-7151, para 61.
[6] Ibid, para 56.

9.1 LIMITATION OF JUDICIAL REVIEW TO POINTS OF LAW?

This section addresses the question whether Article 39 of Directive 2005/85/EC read in the light of the EU right to an effective remedy allows the Member States to maintain or introduce a system in which the facts underlying the asylum decision are assessed by a non-judicial body, while the appeal before the court or tribunal within the meaning of Article 39 of Directive 2005/85/EC will be limited to points of law. Article 46(3) of Directive 2013/32/EU explicitly provides that the court or tribunal examining the appeal against the negative asylum decision in first instance should address both facts and points of law.

The 2010 research of the United Nations High Commissioner for Refugees (UNHCR) showed that in a majority of the Member States surveyed the judicial body, competent to review negative decisions on applications for international protection, has jurisdiction to review questions of both fact and law.[7] However, in Belgium and the United Kingdom the appeal body did not have full jurisdiction over some categories of decisions.[8] In such cases the judicial review was limited to the legality of the decision. In Greece the appeal body, the Council of State, only had jurisdiction to review the legality of the decision by the determining authority and did not review the facts. In Slovenia the facts of an asylum case were also not reviewed by a court or tribunal.[9]

9.1.1 Case Law by the Court of Justice

The Court of Justice held in *Samba Diouf* that the national court within the meaning of Article 39 of Directive 2005/85/EC should be able 'to review the merits of the reasons which led the competent administrative authority to hold the application for international protection to be unfounded or made in bad faith'.[10] In *Samba Diouf* the national court was potentially prevented from reviewing the reasons underlying the decision to process an asylum claim in an accelerated procedure, in the context of the appeal against the decision to reject the asylum application.[11] In that case the reasons for processing the asylum claim in accelerated procedure were identical to the reasons for rejecting the asylum claim. As a result, the national court was potentially not allowed to review the reasons underlying the rejection of the asylum claim. According to the Court of Justice such a situation 'would render review of the legality of the asylum decision impossible, as regards both the facts and the law'.[12] It should be concluded from this that in

[7] UNHCR, *Improving Asylum Procedures* (n 4) s 16, 461.

[8] Ibid, s 16, 461–62. In Belgium this applies to decisions of the Aliens office relating to the preliminary examination of subsequent applications or asylum applications from EU citizens.

[9] Ibid, s 16, 463.

[10] *Samba Diouf* (n 5) para 61.

[11] The referring court and the representative of the Luxembourg Government disagreed on this point.

[12] *Samba Diouf* (n 5) para 57.

asylum cases the national court or tribunal is expected to review factual issues such as whether the applicant has presented false information.

The conclusion that a court or tribunal within the meaning of Article 39 of Directive 2005/85/EC should review the facts is reinforced by the fact that the Court of Justice in *Samba Diouf* referred to its judgment in *Wilson*.[13] It follows from this judgment that under EU law a 'court or tribunal' should be able to review both fact and law. In *Wilson* the Court was asked by a national court to interpret Article 9 of Directive 98/5,[14] which requires a remedy before a court or tribunal in accordance with the provisions of domestic law.[15] In the *Wilson* case the facts were reviewed in first and second instance by non-judicial bodies, which, according to the Court of Justice, could not be considered impartial. Therefore, they did not fulfil the requirements for a court or tribunal as defined by Community law.[16] The Court of Justice established that the jurisdiction of the *Cour de Cassation*, deciding in last instance, was limited to questions of law, so that it did not have full jurisdiction. The Court of Justice ruled that the *Cour de Cassation* could not be considered a court or tribunal as required by Article 9 of the said Directive.[17] It is important to note that the Court of Justice in *Wilson* referred to the 'full jurisdiction test' applied by the ECtHR in cases concerning Article 6 European Convention on Human Rights (ECHR), which will be discussed in the next section.[18]

9.1.2 Obligations Stemming from the ECHR, CAT and ICCPR

The Court of Justice's rulings in *Samba Diouf* and *Wilson* are in line with the ECtHR's interpretation of the term 'court or tribunal' under Article 6 ECHR. Under Article 6(1) ECHR a body can only be considered a court or tribunal within the meaning of Article 6(1) ECHR if it addresses both questions of fact and questions of law.[19] In *Le Compte, Van Leuven and De Meyere* the ECtHR considered that questions of fact and questions of law

> are equally crucial for the outcome of proceedings relating to 'civil rights and obligations'. Hence the right to a court and the right to a judicial determination of the dispute cover questions of fact just as much as questions of law.[20]

[13] Ibid, para 57.

[14] Dir 98/5/EC to facilitate practice of the profession of lawyer on a permanent basis in a Member State other than that in which the qualification was obtained [1998] OJ L77/36.

[15] Case C-506/04 *Wilson* [2006] ECR I-8613, para 60.

[16] In this case: the Disciplinary and Administrative Committee in first instance, or the Disciplinary and Administrative Appeals Committee in appeal.

[17] *Wilson* (n 15) paras 61–62.

[18] Widdershoven states that the Court of Justice in *Samba Diouf* implicitly applied the 'full jurisdiction test' by setting requirements to judicial review. RJGM Widdershoven, 'Case C-69/10, *Samba Diouf* [2011]' (2011) *AB Rechtspraak Bestuursrecht* no 2011/304, para 4.

[19] ECtHR 7 November 2002, *Veeber v Estonia*, no 37571/97, para 70.

[20] ECtHR (Plen) 23 June 1981, *Le Compte, Van Leuven and De Meyere v Belgium*, no 6878/75, para 51.

The ECtHR assesses the overall fairness of the procedure. It accepts that the procedure does not need to be conducted at each of its stages before tribunals meeting the requirements of Article 6(1) ECHR. Demands of flexibility and efficiency, which are fully compatible with the protection of human rights, may justify the prior intervention of administrative, professional or judicial bodies which do not fully satisfy the requirements set by Article 6 ECHR.[21] If the proceedings before a certain body do not comply with those requirements, no violation of Article 6 will be found if another remedy is available which does provide the safeguards required by Article 6(1) ECHR and has full jurisdiction.[22] Courts which only have jurisdiction to assess the lawfulness of a decision do not comply with the full jurisdiction test. In *Zumtobel*, for example, the Court considered that the Constitutional Court, which could inquire into the contested proceedings only from the point of view of conformity with the Constitution and could not examine all the relevant facts, did not have full jurisdiction.[23]

The ECtHR found violations of Article 6 ECHR in cases where the domestic courts or tribunals were precluded from determining a central issue in dispute and had considered themselves bound by the prior findings of administrative bodies.[24] In *Terra Woningen*, for example, the Dutch District Court decided to set the rent for an apartment owned by the applicant at the legal minimum on the ground that the Provincial Executive had designated the area as one where soil cleaning was required. The Court did not go into the question whether the Provincial Executive had acted correctly in making this decision. According to the ECtHR the court, by doing so, deprived itself of jurisdiction to examine facts which were crucial for the determination of the dispute. It therefore found a violation of Article 6 ECHR.[25] In *Chevrol* a violation of Article 6 ECHR was found because the French *Conseil d'Etat* considered itself to be bound by an opinion of the Minister of Foreign Affairs concerning the applicability of a treaty between France and Algeria. It was 'thereby voluntarily depriving itself of the power to examine and take into account factual evidence that could have been crucial for the practical resolution of the dispute before it'.[26]

The ECtHR's case law under Article 13 ECHR indicates that in asylum cases an independent body should review both facts and law. According to the ECtHR 'the notion of an effective remedy under Article 13 requires independent and rigorous scrutiny of a claim that there exist substantial grounds for fearing a real risk

[21] Ibid, para 51.

[22] See, eg ECtHR 22 November 1995, *Bryan v the United Kingdom*, no 19178/91, para 40.

[23] ECtHR 21 September 1993, *Zumtobel v Austria*, no 12235/86, para 30. See also *Veeber* (n 19) para 71, ECtHR 20 June 2002, *Koskinas v Greece*, no 47760/99, para 30.

[24] ECtHR 21 July 2011, *Sigma Radio Television*, nos 32181/04 and 35122/05, para 157, ECtHR 31 July 2008, *Družstevní Záložna Pria et al v the Czech Republic*, no 72034/01, para 111. See also ECtHR 28 June 1990, *Obermeier v Austria*, no 11761/85.

[25] ECtHR 28 November 1998, *Terra Woningen v the Netherlands*, no 20641/92, paras 52–55. See also ECtHR 24 November 2005, *Capital Bank AD v Bulgaria*, no 49429/99.

[26] ECtHR 13 February 2003, *Chevrol v France*, no 49636/99, para 82.

of treatment contrary to Article 3'.[27] It is hard to imagine that 'rigorous scrutiny' can be provided by an authority which is only competent to rule on points of law. The case law of the ECtHR under Articles 3 and 13 ECHR, which will be discussed in section 9.2.2, clearly shows that the national authority must review the facts underlying the decision on the claim based on Article 3 ECHR.[28]

Furthermore, it may be derived from the subsidiary role of the ECtHR and the UN Committees that national courts should assess the facts underlying a claim based on the principle of *refoulement*.[29] The ECtHR has stated in its case law that it 'is sensitive to the subsidiary nature of its role and must be cautious in taking on the role of a first instance tribunal of fact, where this is not rendered unavoidable by the circumstances of a particular case'.[30] Likewise, the Committee against Torture (ComAT) and the Human Rights Committee (HRC) have considered in many cases that it is for the courts of the State parties to the Convention, and not the Committee, to evaluate facts and evidence in a particular case.[31]

9.1.3 Subconclusion: Limitation of Judicial Review to Points of Law?

It follows from the judgments of the Court of Justice in *Samba Diouf* and *Wilson* that a court or tribunal, as required by Article 39 of Directive 2005/85/EC, should review both points of law and points of fact. This view is supported by the case law of the ECtHR under Article 6 ECHR, which requires a court or tribunal to have 'full jurisdiction'. Furthermore, a judicial review which is limited to points of law cannot be considered a rigorous scrutiny as required by the ECtHR in *refoulement* cases. A system in which the facts are established by the administrative authorities and cannot be reviewed by a court or tribunal should therefore be considered

[27] See, eg ECtHR 11 July 2000, *Jabari v Turkey*, no 40035/98, para 50. See also Council of Ministers of the Council of Europe, *Twenty Guidelines on Forced Return* (4 May 2005) www.refworld.org/docid/42ef32984.html accessed 25 September 2013, guideline no 5(2).

[28] The view of the ComAT on this issue is not clear. In ComAT 6 December 2006, *SPA v Canada*, no 282/2005, para 7.4 and ComAT 15 November 2007, *LZB v Canada*, no 304/2006, para 6.6, the ComAT seems to accept that national courts only review the legality of asylum decisions. However, in a more recent case the Committee required a judicial review of the merits, rather than merely of the reasonableness, of decisions to expel an individual where there are substantial grounds for believing that the person faces a risk of torture. ComAT 8 July 2011, *Nirmal Singh v Canada*, no 319/2007, para 8.9.

[29] R Bruin, 'Geen lijdelijke rechter' (2003) 19 *Nieuwsbrief Asiel- en Vluchtelingenrecht* 572; L Wildhaber, *The Place of the European Court of Human Rights in the European Constitutional Landscape*, Address at the Conference of European Constitutional Courts, XIIth Congress 2002 (www.confcoconsteu.org) accessed 10 January 2014, 3.

[30] ECtHR 21 February 2002, *Matyar v Turkey*, no 23423/94, para 108. See also Wildhaber, ibid, 2, where he states that 'European control is a fail-safe device designed to catch the ones that get away from the rigorous scrutiny of the national bodies'.

[31] See, eg *SPA* (n 28) para 7.6 and HRC 18 November 1993, *Kindler v Canada*, no 470/1991, para 6.6. See also Bruin, 'Geen lijdelijke rechter' (n 29) 574.

contrary to Article 39 of Directive 2005/85/EC. Such a system is also not allowed under Article 46(3) of Directive 2013/32/EU.

9.2 THOROUGH REVIEW OF THE ASSESSMENT OF THE FACTS

The Court of Justice considered in *Samba Diouf* that Article 39 of Directive 2005/85/EC, read in the light of the EU right to an effective remedy, requires that the reasons which led the competent authority to reject the asylum application as unfounded should be the subject of a 'thorough review' by the national court.[32] The Court of Justice has thus brought the intensity of judicial review within the scope of the EU right to an effective remedy and with regard to this aspect has limited the procedural autonomy of the Member States.[33] Article 46(3) of Directive 2013/32/EU provides that judicial review by the national court should be 'full'.

In this section it will be examined what a 'thorough' or 'full' review should actually entail. Does it require that the national court substitute its own assessment of the facts with the assessment of the determining authority? Or is a reasonability test of the determining authority's establishment of the facts, including its credibility assessment, sufficient? These questions will be addressed taking into account the case law of the Court of Justice in other fields of EU law as well as the case law of the ECtHR under Articles 3 and 13 ECHR in *non-refoulement* cases and with regard to the 'full jurisdiction' test under Article 6 ECHR.

This section addresses the required intensity of the judicial review of two elements of the asylum decision: (1) the establishment of the facts; and (2) the question whether, on the basis of these facts, the asylum seeker qualifies for protection following the criteria of the Qualification Directive. The intensity of review of these two elements may differ in theory. The Dutch courts, for example, are of the opinion that a limited (marginal) judicial review needs to be applied to the establishment of the facts, while a more rigorous judicial review should be applied to the qualification question.[34] However, in practice, these two aspects of the asylum decision often overlap.[35] In the case law of national and international courts they have regularly not been clearly distinguished. Therefore, the required intensity of judicial review of both aspects will be assessed together.

[32] *Samba Diouf* (n 5) para 56.

[33] See also Widdershoven, 'Case C-69/10' (n 18) para 3.

[34] See, eg Administrative Jurisdiction Division of the Council of State 27 January 2003, no 200206297/1, ECLI:NL:RVS:2003:AF5566.

[35] For example, the question of whether it is plausible that an asylum seeker attracted the special, negative attention of the authorities of the country of origin may be regarded a factual question, but also a qualification question. The same applies to the question of whether the alleged discrimination would cause such a severe restriction of the means of existence that it would prevent the asylum seeker from functioning socially.

In most asylum cases, fact-finding is difficult due to a lack of evidence. In many asylum cases the establishment of the facts consists largely of an assessment of the credibility of the asylum applicant's statements.[36] Some courts may be of the opinion that the determining authority is better equipped to evaluate the evidence and assess the credibility of an asylum account than the court.[37] Therefore, the determining authority should be granted wide discretion and judicial review should be limited to the reasonableness of its decision. The Dutch Council of State, for example, has considered that the determining authority has a margin of appreciation in assessing the credibility of the asylum account.

> It [the decision making authority] assesses the credibility of the asylum account on the basis of extended interviews and a comparison with all it knows of the situation in the country of origin on the basis of country reports and other objective sources and the research done, and the considerations made before in connection with the interviews of other asylum seekers in a comparable situation. This overview enables him to make this assessment in a comparing and therefore objective way. The court is not capable to assess the credibility in a comparable manner. That does not mean that the minister's considerations are not subjected to a judicial review. The standard in the assessment that has to be made is, however, not the judge's own opinion on the credibility of the asylum seekers narrative, but the question whether there is ground for the opinion that the minister … reasonably could not have come to his opinion about the credibility of the narrative. This is irrespective of the fact that the process of decision-making should meet the demands of due process and motivation as required by law, and that the judge must assess the decision by these standards.[38]

However, some judges think differently on the intensity of the judicial review required in asylum cases. A judge of the English Court of Appeal, for example, considered that the court should subject the Secretary of State's decision to rigorous examination. In this judge's opinion this examination must include consideration of the underlying factual material to see whether it compels a different conclusion to that arrived at by the Secretary of State. He asserted:

> [T]his is not an area in which the Court will pay any especial deference to the Secretary of State's conclusion on the facts. In the first place, the human right involved here—the right not to be exposed to a real risk of Article 3 treatment—is both absolute and fundamental: it is not a qualified right requiring a balance to be struck with some competing social need. Secondly, the Court here is hardly less well placed than the Secretary of State himself to evaluate the risk once the relevant material is before it. Thirdly, whilst I would reject the applicant's contention that the Secretary of State has knowingly misrepresented

[36] See ch 8, section 8.4 in this volume.

[37] See also Schuurmans, who states that a reasonableness test is (also) advocated for cases where it is inherently difficult to objectify the facts, as in asylum cases. Y Schuurmans, 'Review of Facts in Administrative Law Procedures; A European Community Law Perspective' (2008) 1 *Review of European Administrative Law* 5, 9.

[38] Administrative Jurisdiction Division of the Council of State 27 January 2003, no 200206297/1. This text is translated from Dutch into English by the author. See also UNHCR, *Improving Asylum Procedures* (n 4) s 16, 49–50.

> the evidence or shut his eyes to the true position, we must, I think, recognise at least the possibility that he has (even if unconsciously) tended to depreciate the evidence of risk and, throughout the protracted decision-making process, may have tended also to rationalise the further material adduced so as to maintain his pre-existing stance rather than reassess the position with an open mind. In circumstances such as these, what has been called the 'discretionary area of judgment'—the area of judgment within which the Court should defer to the Secretary of State as the person primarily entrusted with the decision on the applicant's removal ...—is decidedly a narrow one.[39]

This judge is of the opinion that the court is as well placed as the determining authority to evaluate the risk of *refoulement* on the basis of the facts. Furthermore, he mentioned two other reasons why judicial scrutiny of the facts should be rigorous: the fact that an absolute and fundamental right, the prohibition of *refoulement*, is involved, and the risk that the determining authority would not approach the case with an open mind.

As will be shown in section 9.2.2.2, the ECtHR has accepted that, as a general principle, the national authorities are best placed to assess the facts and, more particularly, the credibility of witnesses since it is they who have had an opportunity to see, hear and assess the demeanour of the individual concerned. However, this does not prevent the ECtHR from making its own credibility assessment if necessary.[40] Before turning to the ECtHR's case law concerning the intensity of judicial review under the right to an effective remedy and the right to a fair trial, the relevant case law of the EU Courts will be examined.

9.2.1 Case Law by the EU Courts

As mentioned above, the Court of Justice considered in *Samba Diouf* that the EU right to an effective remedy requires a thorough judicial review by a national court of the reasons underlying the decision to reject the asylum application.[41] These reasons may include issues relating to the establishment of the facts, notably the fact that the applicant's asylum account is considered to be implausible. This would imply that the requirement of a 'thorough judicial review' also applies to the evaluation of the evidence and the credibility assessment made by the determining authority.

How the term 'thorough judicial review' (or 'full judicial review') must be interpreted cannot be derived from the case law concerning national decisions in other fields of EU law. The Court of Justice has directly addressed the required intensity of judicial review by the national courts in a very limited number of cases. It was

[39] This consideration was cited in ECtHR 6 February 2001, *Bensaid v the United Kingdom*, no 44599/98, para 28.

[40] ECtHR 9 March 2010, *RC v Sweden*, no 41827/07, para 52.

[41] *Samba Diouf* (n 5) para 56.

generally assumed that the intensity of judicial review falls within the procedural autonomy of the Member States.[42] It should be remembered, however, that the way in which national decisions are reviewed by the national court may not render the exercise of a right granted by EU law impossible or excessively difficult.[43]

Some indications for the requirements regarding the intensity of judicial review which follow from the EU right to an effective remedy may be derived from the case law concerning appeals against decisions of the EU Institutions before the EU Courts. In such cases the General Court (like the former Court of First Instance (CFI)) has exclusive jurisdiction to find the facts. The Court of Justice only assesses points of law and examines whether the clear sense of the evidence is distorted.[44] Arguably, the General Court and the Court of Justice in this case law show the level of intensity of judicial review which is required in order to guarantee effective judicial protection. A method of judicial review applied by a national court which is much more restrictive than the method applied by the General Court in similar cases may lead to a violation of the EU right to an effective remedy.[45]

The Court of Justice has recognised that the case law concerning the intensity of judicial review of decisions of the EU Institutions may be considered relevant in the national context. Tridimas states: '*Upjohn* illustrates a tendency to view Community and national authorities as part of one and the same constitutional structure and subject them to equivalent standards of accountability.'[46] In *Upjohn* the Court of Justice held with regard to the principle of effectiveness that the national courts are not required to apply a more extensive judicial review than that carried out by the Court of Justice in similar cases. As a result, the national court was not required to substitute its assessment of the facts and, in particular, of the scientific evidence relied on in support of the decision for the assessment made by the national determining authority.[47] It is questionable whether the reasoning in *Upjohn* can be applied *a contrario*, meaning that the national courts are not allowed to apply a less rigorous judicial review than the EU Courts in similar cases.[48] This does not follow from the judgment in *Upjohn*. Some authors derived from the judgment in *Upjohn* that judicial review on the merits is not required by

[42] Schuurmans, 'Review of Facts in Administrative Law Procedures' (n 37) 30. JS Delicostopoulos, 'Towards European Procedural Primacy in National Legal Systems' (2003) 9 *European Law Journal* 599, 602.

[43] Case C-120/97 *Upjohn Ltd* [1999] ECR I-223, para 32; Case C-467/01 *Eribrand* [2003] ECR I-6471, para 62. See also Schuurmans, (n 37) 30 and 32.

[44] Schuurmans, ibid, 16. See for the jurisdiction of the General Court Art 256 TFEU.

[45] See also Schuurmans, ibid, 34.

[46] T Tridimas, *The General Principles of Community Law* (Oxford, Oxford University Press, 2006) 449.

[47] *Upjohn* (n 43) paras 35–37. See Schuurmans (n 37) 16 and JH Jans, R de Lange, S Prechal and RJGM Widdershoven, *Europeanisation of Public Law* (Groningen, Europe Law Publishing, 2007) 91.

[48] Schuurmans (n 37) 32.

EU law and that a legality review should be considered sufficient.[49] Nevertheless, it should not be ruled out that the intensity of judicial review applied by the EU Courts may be relevant in order to establish the minimum level of intensity of judicial review which the national courts are required to apply in similar cases according to the right to an effective remedy.[50]

It is contended here that the case law of the CFI and the Court of Justice concerning the intensity of judicial review of the establishment of the facts in cases concerning complex assessments should be considered particularly relevant. Complex assessments by the EU Institutions take place in various fields of law and can have a different character.[51] They may, for example, concern medical issues or complex economic assessments, as in the cases of *Pfizer* and *Tetra Laval* which will be discussed in detail in this section.[52]

It is difficult to find facts objectively in both asylum cases and EU decisions involving complex assessments.[53] In asylum cases this is due to the general lack of documentary evidence. In cases involving complex assessments this is because the decision is based on (often contradicting) scientific data or expert reports. In both types of cases it is accepted (with regard to asylum cases at least by some national courts) that because of the difficulties in establishing the facts, determining authorities should enjoy discretion and judicial review should be limited.[54] The determining authorities are considered to be better placed to establish and evaluate the facts than the court, because they have the specific expertise necessary for this task.[55]

The Court of Justice's settled case law requires that, where an EU authority is required to make complex assessments in the performance of its duties, it has wide discretion, which also applies, to some extent, to the establishment of the factual basis of its action.[56] The EU judicature must restrict itself to examining the

[49] See Jans et al, *Europeanisation of Public Law* (n 47) 93–94 and Delicostopoulos, 'Towards European Procedural Primacy' (n 42), 602.

[50] Schuurmans (n 37) 16 and 32. Schuurmans recognises, however, that such a violation will not easily be established. She also notes at 34 that a very limited review of fact-finding may involve the risk of the courts making an error in reviewing the facts and evidence, for which the Member State may be held liable.

[51] Schuurmans states that 'an assessment of the facts is complex, for example, where complicated economic or social assessments must be made, or where an assessment is otherwise based on specific scientific data'. Schuurmans (n 37) 19.

[52] Case T-13/99 *Pfizer Animal Health SA v Council* [2002] ECR II-3305 and Case C-12/03 P *Commission v Tetra Laval* [2005] ECR I-987. See also E Barbier de la Serre and A Sibony, 'Expert Evidence Before the EC Courts' (2008) 45 *Common Market Law Review* 941, 953.

[53] Schuurmans (n 37) 27.

[54] For criticism on the limited judicial review of technical issues, see Barbier de la Serre and Sibony, 'Expert Evidence' (n 52) 894.

[55] Ibid, 955; J Schwartze, 'Judicial Review of European Administrative Procedure' (2004) 68 *Law and Contemporary Problems* 85, 95; P Craig, *EU Administrative Law* (Oxford, Oxford University Press, 2006) 469.

[56] *Pfizer Animal Health SA* (n 52) para 168 and Case 138/79 *SA Roquette Frères* [1980] ECR 3333, para 25. See also Schuurmans (n 37) 19. See for criticism on this case law Barbier de la Serre and Sibony (n 52) 956–57.

accuracy of the findings of fact and law made by the authority concerned and to verifying, in particular, that the action taken by that authority is not vitiated by a manifest error or a misuse of powers and that it did not clearly exceed the boundaries of its discretion.[57] In cases involving complex assessments the EU Courts thus apply a limited judicial review of the fact-finding by the EU Institutions. How can the case law concerning this limited review be relevant for the interpretation of the required 'thorough' or 'full' judicial review in asylum cases?

The CFI's case law concerning cases involving complex assessments shows that in practice this limited form of judicial review is quite rigorous.[58] In several cases concerning the lawfulness of a penalty for the infringement of competition rules the Court of Justice considered the EU Courts 'cannot use the Commission's margin of discretion ... as a basis for dispensing with the conduct of an in-depth review of the law and of the facts'.[59] Furthermore, the EU Courts have tested the EU Institutions' decisions against procedural safeguards. The Court of Justice may use this method of judicial review as a source of inspiration for the interpretation of the term 'thorough judicial' review in asylum cases. Arguably, judicial review which offers a lower intensity of judicial review than the limited review performed by the EU Courts in cases involving complex assessments cannot be considered a thorough judicial review. One must be very cautious in applying the case law concerning complex assessments directly to asylum cases. However, it is possible to draw some general guidelines from this case law which are relevant for asylum cases.[60]

First, the method of review of the facts in cases involving complex assessments will be addressed. The final part of this section will examine the judicial review by the EU Courts of the procedural guarantees offered during the proceedings.

Judicial Review of the Facts in Cases Involving Complex Assessments

In cases involving complex assessments judicial review by the General Court of the way in which the EU Institutions assessed and evaluated the facts is limited. The EU judicature is not entitled to substitute its assessment of the facts for that of the EU Institutions.[61] Instead, it must confine itself to ascertaining whether the exercise by the institutions of their discretion in that regard is vitiated by a manifest

[57] *Upjohn* (n 43) para 34.

[58] Schuurmans (n 37) 25.

[59] Case C-199/11 *Otis* [2012] para 61 and Case C-386/10 P *Chalkor* [2011] para 62. For commentary, see A Sibony, 'Case C-272/09 P, *KME Germany and others v Commission* [2011]' (2012) 49 *Common Market Law Review* 1977.

[60] The intensity of judicial review that national courts are required to supply is influenced directly by the degree of discretion Member States enjoy in their implementation of the EC measure in question. A Ward, *Judicial Review and the Rights of Private Parties in EU Law* (Oxford, Oxford University Press, 2007) 175. The importance of the interests at stake may also influence the required intensity of judicial review. Schuurmans (n 37) 33.

[61] See, eg *Upjohn* (n 43) para 34 and Case T-201/04 *Microsoft* [2007] ECR II-1491, para 88.

Barbier de la Serre and Sibony state that for that reason EU Courts are reluctant to ask for an expert report in cases involving complex assessments. Barbier de la Serre and Sibony (n 52) 953–55.

error or a misuse of powers or whether the institutions clearly exceeded the bounds of their discretion (a reasonableness test).[62] This does not mean, however, that the review by the EU judicature does not closely examine the fact-finding.[63] Several authors have argued that although the wording of the reasonableness test has remained the same, the EU Courts have entered into more rigorous scrutiny of the facts.[64] The Courts have more readily accepted a manifest error.[65] In this section two judgments will be examined in which the EU Courts have applied the intensified reasonableness test. These cases do not necessarily represent the general view of the EU Courts.[66] However, they have been mentioned in literature as leading cases,[67] which should be considered to provide important guidance for national administrative proceedings.[68]

Pfizer Animal Health SA v Council

The first striking example of an intensive review applied by the Court of First Instance in the context of the reasonableness test, is the judgment in *Pfizer* which was discussed in chapter eight, section 8.5.1 on expert reports. In this case a regulation was contested, by which the authorisation of an additive in feeding stuffs, viginiamycin, was withdrawn. The Council took the view that the use of viginiamycin, which was produced by Pfizer, involved a risk to human health. It was, therefore, necessary to withdraw the authorisations relating to the use of the product. The Council had drawn attention in its arguments to the fact that the decision to withdraw the authorisation of a certain additive was based on extremely complex scientific and technical assessments, over which scientists had widely diverging views. Pfizer argued that the contested regulation should be annulled, since the Community institutions had made errors in the analyses of the risks to human health and their application of the precautionary principle. In its view the Community Institutions made errors in their analysis of the various items of scientific evidence, including disregarding the conclusion of an expert opinion which was in favour of Pfizer.

The CFI recognised that the Council enjoyed broad discretion in taking the decision because the case concerned the common agricultural policy, the Community

[62] See, eg *Pfizer Animal Health SA* (n 52) para 169.

[63] Schuurmans (n 37) 30.

[64] Craig, *EU Administrative Law* (n 55) 446–47. Craig describes the early case law of the Court of Justice regarding judicial review of fact and discretion at 439–44. See also Schuurmans (n 37) 20 and Schwartze, 'Judicial Review' (n 55) 100.

[65] Craig, (n 55) 447; Schuurmans (n 37) 20.

[66] Craig shows that judicial review of fact in recent cases concerned with common policies, State aids and structural funds are more far-reaching than the early case law, but is still significantly less intensive than in the risk regulation and merger cases like *Pfizer* and *Tetra Laval*. Craig (n 55) 458. See with regard to the discussion the compatibility of the intensity of judicial review of competition law sanctions with the right to fair trial Sibony, 'Case C-272/09 P'(n 59).

[67] Craig considers *Pfizer* and *Tetra Laval* to be 'prominent examples' of the EU Court's modern approach. Craig (n 55) 447.

[68] See also Schuurmans (n 37) 25.

institutions had to determine the level of risk deemed unacceptable for society and the Community authority was required to make complex assessments in the performance of its duties. Therefore, judicial review of the findings of fact had to be limited to the reasonableness test.[69] However, the CFI set out detailed requirements against which expert evidence should be tested. These requirements follow from the principles of excellence, transparency and independence.[70] The CFI held, for example, that the competent Community Institution must prepare for the expert the factual questions which need to be answered before it can adopt a decision and assess the probative value of the opinion delivered by the committee.[71] Furthermore, it set out the conditions in which the Community Institution may disregard (part of) an expert opinion. Subsequently, the Court reviewed the reasons why the Community Institutions chose to use certain parts of expert reports and to disregard others. It also tested whether the Institution took into account the fact that certain expert reports had methodological limitations and were therefore of less value. The CFI concluded that the Community Institutions did not make manifest errors when they made findings in respect of the relevant facts.[72]

Commission v Tetra Laval

In *Tetra Laval* the Court of Justice indicated specifically what the reasonableness test of the facts in cases involving complex assessments entails. The Court considered that the fact that a decision must be subject to a limited form of judicial review does not mean that the Community judicature must refrain from reviewing the Commission's interpretation of information. Not only must the Community judicature establish whether the evidence relied on is factually accurate, reliable and consistent, but also whether that evidence contains all the information which must be taken into account in order to assess a complex situation, and whether it is capable of substantiating the conclusions drawn from it.[73] This consideration was also used by the CFI and the General Court in later cases concerning other fields of EU law.[74]

[69] *Pfizer Animal Health SA* (n 52) paras 166–69 and 323.

[70] See also ch 8, section 8.5.1.

[71] *Pfizer Animal Health SA* (n 52) para 198.

[72] Ibid, para 311. On this case, see also Craig (n 55) 447–52.

[73] *Commission v Tetra Laval* (n 52) para 39. Costello states that with this requirement, the Court of Justice emphasised the need for intensive review. Costello, 'The European Asylum Procedures Directive' (n 3) 31.

[74] See eg Case C-525/04 P *Spain v Lenzing* [2007] ECR I-9947, para 57 (State Aid); Case T-284/08 *People's Modjahedin Organization of Iran v Council* [2008] ECR II-3487, para 55 (EU measures freezing the funds of persons or organisations suspected of involvement in terrorist activities); Case T-187/06 *Schräder v CPVO* [2008] ECR II-3151, para 61 (Intellectual Property); and Case T-475/07 *Dow AgroSciences Ltd v Commission* [2011] ECR II-5937, para 153 (Agriculture). See also Sibony (n 59).

In *Tetra Laval* the Court of Justice rejected the Commission's complaint that the CFI had exceeded the limits of its power of review.[75] The Court concluded that the CFI did not err in law when it set out the tests to be applied in the exercise of its power of judicial review or when it specified the quality of the evidence which the Commission is required to produce in order to demonstrate that the requirements set by Community legislation are satisfied.[76]

The Commission had declared the merger of Tetra Laval BV with another company incompatible with the common market as the new entity would obtain a dominant position in the PET market.[77] The CFI held that the Commission had committed manifest errors of assessment in its findings as to leveraging and the strengthening of Tetra's dominant position and therefore annulled the contested decision. It took into account that the Commission admitted that its forecast in the contested decision with regard to the increase in the use of PET for packaging UHT milk was exaggerated. Furthermore, it found that the evidence produced by the Commission was unfounded by stating that, of the three independent reports cited by the Commission, only one contained information on the use of PET for milk packaging. It also showed that the evidence produced by the Commission was unconvincing by pointing out that the increase forecast in the report relied on by the Commission was of little significance and that the Commission's forecast was inconsistent with the undisputed figures in other reports. According to the CFI, the Commission's analysis was incomplete which made it impossible to confirm its forecasts, given the differences between those forecasts and the forecasts made in other reports.[78]

In the context of asylum cases, the considerations of the Court of Justice in *Tetra Laval* regarding the intensity of judicial review of prospective analysis are interesting.[79] The Court of Justice stressed that in the case of a prospective analysis a judicial review of the evidentiary assessment performed by the EU Institution is especially important.[80] According to the Court a prospective analysis of the kind necessary in merger control must be carried out with great care. The reason for that is that it does not entail the examination of past events—for which many

[75] The Commission argued before the Court of Justice that the CFI required it, when adopting its decision, to satisfy a standard of proof and to provide a quality of evidence in support of its line of argument which are incompatible with the wide discretion it enjoys in assessing economic matters.

[76] *Commission v Tetra Laval* (n 52) paras 42–45. For this case see also Craig (n 55) 453–57.

[77] The Commission's decision was based on Art 2 of Council Reg (EEC) no 4064/89 of 21 December 1989 on the control of concentrations between undertakings [1989] OJ L395/1, corrected version in OJ L257/13, as amended by Council Reg (EC) No 1310/97 of 30 June 1997 OJ L180/1.

[78] *Commission v Tetra Laval* (n 52) para 46. Schwartze deemed the Court's thorough and detailed analysis of all the facts and legal arguments used in the Commission's decisions, despite the complexity of the issue, remarkable. Schwartze (n 55) 99. Schwartze mentions two other merger cases in which the CFI concluded that the Commission made manifest errors in the establishment of the facts: Case T-310/01 *Schneider Electric v Commission* [2002] ECR II-4071 and Case T-342/99 *Airtours v Commission* [2002] ECR II-2585. For *Airtours* see also Craig (n 55) 452–53.

[79] Costello remarks that the Court's reasoning here has a striking, if unexpected, parallel with the asylum context. Costello (n 3) 31.

[80] *Commission v Tetra Laval* (n 52) para 39.

items of evidence are often available, which make it possible to understand the causes—or of current events, but rather a prediction of events which are more or less likely to occur in the future. The prospective analyses make it necessary to envisage various chains of cause and effect with a view to ascertaining which are the most likely. However, the chains of cause and effect are dimly discernible, uncertain and difficult to establish. That being so, the quality of the evidence produced by the Commission in order to establish that it is necessary to adopt a decision declaring the concentration incompatible with the common market is particularly important. After all, that evidence must support the Commission's conclusion that, if such a decision were not adopted, the economic development envisaged by it would be plausible.

One could argue that asylum cases also involve a prospective analysis: there is a question of whether the asylum seeker has a well-founded fear of persecution or runs a real risk of torture or inhuman or degrading treatment, if expelled to his country of origin. Therefore, the argument that decisions involving prospective analysis require a stricter judicial review may also be used in asylum cases. Costello states that 'the asylum process, with "essays in prediction" at its core, is similarly fraught', and that the reasoning in *Tetra Laval* 'suggests that a strict standard of review should be demanded as a matter of EC law'.[81] It should be noted that in asylum cases the chains of cause of past events are also 'dimly discernible, uncertain and difficult to establish'. It is often not clear by whom or for what reason applicants were subjected to threats of persecution or serious harm in their country of origin. This could be a further argument for a thorough judicial review of fact-finding in asylum cases.

Judicial Review of the Procedural Guarantees Offered during the Proceedings

The EU Courts have recognised that a limited judicial review should be (partly) compensated by procedural guarantees granted during the administrative proceedings, such as the right to be heard and the right to know the reasons for the decision.[82] Schwartze notes that 'today, allowing the administration discretionary powers appears permissible only if discretion is exercised in strict observance of procedural guarantees'.[83] In *Technische Universität München* the CFI held that in

[81] Costello (n 3) 31.

[82] See, eg Case C-269/90 *Technische Universität München* [1990] ECR I-5469, para 14; *Pfizer Animal Health SA* (n 52) para 171, *Spain v Lenzing* (n 74) para 58; Case T-228/02 *Organization des Modhahedines du peuple d'Iran v Council* [2007] ECR II-4665, paras 154–55; and Case T-306/01 *Yusuf and Al Barakaat International Foundation v Council and Commission* [2005] ECR II-3533, paras 326–27. See also Schwartze (n 55) 94–96; J Ponce, 'Good Administration and Administrative Procedures' (2005) 12 *Indiana Journal of Global Legal Studies* 551, 583; and Barbier de la Serre and Sibony (n 52) 955–56.

[83] Schwartze (n 55) 95–96.

cases entailing complex technical evaluations, where the Commission has a power of appraisal in order to be able to fulfil its tasks:

> Respect for the rights guaranteed by the Community legal order in administrative procedures is of even more fundamental importance. Those guarantees include, in particular, the duty of the competent institution to examine carefully and impartially all the relevant aspects of the individual case, the right of the person concerned to make his views known and to have an adequately reasoned decision. Only in this way can the Court verify whether the factual and legal elements upon which the exercise of the power of appraisal depends were present.[84]

The CFI thus only considers itself able to perform its judicial review effectively when certain procedural guarantees in the administrative phase have been respected.[85] In *Technische Universität München* the procedural guarantees in this sense included rules on investigation, the right to be heard, and the duty to state reasons for the decision.[86] In later cases in which a limited judicial review was applied the CFI also referred to the importance of procedural guarantees including the obligation to state reasons, the obligation for the competent institution to examine carefully and impartially all the relevant elements of the individual case[87] and the right to a fair hearing.[88]

Subconclusion: Case Law of the EU Courts

The Court of Justice ruled in *Samba Diouf* that Article 39 of Directive 2005/85/EC requires 'thorough' judicial review of the reasons for rejecting an asylum claim. The Court has not addressed the question whether such review requires the national court or tribunal to carry out its own assessment of the facts or allows a reasonability test of the determining authority's establishment of the facts. Article 46(3) of Directive 2013/32/EU requires a 'full' judicial review of the negative asylum decision, without further explaining the required intensity of such review.

It was argued in this section that the EU Courts' case law with regard to complex assessments may provide guidance in finding an answer to the question how intense judicial review in asylum cases must be. In both asylum cases and EU decisions involving complex assessments it is difficult to find the facts objectively and therefore the determining authority is considered to be better placed than the court to establish and evaluate the facts. The Court of Justice has itself recognised

[84] *Technische Universität München* (n 82) para 14.

[85] See also Schuurmans (n 37) 28. She states that: 'by setting clear and strict requirements on the administration's investigation of the facts and the statement of reasons underlying the factual assessment, the Community courts are able to guarantee that their test of reasonableness actually provides legal protection'.

[86] *Technische Universität München* (n 82) paras 22–26. See also Schwartze (n 55) 95.

[87] *Spain v Lenzing* (n 74) para 58; *Pfizer Animal Health SA* (n 52) para 171; Case C-16/90 *Nölle* [1991] para 13.

[88] *Organization des Modhahedines du peuple d'Iran v Council* (n 82) paras 154–55. See further ch 10, section 10.4.

in *Upjohn* that the intensity of review carried out by the EU Courts is to a certain extent normative for the intensity of the review which is carried out by national courts in similar cases.[89]

On the basis of the EU Courts' judgments concerning EU decisions involving complex assessments it is impossible to define the exact level of intensity of judicial scrutiny of the assessment of the facts which should be applied in asylum cases. It can certainly not be derived from this case law that national courts are obliged to substitute their assessment of the facts underlying the asylum claim for that of the determining authority. In cases involving complex assessments the EU Institutions have wide discretion which also applies, to some extent, to fact-finding. As a result, the EU judicature restricts itself to examining the accuracy of the findings of fact and to verifying, in particular, that the action taken by that authority is not vitiated by a manifest error. This section showed, however, that in practice, notably in the cases of *Pfizer* and *Tetra Laval*, this limited form of judicial review turns out to be quite rigorous. The General Court establishes whether the evidence relied on is factually accurate, reliable and consistent and whether that evidence contains all the information which must be taken into account in order to assess a complex situation and whether it is capable of substantiating the conclusions drawn from it. In *Tetra Laval*, the Court of Justice held that judicial review of the evidentiary assessment by an EU Institution is particularly necessary in cases requiring a prospective analysis in which the chains of cause are dimly discernible, uncertain and difficult to establish. This consideration may also be considered relevant for asylum cases, because in these cases the causes of future as well as past events are often difficult to establish. Furthermore, the EU Courts have held that a limited form of judicial review, such as that applied in cases involving complex assessments, should be compensated by procedural guarantees granted during the administrative proceedings.

It is argued here that a form of judicial review which offers a less intense review than that undertaken by the EU Courts in cases involving complex assessments cannot be considered a thorough or full judicial review. It should be remembered in this context that EU fundamental rights are involved in asylum cases, which require a high level of procedural protection. On the basis of the case law concerning complex assessments, it is contended that the court or tribunal within the meaning of Article 39 of Directive 2005/85/EC and Article 46 of Directive 2013/32/EU should at least establish whether the evidence relied on in the asylum decision is factually accurate, reliable and consistent, whether that evidence contains all the information which must be taken into account in order to assess the risk of *refoulement*, and whether it is capable of substantiating the conclusions drawn from it. Furthermore, this court or tribunal should ensure that the procedural rights of the applicant guaranteed by the Procedures Directive have been respected. As will be shown in section 9.2.2, this (minimum) level of intensity of

[89] See n 43.

judicial review would also comply with the requirement of 'close and rigorous' scrutiny which follows from Articles 3 and 13 ECHR.

9.2.2 Obligations Stemming from the ECHR, CAT and ICCPR

More specific guidelines for the intensity of judicial review of the facts in asylum cases may be derived from the ECtHR's case law and the views of the ComAT and the HRC. Two strands of case law are important. First, the case law regarding the right to an effective remedy and the right to a fair trial which directly addresses the level of intensity of judicial review which should be applied by the national court, should be examined. The case law concerning Articles 3 and 13 ECHR sets out standards as to the intensity of judicial review specifically required in asylum cases. The case law under Article 6 ECHR, which concerns the intensity of judicial review in other sorts of administrative cases, is also important. It is relevant to know whether this case law sets higher standards as to the required level of intensity of judicial review than the case law under Articles 3 and 13 ECHR. If that is the case, those higher standards may inspire the EU right to an effective remedy, even if applied in asylum cases.[90]

Secondly, the case law which reveals the way in which the ECtHR itself reviews *non-refoulement* cases should be addressed. It is contended that the subsidiary role of the ECtHR precludes the review from being performed by the national courts in *non-refoulement* cases is much more limited than the review performed by those bodies.[91] It would undermine the subsidiary role of the ECtHR if asylum applicants felt obliged to complain before that court, because the national court gives fewer guarantees for conformity of deportations with Article 3 than the ECtHR.[92] The ECtHR would then become 'an appeal tribunal from the asylum and immigration tribunals of Europe'.[93]

In that context it is important to note that the ECtHR seems to suggest that the standard of review performed by the Court itself is normative for the standard of review which is constituted by the national courts. The ECtHR uses the same term 'rigorous scrutiny' for the standard of review which it applies itself in Article 3 cases, as well as for the standard of review it requires domestic courts to

[90] See further ch 4, section 4.3.2.

[91] See also Spijkerboer, 'Subsidiarity and "Arguability"' (n 1) 68–69. For the case law concerning the subsidiary role of the ECtHR and the UN Committees as a source of inspiration, see also ch 4, section 4.3.1.

[92] Spijkerboer, ibid, 68.

[93] According to former President of the ECtHR Costa this is exactly what the ECtHR is not. See President of the ECtHR, Statement concerning Requests for Interim Measures (Rule 39 of the Rules of Court) (11 February 2011) www.coe.int/t/dghl/standardsetting/cddh/gt-gdr-c/GT-GDR-C(2012)005_Statement%20of%20the%20ECtHR%20President%20on%20Interim%20Measures.pdf accessed 25 September 2013. See also Council of Europe, Izmir Declaration (26–27 April 2011) www.echr.coe.int/Documents/2011_Izmir_FinalDeclaration_ENG.pdf accessed 25 September 2013, 3.

apply in Article 3 cases.[94] Furthermore, in *Smith and Grady* the ECtHR explicitly established a link between the standard of review applied by the court and that which should be applied by the national courts. In that case it considered that in the cases of *Soering* and *Vilvarajah* 'the Court found that the test applied by the domestic courts in applications for judicial review of decisions by the Secretary of State in extradition and expulsion matters *coincided with the Court's own approach under Article 3 of the Convention*' (emphasis added). Therefore, *Soering* and *Vilvarajah* could be contrasted to the applications in *Smith and Grady* in which the national court did not test the contested decision against the requirements set by Article 8 ECHR.[95] In *Soering* and *Vilvarajah* the Court did not find a violation of Article 13 ECHR but it did in *Smith and Grady*.

In this section the case law regarding the right to an effective remedy and the subsidiary role of the supervising bodies will be discussed first, as this case law specifically concerns asylum cases. Finally, the requirements under Article 6 ECHR will be briefly addressed.

9.2.2.1 Intensity of Judicial Review under the Right to an Effective Remedy

According to the ECtHR, the effectiveness of a remedy within the meaning of Article 13 imperatively requires 'close scrutiny by a national authority and independent and rigorous scrutiny of any claim that there exist substantial grounds for fearing a real risk of treatment contrary to Article 3'.[96] These requirements follow from the importance which the Court attaches to Article 3 ECHR and the irreversible nature of the damage which may result if the risk of torture or ill-treatment materialises.

In *MSS* the ECtHR concluded for the first time that the standard of judicial review applied by a national court did not comply with the requirements of close and rigorous scrutiny. The judgment concerned the extremely urgent procedure before the Belgian Aliens Appeal Board in which the execution of an expulsion measure could be stayed. In this procedure, the Aliens Appeal Board verified that the administrative authority's decision relied on facts contained in the administrative file, that in the substantive and formal reasons given for its decision it did not, in its interpretation of the facts, make a manifest error of appreciation, and that it did not fail to comply with essential procedural requirements or with statutory formalities required on pain of nullity, or exceed or abuse its powers.[97]

The ECtHR considered that the extremely urgent procedure had to comply with the requirements concerning the scope of the scrutiny following from Article 13 ECHR. 'The contrary would amount to allowing the States to expel the individual

[94] Spijkerboer (n 1) 63–64.
[95] ECtHR 27 December 1999, *Smith and Grady v the United Kingdom*, no 33985/96, para 138.
[96] See ECtHR (GC) 21 January 2011, *MSS v Belgium and Greece*, no 30696/09, para 293 and *Jabari* (n 27) para 50.
[97] *MSS* (n 95) para 141.

concerned without having examined the complaints under Article 3 as rigorously as possible.'[98] According to the ECHR the extremely urgent procedure did not comply with the requirement of rigorous scrutiny for several reasons. First, as was also recognised by the Belgian Government, this procedure reduced the rights of the defence and the examination of the case to a minimum. The examination of the complaints under Article 3 by the Aliens Appeal Board could, according to the ECtHR, not be considered 'thorough'. The examination was limited to verifying whether the persons concerned had produced concrete proof of the irreparable nature of the damage that might result from the alleged potential violation of Article 3. The burden of proof was thus increased to such an extent as to hinder the examination on the merits of the alleged risk of a violation. Furthermore, the Aliens Appeals Board did not always take into account new material submitted by the applicant.[99]

Another case in which the ECtHR (briefly) addressed the intensity of judicial review by the national court was *Abdulkhakov*. In this case the ECtHR had doubts whether the risk of *refoulement* had been subject to rigorous scrutiny. It considered that it was 'struck by the summary reasoning adduced by the domestic courts and their refusal to assess materials origination from reliable sources'.[100]

It follows from these judgments that within the meaning of Article 13 ECHR the national authority should examine the alleged risk of a violation of Article 3 ECHR on the merits, including the evidence underlying the asylum claim and decision. It cannot limit its examination to compliance with procedural requirements and the existence of manifest errors.

In several cases against the UK the ECtHR held that the appeal against an extradition order, a deportation order or a refusal to grant asylum provided by the British court did meet the requirements of Article 13 ECHR.[101] The British national court could review the exercise of the Secretary of State's discretion on the basis that it was tainted with illegality, irrationality or procedural impropriety. Irrationality was determined on the basis of the Wednesbury principles, administrative principles set out in the UK's case law. The test in an extradition or expulsion case would be that no reasonable Secretary of State could have made an order for return in the circumstances.

In its judgments the ECtHR stressed that, although the domestic courts would not reach findings of fact for themselves, the judicial review by the English court was careful, detailed and rigorous. In *Soering* the Court considered that 'it was satisfied that the English courts can review the "reasonableness" of an extradition

[98] Ibid, para 388.

[99] Ibid, paras 389–90.

[100] ECtHR 2 October 2012, *Abdulkhakov v Russia*, no 14743/11, para 148.

[101] ECtHR (Plen) 7 July 1989, *Soering v the United Kingdom*, no 14038/88, ECtHR, 30 October 1991; *Vilvarajah et al v the United Kingdom*, nos 13163/87; 13164/87; 13165/87; 13447/87; 13448/87; ECtHR 2 May 1997, *D v the United Kingdom*, no 30240/96, ECtHR (Adm) 7 March 2000; *TI v the United Kingdom*, no 43844/98; ECtHR 6 February 2001, *Bensaid* (n 39); and ECtHR 6 March 2001, *Hilal v the United Kingdom*, no 45276/99. See also Spijkerboer (n 1) 66–68.

decision in the light of the kind of factors relied on by Mr Soering before the Convention institutions in the context of Article 3'.[102] The ECtHR was of the opinion that an application for judicial review arguing 'Wednesbury unreasonableness' on the basis of the same material that he adduced before the court in relation to his treatment while staying in death row 'would have been given "the most anxious scrutiny" in view of the fundamental nature of the human right at stake'. Therefore, Article 13 ECHR had not been violated.[103]

In *Vilvarajah* the ECtHR took into account that the English courts had stressed their special responsibility to subject administrative decisions in asylum cases to the closest scrutiny where an applicant's life or liberty may be at risk.[104] It stated:

> While it is true that there are limitations to the powers of the courts in judicial review proceedings the Court is of the opinion that these powers, exercisable as they are by the highest tribunals in the land, do provide an effective degree of control over the decisions of the administrative authorities in asylum cases and are sufficient to satisfy the requirements of Article 13.[105]

The ECtHR based its conclusion that the judicial review of asylum cases in England is in fact a rigorous one on several decisions by the House of Lords and other national courts. In *Soering*, for example, the ECtHR referred to a judgment by the House of Lords in which Lord Bridge stated that within the limitations of the Wednesbury principles the court must 'be entitled to subject an administrative decision to the most rigorous examination to ensure that it is in no way flawed, according to the gravity of the issue which the decision determines'[106] if 'an administrative decision under challenge is said to be one which may put the applicant's life at risk, the basis of the decision must surely call for the most anxious scrutiny'. Lord Templeman argued in the same judgment that 'where the result of a flawed decision may imperil life or liberty a special responsibility lies on the court in the examination of the decision-making process'.[107] In *Vilvarajah* the Court referred to a case in which the High Court judge quashed the decision on the ground that the Secretary of State, in reaching his decision, 'took into account matters which ought not to have been taken into account and failed to take into account matters he should'.[108]

[102] *Soering* (n 101) para 121.

[103] Ibid, para 122.

[104] See ECtHR 8 July 2003, *Hatton et al v the United Kingdom*, no 36022/97, para 140; *Bensaid* (n 39) paras 55–56 and ECtHR 6 March 2001; *Hilal v the United Kingdom*, no 45276/99, paras 37 and 77–79.

[105] ECtHR 30 October 1991, *Vilvarajah et al v the United Kingdom*, nos 13163/87, 13164/87, 13165/87, 13447/87 and 13448/87, para 126.

[106] *Soering* (n 101) para 35.

[107] Ibid, para 35.

[108] *Vilvarajah* (n 105) para 91. The ECtHR also mentioned a case in which the judges stressed that in refugee cases the court is entitled to, and should, subject administrative decisions to rigorous examination. See also *Bensaid* (n 39) para 28.

The ECtHR has thus accepted that the national authority within the meaning of Article 13 ECHR does not reach findings of fact for itself. However, it follows from *MSS* that the national authority needs to enter into a thorough examination of the evidence underlying the asylum claim. This also follows from the fact that in the cases against the UK it was only after the ECtHR established that the review performed by the British courts was in fact a rigorous one, that it deemed the complaints under Article 13 ECHR unfounded. By assessing the actual test performed by the British courts in detail, the Court underlined the importance it attached to a rigorous review of Article 3 cases. It is, however, not possible on the basis of this case law to precisely define the minimum level of intensity of judicial review which should be applied in *refoulement* cases.[109] In order to gain a better understanding of the meaning of a 'rigorous scrutiny' it is, therefore, useful to take a look at the way the ECtHR itself reviews *refoulement* cases. This will be examined in section 9.2.2.2.

The View of the ComAT

The view of the ComAT with regard to the required intensity of review of asylum decision has not been consistent. In several cases against Canada the Committee accepted a very limited form of judicial review.[110] However, in its more recent view in *Singh*, as well as in its Concluding Observations regarding Canada, the Committee's standards were more stringent. It held that a State party 'should provide for judicial review of the merits, rather than merely of the reasonableness, of decisions to expel an individual where there are substantial grounds for believing that the person faces a risk of torture'.[111] In *Singh* it considered that Article 22 CAT had been violated because judicial review by the Canadian Court did not include a review on the merits of the complainant's claim that he would be tortured upon return. The Canadian Federal Court, the only judicial body to which the applicant had access, could only quash a decision of the Immigration Refugee Board

> if satisfied that: the tribunal acted without jurisdiction; failed to observe a principle of natural justice or procedural fairness; erred in law in making a decision; based its decision on an erroneous finding of fact; acted, or failed to act, by reason of fraud or perjured evidence; or acted in any other way that was contrary to law.[112]

The standard that the Court applied to the credibility of the findings of the Immigration Refugee Board was that of 'patent reasonableness'. The applicant in *Singh* contended that the Federal Court had established jurisprudence that if the

[109] See also Spijkerboer (n 1) 68, where he states that the ECtHR has 'never stated that the former British review system constitutes the bottom line of what is still acceptable'.

[110] See, eg *SPA* (n 28) para 7.4 and *LZB* (n 28) para 6.6, where the Committee considered that the appeal by the Federal Court is not a mere formality and that the court may, in appropriate cases, look at the substance of a case.

[111] *Nirmal Singh* (n 28) para 8.9. See also ComAT, Concluding Observations on Canada (7 July 2005, CAT/C/CR/34/CAN), para 5(c).

[112] *Nirmal Singh* (n 28) para 8.8.

Immigration Refugee Board decided a refugee claimant is not credible, than their story could not be a base for preventing their deportation, even when there is substantial evidence of an error in judgment. In the case of *Singh*, the Federal Court concluded that the decision was not patently unreasonable, largely on grounds of the delay in claiming refugee status after arrival in the country and failure to provide credible or trustworthy evidence as to the complainant's background information in India.[113]

In its Concluding Observations of May 2007 regarding the Netherlands, the Committee recommended that the appeal procedures entail an adequate review of rejected applications and permit asylum applicants to present facts and documentation which could not be made available, with reasonable diligence, at the time of the first submission.[114] This implies that the national court is supposed to review the facts, including new evidence.

9.2.2.2 The Subsidiary Role of the ECtHR, ComAT and HRC in Asylum Cases

This section addresses the intensity of review applied by the ECtHR and, briefly, the UN Committees. It will be shown that the ECtHR generally applies a rigorous scrutiny of the facts and evidence relevant to the claim of a risk of *refoulement*. However, the ECtHR has not always been consistent in this respect, paying more deference to the assessment of the risk of *refoulement* by the national authorities in some recent cases. The ComAT and particularly the HRC, do not usually interfere in the establishment of the facts by the State authorities. In some cases the ComAT has concluded that the applicant's asylum account should be considered credible, while the State authorities did not. The reason for that seems to be that in those cases the State authorities failed to take into account important facts or evidence, notably medical reports.

Rigorous Scrutiny of Claims of Refoulement *by the ECtHR*

According to the ECtHR's standing case law the ECtHR itself applies a 'rigorous scrutiny' to claims of a risk of *refoulement*:

> The Court's examination of the existence of a risk of ill-treatment in breach of Article 3 … at the relevant time must necessarily be a rigorous one in view of the absolute character of this provision and the fact that it enshrines one of the fundamental values of the democratic societies making up the Council of Europe.[115]

[113] Ibid, para 2.10.

[114] ComAT, Concluding Observations on the Netherlands (3 August 2007, CAT/C/NET/CO/4) para 7.

[115] *Vilvarajah* (n 104) para 108. See also ECtHR (GC) 28 February 2008, *Saadi v Italy*, no 37201/06, para 142.

In *Salah Sheekh* the ECtHR considered that in assessing an alleged risk of treatment contrary to Article 3 in respect of aliens facing expulsion or extradition, 'a full and *ex nunc* assessment is called for'.[116]

At the same time, particularly in recent cases, the ECtHR has stressed its subsidiary role. It considers that 'it must be cautious in taking on the role of a first-instance tribunal of fact' and that 'it is not its task to substitute its own assessment of the facts for that of the domestic courts'. According to the Court, 'in normal circumstances it requires cogent elements to lead it to depart from the findings of fact reached by those courts'.[117] The ECtHR in recent cases pays more attention to the quality of the national asylum proceedings[118] including the intensity of judicial review by the national courts.[119] In some cases it only establishes that the national authorities carefully examined the risk of *refoulement* and does not (explicitly) conduct its own assessment of the facts of the case and the risk of *refoulement*. In its judgment in *Husseini*, for example, the ECtHR considered that the Swedish Migration Board and the Aliens Appeals Board

> conducted a thorough examination of the applicant's case, which entailed that the applicant was heard three times. Before both instances the applicant was assisted by appointed counsel. The national authorities had the benefit of seeing, hearing and questioning the applicant in person and of assessing directly the information and documents submitted by him, before deciding the case. The Court finds no reason to conclude that their decisions were inadequate or that the outcome of the proceedings before the two instances was arbitrary. Furthermore, there are no indications that the assessment made by the domestic authorities was insufficiently supported by relevant materials or that the authorities were wrong in their conclusion that there were no substantial grounds for finding that the applicant would risk being persecuted upon return to Afghanistan.[120]

This and similar recent judgments potentially reflect a new approach of the ECtHR, which is intended to ensure that it does not act as a fourth instance court, in conformity with the Izmir Declaration.[121]

Recent case law also shows, however, that the ECtHR (still) enters into a rigorous scrutiny if it finds it necessary. In several cases, it first established that the State authorities had not carried out an adequate assessment of the risk of *refoulement*

[116] ECtHR 11 January 2007, *Salah Sheekh v the Netherlands*, no 1948/04, para 136.

[117] *Abdulkhakov* (n 100) para 137. See also ECtHR 23 September 2010, *Iskandarov v Russia*, no 17185/05, para 106.

[118] For older cases in which the ECtHR referred to the quality of the national asylum proceedings before conducting its own assessment of the facts, evidence and credibility of the asylum account, see eg ECtHR (Adm) 16 March 2004, *Nasimi v Sweden*, no 38865/02 and ECtHR (Adm) 2 February 1999, *JED v the United Kingdom*, no 42225/98.

[119] In several recent judgments such as *MSS* (n 95); ECtHR 2 February 2012, *IM v France*, no 9152/09; and ECtHR (GC) 23 February 2012, *Hirsi Jamaa et al v Italy*, no 27765/09, the ECtHR under Art 13 ECHR performed a strict review of the procedural safeguards in place.

[120] ECtHR 13 October 2011, *Husseini v Sweden*, no 10611/09, paras 86–87. See also, eg ECtHR 20 October 2011, *Samina v Sweden*, no 55463/09, paras 54–55 and ECtHR (Adm) 19 February 2013, *Atayeva and Burman v Sweden*, no 17471/11.

[121] Izmir Declaration (n 93) 3.

before proceeding with its own assessment.[122] However, in other cases the ECtHR conducted its own assessment of the facts and evidence of the case without explicitly considering the quality of the national asylum proceedings[123] or even after it had concluded that the national proceedings provided sufficient guarantees.[124] The Court does not always indicate why it has made a fresh and rigorous examination of the facts. In several cases it considered that in extradition and deportation cases it needed to examine whether the assessment made by the authorities of the Contracting State was adequate and sufficiently supported by domestic materials as well as by materials originating from other reliable and objective sources, where an applicant had provided reasoned grounds which cast doubt on the accuracy of the information relied on by the respondent government.[125] Baldinger suggests that apart from insufficient national proceedings, new facts or circumstances which casts doubt on the information relied on by the government and disrespect of the national authorities for the absolute nature of the prohibition of *refoulement* may be grounds for the ECtHR to conduct an independent examination of the facts and credibility of the asylum account.[126]

FN is an example of a case in which the ECtHR conducted its own examination of the facts and credibility of the asylum account and departed from the findings of the national authorities. In this case the ECtHR found 'no indications that the domestic proceedings lacked effective guarantees to protect the applicants against arbitrary *refoulement* or were otherwise flawed'.[127] Nevertheless, the ECtHR continued by examining whether the information presented before the Court would lead it to depart from the domestic authorities' conclusions. Indeed, in this case the ECtHR found reasons to depart from the Swedish authorities' assessment of the facts. Unlike the Swedish authorities it considered that the applicants' responses to some of the Swedish authorities' grounds for questioning the documents he submitted credible and, moreover, supported by information from international sources. Furthermore, it found that the Swedish authorities should have attached more weight to several other documents (including employment books and a birth certificate) submitted by the applicant. Finally, even though it recognised that the applicants had given certain contradictory and inconsistent information about what happened to them in Uzbekistan, and that they seem to have added to their accounts, it considered that they had maintained the essence of their asylum account. The Court concluded for these reasons, as well as the

[122] See, eg ECtHR 28 March 2013, *IK v Austria*, no 2964/12, para 75; ECtHR 5 February 2013, *Zokhidov v Russia*, no 67286/10, para 131; and ECtHR 8 November 2011, *Yakubov v Russia*, no 7265/10.

[123] ECtHR 18 April 2013, *MOM v France*, no 18372/10 In this case the ECtHR departed from the findings of the French authorities with regard to evidence and credibility.

[124] See, eg ECtHR 28 June 2012, *AA v Sweden*, no 14499/09, para 77.

[125] See, eg ECtHR 25 April 2013, *Savriddin Dzhurayev v Russia*, no 71386/10, para 156.

[126] HJM Baldinger, *Rigorous Scrutiny versus Marginal Review* (Nijmegen, Wolf Legal Publishers, 2013) 248.

[127] ECtHR 18 December 2012, *FN v Sweden*, no 28774/09, para 70.

fact that the applicants were brought to the attention to the Uzbek authorities and information concerning the situation in Uzbekistan, that the expulsion of the applicants would violate Article 3 ECHR.

In many earlier judgments the ECtHR also did not pay deference to the asylum decision made by the national authorities.[128] Instead it established itself whether the applicant's personal situation was such that his expulsion or extradition would contravene Article 3 of the Convention.[129] In those judgments the ECtHR assessed the credibility of the applicant's asylum account and the facts and evidence in the case.[130] In several cases the ECtHR attached weight to the fact that national authorities had knowledge and experience in the assessment of asylum applications submitted by certain groups of asylum applicants.[131] This did not mean, however, that the ECtHR did not apply a rigorous scrutiny.[132]

In *RC*, for example, there was a dispute between the parties as to the facts of the case and the credibility of the applicant's asylum account. The ECtHR acknowledged that it is often difficult to establish the pertinent facts precisely. It accepted that 'as a general principle, the national authorities are best placed to assess not just the facts but, more particularly, the credibility of witnesses since it is they who have had an opportunity to see, hear and assess the demeanour of the individual concerned'.[133] Nevertheless, the Court did not share the conclusion of the government that the information provided by the applicant was such as to undermine his general credibility. The ECtHR thus replaced its own assessment of the credibility of the asylum account for that of the Swedish (administrative and judicial) authorities.

In most asylum cases, the Court assesses the credibility of the applicant's asylum account on the basis of information, for example, reports of interviews, which came to light during the national asylum procedure, and the statements made by the applicant during the proceedings before the ECtHR.[134] In *Said*

[128] For earlier cases in which the ECtHR seems to apply a marginal review, see ECtHR (Adm) 26 October 2000, *Damla v Germany*, no 61479/00 and ECtHR (Adm) 22 September 2005, *Kaldik v Germany*, no 28526/05. In these decisions it used a standard text block which is normally used in cases concerning Art 6 ECHR. See also ECtHR (Adm) 14 September 2000, *Chentiev and Ibragimov*, nos 21022/08, 51946/08.

[129] In several cases the ECtHR mentioned 'the need to examine all the facts of the case'. See, eg ECtHR 17 July 2008, *NA v the United Kingdom*, no 25904/07, para 113. However, the ECtHR does not itself examine the actual asylum applications or verify how the States honour their obligations under the Geneva Convention. See *MSS* (n 95) para 286.

[130] These include cases in which the Court concluded that Art 3 had been violated (see, eg *Hilal* (n 104) ECtHR 5 July 2005, *Said v the Netherlands*, no 2345/02 and ECtHR 26 July 2005, *N v Finland*, no 38885/02) but also cases, which were declared manifestly unfounded. See, eg *Nasimi* (n 118) and ECtHR (Adm) 8 March 2007, *Collin and Akaziebie v Sweden*, no 23944/05.

[131] *Vilvarajah* (n 105) para 114, ECtHR (Plen) 20 March 1991, *Cruz Varas et al v Sweden*, no 15576/89, para 81; ECtHR (Adm) 22 June 2004, *F v the United Kingdom*, no 17341/03; and EComHR 8 April 1993, *MPG v Sweden*, no 20981/92.

[132] See also Spijkerboer (n 1) 64–66.

[133] *RC* (n 40) para 52.

[134] See, eg *Hilal* (n 104) ECtHR (Adm) 6 September 2007; *M v Sweden*, no 22556/05; and ECtHR (Adm) 17 January 2006, *Bello v Sweden*, no 32213/04.

the ECtHR considered that it 'must proceed, as far as possible to an assessment of the general credibility of the statements made by the applicant before the Netherlands authorities and during the present proceedings'.[135] In *N* the ECtHR went as far as to appoint two of its members as delegates in order to take oral evidence from the applicant, his wife, and several other persons. Based on this assessment, the Court concluded that the applicant's account of his background in the Democratic Republic of the Congo should be considered sufficiently consistent and credible.[136] The ECtHR noted that the position of the Court did not contradict in any respect the findings of the Finnish courts. Neither was there any indication that the initial asylum interview had been in any way rushed or otherwise conducted in a superficial manner.[137]

In many cases the Court included country of origin information[138] or other information in its assessment which it had obtained itself.[139] The Court considered:

> In its supervisory task under Article 19 of the Convention, it would be too narrow an approach under Article 3 in cases concerning aliens facing expulsion or extradition if the Court, as an international human rights court, were only to take into account materials made available by the domestic authorities of the Contracting State concerned, without comparing these with materials from other reliable and objective sources.[140]

It should, therefore, be concluded that the ECtHR has in many cases applied a rigorous scrutiny in claims under Article 3 ECHR, and that it does not hesitate to assess the credibility of an asylum account or to gather evidence on its own initiative.[141] This applies even if the asylum claim was properly assessed by the national determining authority and courts. It follows from the subsidiary role of the court that the national courts should perform a judicial scrutiny, which is at least as rigorous as the ECtHR's review.

The UN Committees' Subsidiary Role

The ComAT pays more deference to the findings of the State authorities than the ECtHR. It has stressed many times that it is not an appellate, quasi-judicial or administrative body and that it must, therefore, give considerable weight to findings of fact made by the organs of the State party.[142] While assessing a case, the Committee determines whether the State party's review of the complainant's case

[135] *Said* (n 130) para 50.

[136] *N* (n 130) paras 152–56. See also ECtHR 9 October 1988, *Hatami v Sweden*, no 32448/96, para 25.

[137] *N* (n 130) para 157.

[138] See, eg ECtHR 8 April 2008, *Nnyanzi v the United Kingdom*, no 21878/06, para 63.

[139] See, eg *Hilal* (n 104) para 60 and *NA* (n 129) para 119.

[140] *Salah Sheekh* (n 116) para 136. See also ECtHR 12 May 2010, *Khodzayev v Russia*, no 52466/08, para 96.

[141] See also Spijkerboer (n 1) 64–66.

[142] See, eg ComAT 3 July 2011, *TD v Switzerland*, no 375/2009, para 7.7. See also ComAT, General Comment No 1 (1997, A/53/44), para 9(a).

was deficient in this respect.[143] In many cases the ComAT followed the assessment made by the authorities of the State and declared the complaint unfounded.[144] In a view concerning a complaint against the Netherlands, for example, the Committee considered:

> The relevant evidence regarding the complainant's history in Turkey, together with his activities inside and outside Turkey has been considered by the Dutch authorities. The Committee is not in a position to challenge their findings of fact, nor to resolve the question of whether there were inconsistencies in the complainant's account. Consistent with the Committee's case law, due weight must be accorded to findings of fact made by government Authorities.[145]

Nevertheless, the ComAT stressed in some cases that it has the power of free assessment of the facts arising in the circumstances of each case.[146] It must assess the facts and evidence in a given case, once it has been ascertained that the manner in which the evidence was evaluated was clearly arbitrary or amounted to a denial of justice.[147] In *Dadar*, the ComAT considered that the argument submitted by the State party that the Committee is not a fourth instance, cannot prevail over the absolute prohibition enshrined in Article 3 of the Convention.[148] Therefore, the Committee sometimes evaluates evidence and assesses the credibility of the asylum account itself. Indeed, in some cases it has reached a different conclusion on these issues to that of the national authorities.[149]

The Committee does not explain why it considers that the manner in which the evidence was evaluated, was or was not clearly arbitrary. However, it is striking that in many of the cases in which the Committee reached a different conclusion to the State authorities with regard to the credibility of the applicant's asylum account, the State authorities had failed to take into account important facts or evidence.[150] Specifically, in many of those cases medical reports had not been taken into account as evidence in the national procedure or the Committee

[143] ComAT 21 November 2003, *AR v the Netherlands*, no 203/2002, para 7.6, ComAT 15 May 2008, *MJAMO et al v Canada*, no 293/2006, para 10.5. The ComAT referred to its General Comment No 1 (n 141) para 9.

[144] See, eg ComAT 14 May 2003, *AA v the Netherlands*, no 198/2002 and ComAT 11 May 2004, *AK v Australia*, no 148/1999.

[145] ComAT 14 May 2004, *SG v the Netherlands*, no 135/1999, para 6.6.

[146] See, eg *TD* (n 141) para 7.7. See also General Comment No 1 (n 142) para 9(b).

[147] *SPA* (n 28) para 7.6 and ComAT 12 May 2003, *GK v Switzerland*, no 219/2002, para 6.12. In *MJAMO* (n 143) para 10.5 the ComAT also seems to require that the domestic courts had clearly violated their obligations of impartiality.

[148] ComAT 5 December 2005, *Dadar v Canada*, no 258/2004, para 8.8.

[149] See, eg ComAT 25 November 2011, *Eftekhary v Norway*, no 312/2007.

[150] Baldinger, *Rigorous Scrutiny versus Marginal Review* (n 125) 149; KW Wouters, *International Legal Standards for the Protection from Refoulement* (Antwerp, Intersentia, 2009) 492; M Nowak and E McArthur, *The United Nations Convention against Torture: A Commentary* (Oxford, Oxford University Press, 2008) 223.

judged that the applicant's medical problems could explain inconsistencies in their statements.[151]

The HRC also generally respects the assessment of the facts by the national authorities.[152] For example, in *Kindler*, an extradition case, the HRC 'reiterates its constant jurisprudence that it is not competent to re-evaluate the facts and evidence considered by national courts. The Committee may verify whether the author was granted all the procedural safeguards provided for in the Covenant'.[153] Wouters states that the HRC allows itself a prominent role in the assessment of facts and evidence only when there is bad faith, abuse of power, or other arbitrariness on the part of the State.[154] There are very few cases in which the HRC concluded that Articles 6 or 7 ICCPR would be violated upon return.[155] *Hamida* is a rare example of a case in which the Committee assessed the facts and evidence itself and came to a different conclusion to the State authorities as to the credibility of the applicant's account.[156] In some cases the HRC concluded that expulsion of a person would violate Article 7 ICCPR because insufficient procedural guarantees had been offered by the State authorities,[157] further analysis should have been carried out,[158] or the State authorities had failed to comment on the applicant's fairly detailed account of why in his opinion a risk of *refoulement* existed.[159]

The deferential position of the UN Committees vis-à-vis the examination of the asylum claim by the State authorities can be explained by their concern to maintain their subsidiary role. It does not mean that they are of the opinion that national courts should not be in the position, or are not required, to apply a rigorous scrunity to the facts in an asylum case. Furthermore, if necessary in the light of the seriousness of the case, the ComAT and the HRC enter into an assessment of the relevant evidence and the credibility of the asylum account. The prohibition of *refoulement* thus prevails over the need to ensure the subsidiary role of the UN Committees.

[151] See, eg ComAT 16 December 1998, *Halil Haydin v Sweden*, no 101/97, paras 6.6 and 6.7 ComAT 25 May 2002, *Chedli Ben Ahmed Karoui v Sweden*, no 185/2001, para 10, ComAT 17 December 2004, *Enrique Falcon Ríos v Canada*, no 133/99, paras 8.4–8.5, ComAT 22 January 2007, *CT and KM v Sweden*, no 279/2005, para 7.5 and ComAT 22 January 2007, *VL v Switzerland*, no 262/2005, para 8.8.

[152] Wouters, *International Legal Standards* (n 149) 397.

[153] *Kindler* (n 31) para 6.6. See also HRC 6 December 2002, *Zheludkova v Ukraine*, no 726/1996, para 5.3, HRC 20 August 2004, *Perterer v Austria*, no 1015/2001, para 10.5.

[154] Wouters (n 149) 397. He refers among others to HRC 3 April 2007, *PK v Canada*, no 1234/2003, para 7.3.

[155] Wouters (n 149) 367.

[156] HRC 13 April 2010, *Hamida v Canada*, no 1544/2007, para 8.7. See also Baldinger (n 125) 94–97.

[157] HRC 15 June 2004, *Ahani v Canada*, no 1051/2002, para 10.7.

[158] HRC 9 May 2011, *Pillai v Canada*, no 1763/2008, para 11.4.

[159] HRC 9 December 2004, *Byahuranga v Denmark*, no 1222/2003, para 11.3.

9.2.2.3 The Right to a Fair Trial

When assessing whether a court or tribunal complies with the 'full jurisdiction' requirement, the ECtHR tests whether the court considered the submissions of the applicant 'on their merits, point by point, without ever having to decline jurisdiction in replying to them or in ascertaining various facts'.[160] The ECtHR applies this test on a case-by-case basis, carrying out an examination of both the case file and the relevant provisions of national law.[161]

Article 6(1) ECHR does not necessarily require a judicial body to substitute its own decision for that of the administrative authorities; on certain conditions it may pay deference to the administrative decision. The ECtHR considered that in assessing the sufficiency of the judicial review available to the applicant 'it is necessary to have regard to matters such as the subject-matter of the decision appealed against, the manner in which that decision was arrived at and the content of the dispute, including the desired and actual grounds of appeal'.[162] These three factors, to which the ECtHR referred in many cases, will be addressed separately in this section.

The Subject Matter of the Decision

The ECtHR finds that in areas of law in which the administrative authorities exercise discretion or where special knowledge or experience is needed to take a decision, judicial bodies may limit their review to an assessment of the reasonableness of the decision.[163] They do not need to substitute their own findings of fact for those of the administrative authorities and are, therefore, not obliged to hold a full court hearing on both facts and law.[164] Areas of law in which administrative authorities, according to the ECtHR, typically exercise discretion include town and country planning and environmental protection.[165] These specialised areas of the law involve the exercise of discretion involving a multitude of local factors inherent in the choice and implementation of policies.[166] Furthermore, the issues to be determined in such areas require a measure of professional knowledge or experience.[167]

[160] See, eg *Zumtobel* (n 23) para 32.

[161] See, eg *Družstevní Záložna Pria* (n 24) para 107; ECtHR 4 October 2001, *Potocka et al v Poland*, no 33776/96, para 54; *Zumtobel* (n 23) para 32. This makes it difficult to establish the exact purport of judgments and the precise contents of the Court's doctrine. See ECtHR 26 April 1995, *Fischer v Austria*, no 16922/90, dissenting opinion of Judge Martens, para 15.

[162] *Bryan* (n 22) para 45.

[163] Ibid, para 44.

[164] See ECtHR (GC) 28 May 2002, *Kingsley v the United Kingdom*, no 35605/97, para 53.

[165] ECtHR 28 July 2005, *Alatulkkila v Finland*, no 33538/96, para 52; and *Bryan* (n 22) para 47. See also ECtHR (GC) 18 January 2001, *Jane Smith v the United Kingdom*, no 25154/94; and ECtHR (GC) 18 January 2001, *Chapman v the United Kingdom*, no 27238/95.

[166] *Alatulkkila* (n 164) para 52.

[167] ECtHR 27 October 2009, *Crompton v the United Kingdom*, no 42509/05, para 73.

In cases in which no specialised knowledge is required to take the decision, and where the factual findings cannot be said 'to be merely incidental to the reaching of broader judgments of policy or expediency which it was for the democratically accountable authority to take', limited judicial review is not allowed under Article 6 ECHR.[168] *Tsfayo*, for example, concerned the decision by a local authority to refuse a claim for backdated housing and council tax benefit. The reason given for the refusal was that the applicant had failed to show 'good cause' for her delay in making the claim. According to national case law, the concept of 'good cause' involved an objective judgment as to whether the individual claimant, with his or her characteristics such as language and mental health, did what could reasonably have been expected of him or her. The applicant challenged the decision before the Housing Benefit and Council Tax Review Board (HBRB). This body was directly connected to the local authority which refused the claim. The applicant gave evidence to the HBRB as to the moment she realised that anything was amiss with her claim for housing benefit. The HBRB found her explanation to be unconvincing and rejected the claim. The court before which the HBRB's decision could be appealed did not have jurisdiction to rehear the evidence or substitute its own views as to the applicant's credibility; it only assessed whether the decision was unreasonable or irrational. According to the ECtHR, the dispute in this case concerned a 'simple question of fact' namely whether there was 'good cause' for the applicant's delay in making a claim. No specialist expertise was required to determine this issue, nor did the facts fall within the scope of the authorities' discretionary power.[169] As the HBRB lacked independence and essential procedural guarantees, while the intensity of the judicial review before the High Court was limited, Article 6 ECHR had been violated.[170] Article 6 ECHR thus requires that simple questions of fact should, unlike complex policy assessments, be subjected to full judicial review.

The Manner in which the Disputed Decision was Arrived at

When examining the sufficiency of the review performed by the national court, the ECtHR takes into account the guarantees offered during the administrative proceedings. In several cases the ECtHR found that the proceedings before the administrative body did not fully comply with the requirements of Article 6(1) ECHR, but could nevertheless be qualified as 'quasi-judicial'. In *Bryan* the ECtHR pointed at the uncontested safeguards attending the procedure before the Housing and Planning Inspector, namely

> the quasi-judicial character of the decision-making process; the duty incumbent on each inspector to exercise independent judgment; the requirement that inspectors must not be subject to any improper influence; the stated mission of the Inspectorate to uphold

[168] Ibid, paras 73 and 77.

[169] ECtHR 14 November 2006, *Tsfayo v the United Kingdom*, no 60860/00, para 46.

[170] Ibid. See also *Crompton* (n 166) para 77.

> the principles of openness, fairness and impartiality ... Further, any alleged shortcoming in relation to these safeguards could have been subject to review by the High Court.[171]

In *Kingsley*, the ECtHR took into account that a hearing took place; that the applicant could call evidence, consider the various elements of the case against him and comment on the way the proceedings should take place; and that the applicant was represented by counsel.[172] In the *Tsfayo* case referred to above, in which a violation of Article 6 ECHR was found, the ECtHR put significant weight on the fact that the determining authority (the HBRB) was not merely lacking in independence from the executive, but was directly connected to one of the parties to the dispute. According to the ECtHR, the safeguards built into the HBRB procedure were not adequate to overcome this fundamental lack of objective impartiality.[173] The notion that the overall fairness should be assessed thus also comes to the fore when assessing whether the intensity of judicial review was sufficient in the light of Article 6 ECHR.

The Content of the Dispute

Finally, the ECtHR assesses whether (in spite of the limited jurisdiction of the court) the grounds of appeal submitted by the applicant were adequately addressed by the national court. In *Bryan*, for example, the ECtHR considered that the applicant's submissions 'went essentially to questions involving "a panoply of policy matters such as development plans, and the fact that the property was situated in a green belt and a conservation area"'. According to the ECtHR, the High Court had jurisdiction to entertain the grounds of the applicant's appeal and his submissions were adequately dealt with point by point.[174] *Crompton* concerned a dispute regarding the level of compensation which had to be offered to the applicant following his discharge from the army. The level of compensation was decided on by the Army Board, a body composed of members of the armed forces, which could not be considered independent. The ECtHR found that the High Court had sufficiency of review to remedy the lack of independence of the Army Board, although the court could not substitute its own view as to an appropriate award in the circumstances of the case. The ECtHR found it sufficient that the court could and did examine both the method of calculation of the compensation and the base figures used for the calculation. In the applicant's case it found the base figure to be inaccurate and required the Army Board to review

[171] *Bryan* (n 22) para 46.

[172] *Kingsley* (n 164) para 54. In this case the ECtHR found a violation of Art 6 ECHR because the court could not quash the impugned decision and remit the case for a new decision by an impartial body.

[173] *Tsfayo* (n 169) para 47.

[174] *Bryan* (n 22) para 47. See also *Potocka* (n 161) para 58. For a different view, see ECtHR 9 January 2013, *Volkov v Ukraine*, no 21722/11, paras 127–228.

the calculation.[175] It should be concluded that Article 6 ECHR requires that the grounds for appeal are addressed on the merits by a court or tribunal.

9.2.3 Subconclusion: Thorough Review of the Assessment of the Facts

On the basis of the examination of the EU Courts and the case law of the ECtHR it is not possible to define the precise level of intensity of judicial review, which should be offered by the 'thorough' review required by Article 39 of Directive 2005/85/EC and the 'full' judicial review required by Article 46(3) of Directive 2013/32/EU. It should be concluded, however, that the Member States do not have full discretion to determine how intense the judicial scrutiny of an asylum decision must be. The terms 'thorough' and 'full' already suggest that national courts cannot pay much deference to the determining authority's assessment of the asylum claim. Furthermore, both the case law of the EU Courts and the ECtHR show that a review of an asylum decision which limits itself to a pure reasonableness test, does not comply with the right to an effective remedy.

It may be derived from the case law of the EU Courts in cases involving complex assessments, that the right to an effective remedy requires, even in cases in which the determining authority has wide discretion, that a court carries out a meaningful examination of the facts and evidence. It must examine whether the evidence relied on is factually accurate, reliable and consistent, whether that evidence contains all the information which must be taken into account in order to assess a complex situation, and whether it is capable of substantiating the conclusions drawn from it. A limited form of judicial review of the decision must be compensated by an intensive review of the procedural guarantees offered in the administrative phase, such as the right to be heard or the duty to state reasons. It is hard to imagine that a judicial review which is less intensive than the limited review carried out by the CFI/General Court in cases involving complex assessments can be considered 'thorough' or 'full'.

The ECtHR's case law makes clear that the need to prevent irreparable harm requires rigorous scrutiny by an independent authority of a claim of a risk of *refoulement*. It follows from the ECtHR's judgments in *MSS* and the many cases against the UK that under Article 13 ECHR the national authority must enter into a thorough examination of the facts and evidence underlying the asylum claim. This can also be derived from the intensity of the review carried out by the ECtHR itself in *refoulement* cases. Notably, the ECtHR, if necessary, replaces its own assessment of the evidence and the credibility of the applicant's asylum account for that of the determining authority and gathers (country of origin) information on its own initiative. The subsidiary role of the ECtHR would be seriously

[175] *Crompton* (n 167) paras 78–79. See also *Fischer* (n 161) para 34; *Zumtobel* (n 23) para 32; EComHR 9 December 1997, *Wickramsinghe v the United Kingdom*, no 31503/96.

undermined if judicial scrutiny by the national court gave fewer guarantees for conformity of an asylum decision with Article 3 ECHR than the ECtHR's own review.[176] The ComAT has confirmed, in its recent view in *Singh* and in its Concluding Observations with regard to Canada, that a very limited review of the facts of an expulsion decision, including the credibility of the applicant's asylum account (patent unreasonableness) is not allowed.

Under Article 6 ECHR, national courts are not allowed to apply a reasonableness test to simple questions of fact which do not fall within the scope of the administrative authorities' discretion and for which no special knowledge or experience is required. In such cases the court must have jurisdiction to rehear the evidence or to substitute its own views. It is contended here that the assessment of the credibility of the asylum applicant cannot be considered 'a simple question of fact'.[177] Therefore, it cannot be argued on the basis of this case law that the EU right to an effective remedy requires national courts or tribunals within the meaning of Article 39 of Directive 2005/85/EC and Article 46 of Directive 2013/32/EU to substitute their own findings of fact for that of the determining authority. The ECtHR has held under Article 6 ECHR that where the dispute concerns the exercise of discretionary judgment by the administrative authorities and the proceedings before these authorities offer important procedural guarantees, the national court may limit its review to a reasonableness test. However, the grounds of appeal must be addressed on their merits and point by point by this court. This also applies to the review of findings of fact.[178] It should thus be concluded that Article 6 ECHR sets important standards as to the intensity of judicial review. However, these standards do not appear to require a higher level of intensity of judicial review than the rigorous scrutiny required by Articles 3 and 13 ECHR in asylum cases.

How the Member States guarantee the required minimum level of intensity of judicial review falls within their procedural autonomy. They may choose a solution which best fits with their administrative legal system and their views on the division of powers between the legislator, administration and judiciary. The national courts are not obliged to replace their own assessment of the facts or evidence underlying the asylum claim for that of the determining authority. They may also choose to focus on the quality of the asylum decision and to give weight to the observance of procedural guarantees during the administrative phase.

[176] Spijkerboer (n 1) 68.

[177] See ch 8, section 8.5. See also the ECtHR's own recognition that the national authorities who had an opportunity to see, hear and assess the demeanour of the applicant are best placed to assess the credibility of the applicant's asylum account.

[178] *Bryan* (n 22) para 47.

9.3 THE RELEVANT MOMENT IN TIME: *EX TUNC* OR *EX NUNC* REVIEW?

A final important question relating to the standard of judicial review is whether the national court should or may restrict itself to a review of the contested decision and its underlying facts, or whether it should take into account grounds for asylum, facts, circumstances or evidence (hereafter referred to as new elements and findings[179]) which emerged or were submitted after the issuing of an asylum decision.[180] The UNHCR noted in 2010 that in some Member States there are no restrictions on the right to submit new elements and findings during the appeal stage,[181] while there are restrictions in other Member States.[182]

Directive 2005/85/EC

Article 39 of Directive 2005/85/EC does not require the national court or tribunal to take into account elements or findings submitted during the appeal stage. Article 32 of this Directive gives Member States the opportunity to examine further representations by the applicant or the elements of a subsequent asylum application in the framework of the examination of the decision under review or appeal, 'insofar as the competent authorities can take into account and consider all the elements underlying the further representations or subsequent application within this framework'. Article 32 also gives the option of a special procedure for subsequent asylum applications, which can be applied after the administrative decision or a final decision on the previous asylum application has been taken. A subsequent application for asylum shall first be subject to a preliminary examination as to whether, after the decision on the previous asylum application has been reached, new elements or findings relating to the examination have arisen or have been presented by the applicant.[183] Only if new elements or findings which add significantly to the likelihood of the applicant qualifying as a refugee have been presented are the Member States obliged to further examine the application in conformity with the guarantees laid down in Chapter II of the Directive.[184] Member States may decide to further examine the application only if the applicant

[179] See for relevant elements Art 4(1) and (2) Dir 2011/95/EU.

[180] Spijkerboer notes that 'the issue of which moment in time is relevant is related to the position of courts vis à vis the administration. If the position of courts is not to decide on the merits of asylum claims, but to decide on the legality of the administrative decision, then an *ex nunc* assessment is problematic, because courts may take into account evidence of which the administration could not have been aware. Only if courts are competent to assess the substantive merit of an asylum application themselves, would an ex nunc assessment be a plausible option'. Spijkerboer (n 1) 53.

[181] Bulgaria, Finland, France, Germany and with regard to regular rejections, Italy and the UK.

[182] Belgium, Czech Republic, Germany and with regard to applications rejected as irrelevant or manifestly unfounded, the Netherlands and Slovenia. UNHCR, *Improving Asylum Procedures* (n 4) s 16, 55–56.

[183] Art 32(3) Dir 2005/85/EC.

[184] Art 32(4) Dir 2005/85/EC. According to Art 32(5) Dir 2005/85/EC Member States may, in accordance with national legislation, further examine a subsequent application where there are other reasons why a procedure has to be re-opened.

concerned was, through no fault of his own, incapable of asserting the new elements or finding in the previous procedure, in particular by exercising his or her right to an effective remedy pursuant to Article 39 of Directive 2005/85/EC.[185] The Member States may thus require asylum applicants to raise new facts and evidence during the appeal stage if the national court is competent to take into account such facts and evidence.

Directive 2013/32/EU

Article 46(3) of Directive 2013/32/EU explicitly requires an *ex nunc* judicial review of the asylum decision by a court or tribunal, but does not exactly explain what an *ex nunc* assessment means. The text of Article 32(1) of Directive 2005/85/EC was maintained in Article 40(1) of Directive 2013/32/EU. This could indicate that a court or tribunal performing an *ex nunc* judicial review may not be able 'to take into account and consider all the elements underlying the further representations' and that sometimes such elements should be submitted in a subsequent asylum procedure.

In this section it is argued on the basis of the case law of the Court of Justice and the ECtHR that the EU right to an effective remedy requires that the national court or tribunal of Article 39 of Directive 2005/85/EC perform an *ex nunc* assessment of a claim of a risk of *refoulement* and takes into account new elements and findings which had been submitted (or emerged) after the first decision on the asylum application. In the light of the principle of procedural autonomy Member States may chose how they guarantee that such an *ex nunc* assessment is carried out. One option is that the court or tribunal takes into account relevant new facts and evidence in the appeal against the negative decision on the asylum claim. This option seems to be required by Article 46(3) of Directive 2013/32/EU. Another option which may be allowed by Article 39 of Directive 2005/85/EC is that Member States allow asylum applicants full consideration on the merits of a subsequent asylum application on the basis of relevant new elements or findings. The decision on this application should then be open to review by the national court or tribunal within the meaning of Article 39 of Directive 2005/85/EC. Systems in which relevant new elements and findings cannot be taken into account by the court in the context of the appeal in a first or a subsequent asylum procedure should be considered contrary to EU law.

9.3.1 The Case Law of the Court of Justice

The Court of Justice has not yet addressed whether a 'thorough review' by the national court or tribunal should include new elements and findings submitted during the appeal stage. The only judgment which addresses the relevant moment

[185] Art 32(6) Dir 2005/85/EC.

of the assessment of the existence of a fear of persecution is *Salahadin Abdullah.* This case concerned the withdrawal of refugee status. In a procedure in which the refugee status is withdrawn, the refugee may rely on a reason for persecution other than that accepted at the time when refugee status was granted. The Court of Justice considered in *Salahadin Abdullah* that Article 4(4) of the Qualification Directive requires the determining authorities to take into account acts or threats of persecution connected to this other reason of persecution. The Court seems to be of the opinion that this applies even if the acts or threats of persecution occurred in the country of origin before the asylum application was lodged but were not mentioned by the applicant in the asylum procedure.[186] This implies that if the Member State authorities intend to withdraw a refugee status an *ex nunc* assessment needs to take place. This judgment does not address the question whether a national court should take into account facts or evidence submitted after the decision by the determining authority. However, it may indicate that an applicant's statements, in particular those regarding previous persecution, cannot be excluded from the assessment of the risk of future persecution or serious harm on the sole ground that the applicant could and should have submitted them earlier.

Furthermore, the Court of Justice has made clear in *Byankov* that a national procedural rule which prevents a final decision from being reviewed or withdrawn when it is shown on the basis of a new judgment of the Court of Justice that this decision is contrary to EU law, may violate the principle of effectiveness.[187] National procedural rules which limit the national court's powers to examine (final) decisions on the basis of new elements or findings in order to ensure the principle of legal certainty may thus be contrary to EU law.

The judgment in *Orfanopoulos and Oliveiri* is particularly relevant for the question whether national courts should take into account new elements or findings in their examination of the appeal against the rejection of the asylum application. In this case the Court of Justice addressed the standard of judicial review of expulsion measures against EU citizens on public policy grounds.[188] The Court has held that in order to expel an EU citizen under the exception based on reasons of public policy, the competent national authorities must assess, on a case-by-case basis, whether the measure or the circumstances which gave rise to that expulsion order prove the existence of personal conduct constituting a *present* threat to the requirements of public policy. The Court recognised in *Orfanopoulos and Oliveiri* that, in practice, circumstances may arise between the date of the expulsion order and that of its review by the competent court, which point to the cessation or the substantial diminution of the threat which the conduct of the person ordered

[186] Joined Cases C-175/08, C-176/08, C-178/08 and C-179/08 *Salahadin Abdulla* [2010] ECR I-1493, para 97.

[187] Case C-249/11 *Byankov* [2012].

[188] Case C-482/01 *Orfanopoulos and Oliveiri* [2004] ECR I-5257, paras 77–82. See also Case C-467/02 *Cetinkaya* [2004] ECR I-10895, para 47.

to be expelled constitutes to the requirements of public policy. According to the Court, derogations from the principle of freedom of movement for workers must be interpreted strictly, and thus the requirement of the existence of a present threat must, as a general rule, be satisfied at the time of the expulsion. For that reason, in reviewing the lawfulness of the expulsion of an EU citizen, a national practice whereby the national courts may not take into consideration factual matters which occurred after the final decision of the competent authorities which may point to the cessation or the substantial diminution of the present threat to public policy, is liable to adversely affect the right to freedom of movement to which nationals of the Member States are entitled, particularly their right not to be subjected to expulsion measures save in the extreme cases provided for by EU law. According to the Court, that is particularly relevant if a lengthy period has elapsed between the date of the expulsion order and that of the review of that decision by the competent court. The principle of effectiveness thus requires courts to perform an *ex nunc* review of the threat to public policy posed by an EU citizen against whom an expulsion measure was taken.[189]

Asylum cases and cases in which an EU citizen will be expelled for reasons of public policy have two important things in common. First, it needs to be established at the time of expulsion whether there is a *present* threat: in asylum cases it concerns a present threat of *refoulement*, in cases of EU citizens a present threat of a person to the requirements of public policy. Furthermore, in both types of cases a fundamental EU right is at stake. In *Orfanopoulos* the Court of Justice held that the effective exercise of the freedom of movement requires an *ex nunc* assessment of the present threat by the national court. It is not a big step to argue in analogy with this judgment that the effective exercise of the EU right to asylum and the EU prohibition of *refoulement* requires an *ex nunc* assessment by the national court of the present threat (the real risk) of *refoulement*. This would imply that new elements or findings which were submitted or which emerged after the rejection of the asylum claim by the determining authority should be taken into account by the national court or tribunal within the meaning of Article 39 of Directive 2005/85/EC and Article 46 of Directive 2013/32/EU. The need for an *ex nunc* assessment of the risk of *refoulement* by the national court is, as will be explained in section 9.3.2, confirmed by the case law of the ECtHR.

It cannot be assumed from *Orfanopoulos and Oliveiri*, however, that Member States are not allowed to choose a system, explicitly allowed by Directive 2005/85/EC, in which new elements or findings are considered during a subsequent asylum procedure. The procedural rules governing these subsequent proceedings, however, may not undermine the effectiveness of the EU right to asylum and the prohibition of *refoulement*. This means that the applicant may not be expelled until the national court has ruled on the appeal in the subsequent procedure.[190]

189 The Court of Justice refers to the principle of effectiveness in para 80 of the judgment.
190 See further ch 6.

Furthermore, elements or findings which support the existence of a risk of *refoulement* should not be excluded from the assessment of this risk for the sole reason that they could have been submitted earlier in the procedure.[191] Finally, the total duration of the asylum procedures may not violate the right to good administration[192] or undermine the effectiveness of the remedy required by Article 39 of Directive 2005/85/EC.[193]

Article 46(3) of Directive 2013/32/EU seems to require that all new elements and findings which are submitted to the court or tribunal within the meaning of Article 46(1) of this Directive during the appeal proceedings must be taken into account by this court or tribunal. However, as was remarked before, the text of Article 40(1) of the Directive does not exclude some new elements or findings from being examined in a subsequent asylum procedure.

9.3.2 Obligations Stemming from the ECHR, CAT and ICCPR

The principle of *non-refoulement* requires the ECtHR to carry out a 'full and *ex nunc* assessment' of the case. In cases in which the applicant has not yet been expelled, the material point in time for the examination of the risk of *refoulement* is that of the Court's consideration of the case. The ECtHR stated that 'even though the historical position is of interest in so far as it may shed light on the current situation and its likely evolution, it is the present conditions which are decisive'.[194] Such *ex nunc* assessment also requires that evidence or information that has come to light after the final decision must be taken into account by the domestic authorities. In *Salah Sheekh* the Court considered that in assessing an alleged risk of treatment contrary to Article 3 in respect of aliens facing expulsion or extradition, a full and *ex nunc* assessment is called for as the situation in a country of destination may change over time.[195]

In practice, the Court takes account of recent information, among others country of origin information.[196] It also includes new statements or evidence adduced by the applicant in its assessment. In *Hilal*, for example, the Court took into account statements made by the applicant's wife during asylum proceedings

[191] The exclusion from the assessment of evidence which supports the existence of a real risk of *refoulement* on pure procedural grounds undermines the effectiveness of the absolute prohibition of *refoulement*.

[192] See Arts 23(2) Dir 2005/85/EC and 31(2) Dir 2013/32/EU which require that the asylum procedure is concluded as soon as possible. Art 31(3)–(6) Dir 2013/32/EU, which provides for time limits for the asylum procedure. See also Joined Cases C-411/10 and C-493/10 *NS and ME et al* [2011] para 98.

[193] Art 47 of the Charter requires a fair and public hearing within a reasonable time.

[194] See *Said* (n 130) para 48.

[195] *Salah Sheekh* (n 116) para 136. See also *NA* (n 129) para 112; ECtHR 10 February 2011, *Dzhaksybergenov v Ukraine*, no 12343/10, para 36; ComAT 8 July 2011, *Chahin v Sweden*, no 310/2007, paras 9.4 and 9.6; and ComAT 1 July 2011, *Jahani v Switzerland*, no 357/2008, para 9.4.

[196] See, eg *NA* (n 129) para 119.

which started after the applicant had lodged a complaint before the Court.[197] Furthermore, it included in its assessment several documents which were submitted by the applicant to the British Secretary of State after the first decision on the asylum request. These documents were examined by the Secretary of State and the national courts but were not considered relevant because they believed that there was an 'internal flight solution' where the applicant could safely live.[198]

The ECtHR has not explicitly considered that national courts should, like the ECtHR itself, include new elements or findings in their review of an asylum or expulsion decision. However, in *MSS* the ECtHR did take into account in its assessment of the effectiveness of the extremely urgent procedure before the Aliens Appeals Board that the Aliens Appeal Board did not always take into account materials submitted by applicants after their interviews with the Aliens Office. According to the ECtHR this was one of the reasons why these applicants were prevented from establishing the arguable nature of their complaints under Article 3 of the Convention. In this case the applicant could be transferred to Greece immediately after the Alien Appeal Board's decision. There was thus no opportunity to submit new evidence at a later stage.

In *IK* the ECtHR was not persuaded that the applicant's grievance had been thoroughly examined by the Austrian authorities, because these (administrative and judicial) authorities failed to take into account an important new development in the applicant's subsequent asylum proceedings. This new development concerned the fact that the applicant's mother had been awarded refugee status after the Austrian Asylum Court had considered that claim to be credible and convincing and that there was a considerable risk of persecution. This was relevant to the applicant's case as he relied on the same asylum account as his mother. The Austrian authorities found that his asylum motives had been sufficiently thoroughly dealt with in his first proceedings (in which the credibility of the applicant's statements were deemed incredible) and dismissed his request as *res judicata*. This case shows that relevant new elements or findings must be taken into account by the national court at some stage of the asylum proceedings and cannot be ignored on procedural grounds.[199]

Furthermore, one may argue in the light of the subsidiary role of the ECtHR that the fact that the Court assesses claims under Article 3 ECHR *ex nunc* obliges national courts to do the same. Otherwise applicants would be obliged to lodge a complaint before the ECtHR in order to have the new elements or findings assessed.[200] The ECtHR's case law does not, however, prevent States from choosing

[197] *Hilal* (n 104) para 66.

[198] See also Spijkerboer (n 1) 56. It should be noted, however, that the ECtHR sometimes holds the fact that statements and/or evidence are submitted at a late stage of the procedure against the applicant. See further ch 8, sections 8.5 and 8.6.

[199] *IK* (n 121).

[200] See also Spijkerboer (n 1) 57. The ComAT and HRC often ensure their subsidiary role by refusing to include these new facts and circumstances in their assessment. Instead, they grant the State authorities an opportunity to evaluate the new evidence in a new asylum procedure and declare the

to oblige an applicant to submit a new application on the basis of the new facts, while the decision on this application including the assessment of the new facts and circumstances will be tested by the national court.[201]

9.3.3 Subconclusion: The Relevant Moment in Time

Directive 2005/85/EC allows the national courts or tribunals of the Member States to take into account facts and evidence submitted after the decision by the determining authority, but does not require them to do so. The new facts or evidence may, according to Article 32 of the Directive also be assessed in a subsequent asylum procedure. This gives the determining authority the opportunity to first assess the risk of *refoulement* in the light of these new elements or findings. Both options seem to comply with the case law of the Court of Justice and the ECtHR, provided that at one stage of the procedure, before the expulsion of the applicant, the national court or tribunal reviews the asylum decision while taking into account all relevant available elements and findings. Furthermore, the examination of new elements or findings in a subsequent asylum procedure should not lead to considerable delays in the processing of the case.

The *ex nunc* review required by Article 46(3) of Directive 2013/32/EU arguably entails, in principle, the court or tribunal within the meaning of Article 46 taking into account all relevant new elements and findings. Article 40(1) of the Directive, however, leaves open the possibility that some new elements or findings can only be submitted in subsequent asylum proceedings.

Both the Court of Justice's judgment in *Orfanopoulos and Oliveiri* and the ECtHR's case law make clear that the assessment of an actual, present threat at the moment of expulsion requires an *ex nunc* assessment by the national court. The absolute nature of the prohibition of *refoulement* prevents relevant facts or evidence from being taken into account by the national court on the sole ground that they should have been submitted earlier in the procedure. This may be derived from the Court of Justice's judgment in *Salahadin Abdullah* but also from the EU principle of effectiveness. The effectiveness of the EU prohibition of *refoulement* would be seriously undermined if facts or evidence supporting the existence of a risk of *refoulement* were excluded from the national court's assessment, only because they were submitted in a later stage of the procedure.[202] Furthermore, the subsidiary role of the ECtHR would be endangered if applicants were obliged to lodge a complaint before the ECtHR in order to have the risk of *refoulement*

complaints before the Committees inadmissible. See, eg ComAT 2 May 1995, *AE v Switzerland*, no 24/1995 and HRC 10 August 2006, *Dawood Khan v Canada*, no 1302/2004.

[201] Note that the ECtHR took into account in *Bahaddar* that the applicant could lodge a fresh application to remedy the violation of Art 3 ECHR and therefore did have an effective remedy at his disposal. ECtHR 19 February 1998, *Bahaddar v the Netherlands*, no 25894/94.

[202] See further ch 8, section 8.6.

examined in the light of all available facts or evidence, including those submitted in a later stage of the asylum procedure.

9.4 SYNTHESIS OF FINDINGS

National rules and practice regarding the standard of judicial review depend on the vision on the division of tasks between the legislator, administration and judiciary. The EU legislator, the EU Courts and the ECtHR are, in the light of the procedural autonomy of the Member States, hesitant to set requirements with respect to the standard of review by national courts. However, the Court of Justice in *Samba Diouf* has brought the scope and intensity of judicial review within the scope of the EU right to an effective remedy. This right requires a thorough judicial review of the reasons which lead the determining authority to reject the asylum claim as unfounded.[203] Article 46(3) of Directive 2013/32/EU states that an effective remedy should provide for a 'full and *ex nunc* examination of both facts and points of law'. This chapter examined how the term 'thorough' or 'full and *ex nunc*' judicial review should be interpreted. The following conclusions were drawn:

Scope of Judicial Review

— It follows from the Court of Justice's judgments in *Samba Diouf* and *Wilson* that a court or tribunal as required by Article 39 of Directive 2005/85/EC should review both points of law and points of fact.[204] This view is supported by the case law of the ECtHR under Article 6 ECHR, which requires a court or tribunal to have 'full jurisdiction'.[205] A judicial review which is limited to points of law only cannot be considered a rigorous scrutiny as required by the ECtHR in *refoulement* cases.[206] Article 46(3) explicitly states that judicial review should include points of law and points of fact.

— A system in which the facts are established by the administrative authorities and cannot be reviewed by a court or tribunal should therefore be considered contrary to Article 39 of Directive 2005/85/EC and Article 46(3) of Directive 2013/32/EU.

[203] *Samba Diouf* (n 5) paras 56 and 61.

[204] *Samba Diouf* (n 5) para 57; *Wilson* (n 15) para 60.

[205] See, eg *Le Compte, Van Leuven, De Meyere v Belgium* (n 20) para 51.

[206] For example, the ECtHR mentioned the requirement of a rigorous scrutiny in *Jabari* (n 27) para 50.

Intensity of Judicial Review

— It should be derived from the case law of the EU Courts and the ECtHR's that the thorough judicial review demanded by Article 39 of Directive 2005/85/EC and the full judicial review within the meaning of Article 46(3) of Directive 2013/32/EU requires as a minimum that the national court or tribunal assesses the claim of a risk of *refoulement* on its merits. It should carefully examine the facts and evidence underlying the asylum claim. A reasonableness test in which wide discretion is afforded to the determining authority's fact-finding, including the assessment of the applicant's credibility, is not allowed.
— National courts are not obliged to replace their own assessment of the facts for that of the determining authority. They may choose to focus on the quality of the asylum decision and the procedural fairness of the asylum procedure.
— The EU Courts have shown in cases involving complex assessments that a limited form of judicial review should entail an assessment whether the evidence relied on is factually accurate, reliable and consistent, whether that evidence contains all the information, which must be taken into account in order to assess a complex situation and whether it is capable of substantiating the conclusions drawn from it.[207] Furthermore, the EU Courts ensure that procedural guarantees were strictly observed during the administrative procedure.[208] Arguably the judicial scrutiny carried out by the EU Courts shows the minimum level of judicial review necessary in order to ensure the EU right to an effective remedy. This level of intensity of judicial review may, therefore, be considered to be normative for judicial review by national courts in similar cases.[209]
— Asylum cases can be considered similar to cases involving complex assessments, in the sense that in both types of cases it is difficult to find the facts objectively. Therefore, the thorough review required in asylum cases cannot be less intensive than the limited form of judicial review in cases concerning complex assessments.
— The ECtHR made clear in *MSS* and in several cases against the UK that the national authority within the meaning of Article 13 ECHR must enter into a thorough examination of the facts and evidence underlying the asylum claim.[210] This should also be derived from the high level of intensity of the review the ECtHR itself has carried out in *refoulement* cases.[211] If national

[207] *Commission v Tetra Laval* (n 52) para 39.
[208] *Technische Universität München* (n 82) para 14.
[209] See also Schuurmans (n 37).
[210] *MSS* (n 96) paras 389–90 and (among others) *Soering* (n 101) para 121–22 and *Vilvarajah* (n 105) para 125–26.
[211] See, eg *FN* (n 127); *N* (n 130); and *Said* (n 130).

courts carry out a more limited judicial review than the ECtHR that would undermine the subsidiary role of the ECtHR.[212]

The Relevant Moment of Time

— Article 39 of Directive 2005/85/EC read in the light of the EU right to an effective remedy requires that the national court should at one stage of the asylum procedure, before the expulsion of the applicant, review the asylum decision on the basis of all relevant available facts and evidence. This includes all relevant evidence which is submitted in a later stage of the asylum procedure (after the first administrative decision on the asylum application). Article 46(3) of Directive 2013/32/EU explicitly requires an *ex nunc* judicial review by the national court in first instance.
— The effectiveness of the EU prohibition of *refoulement* would be undermined if relevant facts or evidence cannot be taken into account by the national court on the sole ground that they should have been submitted earlier in the procedure. This was derived from the judgment of the Court of Justice in *Orfanopoulos and Oliveiri* and the case law of the ECtHR which show that the assessment of an actual, present threat at the moment of expulsion requires an *ex nunc* assessment by the national court.[213]

[212] See also Spijkerboer (n 1) 68–69.
[213] *Orfanopoulos* (n 188) paras 77–82; *Salah Sheekh* (n 116) para 136; *IK* (n 122).

10

The Use of Secret Information in Asylum Cases

IN SOME ASYLUM cases (part of) the establishment of the facts is based on evidence gathered by the authorities which is not made available to the asylum seeker concerned or his legal representative. This information may be kept secret for several reasons. State authorities may refuse to reveal the identity and function of the sources of the information in order to protect those sources or the international relations with the country of origin of those sources. States may also want to protect the methods they use for assessing the credibility of individual asylum accounts. In some Member States legal advisers may not have access to country of origin information relied on by the determining authority.[1] Finally, information may be kept secret for national security reasons.[2] Member States generally do not disclose information regarding investigations into terrorism or organised crime in asylum or expulsion proceedings.

The fact that a person is involved in terrorism may lead to a risk of *refoulement* upon return to his country of origin.[3] Information concerning this person's terrorist activities may thus be relevant for the assessment of the risk of *refoulement*. However, information regarding the danger of an asylum seeker for national security of the State in which he claimed asylum cannot be included in the question whether a person is in need of protection on the basis of the EU prohibition of *refoulement*. The European Court of Human Rights (ECtHR) ruled several times that the risk of a violation of Article 3 European Convention of Human Rights (ECHR) upon expulsion cannot be balanced against national security concerns. Therefore, national security concerns and evidence substantiating such concerns cannot lead to the refusal of protection against *refoulement*. Furthermore, they cannot justify a limitation of the right to an effective remedy against a decision on

[1] The Commission mentions Lithuania and Spain as examples. Commission, 'Report from the Commission to the European Parliament and the Council on the Application of Directive 2005/85/EC of 1 December 2005 on Minimum Standards on Procedures in Member States for Granting and Withdrawing Refugee Status' COM (2010) 465 final, 8.

[2] According to the Commission, evaluation of the Procedures Directive of September 2010, limitations to the right of access to the file for legal representatives (Art 16 Dir 2005/85/EC) on national security grounds are applicable in Cyprus, Greece, Ireland, Lithuania, the Netherlands, Spain and the UK. Commission Report (n 1) 8.

[3] See, eg ECtHR (GC) 28 February 2008, *Saadi v Italy*, no 37201/06.

the existence of a risk of *refoulement*.[4] As the Court of Justice respects the ECHR when interpreting EU asylum law, it should be assumed that the same applies to the EU prohibition of *refoulement*.

National security concerns may play a role in the decision whether a person may be excluded from an EU refugee or subsidiary protection status. According to EU law, a person may be excluded from such a status if there are serious reasons for considering that he committed a serious crime or is currently involved in terrorist or other criminal activities.[5] Secret evidence substantiating such serious reasons or such involvement may thus be used in the assessment of a person's EU right to an asylum status and may affect his procedural rights.[6] As decisions regarding the exclusion of a person from an asylum status fall outside the scope of this study, they will not be specifically addressed in this chapter.[7] However, the conclusions drawn in this chapter are also relevant for these decisions.

It is very difficult for the person concerned to challenge a decision which is based on secret information or on information of which the sources are not known to him. It is, therefore, often argued that the right to adversarial proceedings and the principle of equality of arms are violated in these cases. Moreover, the court reviewing the decision is sometimes not given access to all the information underlying the challenged decision. This undermines the effectiveness of judicial review. Under EU law several other rights and principles play a role in cases concerning secret information, such as the right of access to the file, the right to be heard and the duty to state reasons which are all interlinked.[8]

A separate chapter on the issue of the use of secret evidence is included in this book, because in the case law regarding this issue the three basic concepts discussed in chapter four, section 4.5 are clearly important. The most obvious aspect in cases concerning secret information is that the interests of the party concerned in adversarial proceedings and equality of arms must be balanced against the interests of the State and/or third parties to keep certain information secret. Secondly, it is accepted, particularly in the case law of the ECtHR, that limitations to the right to adversarial proceedings may be justified, as long as they are counterbalanced by compensation techniques. An example which will be discussed in several sections of this chapter is the use of special security-cleared counsels who have access to the secret evidence and can plead on behalf of the party concerned (special advocate proceedings). The question whether the ECHR has been violated thus depends on the fairness or effectiveness of the procedure seen as a whole. Finally, the nature of the case seems to determine the level of procedural guarantees required.

[4] Ibid and ECtHR (GC) 25 October 1996, *Chahal v the United Kingdom*, no 22414/93.

[5] Arts 12(2), 14(4a) and 17 Dir 2011/95/EU.

[6] See, eg M Bliss, 'Serious Reasons for Considering: Minimum Standards of Procedural Fairness in the Application of the Article 1F Exclusion Clauses' (2000) 12 *International Journal of Refugee Law* 92, 120–23.

[7] See ch 1, section 1.5 in this volume.

[8] See also ch 4, section 4.2 in this volume.

In this chapter it will be argued that although EU legislation, in particular Directive 2005/85/EC, allows for the use of secret information in asylum cases, the Member States' discretion is limited by the EU right to be heard, the duty to state reasons and the right to an effective remedy. The explicit possibility, left open by Directive 2005/85/EC, to withhold relevant information from the national court deciding the appeal against a negative asylum decision, clearly infringes the right to an effective remedy and should, therefore, be considered void.

The two main sources addressed in this chapter are the case law of the Court of Justice and CFI/General Court and that of the ECtHR. The EU Courts addressed the use of secret evidence mainly in competition cases and EU sanction cases in which the funds and economic resources of persons and organisations are frozen. The ECtHR has ruled on this issue in very different cases, regarding civil rights and obligations, criminal charges, secret surveillance, detention and expulsion. It will be shown that the case law of these courts on the one hand show clear parallels, and at the same time complement each other. This chapter attempts to derive from this case law one set of procedural standards for asylum cases in which secret evidence is used.

10.1 THE USE OF SECRET INFORMATION UNDER EU LAW

Article 41(2)(b) of the Charter includes 'the right of every person to have access to his or her file, while respecting the legitimate interests of confidentiality and of professional and business secrecy'. The right of access to the file had already been recognised as a general principle of EU law by the EU Courts. According to the EU Courts, the right of access to the file is 'one of the procedural safeguards intended to protect the rights of the defence and to ensure, in particular, that the right to be heard can be exercised effectively'.[9] The right of access to the file is also linked to the obligation to state reasons and the right to an effective remedy as well as to the principles of equality of arms and adversarial proceedings. In all proceedings in which EU sanctions are imposed the rights of the defence must be respected in administrative as well as appeal proceedings.[10]

Directive 2005/85/EC

Article 16 of Directive 2005/85/EC explicitly accepts that the asylum applicant and his legal representative, and in cases concerning national security, also the court or tribunal examining the appeal against a negative asylum decision, may be refused access to (part) of the file underlying the asylum decision. This suggests that the

[9] Case T-53/03 *BPB v Commission* [2008] ECR II-1333, para 31; Case T-170/06 *Alrosa v Commission* [2007] ECR II-2601, para 197; and Case T-36/91 *Imperial Chemical Industries v Commission* [1995] ECR II-1847, para 69.

[10] See, eg *BPB v Commission* (n 9) para 40; Case T-228/02 *Organisation des Modjahedines du peuple d'Iran v Council* [2006] ECR II-4665, para 94; Case C-417/11 P, *Council v Bamba* [2012].

asylum decision may be (partly) based on secret information. Article 16(1) of Directive 2005/85/EC provides that the legal representative may be refused access to information in the asylum seeker's file, where disclosure of information or sources would jeopardise national security, the security of the organisations or person(s) providing the information, or the security of the person(s) to whom the information relates, or where the investigative interests relating to the examination of applications of asylum by the competent authorities of the Member States, or the international relations of the Member States would be compromised. In these cases, access to the information or sources in question shall be available to the authorities (a court or tribunal) which provide the effective remedy required by Article 39 of Directive 2005/85/EC. The access of the court or tribunal to this information may, however, be precluded in cases of national security.

Directive 2013/32/EU

Article 23(1) of Directive 2013/32/EU allows Member States to refuse access to (part of) the file to the applicant and his legal representative on the same grounds as those mentioned in Article 16 of Directive 2005/85/EC. However, Article 23(1) requires the Member States to make access to secret information or sources available to the court or tribunal within the meaning of Article 46 of the Directive to provide for an effective remedy. Furthermore, Article 23(1) states that Member States should establish in national law procedures guaranteeing the respect of the applicant's rights of defence. The provision explains that:

> Member States may, in particular, grant access to such information or sources to a legal adviser or other counsellor who has undergone a security check, insofar as the information is relevant for examining the application or for taking a decision to withdraw international protection.

The provision here refers to the special advocate procedure which is applied in the UK in addition to Canada and New Zealand. This procedure will be further discussed in this chapter.

Directive 2011/95/EU

Article 4 of Directive 2011/95/EU does not mention the use of evidence which is not, or is only partly, disclosed to the asylum applicant. Noll states, however, that the examining authorities' obligation to assess the relevant elements of the asylum claim in cooperation with the applicant laid down in Article 4(1) of the Qualification Directive, may imply that classified investigative material which cannot be shared with the applicant must be excluded from the basis for a decision in the case.[11]

[11] G Noll, *Evidentiary Assessment and the EU Qualification Directive, New Issues in Refugee Research, Working Paper No 117* (Geneva, UNHCR) 7.

Relevant Case Law of the EU Courts

The EU Courts have applied the right of access to the file and its related rights and principles in cases concerning several very different fields of EU law. In all these cases, the EU Courts seem to apply the same standards. The case law developed under the right of access to the file in one field of EU law should, therefore, be considered relevant for other fields of EU law, including asylum law.[12] The Court of First Instance (CFI), for example, referred in its judgments concerning EU sanctions to its earlier case law in competition law cases. Violations of the right of access to the file and the rights of the defence are assessed on a case-by-case basis,[13] which gives the EU Courts the opportunity to take the nature of the case into account.[14]

In asylum cases the national courts are confronted with decisions which are (partly) based on confidential information. In several recent cases the Court of Justice has ruled which requirements follow from the right to an effective remedy, with respect to judicial review by national courts in cases in which secret information is used. These cases will be discussed in section 10.2.

Most of the case law regarding the use of secret information, however, concerns decisions of the EU Institutions which were reviewed by the CFI or the General Court and (in some cases) eventually by the Court of Justice. It may be assumed that the CFI's case law regarding the right of access to the file and related rights and principles is also relevant for national courts dealing with decisions based on confidential information. Notably, in its preliminary ruling in *ZZ* concerning the restriction of free movement of an EU citizen on grounds of public security, the Court of Justice referred several times to its judgment in *Kadi I* which concerned a direct appeal before the EU Courts against an EU sanction.[15] The EU rights and principles applied in these cases, such as the rights of the defence and the right to an effective remedy, also apply in the national context. Furthermore, as will be shown in the following sections, the principles set out by the Court of Justice in cases concerning judicial review by national courts are in line with the principles applied by the EU Courts in appeals against decisions by EU Institutions. In the *Kadi II* judgment the Court of Justice referred several times to its judgment in *ZZ*.[16] Therefore, section 10.3 discusses the case law concerning economic issues, particularly competition law. Section 10.4 examines the case law regarding EU sanctions freezing the funds of persons and organisations. Confidential

[12] See Craig who states, with regard to Case T-42/96 *Eyckeler* [1998] ECR II-401 which concerned customs decisions: 'The ease with which the CFI reasoned by analogy from competition to customs, signifies the generalization of access to the file as an aspect of the right to be heard, irrespective of the subject-matter area in question, and this is in accord with the formulation in the Charter of Fundamental Rights.' P Craig, *EU Administrative Law* (Oxford, Oxford University Press, 2006) 367.

[13] *BPB v Commission* (n 9) para 33.

[14] See, eg Case T-221/95 *Endemol* [1999] para 68.

[15] Case C-300/11 *ZZ* [2013] paras 53, 54 and 57. See also Case C-450/06 *Varec* [2008] ECR I-581, Opinion of AG Sharpston, para 61.

[16] Joined Cases C-584/10 P, C-593/10 P and C-595/10 P *Commission et al v Kadi* [2013] paras 100, 101, 120 and 125–29.

information may also play a role in other fields of EU law such as customs decisions or civil service cases. I chose to limit this chapter to competition cases and EU sanction cases. In competition cases the EU Courts developed a comprehensive body of case law concerning the right of access to the file. In EU sanction cases, as in asylum cases, the limitation of the right of access to the file for reasons of national security plays an important role.

The EU Courts have recognised in their case law that the right of access to the file is not absolute. EU Institutions may refuse to disclose documents containing business secrets, internal documents, and information which should remain confidential in order to protect the sources that provided the documents or information or for reasons of national security. In those situations the interests in not disclosing relevant information must be balanced against the rights of the defence.

Relevance of the ECHtR's Case Law

The EU Courts in direct appeals against decisions of EU Institutions sometimes refer to the case law of the ECtHR when addressing the right of access to the file and the rights of the defence.[17] Furthermore, the Court of Justice has indicated in *Varec* that national procedures in which confidential information plays a role must comply with the requirements following from Article 6 ECHR.[18] The references to the ECtHR's case law are, however, random and incomplete. It is striking that in two important judgments of the Court of Justice concerning the use of secret evidence and the EU right to an effective remedy, in *Kadi II* and *ZZ*, no mention is made of the ECtHR's case law, and in particular its judgment in *A and others*. In *Kadi II* the General Court had referred extensively to the criteria set out ECtHR's judgment in *A and others*.[19]

Nonetheless, there are clear parallels between the case law of the EU Courts and that of the ECtHR. It is conceivable that in the future the case law of the ECtHR will help the EU Courts to fill in some of the existing gaps in their jurisprudence concerning the use of confidential information. Section 10.5 will address the ECtHR's case law extensively, in order to understand which minimum standards are set by this Court.

[17] See, eg Cases C-402/05 P and C-415/05 P *Kadi and Al Barakaat v Council and Commission* [2008] ECR I-6351, para 344 and *Modjahedines du peuple d'Iran v Council* (n 10) paras 119 and 158.

[18] *Varec* (n 15) paras 44–48 and Case T-47/03 *Sison v Council* [2007] ECR II-73, para 166. In *ZZ* (n 15) however, strikingly, and differing from AG Bot's Opinion, the Court made no references to the ECtHR's case law.

[19] Case T-85/09 *Kadi v Commission* [2010] ECR I-6351, paras 175–76.

10.2 OBLIGATIONS FOR THE NATIONAL COURTS OF MEMBER STATES UNDER EU LAW

The most important case in which the Court of Justice directly addressed the requirements following from Article 47 of the Charter in cases pending before a national court in which secret information is used, is *ZZ*. This case concerned the decision by the UK to cancel the right of residence of a French national (ZZ) on the ground that his presence was not conducive to the public good, and to exclude him from the UK. In September 2006 ZZ travelled to the UK where a decision refusing him admission was taken on grounds of public security. He appealed the decision refusing entry before the Special Immigration Appeals Commission (SIAC). During the appeal proceedings, the Secretary of State refused to disclose the evidence on which the refusal of entry was based. The SIAC assessed in a closed session whether the non-disclosure of the evidence was justified. The hearing of the appeal itself took place in open and closed sessions. During the closed sessions ZZ and his personal advisers were absent, but ZZ was represented by two special advocates. These security-cleared counsels had access to the non-disclosed evidence and argued the case on his behalf. The SIAC gave an 'open' judgment and a 'closed' judgment, which was provided only to the Secretary of State and ZZ's special advocates. In its open judgment, the SIAC made clear that most of the evidence against ZZ had remained secret and that the disclosed information did not concern 'the critical issues'. The SIAC dismissed the appeal. It was satisfied that ZZ was involved in activities of the Armed Islamic Group network and in terrorist activities in 1995 and 1996. It found that items which ZZ admitted owning or to have owned had been discovered in 1995 in Belgium, in premises rented by a known extremist where a quantity of arms and ammunition were also found. The SIAC found that the personal conduct of ZZ represented a genuine present and sufficiently serious threat to public security, which outweighed ZZ's right to enjoy family life in the UK. The further reasons for this decision were only mentioned in the closed decision. ZZ appealed the SIAC's decision before the Court of Appeal, which referred a question for preliminary ruling to the Court of Justice. This question (as rephrased by the Court of Justice) was whether:

> Article 30(2) of Directive 2004/38, read in the light in particular of Article 47 of the Charter, must be interpreted as requiring a national court hearing an appeal of a Union citizen against a decision refusing entry taken under Article 27(1) of that directive to ensure that the essence of the public security grounds which constitute the basis of that decision is disclosed to the person concerned where the competent national authority contends before that court that such disclosure is contrary to the interests of State security.[20]

Article 30(1) of Directive 2004/38/EC states that EU citizens and their family members shall be notified in writing of any decision restricting their freedom

[20] *ZZ* (n 15) para 40.

of movement for reasons of public policy, public security or public health, in such a way that they are able to comprehend its content and the implications for them. Article 30(2) of the Directive, moreover, provides that these persons 'shall be informed, precisely and in full, of the public policy, public security or public health grounds on which the decision taken in their case is based, unless this is contrary to the interests of State security'. According to Article 31 of Directive 2004/38/EC, persons concerned shall have access to judicial and, where appropriate, administrative redress procedures against this decision.

The Right to an Effective Remedy

The Court of Justice noted that it was not in dispute that ZZ was not informed precisely and in full of the grounds that constituted the basis of the decision refusing entry. It considered that the possibility to derogate from the obligation to inform a person precisely and in full of the grounds for the restriction of his freedom of movement in the interests of State security must be interpreted restrictively. The Court went on to interpret this provision in the light of the right to an effective remedy as laid down in Article 47 of the Charter. First, the Court of Justice referred to its standing case law concerning the statement of reasons. It considered that the person concerned:

> must be able to ascertain the reasons upon which the decision taken in relation to him is based, either by reading the decision itself or by requesting and obtaining notification of those reasons … so as to make it possible for him to defend his rights in the best possible conditions and to decide, with full knowledge of the relevant facts, whether there is any point in his applying to the court with jurisdiction, and in order to put the latter fully in a position in which it may carry out the review of the lawfulness of the national decision in question[21]

Secondly, the Court referred to the right to adversarial proceedings and stated that the right to an effective remedy would be infringed 'if a judicial decision were founded on facts and documents which the parties themselves, or one of them, have not had an opportunity to examine and on which they have therefore been unable to state their views'.[22]

Limitations to the Right to an Effective Remedy

The Court of Justice recognised that the right to an effective remedy may be subjected to limitations. It referred to Article 52(1) of the Charter which provides that such limitations must respect the essence of Article 47, must be proportionate and necessary and genuinely meet objectives of general interest recognised by the EU. It accepted that State security reasons may prove it necessary not to disclose certain information to the person concerned in both in administrative

[21] Ibid, para 53.
[22] Ibid, para 55.

and judicial proceedings.[23] However, non-disclosure is only justified when it is 'strictly necessary' and only in 'exceptional cases'.[24] The Court thus applies a very high standard. This high standard is also applied by the ECtHR in criminal cases under Article 6 ECHR.[25]

Judicial Review of the Reasons for Non-disclosure

The Court of Justice stresses several times, and in different wordings, that it not up to the administrative authorities alone to decide whether reasons of State security prevent the disclosure of information (that is, reasons for the decision as well as evidence underlying the decision).[26] Member States are required 'to provide for effective judicial review … of the existence and validity of the reasons invoked by the national authority with regard to State security…'.[27] The national court must verify whether reasons of State security stand in the way of precise and full disclosure of the grounds on which the decision in question is based and of the related evidence. This judicial review must be independent and extend to all the matters of law and fact.[28] It is up to the administrative authorities to prove that State security would in fact be compromised by precise and full disclosure to the person concerned of the grounds which constitute the basis of the decision and of the related evidence. According to the Court 'there is no presumption that the reasons invoked by a national authority exist and are valid'.[29]

If the national court concludes that the reasons of State security invoked by the administrative authorities do not stand in the way of precise and full disclosure to the person concerned of the grounds on which the decision is based, it must give them the opportunity to disclose the missing grounds and evidence to the person concerned. 'If that authority does not authorise their disclosure, the court proceeds to examine the legality of such a decision on the basis of solely the grounds and evidence which have been disclosed.'[30]

Judicial Review of the Content of the Decision

The Court of Justice stated that Member States must ensure that the national court performing the judicial review required by Article 31 of Directive 2004/38/EC is able to examine both all the grounds and the related evidence on the basis of

[23] Ibid, paras 54 and 57. In *Varec* (n 15) paras 47 and 51 the Court also accepted in the context of contract award procedures that the in some cases it may be necessary to withhold certain information from the parties in order to preserve the fundamental rights of a third party or to safeguard an important public interest.

[24] *ZZ* (n 15) paras 57 and 69.

[25] See section 10.5.3.

[26] See also *Varec* (n 15) para 55, and Case C-438/04, *Mobistar* [2006] ECR I-6675, para 43.

[27] *ZZ* (n 15) para 58.

[28] Ibid, paras 60 and 62.

[29] Ibid, para 61.

[30] Ibid, para 63.

which the decision was taken.[31] This implies that the national court must receive the evidence underlying the contested decision. This is in line with the Court of Justice's earlier judgments in *Varec* and *Mobistar* where it held that national courts should have at their disposal all the information necessary in order to decide in full knowledge of the facts on the merits of the appeal, including confidential information.[32]

Balancing State Security and the Right to an Effective Remedy

If the national court finds that State security does stand in the way of disclosure of the grounds of the decision to the person concerned, judicial review of the legality of the decision must be carried out 'in a procedure which strikes an appropriate balance between the requirements flowing from State security and the requirements of the right to effective judicial protection'.[33] To that end:

> the court with jurisdiction in the Member State concerned must have at its disposal and apply techniques and rules of procedural law which accommodate, on the one hand, legitimate State security considerations regarding the nature and sources of the information taken into account in the adoption of such a decision and, on the other hand, the need to ensure sufficient compliance with the person's procedural rights, such as the right to be heard and the adversarial principle.[34]

Any interference with the exercise of the right to an effective remedy must be limited to that which is strictly necessary. The Court of Justice gives some indications as to the guarantees which should be offered in such procedure. The procedure must ensure, to the greatest possible extent that the adversarial principle is complied with. This must enable the person concerned to contest the grounds on which the decision in question is based and to make submissions on the evidence relating to the decision. With regard to the *grounds* (reasons) for the decision the Court considers that 'the person concerned must be informed, in any event, of the essence of the grounds on which a decision refusing entry … is based….'[35] According to the Court 'the necessary protection of State security cannot have the effect of denying the person concerned his right to be heard and, therefore, of rendering his right of redress as provided for in Article 31 of that directive ineffective'.[36] Thus, as a minimum, the statement of reasons must explain the essence of the case against the person concerned. If the administrative authorities fail to comply with this requirement, the national court must decide which consequences follow from this failure.[37] The Court of Justice does not explain,

[31] Ibid, para 59.
[32] *Mobistar* (n 26) para 40, *Varec* (n 15) para 53 and K Von Papp, 'Case C-450/06, *Varec* [2008]' (2009) 46 *Common Market Law Review* 991, 996.
[33] Ibid, para 64.
[34] Ibid, para 57.
[35] Ibid, para 65. The Court here disagreed with AG Bot in para 80 of his Opinion.
[36] Ibid, para 65.
[37] Ibid, para 68.

however, what constitutes the essence of a case. Arguably, the case law of the EU Courts in EU sanction cases, as well as the case law of the ECtHR, may provide some guidance in this respect.

By requiring the disclosure of the essence of the case the Court of Justice seems to follow the ECtHR's judgment in *A and others*, even though it does not refer to it in its judgment. This is striking because the *A and others* case concerned the detention of persons who were suspected of terrorist activities (Article 5(4) ECHR), whereas *ZZ* concerned the expulsion of EU citizens. Apparently, the Court of Justice reads the strict guarantees applicable in detention cases and criminal cases into Article 47 of the Charter and applies them in the context of the expulsion of an EU citizen.

The Court finds that a different balancing test applies to the *evidence* underlying the decision. The non-disclosure of evidence may be justified. It stated:

> In certain cases, disclosure of that evidence is liable to compromise State security in a direct and specific manner, in that it may, in particular, endanger the life, health or freedom of persons or reveal the methods of investigation specifically used by the national security authorities and thus seriously impede, or even prevent, future performance of the tasks of those authorities.[38]

However, the non-disclosure of evidence may have consequences for the evidentiary value of this evidence. The national court must assess:

> whether and to what extent the restrictions on the rights of the defence arising in particular from a failure to disclose the evidence and the precise and full grounds on which the decision … is based are such as to affect the evidential value of the confidential evidence.[39]

The Court does not address the fairness of the special advocate procedure applied in the proceedings before the SIAC in the *ZZ* case. The SIAC remarked that most of the evidence against ZZ had remained secret and that the disclosed information did not concern the critical issues of the case. Therefore, arguably the essence of the case had not been disclosed to ZZ and the right to an effective remedy guaranteed by Article 47 of the Charter may thus have been violated.[40] It will be shown in section 10.5.4 that the ECtHR also found that the special advocate procedure applied in the UK does not always accurately compensate limitation to the right to adversarial proceedings.

In *Varec* and *Mobistar*, which concerned the protection of business secrets, the Court held that the principles of the protection of confidential information and of business secrets must be observed in such a way as to reconcile it with the right to effective legal protection and the rights of the defence of the parties to

[38] Ibid, para 66.
[39] Ibid, para 67.
[40] AG Bot concluded in his Opinion that the national proceedings complied with the right to an effective remedy. *ZZ* (n 15) opinion of AG Bot, para 100.

the dispute.[41] We will see in the next section that this terminology is also used by the EU Courts in direct appeals against Commission decisions in competition cases. It means, for example, that a non-confidential version or summaries of confidential documents or a list of documents contained in the file is provided to the parties concerned.

10.3 COMPETITION CASES AND THE PROTECTION OF BUSINESS SECRETS

In competition cases, the EU Courts have set out the general principles with regard to cases in which the protection of confidential information on the one hand, and the rights of the defence of the parties concerned on the other hand, collide. Such cases concern, for example, the imposition by the Commission of a fine on one or more companies for participating in a concerted practice and/or abusing their dominant position, or the refusal to give permission for a merger. The Commission's decisions are often (partly) based on information provided by other companies.[42] Those companies may wish to remain anonymous or may request the Commission to ensure the confidentiality of documents containing business secrets. The EU Courts have held that in such cases the right to confidentiality must be balanced against and reconciled with the rights of the defence, in particular the right of access to the file and the right to be heard.

The case law which will be discussed in this section concerns decisions by the Commission and their review by the CFI/General Court and subsequently the Court of Justice.[43] Furthermore, some references will be made to the Commission Notice on the rules for access to the Commission file in certain competition cases (the Commission Notice).[44]

10.3.1 The Right of Access to the File

In competition cases, the legality of the use of confidential information is usually addressed under the right of access to the file and the right to be heard. The purpose of providing access to the file in competition cases is to enable the addressees

[41] *Varec* (n 15) para 52. See also *Mobistar* (n 26) para 40.

[42] For the special problems which characterise the production of evidence in competition cases, see Case C-411/04 P *Salzgitter Mannesmann v Commission* [2007] ECR I-959, Opinion of AG Geelhoed, paras 52–59.

[43] For the purpose of gathering relevant case law I have used R Barents, *Directory of EC Case Law on Competition* (Alphen aan den Rijn, Kluwer Law International, 2007) 568–89.

[44] Commission Notice on the rules for access to the Commission file in cases pursuant to Arts 81 and 82 of the EC Treaty, Arts 53, 54 and 57 of the EEA Agreement, and Council Reg (EC) No 139/2004 [2005] OJ C-325/7. For the procedure before the Commission, see also Commission Decision of 23 May 2001 on the terms of reference of hearing officers in certain competition proceedings [2001] OJ L162/21.

of statements of objections to examine evidence in the Commission's file so that they are in a position to express their views effectively on the conclusions reached by it in its statement of objections on the basis of that evidence.[45] The right of access to the file is justified by the need to ensure that the undertakings in question are able to defend themselves properly against the objections raised in that statement.[46] During the administrative procedure, the party concerned must be able to make known its views on the truth and relevance of the facts, charges and circumstances relied on by the Commission.[47]

When taking a decision adversely affecting a party the EU Institutions are obliged to provide access to the file to this party.[48] The 'file' consists of all information relevant to the defence of the interests of the party concerned.[49] It thus includes both inculpatory and exculpatory evidence.[50] The rights of the defence of the party concerned have only been infringed if the non-disclosure of the documents in question might have influenced the course of the procedure and the content of the decision to the applicant's detriment.[51] The Commission is allowed to preclude from the administrative procedure evidence which has no relation to the allegations of fact and of law in the statement of objections and which therefore has no relevance to the investigation.[52] In order to ascertain whether the non-disclosure of a document could have harmed the defence during the administrative procedure, a distinction should be made between inculpatory and exculpatory evidence.[53]

Inculpatory Evidence

The right of access to the file is not an end in itself, but is intended to protect the rights of the defence.[54] Therefore, the Commission is under no obligation to disclose to the undertakings concerned the inculpatory evidence upon which it does not rely in its decision in support of the complaints.[55] 'A document can be

[45] See, eg Case C-51/92 P *Hercules Chemicals v Commission* [1999] ECR I-4235, para 75.

[46] See, eg *Endemol v Commission* (n 14) para 65.

[47] *Imperial Chemical Industries v Commission* (n 9) para 69.

[48] See also A Erlandsson, 'The Defendant's Right of Access to the Commission's File in Competition Cases' (1998) 25 *Legal Issues of Economic Integration* 139, 145–46.

[49] See, eg Case C-49/88 *Al-Jubail* [1991] ECR I-3187, para 17 (anti-dumping case).

[50] Erlandsson, 'The Defendant's Right of Access' (n 48) 146. According to the Commission Notice on the rules for access to the Commission file (n 44) the parties will in principle be granted access to all documents making up the Commission's file. This file consists of all documents which have been obtained, produced and/or assembled by the Commission Directorate for Competition, during the investigation.

[51] *Imperial Chemical Industries v Commission* (n 9) para 78.

[52] This is also called the objective link criterion. See, eg Joined Cases C-204/00 P, C-205/00 P, C-211/00 P, C-213/00 P, C-217/00 P and C-219/00 P *Aalborg Portland et al v Commission* [2004] para 126.

[53] Ibid, para 130.

[54] *Hercules Chemicals v Commission* (n 45) para 76.

[55] Joined Cases T-191/98, T-212/98 to T-214/98 *Atlantic Container Line et al v Commission* [2003] ECR II-3275, para 377.

regarded as a document that incriminates an applicant only where it is used by the Commission to support a finding of an infringement in which that party is alleged to have participated.'[56] In *BPB*, for example, the CFI considered that information provided by an anonymous informant, which was not disclosed to the undertaking concerned, was a factor triggering the Commission's investigations. However, no objection in the statement of objections or the contested decision was based solely on the information provided by this informant. For that reason, and because the confidentiality of the information was justified, the rights of the defence and the principle of equality of arms had not been violated.[57]

Inculpatory documents that have not been communicated to the undertakings concerned during the administrative procedure are not admissible as evidence. Therefore, they must be excluded as evidence, if the Commission relied on them in its decision.[58] The decision must only be annulled if the other evidence underlying the decision does not meet the required standard of proof.[59] The party concerned must show that the result at which the Commission arrived in its decision would have been different if the document(s) which were not communicated to it had to be disallowed as evidence.[60] A document containing incriminating evidence does not automatically need to be excluded if only part of the information included in it must remain confidential. (See further section 10.3.3.)[61]

Exculpatory Evidence

The party concerned must have access to documents which are or might be capable of substantiating its defence. However, according to the CFI, the rights of the defence have only been infringed if it has been established that the non-disclosure of the documents in question

> might have influenced the course of the procedure and the content of the decision to the applicant's detriment. The possibility of such an influence can therefore be established if a provisional examination of some of the evidence shows that the documents not disclosed might in the light of that evidence have had a significance which ought not to have been disregarded.[62]

[56] *BPB v Commission* (n 9) para 32.

[57] Ibid, paras 32–38.

[58] Ibid, para 41. See also Case C-62/86 *AKZO* [1991] ECR I-3359, paras 21 and 24 and Case 107/82 *AEG* [1983] ECR 3151, paras 24–25.

[59] *AEG* (n 58) para 30.

[60] Case C-407/08 P *Knauf Gips v Commission* [2010] ECR I-6375, para 13. See also Case T-410/03 *Hoechst v Commission* [2008] ECR II-881, para 146; *BPB v Commission* (n 9) para 45; and Erlandsson (n 48) 172.

[61] *Salzgitter Mannesmann v Commission* (n 42) para 44. For a different view, see *AEG* (n 58) paras 23–24.

[62] *Imperial Chemical Industries v Commission* (n 9) para 78. See also *Knauf Gips v Commission* (n 60) para 23, *Hercules Chemicals v Commission* (n 45) para 80 and Case T-161/05 *Hoechst v Commission* [2009] ECR II-3555, para 166.

Thus, the undertaking concerned must 'establish not only that it did not have access to certain exculpatory evidence, but also that it could have used that evidence for its defence'.[63] In this regard applicants

> cannot be required to set out in their application detailed arguments or a consistent body of evidence to show that the outcome of the administrative procedure might have been different if they had had access to certain documents which were in fact never disclosed to them. Such an approach would in effect amount to requiring a *probatio diabolica*.[64]

The applicant should, however, adduce prima facie evidence that the undisclosed documents would be useful to its defence.[65]

In some cases the CFI granted the undertaking access to non-confidential versions of the non-disclosed documents and invited it to show how the non-disclosure of these documents could have harmed its defence.[66] In *Solvay* the undertaking concerned argued that certain documents could have contained information which it could have used for its defence. However, these documents had gone missing. The Court of Justice noted that Solvay could have found in the missing sub-files evidence originating from other undertakings, which would have enabled it to offer a different interpretation of the facts from that adopted by the Commission, which could have been of use for its defence. It furthermore ruled that since Solvay had not had access to those documents, and their content was neither certain nor capable of being ascertained, Solvay could not be required 'to state the arguments which it would have raised had those documents been available to it—something which was materially impossible for it to know'.[67]

The CFI, and in appeal cases, the Court of Justice, examine whether a document, which is relevant and therefore should have been disclosed to the undertaking concerned, was of use to this undertaking's defence.[68] In this examination the strength of the (disclosed) evidence relied on by the Commission and that of the positions of the party concerned are taken into account.[69] The CFI concluded in many cases that the evidence could not have been capable of substantiating the undertaking's defence and that, therefore, no violation of the rights of the defence

[63] *Knauf Gips v Commission* (n 60) para 24. See also *Aalborg Portland et al v Commission* (n 52) para 133; *BPB v Commission* (n 9) para 55; and *Hoechst v Commission* (n 60) para 146.

[64] Case T-587/08 *Fresh Del Monte Produce, Inc v Commission* [2013] para 689.

[65] Ibid, para 690.

[66] See, eg Case T-52/03 *Knauf Gips v Commission* [2008] ECR II-115, para 68; *Hoechst v Commission* (n 60) para 150; and Case T-7/89 *Hercules Chemicals v Commission* [1991] ECR II-1711, para 56.

[67] Case C-109/10 P *Solvay SA v Commission* [2011] ECR I-10329, para 63.

[68] See, eg *Imperial Chemical Industries v Commission* (n 9) para 87, where the CFI concluded that some documents which were not disclosed to the undertaking concerned were capable of substantiating its defence. See also *Knauf Gips v Commission* (n 60) para 25.

[69] See, eg *Imperial Chemical Industries v Commission* (n 9) paras 87–109 and *Aalborg Portland et al v Commission* (n 52) paras 156–64.

occurred.[70] If an infringement of the rights of the defence has been established, the decision must be annulled.

According to the EU Courts it cannot be for the Commission alone to decide which documents are useful for the defence of the undertaking.[71] This follows from the principle of equality of arms, which presupposes that in a competition case the knowledge which the undertaking concerned has of the file used in the proceeding is the same as that of the Commission.[72] In *Imperial Chemical Industries* the CFI considered that where difficult and complex economic appraisals are to be made, the Commission must give the advisers of the undertaking concerned the opportunity to examine documents which may be relevant so that their probative value for the defence can be assessed. This is particularly important in proceedings where documents may just as easily be interpreted in a way favourable to the undertakings concerned as in an unfavourable way.[73] The CFI considered that

> in such circumstances any error made by the Commission's officials in categorizing as 'neutral' a given document which, as an item of irrelevant evidence, will not then be disclosed to the undertakings, must not be allowed to impair their defence.[74]

Obligation to Request Access to the File

It seems to follow from the CFI's case law that the Commission is obliged to ensure on its own initiative that the rights of the defence are respected and thus that the party concerned has access to the documents included in the investigation file.[75] The undertaking is thus not required to request the Commission to be granted access to the file.[76] When the undertaking does request access to documents which were not communicated to it, it must specify which documents it wishes to have access to and for what reasons.[77] The CFI held that the Commission is not required to make available, on its own initiative, documents which are not in its investigation file and which it does not intend to use against the parties concerned in the final decision. An undertaking which learns during the administrative procedure that the Commission has documents which might be useful for its defence and wishes to inspect them must make an express request to the Commission for access to those documents. If the applicant fails to make such a request during the

[70] See, eg *Aalborg Portland et al v Commission* (n 52) paras 158–64; Case T-151/07, *Kone v Commission* [2011] ECR II-5313, paras 152–56; and Case T-191/06 *FMC Foret v Commission* [2011] ECR II-2959, paras 300–14.

[71] See, eg *Aalborg Portland et al v Commission* (n 52) para 126 and Case 107/82, *AEG* [1983] para 24.

[72] *Imperial Chemical Industries v Commission* (n 9) para 93.

[73] Ibid, paras 91–92 and 111.

[74] Ibid, para 92.

[75] See, eg Case T-49/88 *Al-Jubail Fertilizer* v *Council* [1991] para 17.

[76] *Imperial Chemical Industries v Commission* (n 9) para 96. See Erlandsson (n 48) 166.

[77] *BPB v Commission* (n 9) para 33.

administrative procedure, his right to do so is barred in any action for annulment brought against the final decision.[78]

Access to the File in Practice

According to the Commission Notice, access to the file may be provided in several ways: by means of electronic data storage device; through copies of the accessible file on paper sent to the parties by mail; by inviting the parties to examine the accessible file on the Commission's premises or a combination of those methods.[79]

10.3.2 The Right to Confidentiality

The EU Courts have accepted that the confidentiality of the following documents or information may be justified in competition cases:

- documents containing other companies' business secrets;
- internal documents of the Commission; and
- other confidential Information disclosed to the Commission subject to an obligation of confidentiality, such as information enabling complainants to be identified.[80]

Protection of Business Secrets

Article 41 of the Charter explicitly mentions that business secrets must be respected.[81] The EU Courts have also recognised the protection of business secrets as a general principle of EU law.[82] According to the Commission, a business secret is information about an undertaking's business activity, disclosure of which could result in serious harm to that undertaking.[83] The protection of business secrets helps the Commission to achieve the objectives of competition law. It should make it easier for the Commission to obtain information from third undertakings.[84] The Court of Justice held in *AKZO* that a third party who has submitted a complaint may not in any circumstances be given access to

[78] *Fresh Del Monte Produce, Inc v Commission* (n 64) para 657; Case T-186/06 *Solvay v Commission* [2011] ECR II-2839, para 227.

[79] Commission Notice on the rules for access to the Commission file (n 44) para 44.

[80] See, eg *Hoechst v Commission* (n 60) para 145, *BPB v Commission* (n 9) para 36 and *Endemol v Commission* (n 14) para 66. See also the Commission Notice on the rules for access to the Commission file (n 44) and Art 4 of Reg (EC) No 1049/2001 of the European Parliament and of the Council of 30 May 2001 regarding public access to European Parliament, Council and Commission documents [2001] OJ L145/43.

[81] See also Art 339 TFEU.

[82] See, eg *Imperial Chemical Industries v Commission* (n 9) para 98, and for the national context *Varec* (n 15) para 49.

[83] Commission Notice on the rules for access to the Commission file (n 44) para 18.

[84] Erlandsson (n 48) 148.

documents containing business secrets.[85] However, in later cases, the EU Courts accepted that the right to confidentiality must be balanced against the rights of the defence. (See further section 10.3.3.)

Internal Commission Documents

Internal documents are not to be communicated to the parties concerned unless the circumstances of the case are exceptional and the parties concerned show the need to do so. According to the CFI, the restriction on access to internal documents is justified by the need to ensure the proper functioning of the institution concerned.[86] The Commission Notice states that internal documents can be neither inculpatory nor exculpatory. The restriction of access to internal documents, therefore, does not prejudice the proper exercise of the parties' rights of the defence.[87]

Other Confidential Information

The CFI has held that 'in the case of information supplied on a purely voluntary basis, accompanied by a request for confidentiality in order to protect the informant's anonymity, an institution which accepts such information is bound to comply with such a condition'.[88] According to the CFI 'the Commission's ability to guarantee the anonymity of certain of its sources of information is of crucial importance with a view to ensuring the effective prevention of prohibited anti-competitive practices'.[89] The EU Courts have recognised 'that an undertaking holding a dominant position on the market might adopt retaliatory measures against competitors, suppliers or customers who have collaborated in the investigation carried out by the Commission'. [90] Therefore, third-party undertakings which submit documents to the Commission in the course of its investigations and consider that as a result reprisals might be taken against them, can do so only if they know that account will be taken of their request for confidentiality.

10.3.3 Confidentiality versus Access to the File

It follows from the above that the Commission may face a dilemma of whether it should keep certain information confidential and therefore refrain from using

85 Case 53/85 *AKZO Chemie BV and AKZO Chemie UK v Commission* [1986] ECR 1965, para 28.

86 *Hoechst v Commission* (n 60) para 165, Order of 10 December 1997 in Joined Cases T-134/94, T-136/94, T-137/94, T-138/94, T-141/94, T-145/94, T-147/94, T-148/94, T-151/94, T-156/94 and T-157/94 *NMH Stahlwerke et al v Commission* [1999] paras 35–36.

87 Commission Notice the rules for access to the Commission file (n 44) para 12.

88 *BPB v Commission* (n 9) para 36.

89 Ibid, para 36.

90 Case C-310/93 P *BPB and Britisch Gypsum v Commission* [1995] ECR I-865, para 26. See also Commission Notice on the rules for access to the Commission file (n 44) para 19.

it as evidence, or disclose the information with the risk of seriously harming the interests of the company which provided the information.[91] The Commission has recognised that in proceedings under Articles 81 and 82 of the former EC Treaty the qualification of a piece of information as confidential is not a bar to its disclosure if such information is necessary to prove an alleged infringement or could be necessary to exonerate a party. In that case the need to safeguard the rights of the defence of the parties may outweigh the concern to protect the confidential information of other parties. The Commission assesses whether those circumstances apply to any specific situation, taking into account: the relevance of the information; whether the information is indispensable; the degree of sensitivity involved; and the preliminary view of the seriousness of the alleged infringement. When the Commission intends to disclose information, the person or undertaking in question gets the opportunity to provide a non-confidential version of the information. The non-confidential information must have the same evidential value as the confidential version.[92]

According to the EU Courts, the rights of the defence must be balanced against the right of other economic operators to the protection of their confidential information and their business secrets.[93] If an inculpatory or exculpatory document contains genuine business secrets or cannot be disclosed for one of the other reasons mentioned above, a solution must be sought in which the right of confidentiality and the rights of the defence are reconciled.[94] The communication of a non-confidential version or a summary of the document is the most important solution proposed by the CFI. Furthermore, the Commission may provide a list of documents contained in the Commission's file before granting access to (non-confidential versions) of those documents.

Non-confidential Versions or Summaries

According to the CFI, the Commission can protect the business secrets or other confidential information of third parties by deleting the sensitive passages from the copies of the documents sent to the applicant.[95] This could also imply that the identity of the source of the information is not disclosed. A non-confidential summary must be sufficiently precise.[96] According to the Commission Notice, 'the non-confidential versions and the descriptions of the deleted information must be established in a manner that enables any party with access to the file to

[91] See also Erlandsson (n 48) 158.

[92] Commission Notice on the rules for access to the Commission file (n 44) paras 24 and 25.

[93] *Imperial Chemical Industries v Commission* (n 9) para 98. See for the national context *Varec* (n 15) para 51 and *Mobistar* (n 26) para 40.

[94] See, eg *Endemol v Commission* (n 14) para 67.

[95] *Imperial Chemical Industries v Commission* (n 9) para 102. It is not clear whether such non-confidential summaries must be provided by the Commission of its own initiative, or on the party's request. *BPB and British Gypsum v Commission* (n 90) para 31 seems to suggest that such summaries must be requested.

[96] See *Hoechst v Commission* (n 60) para 154.

determine whether the information deleted is likely to be relevant for its defence and therefore whether there are sufficient grounds to request the Commission to grant access to the information claimed to be confidential'.[97]

The CFI held in several cases that the provision of non-confidential versions of evidence underlying the contested decision did not infringe the rights of the defence. However, the weight of the evidence may be reduced because of the fact that certain information is not communicated to the undertaking concerned. In *Endemol*, a concentration case, the Commission provided non-confidential summaries of some independent television producers' replies to the Commission's questionnaires. These summaries concealed the identity of those producers. The CFI noted that the replies to the questionnaires contained only the views of the third parties on the likely consequences of the concentration. 'The non-confidential summaries made those views clear. It was thus not necessary to know the identity of the third parties in question in order to be able to challenge the views expressed.'[98]

In *Salzgitter Mannesmann* the Court of Justice held that the CFI rightly allowed a document as incriminating evidence, while the identity of the author and the person who transmitted it to the Commission were not disclosed to the party concerned. The Court referred to the following three circumstances. First, it pointed to the fact that the CFI in assessing the credibility of the document took into account the anonymous origin of that document. According to the CFI the credibility of that document was necessarily reduced by the fact that the context in which it was drafted was largely unknown and the Commission's assertions in that regard could not be verified. Secondly, the CFI held that evidence of anonymous origin cannot in itself establish the existence of an infringement of EC competition law. In this case the anonymous statements were supported by other evidence and they were only of ancillary importance. Finally, the Court took into account that the party concerned was given opportunity to comment on the document and to put forward its arguments on the probative value of that document in the light of its anonymous origin.[99]

In *Hoechst* the CFI held that the non-confidential version of relevant documents in the form made available to the undertaking concerned bore 'a close relationship to a failure to disclose' those documents. The Court took into account that the documents consisted of 101 pages virtually all of which were blank and marked 'Business secrets'. No summary of the content of the documents was provided during the administrative proceedings. Only a list setting out the date, sender and addressee of the documents and where appropriate the subject matter was

[97] Commission Notice on the rules for access to the Commission file (n 44) para 38.

[98] *Endemol v Commission* (n 14) paras 71–72.

[99] *Salzgitter Mannesmann v Commission* (n 42) paras 46–50 and the Opinion of AG Geelhoed in this case, paras 62–65.

provided.[100] In *Alrosa* some third party observations submitted to the Commission were essential for the Commission's decision as it changed its initial position on the basis of them. Alrosa only received a summary of the Commission's conclusions drawn from these observations and non-confidential summaries of the observations themselves. The non-confidential version of the third party observations requested by Alrosa was supplied at a moment when it was impossible for Alrosa to provide an effective reply to them. According to the CFI Alrosa was therefore not given the opportunity to fully exercise its right to be heard.[101]

List of Documents

If protecting a third company's business secrets or other sensitive information by preparing non-confidential versions of all the documents in question proves difficult, the Commission could send to the party concerned a list of documents contained in the Commission's file.[102] Then the party concerned can request access to specific documents on that list. Those documents or, if necessary, non-confidential versions of them, should be provided to the party concerned. The purpose of having a list as proposed by the CFI is that the information contained in it 'should provide to the applicant information sufficiently precise to enable it to ascertain, with knowledge of the facts, whether the documents described were likely to be relevant for its defence'.[103] In several cases the Commission sent the party concerned a list of documents contained in the Commission's file. In *Endemol* the CFI held that the table of the file contents presented by the Commission did not infringe the rights of the defence. In that case the Commission had prepared a summary list of all 279 documents which made up the file. First, that list gave a breakdown of the documents by type (annual reports, internal notes, requests for information and so forth). Secondly, the list indicated, for each document or group of documents, whether it was accessible to the companies concerned, partially accessible to them, confidential or not relevant.[104]

10.3.4 Judicial Review

In appeals against Commission decisions in competition cases the General Court (like the former CFI) may request the Commission to submit its file including all confidential evidence.[105] In order to enable the CFI to determine whether

[100] *Hoechst v Commission* (n 60) para 152. The Court did not find a violation of the right of access to the file because the documents concerned could not have changed the Commission's conclusions.

[101] *Alrosa v Commission* (n 9) paras 196–203.

[102] See also the Commission Notice on the rules for access to the Commission file (n 44) para 45.

[103] *Imperial Chemical Industries v Commission* (n 9) para 104. See also *Hoechst v Commission* (n 60) para 154.

[104] *Endemol v Commission* (n 14) para 78.

[105] See Art 24 of Protocol (No 3) on the Statute of the Court of Justice of the European Union [2008] OJ C115/210.

it is conducive to proper conduct of the procedure to order the production of certain documents, the undertaking should identify the documents requested and provide the Court with at least minimum information indicating the utility of those documents for the purposes of the procedure.[106] The Commission may request the Court not to disclose the confidential information to the applicant undertaking.[107]

The Court first carries out a comparative and provisional analysis of the probative value of the documents that were not disclosed and of the evidence that the Commission regards as sufficient to lead to the findings made in its decision.[108] During this procedure the Court does not disclose the documents concerned to the applicants.[109] In its analysis the Court establishes whether the non-disclosure of the documents in question might have influenced the course of the procedure and the content of the decision to the applicant's detriment.[110] Documents which are not relevant to the applicant's defence are left out of the Court's file. They remain wholly extraneous to the proceedings and are not taken into consideration by the Court.[111]

In some cases the Court examines whether the (partial) non-disclosure of the relevant evidence is justified.[112] During this examination the Court guarantees the confidentiality of the evidence submitted by the Commission.[113] If the confidentiality is not justified, the Court will disclose the confidential evidence to the parties concerned.[114] If confidentiality is justified, a non-confidential version of the evidence may be made available to the applicant.

Then the court assesses, according to the principles set out above, whether the rights of the defence are infringed and whether the decision should be annulled. Where a document has not been disclosed to the applicant, the Court does not take that document into account.[115] The Court examines whether the decision can be based on the non-confidential evidence. If, during the administrative proceedings, the applicant only had access to a non-confidential version of a document, the Court examines whether this amounts to an infringement of the rights of the

[106] Case C-185/95 P *Baustahlgewebe v Commission* [1998] ECR I-8417, para 93.

[107] See, eg the CFI's Order in *NMH Stahlwerke et al v Commission* (n 86) para 37.

[108] *Aalborg Portland et al v Commission* (n 52) para 132.

[109] Art 67(3) of the Consolidated Version of the Rules of Court of the General Court (2010/C 177/02) [2010], OJ C177/37.

[110] *Imperial Chemical Industries v Commission* (n 9) para 78. See also the CFI's Order in *NMH Stahlwerke et al v Commission* (n 86) para 40.

[111] See, eg the CFI's Order in *NMH Stahlwerke et al v Commission* (n 86) para 33 and *Hoechst v Commission* (n 60) paras 169–71.

[112] See, eg *Endemol v Commission* (n 14) para 69 and *Imperial Chemical Industries v Commission* (n 9) para 102. This also follows from Art 67(3) of the Consolidated Version of the Rules of Court of the General Court (n 109). In Case T-44/00, *Mannesmannröhren-Werke v Commission* [2004] ECR II-2223, paras 81–99 the CFI did not assess whether the non-disclosure of the names of the sources of relevant information was justified.

[113] See Art 67(3) of the Consolidated Version of the Rules of Court of the General Court (n 109).

[114] See, eg CFI's Order in *NMH Stahlwerke et al v Commission* (n 86).

[115] See Art 67(3) of the Consolidated Version of the Rules of Court of the General Court (n 109).

defence.[116] Where possible exculpatory documents are not disclosed to applicant, the rights of the defence are violated and the decision will be annulled.

An infringement of the rights of the defence which occurred during the administrative procedure cannot be regularised during the proceedings before the General Court or the Court of Justice.[117] The Court of Justice gives two reasons for this. The first is that the examination undertaken by the General Court is limited to review of the pleas in law put forward. Therefore, it has neither the object nor the effect of replacing a full investigation of the case in the context of an administrative procedure. Secondly, the Court of Justice finds that the belated disclosure of documents in the file does not put the undertaking back into the situation it would have been in, if it had been able to rely on those documents in presenting its written and oral observations to the Commission.[118] If during the administrative procedure the applicant had been able to rely on documents which might exculpate it, it might have been able to influence the Commission's assessment. Therefore, the Court cannot rule out the possibility that the Commission would have found the infringement to be shorter and less serious and would, consequently, have fixed the fine at a lower amount.[119]

10.3.5 Subconclusion: The Use of Secret Information in EU Competition Cases

In competition cases, the EU Courts attach great importance to both the rights of the defence and the protection of confidential information, particularly business secrets. They recognise that the disclosure of business secrets or other confidential information may cause an undertaking serious harm. On the other hand, the Courts have accepted that the refusal to communicate evidence to the undertaking which is the object of a Commission decision (for example to impose a fine), may harm the rights of the defence. The fact that a relevant document has not been disclosed to the undertaking concerned has severe consequences. Inculpatory documents which were not communicated to the undertaking should be excluded as evidence. The rights of the defence are infringed where exculpatory documents have not been disclosed which might have influenced the course of the procedure and the content of the decision to the applicant's detriment. The undertaking must be able to assess itself whether information is relevant to its defence. It should substantiate before the General Court that the documents may have changed the Commission's conclusions. In several cases the undertaking did

[116] See, eg *Endemol v Commission* (n 14) para 72.

[117] See, eg *Aalborg Portland et al v Commission* (n 52) para 104 and *Imperial Chemical Industries v Commission* (n 9) para 108.

[118] Case C-110/10 P *Solvay SA v Commission* [2011] ECR I-10439, para 51 and *Hercules Chemicals v Commission* (n 45) paras 78–79.

[119] *Imperial Chemical Industries v Commission* (n 9) paras 108 and 113.

not succeed in doing so. In its assessment the General Court takes into account the strength of the (disclosed) evidence relied on by the Commission and that of the undertaking's positions.

The Commission does not necessarily need to choose between the protection of confidential information and the rights of the defence. According to the EU Courts, in competition cases those two interests must be balanced against each other. A compromise, such as the provision of non-confidential versions of documents is permissible. Such summaries must provide sufficiently precise information to enable the party concerned to determine whether the deleted information is likely to be relevant for its defence and to express its views on it.

The General Court plays an active role in reviewing competition decisions in which it is claimed that the rights of the defence have been infringed because confidential information has not been disclosed to the undertaking concerned. It assesses whether the information concerned could be relevant for the undertaking's defence. In some cases it examines whether the (partial) non-disclosure of the relevant information is justified. Finally, it rules whether the rights of the defence have been infringed because possible exculpatory evidence has not been disclosed. It also decides whether, after exclusion of the inculpatory evidence not disclosed to the undertaking, the remaining non-confidential evidence is sufficient to support the decision.

10.4 EU SANCTIONS AND THE PROTECTION OF NATIONAL SECURITY

This section will discuss two types of EU sanctions which often concern the freezing of funds and assets of persons, companies or organisations (henceforth EU sanctions): EU sanctions aimed at persons or groups allegedly involved in terrorist activities (anti-terrorism sanctions); and EU sanctions which target third States. Decisions in both categories of EU sanctions are often partly based on confidential information; the statement of reasons is concise and the right of the party concerned to be heard restricted. The Court of Justice has made clear that the same EU rights and principles apply to both types of EU sanctions.[120]

Since 11 September 2001, the EU has taken measures to combat terrorism. It has engaged in sanctions freezing the funds and assets of persons who commit and/or facilitate terrorist acts and those of groups and entities owned or controlled by or acting on behalf of such persons.[121] Anti-terrorism sanctions are often based on information which is not disclosed to the person or entity concerned and sometimes not even to the EU Institutions and EU Courts. This information, and other

[120] *Council v Bamba* (n 10). See also M Wimmer, 'Individual Sanctions and Fundamental Rights Standards: *Bamba*' (2013) 50 *Common Market Law Review* 1119, 1125–27.

[121] C Koedooder and N de Lang, 'Anti-terrorist Blacklisting in the European Union, The Influence of National Procedures on the Judgments of the Court of First Instance of the European Communities' (2009) 36 *Legal Issues of Economic Integration* 313.

information underlying the anti-terrorism sanction, is usually kept confidential in the interest of the security and the conduct of the international relations of the Member States and/or the EU.

The EU has also imposed sanctions on third States (such as Burma, Iran and the Côte d'Ivoire), their regimes, supporters and persons associated with them. The objective of these sanctions is 'to bring about a change in policy or activity by the target country, part of country, government, entities or individuals', in line with the Common Foreign and Security Policy.[122] Such sanction decisions are usually based on an assessment through diplomatic channels (EU Heads of Mission) or on public information.[123]

In many of the EU sanction cases which have been ruled by the EU Courts the person or entity concerned complained about a (total) lack of reasons for the decision, the fact that the evidence underlying the decision had not been notified to it, and that it did not, therefore, have the opportunity to defend itself. The EU Courts in their rulings have referred to three principles in particular: the right to be heard; the obligation to state reasons; and the right to an effective remedy. The requirements derived from these three principles will be discussed in sections 10.4.2 to 10.4.4.

The same general principles are used in EU sanction and competition cases. As stated in the introduction to this chapter, the CFI in EU sanction cases referred to relevant case law in competition cases. However, there are also some important differences between the EU Courts' approaches in these cases. This section will show that the limitations to the rights of the defence allowed in EU sanction cases seem to be more far-reaching than in competition cases. The reason for this potentially relates to the nature of the case and the grounds for not disclosing relevant evidence. Furthermore, the fact that the scope of judicial review of (autonomous) EU sanctions on the EU level is fairly limited as a result of a division of tasks between the national and EU level (as explained in section 10.4.1), may play a role.

The case law concerning EU sanctions is less developed than in competition cases. The EU Courts have not yet addressed in detail the question how the rights of the defence must be balanced against the protection of the safety and the conduct of the international relations of the Member States and/or the EU. In several recent cases the EU Courts have given explanations on the sufficiency of the statement of reasons, which may be relevant to identify what constitutes 'the essence' of a case.

[122] Council's Guidelines on implementation and evaluation of restrictive measures (sanctions) in the framework of the EU Common Foreign and Security Policy, Document 17464/09, 15 December 2009, para 4.

[123] Wimmer, 'Individual Sanctions' (n 120) 1128. See also Council's Guidelines on implementation and evaluation of restrictive measures (n 122) paras 6 and 24.

10.4.1 Legal Framework and Scope of Judicial Review

Before turning to an examination of the case law of the EU Courts, some comments will be made concerning the relevant legal framework and the possibility of judicial review of EU sanctions. There are two strands of EU sanctions:[124] those designated to give effect to resolutions issued by the United Nations Security Council[125] and autonomous EU sanctions.[126] The legal basis for the EU sanctions could be found in Articles 60, 301 and 308 of the former EC Treaty.[127] Since the entrance into force of the Treaty of Lisbon, the sanctions are based on Articles 75 and 215 TFEU.

The EU sanctions which will be discussed in this section are adopted following different procedures. This has consequences for the scope of judicial review performed by the EU Courts. Arguably, the scope of judicial review influences the way in which the EU Courts apply the obligation to state reasons and the right to be heard in an individual case. It is, therefore, necessary to explain the procedures which are followed and the scope of judicial review applied in EU sanction cases before turning to the EU Courts' interpretation of relevant EU procedural rights and principles in those cases.

This section addresses anti-terrorism sanctions which are based on UN Security Council Resolutions as well as autonomous anti-terrorism sanctions. Both the procedure for imposing anti-terrorism sanctions based on UN Security Council Resolutions and the procedure for taking autonomous anti-terrorism sanctions take place at two levels: the UN level and the EU level, or the national level and the EU level. The cases examined in this section which concern EU sanctions against third States are all autonomous EU sanctions, in which the decision is taken only at the EU level.

10.4.1.1 Anti-terrorism Sanctions based on UN Security Council Resolutions

The EU sanctions which give effect to UN Security Council Resolutions are preceded by a Security Council decision to place a person or entity on the terrorist list.[128] Following this decision the Council draws up a list of suspected terrorists

[124] CC Murphy, 'Fundamental Rights and Security, The Difficult Position of the European Judiciary' (2010) 16 *European Public Law* 289, 301.

[125] See, eg *Kadi and Al Barakaat v Council and Commission* (n 17); Case T-318/01 *Othman v Council and Commission* [2009] ECR II-1627; and Joined Cases C-399/06 P and C-403/06 P *Hassan and Ayadi v Council and Commission* [2009] ECR I-11393.

[126] See, eg *Modjahedines du peuple d'Iran v Council* (n 10); *Sison v Council* (n 18).

[127] *Kadi and Al Barakaat v Council and Commission* (n 17) paras 158–236. See also Murphy, 'Fundamental Rights and Security' (n 124) 301–304, T Tridimas and JA Gutierrez-Fons, 'EU Law, International Law and Economic Sanctions against Terrorism: The Judiciary in Distress?' (2008) 32 *Fordham International Law Journal* 660, 664–79 and C Eckes, 'Case T-228/02, *Modjahedines du people d'Iran v Council* [2006]' (2007) 44 *Common Market Law Review* 1117, 1121. For sanctions against third States see, however, Case C-376/10 P *Tay Za* [2012].

[128] See Art 4 of Common Position on the application of specific measures to combat terrorism (2001/931/CFSP) [2001] OJ L344/93 and Art 7(1) of Council Reg No 881/2002 imposing certain specific restrictive measures directed against certain persons and entities associated with Usama bin

and subsequently issues a regulation which is applied to the individual included in the list.[129] Little is known about the procedure of listing individuals suspected of terrorist activities at the UN level. Suspects must be identified based on information provided by States and regional organisations. Individuals do not have the opportunity to be heard before or after the listing and they have no right to appeal the decision to place them on the UN list.[130] Furthermore, the Security Council does not communicate the reasons and evidence justifying his appearance on the list to the person concerned.[131] In both *Kadi I* and *Kadi II* the Court of Justice found that the procedure at the UN level clearly fails to offer guarantees of effective judicial protection.[132]

Because of the failures in the proceedings at the UN level, the EU Courts held that EU sanctions which are directly based on Security Council Resolutions should be subjected to a full judicial review by the EU Courts. Furthermore, the EU Courts test whether the proceedings followed comply with EU fundamental rights, such as the rights of the defence and the right to an effective remedy.[133] The review of the EU Courts must extend to whether rules as to procedure and rules as to competence, including whether or not the legal basis is adequate, are observed.[134] Furthermore, the EU Courts must review the factual basis of the decision to impose restrictive measures.[135] The EU Courts do not review the legality of the Security Council decision itself.[136]

10.4.1.2 Autonomous Anti-terrorism Sanctions

Autonomous EU sanctions are based on information of the Member States. According to Article 1(4) of Common Position 2001/931 the list in its annex

> shall be drawn up on the basis of precise information or material in the relevant file which indicates that a decision has been taken by a competent authority in respect

Laden, the al-Qaida network and the Taliban, and repealing Council Reg (EC) No 467/2001 prohibiting the export of certain goods and services to Afghanistan, strengthening the flight ban and extending the freeze of funds and other financial resources in respect of the Taliban of Afghanistan.

[129] Koedooder and de Lang, 'Anti-terrorist Blacklisting in the European Union' (n 121) 319.

[130] Ibid, 316–17. See also *Kadi and Al Barakaat v Council and Commission* (n 17) paras 319–25.

[131] *Kadi and Al Barakaat v Council and Commission* (n 17) para 325. Tzanou and El Droubi mention that in *Othman* the Court of First Instance seems to endorse the applicant's view that the Security Council's decision to include him on the terrorist list is a political decision, taken in a wholly non-judicial manner, without any regard to the rules of evidence or of fairness. M Tzanou and S El Droubi, 'Case T-318/01, *Othman v Council* [2009]' (2010) 47 *Common Market Law Review* 1233, 1240.

[132] *Kadi and Al Barakaat v Council and Commission* (n 17), para 322; *Commission et al v Kadi* (n 16) para 133. See also HJ Hooper, 'Liberty before Security: Case T-85/09 *Yassin Abdullah Kadi v Commission (No 2)* [2010]' (2012) 18 *European Public Law* 457.

[133] *Commission et al v Kadi* (n 16) para 118. *Kadi and Al Barakaat v Council and Commission* (n 17) para 326.

[134] *Commission et al v Kadi* (n 16) para 117.

[135] Ibid, para 119.

[136] *Kadi and Al Barakaat v Council and Commission* (n 17) para 286. On this issue, see also Tridimas and Gutierrez-Fons, 'EU Law, International Law' (n 127) 679–702.

> of the persons, groups and entities concerned, irrespective of whether it concerns the instigation of investigations or prosecution for a terrorist act, an attempt to perpetrate, participate in or facilitate such an act based on serious and credible evidence or clues, or condemnation for such deeds.

The term 'competent authority' shall mean a judicial authority, or, where judicial authorities have no competence in the area covered by this provision, an equivalent competent authority in that area.[137]

Before imposing an EU sanction, the EU Institutions must first decide whether a national decision as described in Article 1(4) of Common Position 2001/931 has been taken. Secondly, they must assess whether the inclusion of the person or entity concerned on the EU terrorist list is still justified.[138] When performing this second assessment the EU Institutions enjoy broad discretion.[139] As a result, the review by the CFI of this decision is limited.[140] The CFI has stressed, however, that it does review the Council's interpretation of the relevant facts and that review of the observance of certain procedural guarantees is of fundamental importance.[141]

The Council should generally refrain from testing the legality of the national decision underlying the EU sanction. In *PMOI I* the CFI considered:

> [I]t is not for the Council to decide whether the proceedings instigated against the party concerned and resulting in that decision as provided for by national law of the Member State were correctly conducted or whether the fundamental rights of the party concerned were respected by the national authorities. That power belongs exclusively to the national courts or as the case may be to the European Court of Human Rights.[142]

In addition, where the EU sanction is based on a national decision concerning investigations or prosecutions, rather than on a conviction or a sentence, the Council should

> defer as far as possible to the assessment conducted by the competent national authority, at least where it is a judicial authority, both in respect of the issue of whether there are 'serious and credible evidence or clues' on which the decision is based and also in respect of recognition of potential restrictions on access to that evidence or those clues legally justified under national law.[143]

[137] With regard to the interpretation of Art 1(4) of Common Position 2001/931 (n 128) see Joined Cases C-539/10 P and C-550/10 P *Stichting Al-Aqsa v Council* [2012].

[138] See, eg Case T-284/08 *People's Modjahedin Organization of Iran v Council* [2008] ECR II-3487, para 51.

[139] *Modjahedines du peuple d'Iran v Council* (n 10) para 159 and Case T-49/07 *Fahas v Council* [2010] ECR II-5555, para 57.

[140] The CFI stressed that this limited review applies, especially, to the Council's assessment of the factors as to appropriateness on which decisions to freeze funds are based. *Modjahedines du peuple d'Iran v Council* (n 10) para 159.

[141] Case T-256/07 *People's Modjahedin Organization of Iran v Council* [2008] ECR II-3019, paras 138–39.

[142] *Modjahedines du peuple d'Iran v Council* (n 10) para 121 and *Sison v Council* (n 18) para 168.

[143] *Modjahedines du peuple d'Iran v Council* (n 10) para 124; *Sison v Council* (n 18) para 171; and *People's Modjahedin Organization of Iran v Council* (n 141) para 133.

This follows from the duty of sincere cooperation which is currently laid down in Article 4(3) TEU. The CFI only allows for the possibility of review of the national decision on the EU level, if the national decision is not taken by a competent authority within the meaning of Article 4(1) of Common Position 2001/931.[144] This may also apply if the national decision is a decision to investigate or prosecute (and thus not a conviction and sentence) taken by an authority which is not a judicial authority and which is not subject to judicial review at the national level.[145]

As a result, the EU Courts generally only review whether the Council's burden of proof is met and the rights of the defence are respected with regard to two aspects of the decision to impose an EU sanction: the establishment that there is (1) a national decision which (2) justifies inclusion on the EU terrorist list and thus the imposition of an EU sanction.[146] They do not engage in the question whether the person or entity concerned can be considered to be involved in terrorism.

This does not mean that the rights of the defence are not ensured in cases concerning autonomous anti-terrorism sanctions. It is for the national determining authority and courts to examine the (confidential) evidence underlying the national decision and to ensure that the rights of the defence are respected in the procedure which lead to the decision mentioned in Article 4(1) of Common Position 2001/931.

> It is precisely those safeguards of the rights of the defence which exist at national level, subject to effective judicial review, which relieve the Community institutions of any obligation to provide fresh safeguards at Community level in relation to the same subject-matter.[147]

In this context the CFI referred to the ECtHR's judgment in *Tinnally* concerning the rights of the defence under Article 6 ECHR, which will be discussed in section 10.5.[148]

10.4.1.3 Autonomous Sanctions against Third States

Autonomous EU sanctions against third States are only taken at the EU level and can thus only be appealed before the EU Courts. According to the General

[144] *Modjahedines du peuple d'Iran v Council* (n 10) para 125 and *Sison v Council* (n 18) para 172.

[145] *Modjahedines du peuple d'Iran v Council* (n 10) para 124 ('at least where it is a judicial authority') and *Sison v Council* (n 18) para 171, *People's Modjahedin Organization of Iran v Council* (n 141) para 145. See also A Gattini, 'Joined Cases C-402/05 P and C-415/05 P, *Kadi and Al Barakaat* [2008]' (2009) 46 *Common Market Law Review* 213, 239.

[146] See, eg *Modjahedines du peuple d'Iran v Council* (n 10) para 146.

[147] *Kadi v Commission* (n 19), para 186. See also *People's Modjahedin Organization of Iran* (n 141) paras 145–46.

[148] *Sison v Council* (n 18) para 166. For criticism on this case-law, see E Spaventa, 'Joined Cases T-256/07, *People's Modjahedin Organization of Iran* [2008] and T-284/08, *People's Modjahedin Organization of Iran* [2008]' (2009) 46 *Common Market Law Review* 1239, 1256–60.

Court, the judicial review of the lawfulness of an autonomous EU sanction where restrictive measures are imposed on an entity, 'extends to the assessment of the facts and circumstances relied on as justifying it, and to the evidence and information on which that assessment is based'.[149] This means that a full judicial review is applied by the EU Courts.

10.4.2 The Right to be Heard

The general principles developed in cases regarding other fields of EU law also apply to EU sanctions.[150] The right to be heard requires that the person or entity concerned is informed of the evidence used against him to justify the restrictive measures imposed on him and that he is enabled to effectively make known his view on this evidence.[151] The right to be heard does not give the party concerned the right to a formal hearing: it is sufficient that it has the opportunity to submit written observations.[152] The General Court held that the Council is not obliged to spontaneously grant access to the documents in its file. It is only on the request of the party concerned that the Council is required to provide access to all non-confidential official documents concerning the measure at issue. It is only obliged to communicate sufficiently precise information, enabling the entity concerned to make its point of view on the evidence adduced against it by the Council known to advantage.[153]

In the context of autonomous anti-terrorism sanctions, the right to be heard has a fairly limited purpose. In the case of an initial decision to freeze funds, the right to be heard requires, in principle, first, that the person or entity concerned be informed by the Council of the specific information or material in the file which indicates that a national decision has been taken in respect of it by a competent authority of a Member State. Furthermore, where applicable, any new material which has not yet been assessed by a competent authority at the national level must be communicated to the person or entity concerned.[154] In the case of a subsequent decision to freeze funds, observance of the right to be heard requires, that the party concerned be informed of the information or material in the file which, in the view of the Council, justifies maintaining it in the disputed lists, and also, where applicable, of any new material which has not yet been assessed by a

[149] Case T-494/10 *Bank Saderat Iran* [2013] para 105.

[150] *Modjahedines du peuple d'Iran v Council* (n 10) paras 91–93.

[151] *Kadi and Al Barakaat v Council and Commission* (n 17) para 348.

[152] *People's Modjahedin Organization of Iran v Council* (n 141) para 93.

[153] Case T-492/10 *Melli Bank plc v Council* [2013] para 73 and Case T-390/08 *Bank Melli Iran v Council* [2009] ECR II-3967, para 97 which was confirmed by Case C-548/09 P *Bank Melli Iran* [2011].

[154] Tridimas and Gutierrez-Fons state that the 'CFI appears to leave itself here sufficient margin of manoeuvering to intervene in exceptional circumstances'. They state that it is not clear, however, whether it is open to the applicant to argue in all cases that the national proceedings were defective. Tridimas and Gutierrez-Fons (n 127) 712–13.

competent authority at the national level.[155] In the proceedings on the EU level, the right to be heard, therefore, does not extend to the evidence underlying the national decision on which the anti-terrorism sanction is based.

In proceedings concerning anti-terrorism sanctions which are based on UN Security Council Resolutions, the right to be heard requires first, that the summary of reasons provided by the Sanctions Committee which is the basis for the EU sanction at least, is disclosed to the person or entity concerned. Secondly, the person or entity concerned must be able 'to defend his rights under the best possible conditions and to decide, with full knowledge of the relevant facts, whether there is any point in bringing an action before the Court of the European Union'.[156] Finally, the EU Institution must examine carefully and impartially whether the reasons alleged are well founded in the light of these observations and any exculpatory evidence produced by the person or entity concerned.[157] If necessary, the EU Institution must ask the Sanctions Committee or the Member of the UN which proposed the listing of the person or entity concerned, to disclose information or evidence.[158]

10.4.2.1 Possible Limitations to the Right to be Heard

The EU Courts have accepted that far-reaching limitations of the right to be heard may be justified in EU sanction cases. These limitations regard the moment in the procedure at which the hearing takes place as well as the disclosure of evidence.

As to the moment of the hearing, both Courts held that EU authorities are not obliged to hear the party concerned (and therefore to notify the evidence adduced against it) before imposing an EU sanction.[159] A measure freezing the funds or a person or entity must by its very nature take advantage of the effect of surprise and be applied with immediate effect. The Council and the Member States have pointed at the fact that the party concerned could have taken advantage of the time period allowed to it to submit its comments to transfer those funds out of the Union.[160] These considerations do not apply to subsequent decisions to impose an EU sanction 'as the surprise effect is no longer necessary in order to ensure that the measure is effective'. Therefore, such a decision 'must, in principle, be preceded by notification of the incriminating evidence and by allowing the person or entity concerned an opportunity of being heard'.[161] Moreover, the Council must ensure

[155] *Modjahedines du peuple d'Iran v Council* (n 10) para 126. See also Tridimas and Gutierrez-Fons (n 127) 709.

[156] *Commission et al v Kadi* (n 16) para 111.

[157] *Commission et al v Kadi* (n 16) para 135. See also paras 110–14.

[158] Ibid, para 115.

[159] *Kadi and Al Barakaat v Council and Commission* (n 17) paras 338–41.

[160] *Modjahedines du peuple d'Iran v Council* (n 10) para 81.

[161] Case C-27/09 P *French Republic v People's Mojahedin Organization of Iran* [2011] para 62.

that the person or entity concerned can be notified of the information in question in good time so that it is able effectively to make known its point of view.[162]

Secondly, the EU Courts accepted that 'overriding considerations to do with safety or the conduct of the international relations of the Community and of its Member States may militate against the communication of certain matters to the persons concerned and, therefore, against their being heard on those matters'.[163] According to the CFI, such restrictions are consistent with the constitutional traditions of the Member States and the ECtHR's case law under Article 6 ECHR.[164] In anti-terrorism sanction cases the refusal to disclose evidence, in the view of the CFI, applies above all to the 'serious and credible evidence or clues' on which the national decision to instigate an investigation or prosecution is based, in so far as they may have been brought to the attention of the Council. However, the CFI also finds it

> conceivable that the restrictions on access may concern the specific content or the particular grounds for that decision, or even the identity of the authority that took it. It is even possible that, in certain, very specific circumstances, the identification of the Member State or third country in which a competent authority has taken a decision in respect of a person may be liable to jeopardise public security, by providing the party concerned with sensitive information which it could misuse.[165]

10.4.2.2 Possible Compensation for the Absence of a Hearing

If the evidence has not been disclosed to the person or entity concerned during the administrative proceedings this evidence must be notified to it, in so far as reasonably possible, either concomitantly with, or as soon as possible after, the adoption of the initial decision to freeze funds. A hearing does not need to be conducted immediately after the decision 'in the light of the possibility that the parties concerned also have immediately to bring an action before the CFI, which also ensures that a balance is struck between observance of the fundamental rights of the persons included in the disputed list and the need to take preventive measures in combating international terrorism'.[166] Unlike in competition cases, in EU sanction cases the absence of a hearing during the administrative phase in a first decision to freeze funds can thus be compensated during the appeal phase.[167]

[162] *Bank Saderat Iran* (n 149) para 77.

[163] *Kadi and Al Barakaat v Council and Commission* (n 17) para 342 and *Modjahedines du peuple d'Iran v Council* (n 10) para 133.

[164] The CFI here referred to the judgments in *Chahal* (which did not concern Art 6 ECHR) and *Jasper*. Both cases will be discussed in section 10.5.

[165] *Modjahedines du peuple d'Iran v Council* (n 10) para 136.

[166] Ibid, paras 129–30. See also *Bank Melli Iran v Council* (n 153) para 98.

[167] This also follows from *Kadi and Al Barakaat v Council and Commission* (n 17) para 337.

During the appeal the EU Courts can use techniques which accommodate the rights of the defence and concern legitimating non-disclosure of evidence.[168]

10.4.2.3 Application to Specific Cases

As mentioned above, in many of the EU sanction cases before the EU Courts the party concerned did not have access to the evidence underlying the contested decision and a violation of the right to be heard was found. In some autonomous anti-terrorism sanction cases the Council even refused to inform the applicant of the identity of the Member State which was the author of the national decision underlying the EU sanction.[169]

Anti-terrorism Measures based on UN Security Council Resolutions

In *Kadi I* the Court of Justice considered that the applicable EU legislation on which the EU sanction was based did not provide for a procedure for communicating the evidence justifying the inclusion of the names of the persons concerned in the terrorist list and for hearing those persons, either at the same time as that inclusion or later. Furthermore, it took into account that the Council at no time informed the appellants of the evidence adduced against them that allegedly justified the inclusion of their names for the first time in the list. The Court concluded that

> because the Council neither communicated to the appellants the evidence used against them to justify the restrictive measures imposed on them nor afforded them the right to be informed of that evidence within a reasonable period after those measures were enacted, the appellants were not in a position to make their point of view in that respect known to advantage.[170]

Therefore, the appellants' rights of the defence, in particular his right to be heard, were not respected.[171]

The approach of the EU Courts applied in *Kadi* seems to be different than that applied in several cases concerning autonomous anti-terrorism sanctions. In those cases the General Court does not seem to set very high standards as regards the right to be heard. This difference may be explained by the fact that in cases regarding autonomous EU anti-terrorism sanctions it is up to the national

[168] *Commission et al v Kadi* (n 16) para 125 and *Kadi and Al Barakaat v Council and Commission* (n 17) para 344. See further section 10.4.4.3.

[169] *Sison v Council* (n 18) para 209.

[170] *Kadi and Al Barakaat v Council and Commission* (n 17) paras 345–48. See also *Othman v Council and Commission* (n 125) paras 82–85.

[171] See also *Modjahedines du peuple d'Iran v Council* (n 10) paras 160–62 and *People's Modjahedin Organization of Iran v Council* (n 138) paras 36–37, where the CFI held that the right to be heard was violated because the Council adopted a subsequent decision to impose an EU sanction without first informing the applicant of the new information or new material in the file, which in its view, justified maintaining it on the list.

courts to ensure the rights of the defence with respect to the allegations of involvement in terrorist activities, while at the UN level no judicial review of the decision to place a person on a terrorist list takes place.

Autonomous Anti-terrorism Sanctions

In *Sison I* the CFI considered that the Council should have communicated the national decisions to Sison as they were official acts adopted at the end of public judicial proceedings to which the applicant had been a party. It was thus not necessary to keep those decisions confidential.[172] In the *PMOI II* judgment, however, the CFI found with regard to one of the two subsequent decisions to impose an EU sanction that the right to be heard had not been violated. It first took into account that the Council communicated to the applicant a number of documents from the file. As regards the documents, which were not notified to the applicant, the Council explained that it was not in a position to forward them to the applicant, because the State which had provided them had not consented to their disclosure. Furthermore, the CFI referred to the fact that the applicant had challenged neither that refusal to communicate certain incriminating documents, nor the reasons put forward to justify it. Secondly, the CFI held that the Council placed the applicant in a position to make its case properly regarding the evidence incriminating it, an opportunity to which it in fact availed itself on several occasions.[173]

In *PMOI II* the CFI also indicated that the Council's duty to show that it took into account the submissions of the party concerned is limited. The party concerned complained that the Council had not in any way sought to respond to the criticism levelled at it and that it had taken no account of the exculpatory material produced by it. The CFI held that the rights of the defence had not been violated on this ground. It inferred from the Council's letters and the fact that the applicant's submission had been communicated to the delegations of the Member States before the decision had been adopted, that due account had been made of the applicant's submissions. Moreover, it stated that the Council was not obliged to reply to the applicant's observations in the light of the documents submitted by the applicant, if it thought that they did not warrant the conclusions that the applicant claimed to infer from them. The fact that the statement of reasons did not address the applicant's submissions, but was rather a word-for-word repetition of the initial statement of reasons 'in itself means only that the Council maintained its point of view'. In the absence of any other relevant evidence, as was the case here, 'such similarity of texts does not establish that the Council failed, when assessing the case, to afford proper consideration to the arguments put forward

[172] *Sison v Council* (n 18) para 212.

[173] *People's Modjahedin Organization of Iran* (n 141) paras 91–92.

by the party concerned in arguing its case'. According to the CFI, the Council did give a specific reply to the applicant's main argument.[174]

10.4.3 The Obligation to State Reasons

The Court of Justice in EU sanction cases refers to its standing case law regarding the obligation to state reasons.[175] In principle, therefore, the requirements following from the obligation to state reasons recognised by the EU Courts in other fields of EU law, also apply to EU sanctions. The Council had argued in the *PMOI I* case that the material conditions regarding the obligation to state reasons in the fight against terrorism are not the same as those existing in other areas, such as competition.[176] The EU Courts did not agree with the Council. In their view, the obligation to state reasons constitutes an essential principle of EU law which may be derogated from only for compelling reasons. The Court of Justice stresses that where the person concerned is not afforded the opportunity to be heard before the adoption of an initial decision to freeze funds

> compliance with the obligation to state reasons is all the more important because it constitutes the sole safeguard enabling the person concerned, at least after the adoption of that decision, to make effective use of the legal remedies available to him in order to challenge the lawfulness of that decision.[177]

The statement of reasons for a decision to freeze funds must 'identify the actual and specific reasons why the EU Institution considers, in the exercise of its discretion, that that measure must be adopted in respect of the person concerned'.[178] On the other hand, however, the Court of Justice considered that it is not necessary for the reasoning to go into all the relevant facts and points of law.[179] In addition a detailed response to all the comments made by the party concerned is not necessary.[180] '[T]he reasons given for a measure adversely affecting a person are sufficient if that measure was adopted in a context which was known to that person and which enables him to understand the scope of the measure concerning him.'[181] At least one of the reasons mentioned in the decision must constitute

[174] Ibid, paras 94–96. See also *Fahas v Council* (n 139) para 49.

[175] *Kadi and Al Barakaat v Council and Commission* (n 17) para 350 (anti-terrorism sanction based on an UN resolution), *Stichting Al-Aqsa v Council* (n 137) paras 138–39 (autonomous anti-terrorism sanction) and *Council v Bamba* (n 10) paras 49–54 (autonomous sanction against a third State). See further ch 4, section 4.4.3 in this volume.

[176] *Modjahedines du peuple d'Iran v Council* (n 10) para 83.

[177] *Council v Bamba* (n 10) para 51.

[178] Ibid, para 52. See also Joined *Commission et al v Kadi* (n 16) para 116.

[179] *Stichting Al-Aqsa v Council* (n 137) para 140; *Council v Bamba* (n 10) para 53.

[180] *Commission et al v Kadi* (n 16) para 116.

[181] *Council v Bamba* (n 10) para 54.

a sufficient basis for the decision. In the absence of any such reason the decision must be annulled.[182]

In autonomous anti-terrorism sanctions the statement of reasons for a decision to impose an EU sanction must show first that the conditions for taking the decision, set out in Article 4 of Common Position 2001/931, are met. It must, therefore, indicate which national decision underlies the decision imposing the EU sanction.[183] If the Council based its decision on information communicated by the Member States, which has not been assessed by a national authority, it must indicate why it considers that this information justifies the inclusion of the person concerned on the list.[184] Subsequent decisions to freeze funds must indicate the actual and specific reasons why, after a re-examination, the Council considered that there were still grounds for the EU sanction.[185] The EU Institutions do not need to explain why they find that a person who is considered to be involved in terrorism should have their funds frozen, as the freezing of the funds of persons involved in terrorist acts constitutes the rule.[186]

10.4.3.1 Possible Limitations to the Statement of Reasons

Exceptions to the obligation to indicate the actual and specific reasons for the EU sanction are allowed under exceptional circumstances. First, the General Court has considered that a detailed publication of the complaints put forward against the parties concerned might conflict with the overriding considerations of public interest concerning the security of the EU and its Member States, or the conduct of their international relations. Moreover, it may jeopardise the legitimate interests of the persons and entities in question, in that it would be capable of causing serious damage to their reputation. In such a situation, the Court may find, exceptionally, that only the operative part of the decision and a general statement of reasons need be in the version of the decision to freeze funds published in the Official Journal. The actual, specific statements of reasons for that decision must, however, be formalised and brought to the knowledge of the parties concerned by other appropriate means.[187]

Secondly, the CFI has held that the overriding considerations concerning the security of the Community and its Member States, or the conduct of their

[182] *Commission et al v Kadi* (n 16) para 130. See also *Bank Saderat Iran* (n 149) para 101.

[183] *Stichting Al-Aqsa* (n 137) para 142.

[184] Tridimas and Gutierrez-Fons (n 127) 716–17. According to them this formulation appears to suggest that the Council is under an obligation to show that it was satisfied that the national authority assessed the evidence.

[185] *Sison v Council* (n 18) para 217. If the grounds of a subsequent EU sanction are in essence the same as those already relied on when a previous decision was adopted, a mere statement to that effect may suffice, particularly when the party is a group or entity. See also Case T-341/07, *Sison v Council II* [2009] ECR II-3625, para 60 and Case T-253/04, *KONGRA-GEL et al v Council* [2008] ECR II-46, para 97.

[186] *Stichting Al-Aqsa* (n 137) para 144.

[187] *Modjahedines du peuple d'Iran v Council* (n 10) para 147.

international relations, may preclude disclosure to the parties concerned of the specific and complete reasons for the initial or subsequent decision to freeze their funds. The considerations regarding the restrictions of the right to a fair hearing (set out in section 10.4.2.1) also apply to the restriction of the obligation to state reasons. Furthermore, the CFI drew inspiration from Article 30(2) of Directive 2004/38/EC and the case law applicable to that provision.[188] This provision states that

> the persons concerned shall be informed, precisely and in full, of the public policy, public security or public health grounds on which the decision restricting the freedom of movement and residence of a citizen of the Union or a member of his family taken in their case is based, unless this is contrary to the interests of State security.

According to the case law of the Court of Justice the State concerned must, when notifying an individual of such a restrictive measure give him a precise and comprehensive statement of the grounds for the decision, to enable him to take effective steps to prepare his defence.[189]

10.4.3.2 Possible Compensation for a Lack of Reasons

The statement of reasons must in principle be notified to the person concerned at the same time as the decision adversely affecting him or at least as soon as possible after that decision.[190] In *Kadi I* the Court of Justice did not seem to exclude that the infringement of the obligation to state reasons be remedied during the appeal before the EU Courts.[191] As was pointed out in chapter four, section 4.4.3, it is the EU Courts' standing case law that the failure to state the reasons cannot be remedied by the fact that the person concerned learns the reasons for the act during the proceedings before the EU Courts. The General Court has followed this case law in cases concerning EU sanctions.[192] It has held that the possibility of regularising a statement of reasons after an action has been started might prejudice the right to a fair hearing. The reason for that is that the applicant would only have the reply in which to set out his pleas contesting the reasons which he would not know until after he had lodged his application. The principle of equality of the parties before the EU Courts would accordingly be affected. In *KONGRA-GEL*

[188] Ibid, para 147. Dir 2004/38/EC of the European Parliament and of the Council of 29 April 2004 on the right of citizens of the Union and their family members to move and reside freely within the territory of the Member States amending Reg (EEC) No 1612/68 and repealing Dirs 64/221/EEC, 68/360/EEC, 72/194/EEC, 73/148/EEC, 75/34/EEC, 75/35/EEC, 90/364/EEC, 90/365/EEC and 93/96/EEC [2004] OJ L 158/77. See also section 10.2.

[189] *Modjahedines du peuple d'Iran v Council* (n 10) paras 148–50.

[190] *Kadi and Al Barakaat v Council and Commission* (n 17) para 336.

[191] Ibid, para 350. For a critique, see Tridimas and Gutierrez-Fons (n 127) 700. They state that if process rights are to have any meaning, it is difficult to see how the requirement of reasoning can be complied with retrospectively.

[192] Case T-421/11 *Qualitest FZE* [2012] para 43.

the CFI held that the Council did not comply with the obligation to state reasons, by providing a statement of reasons after the adoption of the decision imposing the EU sanction and after the appeal before the CFI had been lodged. According to the Council, it provided the statement as soon as reasonably possible after the contested decision in the light of the guidance provided by the *PMOI I* judgment. According to the CFI, the Council's argument was based on the mistaken premise that the statement of reasons can be provided after the action before the EU Courts has commenced.[193]

10.4.3.3 Application to Specific Cases

Autonomous Anti-terrorism Sanctions

The duty to state reasons in autonomous anti-terrorism sanctions is rather limited as it extends only to the question whether there is a national decision which justifies such sanction. Nevertheless, in several cases the CFI annulled an EU anti-terrorism sanction because the decision did not comply with the requirement to state reasons. The CFI sometimes based its annulment of the EU sanction solely on this ground.[194] In some cases there was no statement of reasons. In *Sison I* the CFI concluded that the contested decision did not comply with the obligation to state reasons

> for they do no more than state … that it is 'desirable' or that it has been 'decided' to adopt an up-to-date list of the persons, groups and entities to which Regulation (EC) No 2580/2001 applies. Such general and formulaic wording is tantamount to a total failure to state reasons.[195]

The CFI held in this case that the decision should have at least mentioned the national court judgments on which the decision was based.[196] Furthermore, it ought to have indicated, subject to the possibly their being confidential, the main reasons why the Council took the view, in the exercise of its discretion, that the applicant was to be the subject of such a decision on the basis of those judgments.[197]

In some later cases the EU Courts did not find a violation of the duty to state reasons. In the *PMOI II* case the CFI found that the Council sent to the applicant 'a statement clearly and unambiguously explaining the reasons which, in its opinion, justified the applicant's continued inclusion in the list at issue'. It took into account that the statement contained specific examples of acts of terrorism referred to in the relevant EU provisions for which the applicant was said to be

[193] *KONGRA-GEL et al v Council* (n 185) para 100. See also *People's Modjahedin Organization of Iran* (n 141) para 90 and *Sison v Council II* (n 185) para 182.

[194] Tridimas and Gutierrez-Fons (n 127) 721.

[195] *Sison v Council* (n 18) para 216. See also Case T-327/03, *Stichting Al Aqsa v Council* [2007] ECR II-79, para 55.

[196] See also *Stichting Al Aqsa v Council* (n 195) paras 60–64 and *Modjahedines du peuple d'Iran v Council* (n 10) para 166.

[197] *Sison v Council* (n 18) para 217. See also *KONGRA-GEL et al v Council* (n 185) para 98.

responsible. Furthermore, the CFI referred to the fact that the decision stated that, because of those acts, a decision had been taken by a competent authority of the UK to proscribe the applicant as an organisation concerned in acts of terrorism and that that decision was subject to review under the applicable UK legislation and that it was still in force.[198] In the same judgment, however, the CFI held that the statement of reasons with regard to a later decision to continue the EU sanction was obviously insufficient as it did not make it possible to grasp how far the Council took into account a new national decision, in which it was held that the organisation concerned was no longer concerned in terrorism.[199] Moreover, the CFI took into account that the decision did not explain the specific reasons why the Council took this view in spite of this decision that the continued inclusion of the applicant on the terrorist list remained justified.[200] In *Stichting Al-Aqsa* the Court of Justice considered that the statement of reasons set out the individual and specific reasons which led the Council to consider, on the basis of information considered to be reliable by a national authority, that the appellant was involved in the financing of terrorism. Such elements were sufficient to enable the appellant to understand the accusations made against it. The statement of reasons mentioned that Al-Aqsa was raising funds for certain organisations which belonged to the Palestinian movement Hamas, which appeared on the EU list of groups involved in terrorist acts. Some of those organisations made funds available for the commission, or for facilitation in the commission, of terrorist acts. The decision also indicated on which decision made by the Dutch authorities the EU sanction was based.[201]

Anti-terrorism Sanctions based on UN Security Council Resolutions

In cases concerning anti-terrorism sanctions based on UN Security Council Resolutions and sanctions against third States the EU Courts had the opportunity to assess the statement of reasons provided by the EU Institutions with regard to the allegations against the party concerned justifying the EU sanction. It is useful to examine the considerations of the EU Courts in some detail, as they may give indications as to what these Courts consider to be the essence of the case.

Was the General Context of the Decision known to the Applicant?

When assessing the sufficiency of the statement the Court of Justice takes into account whether the applicant was aware of the general context of the restrictive

[198] *People's Modjahedin Organization of Iran* (n 141) para 90. See also *Sison v Council II* (n 185) para 64.

[199] The national authority held that there was such a lack of evidence that the decision to proscribe the organisation could be defined as unreasonable and perverse. *People's Modjahedin Organization of Iran* (n 141) para 90. See also *Sison v Council II* (n 185) para 184.

[200] *People's Modjahedin Organization of Iran* (n 141) para 90. See also *Sison v Council II* (n 185) paras 177–85.

[201] *Stichting Al-Aqsa v Council* (n 137) paras 138–43.

measures concerned. In *Bamba* the Council decided to freeze the funds of the Director of a newspaper in Côte d'Ivoire as part of restrictive measures against persons who were obstructing the processes of peace and national reconciliation in Côte d'Ivoire, and in particular those who were jeopardising the proper outcome of the electoral process of 2010. The decision mentioned the following grounds: 'Director of the Cyclone group which publishes the newspaper "Le Temps": Obstruction of the peace and reconciliation processes through public incitement to hatred and violence and through participation in disinformation campaigns in connection with the 2010 presidential election.' The Court of Justice considered that the statement of reasons must be 'appropriate to the act at issue and the context in which it was adopted'.[202] It referred to the fact that the general context (the serious situation in Côte d'Ivoire and the threats posed to international peace and security) of the restrictive measures must have been familiar to Bamba in view of her personal and professional position.

Specificity of the Statement of Reasons

The EU Courts also examine whether the statement of reasons contains only general allegations or specific information which the applicant may be able to contest. Generally, a statement of reasons which refers to specific acts, names of persons or organisations involved in such acts, dates or periods, or other details, are considered sufficient by the EU Courts. The role of the person or entity concerned in terrorist activities must also be identified.[203] In *Bamba*, for example, the Court of Justice stated that the decision 'identifies the actual and specific evidence, in terms of professional position, publishing group, newspaper and types of activities and press campaigns covered' which lie at the basis of the Council's view that Bamba was involved in obstructing the process of peace and reconciliation in Côte d'Ivoire.[204] The court agrees with the Council that Bamba should have known that:

> by alluding, in the contested acts, to her position as director of the group which publishes the newspaper *Le Temps*, the Council intended to highlight the power to influence and the responsibility which might be supposed to result from that position as regards the editorial line of that newspaper and the content of press campaigns allegedly run by that newspaper during the Ivorian post-electoral crisis.[205]

The Court of Justice concluded that Bamba was placed in a position to effectively dispute the merits of the contested acts.

[202] Case T-86/11 *Bamba* [2011] ECR II-2749, para 53.

[203] *Commission et al v Kadi* (n 16) paras 143–50. See also, eg *Bank Saderat Iran* (n 149) paras 63–72 and Case T-496/10, *Bank Mellat v Council*, paras 66–77.

[204] *Council v Bamba* (n 10) para 56.

[205] Ibid, para 58. The approach of the General Court in this case was different and it concluded that the duty to state reasons had been violated. See Case T-86/11 *Bamba* [2011] ECR II-2749, para 52. See also Wimmer (n 120) 1127–29.

In *Bank Melli Iran* the General Court found that the decision to freeze the funds of the bank because of its support for nuclear proliferation was sufficiently reasoned. It referred to the fact that the Council mentioned:

> first, the kind of support lent by the applicant, namely providing financial services, including opening letters of credit and maintaining accounts, secondly, the activities linked to nuclear proliferation involved by those services, namely the purchase of sensitive materials, and, thirdly, the beneficiaries of the support provided by the applicant, that is to say, the eight entities designated by name.[206]

Several examples of insufficient statements of reasons can be also found in the case law of the EU Courts. In *Kadi II* the Court of Justice found that

> the allegation that Mr Kadi had been the owner in Albania of several firms which funnelled money to extremists or employed those extremists in positions where they controlled the funds of those firms, up to five of which received working capital from Usama bin Laden, is insufficiently detailed and specific given that it contains no indication of the identity of the firms concerned, of when the alleged conduct took place and of the identity of the 'extremists' who allegedly benefitted from that conduct.[207]

In *Qualitest FZE* the only reason given for the decision to freeze the funds of a company was that the company was 'Involved in procurement of components for Iranian nuclear programme.' According to the General Court this sentence merely paraphrased the legal basis for the decision and did not enable the party concerned 'to understand the reasons for adopting those measures and the Court to exercise its power of review'.[208]

The EU Courts have indicated in several cases which defences could have been or were actually raised by the parties concerned. In *Bamba* the Court of Justice mentioned several ways in which she could have disputed the allegations against her, namely by denying:

— her position as director of the group which publishes the newspaper *Le Temps*;
— the existence of the campaigns; or
— any responsibility in connection with those campaigns.

or by disputing the relevance of all or any of those facts or their classification as obstructions to the process of peace and reconciliation in Côte d'Ivoire capable of justifying the use of restrictive measures against her.[209]

In *Fulmen and Fereydoun Mahmoudian* the General Court considered that the sufficiency of the statement of reasons provided was confirmed by the content of the applications of the parties concerned as they precisely addressed the

206 *Bank Melli Iran v Council* (n 153) para 84.
207 *Commission et al v Kadi* (n 16) para 141.
208 Case T-421/11 *Qualitest FZE* [2012] paras 36 and 39.
209 *Council v Bamba* (n 10) para 59.

allegations against them.[210] In *Qualitest FZE* on the other hand, the General Court found that the contents of the pleadings of the addressee of the decision confirmed its judgment that the statement of reasons of the decision was insufficient. These pleadings included denials of a general nature, 'thus reflecting the fact that the applicant was unaware of the actual and specific allegations of the Council in its regard.' The Court notes that where the party concerned responds to specific factual matters referred to by the Council in the defence, the party's reply was also more specific.[211]

Separation of Statement of Reasons and Underlying Evidence

The Court of Justice separates the question of the statement of reasons from the evidence of the alleged conduct which underlies the decision to impose restrictive measures. The examination of the merits of the statement of reasons should consist of ascertaining whether the evidence relied on by the Council is established and whether it is capable of justifying the adoption of those measures.[212] That implies that the EU Courts assess the decision in the light of the underlying evidence. In some cases there was no evidence of the allegations against the party concerned, which lead to the annulment of the decision.[213] In *Kadi II* the Court of Justice found that the statement of reasons for the decision to impose sanctions on Kadi were sufficient (except for one ground). The Court then analysed the defences raised by Kadi and the evidence submitted by the Commission and concluded that none of the allegations against Kadi justified the adoption of the EU sanction.[214]

10.4.4 The Right to an Effective Remedy

It was explained in section 10.4.1 that decisions imposing EU sanctions may be subjected to judicial review by the EU Courts. The scope of judicial review performed by the EU Courts differs, however, with respect to the different types of EU sanctions.[215] The intensity of judicial review also varies according to the type of EU sanction.

[210] Joined Cases T-439/10 and T-440/10 *Fulmen and Fereydoun Mahmoudian v Council* [2012] para 53.

[211] Case T-421/11 *Qualitest FZE* [2012] para 40.

[212] *Council v Bamba* (n 10) paras 60–61. See also Case C-548/09 P *Bank Melli Iran* [2011] para 88.

[213] See, eg Case T-509/10, *Manufacturing Support & Procurement Kala Naft Co v Council* [2012] paras 123–24.

[214] *Commission et al v Kadi* (n 16) paras 151–63.

[215] *Kadi and Al Barakaat v Council and Commission* (n 17) para 343 and *Modjahedines du peuple d'Iran v Council* (n 10) para 156.

Autonomous Anti-terrorism Sanctions

In cases regarding autonomous anti-terrorism sanctions the Council enjoys broad discretion in its assessment of the matters to be taken into account for the purpose of imposing EU sanctions. As a result, the scope of judicial review is limited. Specifically, the EU Courts may not substitute their assessment of the evidence, facts and circumstances justifying the adoption of such measures for that of the Council.[216] However, the CFI also held

> that does not mean that the Court is not to review the interpretation made by that institution of the relevant facts .... The Community judicature must not only establish whether the evidence relied on is factually accurate, reliable and consistent, but must also ascertain whether that evidence contains all the relevant information to be taken into account in order to assess the situation and whether it is capable of substantiating the conclusions drawn from it.[217]

The existence of a national decision on which the EU sanction should be based, for example, is subjected to (more) rigorous review.[218] The Court pays more deference to the EU Institution's assessment of the factors as to appropriateness on which decisions to freeze funds are based.[219]

Anti-terrorism Measures which are based on UN Security Council Resolutions

In cases regarding anti-terrorism measures which are based on UN Security Council Resolutions, the EU Courts pay much less deference to the decision of the EU Institution. They subject the decision, including the facts and evidence underlying the decision, to a full judicial review.

> That entails a verification of the allegations factored in the summary of reasons underpinning that decision ... with the consequence that judicial review cannot be restricted to an assessment of the abstract cogency in the abstract of the reasons relied on, but must concern whether those reasons, or, at the very least, one of those reasons, deemed sufficient in itself to support that decision, is substantiated.[220]

In *Kadi II* the Court of Justice went into the details in its assessment of the allegations against Kadi, the evidence underlying these allegations, and the defences raised by Kadi.[221]

216 *Modjahedines du peuple d'Iran v Council* (n 10) para 159. Here the CFI referred to the ECtHR's case law in *Leander* (n 280) and ECtHR 20 June 2002, *Al-Nashif v Bulgaria,* no 50963/99. In other judgments concerning EU sanctions in which the same consideration is used, the CFI referred to its standing case law concerning the intensity of judicial review in other fields of EU law, such as Case C-525/04 P *Spain v Lenzing* [2007]. See, eg *People's Modjahedin Organization of Iran* (n 141) paras 138–39 and *People's Modjahedin Organization of Iran v Council* (n 138) para 55.

217 *Kadi v Commission* (n 19) para 142. The General Court referred by analogy to Case C-525/04 P, *Spain v Lenzing* [2007] a State aid case. With regard to the intensity of judicial review performed by the EU Courts see also ch 9, section 9.2.1 in this volume.

218 See, eg *People's Modjahedin Organization of Iran v Council* (n 138).

219 Case T-256/07, *People's Modjahedin Organization of Iran* [2008] ECR II-3019, para 138.

220 *Commission et al v Kadi* (n 16) para 119.

221 Ibid, paras 151–65.

EU Sanctions against Third States
In cases concerning EU sanctions against third States the EU Courts also perform a full judicial review, which includes the factual basis of the decision to impose an EU sanction.[222]

10.4.4.1 Disclosure of Evidence to the EU Courts

The CFI has considered in several cases that the right to an effective remedy is violated if it does not receive the evidence underlying the contested decision.[223] The CFI held in the *PMOI III* case that

> the Council is not entitled to base its funds-freezing decision on information or material in the file communicated by a Member State, if the said Member State is not willing to authorise its communication to the Community judicature whose task is to review the lawfulness of that decision.[224]

The Court of Justice recognises that where the EU Institution refuses to send the relevant confidential evidence to the Court, the Court is not able to conduct its judicial review.[225] However, it does not seem to be of the opinion (at least in cases concerning EU sanctions based on UN Security Council Resolutions) that all the information on which the decision to impose the EU sanction is based should be disclosed to the Court. In *Kadi II* the Court held that the EU Courts must, if it is necessary to carry out their judicial review of the decision, request the EU Institution to produce the evidence, confidential or not, relevant to such an examination. The information or evidence provided by this institution should support the reasons relied on against the person concerned. According to the Court, there is, however, no requirement that this institution produces before the EU Courts all the information and evidence underlying the reasons alleged in the summary provided by the Sanctions Committee.

If the competent EU Institution finds itself unable to comply with the EU Court's request to provide evidence or information, it is the duty of those Courts to base their decision solely on the material which has been disclosed to them.[226] In cases concerning EU sanctions based on UN Security Council Resolutions the open material consists of the indications contained in the narrative summary of reasons provided by the Sanctions Committee, the observations and exculpatory evidence that may have been produced by the person concerned and the response of the competent EU Institution. 'If that material is insufficient to allow a finding

[222] *Bank Saderat Iran* (n 149) para 105.
[223] *Modjahedines du peuple d'Iran v Council* (n 10) para 155, where the CFI held that it must be able to review the lawfulness and the merits of the measures to freeze funds 'without it being possible to raise objections that the evidence and information is secret or confidential'. See also eg *Sison v Council* (n 18) para 202.
[224] *People's Modjahedin Organization of Iran v Council* (n 138) para 73.
[225] *Kadi and Al Barakaat v Council and Commission* (n 17) para 351.
[226] *Commission et al v Kadi* (n 16) para 123.

that a reason is well founded, the Courts of the European Union shall disregard that reason as a possible basis for the contested decision to list or maintain a listing.'[227]

The Court of Justice here seems to take into account the fact that the evidence underlying the decision to impose sanctions on the UN level, may be based on information provided by UN members which may not be accessible for the EU Institutions. The Court of Justice does not address the question of potential exculpatory evidence which may have been sent to the Sanctions Committee by a UN member which is not disclosed to the person or entity concerned.

10.4.4.2 Possible Limitations to the Right to an Effective Remedy

If the EU Institution does provide relevant information or evidence to the EU Courts it is up to the EU Court to review whether it sufficiently supports the allegations against the person or entity concerned. The Court of Justice accepts that also during appeal 'overriding considerations to do with the security of the European Union or of its Member States or with the conduct of their international relations may preclude the disclosure of some information or some evidence to the person concerned'.[228] It is up to the EU Courts to decide whether the reasons relied on by the EU Institution to preclude disclosure are sufficient. If the EU Court concludes that non-disclosure of (part of) the evidence or information is not justified it will give the EU Institution the opportunity to make such a disclosure. If the EU Institution refuses to comply with the EU Court's request for disclosure, the evidence or information concerned will be excluded from the Court's assessment. On the other hand, if the EU Courts conclude that non-disclosure of the information or evidence produced before the EU Court is justified, this Court must

> strike an appropriate balance between the requirements attached to the right to effective judicial protection, in particular respect for the principle of an adversarial process, and those flowing from the security of the European Union or its Member States or the conduct of their international relations.[229]

10.4.4.3 Possible Compensation for Limitations to the Rights of the Defence during the Appeal

In *Kadi I* the Court of Justice stated that if certain evidence cannot be communicated to the parties during the appeal phase

> it is none the less the task of the Community judicature to apply, in the course of the judicial review it carries out, techniques which accommodate, on the one hand,

227 Ibid, para 123.
228 Ibid, para 125.
229 Ibid, para 128.

> legitimate security concerns about the nature and sources of information taken into account in the adoption of the act concerned and, on the other, the need to accord the individual a sufficient measure of procedural justice.[230]

The Court of Justice referred in *Kadi I* to the ECtHR's case law in *Chahal*, in which such techniques were mentioned for the first time by the ECtHR. It concerned the use of special advocates who act on behalf of the party to which certain information is not disclosed and who can examine and comment on this information. Apparently the Court of Justice found that it should apply such techniques if they were necessary to compensate the limitations of the party's rights of the defence. After the judgment in *Kadi I*, the ECtHR further addressed the special advocate procedure applied in the UK in the judgment in *A and others*. It found that this procedure does not always adequately ensure the right to an adversarial procedure.[231] This may be the reason why in *Kadi II* the Court of Justice did not refer to the special advocate procedure and considered instead that 'it is legitimate to consider possibilities such as the disclosure of a summary outlining the information's content or that of the evidence in question'.[232]

Application to Specific Cases

Because of the strict relationship between the right to be heard, the obligation to state reasons, and the right to an effective remedy, the EU Courts found a violation of the right to an effective remedy in all cases in which those first two rights had been infringed. According to the Courts, the applicants were not able to defend their rights with regard to the evidence underlying the decision in satisfactory conditions before the Court.[233] In the *Bank Melli Iran* and *Fahas* cases, in which the right to be heard and the obligation to state reasons were not violated, the CFI did not find a violation of the right to an effective remedy.[234]

In most anti-terrorism sanction cases the Council had taken the opinion that confidential evidence underlying the EU sanction could not be disclosed to the EU Courts. The Court of Justice has criticised this 'fundamental position' adopted by the Council.[235] In *PMOI III* the CFI considered that the Council had not explained why the production of relevant information or material in the file would violate the principle of confidentiality, whereas their production to the members of the Council, and thus to the governments of the 26 other Member States, did not.[236] In cases in which the confidential evidence was not disclosed

[230] *Kadi and Al Barakaat v Council and Commission* (n 17) para 344.

[231] This judgment will be discussed in section 10.5.4.

[232] *Commission et al v Kadi* (n 16) para 129.

[233] See, eg *Kadi and Al Barakaat v Council and Commission* (n 17) para 349; *Modjahedines du peuple d'Iran v Council* (n 10) para 158; *Sison v Council* (n 18) para 165; *Othman v Council and Commission* (n 125) para 86; and *Stichting Al Aqsa v Council* (n 195) para 64.

[234] *Bank Melli Iran v Council* (n 153) para 106; *Fahas v Council* (n 139) paras 59–62.

[235] *Kadi and Al Barakaat v Council and Commission* (n 17) para 350.

[236] *People's Modjahedin Organization of Iran v Council* (n 138) paras 72 and 76.

to the EU Court the violation of the applicant's right to be heard was not remedied during the appeal proceedings before these Courts.[237] Furthermore, the EU Courts found that they were not able to undertake the review of the lawfulness of the contested decision.[238]

10.4.5 Subconclusion: The Use of Secret Information in EU Sanction Cases

In their judgments the EU Courts made clear that in cases concerning EU sanctions aiming at combating terrorism or EU sanctions which target third States, EU fundamental rights, such as the rights of the defence and the right to an effective remedy, must also be respected. Limitations to these rights are allowed to ensure the effectiveness of the EU sanctions or to protect the security of the EU or of its Member States or the conduct of their international relations. Most importantly, the right to be heard does not need to be respected before the EU sanction is first imposed and the specific and complete reasons for the decision and the evidence and information underlying the decision does not always need to be disclosed to the person or entity concerned.

It its case law concerning anti-terrorism sanctions based on UN Security Council Resolutions and EU sanctions against third States, the EU Courts have indicated which factors are relevant when assessing the sufficiency of the statement of reasons. First, it should be examined whether the applicant was aware of the general context of the restrictive measures concerned.[239] Secondly, the specificity of the reasons should be taken into account. A statement of reasons which refers to specific acts, names of persons or organisations involved in such acts, dates or periods, or other details is considered sufficient by the EU Courts.[240] At least one of the reasons given for the decision must be sufficient to support the decision.[241] This case law of the EU Courts may be used to identify what constitutes the essence of the case against a person or entity. This is relevant because the Court of Justice considered in *ZZ* with regard to proceedings before national courts that Article 47 of the Charter requires that the essence of the grounds which constitute the basis of that decision must be disclosed to the person concerned.[242] In cases concerning autonomous anti-terrorism sanctions the scope of the duty to state reasons is rather limited, because the factual basis of the allegation that a person or entity is involved in terrorism is reviewed only at the national level.

[237] *Kadi and Al Barakaat v Council and Commission* (n 17) para 350.

[238] See, eg *Kadi and Al Barakaat v Council and Commission* (n 17) para 351, *Modjahedines du peuple d'Iran v Council* (n 10) para 166, *People's Modjahedin Organization of Iran v Council* (n 138) para 76. For a different view, see *Bank Melli Iran v Council* (n 153) para 106, where the CFI held that it was in a position to carry out a full review.

[239] *Council v Bamba* (n 10) para 54.

[240] *Commission et al v Kadi* (n 16) paras 143–50.

[241] Ibid, para 130.

[242] *ZZ* (n 15) para 40. See section 10.2.

In cases concerning autonomous anti-terrorism sanctions the scope of judicial review by the EU Courts is rather limited because national authorities and courts decide on the factual basis of the allegations against a person or entity. Nevertheless, the EU Courts do review whether the proceedings on the EU level complied with EU fundamental rights and whether the Council has met its burden of proof. In anti-terrorism sanctions which are based on UN Security Council Resolutions and sanctions against third States, the EU Courts apply a full judicial review.

The EU Courts have made clear that in order to be able to perform judicial review effectively they must receive the evidence and information underlying the contested decision from the EU Institution. If the EU Institution refuses to disclose information or evidence to the EU Court, this Court must assess whether the open material provides sufficient support for the allegations against the person or entity concerned. Where the EU Institution provides secret information or evidence to the EU Court, the Court must decide whether it is justified in refusing to disclose this information or evidence to the person or entity concerned. Evidence or information which is not disclosed to the person even though the Court finds that such non-disclosure is not justified, should be disregarded. If the Court allows the non-disclosure of evidence or information, the limitations of the right of the defence of the person or entity concerned must be compensated, for example, by using non-confidential summaries of documents.[243]

It is striking that the Court of Justice has barely made references to the ECtHR's case law concerning the use of secret information in its recent judgments. Nevertheless, the case law of the Court of Justice and the ECtHR show important parallels. In the next section the ECtHR's case law will be discussed.

10.5 THE USE OF SECRET INFORMATION UNDER INTERNATIONAL LAW

The use of secret information has been addressed by the ECtHR, the Committee against Torture (ComAT), the Human Rights Committee (HRC) and the UN High Commissioner for Refugees (UNHCR). The body of case law under the ECHR provides by far the most developed standards and will therefore be discussed at length in this section. First, however, a brief overview will be given of the views of the other supervising bodies.

The ComAT and HRC have addressed the use of secret information in a few individual cases. In *Agiza* the ComAT considered that national security concerns might justify some adjustments being made to the particular process of review. However, the mechanism chosen must continue to satisfy the requirements of effective, independent and impartial review. In *Agiza* a violation of the procedural

[243] *Commission et al v Kadi* (n 16) paras 120–30.

requirements under Article 3 CAT had occurred as no such review was available.[244] In its Concluding Observations of June 2012 regarding Canada, the ComAT noted that Canada continued to engage in deportations, extraditions or other removals, in practice, often using security certificates under the Immigration and Refugee Law Protection Act which could result in violations of the principle of *refoulement*. Furthermore, the Committee expressed its concerns with respect to the special advocate procedure applied in Canada. It noted in particular that special advocates have a very limited ability to conduct cross-examinations or to seek evidence independently. Furthermore, it stated that

> individuals subject to security certificates have access to a summary of confidential evidence concerning them and cannot directly discuss full content with their special advocates. Accordingly, the advocates cannot properly know the case against them or make full answer or defence in violation of the fundamental principles of justice and due process.[245]

The Committee recommends that the use of security certificates be extensively ensured. As will be explained in section 10.5.4 the ECtHR has raised similar objections against the special advocate procedure applied by the UK.

The *Ahani* case decided by the HRC concerned a person who was to be expelled for national security reasons. The Committee considered that because of the issues of national security that were involved, it was not persuaded that the procedure before the Canadian Federal Court in which the reasonableness of the security certificate was assessed, was unfair to the author. Nor did the Committee 'discern on the record any elements of bad faith, abuse of power or other arbitrariness which would vitiate the Federal Court's assessment'. The Committee took into account that, in the Canadian Federal Court's 'reasonableness' hearing on the security certification, the author was provided with a summary, redacted for security concerns, reasonably informing him of the claims made against him. Furthermore, the Committee noted that the Federal Court was conscious of the 'heavy burden' upon it to assure through this process the author's ability to be aware of and respond appropriately to the case made against him, and the author was able to, and did, present his own case and cross-examine witnesses.[246] The Committee did find a violation of Article 13 ICCPR regarding the appeal against the deportation order before the Canadian Supreme Court. The reason was that the Supreme Court did not grant the applicant enhanced procedural protections, including provision of all information and advice on which the Minister intended to rely, receipt of an opportunity to address the evidence in writing and to be given written reasons by the Minister, because he had not made out a prima facie risk of *refoulement*. Such guarantees

[244] ComAT 20 May 2005, *Agiza v Sweden*, no 233/2003, para 13.8.

[245] ComAT, Concluding Observations on Canada (25 June 2012, CAT/C/CAN/CO/6) para12. See also Concluding Observations on New Zealand (19 May 2009, CAT/C/NZL/CO/5).

[246] For a description of the procedure, see para 2.3 of the judgment.

were provided in another, similar case before the Supreme Court in which a prima facie case risk was apparent.[247]

Anonymous Sources

In two complaints against Sweden before the ComAT, a report was drawn up by the Swedish embassy in Ankara in which it was concluded that part of the applicants' asylum account was not true and/or documents provided by them were not authentic. Both reports were based on information obtained from anonymous sources and the applicants complained that they were, therefore, unable to effectively challenge the findings contained in the reports. In one case the ComAT refused to take the report into account because it had been submitted by the State authorities after the national proceedings had been concluded. As a result, 'the applicant had not had an opportunity either to contest the information provided therein or to challenge the investigator whose name has not been revealed before the domestic authorities'.[248] In the other case the Committee did not deem the applicants' complaint regarding the use of anonymous sources to be well founded. Instead, it considered that the applicants had failed to disprove the State's findings regarding the authenticity of the documents adduced by them.[249] The Committee thus seems to accept that information provided by anonymous sources is included in the assessment of the credibility of an asylum account.

Secret Information in Article 1F Proceedings

Finally, the UNHCR addressed the use of secret information in proceedings in which a person is excluded from refugeeship on the basis of Article 1F of the Refugee Convention. According to the UNHCR, such an exclusion should not be based on sensitive evidence that cannot be challenged by the individual concerned. It accepts, however, that 'exceptionally, anonymous evidence (where the source is concealed) may be relied upon, but only where this is absolutely necessary to protect the safety of witnesses and the asylum-seeker's ability to challenge the substance of the evidence is not substantially prejudiced'. Furthermore, the UNHCR states that 'secret evidence or evidence considered in camera (where the substance is also concealed) should not be relied upon to exclude. Where national security interests are at stake, these may be protected by introducing procedural safeguards which also respect the asylum-seeker's due process rights.'[250]

[247] HRC 15 June 2004, *Ahani v Canada*, no 1051/2002.

[248] ComAT 21 November 2008, *EJ et al v Sweden*, no 306/2006.

[249] ComAT 2 May 2007, *ERK and YK v Sweden*, nos 270/2005 and 271/2005, paras 2.7, 5.4 and 7.5. The applicants only stated with regard to the embassy report that the discrepancies in the documents were merely 'alleged formal errors' and that they lack the means and necessary legal expertise to make any further comments.

[250] UNHCR, *Guidelines on International Protection No 5: Application of the Exclusion Clauses: Article 1F of the 1951 Convention relating to the Status of Refugees* (4 September 2003, HCR/GIP/03/05) www.refworld.org/docid/3f5857684.html accessed 26 September 2013, para 36.

Conclusion

It should be concluded that the supervising bodies mentioned above find that expulsion measures based on national security should be subjected to judicial review. They accept, however, that national security reasons or other interests of the State may limit the procedural guarantees offered in asylum or deportation proceedings. It does not follow from these views to what extent procedural safeguards may be limited. The ECtHR's case law discussed in the following section provides more guidance on this point.

10.5.1 The ECtHR's Case Law on Secret Information

The ECtHR has addressed the use of confidential information in complaints under several provisions of the Convention and in very different types of cases. In such complaints the Court usually examines whether the right of adversarial proceedings (and sometimes the right to equality of arms) has been complied with. The right to adversarial proceedings has been recognised under Articles 5(4), 6(1) civil and criminal limb, 8, 9, 13 ECHR and Article 1 of Protocol 7 ECHR.[251] Cases falling within the scope of Articles 5(4), 6(1) civil limb and 8 ECHR often concern measures which are intended to protect the national security of the State. Examples include detention of persons suspected of being involved in terrorist activities, secret surveillance of persons, the issuing of certificates by the State relating to a person's danger for national security, which may result in a person losing or not obtaining a job, or the expulsion or non-admission of persons on national security grounds. In these cases (some of) the evidence underlying the decision to take such measures are not disclosed to the person concerned for national security reasons. In criminal cases, evidence may not be disclosed to the accused in order to protect witnesses or the State's interest in keeping secret police methods of investigation of crime.

The case law of the ECtHR only concerns the guarantees which should be offered during the (appeal) proceedings before a national court (Articles 5 and 6) or a national independent authority (Article 13). This is, therefore, different from the case law of the EU Courts examined in the previous sections, which also regarded the guarantees required during the administrative proceedings before the EU Institutions.

The ECtHR has recognised that the national court or independent authority dealing with an appeal against a decision may need to afford a wide margin of appreciation to the executive in matters of national security. However, this does

[251] This follows from the fact that Art 1 of Protocol 7 requires that the expulsion of an alien lawfully resident is 'in accordance with the law'. The phrase 'in accordance with the law' has a similar meaning throughout the Convention and its Protocols. Under Arts 8 and 9 the Court held that the right to adversarial proceedings flows from this requirement. See ECHR 24 April 2008, *CG et al v Bulgaria*, no 1365/07, para 73. This section will not further address Art 9 ECHR and Art 1 of Protocol 7 ECHR.

not mean that as soon as the executive has chosen to invoke the term 'national security' the decision may escape any review by the court or independent authority.[252] Under Article 6 ECHR the ECtHR held that the right to submit a dispute to a court or tribunal in order to have a determination of questions of both fact and law cannot be displaced by the *ipse dixit* of the executive.[253] The Court has also held under Articles 8, 9 and 13 ECHR that a national independent authority must be able to review whether invoking national security as the basis for measures against a person is reasonable and not arbitrary.[254] The existence of a meaningful and independent review of measures is a necessary guarantee against arbitrariness and abuse of power.[255] In several cases the ECtHR found a violation of Articles 6(1), 8, or 13 ECHR because the national court or independent authority could not review the decision that the person concerned was a danger to national security, did not examine relevant facts and evidence and in some cases confined itself to 'a purely formal examination'.[256]

According to the Court, the limits of the notion of national security should not be stretched beyond its natural meaning.[257] In *CG* the ECtHR held that drugs offences are not capable of impinging on the national security of Bulgaria and cannot serve as a sound factual basis for the conclusion that, if not expelled, the applicant would present a national security risk in the future.[258] This was also found with regard to allegations of human trafficking in *Raza*.[259] In several cases the ECtHR was prevented from assessing whether the measure could be justified in the light of national security because the State failed to provide it with relevant documents.[260]

[252] See, eg with regard to Art 13 ECHR *Al-Nashif* (n 216) paras 94 and 137. The ECtHR considered with regard to Art 5 ECHR that 'national authorities cannot do away with effective control of lawfulness of detention by the domestic courts whenever they choose to assert that national security and terrorism are involved'. See also ECtHR 26 July 2011, *Liu v Russia*, no 29157/09, para 88.

[253] ECtHR 10 July 1998, *Tinnelly and McElduff et al v the United Kingdom*, nos 20390/92 and 21322/92, para 77. See also ECtHR 30 October 2001, *Devlin v the United Kingdom*, no 29545/95, para 31 and ECtHR 19 March 2002, *Devenney v the United Kingdom*, no 24265/94, para 28.

[254] *Al-Nashif* (n 216) paras 124 (Art 8) and 137 (Art 13). See *Nolan and K v Russia*, no 2512/04, para 71.

[255] See, eg ECtHR (Adm) 1 March 2005, *Haliti v Switzerland*, no 14015/02. See also ECtHR 8 June 2006, *Lupsa v Romania*, no 10337/04, paras 38 and 42 and ECtHR 26 July 2011, *M et al v Bulgaria*, no 41416/08, para 102.

[256] See, eg *Al-Nashif* (n 216); *Liu v Russia* (n 252) (Arts 8 and 13 ECHR) para 89; *CG* (n 251) paras 47 and 50 (Art 8 and Art 1 of Prot 7) *Lupsa* (n 255) para 41 (Art 8); *Tinnelly and McElduff* (n 253) paras 75 and 77 (Art 6).

[257] *CG* (n 251) para 43.

[258] Ibid, para 43.

[259] ECtHR 11 February 2010, *Raza v Romania*, no 31465/08, para 53. See also ECtHR 16 December 2008, *Gulijev v Lithuania*, no 10425/03, para 46 and under Art 9 ECHR: *Nolan and K v Russia* (n 254) para 72.

[260] See, eg *Saadi* (n 3).

It is important to remember that national security concerns cannot justify the expulsion of a person to a country where he runs a real risk of *refoulement.*[261] Secret evidence substantiating that a person poses a risk to national security, therefore, cannot play a role in the rigorous scrutiny required in Article 3 ECHR cases. In its judgment in *A* the ECtHR found that the expulsion of the applicant would violate Article 3; secret evidence had been used by the national authorities to justify the refusal of an asylum status. This evidence had not been included in the assessment of whether expulsion of the applicant would infringe Article 3 ECHR. The ECtHR did not find a violation of Article 13 ECHR reiterating that the right to political asylum is not explicitly protected by either the ECHR or its Protocols. It considered that the secret materials did not, as such, concern the applicant's fear of being subjected to ill-treatment in Libya, but whether he was posing a threat to the national security of the Netherlands. The fact that this information was disclosed (with the applicant's permission) to the national courts which also reviewed the decision regarding the risk of *refoulement* did not, in the ECtHR's view, compromise the independence of those courts.[262]

As noted in the introduction to this chapter, secret evidence may also be used by national authorities in order to assess the credibility of the asylum seeker or establish the facts. The ECtHR has ruled in two asylum cases in which the government relied on country of origin information provided by anonymous sources.[263] These cases will be discussed further in section 10.5.4.

Asylum cases in which secret information is used to establish the facts are comparable to criminal cases. In both types of cases the national court or authority must review the facts rigorously. In expulsion or other cases falling within the scope of Article 8 ECHR the situation is different. In such cases secret evidence is used in order to justify an interference with the right to family life. National authorities enjoy a wide margin of appreciation when deciding whether national concerns exist and whether they justify the interference with the right to private or family life. National courts may, therefore, defer to those decisions. It may thus be expected that the ECtHR will follow its case law concerning criminal cases under Article 6 ECHR in asylum cases in which secret evidence is used in the assessment of the risk of *refoulement*. It will be noted in section 10.5.2 that the ECtHR has already applied the guarantees required by the criminal limb of Article 6(1) ECHR to detention and administrative cases, taking into account the nature of the case.

[261] *Chahal* (n 4) para 151.

[262] ECtHR 20 July 2010, *A v the Netherlands*, no 4900/06, para 160.

[263] ECtHR 22 September 2011, *HR v France*, no 64780/09, para 61 and ECtHR 2 June 2011, *Sufi and Elmi v the United Kingdom*, nos 8319/07 and 11449/07, paras 233–34.

10.5.2 The Right to Adversarial Proceedings: Level of Procedural Protection

The ECtHR has recognised that all procedures governed by Articles 5(4),[264] 6,[265] 8[266] and 13[267] ECHR must be adversarial and that in those proceedings the principle of equality of arms must be respected.[268] The principle of adversarial proceedings entails that the parties to a trial have knowledge of and are able to comment on all the evidence adduced or observations filed.[269] In criminal cases the right to an adversarial trial means 'that both prosecution and defence must be given the opportunity to have knowledge of and comment on the observations filed and the evidence adduced by the other party'.[270] The ECtHR also held that 'failure to disclose to the defence material evidence which contains such particulars as could enable the accused to exonerate himself or have his sentence reduced would constitute a refusal of facilities necessary for the preparation of the defence' and therefore a violation Article 6(3)(b) ECHR.[271]

The principle of equality of arms 'requires each party to be given a reasonable opportunity to present his case under conditions that do not place him at a substantial disadvantage vis-à-vis his opponent'.[272] The general requirements derived from both principles seem to be the same for all cases (civil, criminal or other) governed by the ECHR.[273] As will be further explained below, the specific application of those principles may, however, differ according to the nature of the case. Almost all case law examined below addresses the issue of non-disclosure of evidence under the right to adversarial proceedings and not under the right to equality of arms.[274] Therefore, in the following sections reference will be only made to the right to adversarial proceedings.

[264] ECtHR (GC) 19 February 2009, *A et al v the United Kingdom*, no 3455/05, para 204.

[265] In some cases under Art 6 the ECtHR examined the complaints regarding the use of secret evidence under the right of access to court. See, eg *Tinnelly and McElduff* (n 253) and *Devenney* (n 253) no 24265/94.

[266] In Art 8 cases the right to adversarial proceedings is usually derived from the 'quality of law criterion' which follows from the requirement that an interference with the right to family or private life must be 'in accordance with the law'. In ECtHR 19 October 2010, *Özpinar v Turkey*, no 20999/04, the Court took into account the lack of adversarial proceedings in the proportionality test under Art 8.

[267] See *Al-Nashif* (n 216) paras 123 and 137.

[268] Trechsel notes that in the ECtHR's case law, the right to adversarial proceedings is not always clearly separated from the principle of equality of arms. S Trechsel, *Human Rights in Criminal Proceedings* (Oxford, Oxford University Press, 2005) 90.

[269] ECtHR (GC) 22 January 1996, *Lobo Machado v Portugal*, no 15764/89, para 31.

[270] See ECtHR (GC) 16 February 2000, *Fitt v the United Kingdom*, no 29777/96, para 21. See also D Harris, M O'Boyle, C Warbrick and E Bates, *Law of the European Convention on Human Rights* (Oxford, Oxford University Press, 2009) 254 and Trechsel, *Human Rights in Criminal Proceedings* (n 267) 90.

[271] ECtHR 6 March 2012, *Leas v Estonia*, no 59577/08, para 81.

[272] ECtHR 27 October 1993, *Dombo beheer v the Netherlands*, no 14448/88, para 33. See also ch 4, section 4.3.7 in this volume.

[273] ECtHR 27 January 1997, *Nideröst-Huber v Switzerland*, no 18990/91. See also E Van Kempen, 'De omgang met geheim bewijs in de vreemdelingenrechtelijke procedure' (2009) 24 *Migrantenrecht* 434, 437.

[274] See also Trechsel (n 267) 101.

Relevance of the Nature of the Case

The level of procedural protection under the right to adversarial proceedings depends on the nature of the case. Arguably, the highest level of protection is offered in criminal cases falling within the scope of Article 6(1) and (3) ECHR. The ECtHR also decided to apply these high standards in some cases falling within the scope of the civil limb of Article 6 and even other provisions of the Treaty. In *A and others* the ECtHR considered that because a suspicion of terrorism was the reason for the detention and

> in view of the dramatic impact of the lengthy—and what appeared at the time to be indefinite—deprivation of liberty on the applicants' fundamental rights, Article 5 § 4 must import substantially the same fair trial guarantees as Article 6 § 1 in its criminal aspect.[275]

In *Pocius* and *Aksoy*, both cases falling within the scope of the civil limb of Article 6 ECHR, the Court also applied these guarantees while referring to the circumstances of the case. In *Pocius* the applicant had contested being implicated in criminal activities as a ground for listing his name in an operational records file, as a result of which the applicant's permit to keep and carry a firearm had been revoked.[276] The *Aksoy* case concerned disciplinary proceedings against a nurse who was working for a military academy of medicine in Turkey.[277]

With regard to Article 5(4) ECHR, the Court held that this provision 'does not impose a uniform, unvarying standard to be applied irrespective of the context, facts and circumstances. According to the Court, the Article 5(4) procedure does not always need to meet the standards required under the civil and criminal limb of Article 6 ECHR. However, it must have a judicial character and provide guarantees appropriate to the type of deprivation of liberty in question. The procedure must be adversarial and must ensure equality of arms. In detention on remand cases the detainee must have the opportunity to effectively contest the basis of the allegations against him, which means, amongst other things, that he must have access to documents in the case file which form the basis of the prosecution case against him.[278] In remand cases as well other cases in which a suspicion against the detainee is the ground for detention (as in *A and others*) and/or the detention has great impact on the detainee, Article 6 ECHR standards are incorporated into Article 5(4) ECHR.[279] It may thus be assumed that in other kinds of detention cases, lower standards may apply.

275 *A et al v UK* (n 264) para 217.

276 *Pocius* (n 295) para 53. See also ECtHR 6 July 2010, *Užukauskas v Lithuania*, no 16965/04, para 47.

277 ECtHR 31 October 2006, *Aksoy v Turkey*, no 59741/00, para 27. Also in other cases the Court referred to the important consequences of a measure for the applicants, without that explicitly leading to higher procedural guarantees. See, eg *Devenney* (n 253) para 27 and ECtHR 13 December 2007, *Dagtekin v Turkey*, no 70516/01, para 34.

278 *A et al v UK* (n 264), paras 203–204.

279 Ibid, para 217.

The lowest standards seem to apply to cases concerning secret surveillance and the use of secret information for screening job candidates who would have access to sensitive information governed by Article 13 ECHR. In these cases the ECtHR accepted that a remedy must be 'as effective as can be'. According to the ECtHR, it is inherent in any system of secret surveillance or secret checks that there would be a restricted scope for recourse. Such a system can only function if the individual concerned remained unaware of the measures affecting him.[280] In those cases the Court did not find a violation of Article 13 ECHR although the available remedies only had limited effectiveness.[281]

Limited Application of the Requirement of a Remedy which is 'as effective as can be'

In *Al-Nashif*, the ECtHR also distinguished cases regarding the expulsion of aliens on national security grounds falling within the scope of Article 8 ECHR from cases concerning secret surveillance and the use of secret information for screening job candidates. It considered that in expulsion cases, reconciling the interest of preserving sensitive information with the individual's right to an effective remedy is obviously less difficult than in secret surveillance cases.[282] In none of the later expulsion cases the Court applied the 'as effective as can be' criteria. It may, therefore, be assumed that in *expulsion* cases stricter procedural guarantees are required under Articles 8 and 13 than in cases concerning secret surveillance or secret checks.[283]

Finally, in *Tinnelly and others* the ECtHR considered that the requirement of a remedy which is 'as effective as can be' cannot apply to civil cases falling within the scope of Article 6(1) ECHR. The Court stressed in this respect

> that the requirements of an 'effective remedy' for the purposes of Article 13 of the Convention are less strict than those of Article 6 § 1. For this reason, the Government's assertion that the access enjoyed by the applicants was as effective as could be in the circumstances cannot be sustained.[284]

Article 6(1) ECHR thus offers more protection than Article 13. It does not directly follow from the case law whether, and if so with regard to which aspects, the civil limb of Article 6(1) ECHR offers less protection than its criminal limb with regard to the use of confidential information.

[280] ECtHR 26 March 1987, *Leander v Sweden*, no 9248/81, paras 78 and 84 and ECtHR (Plen) 6 September 1978, *Klass v Germany*, no 5029/71, para 69. See also *Al-Nashif* (n 216) paras 136–37.

[281] *Leander* (n 280) para 84 and *Klass* (n 280) paras 70–72.

[282] *Al-Nashif* (n 216) para 137.

[283] The level of protection guaranteed under Arts 8 and 13 ECHR in expulsion cases seems to be the same.

[284] *Tinnelly and McElduff* (n 253) para 77.

Level of Procedural Protection under Article 3 ECHR

The Court suggests in *Chahal* that the procedural safeguards under Article 3 are stronger than those derived from Article 13 in *Klass* and *Leander*. It considered in *Chahal* that:

> it must be borne in mind that these cases concerned complaints under Articles 8 and 10 of the Convention ... and that their examination required the Court to have regard to the national security claims which had been advanced by the Government. The requirement of a remedy which is 'as effective as can be' is not appropriate in respect of a complaint that a person's deportation will expose him or her to a real risk of treatment in breach of Article 3 ... where the issues concerning national security are immaterial.[285]

This consideration obviously refers to the fact that Article 3 ECHR is absolute and that national security issues cannot play a role in the assessment of whether a person's expulsion violates this provision. However, it may also be derived from this consideration that a remedy which is 'as effective as can be' will never be sufficient in cases concerning Article 3 ECHR. Instead, a rigorous scrutiny must take place.[286] In *Othman*, a case in which the applicant claimed that his extradition would violate Article 3 ECHR, the ECtHR considered that the standards developed under Article 13 ECHR in *CG*, *A v the Netherlands* and *Kaushal* applied.[287] The ECtHR did not agree with the applicant that 'there is an enhanced requirement for transparency and procedural fairness' in extradition cases where diplomatic assurances are being relied upon. 'As in all Article 3 cases, independent and rigorous scrutiny is what is required.'[288] The ECtHR found that the *Othman* case was different from the *A and others* case because the secret information relief upon in *Othman* did not concern allegations against the applicant.

10.5.3 Limitations of the Right to Adversarial Proceedings

In all types of cases, the ECtHR has recognised that the right to adversarial proceedings may be limited in special circumstances. In *Othman*, the ECtHR held that national courts may consider closed evidence on safety of return, provided that the evidence has been disclosed to a special advocate. In this case the national courts discussed in a closed session the process by which a Memorandum of Understanding (MoU) between the UK and Jordan had been agreed. This MoU set out a series of assurances of compliance with international human rights standards, which would be adhered to when someone was returned from one State to another. The extent to which the MoU would mitigate the risk of torture was

[285] Chahal (n 4) para 150.
[286] Ibid, para 151.
[287] ECtHR 2 September 2010, *Kaushal et al v Bulgaria*, no 1537/08.
[288] ECtHR 17 January 2012, *Othman v the United Kingdom*, no 8139/09, para 219. See also ch 5, section 5.5.4 in this volume.

also discussed in the applicant's absence.[289] In criminal cases, the ECtHR held that the entitlement to disclosure of relevant evidence is not an absolute right. There may be reasons, such as the need to preserve the fundamental rights of another individual or to safeguard an important public interest, which justify a limitation of this right.[290] Under the civil limb of Article 6 ECHR the Court has held that a limitation of the right of access to court is not compatible with the Convention if it does not pursue a legitimate aim.[291] In *Al-Nashif* the Court considered in its ruling under Articles 8 and 13 ECHR that certain limitations on the type of remedies available to the individual may be justified where national security considerations are involved. Nevertheless, the remedy must remain effective in practice as well as in law.[292]

The ECtHR has identified several interests which may justify limitations of the right to adversarial proceedings. In *Sufi and Elmi* the ECtHR recognised, with regard to sources providing country of origin information for the purpose of the assessment of asylum cases, that 'where there are legitimate security concerns, sources may wish to remain anonymous'.[293] Similarly, the ECtHR has considered that the need to protect witnesses at risk of reprisals may justify a limitation of the right to adversarial proceedings.[294] The same applies to the need to keep secret police methods of investigation of crime.[295] In *van Mechelen and others*, a criminal case, the ECtHR accepted that it was necessary to preserve the anonymity of an agent deployed in undercover activities for his own or his family's protection so as not to impair his usefulness for future operations.[296] In *Mirilashvili*, another criminal case, the ECtHR considered that the aim of organising criminal proceedings in such a way as to protect information about the details of undercover police operations could legitimise the limitation to the right to adversarial proceedings.[297]

Furthermore, the ECtHR has accepted under several provisions that limitations may be justified in order to protect national security.[298] In *A and others*, for example, which concerned the indefinite detention of persons suspected of involvement in terrorist activities, the Court pointed to the fact that 'the activities and

[289] See, eg *Othman* (n 287) paras 23, 26 and 219.

[290] See, eg *Fitt* (n 269) para 45.

[291] *Tinnelly and McElduff* (n 253) para 72.

[292] *Al-Nashif* (n 216) paras 123 and 137.

[293] *Sufi and Elmi* (n 263) para 233.

[294] ECtHR 15 December 2011, *Al-Khawadja and Tahery v the United Kingdom*, nos 26766/05 and 22228/06, paras 120–25 and ECtHR 20 February 1996, *Doorson v the Netherlands*, no 20524/92, para 70.

[295] *Fitt* (n 270) para 45 and ECtHR 6 July 2010, *Pocius v Lithuania*, no 35601/04, para 52.

[296] ECtHR 23 April 1997, *Van Mechelen et al v the Netherlands*, nos 21363/93, 21364/93, 21427/93 and 22056/93, para 57. See also ECtHR (Adm) 17 September 2005, *Haas v Germany*, no 73047/01, where anonymous informants risked becoming the victim of acts of revenge abroad, where German authorities could only protect them to a very limited extent.

[297] ECtHR 11 December 2008, *Mirilashvili v Russia*, no 6293/04, para 202.

[298] See, eg under Art 5 *A et al v UK* (n 264), under Art 6 *Tinnelly and McElduff* (n 253) and under Arts 8 and 13 *Al-Nashif* (n 216).

aims of the al'Qaeda network had given rise to a "public emergency threatening the life of the nation"'. According to the ECtHR, therefore, it must

> be borne in mind that at the relevant time there was considered to be an urgent need to protect the population of the United Kingdom from terrorist attack and ... a strong public interest in obtaining information about al'Qaeda and its associates and in maintaining the secrecy of the sources of such information[299]

Necessity of Non-disclosure

In cases falling within the criminal limb of Article 6(1) or in which the standards accepted under that provision were applied, the Court stated that only such measures restricting the rights of the defence which are 'strictly necessary' are permissible.[300] If a less restrictive measure is sufficient then that measure should be applied.[301] 'Relevant and sufficient' reasons must be adduced by domestic authorities for the use of anonymous witnesses in criminal cases.[302] In *A and others* the ECtHR considered that 'it was essential that as much information about the allegations and evidence against each applicant was disclosed as was possible without compromising national security or the safety of others'.[303] This case law presupposes a very strict test. It is not clear from the ECtHR's case law whether such a strict test also applies to civil cases decided under Article 6(1) ECHR.

Under Articles 8 and 13 ECHR the ECtHR has held that 'there must be some form of adversarial proceedings before an independent body competent to review the reasons for the decision, *if need be with appropriate procedural limitations* on the use of classified information' (emphasis added).[304] This also suggests that limitations on the right to adversarial proceedings, such as the non-disclosure of evidence, are only allowed if necessary.[305]

Assessment of the Necessity of Non-disclosure by the National Court

The ECtHR has held under Articles 6(1) and 5(4) ECHR that the national court should decide whether it is justified to refuse disclosure of evidence to the party concerned.[306] The national court must be also entitled to assess a person's reasons

[299] *A et al v UK* (n 264) paras 216–17.

[300] See, eg *Fitt* (n 270) para 45 and *Pocius* (n 295) para 52.

[301] *Van Mechelen* (n 296) para 58.

[302] See, eg *Doorson* (n 294) para 71.

[303] *A et al v UK* (n 264) para 218.

[304] ECtHR 6 December 2007, *Liu and Liu v Russia*, no 42086/05, para 59 and *Kaushal* (n 287) para 29.

[305] See, *Raza* (n 259) para 55.

[306] According to van Dijk et al the Court 'attaches great importance to the fact that the need for disclosure is under constant assessment of the judge, who may monitor throughout the trial the fairness or otherwise of the disclosed evidence'. P van Dijk, F van Hoof, A van Rijn and L Zwaak (eds), *Theory and Practice of the European Convention on Human Rights* (Antwerp/Oxford, Intersentia, 2006) 2006, 588. See also ECtHR 24 April 2007, *V v Finland*, no 40412/98, para 77.

to request the disclosure of potential exculpatory evidence.[307] The Court found a violation of Article 6(1) ECHR in several criminal cases in which only State authorities (such as the public prosecutor or the security service) assessed the necessity of keeping relevant information secret.[308] In *Mirilashvili* the ECtHR made clear that in the decision on whether evidence should be disclosed to a party the mere involvement of a court is not sufficient.[309] In this case the Court found that the decision-making process was seriously flawed because the domestic court did not analyse whether the disclosure of the materials withheld from the applicant would, at least arguably, have harmed any identifiable public interest.[310] Finally, in several criminal cases, the fact that the national court did review the necessity of the non-disclosure of confidential information was taken into account in the Court's ruling that Article 6(1) ECtHR had not been violated.[311]

In criminal cases the fact that evidence was not revealed to the court in the first instance, which therefore could not examine the necessity of the non-disclosure of this evidence to the applicant, can sometimes be compensated during appeal proceedings.[312] In *Botmeh and Alami* the ECtHR took into account that

> given the extent of disclosure to the applicants of the withheld material by the Court of Appeal,[313] the fact that the court was able to consider the impact of the new material on the safety of the applicant's conviction in the light of detailed argument of their defence council and the fact that the undisclosed material was found by the court to add nothing of significance to what had already been disclosed at trial ... the failure to place the undisclosed material before the trial judge was in particular circumstances of the case remedied by the subsequent procedure before the Court of Appeal.[314]

In contrast, in *Rowe and Davis* the Court did not find the procedure before the appeal court sufficient to remedy the unfairness of the procedure at first instance. The Court took into account the fact that the Court of Appeal had fewer investigating powers than the court of first instance and the possibility that the Court of Appeal was influenced by the jury's verdict of guilty into underestimating the significance of the undisclosed evidence.[315] The ECtHR held that the fact that the Court of Appeal did not examine the non-disclosed material cannot in itself

[307] *Leas* (n 271) para 81.

[308] See, eg ECtHR (GC) 16 February 2000, *Rowe and Davis v the United Kingdom*, no 28901/95, paras 63–66; *Atlan* (n 308) para 44, *Dowsett* (n 308) para 44; and ECtHR 24 September 2007, *Matyjek v Poland*, no 38184/03, para 57.

[309] *Mirilashvili* (n 297) para 197.

[310] Ibid, paras 206–208.

[311] See, eg *Fitt* (n 270) para 47 and *Jasper* (n 311) para 56.

[312] See S Summers, *Fair Trials, The European Criminal Procedural Tradition and the European Court of Human Rights* (Oxford and Portland OR, Hart Publishing, 2007) 120.

[313] The Court of Appeal had disclosed to the applicant a summary of the information contained in one document and it gave an account of the events which had resulted in the fact that the undisclosed material had not been placed before the trial judge.

[314] ECtHR 7 June 2007, *Botmeh and Alami v the United Kingdom*, no 15187/03, para 44. See also ECtHR 16 December 1992, *Edwards v the United Kingdom*, no 13071/87, paras 36–39.

[315] *Rowe and Davis* (n 308) para 65. See also *Atlan* (n 308) para 45; *V* (n 306) para 79; and Trechsel (n 267) 93.

amount to a violation of Article 6(1) ECHR, in the situation that no deficiencies were found in the first instance procedure.[316]

Arguably, also under the civil limb of Article 6(1) ECHR, the executive cannot decide on its own on the necessity of confidentiality of information. This follows from the fact that the ECtHR has held that an applicant's right to submit a dispute to a court or tribunal in order to have a determination of questions of both fact and law cannot be displaced by the *ipse dixit* of the executive.[317]

The Court has not yet considered whether Article 13 ECHR requires (in expulsion measures) that an independent authority rules on the necessity of the non-disclosure of evidence. In most expulsion cases decided under Articles 8 and 13 the national court had not received the confidential documents and/or had not reviewed the facts, still less the necessity of the limitations of the right to adversarial proceedings. It may, however, be expected that the Court does not accept that it is left to the full discretion of the executive authorities to decide whether national security concerns justify the refusal to disclose documents to the applicant. Such discretion could lead to arbitrariness and would not be in line with the ECtHR's case law which implies that the national court should assess whether national security reasons justify limitations to the right to family life.

Examination of Confidential Evidence by the National Court

The national court should assess whether invoking national security as a justification for a certain measure has a reasonable basis in the facts or reveals an interpretation of 'national security' that is unlawful, or arbitrary and contrary to common sense.[318] Furthermore, it must examine the necessity of the non-disclosure of the evidence. This presupposes that the court receives all the relevant evidence from the State.[319] The ECtHR has made clear that the confidential information used by the State authorities should be disclosed to the national court (Articles 5 and 6 ECHR) or independent authority (Article 13 ECHR) hearing the case. If the court has not received all confidential information in the case file it is not in a position to monitor the need for (non-) disclosure, nor it is able to review the facts.[320] In *Tinnelly*, for example, the Court considered that any substantive review of the grounds motivating the issues of a national security certificate would have been impaired because the court assessing the case did not have sight of all the materials on which the Secretary of State based his decision.[321]

[316] ECtHR 11 January 2011, *McKeown v the United Kingdom*, no 6684/05, para 54.

[317] *Tinnelly and McElduff* (n 253) para 77. In *Mirilashvili* (n 297) para 203 the ECtHR distinguished the case from *Tinnelly* when considering that the decision to withhold certain documents was not taken by the prosecution unilaterally.

[318] *Liu v Russia* (n 252) para 88.

[319] *Rowe and Davis* (n 308) paras 63–66.

[320] See, eg *V* (n 306) para 78 and ECtHR 4 November 2010, *Bannikova v Russia*, no 18757/06, para 64.

[321] *Tinnelly and McElduff* (n 253) para 75. See for cases under Arts 8 and 13 ECHR eg *Lupsa* (n 255) para 41 and *Liu and Liu* (n 304) paras 61 and 63.

Assessment of Secret Evidence by the ECtHR

In criminal cases in which the identity of witnesses was not disclosed to the applicant, the ECtHR has itself assessed whether the reasons for such non-disclosure were 'relevant and sufficient'.[322] In criminal cases where evidence has been withheld from the defence of public interest grounds, the ECtHR does not consider it to be its role to decide whether or not such non-disclosure was strictly necessary. As a general rule, it is for the national courts to assess the evidence before them. The ECtHR has noted that in many cases it was not even in a position to perform a balancing test, as it had not been given the information.[323] The ECtHR thus pays deference to the national decision whether certain evidence should be kept confidential for national security reasons.[324] Instead, the ECtHR ensures that, as far as possible, 'the decision-making process complied with the requirements to provide adversarial proceedings and equality of arms and incorporated adequate safeguards to protect the interests of the accused'.[325]

In *Mirilashvili* the Court held that in situations involving 'national security' considerations for withholding documentary evidence, the Court has applied a less exacting standard than in cases concerning the use of anonymous witnesses. The Court considered, however, that 'that standard of scrutiny should not be applied automatically; the Court retains the power to assess independently whether the case involved national security considerations'.[326] In a few cases regarding Article 6 ECHR the Court did indeed examine (at least marginally) whether the non-disclosure of evidence was justified. The Court has generally held with regard to lustration proceedings, 'unless the contrary is shown on the facts of a specific case, it cannot be assumed that there remains a continuing and actual public interest in imposing limitations on access to materials classified as confidential under former regimes'.[327] It is for the government to prove an interest in keeping documents secret.[328] Furthermore, in *Aksoy* the Court considered that the case file did not contain any element which could justify the non-disclosure of the documents on national security grounds or for other relevant reasons.[329] In *A and others*, on the other hand, the Court concluded that on the material before it, the Court had 'no basis to find that excessive and unjustified secrecy was employed in respect of any

[322] See, eg *Doorson* (n 294) para 71 and *Haas* (n 296).

[323] See, eg *Jasper* (n 311) para 53; *Dowsett* (n 308) para 43; and *Pocius* (n 295) para 53.

[324] This is in line with the Court's opinion that the State's enjoy a wide margin of appreciation in their assessment whether national security justifies certain measures against a person, such as expulsion measures (see section 10.5.1). Summers states that the reason for the ECtHR's deference is that the Court is not interested in acting as a Court of fourth instance. Summers, *Fair Trials* (n 311) 118.

[325] See, eg *Jasper* (n 311), para 53; *Dowsett* (n 308) para 43; and ECtHR 6 July 2010 *Pocius v Lithuania*, no 35601/04, para 53.

[326] *Mirilashvili* (n 297) para 196.

[327] *Matyjek* (n 308) para 56.

[328] ECtHR 14 June 2011, *Mościcki v Poland*, no 52443/07, para 44.

[329] *Aksoy* (n 277) para 28. The Court was able to assess the documents withheld to the applicant, as they were sent to the Turkish High Court six years after the (national) proceedings against the applicant were concluded.

of the applicants' appeals or that there were not compelling reasons for the lack of disclosure in each case'.[330]

No cases were found in which the ECtHR addressed its own role in the assessment whether the non-disclosure of evidence to the applicant was justified under Articles 6(1) civil limb and 13 ECHR. In many expulsion cases under Article 13 the State did not send the confidential evidence to the ECtHR, sometimes in spite of its request to do so.[331]

10.5.4 Confidentiality versus the Right to Adversarial Proceedings

If there is an interest which legitimises a limitation to the right to adversarial proceedings, this interest and the right to adversarial proceedings must be balanced against each other. In *Tinnelly*, for example, the Court examined under Article 6(1) ECHR, civil limb

> whether there existed a reasonable relationship of proportionality between the concerns for the protection of national security invoked by the authorities and the impact which the means they employed to this end had on the applicants' right of access to a court or tribunal.[332]

In *A and others* the Court held that the important public interests of the State to maintain the secrecy of the sources of the information about al'Qaeda and its associates had to be balanced against the applicants' right to procedural fairness under Article 5(4) ECHR.[333]

It follows from the ECtHR's case law that the State's interest to protect the national security of the State weighs heavily and may justify important limitations to the right to adversarial proceedings. Less weight may be attached to other State interests such as the prosecution or prevention of crimes which do not affect national security. In *CG* the Court considered:

> While actions taken in the interests of national security may, in view of the sensitivity of the subject-matter and the serious potential consequences for the safety of the community, attract considerably less in terms of guarantees than might otherwise be the case, an expulsion designed to forestall lesser evils such as run-of-the-mill criminal activities may have to be reviewed in proceedings providing a higher degree of protection of the individual.[334]

In several cases the Court stressed the need for procedural safeguards while referring to what was at stake for the applicant.[335] In this section, it will be explained

[330] *A et al v UK* (n 264) para 219.
[331] See, eg *Raza* (n 259) para 5; and *Gulijev* (n 259) para 45.
[332] *Tinnelly and McElduff* (n 253) para 77. In the criminal context, see also *Fitt* (n 270) para 45.
[333] *A et al v UK* (n 264) paras 216–17.
[334] *CG* (n 251) para 45.
[335] *A et al v UK* (n 264) paras 217–18; *Matyjek* (n 308) para 59; *Aksoy* (n 277) para 27; and *Özpinar* (n 266) para 78.

how, in practice, the balance should be struck between the interest in keeping information confidential and the right to adversarial proceedings.

It was noted in sections 10.5.1 and 10.5.3 that national security concerns can never justify evidence underlying the contested decision being withheld from the national court or independent authority. The court must be informed of the reasons grounding the contested decision and it should assess the merits of the case, including the existence of a threat to national security.[336] This assessment by the court or independent authority is not sufficient. Certain procedural guarantees must be offered to the person concerned. The right to adversarial proceedings also requires that the person concerned is (in some way) informed of the decision and the reasons for it.[337] In *Raza* the ECtHR regarded as unwarranted the complete concealment from the public of the entirety of a judicial decision in an expulsion case in which (according to the government) national security issues were at stake.[338]

The Need for Compensation

When performing a balancing test the right to adversarial proceedings of the applicant must be sufficiently guaranteed. In this light in several cases under various provisions of the Convention the ECtHR have addressed possibilities for compensation of limitations of the right to adversarial proceedings, notably the use of special advocates. In its assessment whether the right to adversarial proceedings has been infringed, the Court further takes into account the weight of the confidential evidence and the specificity of the open material in the case at hand. The issues of compensation and weight of confidential evidence will be discussed below.

In criminal cases and in cases in which the Court applied the guarantees flowing from the criminal limb of Article 6 ECHR,[339] the ECtHR held that 'in order to ensure that the accused receives a fair trial any difficulties caused to the defence by a limitation on its rights must be 'sufficiently counterbalanced by the procedures followed by the judicial authorities'.[340] In the Grand Chamber judgments *Jasper* and *Fitt*, the Court was satisfied that the decision-making procedure complied with the requirement of adversarial proceedings, although the defence did not have the opportunity to examine whether the evidence which was not disclosed to it, could be used in its favour. The Court took into account that the national court assessed whether the evidence had to be disclosed to the defence and that this court stated that it would have ordered disclosure if this 'did or might help

[336] See, eg under Art 6(1), civil limb *Tinnelly and McElduff* (n 253) para 77; *Devenney* (n 253) and under Arts 8 and 13 ECHR *Al-Nashif* (n 216).

[337] See *CG* (n 251) para 46; *Lupsa* (n 255) para 58. See under Art (6)(1) civil limb also *Devenney* (n 253) para 27.

[338] *Raza* (n 259) para 53.

[339] See *A et al v UK* (n 264) para 218.

[340] *Fitt* (n 270) para 45; *Jasper* (n 311) para 52; *Doorson* (n 294) paras 72–73.

further the defence'.[341] The national court was in a position to effectively perform this assessment as it was fully versed in all evidence and issues in the case. Furthermore, during the course of the hearing the defence was able to argue the case for disclosure and to hear the arguments of the prosecution court's reasons for not ordering complete disclosure. In *Fitt*, the defence was also provided with a summary of the witness statement which was kept confidential.[342] In these circumstances the Court did not find it necessary for a special advocate to participate in the proceedings.[343]

It should be noted that in *Jasper* and *Fitt* a substantial minority of the Court found that a violation of Article 6(1) ECHR occurred and that a special advocate should be introduced in criminal proceedings in which confidential evidence is used. In their opinion in *Jasper* the dissenters took into account that the defence were not aware of the category of material which the prosecution sought to withhold from them and were not informed of the reasons for the judge's decision that the material should not be disclosed. However, in *Fitt*, where the defence were informed of the category of material which the prosecution sought to withhold and received an edited summary of the material, the dissenters were also of the opinion that the unfairness created by the defence's absence from the ex parte proceedings could not be remedied by the fact that the judge monitored the need for disclosure of the evidence during the trial.[344] In ex parte proceedings such as were applied in *Jasper*, *Fitt* and *Edwards and Lewis*, the judge examined the evidence which the prosecution wanted to keep secret without the presence of the defence counsel. There are three options in such proceedings:

1. the defence is informed of the category of the materials held by the prosecution and is able to make representations to the court;
2. the defence is not informed of the category of those materials; and
3. the defence is not informed of the fact that an ex parte application was made.[345]

In several other cases the Court did not accept the domestic court's decision that there was no need to disclose evidence to the defence. It found a violation of Article 6(1) ECHR because potentially exculpatory evidence was withheld from the applicant.[346]

[341] For a different view, see *Leas* (n 271) para 88.

[342] *Fitt* (n 270) para 47.

[343] Ibid, paras 47–49; *Jasper* (n 311) paras 54–56. See also *McKeaown* (n 316).

[344] See the dissenting Opinions of Judges Palm, Fischbach, Vajić, Thomassen, Tsatsa-Nikolovska and Traja, of Judge Zupančič and of Judge Hedigan with the *Jasper* and *Fitt* cases.

[345] See ECtHR 22 July 2003, *Edwards and Lewis v the United Kingdom*, nos 39647/98 and 40461/98, para 34.

[346] Ibid, para 58. This judgment was confirmed by the Grand Chamber. ECtHR (GC) 27 October 2004, *Edwards and Lewis v the United Kingdom*, nos 39647/98 and 40461/98 and *Rowe and Davis* (n 308) paras 63–65, where it concerned evidence which could have been used to undermine the credibility of a key prosecution witness.

Special Advocates

The use of special advocates or special counsels as a technique to compensate for limitations of the right to adversarial proceedings in cases in which evidence is not disclosed to a party for national security reasons, was first mentioned by the ECtHR in the *Chahal* judgment. In this case intervening parties drew the Court's attention to a system applied in Canada in such cases. The interveners described the system as follows:

> [A] Federal Court judge holds an in camera hearing of all the evidence, at which the applicant is provided with a statement summarising, as far as possible, the case against him or her and has the right to be represented and to call evidence. The confidentiality of security material is maintained by requiring such evidence to be examined in the absence of both the applicant and his or her representative. However, in these circumstances, their place is taken by a security-cleared counsel instructed by the court, who cross-examines the witnesses and generally assists the court to test the strength of the State's case. A summary of the evidence obtained by this procedure, with necessary deletions, is given to the applicant.[347]

In its assessment of the complaint under Article 5(4) ECHR the Court attached significance to the existence of such a system in Canada. In its view this example 'illustrates that there are techniques which can be employed which both accommodate legitimate security concerns about the nature and sources of intelligence information and yet accord the individual a substantial measure of procedural justice'.[348] After the *Chahal* judgment, the UK also introduced a special advocate system.[349] In several later cases under Articles 5(4), 6(1), 8 and 13 ECHR the Court again referred to the existence of special techniques, without expressing itself on the question of whether such system would comply with those provisions.[350]

In *A and others* the ECtHR finally assessed the compatibility with Article 5(4) ECHR of the special advocate procedure introduced in the UK. In the UK the confidential evidence was disclosed only to a special advocate who acted on behalf of the applicant. During the closed sessions before the SIAC the special advocate could make submissions on behalf of the applicant on procedural matters, including the need for (further) disclosure of evidence as well as the substance of the case. From the moment the special advocate had sight of the closed material, he could not have any further contact with the applicant or his representative save with the permission of the SIAC.[351]

The ECtHR ruled that it depends on the circumstances of the case, in particular the specificity of the information disclosed to the party concerned, whether the

[347] Chahal (n 4) para 144.

[348] Ibid, para 131.

[349] D Bonner, 'Checking the Executive? Detention Without Trial, Control Orders, Due Process and Human Rights' (2006) 12 *European Public Law* 45, 54.

[350] See, eg *Al-Nashif* (n 216) paras 95–97 and 137; *Tinnelly and McElduff* (n 253) para 78; *Devenney* (n 253) para 28; and ECtHR 13 December 2007, *Dagtekin v Turkey*, no 70516/01, para 34. See also *A et al v UK* (n 264) paras 209 and 211.

[351] *A et al v UK* (n 264) para 215.

use of a special advocate would sufficiently compensate this party's lack of access to documents. It considered that 'the special advocate could perform an important role in counterbalancing the lack of full disclosure and the lack of a full, open, adversarial hearing by testing the evidence and putting arguments on behalf of the detainee during the closed hearings'.[352] However, the Court also noted 'that the special advocate could not perform this function in any useful way unless the detainee was provided with sufficient information about the allegations against him to enable him to give effective instructions to the special advocate'.[353] The Court concluded in *A and others* that the right to adversarial proceedings had been infringed in respect of several of the applicants. The Court's considerations regarding the nature of the (non-) disclosed evidence will be addressed below.

In *Othman* the applicant argued that, as in *A and others*, his right to adversarial proceedings had been violated during the proceedings before the SIAC even though special advocates were used during the closed sessions. The ECtHR rightly sees a critical difference between the *A and others* case and the *Othman* case. In *Othman* the SIAC did not discuss allegations against Othman in its closed sessions (at least not in so far as the risk of *refoulement* upon return to Jordan was concerned). It heard evidence with regard to the negotiations preceding the agreement of a MoU between the UK and Jordan and the question whether this MoU would take away the risk of *refoulement* upon return to Jordan. The ECtHR finds that 'there is no evidence that, by receiving closed evidence on that issue, SIAC, assisted by the special advocates, failed to give rigorous scrutiny to the applicant's claim'.[354] Neither was there an unacceptable risk of an incorrect result that had not been mitigated by the presence of the special advocates. Finally, the ECtHR considers that the issues (potentially) discussed before the SIAC, such as the United States' interest in the applicant, were of a very general nature. According to the Court there 'is no reason to suppose that, had the applicant seen this closed evidence, he would have been able to challenge the evidence in a manner that the special advocates could not'.[355]

Other Compensation Techniques

As well as the use of special advocates, several other compensation techniques were reviewed by the ECtHR. In *Doorson* the Court found that the limitations to the right to adversarial proceedings were sufficiently counterbalanced as the anonymous witnesses were questioned by an investigating judge who was aware of their identity. The council for the defence was present at this hearing and was in a position to ask questions to the witnesses, which were all answered.[356]

[352] Ibid, para 220.
[353] Ibid, para 220.
[354] *Othman* (n 289) para 223.
[355] Ibid, para 224.
[356] *Doorson* (n 294) para 73.

In several criminal cases the Court took into account that a non-confidential summary of the relevant evidence was sent to the applicant and that the applicant was able to contest the information contained in the summary.[357] In *Botmeh and Alami* the extent of the disclosure to the applicants of the withheld material by the Court of Appeal in a summary was one of the factors which lead to the Court's conclusion that the appeal proceedings complied with Article 6(1) ECHR.[358] In *Haliti*, a case decided under Articles 8 and 13 ECHR, the ECtHR also considered that the national court disclosed documents to the applicant and that it provided summaries of the relevant parts of the undisclosed information. Therefore, according to the Court, the applicant was in a position to contest the allegations against him.[359]

In *Matyjek*, in which the applicant faced lustration proceedings (a criminal charge), the applicant had access to his case file (including confidential information) after the institution of the lustration proceedings. However, the applicant could consult the confidential documents only in the secret registry of the lustration court and was not allowed to make copies of the documents or to take notes out of the registry.[360]

> [T]he accused's effective participation in his criminal trial must equally include the right to compile notes in order to facilitate the conduct of his defence, irrespective of whether or not he is represented by counsel .... The fact that the applicant could not remove his own notes, taken either at the hearing or in the secret registry, in order to show them to an expert or to use them for any other purpose, effectively prevented him from using the information contained in them as he had to rely solely on his memory.[361]

It is important to note that the ECtHR held earlier in this judgment that in lustration proceedings, such as in the case at hand, it cannot be assumed that there remains a continuing and actual public interest in imposing limited access to materials, unless the contrary is shown in a specific case.[362] Therefore, it may be assumed that limitations to the right to adversarial proceedings were addressed more critically by the ECtHR than in cases in which the non-disclosure was justified. However, this judgment does show that the right to adversarial proceedings is seriously limited by the fact that a party cannot make copies or notes of documents used in his case.

[357] *Fitt* (n 270) para 47.

[358] *Botmeh and Alami* (n 314) paras 43–44.

[359] *Haliti* (n 255).

[360] Any notes the applicant took could only be made in special notebooks that were subsequently sealed and deposited in the secret registry. The notebooks could not be removed from this registry and could be opened only by the person who had made them.

[361] *Matyjek* (n 308) para 59. The Court also found a violation of the principle of equality of arms in this case because the State party had unrestricted access to the confidential documents. See also ECtHR 8 June 2010, *Górny v Poland*, no 50399/07, para 37 and ECtHR 31 May 2011, *Zawisza v Poland*, no 37293/09, where the restrictions with regard to taking notes and making copies of documents were also applied to the applicant's lawyers.

[362] See further section 10.5.3.

In *Tinnelly and McElduff*, the ECtHR rejected the State's argument that mechanisms, such as the Independent Commission for Police Complaints and the statutory controls on the activities of the security services, which assured the accountability of the police and the security services in the performance of their intelligence-gathering functions could compensate for the limitations to the applicants' right of access to court.[363]

Limited Weight of Information Supplied by Anonymous Sources

In *Sufi and Elmi* and *HR*, both asylum cases decided under Article 3 ECHR, the ECtHR considered that limited weight should be attached to country of origin information, which was obtained by the State from sources whose identity was not disclosed to the ECtHR. In these cases the ECtHR did not mention the right to adversarial proceedings. However, it may be assumed that the ECtHR did have the protection of this right in mind when deciding the case. The ECtHR held that 'in the absence of any information about the nature of the sources' operations in the relevant area, it will be virtually impossible for the Court to assess their reliability'.[364] In *Sufi and Elmi* the ECtHR found that the description of the sources relied on were vague ('a diplomatic source', or 'a security advisor'). According to the ECtHR, such descriptions give no indication of the authority or reputation of the sources or of the extent of their presence in the region concerned. In *HR* the State authorities consulted Algerian lawyers on the consequences of the lifting of the state of emergency in Algeria. The ECtHR considered that the French Government had not given details concerning the circumstances of this consultation or the identity of the lawyers consulted. Therefore, the ECtHR could not assess their independence vis-à-vis the power in place or the reliability of their statements.[365]

The ECtHR generally exercises caution when considering information from anonymous sources which is inconsistent with the remainder of the information before it. However 'where the sources' conclusions are consistent with other country information, their evidence may be of corroborative weight'.[366] In *Sufi and Elmi* very little other information was available to the ECtHR. Therefore it was impossible for the Court 'to carry out any assessment of the sources' reliability and, as a consequence, where their information is unsupported or contradictory, the Court is unable to attach substantial weight to it'.[367] In *HR* the ECtHR did not attach much, if any, weight to the statements of the anonymous Algerian lawyers. It may be derived from this case law that national courts who do not know the sources of information supporting the asylum decision, should attach limited

[363] *Tinnelly and McElduff* (n 253) para 77.
[364] *Sufi and Elmi* (n 263) para 233.
[365] *HR* (n 263) para 61.
[366] *Sufi and Elmi* (n 263) para 233.
[367] Ibid, para 234.

weight to this information. Asylum decisions cannot be based to a decisive extent only on information provided by anonymous sources.

The judgments in *Sufi and Elmi* and *HR* are in line with the ECtHR's case law concerning anonymous witnesses in criminal cases under Article 6(1) ECHR. In such cases the ECtHR applies the so called 'sole or decisive' rule. This rule implies that

> when a conviction is based solely or to a decisive degree on depositions that have been made by a person whom the accused has had no opportunity to examine or to have examined, whether during the investigation or at the trial, the rights of the defence may be restricted to an extent that is incompatible with the guarantees provided by Article 6.[368]

The question whether the evidence of an anonymous or absent witness is decisive depends on the strength of the supportive evidence: 'the stronger the corroborative evidence, the less likely that the evidence of the absent witness will be treated as decisive'.[369] According to the ECtHR, the sole or decisive rule is based on

> the principle that the greater the importance of the evidence, the greater the potential unfairness to the defendant in allowing the witness to remain anonymous or to be absent from the trial and the greater the need for safeguards to ensure that the evidence is demonstrably reliable or that its reliability can properly be tested and assessed.[370]

The Court stresses that the sole or decisive rule must be applied flexibly and that the fairness of the procedure as a whole must be assessed. This means that the use of the evidence of an anonymous or absent witness as the sole or decisive evidence in a case does not always lead to a violation of Article 6 ECHR. However, in such a situation procedural guarantees should be very strong.[371] In the case of *Al-Khawadja*, a conviction was based to a decisive extent on the statement of a witness who had died and therefore could not be questioned in court. The ECtHR found that there was no violation of Article 6 ECHR, notwithstanding the difficulties caused to the defence by admitting this witness statement and the dangers of doing so. According to the court there were sufficient counterbalancing factors. There were corroborating statements of witnesses who were questioned in court. Moreover, the jury was told that the witness statement should be granted less weight as the witness could not be cross-examined.[372] In the case of *Tahery* the only direct evidence against the applicant was an untested statement of the only prosecution eyewitness. In this case the ECtHR found a violation of Article 6 ECHR because in its opinion the judge's warning to the jury that it is dangerous to rely on untested evidence, however clearly or forcibly expressed, could not be a sufficient counterbalance. The decisive nature of the witness statement in the

[368] *Al-Khawadja and Tahery* (n 294) para 119.
[369] Ibid, para 131.
[370] Ibid, para 139.
[371] *Al-Khawadja and Tahery* (n 294) paras 143–47.
[372] Ibid, paras 153–58. See also *Haas* (n 296).

absence of any strong corroborative evidence in the case 'meant the jury in this case were unable to conduct a fair and proper assessment' of the reliability of the witness's evidence.[373]

The Weight and Specificity of Other Evidence

In *Jasper* and *Fitt* the ECtHR took into account the guarantees in place in the procedure in which it was decided whether or not evidence should be disclosed to the defence. Another important reason for its refusal to accept that a special advocate procedure was necessary in those cases was that the material which was not disclosed did not form any part of the prosecution case and was not put to the jury.[374] In *Botmeh and Alami* the ECtHR took into account that the undisclosed material was found by the domestic court 'to add nothing of significance to what had already been disclosed at trial'.[375]

In *Edwards and Lewis* and *Rowe and Davis* the Court did find a violation of Article 6 ECHR on the basis that (potentially) relevant information was not disclosed to the defence. In *Edwards and Lewis* the Court considered that the undisclosed evidence related or may have related to an issue of fact decided by the trial judge, namely whether the applicants had been the victim of improper incitement by the police. The trial judge had reviewed the undisclosed material and had concluded that he had heard nothing and seen no material which would have assisted the defence in their argument that evidence should be excluded on the basis that the applicant had been entrapped into committing the offence. The ECtHR held that because the applicants were denied access to the evidence, it was not possible for the defence representatives to argue the case of entrapment in full before the judge. Moreover, the non-disclosed evidence (potentially) included allegations which may have undermined the applicants' submissions on entrapment. The applicants and their representatives were not informed about the nature of the evidence and therefore could not defend themselves against these allegations.[376]

In *Rowe and Davis* the Court found a violation of Article 6(1) ECHR on the basis that evidence, which could have been used to undermine the credibility of a key prosecution witness, was withheld by the prosecution from both the defence and the trial judge at first instance, its non-disclosure on grounds of public interest immunity subsequently being ordered by the Court of Appeal following an ex parte hearing. According to the ECtHR, the procedure before the appeal court was

[373] *Al-Khawadja and Tahery* (n 294) paras 159–65.

[374] *Jasper* (n 311) para 55; *Fitt* (n 270) para 48. According to Harris et al the Court was strongly influenced by the fact that the non-disclosed evidence formed no part of the prosecution case and was not put to the jury. Harris et al, *Law of the European Convention on Human Rights* (n 269) 255.

[375] *Botmeh and Alami* (n 314) para 44.

[376] *Edwards and Lewis* (n 345) para 58. This judgment was confirmed by *Edwards and Lewis* (GC) (n 346).

not sufficient to remedy the unfairness caused at the trial by the absence of any scrutiny of the withheld information by the trial judge.[377]

It seems to follow from *Rowe and Davis* and *Edwards and Lewis* that in criminal cases inculpatory evidence and evidence which is potentially relevant to a person's defence should be disclosed. Unlike in *Fitt* and *Jasper*, the ECtHR did not follow the domestic court(s)' ruling that the confidential material would not assist the defence.[378]

In cases in which the requirements flowing from the criminal limb of Article 6(1) ECHR were applied, such as *Pocius* and *A and others*, the weight of the non-disclosed evidence for the outcome of the proceedings was also taken into account.[379] In *A and others* the Court held that the right to adversarial proceedings would be respected in two situations where:

- the evidence was to a large extent disclosed and the open material plays a predominant role in the determination; or
- all or most of the underlying evidence is not disclosed, but the allegations in the open material are sufficiently specific. It must be possible for the applicant to provide his representatives and the special advocate with information with which to refute these allegations.

The judgment gives several examples of sufficiently specific allegations: the allegation that a person attended a terrorist training camp at a stated location between stated dates, detailed allegations about the purchase of specific telecommunications equipment, possession of specific documents linked to named terrorist suspects and meetings with named terrorist suspects with specific dates and places.[380] The ECtHR also held, with regard to Article 8 ECHR, that the allegations against a person must be sufficiently specific.[381]

The procedural requirements under Article 5(4) ECHR would not be satisfied when all or most of the evidence underlying the detention decision is not disclosed and the open material consists purely of general allegations. With regard to several applicants the Court found that the right to adversarial proceedings had been infringed. Two applicants were accused of being involved in fund-raising for terrorist groups linked to al'Qaeda. The link between the money raised and

[377] *Rowe and Davis* (n 308) paras 63–65. See also the summary of this case in *Botmeh and Alami* (n 314) para 38. The undisclosed information concerned, amongst others, person(s) to whom reward money had been paid for information given to the police regarding the applicants.

[378] This may have to do with the fact that in *Edwards and Lewis* and *Rowe and Davis* the ECtHR knew the nature of the evidence withheld from the defence while it did not in *Fitt* and *Jasper*.

[379] *Pocius* (n 295) para 56, where the Court considered that the information contained in the non-disclosed operational records file was deemed to be essential evidence of the applicant's alleged danger to society. See under Art 8 ECHR, *Gulijev* (n 259) para 44, where the Court took into account that the 'secret' report was not only used as evidence, but, according to the information in the case file, it was also the sole ground for not granting the applicant a temporary residence permit. See also *Bannikova* (n 320) para 63.

[380] *A et al v UK* (n 264) para 220.

[381] *Liu v Russia* (n 252) para 90.

terrorism was not disclosed. Therefore, the Court considered that these applicants were not in a position to effectively challenge the allegations against them. The Court reached the same conclusion in respect of two other applicants. The open allegations concerning them were of a general nature—principally that they were members of named extremist Islamist groups linked to al'Qaeda.

In *A and others* the Court did not prevent inculpatory evidence from being disclosed to the detainee, as long as the open allegations were sufficiently precise. In addition, the Court did not address the issue of the potential non-disclosure of exculpatory evidence. The ECtHR seems to be less strict with regard to the actual use of secret information in *A and others* than it is in criminal cases. This may have to do with the strict standard of proof in criminal cases: a person may only be convicted when a crime is proven beyond reasonable doubt. A detention measure is justified where one of the conditions of Article 5(1) is fulfilled.

10.5.5 Subconclusion: The Use of Secret Information under International Law

The ECtHR has addressed the use of secret evidence principally under the right to adversarial proceedings and the principle of equality of arms. These principles apply to all procedures governed by Articles 5(4), 6, 8, 9, 13 and Article 1 of Protocol 7 ECHR. The general requirements following from these principles seem to be the same with regard to all these Articles. However, the level of procedural protection offered by these principles depends on the nature of the case at issue. Arguably, the highest level of protection is required in criminal cases under Article 6 ECHR, while in cases concerning secret surveillance and the screening of job candidates, the remedy within the meaning of Article 13 only needs to be 'as effective as can be'. It is argued here that in asylum cases, in the light of the absolute nature of the prohibition of *refoulement*, a high level of procedural protection is required.

The ECHR has accepted that the right to adversarial proceedings and the principle of equality of arms are not absolute and that there may be legitimate reasons to limit them. Most of the cases assessed by the court concerned measures aimed at protecting the national security of the State. In those cases national security was often also the reason for not disclosing certain relevant information to the parties involved in the proceedings. The ECtHR has accepted that States enjoy a wide margin of appreciation in their assessment of what measures are necessary to protect national security. It also recognised that national security reasons may justify the non-disclosure of evidence to a person affected by such a measure. However, the ECtHR also made clear that States cannot escape judicial review when invoking national security as the basis for a measure or for its refusal to communicate relevant evidence to the party concerned. Sufficient guarantees must be in place to prevent arbitrariness and to ensure that the right to adversarial proceedings and the principle of equality of arms are respected.

From the ECtHR's case law several minimum standards may be withdrawn, which apply to all cases falling within the scope of Articles 5(4), 6, 8, 9, 13 and Article 1 of Protocol 7 ECHR and therefore also to asylum cases:

— Limitations to the right to adversarial proceedings must pursue a legitimate aim. Interests which may justify such limitations are the protection of national security, the need to protect sources of information or witnesses at risk of reprisals, and the need to keep secret police methods of investigation of crime.
— The non-disclosure of relevant evidence should be necessary and appropriate to pursue this legitimate aim.
— The national court must receive the secret evidence. This court should review whether the non-disclosure of evidence is necessary and review on the basis of that evidence the facts and circumstances of the case. Limited weight should be attached to evidence provided by anonymous sources, whose reliability cannot be examined by the court.
— If a legitimate interest justifies the non-disclosure of the evidence to the party concerned, the interest of the State to keep the evidence secret must be balanced against the right to adversarial proceedings. When carrying out this balancing test the nature of the case at issue must be taken into account. Some form of adversarial proceedings must always be guaranteed. Limitations of the right to adversarial proceedings should be compensated, for example by using a special advocate who assesses and comments on secret evidence on behalf of the party concerned or by using non-confidential summaries.
— When assessing whether the right to adversarial proceedings has been complied with, the weight of the non-disclosed evidence and the specificity of the open material should be taken into account. The right to adversarial proceedings will generally not be violated if limited weight was attached to the secret evidence underlying a decision. However, a person is not able to effectively challenge allegations against him if the open material only contains general allegations.

The ECtHR has addressed the use of secret information in only a few asylum cases. In *Sufi and Elmi*[382] and *HR*.[383] it made clear that limited weight should be attached to information provided by anonymous sources, whose reliability and independence cannot be checked by the Court. The ECtHR has not mentioned the right to adversarial proceedings in those cases or addressed the level of procedural protection which should be offered in *refoulement* cases. In *Othman* the ECtHR considered that the standards developed under Article 13 ECHR in its judgments in *CG*, *Kaushal* and *A v the Netherlands* applied to the use of secret information concerning diplomatic assurances between an extraditing State and

[382] *Sufi and Elmi* (n 263) para 233.
[383] *HR* (n 263) para 61.

the receiving State in a case concerning Article 3 ECHR.[384] It is not excluded however, that where allegations against the applicant (for example, as to the credibility of his asylum account) play a role in the assessment of a risk of *refoulement* a higher level of protection should be applied. In the light of the potential severe consequences for the person concerned of expulsion in violation of the prohibition of *refoulement*, it may be argued that in such cases the same fair trial guarantees as those required under the criminal limb of Article 6(1) should apply. This would mean in particular that limitations to the right to adversarial proceedings, in particular where it concerns allegations against the asylum applicant, are only allowed if they are 'strictly necessary'. The ECtHR has applied the fair trial guarantees in other non-criminal cases in the light of the serious nature of the case. One example of such a case is *A and others*, where the ECtHR pointed at 'the dramatic impact of the lengthy—and what appeared at the time to be indefinite—deprivation of liberty'.

In the conclusion I will address the question how the ECHR standards relate to and should be incorporated into the relevant general principles of EU law. As the case law discussed in this chapter only concerns appeal proceedings before national courts, it may inspire the interpretation of the EU right to an effective remedy.

10.6 SYNTHESIS OF FINDINGS

Article 16 of Directive 2005/85/EC provides the legal adviser or other counsellor who assists or represents the asylum applicant with a right of access to such information in the applicant's file as is liable to be examined by the court providing an effective remedy against the asylum decision, insofar as the information is relevant to the examination of the application. This provision allows for limitations to the applicant's right of access to the file on several grounds. It also provides that information may be withheld from the court, as mentioned in Article 39 of Directive 2005/85/EC, on national security grounds.

Article 23(1) of Directive 2013/32/EU also allows Member States to refuse the applicant and his legal representative access to (part of) the file on the same grounds as those mentioned in Article 16 of Directive 20015/85/EC. However, Article 23(1) requires Member States to make access to secret information or sources available to the court or tribunal assessing the appeal against the asylum decision in accordance with Article 46 of the Directive. Furthermore, it states that asylum proceedings must guarantee the applicant's rights of defence, for example by using special advocates.

On the basis of the case law of the EU Courts discussed in this chapter, it should be expected that these provisions will be tested against, and/or interpreted

[384] *Othman* (n 286).

in the light of, the rights of the defence including the right to be heard during the administrative phase and the right to a reasoned decision (Article 41 of the Charter) and the right to an effective remedy (Article 47 of the Charter and Article 39 of Directive 2005/85/EC and Article 46 of Directive 2013/32/EU). The extensive case law of the ECtHR regarding the right to adversarial proceedings and the use of secret evidence provides for important guidance as to the interpretation of these EU rights. The following conclusions should be drawn:

The Right of Access to the File

— According to the case law of the Court of Justice and the ECtHR the rights of the defence can only be infringed if documents *which are relevant to the case* (inculpatory or exculpatory) are not disclosed to the party concerned. No access needs to be provided to information which could not have influenced the course of the asylum proceedings.[385]
— In asylum proceedings secret evidence may be relevant to the assessment of the credibility of the asylum account or the risk of persecution or serious harm upon expulsion to the country of origin (prohibition of *refoulement*).[386]

Legitimate Aim and Necessity of Non-disclosure

— Limitations to the EU right to be heard during the administrative phase, the right to a reasoned decision and the right to an effective remedy may be justified: the limitation must have a *legitimate aim* and it should be *necessary* and *proportionate*. Furthermore, such limitations must respect the essence of those rights and they must genuinely meet objectives of general interest recognised by the Union.[387]
— Article 16(1) of Directive 2005/85/EC and Article 23(1) of Directive 2013/32/EU mention several grounds which may justify the use of secret information in asylum cases: the protection of the security of organisations or of person(s) providing the information or the security of the person(s) to whom the information relates; the investigative interests relating to the examination of applications of asylum by the competent authorities of the Member States; and the international relations or the national security of the Member States. On the basis of the case law of the Court of Justice and the ECtHR it may be

[385] *Imperial Chemical Industries v Commission* (n 9) para 78. The ECtHR refers to 'the entitlement to disclosure of *relevant* evidence' (emphasis added). See, eg *Rowe and Davis* (n 308) para 61.

[386] Secret evidence may also be used in order to exclude a person from refugee status or subsidiary protection status (right to asylum). Exclusion from asylum status falls outside the scope of this study.

[387] *ZZ* (n 15) paras 54 and 57, *Aalborg Portland et al v Commission* (n 52) para 68 and *Kadi and Al Barakaat v Council and Commission* (n 17) para 342. For the ECtHR see *Fitt* (n 270) para 45 and *A et al v UK* (n 264) para 218.

expected that those grounds will be accepted as legitimate aims for keeping information secret in asylum cases.

— Arguably, in the light of the absolute nature of the prohibition of *refoulement*, evidence on which the assessment of the risk of persecution or serious harm is based, may only be kept secret in 'exceptional cases' if this is 'strictly necessary'.[388] This is the same test as that required by the Court of Justice in cases of expulsion of EU citizens and by the ECtHR under Article 6 ECHR in criminal cases.[389]

— It is not solely up to the administrative authorities, but also for the national court within the meaning of Article 39 of Directive 2005/85/EC and Article 46 of Directive 2013/32/EU to decide whether non-disclosure of evidence pursues a legitimate aim and is necessary.[390] Furthermore, the use of secret evidence may not prevent the national court from thoroughly reviewing the risk of *refoulement*.[391]

— The national court must in principle receive all relevant information underlying the asylum decision, including the evidence which was not disclosed to the person concerned.[392] Article 16(1) of Directive 2005/85/EC which allows authorities to refuse disclosure of relevant information to the national court on national security grounds should thus be considered to be at variance with the EU right to an effective remedy and should be declared void.

The Need for Secrecy of Information versus the Right of Access to the File

— The protection of secret information must be observed in such a way as to reconcile it with the EU right to an effective remedy, the right to be heard and the duty to state reasons. The conflicting interests of the parties concerned must be balanced.[393]

— A total lack of disclosure of grounds for the decision and evidence is never allowed. The (asylum) decision should state sufficiently precise reasons in order to enable the applicant to effectively exercise his right to an effective remedy guaranteed by Article 39 of Directive 2005/85/EC and Article 46 of Directive 2013/32/EU.[394] According to the Court of Justice, the statement

[388] *ZZ* (n 15) paras 57 and 69.

[389] *Fitt* (n 270) para 45.

[390] *ZZ* (n 15) paras 58, 60–62 and *Rowe and Davis* (n 308) para 63.

[391] Case C-69/10 *Samba Diouf* [2011] ECR 7151. The required standard of judicial review of the establishment and qualification of the facts is discussed in ch 9, section 9.2 in this volume.

[392] *Mobistar* (n 26) para 40, *Varec* (n 15) para 53. See also the ECtHR's judgments under Arts 6 and 8 and 13 ECHR where the ECtHR held that substantive review of the grounds motivating a decision is impaired when the court assessing a case does not have sight of the material on which the decision is based.

[393] *Varec* (n 15) para 51; *Kadi and Al Barakaat v Council and Commission* (n 17) para 344; and *A et al v UK* (n 264) paras 216–17.

[394] *Modjahedines du peuple d'Iran v Council* (n 10) paras 150–51.

of reasons must as a minimum explain the essence of the case against the person concerned.[395] In this regard, it is relevant whether the applicant was aware of the general context of the restrictive measures concerned.[396] Furthermore, the specificity of the reasons should be taken into account. A statement of reasons which refers to specific acts, names of persons or organisations involved in such acts, dates or periods or other details is considered sufficient by the EU Courts.[397] At least one of the reasons given for the decision must be sufficient to support the decision.[398]

— This does not mean, however, that all inculpatory or potential exculpatory evidence underlying the asylum decision must be fully disclosed to the asylum applicant.[399] In this light the ECtHR's judgment in *A and others* provides for important guidance. It follows from this judgment that the right to adversarial proceedings is not violated where the evidence was to a large extent disclosed to the applicant and the open material plays a predominant role in the determination, or where the allegations in the open material are sufficiently specific. A negative asylum decision based on documents in which most crucial information is not disclosed thus infringes the right to adversarial proceedings.[400]

— It may further be derived from the case law of the EU Courts as well as the ECtHR that the weight which is attached to the confidential material for the decision should be taken into account when assessing whether the rights of the defence have been infringed in an asylum case.[401] For example, a decision that an asylum account is not credible should be considered problematic if it is based only on the statements of an anonymous source.

— The Court of Justice as well as the ECtHR have recognised that the credibility of evidence of anonymous origin is necessarily reduced by the fact that the context in which it was drafted is largely unknown and the administrative authority's assertions in that regard cannot be verified.[402]

Using Compensation Techniques

— Special techniques, such as the use of special advocates, non-confidential summaries or a list of all the documents in the file, may be used in order

395 *ZZ* (n 15) para 68.

396 *Council v Bamba* (n 10) para 54.

397 *Commission et al v Kadi* (n 16) paras 143–50.

398 Ibid, para 130.

399 *ZZ* (n 15) paras 67–68.

400 *A et al v UK* (n 264) para 220.

401 See, eg *Salzgitter Mannesmann v Commission* (n 42) para 47; *A et al v UK* (n 264) para 200; *Al-Khawadja and Tahery* (n 294).

402 *Salzgitter Mannesmann v Commission* (n 42) para 46, *Sufi and Elmi* (n 263) para 233, *HR* (n 263) para 61. See also *ZZ* (n 15) para 67.

to compensate the use of secret information. Anonymous witnesses may be questioned by an (investigative) judge.

- In some EU sanction cases the EU Courts have referred to the special counsel procedure mentioned by the ECtHR. At the time of writing, the EU Courts have not applied such techniques or assessed their compatibility with EU procedural rights. It should be derived from the ECtHR's judgment in *A and others* that a special advocate who could test the non-disclosed evidence and put arguments on behalf of the applicant during closed hearings could perform an important role in counterbalancing the lack of full disclosure and the lack of a full, open, adversarial hearing. However, the Court also held that the special advocate must be able to perform this function in a useful way. This is only possible if the applicant is provided with sufficiently specific information about the allegations against him (see above) in order to give effective instructions to the special advocate.[403]
- Another way to compensate for the non-disclosure of evidence is the use of non-confidential summaries.[404] The information disclosed in such summaries should be sufficiently precise to enable the person concerned to determine whether the deleted information is likely to be relevant for his case and to express his view on it.[405]
- It may be derived from the EU right to be heard that the applicant must be placed in a position to effectively respond to the information underlying the decision before the asylum decision is taken, unless there are specific reasons which justify that a hearing is omitted during the administrative phase. Therefore, compensation techniques such as non-confidential summaries and/or a special advocate system should generally be provided to the asylum applicant during the administrative phase. An infringement of the right to be heard and the duty to state reasons cannot be compensated during the appeal phase.[406]

[403] *A et al v UK* (n 264) para 220.

[404] *Commission et al v Kadi* (n 16) para 129.

[405] Case T-410/03, *Hoechst v Commission* [2008] ECR II-881, para 154.

[406] *Aalborg Portland et al v Commission* (n 52) para 104 and Case C-51/92 P, *Hercules Chemicals v Commission* [1999] paras 78–79. AG Bot suggests in his Opinion in Case C-277/11, *M v Minister for Justice, Equality and Law Reform Ireland*, paras 76–78 that this may be different in asylum cases which are quasi-criminal in nature. In EU sanction cases EU authorities are not required to hear the party concerned before the first decision to freeze funds because this would undermine the effectiveness of the sanction. See *Kadi and Al Barakaat v Council and Commission* (n 17) paras 338–41.

Part III

Conclusions

11

Towards a Common and Fair European Asylum Procedure?

THIS STUDY BEGAN by underlining the importance of adequate and fair procedures for the effective exercise of rights granted under EU law. In the following chapters it was shown that the EU Courts have recognised this importance. The case law of the Court of Justice concerning the EU right to an effective remedy has considerably limited the procedural autonomy of Member States. There is no reason to believe that asylum procedures will escape the influence of the Court of Justice. The need for procedural guarantees is as great in asylum procedures as in any other field of EU law. As AG Bot considered, with regard to the applicability of the EU right to be heard in asylum cases:

> Indeed, in this type of procedure, which inherently entails difficult personal and practical circumstances and in which the essential rights of the person concerned must clearly be protected, the observance of this procedural safeguard is of cardinal importance. Not only does the person concerned play an absolutely central role because he initiates the procedure and is the only person able to explain, in concrete terms, what has happened to him and the background against which it has taken place, but also the decision given will be of crucial importance to him.[1]

This concluding chapter will make some final remarks with regard to the methodology used in this study. It will argue that this methodology is suitable not only to construct the meaning of the EU right to an effective remedy in the context of asylum, but also in other fields of EU law.

Furthermore, this chapter will draw some conclusions as to the achievements that have already been made by the Procedures Directive (Directives 2005/85/EC and 2013/32/EU) and its potential impact in the future. It will be contended that asylum applicants are better off with the Procedures Directive than they would be without it. Section 11.3 contains the full set of procedural standards which were derived from the Procedures Directive and Qualification Directive read in the light of the EU right to an effective remedy. Section 11.4 stresses the importance of the task of national courts and asylum lawyers to apply the Procedures

[1] Case C-277/11 *MM v Minister for Justice, Equality and Law Reform Ireland* [2012] Opinion of AG Bot, para 43.

Directive, and the EU right to an effective remedy in practice and to encourage the courts to refer questions for preliminary ruling to the Court of Justice.

11.1 EU PROCEDURAL LAW: COMMON PRINCIPLES, SPECIFIC APPLICATIONS

The purpose of this study was to discover the meaning of the EU fundamental right to an effective remedy for the legality and interpretation of EU asylum legislation, in particular the Procedures Directive. The meaning of the EU right to an effective remedy in the context of asylum was derived from the EU Courts' case law and relevant sources of inspiration, in particular the case law of the European Court of Human Rights (ECtHR). This has resulted in a set of procedural standards with regard to several key issues of asylum procedures: the right to remain on the territory of the Member State; the right to be heard; and evidentiary issues.

The methodology used in this study to find the meaning of the EU right to an effective remedy is based on the following assumptions:

- The EU right to an effective remedy encompasses common procedural principles which are applicable in all fields of EU law. These principles can be distilled from the case law of the EU Courts' case law concerning a specific procedural topic, irrespective of the material EU legislation at issue. Furthermore, they are inspired by international law, in particular the European Convention on Human Rights (ECHR) and the case law of the ECtHR.
- When applying these common procedural principles to a specific field of EU law regard should be had to three basic concepts:
    1. the interests of the parties involved in the proceedings must be balanced against each other;
    2. the overall fairness of the procedure should be assessed; and
    3. the subject matter of the proceedings should be taken into account.

The following sections will summarise this method of deriving common principles and applying them to a specific field of EU law.

11.1.1 Common Procedural Principles

Article 47 of the Charter applies in its full extent to all cases falling within the scope of EU law. This is also true for the procedural rights closely linked to it, such as the right to be heard and the duty to state reasons. In all fields of EU law, competition, EU sanctions, equal treatment and asylum, similar aspects of EU or national procedures raise questions as to their compatibility with EU procedural rights. In all types of procedures parties may claim, for example, that a lack of suspensive effect of the appeal, limitations of the right to be heard, evidentiary rules or a limited scope or intensity of judicial review, undermined their right to an effective remedy and/or impeded the effective exercise of their rights granted under EU law. The EU Courts' judgments regarding such claims are relevant not only for the specific procedure at issue, but for all procedures in which EU law is invoked. From this case law procedural principles emerge which are applicable to all fields of EU law. This is how the EU Courts' judgments in competition, EU sanction or equal treatment cases, for example, become relevant for the interpretation of the EU right to an effective remedy in asylum cases.

An early sign that the Court of Justice will indeed treat asylum cases like all other cases falling within the scope of EU law, and will apply the same EU procedural principles, can be seen in the judgment in *Samba Diouf*. The Court of Justice in its judgment referred to its judgment in *Wilson* when addressing the scope of judicial review which should be performed by a court or tribunal within the meaning of Article 39 PD. The *Wilson* case concerned the practice of the profession of lawyer in a Member State other than that in which the qualification was obtained.[2] At the same time, the Court of Justice has referred to its judgment in *Samba Diouf* in various cases concerning other fields of EU law.[3] Examples of procedural principles which were derived from the EU Courts' case law in this study include:

- interim protection must be provided by the national court if necessary to ensure the effectiveness of EU law;
- the use of presumptions is permissible as long as the parties concerned are able to submit evidence in order to rebut such presumptions;
- authorities are not allowed to accept only the best possible evidence in support of a claim under EU law;
- a court or tribunal should review both points of fact and points of law; and
- a court must also receive all evidence underlying the contested decision, if (part of) this evidence was not disclosed to (one of) the parties concerned. This court should assess whether the non-disclosure of evidence pursues a legitimate aim and is necessary and proportionate and whether the right to adversarial proceedings is sufficiently guaranteed.

The procedural principles are often of a rather general nature and cannot be directly applied to any EU context. The specific meaning of these principles and the level of protection offered by them, varies according to the special features of the field of EU law at issue and the individual circumstances of the case. This is where the three basic concepts introduced in chapter four, section 4.5 come to the fore.

[2] Case C-506/04 *Wilson* [2006] ECR I-8613.

[3] See, eg Case C-199/11 *Otis* [2012] para 46.

11.1.2 Specific Applications: The Three Basic Concepts

In this study the case law of the ECtHR and the views of the UNHCR, the Committee against Torture (ComAT) and the Human Rights Committee which specifically concern asylum procedures have been used to determine how the procedural principles distilled from the case law of the EU Courts should be applied in the asylum context. With regard to some of the issues discussed, no case law of the EU Courts was available. In this situation the interpretation of the EU right to an effective remedy was only based on the case law of the ECtHR and the views of other supervising bodies.

The three basic concepts introduced in chapter 4, section 4.5 prove helpful in understanding the choices made by the EU Courts when applying procedural rights in a particular case. Moreover, they are useful in predicting how the EU Courts will interpret the EU right to an effective remedy or related procedural rights and principles in a field of EU law or even a particular case. This will be illustrated in the following sections.

11.1.2.1 Balancing of Interests

The EU Courts balance the interests of the parties involved in a procedure when assessing whether EU procedural rights have been infringed. A national procedural rule which limits a party's procedural rights, such as the right of access to court or the right to be heard, must serve a legitimate aim and should be necessary and proportionate. Therefore, the Member State must also be able to justify a procedural rule which limits an applicant's procedural rights granted under EU law in asylum cases.

In this study, the balancing of interests performed by the EU Courts was most visible in chapter ten, which discussed their case law concerning the use of secret information in competition cases and EU sanction cases. In these cases the EU Courts balance the right to be heard, the right to a reasoned decision, and the right to an effective remedy of the addressee of the decision, against the interest served by the non-disclosure of this information. These interests include the protection of business secrets, the protection of witnesses and the international relations or national security of Member States.

It is relevant to note in the context of asylum procedures that both the Court of Justice and the ECtHR have recognised that the procedural rights of a party may be balanced against the Member States' interest to process cases efficiently.[4] The efficiency of asylum procedures is one of the objectives of the Procedures

[4] See, eg Case C-619/10 *Trade Agency Ltd* [2012] paras 57–59 and Case T-237/00 *Reynolds v Parliament* [2004] ECR II-15, para 102, where the Court of Justice held that the degree of precision of the statement of the reasons for a decision must be weighed against practical realities and the time and technical facilities available for making the decision. See also ECtHR 12 November 2002, *Döry v Sweden*, no 28394/95, para 41.

Directive.[5] The Court of Justice recognised in *Samba Diouf* that shorter time limits in asylum procedures (accelerated asylum proceedings) may be justified to ensure 'that unfounded or inadmissible applications for asylum are processed more quickly, in order that applications submitted by persons who have good grounds for benefiting from refugee status may be processed more efficiently'.[6] Similarly, in *IM* the ECtHR considered that Member States must have the means to cope with large numbers of asylum applicants and that accelerated procedures may facilitate the processing of clearly abusive or manifestly unfounded asylum applications.[7]

The Member States' interest in processing asylum claims efficiently and preventing abuse may thus play a significant role in the context of asylum. However, it is conceivable that this interest may never prevail over the interests of the Member States and the asylum applicant in good decisions.[8]

11.1.2.2 The Overall Fairness of the Procedure

The case law discussed in this study also confirms that in the context of the EU right to an effective remedy the overall fairness of the asylum procedure should be examined. A limitation to a procedural right may be compensated by using compensation techniques. A lack of procedural guarantees in one stage of the procedure may be redressed at a later stage of the procedure and vice versa. In this study it was established, for example, that both the EU Courts and the ECtHR accepted that a limited form of judicial review may be (partly) compensated by procedural guarantees in the administrative phase, in particular the right to be heard and the right to know the reasons of the decision.[9] The Court of Justice has held that in EU sanction cases in which secret evidence is used, the absence of a hearing during the administrative phase can be compensated during the appeal phase.[10] Furthermore, both the Court of Justice and the ECtHR have ruled that a limitation of the right to adversarial proceedings can and must be compensated by using compensation techniques such the appointment of a special advocate or the provision of non-confidential summaries. Section 9.3 argued that the lack of an *ex nunc* examination of the asylum decision by the court or tribunal within the meaning of Article 39 of Directive 2005/85/EC may be compensated by a subsequent asylum procedure in which all relevant new facts and evidence are assessed by the determining authority and may be reviewed by the court or tribunal deciding on the appeal.

[5] See recitals 3 and 11 Preamble Dir 2005/85/EC and recitals 4, 8, 11 and 18 Preamble Dir 2013/32/EU.

[6] Case C-69/10 *Samba Diouf* [2011] ECR I-7151, para 65.

[7] ECtHR 2 February 2012, *IM v France*, no 9152/09, para 142.

[8] Ibid, para 147.

[9] See ch 9 sections 9.2.1 and 9.2.2.3.

[10] Case T-228/02 *Organisation des Modjahedines du peuple d'Iran v Council* [2006] ECR II-4665, paras 129–30; Case T-390/08 *Bank Melli Iran v Council* [2009] ECR II-224, para 98; and Joined Cases C-402/05 P and C-415/05 P, *Kadi and Al Barakaat v Council and Commission* [2008] ECR I-6351, para 337.

Several minor deficiencies in the asylum procedure may reinforce each other and lead to a lack of an effective remedy. Some procedural defects will lead directly to a breach of the right to an effective remedy. The clearest example discussed in this study is the lack of an appeal with automatic suspensive effect against the rejection of an asylum claim. The applicant may be expelled before the appeal court has reached its decision and as a consequence may be exposed to irreparable harm in his country of origin.[11] This deficiency cannot be compensated, for example, by a higher appeal with automatic suspensive effect.

The Court of Justice and the national courts should thus assess the compatibility of a procedural rule with the EU right to an effective remedy while having regard to the guarantees offered in the asylum procedure as a whole.

11.1.2.3 The Subject Matter of the Proceedings

Even though the Court of Justice recognised the Member States' interest in efficient asylum procedures, that does not mean that it will allow that Member States to systematically provide for fewer procedural guarantees in asylum cases than in other cases falling within the scope of EU law. On the contrary, the case law of both the Court of Justice and the ECtHR have made clear that the nature of the fundamental rights at stake in asylum cases, notably the absolute prohibition of *refoulement*, requires a high level of procedural protection. The Court of Justice has considered that the assessment of the extent of the risk of *refoulement* 'must, in all cases, be carried out with vigilance and care, since what are at issue are issues relating to the integrity of the person and to individual liberties, issues which relate to the fundamental values of the Union'.[12]

Similarly, the ECtHR under Article 13 ECHR obliges States to provide for significant procedural guarantees in asylum cases, in view of the importance which the Court attaches to Article 3 ECHR and the irreversible nature of the damage which may result if the risk of torture or ill-treatment materialises. As was shown in this study, Articles 3 and 13 ECHR require a remedy with automatic suspensive effect[13] and rigorous scrutiny of the risk of *refoulement* in the administrative phase as well as by an independent authority.[14] The ECtHR's case law shows that States should be flexible when applying evidentiary rules in asylum cases and not expect the asylum applicant to submit a perfectly substantiated and consistent asylum account.[15] The ECtHR imposes a positive obligation on the State to gather certain evidence and expects it to assume the burden of proof in specific situations, for example, where the applicant has submitted medical evidence of past

[11] See ch 6.

[12] Joined Cases C-175/08, C-176/08, C-178/08 and C-179/08 *Salahadin Abdulla* [2010] ECR I-1493, para 90. See also *MM* (n 1) Opinion of AG Bot, para 43.

[13] See ch 6, section 6.3.1.2.

[14] See ch 9, section 9.2.2.1.

[15] See ch 8, section 8.5

torture.[16] Furthermore, in asylum cases the ECtHR demands an *ex nunc* review by an independent authority on the merits of the risk of *refoulement*.[17]

The case law of the Court of Justice and the ECtHR thus indicates that, given the fundamental rights at stake in asylum cases, the standard of procedural protection offered should be higher rather than lower than that offered by general administrative law in a Member State.

Specific Procedural Position of the Person Concerned

The level of procedural protection which should be offered relates not only to the rights at stake for the party concerned, but also to his particular procedural position. The Court of Justice has accepted that the weak position of consumers and dismissed pregnant workers may warrant special procedural guarantees, such as *ex officio* application of EU law and extended time limits.[18] The Court took into account that these persons lack legal expertise and may, therefore, be required to pay high lawyer's fees or may experience difficulties in obtaining proper advice.

The Court of Justice has not yet addressed the question whether special procedural protection is also necessary in asylum cases. It may, however, be expected that the Court of Justice also takes into account the difficult position in which asylum applicants generally find themselves. It should be noted in this context that the ECtHR has recognised that the weak procedural position of asylum applicants warrants specific procedural guarantees in recent judgments. It stressed the need for clear information on the asylum procedure and for access to (free) legal assistance and interpretation services in asylum procedures.[19]

It follows from the case law of the Court of Justice that the compatibility of a procedural rule with the EU right to an effective remedy should not only be examined in general. The application in a particular case of a procedural rule which is generally considered acceptable may violate the EU right to an effective remedy when the specific circumstances of the individual asylum applicant concerned have been taken into account.[20] National courts should therefore examine whether the procedural rule confirms with the EU right to an effective remedy in general terms and when taking account of the specific circumstances of the case.

[16] See ch 8, section 8.2.2.

[17] See ch 9.

[18] Joined Cases C-240/98 to C-244/98 *Océano Grupo Editorial and Salvat Editores* [2000] ECR I-4941, para 26; and Case C-63/08 *Pontin* [2008] ECR I-10467, paras 62 and 65.

[19] See ECtHR (GC) 21 January 2011, *MSS v Belgium and Greece*, no 30696/09, paras 301, 304 and 319; *IM* (n 7) paras 145 and 150; and ECtHR (GC) 23 February 2012, *Hirsi Jamaa et al v Italy*, no 27765/09, para 204.

[20] See, eg *Samba Diouf* (n 6) paras 66–68.

11.1.3 Wider Applicability of the Methodology

The methodology applied in this study in order to discover the meaning of the EU procedural rights is not only pertinent in the EU asylum context. It may be used in any field of EU law in order to determine how the EU right to an effective remedy should be interpreted.

In this study common principles were mainly derived from the case law concerning other fields of EU law than asylum law. This is not surprising, as asylum law has only recently become part of EU law and therefore there is little case law of the Court of Justice concerning asylum procedures. It may be expected, however, that in the future this case law will develop and will itself provide for procedural principles which are relevant to other fields of EU law. For example, lawyers working in the field of competition law may derive procedural principles from the judgments of the Court of Justice concerning asylum procedures and apply them to their specific field. The judgment of the Court of Justice in *Samba Diouf* has already made clear that the intensity of judicial review is an aspect of the EU right to an effective remedy. This is relevant not only for national courts reviewing asylum decisions, but also for national courts ruling in other cases falling within the scope of EU law.[21]

The method used in this study is also suited to find the meaning of the EU right to an effective remedy with regard to all procedural issues. In the asylum context, for example, it may be used to define the meaning of this right for the application of short time limits for decision-making or appeal proceedings (accelerated asylum proceedings) or the right to legal assistance.

11.2 THE PROCEDURES DIRECTIVE: AN IMPORTANT STEP FORWARD

Directives 2005/85/EC and 2013/32/EU played a central role in this study as they provide for minimum standards for many of the procedural issues discussed. Many NGOs and academics were disappointed by the adoption of Directive 2005/85/EC. It is contended here, however, that the adoption of Directive 2005/85/EC should, nevertheless, be regarded as an important step forward. In spite of its shortcomings, the Directive provides for important standards for asylum procedures. Furthermore, the Directive has brought national asylum procedures within the scope of EU law. Consequently asylum procedures fall within the scope of the Charter and general principles of EU law.

Directive 2005/85/EC developed into Directive 2013/32EU which further improved the legal position of asylum applicants. Many of the positive changes in Directive 2013/32/EU seem to have been inspired by the case law of the EU Courts

[21] See, eg *Otis* (n 3). See also RJGM Widdershoven, 'Case C-69/10, *Samba Diouf* [2011]' (2011) *AB Rechtspraak Bestuursrecht* no 2011/304, para 3.

and the ECtHR concerning the right to an effective remedy. As a result, this case law has been partly incorporated in Directive 2013/32/EU.

This section will briefly evaluate the potential consequences of the adoption of the Procedures Directive for the level of procedural protection offered to asylum applicants. Has a fair and efficient common asylum procedure been established? What is the potential of the EU right to an effective remedy? Does the Directive add anything to the existing protection offered by the ECHR?

Directive 2005/85/EC

There are two ways of looking at Directive 2005/85/EC. First, it may be regarded as an ugly creature: a very complex piece of EU legislation which is clearly the result of long and difficult negotiations between Member States who were unwilling to give up their national solutions for dealing effectively with asylum procedures; a directive which contains more derogation provisions than minimum standards and as a result fails to harmonise the asylum procedures in the Member States; and Most importantly, it is a directive which leaves significant protection gaps and consequently creates the risk of violations of international as well as European Law.[22]

Indeed, the Commission and the UNHCR in their research concerning the implementation of the Procedures Directive ascertained that there were still major differences between the asylum procedures of the Member States.[23] As a result, asylum applicants still have very different prospects of finding international protection depending on where in the EU their applications are examined.[24] Both the Commission and the UNHCR were also concerned about the level of protection offered by those asylum procedures. In 2009 in the proposal for the recast of the Procedures Directive which will be discussed below, the Commission noted:

> Contributions received by stakeholders in response to the Green Paper consultation have pointed to the proliferation of disparate procedural arrangements at national level and deficiencies regarding the level of procedural guarantees for asylum applicants which mainly result from the fact that the Directive currently allows Member States a wide margin of discretion. Consequently, the Directive lacks the potential to back up adequately the Qualification Directive and ensure a rigorous examination of applications for international protection in line with international and Community obligations of Member States regarding the principle of *non-refoulement*.[25]

[22] UNHCR, *Improving Asylum Procedures: Comparative Analysis and Recommendations for Law and Practice* (March 2010) www.refworld.org/docid/4c63e52d2.html accessed 25 September 2013, 91.

[23] See, eg Commission, 'Report from the Commission to the European Parliament and the Council on the application of Directive 2005/85/EC' COM (2010) 465 final and UNHCR, *Improving Asylum Procedures* (n 22) 91.

[24] Commission, 'Staff Working Document accompanying the Proposal for a Directive of the European Parliament and of the Council on minimum standards on procedures in Member States for granting and withdrawing international protection' COM(2009) 554, SEC(2009) 1377, 2.

[25] Commission, 'Proposal for a Directive of the European Parliament and of the Council on minimum standards on procedures in Member States for granting and withdrawing international protection (Recast)' COM (2009) 554 (Explanatory Memorandum) 2.

The UNHCR stated in 2010:

> There are many areas in which individual's rights are not respected, not only because of non-observance of the APD [the Procedures Directive], but also in the context of the application of its provisions, in line with the low minimum standards it sets.[26]

In spite of the fact that the Member States are bound by the guarantees contained in the Procedures Directive, the ECtHR has recently found violations of the right to an effective remedy in asylum cases with respect to Austria,[27] Belgium,[28] Bulgaria,[29] the Czech Republic,[30] Cyprus,[31] France,[32] Greece[33] and Italy,[34] and violations of Article 3 ECHR with respect to a number of other States. The violations were caused by (a combination of) a wide variety of procedural shortcomings, ranging from a lack of access to the asylum procedure, a lack of information about the asylum procedure, the absence of free legal aid and/or interpretation services, the limited nature of the personal interview, the lack of a rigorous scrutiny of the claim of *refoulement*, the speed or the long duration of the procedure, the lack of a remedy with automatic suspensive effect and the limited intensity of judicial review.

Furthermore, in some Member States there is strong political pressure to adopt more restrictive migration policies and legislation. This also results in a lowering of procedural guarantees for asylum procedures. In the Netherlands, for example, the right to a remedy with suspensive effect was limited and no longer applies with regard to subsequent asylum procedures in which the applicant failed to submit new facts or circumstances.[35] The Dutch Government also aims to reduce the number of subsequent asylum procedures by restricting free legal aid in such procedures.[36] In November 2011, French Interior Minister Claude Gueant announced reforms to the asylum system in France including a reduction in the asylum budget and a shortening of the time frame within which asylum applications must be made. The number of safe countries of origin would also be increased.[37] Belgium introduced a list of safe countries of origin in November 2011. Asylum

[26] UNHCR, *Improving Asylum Procedures* (n 22) 91.

[27] ECtHR 28 March 2013, *IK v Austria*, no 2964/12.

[28] ECtHR 2 October 2012, *Singh v Belgium*, no 33210/11; and *MSS* (n 19).

[29] ECtHR 11 October 2011, *Auad v Bulgaria*, no 46390/10 and ECtHR 26 July 2011, *M et al v Bulgaria*, no 41416/08.

[30] ECtHR 23 June 2011, *Diallo v Czech Republic*, no 20493/07.

[31] ECtHR 23 July 2013, *MA v Cyprus*, no 41872/10.

[32] *IM* (n 7).

[33] *MSS* (n 19).

[34] *Hirsi Jamaa* (n 19).

[35] Besluit van de Minister voor Immigratie en Asiel van 8 februari 2011, WBV 2011/1, houdende wijziging van de Vreemdelingencirculaire 2000, Staatscourant 17 February 2011, No 2838.

[36] Gedoogakkoord VVD-PVV-CDA (30 September 2010) www.rijksoverheid.nl/documenten-en-publicaties/rapporten/2010/09/30/gedoogakkoord-vvd-pvv-cda.html accessed 26 September 2013.

[37] European Council for Refugees and Exiles (ECRE), *Weekly bulletin* (9 December 2011) www.ecre.org/media/news/weekly-bulletin.html accessed 26 September 2013 and Réaction de Forum réfugiés au discours de C Guéant du 25 novembre 2011, La hausse de la demande d'asile légitime était prévisible, www.forumrefugies.org/s-informer/communiques2/la-hausse-de-la-demande-d-asile-legitime-etait-previsible accessed 26 September 2013.

applicants originating from these countries must rebut the presumption of safety in their individual case, within a 15-day asylum procedure.[38]

Directive 2013/32/EU

Directive 2013/32/EU contains significantly higher standards than its predecessor and grants less discretion to Member States. The UNHCR stated in June 2013 that the reformed legislation 'has the potential significantly to contribute to harmonizing asylum systems in the Union'. The recast 'asylum package', including the recast Asylum Procedures Directive, along with the Qualification Directive adopted in 2011, 'has the potential to improve protection standards and practice across the Union'.[39]

The proposal for the recast of Directive 2005/85/EC, which finally resulted in the adoption of Directive 2013/32/EU, was 'informed by developing case law of the Court of Justice of the European Union and the European Court of Human Rights, especially concerning the right to an effective remedy'.[40] Indeed, some of the new provisions of Directive 2013/32/EU reflect the conclusions drawn in this study as to the requirements following from the EU right to an effective remedy. Most importantly, Article 46 of Directive 2013/32/EU requires 'a full and *ex nunc* examination of both facts and points of law' and ensures that the asylum applicant will not be expelled during the appeal proceedings.

Although Directive 2013/32/EU provides a higher level of procedural protection to asylum applicants, it does not establish a *common fair and efficient* asylum procedure. The text of the Directive is still complex and contains opportunities for Member States to derogate from important procedural guarantees. Many provisions will need interpretation by the national courts and the Court of Justice. The UNHCR stated: 'In some cases, the negotiating parties had to strike difficult compromises to reach agreement. As a consequence, some opportunities were missed to fill gaps and clarify overly broad, complex and problematic provisions.'[41]

11.2.1 The Potential Impact of the EU Right to an Effective Remedy

This study has shown that the EU right to an effective remedy laid down in Article 47 of the Charter and recognised by the Court of Justice as a principle

[38] Belgische Kamer van Volksvertegenwoordigers, Wetsontwerp tot wijziging van de wet van 15 december 1980 betreffende de toegang tot het grondgebied, het verblijf, de vestiging en de verwijdering van vreemdelingen, no 1825/011, 24 November 2011. The proposal was adopted by the Chamber and the Senate.

[39] UNHCR, *Moving further toward a Common European Asylum System, UNHCR's Statement on the EU Asylum Legislative Package* (June 2013) www.refworld.org/docid/51de61304.html accessed 26 September 2013.

[40] Commission, 'Amended proposal for a Directive of the European Parliament and of the Council on minimum standards on procedures in Member States for granting and withdrawing international protection (Recast)' COM(2011) 319 final, 4 and the initial Commission proposal (n 25) 6.

[41] UNHCR, *Moving further toward a Common European Asylum System* (n 39).

of EU law may set important limits to the Member States' discretion under Directives 2005/85/EC and 2013/32/EU. Potentially it also provides for additional safeguards. Moreover, this right is an important tool for interpretation of the Directives' provisions and may be used to fill in (protection) gaps. The potential impact of the EU right to an effective right of an effective remedy in the field of asylum procedures should therefore not be underestimated.

Directive 2005/85/EC

The EU right to an effective remedy may provide an answer to some of the main deficiencies in the Directive 2005/85/EC identified by the UNHCR and some NGOs. It was concluded in this study that the provisions of the Directive read in the light of the EU right to an effective remedy requires that the applicant be allowed to stay on the territory of the Member State during first instance and appeal proceedings. In addition, the applicant must have sufficient time and opportunity to lodge an appeal against the rejection of the asylum claim. The possibilities mentioned in Article 12 of Directive 2005/85/EC to derogate from the right to a personal interview may only be used in exceptional cases. This study also contended that the EU right to an effective remedy reflected in Article 39 of Directive 2005/85/EC contains several 'hidden' guarantees. This right requires a thorough and (at one stage of the procedure) *ex nunc* judicial review which, involves, as a minimum, the national court or tribunal assessing the claim of a risk of *refoulement* on its merits, carefully examining the facts and evidence underlying the asylum claim. Furthermore, the right to adversarial proceedings, which is incorporated by the right to an effective remedy, demands that the national court assesses whether the non-disclosure of evidence underlying the asylum decision is justified. Limitations to the right to adversarial proceedings should be compensated, for instance, by using non-confidential summaries or special advocates. It was even argued that the last sentence of Article 16(1) of Directive 2005/85/EC, which allows Member States to withhold relevant information to the national court deciding on the appeal against the asylum decision on national security grounds, must be considered at variance with the EU right to an effective remedy and should, therefore, be declared void by the Court of Justice. These findings remain important for all Member States until the Member States have transposed Directive 2013/32/EU, or the time limit for transposition (20 July 2013) has expired. It should be remembered that the United Kingdom and Ireland did not take part in the adoption of Directive 2013/32/EU and remain bound by Directive 2005/85/EC.

Directive 2013/32/EU

In Directive 2013/32/EU many of the problematic exceptions to procedural rights have been deleted and more guarantees are included. Nevertheless, there are still provisions which need interpretation and which may be tested against the EU right to an effective remedy. In this study the EU right to an effective remedy was used to interpret the term 'full and *ex nunc*' judicial review of Article 46(3) of

Directive 2013/32/EU and the provisions concerning the right to remain on the territory during the appeal laid down in Article 46(6) to (8). Moreover, it was concluded that the right to an effective remedy guaranteed by Article 46 of Directive 2013/32/EU generally requires that the applicant is granted the right to an oral hearing during the appeal proceedings.

Directive 2011/95/EU

Not only the Procedures Directive, but also the Qualification Directive (2011/95/EU) may contribute to the procedural protection of asylum applicants. The principle of effectiveness requires that the clear rights for asylum applicants guaranteed by this Directive, most importantly the right to asylum status for those in need of international protection and the prohibition of *refoulement*, are effectively protected. National procedural rules, including evidentiary rules, may not render the exercise of those rights impossible or excessively difficult. It was concluded in chapter eight that Article 4 of the Qualification Directive and the principle of effectiveness set important standards with regard to the standard and burden of proof, the use of presumptions, and the assessment of the statements and evidence submitted by the applicant.

11.2.2 Broader Protection than the ECHR

The question may be raised whether the Procedures Directive and the fact that asylum procedures are now governed by EU fundamental rights adds anything to the protection regime which had already been developed under the ECHR. In this study, the case law of the ECtHR was used as an important source of inspiration for the EU right to an effective remedy and thus indirectly for the interpretation of the Procedures Directive. In fact, this study refers to a larger number of judgments of the ECtHR than of the EU Courts.

When approaching this question from a purely legal perspective one may argue that the Procedures Directive provides for broader protection than Articles 3 and 13 ECHR for two reasons. First, the Procedures Directive covers many procedural issues, such as the right to information, the right to a personal interview, the right to a reasoned decision on the asylum claim, the right to (free) legal aid and interpretation services, special guarantees for unaccompanied minors, and the right to contact the UNHCR, which at the moment of the adoption of the Directive had scarcely been addressed by the ECtHR in its case law.[42] Potentially inspired by the Procedures Directive, in its assessment under Article 13 ECHR the ECtHR took

[42] See, eg ECtHR 12 April 2005, *Shamayev et al v Georgia and Russia*, no 36378/02, para 458 and (under Art 5(1)) ECtHR 5 February 2002, *Čonka v Belgium*, no 51564/99, para 44.

account of (a lack of) some of these rights in a few recent judgments, such as in *MSS* and *IM*.[43]

Secondly, it should be remembered that the scope of application of the Procedures Directive and the EU right to an effective remedy is wider than that of Article 13 ECHR. Most importantly, the EU right to an effective remedy reflected in Article 39 of Directive 2005/85/EC and Article 46 of Directive 2013/32/EU includes the right to a fair trial.[44] The right to a fair trial guaranteed by Article 6 ECHR does not apply to asylum procedures. In this study the case law of the ECtHR under Article 6 ECHR was used as a source of inspiration for the EU right to a fair trial. This study shows that, particularly with regard to the use of secret information and the right to an oral hearing before a court or tribunal, the case law of the ECtHR provides for important guidance for the interpretation of the EU right to a fair trial. Moreover, the right to an effective remedy guaranteed in Article 39 of Directive 2005/85/EC and Article 46 of Directive 2013/32/EU applies to all asylum cases, irrespective of the merits of the case or the procedure in which it was assessed.[45] Article 13 ECHR applies only to cases of an arguable claim of *refoulement*. Finally, the Procedures Directive and the EU right to an effective remedy apply not only to expulsion decisions, which arguably violate the prohibition of *refoulement*, but also to decisions to exclude a person from the right to an asylum status. The ECHR does not guarantee a right to asylum. Consequently, applicants who are refused asylum but will not be expelled,[46] cannot appeal to Article 13 ECHR.[47]

The Procedures Directive has thus made procedural rights for asylum applicants more visible and provides broader protection than Articles 3 and 13 ECHR.

11.2.3 Supervision and Practical Support for Member States

The fact that asylum procedures are now governed by EU law has also lead to further opportunities to supervise the fairness of Member States' asylum procedures. The Commission started infringement procedures against a number of Member States for a failure to implement Directive 2005/85/EC correctly.[48]

[43] *MSS* (n 19); *IM* (n 7). The ECtHR in these cases referred to the relevant provisions of Directive 2005/85/EC in its description of relevant international and European law or relevant international texts and documents.

[44] See ch 4, section 4.3.2.

[45] It applies to manifestly unfounded and inadmissible cases, cases rejected in a standard procedure, an accelerated or border procedure or a preliminary examination (in case of a subsequent asylum procedure).

[46] This applies, for example, to applicants who are refused an asylum status, because there are serious reasons to believe that they committed a serious crime in their country of origin, who face a real risk of persecution upon return. See Art 12(2) Dir 2011/95/EU.

[47] See, eg ECtHR 20 July 2010, *A v the Netherlands*, no 4900/06, paras 152–53.

[48] The Commission sent a letter of formal notice with regard to the implementation of the Procedures Directive to Belgium, Cyprus, Czech Republic, Estonia, Finland, France, Greece, Ireland,

Furthermore, the development of the Common European Asylum System (CEAS) leads to a strengthening of practical cooperation between the Member States in the field of asylum. This cooperation seeks first to increase convergence but also envisages ensuring the ongoing quality of Member States' decision-making procedures in that area.[49] The most important measure taken in this context was the establishment of the European Asylum Support Office (EASO) in 2010.[50] The purpose of EASO is 'to facilitate, coordinate and strengthen practical cooperation among Member States on the many aspects of asylum and help to improve the implementation of CEAS'. EASO shall, among other functions, organise, promote and coordinate activities relating to country of origin information and establish and develop training for officials working in the field of asylum.[51] Before the establishment of EASO, common EU Guidelines for the processing of country of origin information[52] as well as a common European asylum curriculum had already been developed.[53]

EASO must also 'provide effective operational support to Member States subject to particular pressure on their asylum and reception systems'.[54] Such pressure may be characterised by the sudden arrival of a large number of third-country nationals who may be in need of international protection, and may arise from the geographical or demographical situation of the Member State.[55] EASO may deploy Asylum Support Teams in Member States. These teams shall provide expertise, in particular, in relation to interpreting services, information on countries of origin, and knowledge of the handling and management of asylum cases.[56] Asylum Support Teams were sent to Greece and Luxembourg in 2011 and 2012.[57]

Italy, Lithuania, Malta, Poland, Portugal, Spain and Sweden. In most cases the Commission was satisfied with the information provided by the Member State. The Commission issued a reasoned opinion in regard to Belgium, Cyprus, Ireland, Spain and Sweden. Cases against Belgium and Ireland were referred to the Court of Justice, but were closed before a judgment was rendered. See www.ec.europa.eu/home-affairs/news/infringements/infringements_by_policy_asylum_en.htm accessed 30 August 2013.

[49] See, eg Commission, 'Communication from the Commission to the European Parliament, the Council, the European Economic and Social Committee and the Committee of Regions, Policy Plan on Asylum, An Integrated Approach to Protection across the EU' COM(2008) 360 final.

[50] Reg No 439/2010 of the European Parliament and of the Council of 19 May 2010 establishing a European Asylum Support Office [2010] OJ L132/11 (Reg 439/2010).

[51] Ibid, Arts 4 and 6.

[52] European Union, *Common EU Guidelines for Processing Country of Origin Information (COI)* (April 2008, ARGO project JLS/2005/ARGO/GC/03). These guidelines were developed by a project group, formed by representatives of country of origin information desks from immigration services of several Member States.

[53] The curriculum provides for common vocational training for caseworkers, management officials and policy makers working with asylum matters. The aim of the curriculum is to contribute to the implementation of a Common European Asylum System and to increase the quality of the asylum process in Europe.

[54] Art 2 Reg 439/2010 (n 50).

[55] Ibid, Art 8.

[56] Ibid, Art 14.

[57] EASO, *Work Programme 2012* (September 2011) ec.europa.eu/home-affairs/policies/asylum/docs/easo/EASO_2011_00110000_EN_TRA.pdf and EASO, Operating Plan for the Deployment of

Finally, EASO shall provide 'scientific and technical assistance in regard to the policy and legislation of the Union in all areas having a direct or indirect impact on asylum so that it is in a position to lend its full support to practical cooperation on asylum and to carry out its duties effectively'.[58]

It may be expected that the European Commission's supervisory role (although of a limited nature), practical cooperation, and the support of EASO do indeed promote the fairness of the asylum procedures and enhance the quality of asylum decisions.

11.2.4 Subconclusion: The Procedures Directive, An Important Step Forward

It should be concluded that even though the Procedures Directive does have weaknesses, asylum applicants are better off with the Directive than without it. The Directive provides for important guarantees for asylum procedures and at the same time activated the EU right to an effective remedy in asylum cases. The previous chapters of this study have shown that the potential impact of the Procedures Directive through the EU right to an effective remedy is more significant than many expected at the time of the adoption of the Directive.

11.3 A SET OF EU PROCEDURAL STANDARDS FOR ASYLUM PROCEDURES

The purpose of this study was to derive a set of EU procedural standards for a number of key issues of asylum procedures from EU legislation and the EU right to an effective remedy and related procedural rights and principles. In chapters six to ten, conclusions were drawn as to the procedural guarantees which should be offered with regard to the right to remain, the right to be heard, and evidentiary issues. The main procedural standards should be summarised as follows:

The Right to Remain on the Territory of the Member State during the Asylum Procedure

— An asylum applicant should be allowed to remain on the territory of the Member State:
  1. until the determining authority in first instance has carried out a close and rigorous assessment of the asylum claim;

Asylum Support Teams to Luxembourg (26 January 2012) ec.europa.eu/dgs/home-affairs/what-we-do/policies/pdf/operating_plan_ast_lu_en.pdf accessed 26 September 2013.

[58] Art 2(3) of Reg 439/2010 (n 50).

2. for the time necessary to avail himself of the effective remedy before a court or tribunal within the meaning of Article 39(1) of Directive 2005/85/EC and Article 46(1) of Directive 2013/32/EU; and
3. during the course of the appeal proceedings, until rigorous scrutiny of the claim of a risk of *refoulement* has been performed by the court or tribunal.

— Automatic suspensive effect must be attached by law to either the appeal itself or to a request for interim relief.
— The procedure in which interim relief may be granted by the national court or tribunal on request must comply with important procedural guarantees, such as the rights of the defence, a reasonable burden of proof, and a rigorous scrutiny of a claim of a risk of *refoulement*.

The Asylum Applicant's Right to be Heard on his Asylum Motives

— In principle, every asylum applicant should be heard in a personal interview. Exceptions to this rule are only allowed in exceptional cases.
— If a personal interview is omitted the asylum applicant should be given sufficient opportunity to substantiate his asylum claim, for example, by submitting written statements.
— The determining authorities should investigate whether dependent adults have independent asylum motives which could best be explained in a personal interview.
— Minor asylum applicants should, in principle, be interviewed if they so wish and if their age and maturity permits. Only if an interview is not considered to be in the best interests of the child should an interview be omitted.
— The conditions under which interviews are conducted must allow applicants to present the grounds for their applications in a comprehensive manner.
— The interviewer must ascertain that the applicant is able to understand the language chosen for the interview and that he can express himself effectively in this language.
— If the applicant does not understand the language of the interview a competent and qualified interpreter should be provided free of charge. If no such interpreter is available the determining authority should take this into account when examining the case.
— The interviewer must be competent and properly trained to interview asylum applicants.
— Interviews should be conducted in a gender-sensitive manner.
— Minors should be heard in a child-friendly manner.
— The applicant should be granted the opportunity to comment on the report of the personal interview, particularly if the determining authority intends to reject the asylum application on the basis of the information contained in

the report. To that end, the applicant should have timely access to the report of the interview.

- Member States should at one stage of the administrative procedure hear the asylum applicant on its main conclusions regarding the fact-finding, credibility assessment, and the assessment of the risk of *refoulement* as well as important pieces of evidence on which these conclusions are based.
- An oral hearing should be held before the first instance court or tribunal reviewing the negative decision on the asylum claim, particularly if this court decides on the credibility of the applicant's account and/or where the applicant's personal experiences play an important role.
- The applicant must be able to hear and follow the proceedings before the court or tribunal and generally to participate effectively in them.

The Burden and Standard of Proof and Evidentiary Assessment

- The standard of proof should not be set too high. The applicant may be expected to show that there is a 'reasonable possibility' of future persecution or that there are substantial grounds for believing that he faces a real risk of serious harm.
- In the examining the asylum claim the determining authority should take into account all relevant indicators of a risk of *refoulement.*
- The burden of proof must shift from the applicant to the determining authority if the applicant adduced evidence capable of proving that there are substantial grounds for believing that there is a risk of *refoulement.* In particular, the burden of proof should shift if:
  1. the applicant made a plausible case that he was persecuted or subjected to serious harm in the past;
  2. the applicant substantiated that there would be a risk of *refoulement* in submitting credible statements and/or documents;
  3. country of origin information reports show that serious human rights violations occur in the applicant's country of origin; or
  4. the applicant made a plausible case that he belongs to a group which is at risk.
- The applicant should not be expected to prove negative facts.
- The duty to produce evidence should be shared between the applicant and the determining authority. Article 4(1) of the Qualification Directive requires Member States to cooperate actively with the applicant so that all the elements needed to substantiate the application may be assembled, if the elements provided by an applicant are not complete, up to date or relevant.
- The determining authority must gather precise and up-to-date country of origin information.
- The determining authority should direct that a medical expert report be written if the applicant makes out a prima facie case as to the origin of the scars on his body.

— The determining authority should gather evidence which is accessible to it, but not to the applicant.
— The use of presumptions which are impossible or excessively difficult to rebut is not allowed.
— When assessing the credibility of the applicant's asylum account, the determining authority should focus on the core of the asylum account.
— Asylum applicants should be granted the opportunity to explain the alleged deficiencies in the asylum account.
— As soon as the general credibility of the asylum applicant is established, his statements should, according to Article 4(5) of the Qualification Directive, be accepted as facts, without requiring further evidence.
— All relevant and reliable evidence should be taken into account in the assessment of the asylum claim.
— Expert reports must fulfil the requirements of excellence, independence and transparency.
— Country of origin information reports and medical reports should be accorded significant weight in asylum cases.
— Member States cannot rely only on country of origin information provided by their own Ministries but should also take into account reports issued by reputable human rights organisations, UN agencies and authorities of other States. The weight which should be attached to a country of origin information report depends on the authority and reputation of the author, the seriousness of the investigations by means of which they were compiled, the consistency of their conclusions and their corroboration by other sources.
— The weight which should be accorded to a medical report depends on its quality and conclusiveness.

Judicial Review of the Establishment and Qualification of the Facts

— The national court or tribunal which decides on the appeal against the negative asylum decision should review both points of law and points of fact.
— This court or tribunal should assess the claim of a risk of *refoulement* on its merits.
— It should carefully examine the facts and evidence underlying the asylum claim. A reasonableness test in which wide discretion is afforded to the determining authority's fact-finding, including the assessment of the applicant's credibility is not allowed.
— The national court should at one stage of the asylum procedure, before the expulsion of the applicant, review the asylum decision on the basis of all relevant available facts and evidence. This includes all relevant evidence which is submitted in a later stage of the asylum procedure (after the first administrative decision on the asylum application).

— Relevant facts or evidence cannot be excluded from the assessment by the national court on the sole ground that they should have been submitted earlier in the procedure.

The Use of Secret Information

— Asylum applicants should, in principle, have access to documents which are relevant to their case (inculpatory or exculpatory).
— The non-disclosure of evidence underlying the asylum decision should have a *legitimate aim* and it should be strictly necessary and proportionate. Furthermore, the essence of the EU right to be heard, the duty to state reasons, and the right to an effective remedy must be respected.
— The national court deciding on the appeal against the negative asylum decision should review whether non-disclosure of evidence pursues a legitimate aim and is necessary and proportionate.
— The national court must receive all relevant information underlying the asylum decision, including the evidence which was not disclosed to the person concerned.
— The protection of secret information must be observed in such a way as to reconcile it with the EU right to an effective remedy, the right to be heard, and the duty to state reasons. The conflicting interests of the parties concerned must be balanced.
— The statement of reasons of the asylum decision must as a minimum disclose the essence of the case against the applicant. In order to be sufficiently specific the statement of reasons should mention details of the allegations against the applicant such as names of persons, places and dates. At least one of the reasons given for the decision must be sufficient to support the decision.
— The right to adversarial proceedings is not violated where the evidence had been largely disclosed to the applicant and the open material plays a predominant role in the determination, or when the allegations in the open material are sufficiently specific.
— The weight which is attached to the confidential material for the decision should be taken into account when assessing whether the rights of the defence have been infringed in an asylum case.
— The credibility of evidence of anonymous origin must be considered reduced by the fact that the context in which it was drafted is largely unknown and because the determining authority's assertions in that regard cannot be verified.
— Special techniques may be used in order to compensate the use of secret information, such as the use of special counsels, non-confidential summaries or a list of all the documents in the file. Anonymous witnesses may be questioned by an investigative judge.

— A special advocate who could test the non-disclosed evidence and put arguments on behalf of the asylum applicant during closed hearings could perform an important role in counterbalancing the lack of full disclosure and the lack of a full, open, adversarial hearing. The applicant must be provided with sufficiently specific information about the allegations against him in order to give effective instructions to this special counsel.
— The information disclosed in non-confidential summaries should be sufficiently precise in order to put the applicant in the position to determine whether the deleted information is likely to be relevant for his case and to express his view on it.

11.4 ENFORCING THE EU RIGHT TO AN EFFECTIVE REMEDY IN PRACTICE

This study addressed many procedural aspects of asylum procedures which have so far not been decided by the Court of Justice. The conclusions drawn in this study thus need confirmation; first by the national courts of the Member States and ultimately by the Court of Justice. It is primarily up to the national courts to interpret the Procedures Directive in the light of the EU right to an effective remedy and to test the legality of the Directive against this right. Whether the questions raised in this study will ever be put before the Court of Justice depends to a large extent on the national courts.[59] In this respect the lawyers assisting asylum applicants in EU Member States also play an important role. These lawyers may prompt the national courts to apply the Procedures Directive and the EU right to an effective remedy and urge them to refer questions for preliminary rulings to the Court of Justice.

Reliance on and application of the EU right to an effective remedy is not easy. This study shows that the case law of the EU Courts concerning procedural rights with regard to all fields of EU law is also relevant in the context of asylum procedures. Solid general knowledge of EU law is therefore required in order to be able to interpret this case law and apply it to asylum procedures. Furthermore, it is difficult to disclose relevant case law concerning the right to an effective remedy and related procedural rights because this case law concerns all fields of EU law and the EU Courts have used various terms for the same procedural rights. Hopefully this study will assist asylum lawyers and national courts to discover the potential of EU (asylum) law and to apply this right in an individual case.

[59] The crucial role of the national courts in guaranteeing EU fundamental rights has already been stressed in ch 2, sections 2.5.2 and 2.5.3 in this volume.

11.5 TOWARDS FAIR ASYLUM PROCEDURES IN EUROPE

It does not seem realistic to expect that a common and fair European asylum procedure will be established in the near future. Nevertheless, EU law should be taken seriously by determining authorities, national courts and lawyers representing asylum applicants. The Procedures Directive and the EU right to an effective remedy have the potential to raise the level of protection offered by the asylum procedures of the Member States and at the same time to harmonise those procedures to some extent. It may be that EU law sets different or higher standards for asylum procedures than the ECHR and the case law of the ECtHR. A one-sided focus on the ECHR is, therefore, no longer justified. It is now time for professionals working in the field of asylum to bring the Procedures Directive and the EU right to an effective remedy into action. This study may serve as a source of inspiration for this purpose.

Bibliography

Accetto, M and Zlepnig, S, 'The Principle of Effectiveness: Rethinking Its Role in Community Law' (2005) 11 *European Public Law* 375.

Ackers, D, 'The Negotiations on the Asylum Procedures Directive' (2005) 7 *European Journal of Migration and Law* 1.

Anagnostaras, G, 'The Incomplete State of Community Harmonization in the Provision of Interim Protection by the National Courts' (2008) 33 *European Law Review* 586.

Arnull, A, 'Case C-432/05 *Unibet* [2007]' (2007) 44 *Common Market Law Review* 1763.

—— 'The Principle of Effective Judicial Protection in EU Law: An Unruly Horse?' (2011) 36 *European Law Review* 51.

Baldinger, HJM, *Rigorous Scrutiny versus Marginal Review* (Nijmegen, Wolf Legal Publishers, 2013)

Baratta, R, 'National Courts as "Guardians" and "Ordinary" Courts of EU Law: Opinion 1/09 of the ECJ' (2011) 38 *Legal Issues of Economic Integration* 297.

Barbier de La Serre, E, 'Procedural Justice in the European Community Case-law concerning the Rights of the Defence: Essentialist and Instrumentalist Trends' (2006) 12 *European Public Law* 225.

Barbier de la Serre, E and Sibony, A, 'Expert Evidence Before the EC Courts' (2008) 45 *Common Market Law Review* 941.

Barents, R, *Directory of EC Case Law on Competition* (Alphen aan den Rijn, Kluwer Law International, 2007)

Barkhuysen, T and Emmerik, ML van, 'Ongebonden binding, Verwijzing naar soft law-standaarden in uitspraken van het EHRM' (2010) 35 *NTM/NJCM-Bulletin* 827.

Battjes, H *European Asylum Law and International Law* (Leiden/Boston, Martinus Nijhoff, 2006)

—— 'Legal effects of the Istanbul Protocol' in R Bruin, AM Reneman and E Bloemen (eds), *Care Full, Medico-legal reports and the Istanbul Protocol in asylum procedures* (Utrecht/Amsterdam, Pharos/Amnesty International/Dutch Council for Refugees, 2006)

—— 'ECtHR 21 January 2011, *MSS v Belgium and Greece*, no 30696/09' (2011) *Jurisprudentie Vreemdelingenrecht* no 2011/68

Bliss, M, 'Serious Reasons for Considering': Minimum Standards of Procedural Fairness in the Application of the Article 1F Exclusion Clauses' (2000) 12 *International Journal of Refugee Law* 92.

Bloemen, E, Vloeberghs, E and Smits, C, 'Psychological and Psychiatric Aspects of Recounting Traumatic Events by Asylum Seekers' in E Bloemen, R Bruin and M Reneman (eds), *Care Full, Medico-legal reports and the Istanbul Protocol* (Utrecht/Amsterdam, Pharos/Amnesty International/Dutch Council for Refugees, 2006)

Boeles, P, 'Case C-540/03, *Parliament v Council* [2006]', (2006) *Jurisprudentie Vreemdelingenrecht* no 2006/313.

—— *Fair Immigration Proceedings in Europe* (The Hague/Boston, Martinus Nijhoff, 1997)

—— 'Case Reports of the European Court of Human Rights, the Human Rights Committee and the Committee against Torture' (2008) 10 *European Journal of Migration and Law* 105.

Boeles, P, den Heijer, M, Lodder, G and Wouters, K, *European Migration Law* (Antwerp/Oxford/Portland, Intersentia, 2009)

Boerefijn, I, *The Reporting Procedure under the Covenant on Civil and Political Rights, Practice and Procedures of the Human Rights Committee* (Antwerp/Groningen/Oxford, Intersentia/Hart, 1999)

Bonner, D, 'Checking the Executive? Detention Without Trial, Control Orders, Due Process and Human Rights' (2006) 12 *European Public Law* 45.

Bronckers, MCEJ, 'The Relationship of the EC Courts with other International Tribunals: Non-committal, Respectful or Submissive?' (2007) 44 *Common Market law Review* 601.

Bruin, R, 'Geen lijdelijke rechter' (2003) 19 *Nieuwsbrief Asiel- en Vluchtelingenrecht* 572.

R Bruin and AM Reneman, 'Supervising bodies and medical reports' in R Bruin, AM Reneman and E Bloemen (eds), *Care Full, Medico-legal reports and the Istanbul Protocol in asylum procedures* (Utrecht/Amsterdam, Pharos/Amnesty International/Dutch Council for Refugees 2006)

Bulterman, M, 'Case C-540/03, *Parliament v Council* [2006]' (2008) 45 *Common Market Law Review* 245.

de Jesús Butler, I and de Schutter, O, 'Binding the EU to International Human Rights Law' (2007) 26 *Yearbook of European Law* 277.

Byrne, R, 'Remedies of Limited Effect: Appeals under the Forthcoming Directive on EU Minimum Standards on Procedures' (2005) 7 *European Journal of Migration and Law* 71.

Burbano Herrera, C and Haeck, Y, 'Staying the Return of Aliens from Europe through Interim Measures: The Case-law of the European Commission and the European Court of Human Rights' (2011) 13 *European Journal of Migration and Law* 31.

Cleynenbreugel, P van, 'Case C-69/10, *Samba Diouf* [2011]' (2012) 49 *Common Market Law Review* 327.

Conte, A and Burchill, R, *Defining Civil and Political Rights: The Jurisprudence of the United Nations Human Rights Committee* (Aldershot, Ashgate, 2009)

Costa, JP, 'The Relationship between the European Convention on Human Rights and European Union Law—A Jurisprudential Dialogue between the European Court of Human Rights and the European Court of Justice' (Lecture at the King's College London, 7 October 2008)

Costello, C, 'The European Asylum Procedures Directive in Legal Context, New Issues in Refugee Research, Research Paper No 134' (Geneva, UNHCR, 2006)

—— 'Dublin-case NS/ME: Finally, an end to blind trust across the EU?' (2012) 3 *Asiel & Migrantenrecht* 83

Craig, P, *EU Administrative Law* (Oxford, Oxford University Press, 2006)

Craig, P and de Búrca, G, *EU Law* (Oxford, Oxford University Press, 2003)

Delicostopoulos, JS, 'Towards European Procedural Primacy in National Legal Systems' (2003) 9 *European Law Journal* 599.

Deschamp, B and Dowd, R, 'Review of the use of UNHCR Executive Committee Conclusions on International Protection' (Geneva, UNHCR, 2008)

Dijk, P van, Hoof, F van, Rijn, A van and Zwaak, L (eds), *Theory and Practice of the European Convention on Human Rights* (Antwerp/Oxford, Intersentia, 2006)

Doornbos, N, *Op verhaal komen, Institutionele communicatie in de asielprocedure*, (Nijmegen, Wolf Legal Publishers, 2006)

Dougan, M, *National Remedies Before the Court of Justice, Issues of Harmonisation and Differentiation* (Oxford and Portland OR, Hart Publishing, 2004)

Douglas-Scott, S, 'A Tale of Two Courts: Luxembourg, Strasbourg and the Growing European Rights *Aquis*' (2006) 43 *Common Market Law Review* 629.

Dutheil de la Rochère, J, 'The EU Charter of Fundamental Rights, Not Binding but Influential: the Example of Good Administration' in A Arnull, P Eeckhout and T Tridimas (eds), *Continuity and Change in EU law* (Oxford, Oxford University Press, 2008)

Eckes, C, 'Case T-228/02, *Modjahedines du people d'Iran v Council* [2006]' (2007) 44 *Common Market Law Review* 1117.

Engström, J, 'National Courts' Obligation to Apply Community Law *Ex Officio*—The Court Showing New Respect for Party Autonomy and National Procedural Autonomy?' (2008) 1 *Review of European Administrative Law* 67.

Erlandsson, A, 'The Defendant's right of Access to the Commission's File in Competition Cases' (1998) 25 *Legal Issues of Economic Integration* 139.

Gattini, A, 'Joined Cases C-402/05 P and C-415/05 P, *Kadi and Al Barakaat* [2008]' (2009) 46 *Common Market Law Review* 213.

Gerards, JH, 'Fundamental Rights and other Interests: Should it really make a Difference?' in E Brems (ed), *Conflicts between Fundamental Rights* (Antwerp, Intersentia, 2008) 655.

—— 'Judicial Deliberations in the European Court of Human Rights' in N Huls, M Adams, J Bomhof (eds), *The Legitimacy of Highest Court's Rulings (*The Hague, TMC Asser Press, 2009) 407.

Good, A, 'Expert Evidence in Asylum and Human Rights Appeals: An Expert's View' (2004) 16 *International Journal of Refugee Law* 358.

Goodwin-Gill, GS and McAdam, J, *The Refugee in International Law* (Oxford, Oxford University Press, 2007)

Gorlick, B, 'Common Burdens and Standards: Legal Elements in Assessing Claims to Refugee Status' (2003) 15 *International Journal of Refugee Law* 357.

Grahl-Madsen, A, *The Status of Refugees in International Law* (Leiden, Sijthoff, 1966)

Groussot, X, 'UK Immigration Law under Attack and the Direct Application of Article 8 ECHR by the Court of Justice' (2003) 3 *Non state actors and International Law* 187.

—— *General Principles of Community Law* (Groningen, Europa Law Publishing, 2006)

Haapaniemi, P, 'Procedural Autonomy: A Misnomer' in L Ervo, M Gräns and A Jokela (eds), *Europeanization of Procedural Law and the New Challenges to Fair Trial* (Groningen, Europa Law Publishing, 2009)

Hailbronner, K (ed), *EU Immigration and Asylum Law, Commentary on EU Regulations and Directives* (Munich, CH Beck/Hart Publishing/Nomos, 2010)

Harpaz, G, 'The European Court of Justice and its Relations with the European Court of Human Rights: The Quest for Enhanced Reliance, Coherence and Legitimacy' (2009) 46 *Common Market Law Review* 105.

Harris, D, Ó'Boyle, M, Warbrick, C and Bates, E (eds), *Law of the European Convention on Human Rights* (Oxford, Oxford University Press, 2009)

Hathaway, JC, *The Law of Refugee Status* (Toronto/Vancouver, Butterworths, 1991)

——*The Rights of Refugees under International Law*, (Cambridge, Cambridge University Press, 2005)

Heijer, M den, 'Whose Rights and Which Rights? The Continuing Story of *Non-Refoulement* under the European Convention on Human Rights' (2008) 10 *European Journal of Migration and Law* 277.

—— *Europe and Extraterritorial Asylum*, (Oxford and Portland OR, Hart Publishing, 2012)

——'Joined Cases C-411 & 493/10, *NS and ME and Others v Refugee Applications Commissioner, Minister for Justice, Equality and Law Reform* [2011]' (2012) 49 *Common Market Law Review* 1735.

Herlihy, J, 'Evidentiary Assessment and Psychological Difficulties' in G Noll (ed), *Proof, Evidentiary Assessment and Credibility in Asylum Procedures* (Leiden/Boston, Martinus Nijhoff, 2005)

Herlihy, J , Gleeson, K and Turner, S, 'What Assumptions about Human Behaviour Underlie Asylum Judgments?' (2010) 22 *International Journal of Refugee Law* 351.

Hooper, HJ, 'Liberty before Security: Case T-85/09 Yassin Abdullah Kadi v Commission (No 2) [2010]' (2012) 18 *European Public Law* 457.

Iglesias Sánchez, S, 'The Court and the Charter: The Impact of the Entry into Force of the Lisbon Treaty on the ECJ's Approach to Fundamental Rights' (2012) 49 *Common Market Law Review* 1565.

Jans, JH, Lange, R de, Prechal, S and Widdershoven, RJGM, *Europeanisation of Public Law* (Groningen, Europe Law Publishing, 2007)

Joseph, S, Schultz, J and Castan, M, *The International Covenant on Civil and Political Rights: Cases, Material and Commentary* (Oxford, Oxford University Press, 2004)

Kakouris, CN 'Do the Member States Possess Judicial Procedural Autonomy?' (1997) 34 *Common Market Law Review* 1389.

Kälin, W, 'Supervising the 1951 Convention Relating to the Status of Refugees: Article 35 and Beyond' in E Feller, V Türk and F Nicholson (eds), *Refugee Protection in International Law, UNHCR's Global Consultations on International Protection* (Cambridge, Cambridge University Press, 2003)

Kańska, K, 'Towards Administrative Human Rights in the EU. Impact of the Charter of Fundamental Rights' (2004) 10 *European Law Journal* 296.

Kempen, E van, 'De omgang met geheim bewijs in de vreemdelingenrechtelijke procedure' (2009) 24 *Migrantenrecht* 434.

Kerse, CS, 'General Principles of Community Law: Procedural Guarantees' in U Bernitz and J Nergelius (eds), *General Principles of European Community Law* (The Hague, Kluwer Law International, 2000)

Koedooder, C and Lang, N de, 'Anti-terrorist Blacklisting in the European Union, The Influence of National Procedures on the Judgments of the Court of First Instance of the European Communities' (2009) 36 *Legal Issues of Economic Integration* 313.

Kunoy, B and Mortansson, B, 'Case C-578/08, *Chakroun* [2010]' (2010) 47 *Common Market Law Review* 1815.

Lauterpacht, E and Bethlehem, D, 'The scope and content of the principle of *non-refoulement*' in E Feller, V Türk and F Nicholson (eds), *Refugee Protection in International Law, UNHCR's Global Consultations on International Protection* (Cambridge, Cambridge University Press, 2003)

Lenaerts, K and Gutiérrez-Fons, JA, 'The Constitutional Allocation of Powers and General Principles of EU Law' (2010) 47 *Common Market Law Review* 1629.

McAdam, J, 'The Qualification Directive, An Overview' in K Zwaan (ed), *The Qualification Directive: Central Themes, Problem Issues and Implementation in Selected Member States* (Nijmegen, Wolf Legal Publishers, 2007)

Michelogiannaki, M, 'The Negotiations of Directive 2005/85/EC' in K Zwaan (ed), *The Procedures Directive, Central Themes, Problem Issues and Implementation in Selected Member States* (Nijmegen, Wolf Legal Publishers, 2008)

Murphy, CC, 'Fundamental Rights and Security, The Difficult Position of the European Judiciary' (2010) 16 *European Public Law* 289.

Murray, JL, 'Fundamental Rights in the European Community Legal Order' (2008) 32 *Fordham International Law Journal* 531.

Noll, G (ed), *Proof, Evidentiary Assessment and Credibility in Asylum Procedures*, (Leiden/Boston, Martinus Nijhoff, 2005)

—— *Evidentiary Assessment and the EU Qualification Directive, New Issues in Refugee Research, Working Paper No 117* (Geneva, UNHCR, 2005)

—— 'Evidentiary Assessment in Refugee Status Determination and the EU Qualification Directive' (2006) 12 *European Public Law* 295.

Norman S 'Assessing the Credibility of Refugee Applicants: A Judicial Perspective' (2007) 19 *International Journal of Refugee Law* 273.

Nowak, M and McArthur, E, *The United Nations Convention against Torture: A Commentary* (Oxford, Oxford University Press, 2008)

Oliver, P, 'Case C-279/09, *DEB* [2010]' (2011) 48 *Common Market Law Review* 2023.

Papp, K von, 'Case C-450/06, *Varec* [2008]' (2009) 46 *Common Market Law Review* 991.

Peers, S, 'The second phase of the Common European Asylum System: A brave new world—or lipstick on a pig?' (2013) (www.statewatch.org)

Peers, S and Rogers, N (eds), *EU Immigration and Asylum Law: Text and Commentary* (Leiden/Boston, Martinus Nijhoff, 2006)

Ponce, J, 'Good Administration and Administrative Procedures' (2005) 12 *Indiana Journal of Global Legal Studies* 551.

Popovic, A, 'Evidentiary Assessment and Non-Refoulement' in G Noll (ed), *Proof, Evidentiary Assessment and Credibility in Asylum Procedures* (Leiden/Boston, Martinus Nijhoff, 2005)

Prechal, S, 'Competence Creep and General Principles of Law' (2010) 3 *Review of European Administrative Law* 5.

Prechal, S and Shelkoplyas, N, 'National Procedures, Public Policy and EC Law. From Van Schijndel to Eco Swiss and Beyond' (2004) 5 *European Review of Private Law* 589.

Prechal, S and Widdershoven, RJGM, 'Redefining the Relationship between "Rewe-effectiveness" and Effective Judicial Protection' (2011) 4 *Review of European Administrative Law* 31.

Rabinovici, I, 'The Right to Be Heard in the Charter of Fundamental Rights of the European Union' (2012) 18 *European Public Law* 149.

Reichel, J, 'Between Supremacy and Autonomy' in U Bernitz, J Nergelius and C Cardner (eds), *General Principles of EC Law in a Process of Development* (Alphen aan den Rijn, Kluwer Law International, 2008) 243.

Reneman, AM, 'An EU Right to Interim Protection during Appeal Proceedings in Asylum Cases?' (2010) 12 *European Journal of Migration and Law* 407.

—— 'Access to an Effective Remedy before a Court or Tribunal in Asylum Cases' in E Guild and P Minderhoud (eds), *The First Decade of EU Migration and Asylum Law* (Leiden/Boston, Martinus Nijhoff, 2011) 401.

Rhys Jones, D, 'Medical Evidence in Asylum and Human Rights Appeals' (2004) 16 *International Journal of Refugee Law* 381.

Schermers, HG, 'Joined Cases C-143/88 and C-92/89, *Zuckerfabrik Süderdithmarschen and Zuckerfabrik Soest* [1991]' (1992) 29 *Common Market Law Review* 29 133.

Schermers, HG and Waelbroeck, DF, *Judicial Protection in the European Union* (The Hague, Kluwer, 2001)

Schiek, D, 'The ECJ Decision in *Mangold*: A Further Twist on Effects of Directives and Constitutional Relevance of Community Equality Legislation' (2006) 35 *Industrial Law Journal* 329.

Schuurmans, Y, 'Review of Facts in Administrative Law Procedures; A European Community Law Perspective' (2008) 1 *Review of European Administrative Law* 5.

Schwartze, J, 'Judicial Review of European Administrative Procedure' (2004) 68 *Law and Contemporary Problems* 85.

Schwartze, J, 'European administrative law in the light of the Treaty of Lisbon' (2012) 18 *European Public Law* 285.

Senden, L, *Soft Law in Community Law* (Oxford and Portland OR, Hart Publishing, 2004)

Sibony, A, 'Case C-272/09 P, *KME Germany and others v. Commission* [2011]' (2012) 49 *Common Market Law Review* 1977.

Sinaniotis, D, *The Interim Protection of Individuals before the European and National Courts* (Alphen aan de Rijn, Kluwer, 2006)

Spaventa, E, 'Joined Cases T-256/07, *People's Modjahedin Organization of Iran* [2008] and T-284/08, *People's Modjahedin Organization of Iran* [2008]' (2009) 46 *Common Market Law Review* 1239.

Spielmann, D, 'Human Rights Case Law in the Strasbourg and Luxembourg Courts: Conflicts, Inconsistencies, and Complementarities' in P Alston, MR Bustelo and J Heenan (eds), *The EU and Human Rights* (Oxford, Oxford University Press, 1999)

Spijkerboer, TP, 'ECtHR 20 September 2007, *Sultani v France*, no 45223/05' (2008) *Jurisprudentie Vreemdelingenrecht* no 2008/462.

—— 'Case C-465/07, *Elgafaji* [2009]' (2009) *Jurisprudentie Vreemdelingenrecht* no 2009/111.

—— 'Subsidiarity and "Arguability": the European Court of Human Rights' Case Law on Judicial Review in Asylum Cases' (2009) 21 *International Journal of Refugee Law* 48.

Spijkerboer, TP and Vermeulen, BP, *Vluchtelingenrecht* (Amsterdam/Leersum, Nederlands Centrum Buitenlanders, 1995)

—— *Vluchtelingenrecht* (Nijmegen, Ars Aequi Libri, 2005)

Staffans, I, 'Evidentiary Standards of Inquisitorial versus Adversarial Asylum Procedures in the Light of Harmonization' (2008) 14 *European Public Law* 615.

—— 'Judicial Protection and the New European Asylum Regime' (2010) 12 *European Journal of Migration and Law* 273.

—— *Evidence in European Asylum Procedures* (Leiden/Boston, Martinus Nijhoff, 2012)

Summers, S, *Fair Trials, The European Criminal Procedural Tradition and the European Court of Human Rights* (Oxford and Portland OR, Hart Publishing, 2007)

Schwartze, J, 'Judicial Review of European Administrative Procedures' (2004) *Law and Contemporary Problems* 68, 85.

Thomas, R, 'Assessing the Credibility of Asylum Claims, EU and UK Approaches Examined' (2006) 8 *European Journal of Migration and Law* 79.

Toth, AG, 'Case C-213/89 *Factortame* I [1990]' (1990) 27 *Common Market Law Review* 573.

Trechsel, S, *Human Rights in Criminal Proceedings* (Oxford, Oxford University Press, 2005)

Tridimas, T, *The General Principles of Community Law* (Oxford, Oxford University Press, 2006)

Tridimas, T and Gutierrez-Fons, JA, 'EU Law, International Law and Economic Sanctions against Terrorism: The Judiciary in Distress?' (2008) 32 *Fordham International Law Journal* 660.

Trstenjak, V and Beysen, E, 'European Consumer Protection Law: *Curia Semper Dabit Remedium*?' (2011) 48 *Common Market Law Review* 95.

Türk, V, *UNHCR's Role in Supervising International Protection Standards in the Context of its Mandate* (Geneva, UNHCR, 2010)

Tzanou, M and El Droubi, S, 'Case T-318/01, *Othman v Council* [2009]' (2010) 47 *Common Market Law Review* 1233.

Vedsted-Hansen, J, 'Common EU Standards on Asylum—Optional Harmonisation and Exclusive Procedures?' (2005) 7 *European Journal of Migration and Law* 369.

Ward, A, *Judicial Review and the Rights of Private Parties in EU Law* (Oxford, Oxford University Press, 2007)

Widdershoven, RJGM, 'Case C-69/10, *Samba Diouf* [2011]' (2011) *AB Rechtspraak Bestuursrecht* no 2011/304.

Wildhaber, L, *The Place of the European Court of Human Rights in the European Constitutional Landscape Address at the Conference of European Constitutional Courts, XIIth Congress* (2002)

Wimmer, M, 'Individual Sanctions and Fundamental Rights Standards: *Bamba*' (2013) 50 *Common Market Law Review* 1119.

Witte, B de, 'The Role of the ECJ in Human Rights' in P Alston, MR Bustelo and J Heenan (eds), *The EU and Human Rights* (Oxford, Oxford University Press, 1999)

Wouters, CW, *International Legal Standards for the Protection from Refoulement* (Antwerp, Intersentia, 2009)

Young, AL, 'The Charter, Constitution and Human Rights: Is this the Beginning of the End for Human Rights Protections by Community Law' (2005) 11 *European Public Law* 219.

Zahle, H, 'Competing Patterns for Evidentiary Assessments' in G Noll (ed), *Proof, Evidentiary Assessment and Credibility in Asylum Procedures* (Leiden/Boston, Martinus Nijhoff, 2005)

Index

www.ingramcontent.com/pod-product-compliance
Lightning Source LLC
LaVergne TN
LVHW052219200926
848481LV00001B/156
* 9 7 8 1 5 0 9 9 0 7 4 2 7 *